EXPLORERS TO 1815
TEACHER'S MANUAL

Ned Bustard
Eric Vanderhoof
Christi McCullars
Shea Foster
Emily Fischer
and Aaron Larsen

Veritas Press

www.VeritasPress.com
800-922-5082

Second Edition 2007

Veritas Press

www.VeritasPress.com
800-922-5082

ISBN 978-1-932168-67-9

Printed in the United States of America.

EXPLORERS TO 1815

How to use this Manual

We hope this guide will be helpful as you study the period from Explorers to 1815 this year. You are about to take a journey through the past where you can see God's providence on a daily basis. This study should help build an understanding of the world in which we live and what sacrifices and battles occurred which resulted in the tremendous blessings we now know. God was faithful to His people through the years just as He is today. What a joy it is for young children to come to realize God's faithfulness as they learn from the past.

CUSTOMIZE IT

There are 32 events/people featured in the cards in each of the Veritas Press History Sets. That is approximately one per week. A few of the cards have extra projects which may spread into the following week. Before you begin, also familiarize yourself with the materials in the Appendix. Many of these projects may be used throughout the year. All the projects in this manual are only suggestions, so use your imagination and have fun with your group. You will note that the projects vary in appeal to different ages. You may choose the ones you think are appropriate for your group. The projects are marked in the answer key to indicate if the project is better suited for younger students or older (grades fourth and higher) students. If you are using this series for second grade or below, you may need to do some of it orally for the first six weeks; after that three times a week is usually enough. Remember, the reason for the Explorers to 1815 Memory Song is to help memorize the chronology of the events. It is also good, after the song has been memorized, to have the children recite events in proper order, rather than singing them.

SAMPLE SCHOOL WEEK

Monday: Sing the Explorers to 1815 Memory Song (page 471). You may want to have a student come to the front of the room and hold up the flashcards as the class sings. Present the new card. Read the synopsis on the back and discuss it with the class. Allow different students to read it out loud if you can. Then allow the students to answer questions on the corresponding worksheet. The questions are based on information found on the cards. If you are working with second grade or below, they may need to be asked to do this orally for the first part of the year.

Tuesday: Sing the song. Orally review questions from this card's worksheet and from previous events. Obviously, you cannot review every question every day, so do a sampling. Assign different children different sources from the Priority 1 Resources listed on the card and allow them to look up the information and share it with the class.

Wednesday: Sing the song. Orally review questions from the worksheet. Do one of the projects.

Thursday: Sing the song. Orally review from this week and previous weeks. Discuss how this card relates to those before it. Do another project, if there is one.

Friday: Give test. Use remaining time for class instruction and drill.

EXPLORERS TO 1815

How to use this Manual, Page 2

ENJOYING HISTORY

Having fun makes it easy to learn. Using the cards for games is one way. Ask the children to shuffle them and then see who can get their cards in order the fastest. Or have four to six students mix up their cards and then play Go Fish. This allows them to get familiar with the titles. Or you can get in a large room and see who can use their cards to make their own timeline the fastest. A good way to drill questions in a classroom is to divide the children into two teams and ask questions in order. Teams receive a point for each right answer.

"ONE RING TO BIND THEM . . ."

We have found one of the best ways to file the cards is to laminate them, punch a hole in the top right corner, and keep them on a large ring. The children can add the newest card and also have the previous cards handy. Another idea is to laminate them, put a Velcro strip on the card and on the wall, and start a timeline that children can put up and take down over and over again. An extra set of cards mounted at the other end of the room for a reference timeline is a good idea too.

LITERATURE KIT

To truly send students' imaginations flying, we recommend having the students read historical fiction pertaining to the cards they are studying. The books we find work the best are listed in our catalog as a Literature Kit, following the Priority 1 Resources. In order to encourage children to read books related to classroom work, we suggest a book chart to show points earned for each book read by each student. After receiving a certain number of points, the child may receive a reward, such as a special lunch with his teacher. You could have a mom bring in a special lunch or allow the winners to go out.

GRADING

Each worksheet, test, or writing assignment should receive three grades, one each for Content, Grammar and Linguistics (Spelling). See page 439 in the Appendix for a helpful grading chart.

Content: On a scale of 1 to 15, grade for completeness or the correct answer to a question. This grade is applied to their history grade. If your grading scale is different from 1 to 15, use yours.

Grammar: The child should answer the questions in complete sentences, in which he first restates the question.

Example:

Question: Where did John Cabot believe he had landed?

Answer: John Cabot believed that he had landed in the Indies.

As the year progresses you can grade more strictly for grammar. This grade should be applied to an application grade in grammar, but should not affect history content grades. We suggest application at twenty percent of the overall grammar grade.

Linguistics: The children should spell all words correctly. You should deduct for misspelled words once the rule for spelling a particular word has been mastered. For example: "I before e except after c." Once this

EXPLORERS TO 1815

How to use this Manual, Page 3

has been covered, a child's grade would be reduced if they spelled *receive* as *recieve.* If they are using a history card to do their worksheet, they should be taught that those words should be spelled correctly. This grade would be applied towards a linguistics application grade. Again we suggest twenty percent, but not to affect their history grade.

When you look at the tests you will see that there are not the same number of questions on each test or worksheet. We assign five points per question, with the listings of the chronology receiving two points per item listed. Partial credit may be counted because the questions are essay in nature, and they may have portions correct.

Some students may ask why they are receiving three grades on each paper. We believe that it is important for a student to realize that grammar and linguistics matter in history class as well as in grammar class. All three contribute to helping make students understood by others, and are thus intertwined.

FEEDBACK

We welcome your feedback and comments. We hope that this resource will enrich the education of those children entrusted to you, and will help them understand the comprehensive responsibility that God requires of them.

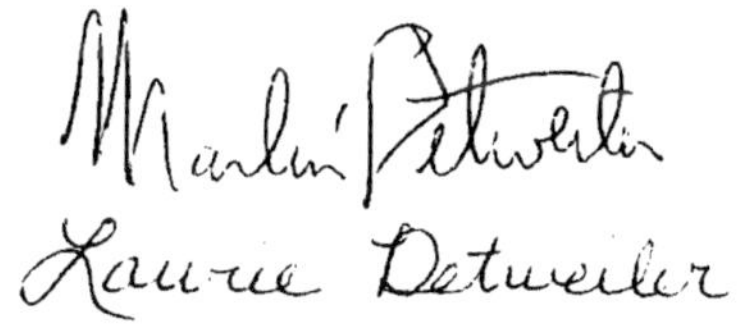

Explorers to 1815
Table of Contents

EXPLORERS TO 1815

Map

The map shown below can be assembled after copying pages 501-515 in the Appendix. Cut out along the solid black lines and tape together by aligning with the light gray interior lines (the panels will overlap—each side of each page is an extra .25"). If you are able, laminating the entire map may prove useful as it will be used throughout the year. For an even larger map, photocopy each page onto tabloid-sized sheets at 140%.

The final page of the map contains medallions representing each of the history cards. Cut the medallions out, and as each flashcard is introduced, read the text on the timeline pages (starting on page 516) to the children and follow the instructions for placing the medallions on the map's corresponding number.

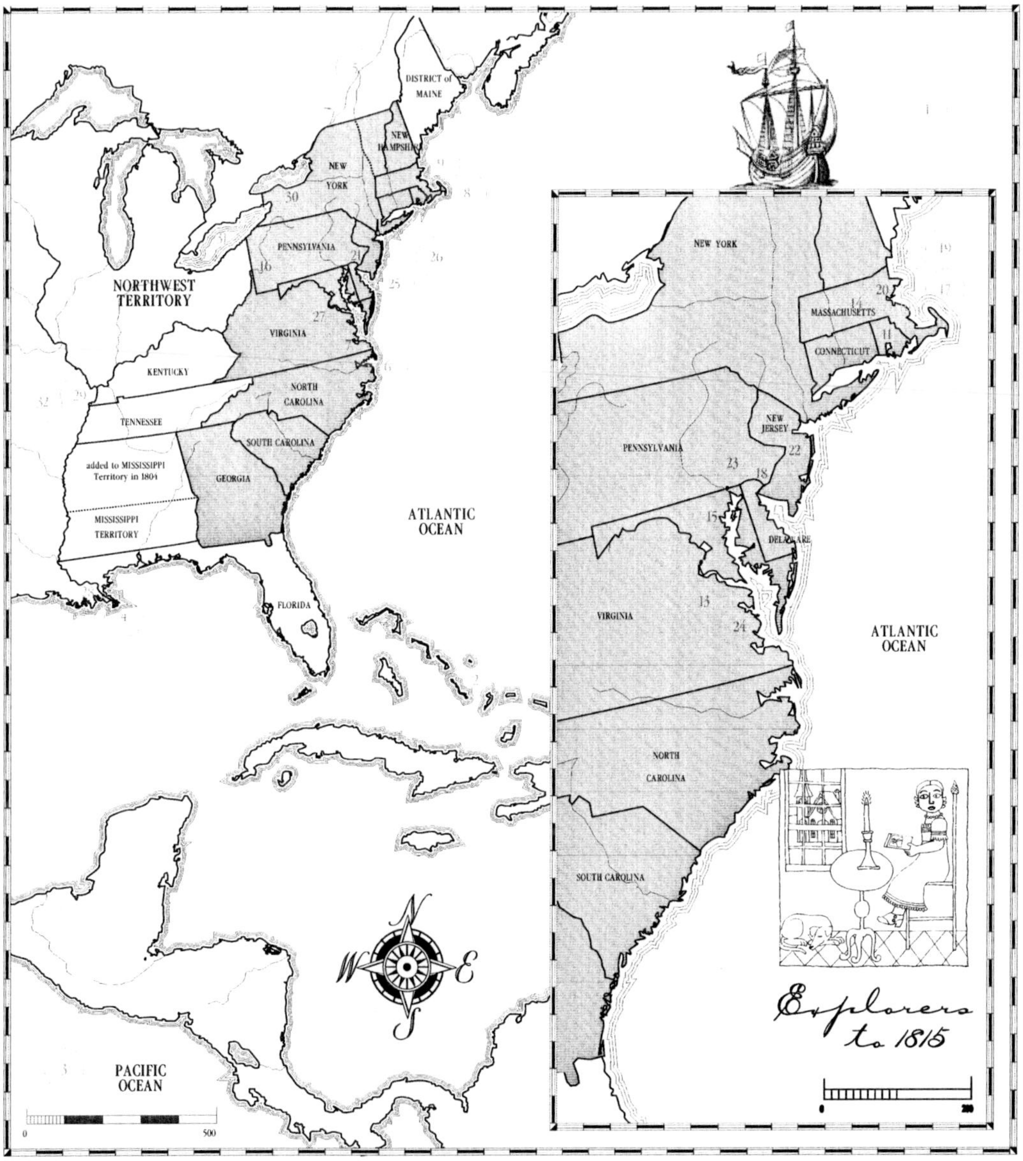

PRINCE HENRY THE NAVIGATOR
Worksheet

1. Of what country was Henry the Navigator a prince?

____

____

2. Where was Prince Henry born? In what year?

____

____

3. What steps did Henry take that helped open the African route to Asia?

____

____

____

4. Using a dictionary if necessary, define *cartography*.

____

____

5. Using a dictionary if necessary, define *astronomy*.

____

____

6. Using a dictionary if necessary, define *navigation*.

____

____

7. How many expeditions did Prince Henry send? How many did he go on himself?

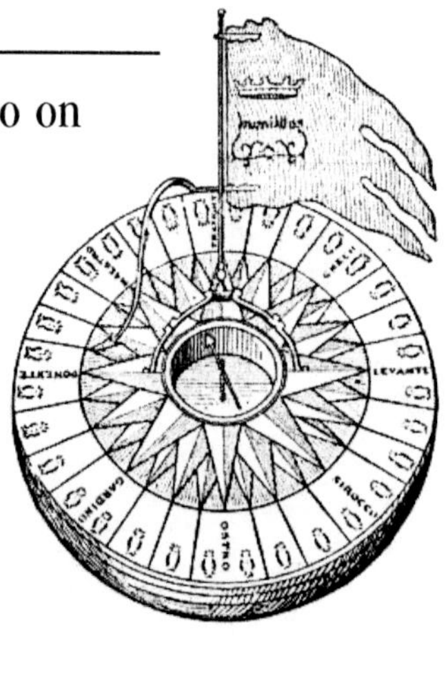

____

____

____

____

PRINCE HENRY THE NAVIGATOR
Project 1—Cartography (Map Making)

Maps of the world looked very different in days past. No one knew that Australia, New Zealand, Antarctica, or the Americas existed. In 1490 Henricus Martellus published a map with seas separating Africa and Asia. The map shown was made by a cartographer named Behaim in 1493. Dotted lines show where the Americas should have been drawn. The viking Leif Ericson had found part of North America and called it Vinland around 1000 A.D., but it is not included on this map. The Isle of St. Brandan is shown near present day Colombia. Saint Brendan the Navigator was an Irish monk who some think landed in the Americas as far south as Florida early in the 6th century A.D., naming the land Hy-Brasil. In 1507 Walseemuller printed a huge world map and put on it a new continent. He named the southern continent "America" after Amerigo Vespucci, who had written about the continent in a writing called *novus mundus* (Latin for "new world").

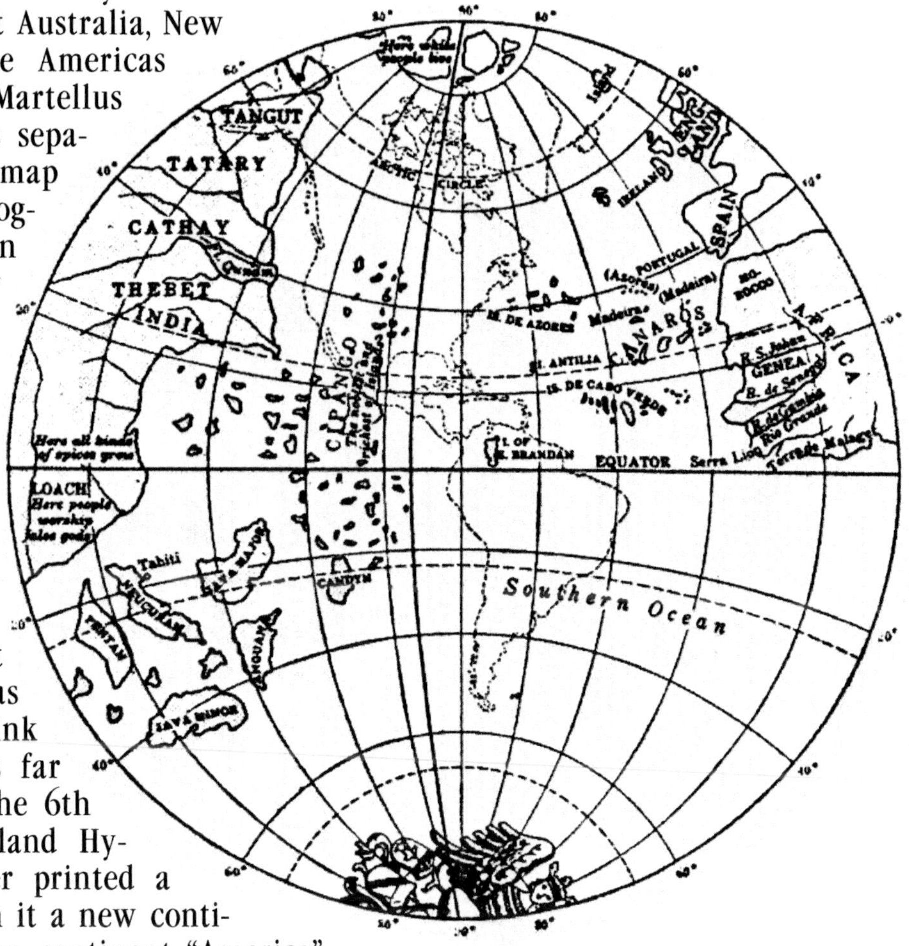

As you can see, it is not easy to make a map of the world around you. To get a feel for this, draw a map of your neighborhood in the space provided on the next page. When you are finished, type in your address at http://maps.google.com and see where you were wrong in placement of landmarks and how the proportions you drew would mislead you if you actually used your map to get around. For example, if you followed your map, would you walk into buildings, or fall into rivers?

Prince Henry the Navigator
Project 2

Prince Henry the Navigator
Test

1. Where was Prince Henry born? In what year?

2. Of what country was Henry the Navigator a prince?

3. What did Henry's school teach?

4. What did Henry's school help to accomplish?

5. How many expeditions did Prince Henry go on himself?

6. Name one of the places reached by Prince Henry's captains.

7. What is a navigator?

8. Define *cartography* and *astronomy*.

Columbus Sails to the New World

Worksheet

1. What was the relationship between Prince Henry the Navigator and Christopher Columbus?

2. What country was home for Columbus?

3. Who funded Columbus's explorations?

4. In what year did Columbus set sail for the new land?

5. How many ships set sail in the voyage? Name them.

6. How many men were on the voyage?

COLUMBUS SAILS TO THE NEW WORLD
Worksheet, Page 2

7. Where did Columbus intend to land? Where did he land?

8. How many voyages did Columbus make? What did he name the place where he landed?

9. Columbus died believing he had reached what country?

10. What did Columbus believe God had called him to do?

Columbus Sails to the New World

Project 1–Journal Entry

Read the following account of Columbus's expedition then write a journal entry summarizing it on the page that follows.

The crusades, the Renaissance, the invention of printing, and the travels of Marco Polo in the East had set people to thinking about matters in the great world beyond the limits of their own little villages or towns. The part of the earth in which the greatest number were interested was India. The reason was the Europeans had learned to enjoy the spices, silks, cottons, and jewels of the East. The old way of bringing these to Europe was up the Red Sea, past Constantinople, and through the Mediterranean to Genoa. Now that the Turks held Constantinople, the eastern Mediterranean was a dangerous place. Just as people were beginning to think they must have the Eastern luxuries, it became more and more difficult to obtain them, and the nation that could find the shortest way to India would soon possess untold wealth.

One man who was thinking most earnestly about India was Christopher Columbus. He was born in Genoa and had been at sea most of his life until he was fourteen. He had read, studied, and thought until he was convinced that the world was round and that the best way to reach China and Japan was not to make the wearisome journey through Asia, but to sail directly west across the Atlantic. He had asked the city of Genoa to provide money for the expedition. He had also asked the King of Portugal, but to no avail. Finally he appealed to Ferdinand and Isabella, king and queen of Spain.

This was why, toward the end of the fifteenth century, a company of learned Spaniards met together at Salamanca to listen to the schemes of a simple, unknown Italian sailor. Columbus told them what he believed. Then they brought forward their objections. "A ship might possibly reach India that way," one said gravely, "but she could never sail uphill and come home again." "If the world is round and people are on the opposite side, they must hang by their feet with their heads down," another declared scornfully. Another objection was that such an expedition that Columbus proposed would be expensive. Moreover he demanded the title of admiral of whatever lands he might discover and one tenth of all precious stones, gold, silver, spices, and other merchandise that should be found in these lands. This was not because he was greedy for money. He was planning to win the Holy Sepulcher at Jerusalem from the Turks, and to do this would require an enormous fortune.

Columbus had formed a noble scheme, but there seemed to be small hope that it would be carried out by Spanish aid, for the Spaniards were waging an important war

Columbus Sails to the New World

Project 1, Page 2

with the Moors (also called Mohammedans or Muslims). The Moors had a kingdom in the south of Spain containing a number of cities. In the capital, Granada, was the palace and fortress of Alhambra, a wonderfully beautiful structure, even in the ruins as it is today. Granada was captured, but even then the Spaniards seemed to have little time to listen to Columbus.

At length he made up his mind to leave Spain and go for aid to the king of France. With his little son Diego he started out on foot. The child was hungry, and so they stopped at the gate of the convent of La Rabido, near the town of Palos, Spain, to beg for the food that was never refused to wayfarers. The prior was a student of geography. He heard the ideas of Columbus, put faith in them, and invited some of his friends to meet the stranger. "Spain must not lose the honor of such an enterprise," the prior declared, and he even went himself to the queen. He had once been her confessor, and she greeted him kindly. King Ferdinand did not believe in the undertaking, but Queen Isabella became thoroughly interested in it. She was Queen of Aragon by her marriage to Ferdinand, but she was Queen of Castile in her own right, and she exclaimed, "I undertake the enterprise for my own crown of Castile, and I will pledge my jewels to raise the necessary funds."

Thus, after eighteen years' delay, the way was opened for Columbus, and he set sail from Palos with three small vessels. Even after they were at sea, Columbus must have felt as if his troubles were just begun, for his sailors were full of fears. They weren't cowards, but no one had ever crossed the Atlantic. There were legends that in one place it was swarming with monsters, and that in another the water boiled with intense heat. There was real danger, also, from the jealous Portuguese, for it was rumored that they had sent out vessels to capture Columbus'ss little fleet. It is a small wonder the sailors were dismayed by the fires of the volcanic peak of Tenerife, but they were almost equally alarmed by every little occurrence. The mast of a wrecked vessel floated by, and they feared it was a sign that their vessel, too would be wrecked. After a while, the magnetic needle ceased to point to the North Star, and they were filled with dread lest they should lose their way on the vast ocean. One night a brilliant meteor appeared, and then they were sure destruction was at hand. The good east wind was sweeping them along gently, but even that worried them, for they feared it would never alter, and how could they get home? Some of them had begun to whisper together of throwing Columbus overboard. Then one day they saw land birds and floating weeds and finally a glimmering light. The sailors were as eager to press onward as their leader.

Early on the following morning land appeared. Columbus, wearing his brilliant scarlet robes and bearing the standard of Spain, was rowed ashore. He fell upon his knees and kissed the ground, thanking God

Columbus Sails to the New World

Project 1, Page 3

most heartily for his care. Then he took possession of the land for Spain. The natives gathered around, and he gave them bells and glass beads. He supposed that he was just off the coast on India, and as he had reached the place sailing west, he called it the West Indies and the people Indians. The island itself he named San Salvador. It is thought to have been one of the Bahamas. He spent some time among the islands, always hoping to come upon the wealthy cities of the Great Khan. At length he returned to Spain, dreaming of future voyages he would make.

When he reached Palos, the bells were rung and people gave up their business to celebrate the wonderful voyage and safe return. Colombus made three other voyages across the ocean, hoping every time to find the rich cities of the East. His enemies claimed he had mismanaged a colony that had been founded in the New World. Another governor was sent out, and he threw the great Admiral into chains. Ferdinand and Isabella were indignant when they knew of this outrage, yet they could not help being disappointed that China had not been found. Neither they nor Columbus dreamed that he had discovered a new continent; and even if they had known it, they would have much preferred finding a way to trade with the distant East.

Columbus Sails to the New World

Project 1, Page 4

Columbus Sails to the New World
Project 2

Trace the route of Columbus's first voyage with a red marker.

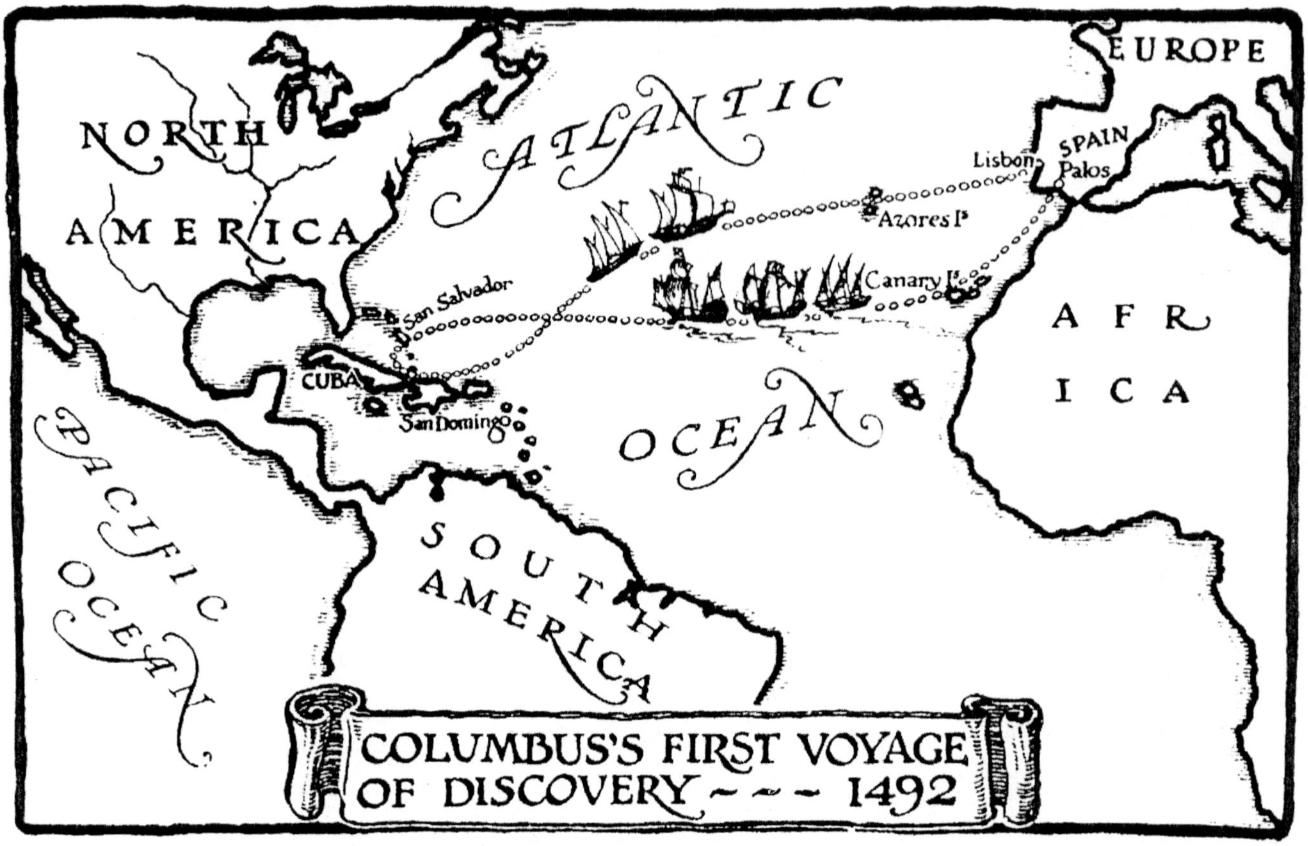

Columbus Sails to the New World

Project 3—A Letter from Columbus

Read Christopher Columbus's letter to the King and Queen of Spain (undated, probably 1494).

Most High and Mighty Sovereigns,

In obedience to your Highness' commands, and with submission to superior judgement, I will say whatever occurs to me in reference to the colonization and commerce of the Island of Espanola, and of other islands, both those already discovered and those that may be discovered hereafter.

In the first place, as regards to the Island of Espanola: Inasmuch as the number of colonists who desire to go thither amounts to two thousand, owing to a land being safer and better for farming and trading, and because it will serve as a place to which they can return and from which they can carry on trade with the neighboring islands:

1. That in the said island there shall be founded three of four towns, situated in the most convenient places, and that the settlers who are there be assigned to the aforesaid places and towns.
2. That for the better and more speedy colonization of the said island, no one shall have liberty to collect gold in it except those who have taken out colonists' papers, and have built houses for their abode, in the town in which they are, that they may live united and in greater safety.
3. That each town shall have its alcalde [mayor] . . . and its notary public, as is the use and custom in Castile.
4. That there shall be a church, and parish priests of friars to administer the sacraments, to perform divine worship, and for the conversion of the Indians.
5. That none of the colonists shall go to seek gold without a license from the governor or alcalde of the town where he lives; and that he must first take oath to return to the place whence he sets out, for the purpose of registering faithfully all the gold he may have found, and to return once a month, or once a week, as the time may have been set for him, to render account and show the quantity of said gold; and that this shall be written down by the notary public before the alcalde, or, if it seems better, that a friar or priest, deputed for that purpose, shall also be present.
6. That all gold thus brought in shall be smelted immediately, and stamped with some mark that shall distinguish each town; and that the portion which belongs to your Highness shall be weighed, and given and consigned to each alcalde in his own town, and registered by the above-mentioned priest or friar, so that it shall not pass through the hands of only one person, and there shall be no opportunity to conceal the truth.

Columbus Sails to the New World

Project 3, Page 2

7. That all gold that may be found without the mark of one of the said towns in the possession of any who has once registered in accordance with the above order shall be taken as forfeited, and that the accuser shall have one portion of it and your Highness the other.
8. That one per centum of all gold that may be found shall be set aside for building churches and adorning the same, and for the support of the priests or friars belonging to them; and, if it should be thought proper to pay any thing to the alcaldes or notaries for their duties, that this amount shall be sent to the governor or measure who may be appointed there by your Highnesses.
9. As regards the division of gold, and the share that ought to be reserved for your Highnesses, this, in my opinion, must be left to the aforesaid governor and treasurer, because it will have to be greater or less according to the quantity of gold that may be found. Or, if it seem preferable, your Highnesses might, for the space of one year, take one half, and the collector the other, and a better arrangement for the division be made afterward.
10. That if the said alcaldes or notaries shall commit, or be privy to any fraud, punishment shall be provided, and the same for the colonists who shall not have declared all the gold they have.
11. That in the said island there shall be a treasurer, with a clerk to assist him, who shall receive all the gold belonging to your Highnesses, and the alcaldes and notaries of the towns shall each keep a record of what they deliver to the said treasurer.
12. As, in the eagerness to get gold, every one will wish, naturally, to engage in its search in preference to any other employment, it seems to me that the privilege of going to look for gold ought to be withheld during some portion of the year, that there may be opportunity to have the other business necessary for the island performed.
13. In regard to the discovery of new countries, I think permission should be granted to all that wish to go, and more liberality used in the matter of the fifth, making the tax easier, in some way, in order that many may be disposed to go on voyages.

I will now give my opinion about ships to the said Island of Espanola, and the order that should be maintained; and that is, that the said ships should only be allowed to discharge on one or two ports designed for the purpose, and should register there whatever cargo they bring or unload; and when the time for their departure comes, that they should sail from these same ports, and

Columbus Sails to the New World
Project 3, Page 3

register all cargo they take in, that nothing may be concealed.

In reference to the transportation of gold from the island to Castile, that all of it should be taken on board the ship, both that belonging to your Highnesses and the property of everyone else; that it should all be placed in one chest with two locks, with their keys, and that the master of the vessel keep one key and some person selected by the governor and treasurer the other; that there should come with the gold, for a testimony, a list of all that has been put into the said chest, properly marked, so that each owner may receive his own; and that, for the faithful performance of this duty, if any gold whatsoever is found outside of the said chest in any way, be it little or much, it shall be forfeited to your Highnesses.

That all the ships that come from the said island shall be obliged to make their proper discharge in the port of Cadiz, and that no person shall disembark or other persons be permitted to go on board until the ship has been visited by the person or persons deputed for that purpose, in the said city, by your Highnesses, to whom the master shall show all that he carries, and exhibit the manifest of all the cargo, it may be seen and examined if the said ship brings any thing hidden and not known at the time of landing.

That the chest in which the said gold has been carried shall be opened in the presence of the magistrates of the said city of Cadiz, and of the person deputed for that purpose by your Highnesses, and his own property be given to each owner.

I beg your Highnesses to hold me in your protection; and I remain, praying our Lord God for your Highnesses' lives and the increase of much greater States.

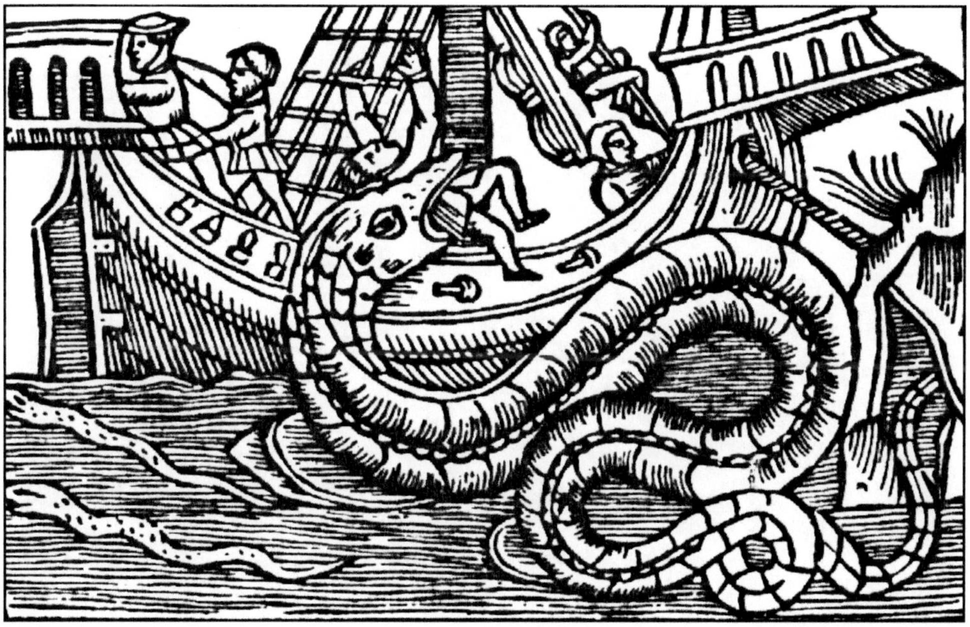

Columbus Sails to the New World

Project 4—Art Study

While Columbus was off sailing to a new world, many instead were focused on the end *of the world. Look at the woodcut on this page by Albrecht Dürer and discuss the following questions.*

1. This print is part of a large series of woodcuts called *The Apocalypse.* How is the date of the publication of this print significant?
2. Can you identify the biblical scene that is described here, including the names of the riders?
3. The woodcut medium is very similar to that of rubber stamps—it prints in lines, not varied tones. How has the artist exploited his chosen medium to show value (light and shade)?

The Four Horsemen from *The Apocalypse* by Albrecht Dürer, 1498

Columbus Sails to the New World

Test

1. In what year did Columbus sail to the new world?

2. Columbus was from what country?

3. Who financed Columbus's voyages?

4. How many ships and men did Columbus take on his first expedition?

5. Where did Columbus actually land? Where did he believe he had landed?

6. What did he name the natives of the land he found?

7. How many voyages did Columbus make to this new land?

Columbus Sails to the New World

Test, Page 2

8. What did Columbus believe God had called him to do?

Review

1. Where was Prince Henry born? What year?

2. Define *cartography.*

3. Define *navigation.*

4. What was Prince Henry's contribution to navigation and cartography?

5. Was Prince Henry the Navigator a navigator?

Magellan Circumnavigates the Earth

Worksheet

1. Who was Ferdinand Magellan?

2. What famous expedition did Magellan command?

3. Who financed this famous voyage?

4. How many ships went on this voyage? Name them.

5. What occurred on the voyage that caused problems for Magellan?
   What was the outcome of these events?

Magellan Circumnavigates the Earth
Worksheet, Page 2

6. What did Magellan discover on this voyage?

____

____

____

7. How many ships returned to Spain? In what year was the return?

____

____

____

____

8. Did Magellan complete the voyage with his crew?

____

____

____

____

Magellan Circumnavigates the Earth

Project 1—Magellan Explores

Read the following account then discuss Magellan's impact on trade. Compare Columbus's first voyage with Magellan's voyage. What are the similarities and differences?

After the death of Columbus, people began to suspect the newly discovered lands were not part of Asia. But the Spaniards were still eager to explore the new world, especially if gold was involved in the explorations. In 1513 Vasco Nuñez de Balboa led a Spanish expedition in Central America. As the Spanish were quarreling over the gold they had found, an Indian chief's son, perhaps wishing to rid his own country of the Spaniards, claimed he could show them an ocean on the shores of Peru that was rich in gold. Balboa and his men crossed the isthmus and, wading fully armed into the water of the Pacific Ocean, took possession of what he called the "South Sea" and all the countries on its coast for the King and Queen of Spain.

With the discovery of the Pacific Ocean on the west coast of Central America, the goal became to find a way by ship through or around America in order to reach the rich trade of India, which the Portuguese had reached by the Cape of Good Hope. The Spanish achieved this goal by an expedition under Ferdinand Magellan. Magellan was a native of Portugal. He served the Portuguese government in the East Indies, and he was in the expedition that discovered the Spice Islands. Having been slighted by the Portuguese government, he renounced his country and entered the service of the King of Spain. In September 1519, Magellan sailed off with five ships in hope of circumnavigating the earth. It was unknown then that it was possible to sail around Cape Horn because South America was thought to reach the South Pole. Magellan was intent on finding a way of getting through South America. On the coast of South America he lost one of his vessels, and he suppressed a mutiny. In October 1520, he entered the straits that now bear his name. His men were very reluctant to continue, and one ship did turn back and sail home. The remaining three ships entered the Pacific Ocean. At the Philippine Islands, Ferdinand Magellan was killed in a battle with the natives. Only one of the five ships, the *Victoria,* succeeded in getting around the world. Only eighteen sick, starving men were alive when the ship reached Spain. Thus ended the first voyage around the globe.

Magellan's route was, indeed, too long for a trade route, and other navigators continued to sail up and down the American coast hoping to find some passage to China, India, and Japan. They did not understand that America was a continent; they believed it might prove to be cut through by straits like the Straits of Magellan, if they could only find them. Several great English navigators tried to discover what they called the Northwest Passage by sailing along the coast of Labrador and into rivers and bays, while the French thought to reach China by passing up the St. Lawrence River and through the Great Lakes. Obviously all these attempts failed, but the explorers were ready to keep trying.

Magellan Circumnavigates the Earth

Project 2–Salt Relief Map

Supplies

cardboard box lid for legal size paper (available from printing companies)

copy of world map (next page)

white glue

pencil

two mixing bowls

spoon

measuring cups

flour

salt

water

food coloring

yarn

Directions

1. Photocopy map up to 120% onto legal size paper then glue the map to the inside of the box lid.
2. Using green dough, cover the land areas.
3. Using blue dough, cover the bodies of water.
4. Allow one week for drying.
5. After drying, cut labels out and glue them in the appropriate places.
6. Glue yarn along Magellan's route.

Salt Dough Recipe

(enough to make three maps)

6 cups of salt

6 cups of flour

2-3 cups of water

Combine salt and flour, mix well. Add two cups of water and mix until smooth. Add remaining water as needed. Divide dough in half. Add green food coloring to one portion and blue to the other. Cover and set aside. (This can be mixed the day before and stored in a refrigerator. It may also be frozen to use later.)

Labels

Pacific Ocean

Atlantic Ocean

Indian Ocean

Asia

China

Japan

Australia

North America

South America

Philippines

Brazil

Europe

Africa

Cape of Good Hope

Magellan Circumnavigates the Earth
Project 3—Art Study

Instead of thinking about a few sailors searching around the world's end, at this time most of the world was busy with other things. Like the Reformation, for example. Look at the engraving on this page by Lucas Chranach the Elder and discuss the following questions:

1. How is Martin Luther dressed in this picture? What does that tell us?
2. What can you tell about the artist's feelings toward Luther? Was he sympathetic toward Luther and his ideas?

Martin Luther as Augustinian Monk by Lucas Cranach the Elder, 1520

Magellan Circumnavigates the Earth

Test

1. What is the date for Magellan Circumnavigates the Earth?

2. Who was Ferdinand Magellan?

3. What famous voyage did Magellan command? Who financed the voyage?

4. How many ships did Magellan command on the voyage?

5. What problem occurred on the voyage? What was the outcome?

6. What did Magellan discover?

MAGELLAN CIRCUMNAVIGATES THE EARTH
Test, Page 2

7. Where did Magellan die?

____

____

____

8. How many ships returned to Spain at the end of the voyage?

____

____

____

9. How long did the trip around the world take?

____

____

____

Review

1. Of what country was Prince Henry a prince?

____

____

____

2. What was Prince Henry's contribution to navigation?

____

____

____

3. What year did Columbus first land in the Bahamas?

____

____

Magellan Circumnavigate the Earth
Test, Page 3

4. Where did Columbus think he was?

5. Why did Columbus want to find a route to the answer to #4?

6. In chronological order list all events studied to date. Next to each place the appropriate date.

Cortés, De Soto, De Leon, and Coronado, the Spanish Explorers

Worksheet

1. What were the dates of the Spanish explorers: Cortés, de Soto, de Leon, and Coronado?

2. What countries had Spain taken over within one hundred years of Columbus's first voyage?

3. What name was given to the period in history that was a result of Spanish exploration during the 1500's?

4. What empire did Hernando Cortés conquer? What happened to the empire?

5. What other lands did Cortés explore?

Cortés, De Soto, De Leon, and Coronado, the Spanish Explorers

Worksheet, Page 2

6. Who discovered the Mississippi River?

___

___

___

7. Who was the first explorer to see the Grand Canyon? What else did he explore?

___

___

___

___

8. Who sailed to Florida in 1513? For what was he searching?

___

___

___

Cortés, de Soto, de Leon, and Coronado, The Spanish Explorers

Project 1—The Lives of the Spanish Explorers

Read the following account and discuss the questions at the end.

Cortés, the Conqueror

Among the millions of people who wondered at the strange stories of the new lands discovered by Columbus was Hernando, a seven-year-old son of a Spanish noble family named Cortés. His young mind was filled with longing for adventure. As soon as he was old enough, Hernando left home to seek his fortune on the island of Santo Domingo in the new world. The governor of this island was pleased with the manner, pluck, and energy of Cortés, and he offered to sell him a large estate on easy terms. But the young Spaniard answered haughtily, "I did not come here to plow fields, I came to get gold."

It was not long before young Cortés saw a chance for adventure. He went with a Spanish governor to settle the island of Cuba. He soon became a favorite of this governor also. An adventurer returned from part of the mainland now called Central America and Mexico with tales of the great wealth of the people called Aztecs, and of the gold mines there.

The governor of Cuba decided to send ships and men to conquer that country and offered the command to Cortés, who worked like a hero to get ready for the campaign. He equipped eleven vessels with six hundred men. A hundred or more of these were sailors and workmen, and the rest were soldiers, some of whom were armed with muskets and some with crossbows. There were fourteen small cannon and sixteen horses in the outfit.

As Cortés was about to sail, the governor of Cuba changed his mind and sent an order to Havana giving the command of the expedition to another officer. But shrewd, young Cortés got wind of this in time and sailed away before the governor's messengers arrived.

The soldiers and other men in the expedition agreed to stand by the brave leader and capture the new country for King Charles of Spain in their name instead of the Cuban governor's. This is exactly what the governor feared Cortés would try to do.

When the Spaniards landed on the continent, the natives were afraid. They had never seen a horse, and they thought the men on horseback were monster human beings with four legs, half man and half horse. Yet they bravely came out of their hiding places to do battle with such frightful invaders. The Spaniards fired a cannon volley and shot their muskets so that several Indians fell dead. "They are gods!" shouted the natives in deadly fear. "They have lightning and thunder in their hands!" It did not take long for Cortés to make terms with these natives, some of whom became allies and interpreters for the Spaniards.

After founding a city at the coast, which he named Villa Rica de la Vera Cruz (Rich City of the True Cross), now called Vera

Cortés, de Soto, de Leon, and Coronado, The Spanish Explorers

Project 1, Page 2

Cruz, Cortés prepared to conquer the empire of the Aztecs with six hundred Spaniards and several thousand Mexican Indians. Montezuma, emperor of the Aztecs, heard of his coming and tried to make him leave the country by sending rich presents from his capital in the mountains. But that did not stop Cortés.

In order to insure victory, the Spanish general committed a brave, though desperate, act. Choosing one ship from his fleet, he manned it and sent a trusted officer back to Spain—not Cuba—with some of Montezuma's presents. With these, Cortés sent other proofs of the wealth of the country which he was about to conquer and add to the empire of King Charles of Spain. After taking from the other ten ships everything the Spaniards could use in the new country, Cortés ordered those vessels burned and sunk.

Thus, having burned their bridges behind them, they had no way of escape but to go forward and fight for their fortunes, their country, and their very lives.

On the march of two hundred miles to Montezuma's capital, the Spaniards beat the Tlascalans in battle and became allies with them against the Aztec tyrant (as the Indians called Emperor Montezuma).

The Indians of the hot countries of America were not so savage as those who lived in the northern parts of the continent, but they had a terrible religious rite which they had learned from the Aztecs. They offered human lives to appease the sun god. Though the Aztecs were a peaceable people otherwise, they often went to war to take prisoners for these terrible sacrifices.

Cortés broke into a temple at one place on the way and murdered the priests who were killing and offering human beings to the sun god. He set up a cross and invited people to become Christians or be killed. In this way he gained many converts from among the frightened Indians.

With Hernando Cortés, this kind of conversion was but a step toward gaining gold and power for himself and for the King of Spain. After many terrible battles, in which he massacred the helpless natives by the thousands, he and his few hundred white men, along with thousands of Indian allies, reached the capital of Montezuma. Built of stone on an island in the midst of a beautiful lake, this civilized city was connected with the mainland by six long stone bridges or causeways. The splendid capital, with its palaces and temples of hewn stone, had much of the beauty of Venice. The city measured twelve miles around. It was then hundreds of years old and proved that the ancient Aztecs knew how to build great stone houses and bridges.

Montezuma, borne on a golden throne on the shoulders of Aztec nobles and officials, came out to meet Cortés. He wore priceless

Cortés, de Soto, de Leon, and Coronado, The Spanish Explorers

Project 1, Page 3

feathers, and his garments were embroidered with many-colored gems. Even his shoes were gold. His courtiers carried carpets to lay down before him, so that his sacred feet should not touch the ground. How the eyes of those greedy Spaniards glittered when they beheld such signs of the great wealth of Montezuma and his people!

The white men were received with great honor. They were served in golden goblets with a strange, rich drink which the Aztecs named cacao. This delicious drink is now called chocolate or cocoa. Montezuma told the Spaniards that their coming had been foretold by the priests for hundreds of years, ever since the visit of a pure white man, a son of the Sun who had come down from the skies. This sun-god had told the Aztecs that he would come again with other sun-gods and reign over the empire forever.

Cortés pretended to be the long-expected "fair god" of the Aztecs, and persuaded Montezuma to visit him in the palace assigned to the Spanish leader and his officers during their stay in the city. The people, who had no reason to believe in the Spanish soldiers, crowded around the sedan chair of their king, crying out against him because he was placing himself in the wicked hands of strangers. Montezuma told them not to fear, for their guests were honorable men and he was sure that all would be well with him. But he soon found that he was not a guest but a prisoner, betrayed by

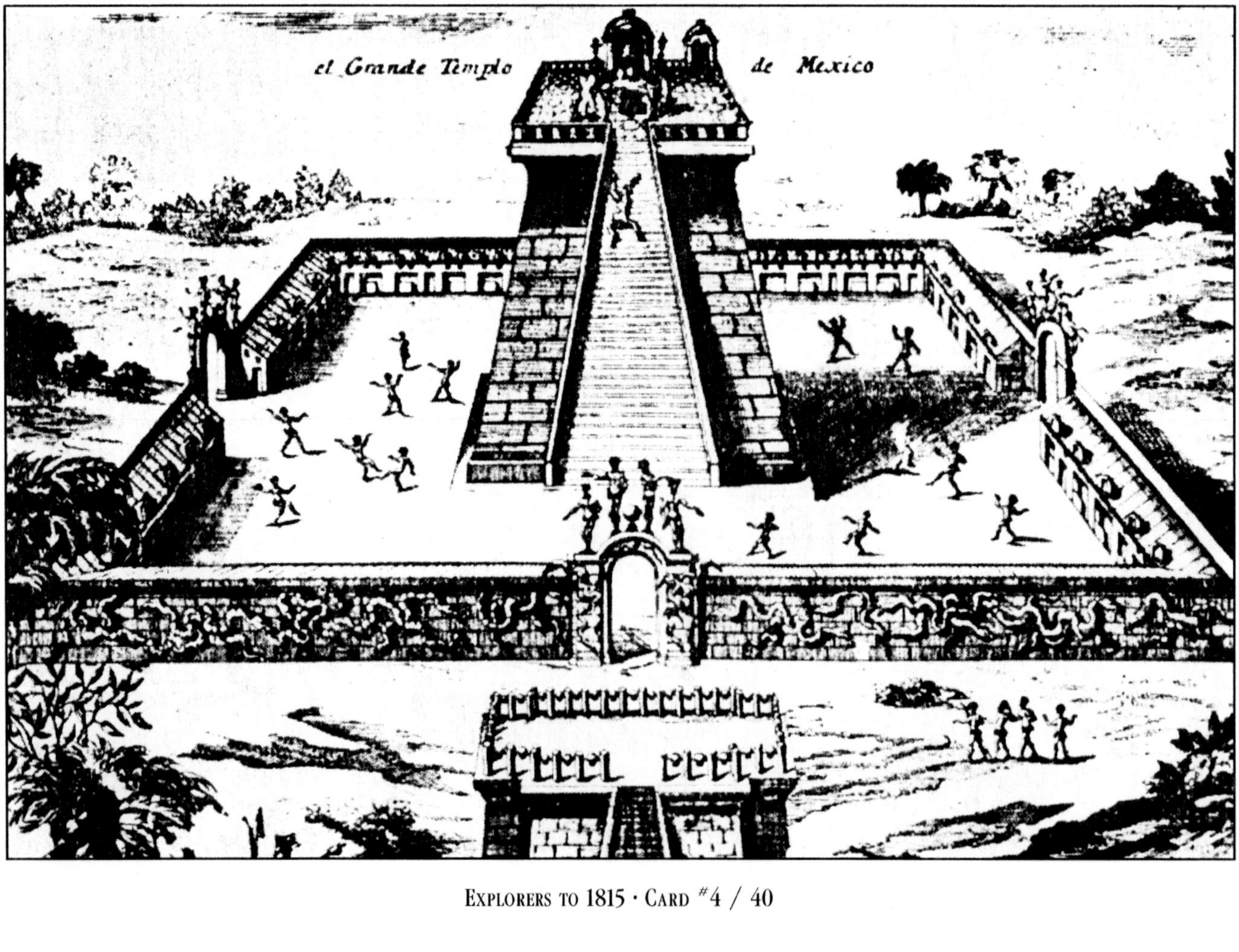

Cortés, de Soto, de Leon, and Coronado, The Spanish Explorers

Project 1, Page 4

a presence of friendship. The Aztecs came again and attacked the palace which Cortés and his men had now turned into a fortress. During the months when the Spaniards held Montezuma as a prisoner, a fierce war was waged with the Aztecs.

While Cortés and his army were in such desperate straits, word came that the governor of Cuba had sent ships and nearly a thousand men to bring the general and his followers back, to be punished as deserters. Cortés and a select band crept out of the capital one dark night, marched hundreds of miles to the coast, and surprised and defeated the army the governor had sent. Then Cortés returned, with all those armed men and many more cannon and horses, to relieve the small garrison he had left to hold the many thousands of Aztecs at bay, and to capture the city of Mexico.

The Aztecs were frightened when they saw the thousand soldiers Cortés now brought up against them, for it looked as if the new troops had come down from the skies to help the Spaniards. When the battle was fiercest, the broken-spirited emperor went out to plead with the natives to stop their fighting. This made them so angry that they hurled stones at him and he died of a broken heart. The hatred of his own people was even harder to bear than Spanish cruelty.

After more fierce fighting, Cortés completed the conquest of Mexico. Years afterward he returned to his old home in Spain, where he was, for a time, treated like a great conqueror. But he suffered in later years from remorse for his treachery and cruelty. When he grew old he was imprisoned through the influence of Spanish enemies.

One day an old, broken man with shaggy gray locks pushed through the crowd around King Charles of Spain, now known as Emperor Charles the Fifth, the most powerful monarch in the world. When the emperor asked the old man who he was, he replied with indignant pride, "I am Cortés, the man who has given you more provinces than your ancestors left you cities."

de Soto, A Gold Hunter in the Southern States

Hernando de Soto was the Spanish grandee, or noble, appointed governor of Cuba and "the Floridas" about twenty-five years after Florida was discovered. It was Ponce de Leon who landed near the southern point of North America on Easter Day 1513 and named that lovely country Florida—Land of Flowers. De Leon had heard a beautiful story that far inland in the heart of the wilderness there was a magic spring that would make young forever all who drank of its sparkling waters. Though he searched long and eagerly, Ponce de Leon discovered no Fountain of Eternal Youth, but he did find endless swamps full of snakes and alligators.

De Soto, the new governor of Florida, made up his mind that Ponce de Leon was a very foolish old man. He ought to have known that there are no such things nowadays as springs of eternal youth. He, Hernando de Soto, was going to show his practical good sense by finding solid, yellow gold—for what good is youth without money to enjoy it with? De Soto was already a very rich man, for he had served under Pizarro, the cruel conqueror of Peru. He had gone home to Spain one of the wealthiest of its grandees in those days of wonderful discoveries and marvelous fortunes. Still Hernando de Soto was not satisfied. He

Cortés, de Soto, de Leon, and Coronado, The Spanish Explorers

Project 1, Page 5

wanted to be like Pizarro or Cortés—to conquer a great country and capture gold mines and vast wealth from its dusky people.

Therefore, on a bright July day, he left Cuba in charge of a high official and sailed away. He and his knights in armor stood on the decks of their nine ships, large and small, and waved farewells to the fair ladies who stood on the castle tower at Havana weeping bitterly, fearing that they would never see their brave lords and knights again.

Governor de Soto and his fleet came to anchor in the harbor now known as Tampa Bay. During the night they were aroused by horrible yells and showers of arrows from the shore. In the morning the Spaniards made a landing, though the natives fought hard to keep them back. Before night they met a man who could be of great use to them. He was a member of a party that, after De Leon's discovery, had gone to Florida to find gold, but had been driven back. This young man, Juan Ortiz, had been captured and kept by the Indians as a slave. A member of De Soto's scouting party tells how they met this poor fellow: "Towards sunset it pleased God that the soldiers described at a distance some twenty Indians painted with a kind of red ointment that they put on when they go to war. They wore many feathers and had their bows and arrows. And when the Christians ran at them, the Indians fled to a hill, and one of them came forth into the path, lifting up his voice and saying in Spanish, "Sirs, for the love of God, slay not me! For I am a Christian like yourselves. I was born in Seville, and my name is Juan Ortiz."

The Spanish governor received Ortiz as if he were his own long-lost son. He made himself very useful because he knew both the Spanish and Indian language, thus he could help the Spaniards talk to the natives.

De Soto now started inland leading a brilliant company of knights and private soldiers, all in bright armor. Over the shining helmets were waving plumes, and many a mailed fist held aloft a rich and beautiful banner. There were hundreds of horsemen and many more men marching on foot. No more richly dressed men and horses ever started out on a crusade to regain possession of the Holy City. But the object of this Spanish quest was gold. Spanish serving men drove along this rich and gay procession four hundred fat hogs. De Soto decided not to risk being starved to death as so many explorers had been. And gamekeepers held in leash, not falcons to catch and kill birds or beasts, but bloodhounds for hunting Indians.

Instead of mountains of rock from which gold could be mined, De Soto's men found swamps. The weather was sultry and moist. Insects got inside their knightly armor and stung them to madness, and venomous serpents coiled around their armored legs. Indians shot poisoned arrows at them from the bushes. Their coats of mail were so heavy that stout knights sank deep into the bogs. They advanced very slowly; they wallowed rather than marched, and their days and nights were spent in weariness and torture.

The fame of the white men went on ahead of them. As De Soto advanced he found the savages on the warpath ready to drive back the invaders. All along their line of march they could hear savage threats in the distance. Juan Ortiz told the Spaniards that the Indians were shouting: "Keep on, robbers and murderers! In Apalachee you will get what you deserve. No mercy will be shown to captives, who will be hung on the highest trees along the trail."

After the Spaniards had marched

Cortés, de Soto, de Leon, and Coronado, The Spanish Explorers

Project 1, Page 6

through the lands of five different chiefs, they found a great chieftain who seemed to wish to make friends with the white men. De Soto gladly accepted, but Juan Ortiz warned him to look out for treachery. The white men were secretly prepared. When the traitor chief gave the signal for his men to attack, the Spaniards raised their battle cry "Santiago" and thousands of savages were killed by a few hundred Spaniards.

Hundreds of Indians took refuge in a lake. Their five good swimmers would lie side by side on the surface like logs, forming a human raft on which the best archer would stand and shoot back at the white men. The fight lasted all day and nearly all night. Before morning all the Indians were killed, captured or put in chains, and divided among the Spaniards as slaves.

The Indians, who at first thought the white men were gods, were now sure they were devils. The boasted village of Apalachee was only a few straw huts on a knoll in the center of a great swamp. And the savages who defended it with bows and arrows were no match for armed Spaniards; the white men killed nearly all of them.

Cold weather came on, and the Spaniards went into winter quarters. A beautiful Indian girl-chief in that region came bringing pearls and gems to De Soto. But he demanded gold. When she understood this she sent men to a far country for the yellow metal he desired so eagerly. De Soto and his men now rejoiced, for they thought they had found the object of their long and painful search. When the red messengers returned the stuff proved not to be gold. It must have been copper ore or "fool's gold."

During the second year of their long march, the Spaniards were led southward to Mabila, which is believed to have stood on the shore of Mobile Bay. This was a huge fortress, the greatest native town the white men had

Cortés, de Soto, de Leon, and Coronado, The Spanish Explorers

Project 1, Page 7

yet seen. Within an immense stockade, or wall of trees on end, stood a number of houses of which would hold hundreds of Indians.

Tuscaloosa, the Mobile chief, set a trap for the Spaniards. The battle which took place here was the worst of all. The Spaniards lost seventy men and forty horses. Then they set fire to the Indians' houses, and the savages perished in the flames.

De Soto's men were heartily sick of fighting. They also despaired of finding gold in the southern swamps. The governor heard that they were plotting to desert him at Mabila and return by boat to Havana. So, instead of waiting for a ship to come from Cuba, he ordered them to march farther into the wilderness. As the prospect of finding gold became more desperate, De Soto seemed to grow more cruel. Indians were beheaded for small offenses; friendly scouts were tortured and sent back with insulting messages to their chiefs.

The farther west the Spaniards went the more bitterly the natives fought and the more successful they were in battle. In one place the Indians burned nearly all the Spaniards' hogs and feasted on roast pork for many days. After terrible wanderings, the few remaining Spaniards came to a wide stream at Chickasaw Bluff, a few miles above the present city of Vicksburg.

Though it is often stated that De Soto discovered the Mississippi, he may not have been the first to see that wide and muddy stream. As he wandered up and down its banks he contracted malarial fever and died miserably. Faithful friends put his body in heavy armor and wrapped that in blankets weighted with sand. Then, on a dark night, they paddled out into the middle of the stream and sank it in a hundred feet of water, where the Indians could not find it and wreak their revenge upon De Soto's remains. His followers attempted to go farther west but became discouraged and descended the Mississippi to the Gulf of Mexico.

Discussion

1. What seems to be the main reason these men risked their lives to explore new territories?
2. How did Cortés cause the Indians to become Christians? Is this method of evangelism biblical?
3. What were the conditions like in the area (now known as Florida) explored by De Soto and his men at that time?

Cortés, De Soto, De Leon, and Coronado
The Spanish Explorers

Project 2–Comparing the Spanish Explorers

Fill in the blanks below with information about the Spanish Explorers using the card and the reading project.

Who:				
What:				
Where:				
Why:				

Cortés, De Soto, De Leon, and Coronado, the Spanish Explorers

Project 3—Gold Masks

The Spanish found gold masks and other valuable items in South America. Consequently, many explorers wanted to look elsewhere for gold in South America. One explorer was Hernando Cortés, who conquered the great Aztec empire.

Below you will find directions to make a mask like those found by the Spanish.

Supplies

one twelve-inch cardboard cake plate (found at a craft supply store)

three nine-inch cardboard cakes plates per mask.

air drying clay

glue sticks, glue gun

fun foam

gold spray paint

scissors

Directions

1. Glue the three nine-inch plates one on top of the other.
2. Glue the nine-inch plates in the center of the twelve-inch plates.
3. Cut out designs from the fun foam and glue them onto the visible portion of the twelve-inch plate.
4. Using clay, form eyes, a nose, and a mouth and glue them on the nine-inch plate.
5. After glue has dried, spray all with gold spray paint.

Cortés, De Soto, De Leon, and Coronado, the Spanish Explorers

Project 4—De Soto and Coronado's Route

Trace De Soto's route (beginning in present-day Florida) through the southeast in blue and Coronado's western route (beginning along the west coast of present-day Mexico) in red.

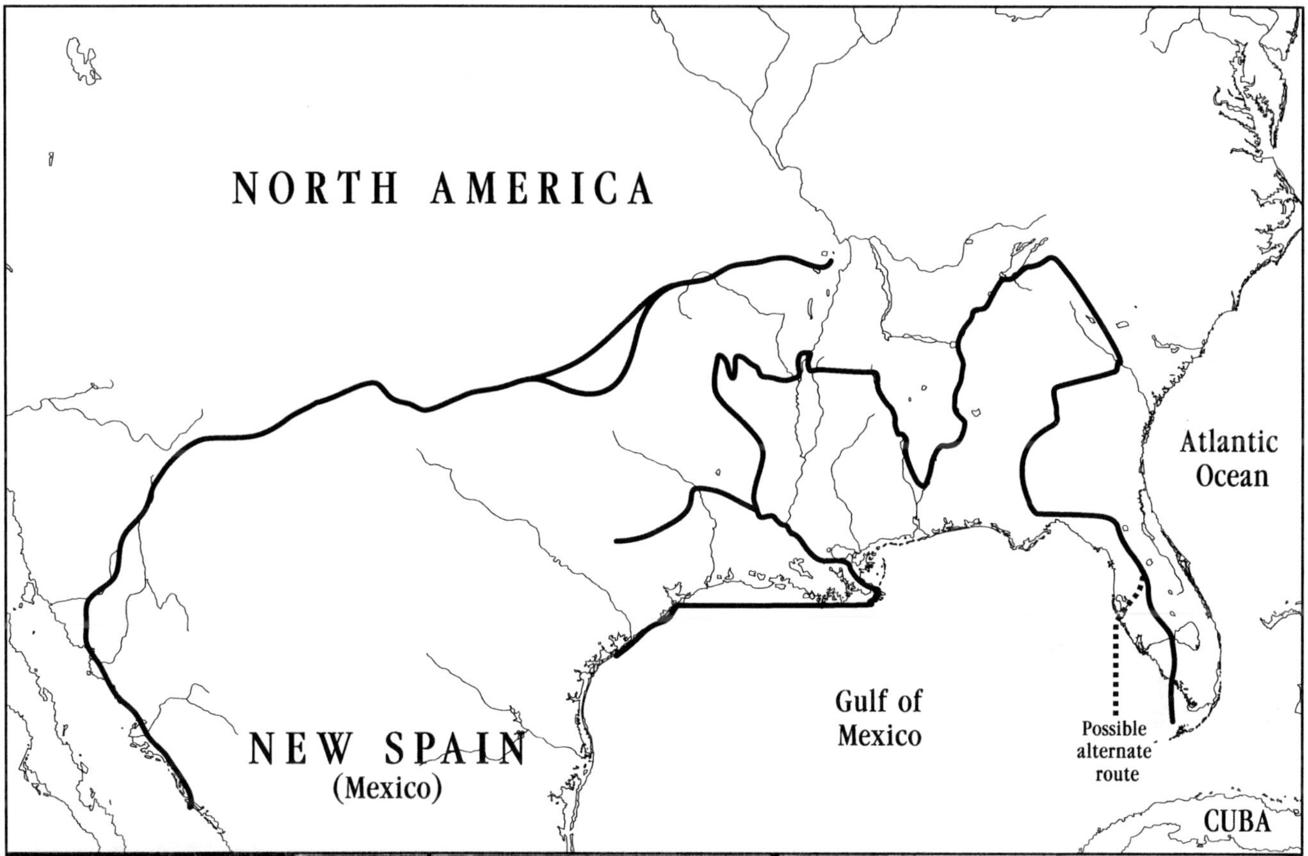

Detail of *Discovery of the Mississippi* by William H. Powell. This painting of de Soto's famous exploration hangs in the U.S. Capitol rotunda.

Cortés, De Soto, De Leon, and Coronado, the Spanish Explorers

Test

1. What name was given to the 1500's because of the Spanish explorers?

2. What lands had Spain conquered in the hundred years following Columbus's first voyage?

3. Who conquered the great Aztec empire? What else did he go on to explore?

4. What did Hernando De Soto discover?

5. Who was the first explorer to see the Grand Canyon? What else did he explore?

6. Where did Ponce De Leon explore? For what was he searching?

Review

1. Where was Prince Henry born? What did he establish?

Cortés, De Soto, De Leon, and Coronado, the Spanish Explorers

Test, Page 2

2. Define cartography.

3. Where did Columbus land on his voyage in 1492? Where did he think he was?

4. What did Columbus believe God had called him to do?

5. What famous voyage did Magellan command?

6. In chronological order list all events studied to date. Next to each place the appropriate date.

Explorers of the Northeast: Cartier, Champlain, and Cabot

Worksheet

1. Who was the first European to reach the coast of North America after the end of Leif Ericson's colonies?

2. Where did the above explorer believe he had reached?

3. Who was Jacques Cartier? What did he investigate?

4. Who was Samuel de Champlain? What did he investigate? What did he discover?

5. What are the dates of the Explorers of the Northeast?

EXPLORERS OF THE NORTHEAST: CARTIER, CHAMPLAIN, AND CABOT

Project 1–John Cabot Discovers North America

Read the following account and discuss the questions at the end.

A DARING SEA CAPTAIN

John Cabot, like Columbus, was born in Genoa, Italy. For all we know, he and Columbus may have been schoolboys together at the same school. At about the time that Columbus was first telling his plans to the king of Portugal, Cabot was living in Venice. He was a merchant and a sea captain. His ships sailed to the ports at the farther end of the Mediterranean Sea and brought back goods from Syria and other distant lands.

Once when he was in one of these ports, he saw a long train of camels that had just arrived from Arabia. The animals were loaded with rich spices which they had brought across the desserts.

"Where did those spices come from?" asked Cabot.

"They came from India," was the answer, "and they have been many months on the way."

This set Cabot to thinking. Was there not some easier and shorter route by which the merchandise of India could be brought to Europe? Columbus and the king of Portugal were trying to solve the same question.

About two years before Columbus made his first voyage, John Cabot left Venice and went with his family to England. He settled in Bristol, which was then the most important of all English seaports. Ships from Bristol often went on long voyages to Norway and Iceland, and some even sailed to Spain and the Mediterranean Sea.

Cabot soon became known as the most daring of all the merchant captains of Bristol. Within twelve months after settling at that port, he sent some ships far out into the Atlantic to search for an island which was said to lie somewhere southwest of Ireland. This was a year before Columbus sailed from Spain. Cabot's ships ventured farther out into the ocean than any others had gone, but they did not discover any land.

When the news was told in England that Columbus really had sailed across the Atlantic and had reached what he believed to be India, the merchants and sailors of Bristol were greatly excited. John Cabot resolved that he would also discover new lands; and King Henry of England very graciously gave him leave "to sail to the east, west, or north, with five ships carrying the English flag, to seek and discover all the islands, countries, regions, or provinces of pagans in whatever part of the world." He was not to sail south lest he should make trouble with Spain.

One thing and then another delayed him. It was not until four years after the return of Columbus from his first voyage that Cabot was ready to sail. He had but one ship, called the *Matthew.* With him went his son

Explorers of the Northeast: Cartier, Champlain, and Cabot

Project 1, Page 2

Sebastian, a young man probably not more than twenty years of age. It was early in May when he sailed from Bristol, and his course was straight west, across the Atlantic.

North America Discovered

The sea was rough and the voyage was tedious and long, but at the end of six weeks a strange, rocky coast was discovered. It was a part of North America. Although the season was almost midsummer, the shore seemed bare and desolate. The *Matthew* sailed along within sight of it for nearly nine hundred miles. Cabot landed now and then and took possession of the country in the name of the king of England. But he found no such beautiful and interesting things as Columbus had discovered farther south. At length he caused the *Matthew* to be turned about, and before the end of July the little vessel and its crew were safe home in Bristol Harbor. Columbus was just then preparing to make his third voyage.

Cabot hastened to London and reported to the king that he had discovered the coast of China. Henry was so highly pleased that he gave the brave captain a present of considerable value in gold, and settled a pension on him for the rest of his life. Cabot himself was the hero of the hour. He dressed himself in silk robes, and was called the Grand Admiral of England; and whenever he walked out in Bristol or London the people ran after him in crowds, like madmen.

Cabot started on another voyage. He believed that if he should sail a little farther south than before, he would discover the rich island of Cipango, or Japan, about which many wonderful stories were afloat. He followed the eastern coast of our country from Maine to Cape Cod and perhaps much farther. But he saw no signs of the wealth and splendor which were said to exist in Japan and India. There were neither cities nor towns nor orchards nor fields. Everywhere there were dense woods, in which wild animals and a few savage men had their homes.

It was not a very promising country, but Cabot, as on his former voyage, took possession of the coast for his master, the king of England. It was this that gave England, in later years, the right to claim the larger part of North America as her own.

Just when Cabot's ship returned to Bristol from his second voyage, we do not know. Indeed, it is supposed by some that he himself died before reaching home, for we do not hear of him again. His son Sebastian became the greatest sea captain of his time, and was for several years in the service of the king of Spain. But it was a long, long time before English ships again visited the wild and wooded shores of North America.

Discussion

1. Name two Italians who had much to do with the discovery of our country.
2. Why was John Cabot so deeply interested in discovering a short way to India?
3. Who saw the mainland of America first, Cabot or Columbus?
4. What countries did Cabot hope to discover?
5. Why was he not better pleased with his discoveries?
6. What claim did England make on account of his discoveries?
7. What was the name of John Cabot's son?
8. What did he become?

Explorers of the Northeast: Cartier, Champlain, and Cabot

Project 2–Model of the Matthew

Follow the directions below to make a tasty model of Cabot's ship, the Matthew*—after you're finished eating the banana split!*

Supplies

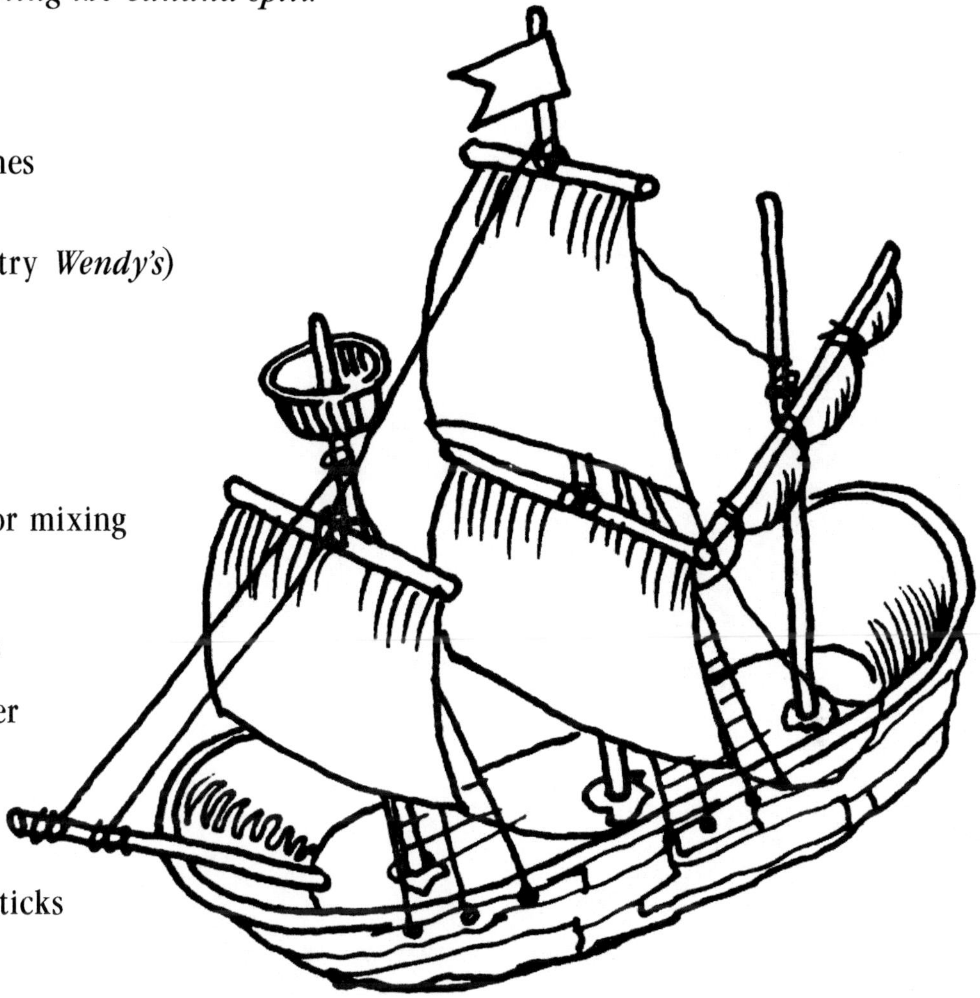

plastic banana split dishes (try *Dairy Queen*)

paper condiment cups (try *Wendy's*)

newspaper

flour

water

large bowl and spoon for mixing

twine

paint and paint brushes

white construction paper

markers

scissors

1/4" wooden dowel or sticks

glue gun

Directions

1. Tear newspaper into 1" x 3" strips. Mix one cup flour to one cup water in bowl (or expand as needed). Dip newspaper strips into flour mixture and cover banana split bowl with wet strips. Apply three layers. Allow to dry.
2. Paint boat and allow to dry.
3. Use glue gun to glue mast in place. Cut sails from construction paper and glue them to mast. Use condiment cup to make a crow's nest. Use twine to create rigging.

Explorers of the Northeast: Cartier, Champlain, and Cabot

Project 3—Journey of Cartier and Champlain

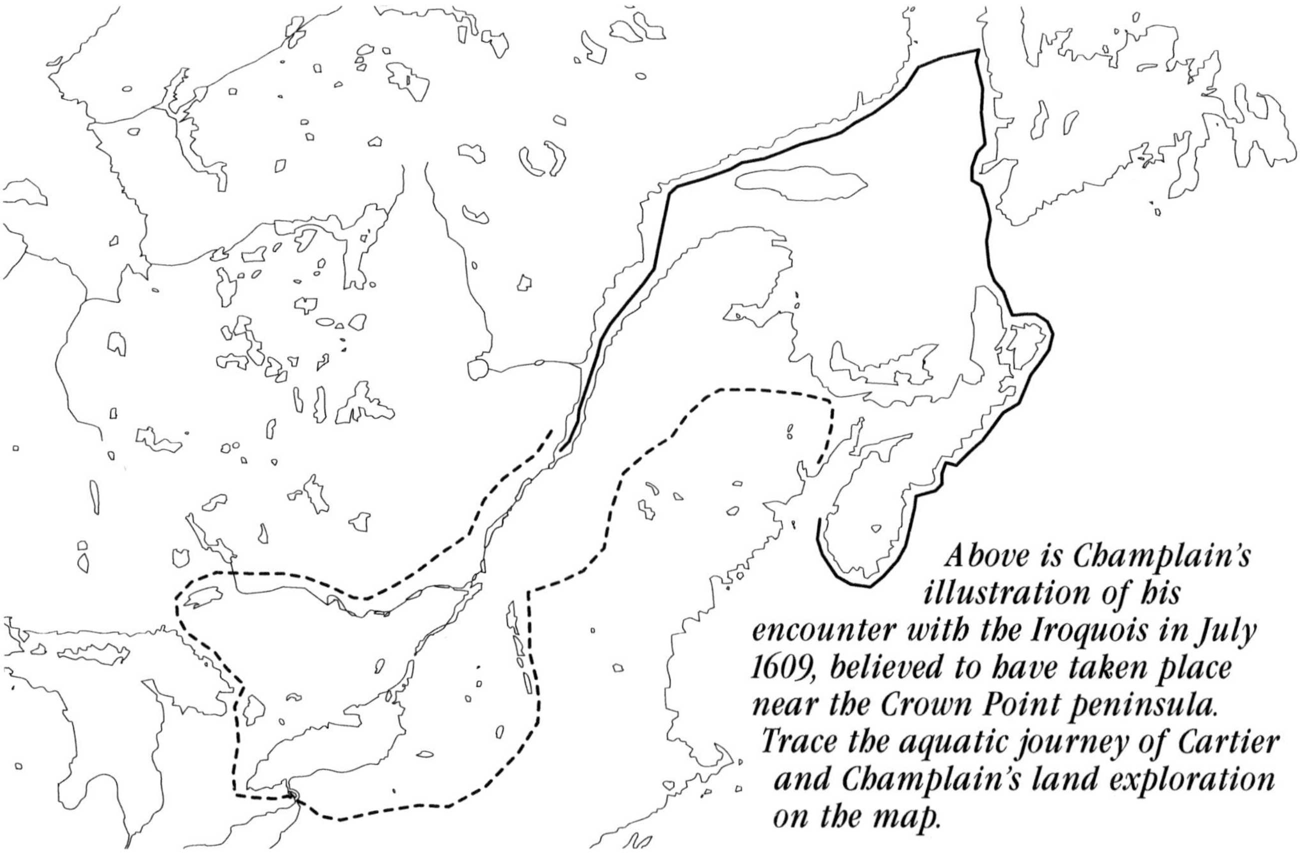

Above is Champlain's illustration of his encounter with the Iroquois in July 1609, believed to have taken place near the Crown Point peninsula. Trace the aquatic journey of Cartier and Champlain's land exploration on the map.

Explorers of the Northeast: Cartier, Champlain, and Cabot

Test

1. From what country was John Cabot? What did he accomplish?

2. Where did John Cabot believe he had landed?

3. What did Jacques Cartier explore?

4. What did Champlain found? What did he discover?

5. What are the dates of the Northeast Explorers?

Review

1. How did Prince Henry take the lead in opening the African trade route to Asia?

Explorers of the Northeast: Cartier, Champlain, and Cabot

Test, Page 2

2. Name the three ships that sailed with Columbus on his voyage in 1492?

___

___

___

3. What was Magellan's major accomplishment?

___

___

___

4. Name the Spanish explorer who conquered the great Aztec Empire.

___

___

5. In chronological order list all events studied to date. Next to each place the appropriate date.

___

___

___

___

___

Raleigh Settles Roanoke

Worksheet

1. Who sent 108 men from England to settle what was then known as Virginia?

2. When was Roanoke settled?

3. Why did Raleigh want to settle this land?

4. Who was the first English child born in America?
   Where was she born?

5. When John White arrived in Roanoke in 1590, what did he find?

6. Why is Roanoke called the "Lost Colony"?

7. Who were the Croatans?

Raleigh Settles Roanoke

Project 1—Life of Walter Raleigh

After completing the reading below, discuss the questions at the end. Then write a letter on the following page pretending to be a colonist in Roanoke writing home to a family member in England describing your hardships and daily routine.

Raleigh as a Boy and Soldier

One of the foremost Englishmen that lived in the time of Drake and Hawkins was Walter Raleigh. He was born in 1552 in a seacoast town in southern England, and he belonged to a family of high social rank. He was a handsome lad of high spirits and fond of all sorts of outdoor life.

But he was especially interested in stories of adventure as they were told by old sailors of his time. One of these sailors, Sir Humphry Gilbert, was a famous explorer. He told about his own adventures, and also, perhaps, about the daring voyages of Hawkins and Drake. These stories stirred the imagination of the active, restless boy.

We know little about his early years, but we are told that he went to the University of Oxford, possibly when only fourteen years of age, and he remained there three years.

But the world of action attracted him more than the quiet life of college. So without waiting to finish his course at Oxford, he went to France and joined the Huguenot army, who were fighting their fellow countrymen, the Catholic party in France. There he remained about six years and then went to Holland to join the Dutch, who were at war with Spain. In this ceaseless campaigning, he mastered the art of war and at the same time learned, like Drake, to hate Spain. During the remainder of his life he did all he could to humble the power of this haughty nation.

In 1578 he joined his half-brother, Sir Humphrey Gilbert, in an expedition to Newfoundland. There they hoped to plant a colony and then to sail and discover the northwest passage to China. But having put to sea, they were attacked by Spaniards, and after the loss of one of their ships and damage to others, they were obliged to return home.

After the failure of this expedition, Raleigh, put in command of a hundred men, went to Ireland to fight against a rebellion there. Here, too, he distinguished himself as a brave soldier.

On his return from Ireland, Raleigh, who was now about twenty-seven years of age, had an opportunity to show a marked courtesy to Queen Elizabeth. One day, as the Queen with her attendants was about to cross a muddy road, Raleigh chanced to be standing nearby. On seeing the Queen hesitate, he took from his shoulders his beautiful velvet cloak and spread it across the way for her Majesty to walk upon. This act of gallantry at once insured the friendship of the Queen. Raleigh soon became one of her greatest favorites.

In appearance he had much to recom-

Raleigh Settles Roanoke

Project 1, Page 2

mend him. He was tall, of shapely figure and handsome features, with dark hair and a high color, and eyes that were expressive and piercing. In conversation he was brilliant and witty, and his dress at court was rich and splendid.

Some of his clothing is described to us. On his hat he wore a pearl-covered band and a black jeweled feather. His shoes, which were tied with white ribbons, were ornamented with jewels worth six hundred pieces of gold. On some occasions he wore a suit of armor made of silver. It was quite the fashion in those days for rich men, as well as women, to dress in this gorgeous manner. Queen Elizabeth herself owned ten hundred and seventy five dresses decked with jewels of great value, and eighty wigs of various colors.

You can easily believe that Raleigh was a very rich man. The Queen made him rich because she was fond of him. She gave him large estates and offices of trust that paid him large sums of money. She also gave him permission to control the sale of special articles of trade; for instance, broadcloth and wines, in order that he might further enrich himself.

Raleigh's Wish to Plant a Colony in America

Although so lavishly supplied, Raleigh did not spend his money altogether foolishly. As a rule he knew how to apply it to good purposes. As the story goes on, you will find that we today owe him much for the attempts he made to establish an English colony in this country. In order to carry out this plan, which was very near his heart, he got permission from the Queen to make discoveries and to take possession of lands not already occupied by any Christian prince. He wished to plant a colony in the country north of Florida. England claimed this land because the Cabots were the first men to discover the mainland of North America.

Before Raleigh's time efforts had been made to settle it, but they were unsuccessful. Now, in 1584, Raleigh fitted out two vessels which he sent over to the New World to find out something about the country. The men in charge of these two vessels brought back to Raleigh as products of the expedition two Indians, some skins of wild animals, and a string of pearls that were as big as large peas. They said they found the Indians in this country friendly and the country itself beautiful. Altogether, they gave so glowing an account of the land they had seen that Queen Elizabeth said it should be called Virginia, in honor of herself, the Virgin Queen.

Raleigh's First Colony

The next year Raleigh sent out a colony of one hundred eight persons. Sir Richard Grenville was the commander of the fleet, and Ralph Lane was the governor of the colony. They landed at Roanoke Island.

This colony met with great misfortunes. They treated the Indians harshly and soon got their ill-will. The story is told that when an Indian stole a silver cup from the colonists, they punished the tribe by burning not only their corn, but the entire Indian village. Such cruelty, of course, made the Indians hate the white man.

Raleigh Settles Roanoke

Project 1, Page 3

But the ill-will of the natives was not the only trouble the colonists had. Provisions ran short, and Grenville sailed to England for more.

During his absence, Lane started out to explore the Roanoke River, of which he had heard wonderful takes from the Indians. They said that this stream flowed through a land rich with minerals, and that its waters came out of a fountain so near the South Sea that in time of storm the waves broke over into the fountain. They also said that near this stream was a town with walls made of pearls.

But Lane and the men who went with him found no such fountain; they found no such town. On the contrary, they suffered great hardships, and suffered so much for want of food that they had to eat dog meat to keep from starving. When Lane returned, everybody felt discouraged, and the future looked gloomy enough. But at this time, Drake, who was on his way to England with a large fleet, arrived and anchored near Roanoke Island. On hearing the condition of the colonists, he offered to leave a part of his fleet with provisions. But when a heavy storm came up, all the colonists decided that they had wishes to return to England.

Drake took them all aboard, and they sailed for home. They had found no gold, but they carried to England something that had quite as much value as gold or precious stones—tobacco, white potatoes, and Indian corn. An amusing incident is told in connection with the early use of tobacco in England. Raleigh himself was the first to learn to smoke. He procured for himself a pipe of silver shaped like the pipes used by the Indians. One day, shortly after he had begun to smoke, a servant came into his room. Seeing the smoke coming from his master's mouth, the man supposed Raleigh was on fire and, hastily approaching, threw a tankard of ale into his face.

But long before this first cargo of tobacco and other products had arrived in England, in fact only two or three weeks after it had left Roanoke with Drake, Grenville returned with provisions. Finding the island deserted, he left fifteen men, and he himself returned to England.

Raleigh's Second Colony

In 1587 a second colony, under Captain John White, sailed from England for Roanoke. This colony contained one hundred fifty men, seventeen women, and eleven children. Raleigh himself wished to join this colony, but the Queen would not allow him to leave her court. He directed that the colonists should make a settlement at Chesapeake Bay, after first landing at

Raleigh Settles Roanoke

Project 1, Page 4

Roanoke Island to find the fifteen men left there by Grenville. The company landed at Roanoke but could not find the men.

After staying there awhile the sailors refused to sail to the Chesapeake, because the summer was far spent. The colonists were therefore obliged to remain on Roanoke Island.

Like the first colony, they were harsh in their treatment of the Indians and began to have trouble with them. Very soon, too, their provisions began to fail, and they begged Captain White to go to England for fresh supplies.

Unwillingly, he consented, for he did not like to leave the colonists, nor did he wish to separate himself from his little granddaughter, Virginia Dare, who was the first white child born in the New World.

He reached home just as his countrymen were preparing to meet the great Spanish fleet that was coming to attack England. The fleet was called the Spanish Armada. For her defense England needed all the ships that her seamen could muster. The fleet, therefore, which Raleigh had fitted out for the colony had to remain at home.

It was almost three years before Captain White could return to Roanoke. He sailed, then, not on his own vessel, but as a passenger on a merchant-ship bound for the West Indies. When he reached Roanoke, the only traces he could discover of the missing colonists were some chests of books and some maps.

When Captain White had gone to England three years before, the colonists had agreed that if they should leave the place for any reason, they would cut in to the bark of a tree the name of the place to which they were going. If they were in distress they would cut a cross above the name.

Captain White found "Croatoan" cut in a tree in capital letters, but he found no cross. Now, Croatoan is the name of an island near Roanoke. White therefore urged the captain of the vessel to carry him to this island. But as the weather had become stormy, the captain refused to sail farther.

What became of the lost colony no one has ever learned. Years after, however, it was discovered that four men, two boys, and one girl had been adopted into an Indian tribe. The rest of the colonists were probably killed by the Indians. Raleigh sent out five expeditions in search of his lost colony, but without success. It was his strong desire to make a new England in America. It was the great purpose of his life. In his attempts to plant a colony in the New World he spent a sum that would equal millions of dollars.

Discussion

1. What were some of the early adventures of Walter Raleigh?
2. What act of gallantry insured friendship with the Queen of England?
3. Describe Raleigh's appearance.
4. What happened to the first colony on Roanoke Island?
5. What happened to the second colony on Roanoke Island?
6. What behavior may have contributed to the colonists hardships?

Raleigh Settles Roanoke

Project 1, Page 5

Raleigh Settles Roanoke

Test

1. How many men did Sir Walter Raleigh send from England to settle what was then known as Virginia? Why did Raleigh do this?

2. In what year was Roanoke settled?

3. Who was the first English child born in America? Where was the child born?

4. When John White arrived at the colony in 1590, what did he find?

5. What is another name the colony of Roanoke has been given?

6. Who were the Croatans?

Review

1. What is cartography?

Raleigh Settles Roanoke

Test, Page 2

2. On how many voyages did Prince Henry the Navigator travel?

___

___

3. In what year did Columbus land off the coast of Florida in the Bahamas?

___

___

4. Who was the first explorer to see the Grand Canyon?

___

___

5. In chronological order list all events studied to date. Next to each place the appropriate date.

___

___

___

___

___

___

Jamestown is Founded in America
Worksheet

1. After whom was Jamestown, Virginia, named?

2. With how many colonists did Jamestown begin? What was unusual about the colonists?

3. What were the names of the ships the colonists sailed to Jamestown? How long did it take for the ships to arrive in Virginia?

4. What year was Jamestown founded?

5. Why had most of the colonists come to Virginia?

6. What happened to most of the colonists in the first few years of the colony?

Jamestown is Founded in America
Worksheet, Page 2

7. Who was John Smith? What did he tell the colonists?

8. What were the years 1609–1610 known as for this colony? Why was this the case?

9. 5,500 people moved to Jamestown in the first 17 years. How many of these people had died?

10. Who was John Rolfe? What did he contribute to the colony?

Indian chief Powhatan's daughter, Matoaka (nicknamed "Pocahontas") was baptized "Rebecca" in 1614 and then later married John Rolfe. One reason for establishing the colony was the desire of the English to convert the Indians to Christianity. Pocahontas was introduced to the English Queen as the first Christian convert in Virginia.

Jamestown is Founded in Virginia

Project 1—Model Longhouse and Log Cabin

When we compare the way of life of the Indians versus the colonists, we find many differences, especially in the kind of shelter they built. The colonists had come to this country accustomed to living a more luxurious life than was immediately possible in the new world. Many of these settlers had not known hard work. Building shelter was a difficult task. The Indians lived in "wetus" houses or "longhouses" with other families. The houses were built out of wooden poles and branches, covered with mats and long strips of bark. The "longhouses" were more than several hundred feet long and large enough for several families. In the middle of each there was a fireplace on the ground and over the fireplace was a large hole in the roof for smoke to escape.

There was little furniture in a house—the common items were mats, baskets, earthen pots, a stone mortar for pounding corn, and sometimes sleeping platforms covered with animal skins.

When they first arrived, the colonists built a small fort as a defense against the Indians. Then, instead of building houses, they made themselves some rude shelters out of branches of trees or old sails. Soon many colonists fell sick, and by autumn half of the colonists had died. When the cool weather set in their condition improved, and the men erected log cabins for themselves.

One of the first acts in establishing Jamestown was to prepare a place of worship. They used an old sail for a roof to keep off the sun and rain. The seats were logs. A bar of wood nailed to two trees fenced off the pulpit. The colonists soon built a church.

Men were fined if they didn't go to church. One of the reasons for removing a president of the council at Jamestown was that he came to Virginia without a Bible.

Jamestown is Founded in Virginia
Project 1, Page 2

Make a longhouse and a log cabin.

Supplies

brown construction paper

pencil

glue

straw

brown pipecleaners

pint milk or cream containers

air-drying clay

Directions

Log Cabin

1. Cut brown construction paper into the length of the sides of the milk container. Cut into strips of 1-1/2".
2. Roll the paper lengthwise tightly around the pencil to form a log. Glue the edge and remove the pencil.
3. After the logs have dried, glue them to the milk carton.
4. Cover the top of the milk carton with construction paper.

Longhouse

1. Bend 4 pipecleaners into U shapes to form the frame for the longhouse.
2. Stick the U-shaped pipecleaners into the clay.
3. Rip brown construction paper into strips. Glue to the pipecleaners.

JAMESTOWN IS FOUNDED IN VIRGINIA

Project 2—Longhouse and Log Cabin Comparison

Compare the homes of the Indians (top) to the homes of the colonists (bottom).

Jamestown is Founded in Virginia

Project 3–Jamestown and John Smith

After reading the following article, discuss the reasons for failure of this settlement with particular attention paid to the relationship between hard work and reaping what we sow. You may want to use the questions at the end to start your discussion.

It was more than one hundred years after John Cabot made his discovery of American shores, and twenty-two years after Raleigh tried to found a colony at Roanoke, before an English settlement took root and flourished in the New World. This was at Jamestown, Virginia, and the year in which it was begun was 1607. Jamestown, therefore, was the first permanent settlement made by Englishmen in the United States. It survived a desperate struggle against starvation and Indian attacks, and the man who more than anyone else helped to keep it alive was John Smith.

The days of England's courtiers and adventurers were drawing to an end, and Smith was one of the last. His life was filled with so many bold exploits and hairbreadth escapes that he makes a picturesque and interesting figure in our early history.

John Smith was born in Lincolnshire, England, and, as he was early attracted by a life of activity and danger, he joined in the war then raging in Holland. It has been said of him that he could not hear of a fight going on anywhere in the world without taking a hand in it, so we are not surprised to find him next in Hungary fighting the Turks.

Once he was taken prisoner and thrown overboard from a ship, but he escaped by swimming to land. At another time he was robbed, bound, and thrown in to a deep wood to die, but again he managed to escape. When he finally reached England, he heard that another attempt was to be made in America to carry on the work that Raleigh had failed in doing, and Smith at once became interested in the project.

The experiments made by Raleigh and others had proved that planting colonies in America would be a very expensive undertaking. England, however, was not willing to allow Spain to have all this new country, for the idea still prevailed that rich treasures might easily be found in America.

With this fond hope in mind, a body of merchants in London in 1605 formed themselves into a charter organization known as the London Company. They procured from King James a charter giving them the right to establish colonies anywhere in America between Cape Fear and the Potomac River. This royal grant stated that the religion of the settlers must be that of the church in England, that they were to treat the natives kindly, and "use all means in their power to draw them to the true knowledge and love of God."

In fitting out the first expedition of the London Company, Captain John Smith took an active part. In the winter of 1606 three ships set sail from England, and Smith was among the one hundred five men who turned their faces toward Virginia.

The Atlantic was safely crossed, and the colonists reached Virginia early in 1607. They entered Chesapeake Bay and, before landing, sailed thirty miles up a broad and beautiful river. This they named James in honor of their king, and for the same reason the little settlement was called Jamestown.

But England had not yet learned what kind of men were needed for a successful

JAMESTOWN IS FOUNDED IN VIRGINIA
Project 3, Page 2

settlement in the wilderness, where trees must be cut down, houses built, and all kinds of rough work done. Instead of carpenters and laborers, the colony consisted largely of men who called themselves "gentlemen," who had been led to come over by the desire for gold.

The colonists lacked many tools that would have been of great service in tilling the soil, but there were plenty of pickaxes for digging precious metals. The settlers were so confident that these were plentiful in Virginia that they sent a shipload of yellow dirt back to England in the vain hope that it might turn out to be gold.

At first Captain John Smith paid little attention to the management of the settlement, although he was one of the council selected to govern the colony. But as the months passed, it became plain that somebody would have to take charge and make new laws, or all the colonists would perish from hunger and the hostility of the savages. As there seemed to be no one else willing or capable, Smith came forward, was chosen governor, and assumed full command.

One of his first acts was to make the wise rule, "He who will not work shall not eat." As all provisions were kept in a common storehouse where one had to apply for his food, this rule was easily enforced. It had been the custom for the men to help themselves to whatever remained of the scanty store, but now this was changed. Smith taught the "gentlemen" to use tools and to cultivate the land; furthermore, he made them build log houses and fortifications for protection against assaults of the savages.

With a few of his men he explored the Chickahominy River, and traded beads and trinkets with the Indians for corn to feed the half-starved colonists. He still clung to the belief that the Pacific Ocean was not far away, and that he was likely at any time to find it.

While he was out on one of these trading and exploring trips, Smith fell into the hands of hostile savages who were ready to put him to death. But he quickly drew from his pocket a compass and showed his captors the trembling needle that always points to the north. This queer little instrument, so different from anything the natives had ever seen, aroused their child-like wonder. Their curiosity got the better of their thirst for blood, and Smith was taken from one Indian village to another to the astonished savages.

One day, finding himself not far from Jamestown, John Smith wrote on a piece of paper an account of his condition and directed the Indians to carry it to the little

Jamestown is Founded in Virginia
Project 3, Page 3

settlement. The savages learned, to their great surprise, that when the white people had looked at the paper they knew all that had happened. This "talking on paper" appeared to their simple minds as one of the greatest of wonders, and it made them think more highly than ever of their captive.

The Indian tribe into whose hands Smith had fallen had a powerful chief called Powhatan. In one of the books that Captain John Smith wrote long afterward, he told how his life was saved by Powhatan's daughter, Pocahontas, a little Indian maiden about twelve years of age. The savages had at last grown tired of their white prisoner and had decided to kill him. The head of the unhappy Englishman was placed on a block and an Indian stood over him ready to strike the fatal blow. Just at that moment Pocahontas rushed forward, and with tears streaming down her cheeks begged her father to spare the white man's life. The old chieftain, with whom the little maid was a great favorite, ordered the prisoner to be released.

Smith finally succeeded in reaching Jamestown, which had suffered many hardships during his absence. The little settlement was to undergo much more suffering before it became established beyond fear of failure. This, as we have seen, was in a large measure due to the kind of men the settlers were. Smith says of them in his history that they were "better fitted to spoil a community than to begin or help one."

Even with the aid of food that Captain Smith was able to get from the Indians and the fish that could be caught, there was not enough provisions to go around. The river water was not fit to dink, and malaria lurked in the surrounding marshes. Fever broke out, many died, and one hard winter the colonists were forced to eat their horses and dogs. Even by resorting to such extreme measures, there were times when the living were too ill and weak to bury the dead.

Fortunately for the new settlers, more and more people in England were beginning to take an interest in the project of founding a colony in America. At last the settlers rejoiced to see a shipload of men sailing up the James River. Soon other ships came, and some of them brought women and children. More houses were built, more seeds were planted and the little colony was firmly established.

In 1609 Captain Smith returned to England, partly because of an accident and partly because some of the new arrivals were jealous of him, wishing to become governor in his place. So they invented charges against him and thus found an excuse for sending him back.

The charges came to nothing, but Smith never returned to the Jamestown settlement, though he made several voyages to America for the purpose of exploring the coast. He gave the name New England to the shores that he explored, and he carried on a profitable trade with the natives in fish and furs. His maps of the coast of Chesapeake Bay and of New England were so nearly correct that they were in use for more than one hundred years.

The books written in his later days by this able Englishman are very interesting. His descriptions of America were so enthusiastic that they helped attract many immigrants to these shores.

After a life crowded with adventure on land and sea, Captain John Smith died in London when not much more than 50 years of age, and his body lies buried in the church of St. Sepulchre.

In the year 1609 there were four thousand colonists in Virginia. The leaders in the colony, desiring to manage their own affairs,

Jamestown is Founded in Virginia
Project 3, Page 4

appealed to the London Company for permission to elect representatives, or "burgesses," to form an assembly to make laws for the colony. The request was readily granted, and in 1619, in the choir of the little church at Jamestown, the first law-making body in America met. This assembly was afterward called the House of Burgesses.

We shall learn a little later how this first settlement in America came to be burned to the ground. There is now nothing left of Jamestown but a crumbling wall, but the work that Captain John Smith and his companions began did not perish. As we continue to study we shall learn how from the humble beginning at Jamestown, Virginia grew into a rich and prosperous state, and of how much service the Virginians have been in the history of our country.

1. Describe how John Smith's character made him a good leader for the Jamestown colony.
2. To whom did King James grant the charter "for establishing a colony anywhere in America between Cape Fear and the Potomac River"?
3. How were the colonists largely unfit to establish a colony?
4. List the ways that John Smith amazed the Indians.
5. Who saved Smith's life from Chief Powhatan?
6. What contributions did Smith make to future settlements in America?

Jamestown is Founded in Virginia
Project 4—James Fort Model

In 1607 James Fort, later known as Jamestown, was established in the New World. It was built 30 miles upriver from Hampton Roads on a flat peninsula approximately three miles long. It was 420 feet long on the James River side and 300 feet long on the other two sides. It was "triangle-wise, having three Bulwarks, at every corner, like a halfe moone, and four or five pieces of artillery mounted on them."

Supplies

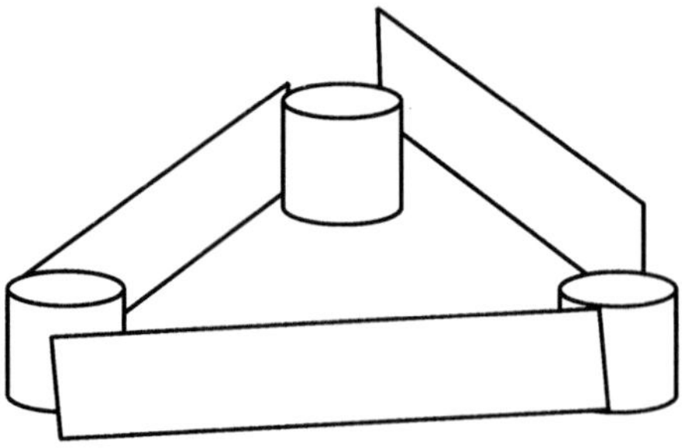

3 empty soup cans

three pieces of cardboard
(one longer than the other two)

glue

popsicle sticks

toothpick

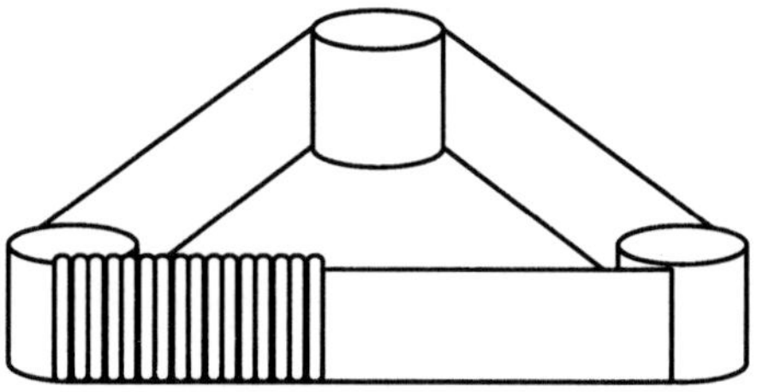

Directions

1. Glue the three boards to the three soup cans.
2. Glue the popsicle sticks around the outside of the fort.
3. Cut out, color and glue the flag to the toothpick and then into a tower.
4. Make a model storehouse, house and a church to place inside the fort.

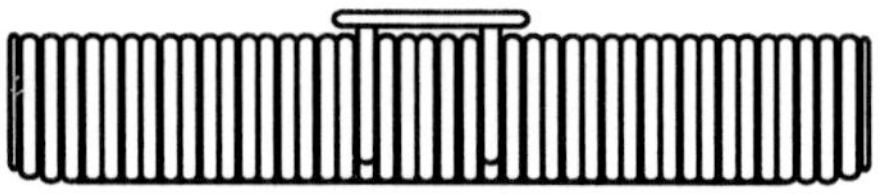

Jamestown is Founded in Virginia
Test

1. In what year was the colony of Jamestown founded?

2. Who was the colony of Jamestown named after?

3. How many people began the colony? What was unusual about them?

4. Why had most of these colonists come to Virginia?

5. Describe what the years 1609 to 1610 were like for the Virginia colonists. Why was this the case? What was this time period in Virginia called?

Jamestown is Founded in Virginia

Test, Page 2

Review

1. Where did Columbus believe he had landed?

2. What did Ferdinand Magellan do that was significant?

3. What did Hernando de Soto discover?

4. Why is Roanoke called the Lost Colony?

5. In chronological order list all events studied to date. Next to each place the appropriate date.

The Mayflower Lands at Plymouth
Worksheet

1. In what month and year did the *Mayflower* land at Plymouth?

____

____

2. Who were the separatists? What did they believe?

____

____

3. Where did the *Mayflower* first land? How long did they stay there before moving on to Plymouth?

____

____

4. The Mayflower ______________________ was an agreement that was signed by ________________ of ________________ men on board to establish an agreement by which they would live in Plymouth.

5. Who led an expedition that resulted in the discovery of a settlement site?

____

____

____

6. What is this site known as?

____

____

____

The Mayflower Lands at Plymouth
Project 1—Booklet: The Pilgrims and the Puritans

Using the information on the card, the following article, and other resources like Of Plymouth Plantation *by William Bradford, www.MayflowerHistory.com, and www.Plimoth.org, have the children create a booklet by answering the questions and illustrating them on each page. You will need to make a copy for each student. Make copies of the following pages, back to back. Cut along the dashed lines and fold along the dotted lines. When the student has completed his answers and pictures, collate and staple along the folded lines.*

From the Mayflower Compact what do we know is the reason these travelers ventured to the New World?

The Pilgrims and the Puritans

What event occurred in 1517 that shook the foundation of the church?

1

What was the name of the document the *Mayflower* passengers signed before settling Plymouth Colony?

18

How many passengers came over on the *Mayflower?*

17

What was the White Horse Tavern? What occurred there?

2

What did the children do on the ship?

15

Who came to rule England in 1558? What did she do to change the church?

4

Who was "Bloody Mary?" What had she done to the state of the Church and particularly Protestants?

3

What did the passengers take along on the ship?

16

What was Foxe's Book of Martyrs?

5

Describe the traveling conditions on the ship.

14

What was the name of the ship on which the Pilgrims ventured to the new World?

13

What was the difference between Queen Elizabeth's and John Foxe's view of the Church?

6

Who went to the Netherlands in 1608 and then to lymouth, Massachusetts in 1620?

11

What did Robert Brown write? How did he differ from Foxe? What resulted from his writings?

8

What two parties had developed in the Church in England by 1570?

7

What united the Puritans and the Pilgrims?

12

Who were the Puritans? What did they believe?

9

Who were the Pilgrims? What did they believe?

10

The Mayflower Lands at Plymouth

Project 1, Page 7—The Pilgrims and the Puritans: Total Reformation for the Glory of God

Read the following article by Samuel T. Logan, Jr., president of Westminster Theological Seminary, Philadelphia, PA —courtesy of Tabletalk.

What's the difference between the Pilgrims and the Puritans? Are they all the same folks? When did the two groups first form? And why did they emerge as distinct religious groups?

Excellent question everyone!

In answering all of the above questions, the year 1517 was especially crucial.

Most know one reason for this—in October of 1517, Martin Luther nailed his theological theses (declarations) to the castle door in Wittenberg, Germany. But 1517 is a crucial year for another reason as well, for in that year, in Boston, England, at a site where now stands an English Pub called Martha's Vineyard, John Foxe was born. To anticipate just a bit, John Bunyan, author of *Pilgrim's Progress,* once said that something John Foxe did, more than any other human action, caused the rise and flourishing of Puritanism.

By 1526, regular (rather subversive) theological discussions were being conducted in the White Horse Tavern in Cambridge. Participants included such future luminaries as Thomas Bilney, Hugh Latimer, Nicholas Ridley, and Thomas Cranmer. Every one of the four was later martyred.

In the meantime, in the late 1520's and early 1530's, Henry VIII was experiencing matrimonial and political difficulties such that, in 1533, he insisted that the Convocation of Canterbury declare his marriage to Catherine of Aragon annulled. In the next year, Henry had the English Parliament declare him the Supreme Head of the Church in England, thus severing all ties with the Roman Church.

While Henry had no particular desire to "reform" the theology of the church, those who had been meeting at the White Horse (and many of their colleagues and supporters) saw this as an opportunity "of the Lord." Perhaps now the Scriptures alone could genuinely become the foundation of the Church and the nation.

Such hopes found little royal support during Henry's lifetime, but when the King died in 1547, his nine-year-old son Edward officially assumed the throne, ruling primarily through the regents, both of whom (first, the Duke of Somerset and then the Duke of Northumberland) had more sympathy for the vision which illuminated those White Horse discussions. The push for the purification of the church and state gained great momentum in England between 1547 and Edward's death in 1553.

But the next Tudor on the throne was Mary Tudor, better known to later generations as "Bloody Mary." Mary wanted nothing more than to return "her" country to the Roman Catholic fold, no matter the cost.

Between 1553 and 1558, Protestant exiles flooded Europe, hoping to escape Mary's sword by gathering in such Protestant bastions as Geneva and Frankfurt. To the latter came 38-year-old John Foxe. Foxe developed a powerful vision of what England could be, if only God's Word were fully and faithfully followed.

Mary's death in 1558 and the accession to the English throne of Mary's Protestant sister Elizabeth reversed the earlier tide and sent Englishmen and Englishwomen home in droves. The seed which became Puritanism received a full shot of theological fertilizer from the pen of John Foxe.

During Mary's reign, hundreds had died

THE MAYFLOWER LANDS AT PLYMOUTH
Project 1, Page 8

for their faith. Would the people of England honor those deaths by seizing the marvelous opportunity the Lord had given England by removing Mary and replacing her with Elizabeth?

Would the people of England now insist that their church and their state be completely purified of all non-Biblical elements so that both institutions (and all people therein) might bring singular honor to the Lord God of Scripture?

These were the questions asked in Foxe's monumental work which we know as *The Foxe's Book of Martyrs.* First published in 1563, Foxe's work was an intense account of the pain suffered by the Marian martyrs and a clarion call to bring both the nation and the church of England into full conformity to the Word of God.

Many of those who shared the dream which had been nurtured at the White Horse Tavern now seized upon Foxe's expression of expectations of His people and insisted, with ever increasing fervor, that both their royal and ecclesiastical leaders direct all English affairs sola Scriptura, according to the Scriptures alone.

Queen Elizabeth I, however, saw things differently. Her vision was of political stability and order. Elizabeth had no interest in any kind of extremism which the theological heirs of those White Horse discussants seemed to her to represent.

England (including the English church) should, in Elizabethan view, be broad and inclusive and should base its life on tradition and reason as well as on the teachings of Scripture.

So, by 1570, there had developed in England two parties 1) those who favored this more rationalistic understanding of church and state, and 2) those who continued to insist that further purification of those two entities was required by Scripture and that England must now seize the spiritual opportunity so brilliantly described by John Foxe. And it was in the midst of this controversy that the term "puritan" began to be regularly used by the first group as a derisive epithet of attack upon the second group.

The 1570's saw the intensification of this conflict with little "progress," at least from the standpoint of the Puritan party. In fact, with the dismissal of Thomas Cartwright from his teaching position at Cambridge for promulgating the heresy of Presbyterianism, it appeared to some Puritans that the cause was being lost and this perception led to the first major split within the Puritan party.

As the Puritan impulse might be primarily associated with (though it actually pre-

The Mayflower Lands at Plymouth

Project 1, Page 9

ceded) *Foxe's Book of Martyrs,* so the "Pilgrim" ethos might be traced appropriately to Robert Browne's book, *Reformation Without Tarrying for Anie,* first published in 1580. Browne might be called a disillusioned Puritan. He shared the vision which informed Foxe's work, but after more than a decade of seeking revival within the English church, he came to the conclusion that it just wan't going to happen. Browne "separated" from the English church and, with like-minded Robert Harrison, started his own congregation in Norwich in 1581.

Thus was formed the "Separatist" movement, a movement which later produced such leaders as John Smyth (whom some regard as the father of English Baptists), John Robinson, William Brewster, and William Bradford. The latter three were directly involved in that group of Separatists which, in 1608, left England for the Netherlands, and then later decided to emigrate to the New World, landing at Plymouth, Massachusetts, in 1620.

Many (probably most) Puritans chose to remain within the English church working for reform, and it was from this group that a much larger group of emigrants left from New England in the late 1620's, establishing their colony at Massachusetts Bay.

The Boston and Plymouth colonies were distinct political and religious entities (at least until the English government combines them in the late 1680's) and, while relations between them were generally friendly, members of both groups were crystal clear on the differences between them.

"Puritans" wanted to remain as part of the English establishment, working for Biblical reforms from within. Even as they emigrated to New England, they affirmed their "Englishness" and saw the main purpose of their new colony as being that of a Biblical witness, a "city on a hill" which would set an example of Biblical righteousness in church and state for Old England and the entire world to see. As deeply committed covenant theologians, they emphasized especially the corporate righteousness of their community before God.

"Pilgrims" wanted to achieve "reformation without tarrying," even if it meant separating from their church and nation. While they continued to think of themselves as English, their emphasis was on their new political identity and spiritual identity. Because of their passionate commitment to the necessity of reformation immediately and without comprise, they emphasized especially strongly individual righteousness before God.

What united Massachusetts Bay and Plymouth and what united both Puritans and Pilgrims was far more significant than what distinguished them. All children of the Reformation, they knew that salvation was by grace alone through faith alone in Christ alone. And they knew this because they took, as their authority, Scripture alone.

They all knew that to God alone must be the glory and, in their different ways, they sought to bring every thought and every action—religious, political, social—captive to the Lordship of Jesus.

Could there be any more important goal for American Christians today?

THE MAYFLOWER LANDS AT PLYMOUTH
Project 2—Passenger List and Mayflower Compact

Read the passenger list recorded by Governor William Bradford in his History of Plimouth Plantation *(the original spelling is maintained here). Then read the Mayflower Compact.*

The names of those which came over first, in ye year. 1620. and were (by the blesing of God) the first beginers, and (in a sort) the foundation, of all the plantations, and Colonies, in New England. (and their families.)

Mr John Carver. Kathrine his wife. Desire Minter; & .2. manservants John Howland. Roger Wilder. William Latham, a boy, & a maid servant, & a child yt was put to him called, Jasper More

Mr William Brewster, Mary his wife, with .2. sons, whose names were Love, & Wrasling. and a boy was put to him called Richard More; and another of his brothers the rest of his children were left behind and came over afterwards.

Mr Edward Winslow Elizabeth his wife, & 2 men servants, caled Georg Sowle, and Elias Sotry; also a little girl was put to him called Ellen, the sister of Richard More.
William Bradford, and Dorathy his wife, having but one child, a sone left behind, who came afterward.

Mr Isaack Allerton, and Mary. his wife; with 3 children Bartholmew Remember, & Mary. and a servant boy, John Hooke.

Mr Samuel fuller; and a servant, caled William Butten. His wife was behind & a child, which came afterwards.

John Crakston and his sone John Crakston

Captain Myles Standish and Rose, his wife

Mr Christpher Martin, and his wife; and 2 servants, Salamon prower, and John Langemore

Mr William Mullines, and his wife; and 2 children Joseph, & priscilla; and a servant Robart Carter.

Mr Wiliam White, and Susana his wife; and one sone caled resolved, and one borne a shipbord caled perigriene ; and 2 servants, named William Holbeck, & Edward Thomson

Mr Steven Hopkins, & Elizabeth his wife; and 2 children, called Giles, and Constanta a doughter, both by a former wife, caled Damaris, & Oceanus, the last borne at sea. And .2. servants, called Edward Doty, and Edward Litster.

Mr Richard Warren, but his wife and children were lefte behind and came afterwards

John Billinton, and Elen his wife: and .2. sones John, & Francis.

Edward Tillie, and Ann his wife: and .2. children that were their cossets; Henery Samson, and Humillity Coper

John Tillie, and his wife; and Eelizabeth their doughter.

Francis Cooke, and his sine John; But his wife & other children came afterwards

Thomas Rogers, and Joseph his sone; his other children came afterwards.

Thomas Tinker, and his wife, and a Son

John Rigdale; and Alice his wife.

James Chilton, and his wife, and Mary their doughter; they had another doughter yt was maried came afterward.

Edward fuller, and his wife; and Samuell their sonne.

John Turner, and .2. sones; he had a

THE MAYFLOWER LANDS AT PLYMOUTH

Project 2, Page 2

doughter came some years after to Salem, wher she is now living.

Francis Eaton. and Sarah his wife, and Samuell their sone, a yong child Moyses fletcher, John Goodman, Thomas Williams, Digerie Priest, Edmond Margeson, Peter Browne, Richard Britterige, Richard Clarke, Richard Gardenar, Gilbart Winslow

John Alden was hired for a cooper, at SouthHampton wher the ship victualed; and being a hopefull yong man was much desired, but left to his owne liking to go, or stay when he came here, but he stayed, and maryed here.

John Allerton, and Thomas English were both hired, the later to goe mr of a shalop here. and ye other was reputed as one of ye company, but was to go back (being a seaman) for the help of others behind. But they both dyed here, before the shipe returned.

Ther were allso other 2 seamen hired to stay a year here in the country, William Trevore; and one Ely. But when their time was out they both returned.

These being about a hundred sowls came over in this first ship; and began this worke, which god of his goodnes hath hithertoo blesed; let his holy name have ye praise.

THE MAYFLOWER COMPACT

The following words are the remaining record of the Mayflower Compact, the document understood to have been a first but temporary agreement for governing the new colony.

> "In ye name of God, Amen. We whose names are underwritten, the loyall subjects of our dread soveraigne Lord, King James, by the grace of God, of Great Britaine, Franc, and Ireland king, defender of the faith, etc.
>
> Having undertaken, for ye glorie of God, and advancemente of ye Christian faith, and honor of our king & countrie, a voyage to plant ye first colonie in ye Northerne parts of Virginia, doe by these presents solemnly & mutualy in ye presence of God, and one of another, covenant & combine our selves togeather into a civill body politick, for our better ordering & preservation & furtherance of ye ends aforesaid; and by vertue hearof to enacte lawes, ordinances, acts, constitutions, & offices, from time to time, as shall be thought most to meet & convenient for ye general good of ye Colonie, unto which we promise all due submission and obedience. In witnes wherof we have hereunder subscribed our names at CapCodd ye 11th. of November, in ye year of ye raine of our soveraigne lord, King James, of England, France, & Ireland ye eighteenth, and of Scotland ye fiftie fourth. Ano: Dom. 1620."

The Mayflower Lands at Plymouth
Project 3—A Letter Home: Voyage to New Plymouth

Write an imaginary letter on the next page from a Pilgrim to his or her relatives in England describing what it was like to make the voyage to the New World on the Mayflower. *Describe what it was like to spend two months in the cramped living quarters that had to be shared with over a hundred other passengers and the time spent at anchor before going ashore at New Plymouth.*

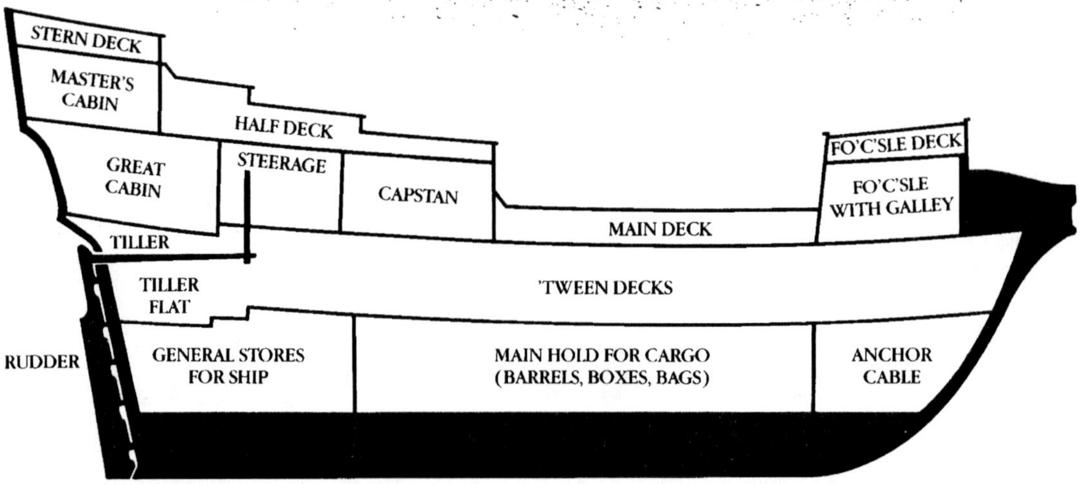

The Mayflower Lands at Plymouth

Project 3, Page 2

The Mayflower Lands at Plymouth
Project 4—Travel Time

It took the *Mayflower* 66 days to travel 3,500 nautical miles at an average speed of two miles an hour or approximately 53 miles per day. The ship had originally intended to take the Pilgrims to Virginia, but because the ship encountered high seas and shoal water, it turned back north to anchor in the hook of what is now Provincetown Harbor. Commercial jets can travel 500 miles an hour. What are some of the speeds of Atlantic crossings today? *Using references or travel books, find out how much time would be required to travel from the East Coast of the United States to London, England, by:*

_______ *cruise ship*
_______ *commercial jet liner*
_______ *military jet*

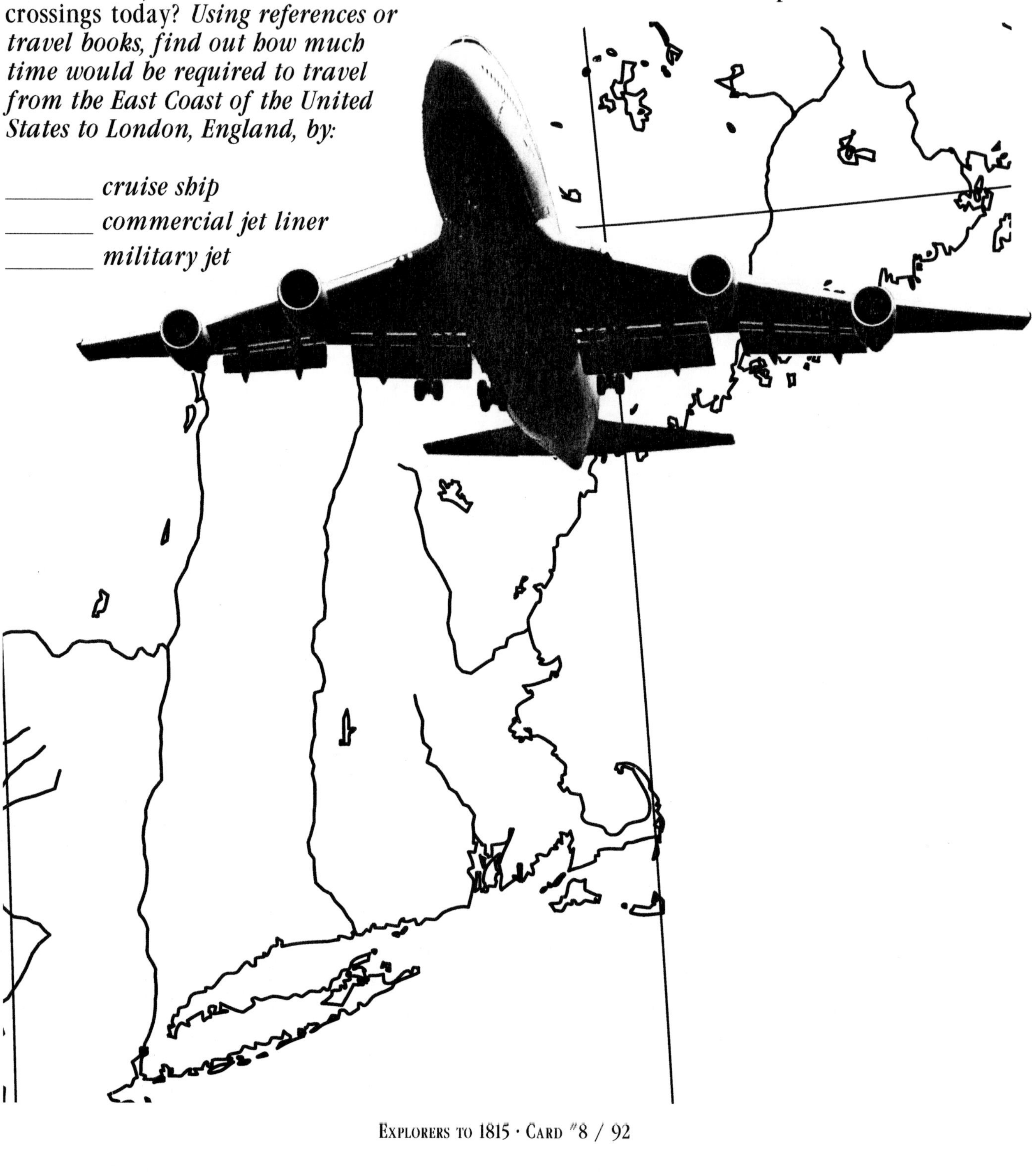

The Mayflower Lands at Plymouth

Project 5—Building the "City on a Hill"

The settlers at Plymouth had their work cut out for them as they tried to build their "City on a Hill." Read the following then try your hand at planning what would be needed for you to build a similar experiment.

Chronology of New Plymouth Expeditions and Construction

1620

November 14	a group of men went ashore from the *Mayflower* to scout a site for the new colony
November 27	second expedition
December 6	18 men set out on the third expedition; they chose New Plymouth as the site for their plantation
December 15	the *Mayflower* weighed anchor from what is today known as Provincetown Harbor
December 16	the *Mayflower* anchored in Plymouth Harbor
December 25	the men began to erect the first building for common use; this common building was finished January 9
December 28	the grounds were measured out for home sites for 19 families and work began on small cottages; a gun platform was built on a hill for the cannons which would be taken from the *Mayflower* before the ship returned to England

1621

February 21	three cannons were brought ashore from the *Mayflower* and placed on the gun platform

Interior Decorating in New Plymouth

The site of New Plymouth was once the location of an Indian village that had been occupied by the Patuxet Indians. Although the entire population of the village had died four years earlier from a plague, the Pilgrims were concerned about the presence of Indians in the area and, to further fortify their small community, they erected a palisade with the fort/meetinghouse at one end overlooking the village. This palisade was begun in February 1622 and took over a month to complete.

New Plymouth was designed as a small and compact settlement. The gun platform overlooked the site of the new Village, and the home sites were laid out in two rows for safety. Each man began the construction of a house for his family although most of the colonists had to spend part of the bitter New England winter in the 20-foot common house. The cramped living conditions and poor diet contributed to sickness (probably pneumonia complicated by scurvy) that began to take its toll in the small community. In two or three months time, half of their company died. Of all the hundred or so persons, scarcely 50 remained and sometimes two or three persons died in a day.

The Mayflower Lands at Plymouth

Project 5, Page 2

In constructing the buildings in New Plymouth, the Pilgrims used the technique that they knew from living in England called post and beam framework with wattle and daub walls. They used large upright posts interwoven with twigs or tree branches and then put a mixture of clay, sand, and straw over it that hardened as it dried. This was also used to build the chimneys for the houses. The outer walls were then covered with clapboard that was cut from timber in the area. The roofs were made of thatch which probably was cattail reeds. These thatched roofs were banned after 1627-28 since they were apt to catch fire from sparks. The roofs of the later homes were covered with wooden shingles.

The floors of the homes were either dirt or clay and were covered with rushes that would be changed occasionally. The windows were covered with oiled linen or paper to keep out the cold and wind but allowing some light to enter the building. The interior of a New Plymouth home was quite sparse by today's standards. The basic furnishings that we think are necessary for a minimum standard of living—tables, chairs, and beds—were not found in all of the early New Plymouth homes. The word *bed* referred to the mattress and *bedstead* was the wooden framework. Not all homes had bedsteads; the bed was sometimes placed directly on the rush-covered floor.

Tables and chairs were also not found in every home. Although some households had no chairs at all, most had a chair for the head of the house and the other members of the family sat on stools, benches, chests, and the floor. Possibly one in every three New Plymouth households had a table of any kind and that was not necessarily a dining table. It is presumed

The Mayflower Lands at Plymouth
Project 5, Page 3

that meals were most often laid out on the top of a chest or barrel that had been covered by a rug and a cloth and the members of the family ate standing up. Most of the New Plymouth homes, however, did have at least one oak chest and some trunks and boxes for storage of personal belongings, food, and tools. These chests and trunks also did double duty as tables and chairs.

There were oil lamps and candlesticks in about a third of the houses in New Plymouth. Probably most of the night time light was provided by the fireplace in each home.

The furnishings that were found in every home were cooking utensils and equipment, barrels, tubs and kegs, trenchers (dishes), platters, spoons, and drinking utensils.

By 1624 New Plymouth had a population of 180 people and 32 houses.

Apparel	Tools	Household Implements	Arms	Food

Pretend you are on a two-month trip to an uninhabited place where there is no plumbing or electricity. List the things needed to start a new life in this uninhabited place. Bring enough food to last until you can plant, grow and harvest your first crops in your new home.

The following pages contain the Inconveniences and the Pilgrims' provisions. These were the lists of necessities that people were advised to bring with them to the Virginia Colonies in 1622, with the exception of food. There is no record of what was actually brought on the *Mayflower*, but this is believed by historians at Plimouth Plantation to be very close to the actual list. There was no standard way of spelling in the 17th century and people spelled words differently than we do today. The lower case *s* that looks like our *f* was used in or at the beginning of words, but the final lower case *s* always looked like the *s* we use today. The *i* and *j* were used interchangeably as were the *u* and *v*. The abbreviations for the cost of provisions are: li.=pounds, s.=shillings, d.=pence

Discussion

How does your list compare with the items found in the list of Pilgrims' Provisions? Was the list made in 1622 more complete than yours? Are tools similar to these still used in construction today? How have these tools improved? What are the disadvantages of the wattle and daub method of building walls and chimneys?

THE INCONVENIENCIES

THAT HAVE HAPPENED TO SOME PERSONS WHICH HAVE TRANSPORTED THEMSELVES

from *England* to *Virginia* , vvithout prouifions neceffary to fuftaine themfelues, hath *greatly hindred the Progreffe of that noble Plantation: For preuention of the like diforders* heereafter, that no man fuffer , either through ignorance or mifinformation; it is thought requifite to publifh this fhort declaration : wherein is contained a particular of fuch neceffaries, *as either priuate families or fingle perfons fhall haue caufe to furnifh themfelues with, for their better fupport at their firft landing in* Virginia;*whereby alfo greater numbers may receiue in part, directions how to prouide themfelues.*

Apparrell.

Apparrell for one man, and fo after the rate for more.

	li.	s.	d.
One Monmouth Cap	00	01	10
Three falling bands	—	01	03
Three fhirts	—	07	06
One wafte-coate	—	02	02
One fuite of Canuafe	—	07	06
One fuite of Frize	—	10	00
One fuite of Cloth	—	15	00
Three paire of Irifh ftockins	—	04	—
Foure paire of fhooes	—	08	08
One paire of garters	—	00	10
One doozen of points	—	00	03
One paire of Canuafe fheets	—	08	00
Seuen ells of Canuafe, to make a bed and boulfter, to filled in *Virginia* 8.s. One Rug for a bed 8.s which with the bed feruing for two men, halfe is	—	08	00
Fiue ells coorfe Canuafe, to make a bed at Sea for two men, to be filled with ftraw, iiij.s. One coorfe Rug at Sea for two men, will coft vj.s. is for one	—	05	00
	04	00	00

Victuall.

For a whole yeere for one man, and fo for more after the rate.

	li.	s.	d.
Eight bufhels of Meale	02	00	00
Two bufhels of peafe at 3.s.	—	06	00
Two bufhels of Oatemeale 4.s.6.d.	—	09	00
One gallon of *Aquauita*	—	02	06
One gallon of Oyle	—	03	06
Two gallons of Vineger 1.s.	—	02	00
	03	03	00

Armes.

For one man but if halfe of your men haue armour it is fufficient fo that all haue Peeces and fwords.

	li.	s.	d.
One Armour compleat, light	—	17	00
One long Peece, fiue foot or fiue and a halfe, neere Musket bore	01	02	—
One fword	—	05	—
One belt	—	01	—
One bandaleere	—	01	06
Twenty pound of powder	—	18	00
Sixty pound of fhot or lead, Piftoll and Goofe fhot	—	05	00
	03	09	06

Tooles.

For a family of 6. perfons and fo after the rate for more.

	li.	s.	d.
Fiue broad howes at 2.s. a piece	—	10	—
Fiue narrow howes at 16.d. a piece	—	06	08
Two broad Axes at 3.s.8.d. a piece	—	07	04
Fiue felling Axes at 18.d. a piece	—	07	06
Two fteele hand fawes at 16.d. a piece	—	02	08
Two two-hand-fawes at 5.s. a piece	—	10	—
One whip-faw, fet and filed with box, file, and wreft	—	10	—
Two hammers 12.d. a piece	—	02	00
Three fhouels 18.d. a piece	—	04	06
Two fpades at 18.d. a piece	—	03	—
Two augers 6.d. a piece	—	01	00
Sixe chiffels 6.d. a piece	—	03	00
Two percers ftocked 4.d. a piece	—	00	08
Three gimlets 2.d. a piece	—	00	06
Two hatchets 21.d. a piece	—	03	06
Two froues to cleaue pale 18.d.	—	03	00
Two hand-bills 20.a piece	—	03	04
One grindleftone 4.s.	—	04	00
Nailes of all forts to the value of	02	00	—
Two Pickaxes	—	03	—
	06	02	08

Houfhold Implements.

For a family of 6. perfons, and fo for more or leffe after the rate.

	li.	s.	d.
One Iron Pot	00	07	—
One kettle	—	06	—
One large frying-pan	—	02	06
One gridiron	—	01	06
Two skillets	—	05	—
One fpit	—	02	—
Platters, difhes, fpoones of wood	—	04	—
	01	08	00

	li.	s.	d.
For Suger, Spice and fruit, and at Sea for 6. men	00	12	06
So the full charge of Apparrell, Victuall, Armes, Tooles, and houfhold ftuffe, and after this rate for each perfon, will amount vnto about the fumme of	12	10	—
The paffage of each man is	06	00	—
The fraight of thefe prouifions for a man, will bee about halfe a Tun, which is	01	10	—
So the whole charge will amount to about	20	00	00

Nets, hookes, lines, and a tent muft be added, if the number of people be greater, as alfo fome kine.

And this is the ufuall proportion that the Virginia *Company doe beftow upon their Tenants which they fend*

Whofoeuer tranfports himfelfe or any other at his owne charge vnto *Virginia,* fhall for each perfon fo tranfported before Midfummer 1625. haue to him and his heires for euer fifty Acres of Land vpon a firft, and fifty Acres vpon a fecond diuifion.

Imprinted at London by FELIX KYNGSTON. 1622.

The Mayflower Lands at Plymouth
Project 5, Page 5

Illustrations of some of the necessities that historians believe the Pilgrims brought to the New World. The food depicted was either brought to America by the Pilgrims or found in Plymouth.

Tools—Tooles
1. Two-man saw
2. Hand Saw
3. Hoe
4. Rope
5. Chisels
6. Fishing Hook
7. Auger
8. Nails
9. Shovel
10. Level
11. Ax
12. Scissors/Shears
13. Square
14. Plane
15. Knife
16. Hammer
17. Measuring Instrument

Utensils—Household Implements

18. Tongs
19. Spit
20. Bellows
21. Kettle
22. Wooden Spoons
23. Spoon
24. Knives
25. Frying Pan
26. Wooden Plates
27. Mortar and Pestle

Arms—Armes

28. Pistol
29. Sword
30. Musket
31. Pike

Food—Victuall

32. Pigs Foot
33. Lamb
34. Apples
35. Beans
36. Nuts
37. Smoked Ham
38. Cabbage
39. Wheat (coarse ground)
40. Cheese
41. Spices
42. Lemons
43. Salt Beef
44. Bread Loaves
45. Salted Codfish (Haberdine)
46. Dried Sausage
47. Chicken
48. Strawberries (preserved)
49. Vinegar
50. Aquavita or Beer
51. Onions
52. Oatmeal

Clothing—Apparrell

53. Coif (woman's cap)
54. Waistcoat
55. Cape
56. Kitted Waistcoat
57. Gloves
58. Suit or Frieze
59. Wool Cap (monmouth)
60. Bed Rug (blanket)
61. Shoes

The Mayflower Lands at Plymouth
Project 6—Games and Clothing

Read over the rules for the following two games. Are the games similar to one you have played? What would be another name for All-Hid?

All-Hid

Two teams (Hiders and Finders) are required for this game. Finders remain at home base while hiders go out to hide themselves. When all are hidden, one of them shouts "all hid!" as a signal for the other team to come look for them. If they can get to home base without being caught, they are free to go out and hide again, but if they are caught, they have to join the finding team and those who caught them may go hide themselves. This game can also be played with one player as "it" and the rest hiders.

Marbles

Draw a circle on the ground. Each player puts an equal number of marbles inside the circle. To begin play, the players take turns shooting marbles at the circle from a designated distance. The player who gets his marble closest to the circle shoots first. The aim of the game is to shoot a marble from outside the circle and knock marbles out of the ring. A player may continue to shoot until he misses and fails to knock any marbles out of the ring. If his shooter marble stays inside the ring, he has to replace any marbles he knocked out.

Review the items shown on the following page, then discuss the following questions:

1. Can you think of any advantages in wearing a coif or hat most of the time?
2. Why would the men wear pants that ended at the knee rather than going down to their shoe tops?
3. What would be some of the disadvantages of wearing long dresses, skirts, cloaks, and capes? What are the advantages?

The Mayflower Lands at Plymouth
Project 6, Page 2

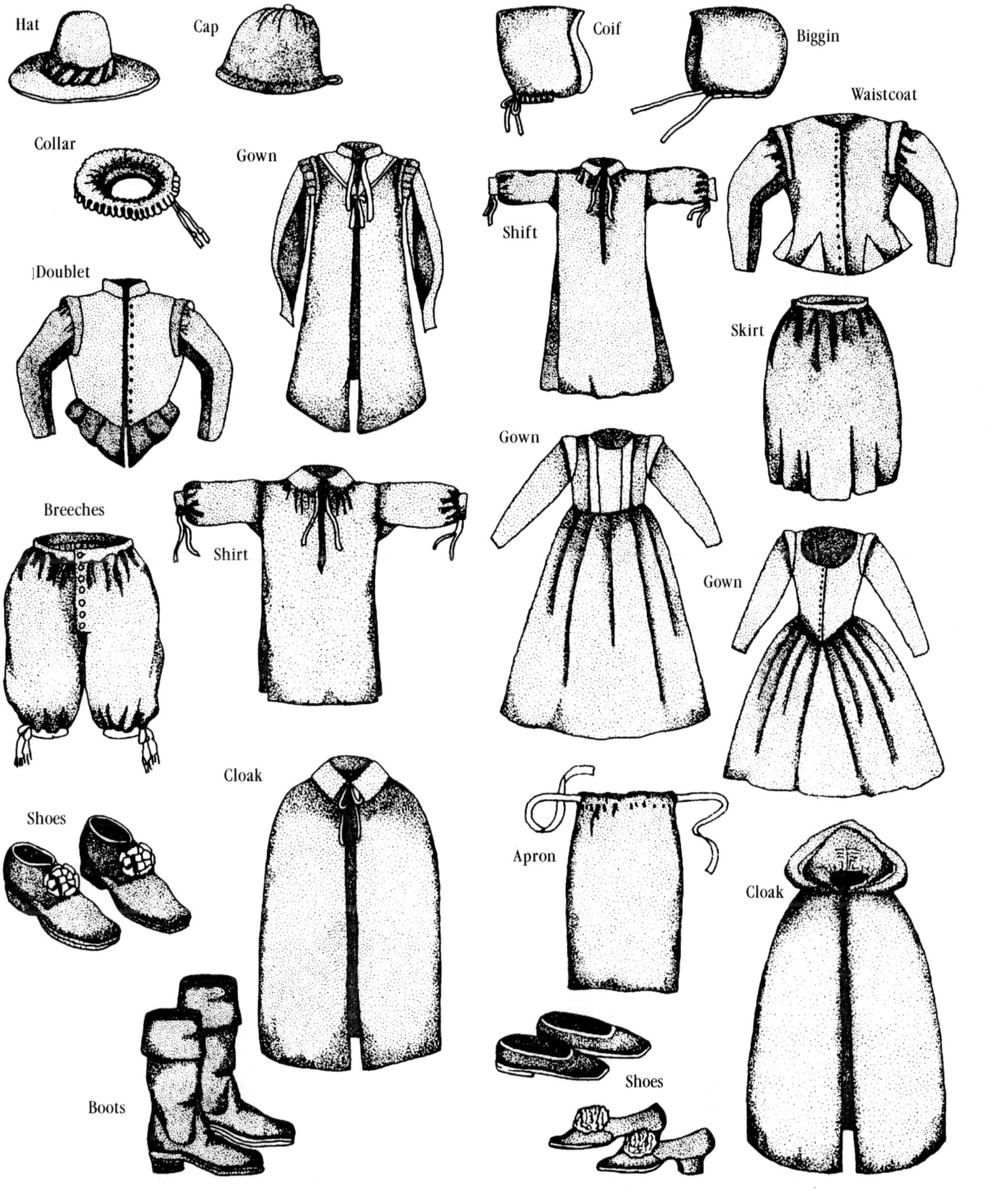

THE MAYFLOWER LANDS AT PLYMOUTH
Literature Unit 1—Voyage to Freedom *by David Gay*

INTRODUCTION THROUGH CHAPTER 2

1. Describe the basic facts of the *Mayflower's* journey. How many miles would they travel, how large was the ship, how many people were on board and how long would the journey take?
2. When did the *Mayflower* leave England, and where was their point of departure?
3. How many ships were leaving England at about the same time, and what were their names?
4. Why did the sailor think the *Speedwell* would not get to its destination?
5. Describe the clothing worn by the men and women pilgrims on their voyage.
6. What was the other name for the pilgrims, and why were they leaving England?
7. What were the names of the members of the Lovelace family. Where had they lived before they boarded the ship for Virginia?
8. What was the last thing the Puritans did before they boarded the ship for their voyage?
9. Each family had to claim its own space in the ship. Describe the living quarters for each of the families. How did they go about marking off an area for their family?
10. What was the third level below deck called. What was kept there?

CHAPTERS 3–7

1. The Lovelace family began their voyage with mixed emotions. What were their reactions to finally being underway on the *Speedwell?*
2. What did it sound like to wake up in their dimly lit, smelly quarters on the ship?
3. How did Matthew Lovelace begin his day?
4. What is the meaning of the word *breakfast?* Describe the Lovelace family's breakfast that first morning out to sea.
5. Describe the scene below decks as the *Speedwell* was enduring its first storm of the voyage.
6. What did Mr. Lovelace tell the other passengers they needed to do during the storm to show their trust in God to the ungodly that were on board the ship?
7. What means was used to prevent people from getting hurt as the ship lurched about in the wild ocean waves?
8. What tune did Mrs. Lovelace sing to calm Prudence's fears during the raging storm. Why did she choose this song in particular?
9. Justice succumbed to the dread sea sickness like many of the other passengers and made an important discovery while trying to find a more comfortable resting position. What was his discovery, and what did his father do about it?
10. When Justice and Prudence slipped away from their napping parents, where did they go and what did they find?

CHAPTER 8–11

1. What was Master Reynolds's plan to take advantage of the Pilgrims?
2. How did Matthew Lovelace find out about the Master's plot, and what did he do?
3. What destination was agreed upon for repairs to the vessel?
4. What stern admonishment did Mr. Lovelace give the captain before departing from his cabin?
5. How did the pilgrims end up moving from the *Speedwell* to the *Mayflower* for their voyage to freedom?
6. What was the difference between the passengers on the *Speedwell* and the ones who were going to be traveling on

The Mayflower Lands at Plymouth

Literature Unit 1—Voyage to Freedom

the *Mayflower*?

7. What nicknames were the passengers given by the crew and townspeople?
8. Mr. Lovelace was not opposed to this new nickname. He felt it was an apt description and hoped that somehow a divine purpose was accomplished by the behavior of the Saints as witnessed by the Strangers. Explain.
9. How did the *Mayflower* get pulled away from the dock?
10. As the ship sailed from port, the Lovelace family watched as England disappeared from view. Mr. Lovelace was saddened by the sight. What were his comments to his family?

Chapters 12–14

1. The children managed to find a place to call their own even in the confining quarters. Where did they go to get away to talk and play?
2. The carpenter told them stories about America. What did he say they'd find in their new home?
3. Who did the carpenter say inhabited the land already, and how did he describe them?
4. The menu for the Lovelace family became very routine. What was their daily meal?
5. Mrs. Lovelace was the teacher for the children. Even though they were at sea, they still had classes every day but Sunday. What did they study?
6. Justice and Prudence were glad that it was dark in their quarters, especially when it came to their meals. Why did they like it dark, rather than bright?
7. There were many things that contributed to the unhealthy living conditions of the ship, not the least of which was the air below decks. Describe the deterioration of their living quarters.
8. The *Mayflower* came into a violent storm while on its voyage. The captain commanded all to stay below decks for their own survival. How did the pilgrims respond to this command?
9. As you remember from the Introduction, several of the characters of this book are real people. Master Reynolds from the *Speedwell* and John Howland from the *Mayflower* really were on board these ships. Mr. Howland nearly cost the group its life. How?
10. Sometimes we think we know better than the people who are giving us instructions. Mr. Howland didn't follow the direct command of the captain and almost cost himself and his friends their lives. How was he rescued?

Chapters 15–19

1. The passengers were able to sleep through some of the storm, and they became unaware of whether it was day or night. Their sleep was interrupted by water splashing into their living quarters on the boat. What did they find was happening?
2. One of the pilgrims brought along a device from his farm that was used by the pilgrims to stop the damage to the ship. What was it called, and how did it work?
3. To what did the captain of the ship attribute the saving of the ship and its passengers? What was the response of the pilgrims?
4. As the storm continued to rage around them and sickness and stench prevailed in the hold of the ship, the captain asked for three men to conference with him. The ship was battered and worn, a floating wreck. What was discussed at this

The Mayflower Lands at Plymouth
Literature Unit 1—Voyage to Freedom

meeting, and what was the outcome?

5. William Butten was one of the authentic members of the crew of the *Mayflower*. He had very definite views of the pilgrims and their belief in God. How did he treat Mr. Howland and the Lovelace children to show his contempt of the pilgrims and their faith?
6. Mr. Lovelace came along just in time to prevent further harm to his children and Mr. Howland. He gave the children specific instructions about how they were to behave toward William Butten. Which passage of Scripture did he read them?
7. William Butten came upon the children alone one day while they were in their favorite haunt. What happened?
8. How was he stopped from harming them?
9. What effect did these encounters have on Justice?
10. Who was responsible for comforting Justice and getting him to rest?

Chapters 20-26

1. All of the occupants of the *Mayflower* were to soon witness the vengeance of God. What happened to William Butten?
2. What suggestions did the sailors make to quiet William and to cure his illness?
3. The crew was well aware of how Butten had mistreated the pilgrims on board, so they were sure none would come to his aid. However, Mr. Lovelace immediately grabbed his Bible and went to the bedside of the sick man. How was he received and what happened?
4. Without fear of William Butten, the children soon found their way back to their favorite spot on the deck. Upon seeing the captain they decided to question him about how long it would be till they arrived in America. How did the captain respond to their quesions?
5. All of the captain's figuring was unnecessary at this point. How did he know they would soon sight land?
6. While still on deck with their father, Justice told his father that they were not going to be landing in Virginia. What he had seen on the captain's charts indicated they were going to be far north of Virginia. His father assured him that he must be mistaken, surely the captain would have told them if they were off course. Who was right?
7. How did Mr. Lovelace handle the news that they were indeed off course? What did the pilgrims do next?
8. They had not traveled very far when a sailor spotted shoals directly in line with their route of travel. The *Mayflower* would surely be tossed about and destroyed along with her occupants. What Bible story did the elderly man review with them, and how did he apply it to this situation?
9. What new decision was reached by the pilgrim group regarding their destination?
10. What month did the pilgrims land, and what were the opposing views of the Lovelace children when their feet were finally set on solid ground again?

THE MAYFLOWER LANDS AT PLYMOUTH
Test

1. What was the month and year the *Mayflower* landed at Plymouth?

____

____

2. How many separatists were on the *Mayflower?* Describe them.

____

____

____

____

3. Where did the *Mayflower* first land? How long did they stay before moving on to Plymouth?

____

____

____

4. What agreement was signed before settling at Plymouth? Who signed it?

____

____

5. Who led an expedition that resulted in the discovery of a settlement site?

____

____

6. What was the name of the other ship that was supposed to accompany the *Mayflower* on the journey? Why was it left behind?

____

____

____

THE MAYFLOWER LANDS AT PLYMOUTH

Test, Page 2

Review

1. What did Prince Henry's school teach?

2. What name was given to the 1500's regarding the Spanish explorers?

3. Where did Jacques Cartier explore?

4. Who were the Croatans?

5. In chronological order list all events studied to date. Next to each place the appropriate date.

Pilgrims Build Plymouth Colony
Worksheet

1. Where is Plymouth Plantation located?

____

____

____

2. What did the Pilgrims bring with them when they came ashore off the Mayflower?

____

____

____

3. What did the Pilgrims believe about God?

____

____

____

4. What caused many deaths the first year?

____

____

____

5. Who was Squanto?

____

____

____

____

6. What happened in November 1621 in Plymouth?

____

____

____

Pilgrims Build Plymouth Colony

Project 1—Letter to a Friend

After reading either Sarah Morton's Day *or* Samuel Eaton's Day *by Kate Waters, write a letter in the space provided to a friend you left behind in Holland when you came to the New World. Be sure to include what you eat and how you spend your days.*

Pilgrims Build Plymouth Colony

Project 2—A Thanksgiving Feast

Plimoth Plantation in Plymouth, Massachusetts, has published a book entitled *The Thanksgiving Primer* that explains in detail how to have an authentic Thanksgiving Feast. *Have the children make costumes and come dressed as Pilgrims or Indians to enjoy this authentic feast.*

Pilgrims Build Plymouth Colony
Test

1. What is the location of Plymouth Plantation?

2. What is the date of the Pilgrims Building Plymouth Colony?

3. What did the Pilgrims bring ashore from the *Mayflower?*

4. What did the Pilgrims believe about God?

5. Why was there so much death the first year in the colony?

6. Who was Tisquantum?

Pilgrims Build Plymouth Colony

Test, Page 2

7. What was the purpose of the celebration the Pilgrims had with the Indians in November of 1621? How long did it last?

Review

1. Who funded Columbus's expedition?

2. Where did Magellan die?

3. Who was the Spanish explorer who discovered Florida?

4. Who funded Cabot's exploration of North America?

Pilgrims Build Plymouth Colony
Test, Page 3

5. In chronological order list all events studied to date. Next to each place the appropriate date.

Massachusetts Bay Colony, Home of the Puritans

Worksheet

1. Massachusetts Bay Colony was one of the first settlements in ______________.
2. Who first established the colony in Salem, Massachusetts?

____

____

____

____

3. What did the Puritans want to do to the Church of England?

____

____

____

____

4. Who led the first group of Puritans to New England in 1628?

____

____

____

5. Who led 1,000 more Puritans to New England in 1630? What was his position in the colony?

____

____

____

____

____

Massachusetts Bay Colony, Home of the Puritans

Worksheet, Page 2

6. What did the person in the previous question believe about the Church of England? What did he believe about the new society they were building?

7. Upon what were the established laws and government of Massachusetts Bay Colony based?

Massachusetts Bay Colony, Home of the Puritans

Project 1—Making a Hornbook

Children were first taught to read during colonial times using a hornbook. A hornbook had the alphabet, sometimes pictures to go with each letter and often the Lord's Prayer at the bottom. They received the name hornbooks because a thin piece of deer horn would be placed over the paper attached to wood to protect it from the constant use of a small child. The children would wear these "books" attached to yarn around their neck or wrist. Not only were they used to teach the children reading, but also to learn to care for their books. If they took good care for their hornbooks, then later on they would be allowed to use real books, which were quite rare and valuable at this time. *Follow the directions below to make your own hornbook.*

Supplies

paper with the look of parchment

clear contact paper

foam board or wood (1/4" thick)

yarn or leather strands

Directions

1. Cut form board or wood according to the pattern.
2. Make a hole in board or wood as illustrated.
3. Cut the "parchment" paper according to the pattern.
4. Copy the alphabet and draw pictures onto the paper. At the bottom of the page copy the Lord's Prayer.
5. Cut and stick laminating materials onto written side of the paper.
6. Glue the paper to the foam board.
7. Place the string through it.

Massachusetts Bay Colony, Home of the Puritans

Project 1, Page 2

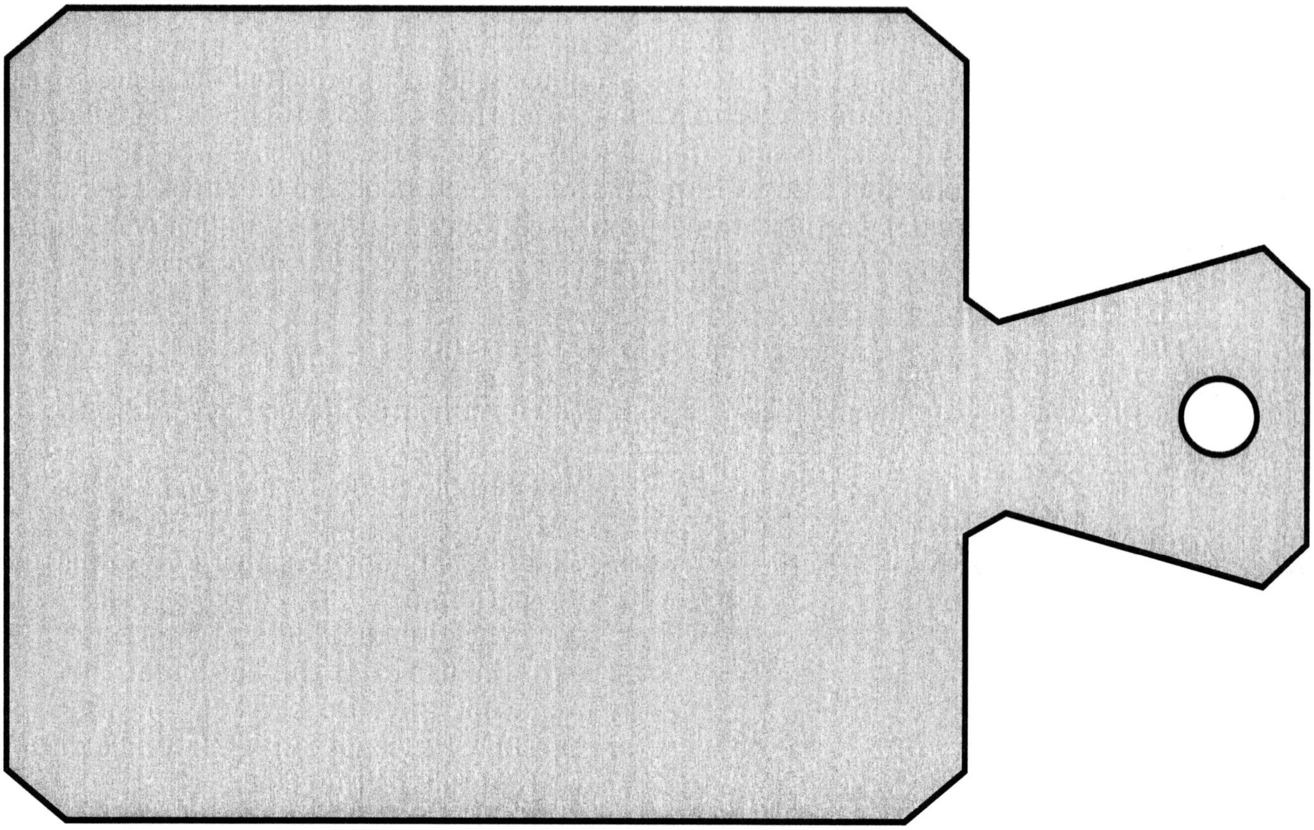

Massachusetts Bay Colony, Home of the Puritans

Project 2—John Winthrop and the Puritans

Read the following then discuss the questions at the end.

John Winthrop
Born 1583—Died 1649

Before 1630 the English had two footholds in the New World—one on the shore of Virginia and the other in what we know now as Massachusetts. Nearly ten years passed after the Pilgrims landed in New England before they were joined by the Puritans. In 1630, the Pilgrim colonists numbered but three hundred in all—a small group to dwell in a wilderness inhabited by savages. They did not regret the step they had taken or falter in their resolve to make America their home, but aching hearts were often hidden by stern faces, and homesick eyes rested lovingly on the dark waters. On the other side lay the mother country, with its well-loved towns, streams, farm lands, homesteads and friends.

But the years of their solitude were drawing to a close, for other Englishmen were coming to keep the Pilgrims company, to form new colonies, and to unite with them in a common defense when the natives became hostile.

Who were these new colonists, and what caused them to come to America? They were called Puritans, because they wished to change, or "purify" some of the forms of the English church service and church government. Neither King James nor Charles I, who succeeded him, would allow any liberty in religion or politics. "I will make them conform to my way," said King James, "or I will harry them out of the land."

Both monarchs were to find that the Pilgrims and the Puritans were willing to be harried out of the land rather than to submit to the harsh laws of their royal rulers. The Puritans, therefore, left England, as the Pilgrims had done, because they desired greater religious and political freedom than it was possible for them to have at home.

While the Pilgrims had been practically cut off from the rest of the world, they managed sometimes to send letters home by the Englishmen who had fisheries on the New England coast. From these letters, as well as from the fishermen themselves, the Puritans heard descriptions of America, of its rich land ready for the plow and of the abundant fish and game and fur-bearing animals. So they, too, decided to come to this new country.

The first of the Puritans came over in 1628 under John Endicott. They settled north of Plymouth, and gave to their little colony the Bible name Salem, meaning "peace." The Indians called this whole region Massachusetts, or the Land of the Blue Hills.

Two years later a company larger by far than any that had yet left England for this country was headed by John Winthrop. He was a gentleman of wealth, a descendant of a fine old family living near Groton, England, and a man of strong religious character. Always deeply religious, he had studied for the ministry, but to please his father he had given it up for the law. He held the office of justice of the peace before he was eighteen years of age.

Massachusetts Bay Colony, Home of the Puritans

Project 2, Page 2

As the years passed John Winthrop grew tired of the despotism of the king. At last, in 1629, he met with about a dozen companions, and after serious discussion they resolved that "for God's glory and the country's good" they would "pass the seas under God's protection to inhabit and continue in New England."

They had little difficulty obtaining from the king a charter granting them permission to establish a new colony with the right to make their own laws. Their corporation was called the Massachusetts Bay Company, and their leader, John Winthrop, was appointed first governor of the Massachusetts colony.

This large Puritan migration which set out in 1630 was very different from that of ten years before. The little *Mayflower* had alone borne the Pilgrims across the Atlantic. This same *Mayflower* was now one of the ships of the Puritan fleet that sailed happily out of Yarmouth Bay; but there were ten others to keep her company. The *Arabella* was the one in which Winthrop crossed.

From March until June they sailed across the ocean. In the eleven ships were seven hundred men and women. There were horses and cattle, tools of many kinds, powder and shot, grain and seed, clothing an provisions.

Far different, too, from the winter desolation of the coast on which the Pilgrims first set foot, was the sight that greeted the Puritans when they arrived in the pleasant summer of 1630. It was the month of June; flowers were holding up their bright faces and filling the air with perfume, strawberries were ripening, and better than all, Endicott and his companions at Salem were waiting to give them welcome.

Winthrop did not remain at Salem but established his own little community at Charlestown. It was soon found, however, that the water there was impure, and many died from its unwholesome effects. Across the river from Charlestown was a piece of land consisting of three hills. This was known as Tri-Mountain, a name afterward shortened to Tremont. To Tri-Mountain Governor Winthrop moved his colony and

Massachusetts Bay Colony, Home of the Puritans

Project 2, Page 3

the place was called Boston, after a fine old city in England, which many of the settlers knew and loved. On the highest of the three hills a beacon light was set to pilot ships coming into the harbor, and from this point beacon fires gave the signal of danger from Indian attacks. It is still called Beacon Hill, and one of Boston's chief thoroughfares is known as Beacon Street.

The Puritans' first winter in New England was almost as severe as had been that of the Pilgrims. The new settlers were not accustomed to the hardships of life in a strange, cold wilderness, and their provisions ran short. One of the men wrote, "Bread was so scarce that sometimes I thought the very crumbs of my father's table would be sweet unto me."

There came a day in midwinter when even Governor Winthrop's corn meal was reduced to a quart, and this he shared with a man poorer than himself. Happily, in that very hour, the hungry Puritans were cheered by the sight of an English ship sailing into the Boston Harbor. More Puritans with an abundant food supply had come to join the colonists.

Although two hundred died during that first winter, Winthrop, calm, courageous, and energetic, never lost heart. He helped with his own hands to do whatever labor was to be performed, and his example of patience and endurance did more than anything else to cheer and save the colony.

Many more immigrants arrived in the spring, the outlook brightened, and from that time the Massachusetts colony steadily grew. During the next ten years more than twenty thousand persons flocked to New England, and settlements were started at Watertown, Roxbury, and other places near Boston.

To each person who subscribed fifty pounds—about two hundred and fifty dollars—toward a colony was given two hundred acres of land, but the Puritans did not depend entirely upon agriculture. They became shipbuilders, engaged in commerce with the West Indies, and established fisheries at Newfoundland which were so successful that the codfish became the emblem of wealth in Massachusetts. Today a golden codfish may be seen in the State Capitol at Boston, showing that it is still a symbol of prosperity. How astonished the Puritans would have been to know that in the year 1905 the codfish catch of North America would be worth more than twelve million dollars.

The custom of holding town meetings, now so general, was first established by the

Massachusetts Bay Colony, Home of the Puritans

Project 2, Page 4

Pilgrims and the Puritans. The town meeting was the beginning of government by the people without the aid of kings. Each colony held its own meeting, in either the church or schoolhouse, and no man was allowed to vote at town meetings unless he was a church member. The colonists selected their own governor, deputy governor, and a council of eighteen men to make the necessary laws. At first the council managed all public affairs, but after a few years there was a General Court or legislature elected to make the laws.

One of the wisest acts of the Puritans, and one which had a far-reaching result, was the early establishment of schools. Many of the colonists were college-bred men, and they desired their children to be educated. They said: "In order that learning may not be buried in the graves of our fathers we will establish free schools." In 1647, only nineteen years after the landing of the Puritans, the General Court passed a law requiring that there should be a school in every town having fifty or more households.

Six years is a very short time in which to establish a town in the shores of a wilderness and bring it to such a condition that a college may be thought of and yet this is exactly what Governor Winthrop and the Puritans in Boston did. Only six years after they landed they set aside a fund for the founding of a college. The amount of money was not large, but two years later John Harvard founded a college in Charlestown, leaving his library and half his estate to aid in carrying out the plan. Such was the beginning of Harvard College.

John Winthrop was more than forty years of age when he came to America. From that time until his death nineteen years later, he never ceased to work for the good of the Massachusetts colony, and for twelve years he served as its governor. In his busy life he found time to write many books, one of them a *History of Massachusetts.*

He died in Boston, deeply loved by his friends in England and America for his devotion to what he believed to be his duty and for his patience and kindness. Someone once said of him: "Among the millions of men descended from those he ruled, there is no one that does not owe much of what is best within him to the benevolent and courageous wisdom of John Winthrop."

Discussion

1. Who were the Puritans? What did they want to do to the Church of England?
2. Who was John Winthrop?
3. How many ships came to the New World in 1630 carrying a large group of Puritans?
4. Describe the first winter the Puritans experienced in the New World.
5. What was the Puritans' view of education?

Massachusetts Bay Colony, Home of the Puritans

Project 3—Considerations and Confessions

Read the following two documents and disscuss the questions at the end.

General Considerations for the Plantation of New England

"*First,* It will be a service unto the Church, of great consequence, to carry the Gospel into those parts of the world, and raise a bulwark against the kingdom of anti-christ, which the Jesuits labor to rear up in all parts of the world.

"*Secondly,* All other Churches of Europe have been brought under *desolations;* and it may be feared that the like judgements are coming upon us; and who knows but God hath provided this place to be a *refuge* for many, whom he means to save out of the General Destruction.

"*Thirdly,* The land grows weary of her inhabitants, insomuch that man, which is the most precious of all creatures, is here more vile and base than the earth he treads upon: children, neighbors and friends, especially the poor, are counted the greatest burdens, which if things were right would be the chiefest earthly blessings.

"*Fourthly,* We are grown to that intemperance in all *excess of riot,* as no mean estate almost will suffice a man to keep sail with his equals, and he that fails in it, must live in scorn and contempt: hence it comes to pass, that all *arts* and *trades* are carried in the deceitful manner, and unrighteous course, as it is almost impossible for a good, upright man to maintain his constant charge, and to live comfortably in them.

"*Fifthly,* The schools of learning and religion are so corrupted, as (besides the unsupportable charge of education) most children, even the best, wittiest, and of the fairest hopes, are perverted, corrupted, and utterly overthrown, by the multitude of evil examples and licentious examples in these seminaries.

"*Sixthly, The whole earth* is the Lord's *garden,* and he hath given it to the sons of Adam, to be tilled and improved by them: why then should we stand starving here for places of habitation, and in the meantime suffer whole countries, as profitable for the use of man, to lye waste without improvement?

"*Seventhly,* What can be a better and nobler work, and more worthy of a Christian, than to erect and support a *reformed particular Church* in its infancy, and unite our forces with such a company of faithful people, as by a timely assistance may grow stronger and prosper; but for the want of it, may be put to great hazards, if not wholly ruined?

"*Eighthly,* If any such as are known to be godly, and live in wealth and prosperity here, shall forsake all this to join with this *reformed* church, and with it ruin the hazard of an hard and mean condition, it will be an example of great use, both for the removing of *scandal* and to give more *life* unto the *faith* of God's people in their prayers for the plantation, and also to encourage others to join the more willingly in it."

A Confession of Faith from the Massachusetts Bay Colony Church

"We covenant with our Lord, and one with another; and we do bind ourselves in the presence of God, to walk together in all his ways, according as he is pleased to reveal Himself unto us in His blessed word of truth; and do explicitly, in the name and

Massachusetts Bay Colony, Home of the Puritans

Project 3, Page 2

fear of God, profess and protest to walk as followeth, through the power and grace of our Lord Jesus Christ.

"We avouch the Lord to be our God, and our selves to be His people, in the truth and simplicity of our spirits.

"We give our selves to the Lord Jesus Christ, and the word of his grace for the teaching, ruling and sanctifying of us in matters of worship in conversation, resolving to cleave unto him alone for life and glory, and to reject all contrary ways, canons, and constitutions of men in his worship.

"We promise to walk with our brethren, with all watchfulness and tenderness, avoiding jealousies and suspicions, back-biting, censuring, secret risings of spirits against them; but in all offences to follow the rule of our Lord Jesus, and to bear and forbear, give and forgive, as he hath taught us.

"In public or private, we will willingly do nothing to the offence of the church; but willing to take advice for our selves and ours, as occasion shall be presented.

"We will not in the congregation be forward to show our own gifts and parts in speaking or scrupling, or there discover the weakness or failings of our brethren; but attend an orderly call thereunto, knowing how much the Lord may be dishonoured, and his gospel, and the profession of it, slighted by our distempers and weaknesses in public.

"We bind our selves to study the advancement of the gospel in all truth and peace; both in regard of those that are within or without it; no way slighting our sister churches, but using their counsel, as need shall be; not laying a stumbling block before any, no, not the Indians, whose good we desire to promote; and so to converse, as we may avoid the very appearance of evil.

"We do hereby promise to carry our selves in all lawful obedience to those that are over us, in Church or Commonwealth, knowing how well pleasing it will be to the Lord, that they should have encouragement in their places, by our not grieving their spirits through our irregularities.

"We resolve to approve our selves to the Lord in our particular callings; shunning idleness as the bane of any state; nor will we deal hardly or oppressingly with any, wherein we are the Lord's stewards.

"Promising also unto our best ability to teach our children and servants the knowledge of God, and of His Will, that they may serve Him also; and all this not by any strength of our own, but by the Lord Christ: whose blood we desire may sprinkle this our covenant made in his name."

Discussion

1. In your own words, rewrite the General Considerations for the Plantation of New England.
2. After reading the Confession of Faith from the Massachusetts Bay Colony Church, summarize each point. Can you think of anything to add that would bring peace to the Lord's church and to the community? If everyone obeys these confessional points, what kind of colony will Massachusetts be? Do any of these points apply to your life? How?

Massachusetts Bay Colony, Home of the Puritans

Project 4—Charter of Massachusetts Bay (1629)

Following is the Charter of the Massachusetts Bay colony, with the original spelling unchanged.

And further, That the said Governour and Companye, and their Successors, maie have forever one common Seale, to be used in all Causes and Occasions of the said Company, and the same Seale may alter, chaunge, breake, and newe make, from tyme to tyme, at their pleasures. And our Will and Pleasure is, and Wee doe hereby for Us, our Heires and Successors, ordeyne and graunte, That from henceforth for ever, there shalbe one Governor, one Deputy Governor, and eighteene Assistants of the same Company, to be from tyme to tyme constituted, elected and chosen out of the Freemen of the saide Company, for the twyme being, in such manner and forme as hereafter in theis Presents is expressed, which said Officers shall applie themselves to take Care for the best disposeing and ordering of the generall buysines and Affaires of, for, and concerning the said Landes and Premisses hereby mentioned, to be graunted, and the plantation thereof, and the Government of the People there. And for the better Execution of our Royall Pleasure and Graunte in this Behalf, Wee doe, by theis presents, for Us, our Heires and Successors, nominate, ordeyne, make, and constitute; our welbeloved the saide Mathewe Cradocke, to be the first and present Governor of the saide Company, and the saide Thomas Goffe, to be Deputy Governor of the saide Company, and the saide Sir Richard Saltonstall, Isaak Johnson, Samuell Aldersey, John Ven, John Humfrey, John Endecott, Simon Whetcombe, Increase Noell, Richard Pery, Nathaniell Wright, Samuell Vassall, Theophilus Eaton, Thomas Adams, Thomas Hutchins, John Browne, George Foxcroft, William Vassall, and William Pinchion, to be the present Assistants to the saide Company, to continue in the saide several Offices respectivelie for such tyme, and in such manner, as in and by theis. Presents is hereafter declared and appointed.

And further, Wee will, and be theis Presents, for Us, our Heires and Successors, doe ordeyne and graunte, That the Governor of the saide Company for the tyme being, or in his Absence by Occasion of Sicknes or otherwise, the Deputie Governor for the tyme being, shall have Authoritie from tyme to tyme upon all Occasions, to give order for the assembling of the saide Company, and calling them together to consult and advise of the Bussinesses and Affaires of the saide Company, and that the saide Governor, Deputie Governor, and Assisants of the saide Company, for the tyme being, shall or maie once every Moneth, or oftener at their Pleasures, assemble and houlde themselves, for the better ordering and directing of their

Massachusetts Bay Colony, Home of the Puritans

Project 4, Page 2

Affaires, and that any seaven or more persons of the Assistants, togither with the Governor, or Deputie Governor soe assembled, shalbe saide, taken, held, and reputed to be, and shalbe a full and sufficient Courte or Assemblie of the saide Company, for the handling, ordering, and dispatching of all such Buysinesses and Occurrents as shall from tyme to tyme happen, touching or concerning the saide Company or Plantation; and that there shall or maie be held and kept by the Governor, or Deputie Governor of the saide Company, and seaven or more of the saide Assistants for the tyme being, upon every last Wednesday in Hillary, Easter, Trinity, and Michas Termes respectivelie forever, one greate generall and solemne assemblie, which foure generall assemblies shalbe stiled and called the foure great and generall Courts of the saide Company.

In all and every, or any which saide greate and generall Courts soe assembled, Wee doe for Us, our Heires and Successors, give and graunte to the saide Governor and Company, and their Successors, That the Governor, or in his absence, the Deputie Governor of the saide Company for the tyme being, and such of the Assistants and Freemen of the saide Company as shalbe present, or the greater nomber of them so assembled, whereof the Governor or Deputie Governor and six of the Assistants at the least to be seaven, shall have full Power and authoritie to choose, nominate, and appointe, such and soe many others as they shall thinke fitt, and that shall be willing to accept the same, to be free of the saide Company and Body, and them into the same to admitt; and to elect and constitute such officers as they shall thinke fill and requisite, for the ordering, mannaging, and dispatching of the Affaires of the saide Governor and Company, and their Successors; And to make Lawes and Ordinances for the Good and Welfare of the saide Company, and for the Government and ordering of the saide Landes and Plantation, and the People inhabiting and to inhabite the same, as to them from tyme to tyme shalbe thought meete, soe as such Lawes and Ordinances be not contrarie or repugnant to the Lawes and Statuts of this our Realme of England.

And, our Will and Pleasure is, and Wee do hereby for Us, our Heires and Successors, establish and ordeyne, That yearely once in the yeare, for ever hereafter, namely, the last Wednesday in Easter Tearme, yearely, the Governor, Deputy-Governor, and Assistants of the saide Company and all other officers of the saide Company shalbe in the Generall Court or Assembly to be held for that Day or Tyme, newly chosen for the Yeare, ensuing by such greater parte of the saide Company, for the Tyme being, then and there present, as is aforesaide. And, if it shall happen the present governor, Deputy Governor, and assistants, by theis presents appointed, or such as shall hereafter be newly chosen into their Roomes, or any of them, or any other of the officers to be appointed for the said Company, to dye, or to be removed from his or their severall Offices or Places before the saide generall Day of Election (whome Wee doe hereby declare for any Misdemeanor or Defect to be removeable by the Governor, Deputy Governor, Assistants, and Company, or such greater Parte of them in any of the publique Courts to be assembled as is aforesaid) That then, and in every such Case, it shall and maie be made lawfull, to and for the Governor, Deputie Governor, Assistants, and Company aforesaide, or such greater Parte

Massachusetts Bay Colony, Home of the Puritans

Project 4, Page 3

of them soe to be assembled as is aforesaide, in any of their Assemblies, to proceade to a new Election of one or more others of their Company in the Roome or Place, Roomes or Places of such Officer or Officers soe dyeing or removed according to their Discretions, And, immediately upon and after such Election and Elections made of such Governor, Deputie Governor, Assistant or Assistants, or any other officer of the saide Company, in Manner and Forme aforesaide, the Authoritie, Office, and Power, before given to the former Governor, Deputie Governor, or other Officer and Officers soe removed, in whose Steade and Place newe shalbe soe chosen, shall as to him and them, cease and determine.

Provided alsoe, and our Will and Pleasure is, That aswell such as are by theis Presents appointed to be the present Governor, Deputie Governor, and Assistants of the said Company, as those that shall succeed them, and all other Officers to be appointed and chosen as aforesaid, shall, before they undertake the Execution of their saide Offices and Places respectivelie, take their Corporal Oathes for the due and faithfull Performance of their Duties in their severall Offices and Places, before such Person or Persons as are by theis Presents hereunder appointed to take and receive the same . . .

And, further our Will and Pleasure is, and Wee doe hereby for Us, our Heires and Successors, ordeyne and declare, and graunte to the saide Governor and Company and their Successors, That all and every the Subjects of Us, our Heires or Successors, which shall go to and inhabite within the saide Landes and Premisses hereby mentioned to be graunted, and every of their Children which shall happen to be borne there, or on the Seas in goeing thither, or retorning from thence, shall have and enjoy all liberties and Immunities of free and naturall Subjects within any of the Domynions of Us, our Heires or Successors, to all intents, Constructions, and Purposes whatsoever, as if they and everie of them were borne within the Realme of England. And that the Governor and Deputie Governor of the saide Company for the Tyme being, or either of them, and any two or more of such of the saide Assistants as shalbe thereunto appointed by the saide Governor and Company at any of their Courts or Assemblies to be held as aforesaide, shall and maie at all Tymes, and from tyme to tyme hereafter, have full Power and Authoritie to minister and give the Oathe and Oathes of Supremacie and Allegiance, or either of them, to all and everie Person and Persons, which shall at any Tyme or Tymes hereafter goe to passe to the Landes and Premisses hereby mentioned to be graunted to inhabite in the same.

And, Wee doe of our further Grace, certen Knowledg and meere Motion, give and graunte to the saide Governor and Company, and their Successors, That it shall and maie be lawfull, to and for the

Massachusetts Bay Colony, Home of the Puritans

Project 4, Page 4

Governor or Deputie Governor, and such of the Assistants and Freemen of the saide Company for the Tyme being as shalbe assembled in any of their generall Courts aforesaide, or in any other Courtes to be specially sumoned and assembled for that Purpose, or the greater part of them (whereof the Governor or Deputie Governor, and six of the Assistants to be alwaies seaven) from tyme to tyme, to make, ordeine, and establishe all Manner of wholesome and reasonable Orders, Lawes, Statutes, and Ordinances, Directions, and Instructions, not contrarie to the Lawes of this our Realme of England, aswell for setling of the Formes and Ceremonies of Government and Magistracy, fitt and necessary for the said Plantation, and the Inhabitants there, and for nameing and setting of all sorts of Officers, both superior and inferior, which they shall find needefull for that Government and Plantation, and the distinguishing and setting forth of the severall duties, Powers, and Lymytts of every such Office and Place, and the Formes pf such Oathes warrantable by the Lawes and Statutes of this our Realme of England, as shalbe respectivelie ministred unto them for the Execution of the said severall Offices and Places; as also, for the disposing and ordering of the Elections of such of the said Officers as shalbe annuall, and of such others as shalbe to succeede in Case of Death or Removeall, and ministring the said Oathes to the newe elected Officers, and for Impositions of lawfull Fynes, Mulcts, Imprisonment, or other lawfull Correction, according to the Course of other Corporations in this our Realme of England, and for the directing, ruling, and disposeing of all other Matters and Thinges, whereby our said People, Inhabitants there, may be soe religiously, peaceablie, and civilly governed, as their good Life and orderlie Conversation, maie wynn nd incite the Natives of Country, to the Knowledg and Obedience of the onlie true God and Saviour of Mankinde, and all Christian Fayth, which in our Royall Intention, and the Adventurers free Profession, is the principall Ende of this Plantation.

Willing, commaunding, and requiring, and by theis Presents for Us, our Heires, and Successors, ordeyning and appointing, that all such Orders, Lawes, Statuts and Ordinances, Instructions and Directions, as shalbe soe made by the Governor, or Deputie Governor of the said Company, and such of the Assistants and Freemen as aforesaide, and published in Writing, under their common Seale, shalbe carefullie and dulie observed, kept, performed and putt in Execution, according to the true Intent and Meaning of the same; and theis our Letters-patents, or the Duplicate or exemplification thereof, shalbe to all and everie such Officers, superior and inferior, from Tyme to Tyme, for the putting of the same Orders, Lawes, Statutes, and Ordinances, Instructions, and Directions, in due execution against Us, our Heires and Successors, a sufficient Warrant and Discharge.

And Wee doe further, for Us, our Heires and Successors, give and graunte to the said Governor and Company, and their Successors by theis Presents, that all and everie such Chiefe Comaunders, Captaines, Governors, and other Officers and Ministers, as by the said Orders, Lawes, Statuts, Ordinances, Instructions, or Directions of the said Governor and Company for the Tyme being, shalbe from Tyme to Tyme hereafter imploied either in the Government of the saide Inhabitants and Plantation, or in the

Massachusetts Bay Colony, Home of the Puritans

Project 4, Page 5

Waye be Sea thither, or from thence, according to the Natures and Lymitts of their Offices and Places respectively, shall from Tyme to Tyme hereafter for ever, within the Precincts and Partes of Newe England hereby mentioned to be graunted and confirmed, or in the Waie by Sea thither, or from thence, have full and Absolute Power and Authoritie to correct, punishe, pardon, governe, and rule all such the Subjects of Us, our Heires and Successors, as shall from Tyme to Tyme adventure themselves in any Voyadge thither or from thence, or that shall at any Tyme hereafter, inhabite within the Precincts and Partes of Newe England aforesaide, not being repugnant to the Lawes and Statutes of our Realme of England as aforesaid . . .

Massachusetts Bay Colony, Home of the Puritans

Test

1. Where was the Massachusetts Bay Colony first established?

2. What did the Puritans believe regarding the Church of England?

3. Who led the first group of Puritans to New England in 1628?

4. Who was John Winthrop? What did he believe about the Church of England and about the new society that was being built?

5. When new laws were established, on what did men like John Cotton base them?

Review

1. What is a navigator?

Massachusetts Bay Colony, Home of the Puritans

Test

2. Who financed Columbus's voyage?

____

____

3. Who was Ferdinand Magellan?

____

____

____

4. What did Hernando de Soto discover?

____

____

5. In chronological order list all events studied to date. Next to each place the appropriate date.

____

____

____

____

____

____

____

____

____

____

ROGER WILLIAMS, FOUNDER OF RHODE ISLAND
Worksheet

1. When did Roger Williams sail from England to New England?

____

____

____

2. Where did Roger Williams preach before accepting a call to the Salem pulpit?

____

____

3. What did he urge people to do concerning the Church of England?

____

____

4. What did Williams believe about the king's power over land in New England?

____

____

____

5. Who examined Williams and asked him to leave the colony?

____

____

6. What colony did Williams and a small group of followers form in 1636?

____

____

7. What did Williams claim about this new colony?

____

____

Roger Williams, Founder of Rhode Island

Project 1—Apple Tree Political Cartoon

It is said that in 1860 some citizens from Providence wanted to build a monument to Roger Williams and his wife Mary. It took a great deal of research because they had been buried in unmarked graves, but when they went to dig the couple up they found that they were in the middle of an old apple orchard. Unfortunately when they unearthed the coffins they only found rotten wood, a few rusty nails and in Mary's grave, a "lock of braided hair." In Roger's resting place they found the roots from a nearby apple tree. Upon closer inspection, they found that the tree had wrapped its way around to where the skull had been, then grew in a straight line where his back bone would have been. At the hips, the root divided and followed the legs down all the way to the heels then turned upwards toward the toes. The apple tree had used the dead body of Roger Williams as fertilizer. Roger Williams, water and sunlight had worked together to help the tree bear apples!

Read Matthew 7:15–23 and then finish this "political cartoon." Political cartoons have been found in newspapers for years and years. The point of such features is to lampoon or highlight a particular point of view for the reader. What kind of apples would Roger's body help to grow?

Roger Williams . . .
A Man *Tolerant*
—of ALL Thyngs

ROGER WILLIAMS, FOUNDER OF RHODE ISLAND

Project 2–Art Study

While Roger Williams was serving his tenure as governor in the backwoods of the Rhode Island colony, Rembrandt was bringing glory to God by making beautiful art. Look at the etching on this page and discuss the following questions.

1. What is happening here? What are the people doing in the background?
2. Who is the focus of the composition?

Christ and the Woman of Samaria by Rembrandt van Rijn, 1657

Roger Williams, Founder of Rhode Island

Test

1. When did Roger Williams sail from England to New England?

2. Where did Roger Williams preach before accepting a call to the Salem pulpit?

3. What did he urge people to do concerning the Church of England?

4. What did Williams believe about the king's power over land in New England?

5. What happened after John Cotton and Thomas Hooker examined Williams?

6. What colony did Roger Williams form in 1636?

7. What did Roger Williams claim about the new colony?

Roger Williams, Founder of Rhode Island

Test, Page 2

Review

1. Of what country was Prince Henry the prince?

2. What did Columbus believe God had called him to do?

3. What did Ponce de Leon explore? For what was he searching?

4. From what country was John Cabot? What did he accomplish?

5. In chronological order list all events studied to date. Next to each place the appropriate date.

Roger Williams, Founder of Rhode Island

Test, Page 3

5. (continued)

Salem Witch Trials
Worksheet

1. What hysteria occurred in Salem in 1692?

2. How many individuals were charged with "covenanting with evil spirits?"

3. How many men and women were hanged? Why?

4. How did the hysteria in Salem begin?

5. How did the government of Massachusetts deal with the accusations?

6. How did the frenzy finally come to an end?

Salem Witch Trials
Project 1—Magnalia Christi Americana

Read the following passage, taken from Magnalia Christi Americana, *in which Cotton Mather quotes the ministers of the province warning those who were trying the accused of witchcraft. As you can see, they were trying to apply biblical principles in their decisions. Read Matthew 18:15–17 and discuss how they were trying to apply this biblical principle.*

"We judge, that in the prosecution of these and all such witchcrafts, there is need of a very critical and exquisite caution: lest by too much credulity for things received only upon the devil's authority, there be a door opened for a long train of miserable consequences, and Satan get an advantage over us; for we should not be ignorant of his devices.

"As in complaints upon witchcrafts, there may be matters of enquiry, which do not amount unto matters of presumption; and there may be matters of presumption, which yet may not be reckoned matters of conviction so 'tis necessary that all proceedings thereabout be managed with an exceeding tenderness towards those that may be complained of: especially if they have been persons formerly of an unblemished reputation.

"When the first enquiry is made into the circumstances of such that may lye under any just suspicion of witchcrafts, we could wish that there may be admitted as little as is possible of such noise, company, and openness as may too hastily expose them that are examined: and that there may nothing be used as a test for the trial of the suspected, the lawfulness whereof may be doubted among the people of God: but that the directions given by such judicious writers as Perkins and Bernard, be consulted in such a case.

"Presumptions, whereupon persons may be committed, and much more convictions, whereupon persons may be condemned as guilty of witchcrafts, ought certainly to be more considerable, than barely the accused person's being represented by a spectre to the afflicted: inasmuch as it is an undoubted and a notorious thing, that a daemon may, by God's permission, appear oven [sic] to ill purposed in the shape of an innocent, yea, and a virtuous man: nor can we esteem alterations made in the sufferers, by a look or touch of the accused, to be an infallible evidence of guilt: but frequently liable to be abused by the devil's legerdemains.

"We know not whether some remarkable affronts given to the devils by our disbelieving of those testimonies whose whole force and strength is from them alone, may not put a period unto the progress of a direful calamity begun upon us, in the accusations of so many persons, whereof, we hope, some are yet clear from the great transgression laid unto their charge."

Salem Witch Trials

Literature Unit 2–The Witch of Blackbird Pond

by Elizabeth George Speare

Chapter 1

1. Where did Kit Tyler grow up?
2. How old was Kit Tyler at the beginning of her adventure?
3. What does it mean that "America was behaving badly underfoot?"
4. What humiliating act did Kit do while in the longboat?
5. Why did Goodwife Cruff believe Kit was a witch?

Chapter 2

1. What was the distance from Saybrook to Wethersfield? How may days did the voyage take?
2. Who was not suspicious of Kit and made the trip bearable?
3. What was required in order to move the Dolphin upriver to Wethersfield?
4. Why did Kit consider the Dolphin filthy?
5. What surprise did Kit tell Captain Eaton?

Chapter 3

1. Why did Kit's spirits sink "lower with each step?"
2. Whom did Aunt Rachel think Kit was?
3. Who resembled the picture Kit had "treasured of her imagined aunt?"
4. What "odd" beverage did Kit drink for breakfast?
5. Why was Uncle Matthew "upset" at Kit's arrival?

Chapter 4

1. Why was Judith so excited?
2. What forbidden extravagance was present with some of Kit's dresses?
3. Kit helped Mercy with what chore?
4. What was the real reason Kit left Barbados?
5. Why was Kit crying in bed?

Chapter 5

1. Why was Uncle Matthew concerned about Kit going to Meeting?
2. Who sat on the stairs in the church building?
3. How long did the sermon last during Kit's first Meeting?
4. What is a "Sabbath house?"
5. Whom did Kit meet after Meeting that caused her to smile?

Chapter 6

1. Why did Kit "insist" that Rev. Bulkeley compliment the meal?
2. Over what did Matthew and Rev. Bulkeley argue?
3. Whom did Kit consider the pivotal member of the Wood family?
4. What caused Judith to drop a spoon?
5. Why did Judith give her blessing to Kit and William?

Chapter 7

1. Why was Kit uncomfortable when William came to call on her?
2. To what position had William been appointed?
3. Why did Kit gain a new respect for William?
4. What did it mean the William was "building a house?"
5. Why did Kit's fingers stiffen from rebellion?

Chapter 8

1. What did Rachel and Mercy make for Kit? Why?
2. What sight made Kit catch her breath?
3. Whose house was at the edge of the Great Meadows?
4. What exciting news did Mercy tell Kit?

Literature Unit 2—The Witch of Blackbird Pond

5. What happened to "change" Matthew Wood?

CHAPTER 9

1. How did Mercy bribe the students into good behavior?
2. How did Kit tell the story of The Good Samaritan?
3. Who was able to get the students back in order?
4. What ornament was noticed by Kit?
5. What did Hannah use to teach Kit a lesson?

CHAPTER 10

1. Why were Hannah Tupper and her husband branded?
2. What did Aunt Rachel want Kit to promise?
3. What had Kit not dared to do for fear of losing control in the classroom?
4. For what was Widow Tupper fined?
5. Who visited Hannah Tupper while kit was there?

CHAPTER 11

1. Why was Mercy not discouraged by the things she was not able to do?
2. What did Prudence Cruff do for Kit?
3. What did Kit want to do for Prudence?
4. Where was Prudence able to keep the hornbook Kit had given her?
5. Whom did Kit discover was in love with John Holbrook?

CHAPTER 12

1. What had Aunt Rachel known all along?
2. With what chore did Kit volunteer to help Nat?
3. What reason did Nat give for the solemn nature of the Puritans?
4. What interest did Kit and Nat have in common?
5. Why did Uncle Matthew think Hannah Tupper should not receive charity from Kit?

CHAPTER 13

1. What event was Judith anticipating with great excitement?
2. Hannah Tupper was accused of what activity?
3. Why was Kit so happy that she "could dance a jig?"
4. What surprising turn of events took place just before the husking bee?
5. What did a red ear of corn signify?

CHAPTER 14

1. What October miracle amazed Kit?
2. What cargo did Nat ask Kit to deliver?
3. What interesting cargo was transported on the Dolphin?
4. What news arrived from Hartford?
5. What news pleased Kit?

CHAPTER 15

1. What were the people going to have to do with their land?
2. What reason did Aunt Rachel give to not be overly concerned about England's control over Connecticut?
3. Why did Judith want to see Gov. Andros?
4. What happened when the draft of wind blew out the candles at the session?
5. Why was Kit proud of her Uncle Matthew?

CHAPTER 16

1. Which holiday was canceled by the new governor?
2. What "outrageous piece of blaspheme" had the rowdy band done?
3. What was done to the three captured ringleaders?
4. What were the three precious objects

Salem Witch Trials

Literature Unit 2—The Witch of Blackbird Pond

Kit had for Prudence?

5. Why had John stopped to say good-bye?

Chapter 17

1. What was done to attempt to get rid of Judith's fever?
2. Who came to the aid of Mercy?
3. Whom did the town blame for the widespread sickness?
4. What was Kit's plan to help Hannah?
5. What was the miracle that saved Kit and Hannah?

Chapter 18

1. For what did Kit thank her Uncle?
2. What did Goodwife Cruff say Hannah had done to escape the fire?
3. What had the townspeople found in the rubble of Hannah Tupper's house?
4. Of what was Kit accused?
5. Who did Kit think would save her?

Chapter 19

1. What made Kit such a sorry sight?
2. Who was noticeably absent from Kit's inquiry?
3. What evidence did the Cruffs present as evidence of Kit's witchcraft?
4. What evidence did Prudence give on behalf of Kit?
5. What charge could Kit have made against Goodwife Cruff?

Chapter 20

1. What didn't Mercy want to miss?
2. What was the reason William gave for not calling on Kit?
3. What excuse did Kit give so she would not have to spend time alone with William?
4. What disheartening news did the militiamen bring?
5. How was Kit able to cope with the cheerless days of winter?

Chapter 21

1. What agreement was reached by John Holbrook and Dr. Bulkeley?
2. What did Kit plan to do with her dresses in the trunks?
3. What "subtle promise" made Kit realize she didn't want to go back to Barbados?
4. Whom did Kit love?
5. What was the name of Nat's new ship?

Salem Witch Trials
Project 2—Arrest Warrant

Read and discuss this actual text of an arrest warrant for Elizabeth Proctor and Sarah Cloyce, dated April 4, 1692.

There Being Complaint this day made (Before us) by capt Jonat Walcott, and Lt Natheniell Ingersull both of Salem Village, in Behalfe of theire Majesties for themselfes and also for severall of their Neighbours Against Sarah Cloyce the wife of peter Cloyce of Salem Village; and Elizabeth Proctor the wife of John Proctor of Salem farmes for high Suspition of Sundry acts of Witchcraft donne or Committed by them upon the bodies of Abigail Williams, and John Indian both of Mr Sam Parris his family of Salem Village, and Mary Walcott daughter of the above said Complainants, And Ann Putnam and Marcy Lewis of the famyly of Thomas Putnam of Salem Village whereby great hurt and dammage hath beene donne to the Bodys of s'd persons above therefore Craved Justice.

You are therefore in theire Majest's names hereby required to apprehend and bring before us Sarah Cloyce the wife of peter Cloyce of Salem Village and Elizabeth Proctor the wife of John Proctor of Salem farmes; on Munday Morneing Next being the Eleventh say of this Instant Aprill aboute Eleven of the Clock, at the publike Meeting house in the Towne, in order to theire Examination Relateing to the premises aboves'd and here of you are not to faile

Salem Witch Trials

Project 3—Death Warrant

Nineteen accused witches were hanged on Gallows Hill

Bridget Bishop
George Burroughs
Martha Carrier
Martha Corey
Mary Easty
Sarah Good
Elizabeth Howe
George Jacobs, Sr.
Susannah Martin
Rebecca Nurse
Alice Parker
Mary Parker
John Proctor
Ann Pudeator
Wilmott Redd
Margaret Scott
Samuel Wardwell
Sara Wildes
John Willard

One accused witch was pressed to death when he failed to plead either guilty or not guilty:

Giles Corey

Other accused witches died in prison:

Sarah Osborn
Roger Toothaker
Lyndia Dustin
Ann Foster

(As many as thirteen others may have died in prison.)

Read and discuss this actual text of a death warrant.

Death Warrant for Sarah Good, Rebecca Nurse, Susannah Martin, Elizabeth Howe, and Sarah Wilds

To George: Corwine Gent'm
High Sheriff of the county of Essex

Whereas Sarah Good wife of William Good of Salem Village Rebecca Nurse wife of Francis Nurse of Salem Village Susannah Martin of Amesbury Widow Elizabeth Howe wife of James Howe of Ipswich Sarah Wild wife of John Wild of Topsfield all of the County of Essex in thier Maj'ts Province of the Massachusetts Bay in New England Att A Court of Oyer; Terminer held by Adjournment for Our Severaign Lord; Lady Kind Wiliam; Queen Mary for the said County of Essex at Salem in the s'd County on the 29th day of June [torn] were Severaly arrigned on Several Indictments for the horrible Crime of Witchcraft by them practised ; Committed On Severall persons and pleading not guilty did for their Tryall put themselves on God; Their Countrey whereupon they were Each of them found; brought in Guilty by the Jury that passed On them according to their respective Indictments and Sentence of death did then pass upon them as the Law directs Execution whereof yet remains to be done: Those are Therefore in thier Maj'ties name William; Mary now King; Queen over England; ca: to will; Command you that upon Tuesday next being the 19th day for [torn] Instant July between the houres of Eight; [torn] in [torn] forenoon the same day you Safely conduct the s'd Sarah Good Rebecca Nurse Susann Martin Elizabeth Howe; Sarah Wild From thier Maj'ties goal in Salem afores'd to the place of Execution; there Cause them; Every of them to be hanged by the Neck untill they be dead and of the doings herein make return to the Clerke of the said Court; this precept and hereof you are not to fail at your perill and this Shall be your sufficient Warrant given under my hand; seale at Boston th 12't day of July in the fourth year of our Soveraigne Lord; Layd Wm; Mary King and Queen

Wm Stoughton
Salem July 19th 1692

Salem Witch Trials
Project 4—Examination and Petition of Mary Easty

Read the actual text from the examination of Mary Easty and her petition for pardon on the following page.

At a Court held at Salem village* 22. Apr. 1692 by the Hon. John Hathorne & Jonathan Corwin.

At the bringing in of the accused severall fell into fits.

Doth this woman hurt you?

[EXAMINERS' NOTE: Many mouths were stopt, & several other fits seized them Abig: Williams said it was Goody Eastie, & she had hurt her, the like said Mary Walcot, & Ann Putman, John indian said her saw her with Goody Hobbs.]

What do you say, are you guilty?

EASTY: I can say before Christ Jesus, I am free.

You see these accuse you. There is a God—Hath she brought the book to you? Their mouths were stopt. What have you done to these children?

E: I know nothing.

How can you say you know nothing, when you see these tormented, & accuse you that you know nothing? Would you have me accuse my self?

E: Yes if you be guilty.

How far have you complyed w'th Satan whereby he takes this advantage ag't you?

E: Sir, I never complyed but prayed against him all my dayes, I have no complyance with Satan in this. What would you have me do?

Confess if you be guilty.

E: I will say it, if it was my last time, I am clear of this sin.

Of what sin?

E: Of witchcraft.

Are you certain this is the woman?

[EXAMINERS' NOTE: Never a one could speak for fits.By and by Ann Putman said that was the woman, it was like her, & she told me her name; It is marvailous to me that you should sometimes think they are bewitcht, & sometimes not, when severall confess that I never knew? Her hands were clincht together, & then the hands of Mercy Lewis was clincht Look now you hands are open, her hands are open. Is this the woman? They made signes but could not speak, but Ann Putman afterwards Betty Hubbard cryed out Oh, Goody Easty, Goody Easty you are the woman, you are the woman Put up her head, for while her head is bowed the necks of these are broken.]

What do you say to this?

E: Why God will know.

Nay God knows now.

E: I know he does.

What did you think of the actions of others before your sisters came out, did you think it was Witchcraft?

E: I cannot tell.

Why do you not think it is Witchcraft?

E: It is an evil spirit, but wither it be witchcraft I do not know,

[EXAMINERS' NOTE: Sevrall said she brought them the Book and then they fell into fits.]

*Most of the early victims and accusers of the 1692 Salem witch trials lived in what was then Salem Village, which is now the town called Danvers, Essex County, Massachusetts. While early depositions and interviews took place in Salem Village starting in February 1692, the actual trials and a majority of depositions and interviews were moved to the nearby Salem Town in May 1692. Salem Town is now simply called Salem and glories in witchcraft: Police cars sport witch logos, Witchcraft Heights Elementary School is the name of a local public school, the Salem High School football team is "The Witches," a statue of Samantha Stephens from *Bewitched* was erected there in 2005, and New Age/Wiccan boutiques riddle the city.

Salem Witch Trials
Project 4, Page 2

The humble petition of mary Eastick unto his Excellency's S'r W'm Phipps to the honour'd Judge and Bench now Sitting in Judicature in Salem and the Reverend ministers humbly sheweth

That whereas your poor and humble petitioner being condemned to die Doe humbly begg of you to take it into your Judicious and pious considerations that your Poor and humble petitioner knowing my own Innocencye Blised be the Lord for it and seeing plainly the wiles and subtility of my accusers by my Selfe can not but Judge charitably of others that are going the same way of my selfe if the Lord stepps not mightily in i was confined a whole month upon the same account that I am condemned now for and then cleared by the afflicted persons as some of your honours know and in two dayes time I was cryed out upon by them and have been confined and now am condemned to die the Lord above knows my Innocence then and Likewise does now as att the great day will be known to men and Angells—I petition to your honours not for my own life for I know that I must die and my appointed time is sett but the Lord he knows it is that if it be possible no more Innocent blood may be shed which undoubtidly cannot be Avoyded In the way and course you goe in I question not but your honours does to the uttmost of your Powers in the discovery and detecting of witchcraft and witches and would not be guilty of Innocent blood for the world but by my own Innocency I know you are in this great work if it be blessed you that no more Innocent blood be shed I would humbly begg of you that your honours would be plesed to examine theis Afflicted Persons strictly and keep them apart some time and Likewise to try some of these confessing wichis I being confident there is severall of them has belyed themselves and others as will appeare if not in this wor[l]d I am sure in the world to come whither I am now agoing and I Question not but youle see and alteration of thes things they my selfe and others have made a League with the Divel we cannot confesse I know and the Lord knowes as will shortly appeare they belye me and so I Question not but they doe others the Lord above who is the Searcher of all hearts knows that as I shall answer att the Tribunall seat that I know not the least thinge of witchcraft therefore I cannot I dare not belye my own soul I beg your honers not to deny this my humble petition from a poor dying Innocent person and I Question not but the Lord will give a blesing to yor endevers

Salem Witch Trials
Project 5—Memorable Providences *by Cotton Mather*

Cotton Mather, minister of the Old North Church in Boston, published a bestselling book on the subject of witchcraft, *Memorable Providences, Relating to Witchcrafts and Posessions,* in 1689 detailing an episode of supposed witchcraft a year earlier involving an Irish washerwoman named Goody Glover. Mather's account, describing the symptoms of witchcraft, was widely read and discussed throughout Puritan New England. The book was in the meager library of Samuel Parris, the Salem minister in whose house began the tragic events of 1692.

Memorable Providences, Relating to Witchcrafts and Possessions. A Faithful Account of many Wonderful and Surprising Things, that have befallen several Bewitched and Possessed Persons in New-England. Particularly, A Narrative of the marvellous Trouble and Releef Experienced by a pious Family in Boston, very lately and sadly molested with Evil Spirits.

Whereunto is added, a Discourse delivered unto a Congregation in Boston, on the Occasion of that Illustrious Providence. As also a Discourse delivered unto the same Congregation; on the occasion of an horrible Self-Murder Committed in the Town. With an Appendix, in vindication of a Chapter in a late Book of Remarkable Providence, from the Columnies of a Quaker at Pen-silvania.

Written by Cotton Mather, Minister of the Gospel, and Recommended by the Ministers of Boston, and Charleston. Printed at Boston in N. England by R.P. 1689. Sold by Joseph Brunning, at his Shop at the Corner of the Prison-Lane next the Exchange.

To the Honorable Wait Winthrop Esq; Sr.

By the special Disposal and Providence of the Almighty God, there now comes abroad into the world a little History of several very astonishing Witchcrafts and Possessions, which partly my own Ocular Observation, and partly my undoubted Information, hath enabled me to offer unto the publick Notice of my Neighbours. It must be the Subject, and not the Manner or the Author of this Writing, that has made any people desire its Publication; For there are such obvious Defects in Both, as would render me very unreasonable, if I should wish about This or Any Composure of mine, O That it were printed in a book! But tho there want not Faults in this Discourse, to give me Discontent enough, my Displeasure at them will be recompensed by the Satisfaction I take in my Dedication of it; which I now no less properly than cheerfully make unto Your Self; whom I reckon among the Best of my Friends, and the Ablest of my readers. Your Knowledge has Qualified You to make those Reflections on the following Relations, which few can Think, and tis not fit that all should See. How far the Platonic Notions of Demons which were, it may be, much more espoused by those primitive Christians and Scholars that we call The Fathers, than they see countenanced in the ensuing Narratives, are to be allowed by a serious man, your Scriptural Divinity, join'd with Your most Rational Philosphy, will help You to Judge at an uncommon rate. Had I on the Occasion before me handled the Doctrin of Demons, or launced forth into Speculations about magical Mysteries, I might have made some Ostentation, that I have read something and thought a little in my time; but it would neither have been Convenient for me, nor Profitable for those plain Folkes, whose Edification I have all along aimed at. I have therefore here but briefly touch't every thing

Salem Witch Trials

Project 5—Memorable Providences, *Page 2*

with an American Pen; a Pen which your Desert likewise has further Entitled You to the utmost Expressions of Respect and Honor from. Though I have no Commission, yet I am sure I shall meet with no Crimination, if I here publickly wish You all manner of Happiness, in the Name of the great Multitudes whom you have laid under ever-lasting Obligations. Wherefore in the name of the many hundred Sick people, whom your charitable and skilful Hands have most freely dispens'd your no less generous than secret Medicines to; and in the name of Your whole Countrey, which hath long had cause to believe that you will succeed Your Honourable Father and Grandfather in successful Endeavours for our Welfare; I say, In their Name, I now do wish you all the Prosperity of them that love Jerusalem. And whereas it hath been sometimes observed, That the Genius of an Author is commonly Discovered in the Dedicatory Epistle, I shall be content if this Dedicatory Epistle of mine, have now discovered me to be,

(Sir) Your sincere and very humble Servant,

C. Mather.

The Introduction

It was once the Mistake of one gone to the Congregation of the Dead, concerning the Survivers, if one went unto them from the dead, they will repent. The blessed God hath made some to come from the Damned, for the Conviction (may it also be for the Conversion) of us that are yet alive. The Devils themselves are by Compulsion come to confute the Atheism and Sadducism, and to reporve the Madness of ungodly men. Those condemned prisoners of our Atmosphere have not really sent Letthers of Thanks from Hell, to those that are on Earth, promoting of their Interest, yet they have been forced, as of old, To confess that Jesus was the Holy one of God, so of late, to declare that Sin and Vice are the things which they are delighted in. But should one of those hideous Wights appear visibly with fiery chains upon him, and utter audibly his roarings and his warnings in one of our Congregations, it would not produce new Hearts in those whom the Scriptures hadled in our Ministry do not effect. However, it becomes the Embassadors of the L. Jesus to leave no stroke untouch't that may conduce to bring men from the power of Satan unto God; and for this cause it, that I have permitted the ensuing Histories to be published. They contain Things of undoubted Certainty, and they suggest Things of Importance unconceivably. Indeed they are only one Head of Collections which in my little time of Observation I have made of Memorable Providences, with Reflections thereupon, to be reserved among other effects of my Diversion from my more state and more weary Studies. But I can with a Contentment beyond meer Patience give those rescinded Sheets unto the Stationer, when I see what pains Mr. Baxtrer, Mr. Glanvil, Dr. More, and several other Great Names have taken to publish Histories of Witchcrafts and Possdessions unto the world. I said, Let me also run after them; and this with the more Alacrity because, I have tidings ready. Go then, my little Book, as a Lackey, to the more elaborate Essays of those learned men. Go tell Mankind, that there are Devils and Witches; and that tho those night-birds least appear where the Day-light of the Gospel comes, yet New-Engl. has had Exemples of their Existence and Operation; and that no only the Wigwams of Indians, where the pagan Powaws often raise

Salem Witch Trials
Project 5—Memorable Providences, *Page 3*

their masters, in the shapes of Bears and Snakes and Fires, but the House of Christians, wh ere our God has had his constant Worship, have undergone the Annoyance of Evil spirits. Go tell the world, What Prays can do beyond all Devils and Witches, and What it is that these Monsters love to do; and through the Demons in the Audience of several standers-by threatned much disgrace to thy Author, if he let thee come abroad, yet venture That, and in this way seek a just Revenge on Them for the Disturbance they have given to such as have called on the Name of God.

Witchcrafts and Possessions.
The First Exemple.

Section I. There dwells at this time, in the south part of Boston, a sober and pious man, whose Name is John Goodwin, whose Trade is that of a Mason, and whose Wife (to which a Good Report gives a share with him in all the Characters of Vertue) has made him the Father of six (now living) Children. Of these Children, all but the Eldest, who works with his Father at his Calling, and the Youngest, who lives yet upon the Breast of its mother, have laboured under the direful effects of a (no less palpable than) stupendous Witchcraft. Indeed that exempted Son had also, as was thought, some lighter touches of it, in unaccountable stabbs and pains now and then upon him; as indeed every person in the Family at some time or other had, except the godly Father, and the suckling Infant, who never felt any impressions of it. But these Four Children mentioned, were handled in so sad and strange a manner, as has given matter of Discourse and Wonder to all the Countrey, and of History not unworthy to be considered by more than all the serious or the curious Readers in this New-English World.

Sect. II. The four Children (whereof the Eldest was about Thirteen, and the youngest was perhaps about a third part so many years of age) had enjoyed a Religious Education, and answered it with a very towardly Ingenuity.' They had an observable Affection unto Divine and Sacred things; and those of them that were capable of it, seem'd to have such a Resentment, of their eternal Concernments as is not altogether usual. Their Parents also kept them to a continual Employnient, which did more than deliver them from the Temptations of Idleness, and as young as they were, they took a delight in it) it may be as much as they should have done. In a word, Such was the whole Temper and Carriage of the Children, that there cannot easily be any thing more unreasonable, than to imagine that a Design to Dissemble could cause them to fall into any of their odd Fits; though there should not have happened, as there did, a thousand Things, wherein it was perfectly impossible for any Dissimulation of theirs to produce what scores of spectators were amazed at.

Sect. III. About Midsummer, in the year 1688, the Eldest of these Children, who is a Daughter, saw cause to examine their Washerwoman, upon their missing of some Linnen which twas fear'd she had stollen from them; and of what use this linnen might bee to serve the Witchcraft intended, the Theef's Tempter knows! This Laundress was the Daughter of an ignorant and a scandalous old Woman in the Neighbourhood; whose miserable Husband before he died, had sometimes complained of her, that she was undoubtedly a Witch, and that whenever his Head was laid, she would quickly arrive unto the punishments due to such an one. This Woman in her daughters Defence bestow'd very bad Language upon the Girl that put her to the Question; immediately upon which, the poor child became variously indisposed in her health, an visited with strange Fits, beyond those that attend an Epilepsy or a Catalepsy, or those that they call The Diseases of Astonishment.

Sect. IV. It was not long before one of her Sisters, an two of her Brothers, were seized, in. Order one after another with Affects like those that molested her. Within a fe weeks, they were all four tortured every where in a manner s very grievous, that it would have broke an heart of stone to have seen their Agonies. Skilful Physicians were consulted for their Help, and particularly our worthy and prudent Friend Dr. Thomas Oakes, who found Himself so affrontcd by the Dist'empers of the children, that he concluded nothing but an hellish Witchcraft could be the Original of these Maladies. And that which yet more confirmed such Apprehension was, That for one good while, the children were tormented just in the same part of their bodies all at the same time together; and tho they saw and heard not one anothers complaints, tho likewise their pains and sprains were swift like Lightening, yet when (suppose) the Neck, or the Hand, or the Back of one was Rack't, so it was at that instant with t'other too.

Sect. V. The variety of their tortures increased continually; and tho about Nine or Ten at Night they alwaies had a Release from their miseries, and ate and slept all night for the most part indifferently well, yet in the day time they were handled with so many sorts of Ails, that it would require of us almost as much time to Relate them all, as it did of them to Endure them. Sometimes they would be Deaf, sometimes Dumb, and sometimes Blind, and often, all this at once. One while their Tongues would be drawn down their Throats; another-while they would be pull'd out upon their Chins, to a prodigious length. They would have their Mouths opened unto such a Wideness, that their Jaws went out of joint; and anon they would clap together again with a Force like that of a strong Spring-Lock. The same would happen to their Shoulder-Blades, and their Elbows, and Handwrists, and several of their joints. They would at times ly in a benummed condition and be drawn together as those that are ty'd Neck and Heels;' and presently be stretched out, yea, drawn Backwards, to such a degree that it was fear'd the very skin of their Bellies would have crack'd. They would make most pitteous out-cries, that they were cut with Knives, and struck with Blows that they could not bear. Their Necks would be broken, so that their Neck-bone would seem dissolved unto them that felt after it; and yet on the sudden, it would become, again so stiff that there was no stirring of their Heads; yea, their Heads would be twisted almost round; and if main Force at any time obstructed a dangerous motion which they seem'd to be upon, they would roar exceedingly. Thus they lay some weeks most pittiful Spectacles; and this while as a further Demonstration of Witchcraft in these horrid Effects, when I went to Praver by one of them, that was very desireous to hear what I said, the Child utterly lost her Hearing till our Prayer was over.

Sect. VI. It was a Religious Family that these Afflictions happened unto; and none but a Religious Contrivance to obtain Releef, would have been welcome to them. Many superstitious proposals were made unto them, by persons that were I know not who, nor

Salem Witch Trials

Project 5—Memorable Providences, *Page 5*

what, with Arguments fetch't from I know not how much Necessity and Experience; but the distressed Parents rejected all such counsils, with a gracious Resolution, to oppose Devils with no other weapons but Prayers and Tears, unto Him that has the Chaining of them; and to try first whether Graces were not the best things to encounter Witchcrafts with. Accordingly they requested the four Miliisters of Boston, with the Minister of Chai-Istown, to keep a Day of Prayer at their thus haunted house; which they did in the Company of some devout people there. Immediately upon this Day, the youngest of the four children was delivered, and never felt any trouble as afore. But there was yet a greater Effect of these our Applications unto our God!

Sect. VII. The Report of the Calamities of the Family for which we were thus concerned arrived now unto the ears of the Magistrates, who presently and prudent y apply'd themselves, with a just vigour, to enquire into the story. The Father of the Children complained of his Neighbour, the suspected ill woman, whose name was Glover; and she being sent for by the Justices, gave such a wretched Account of her self, that they saw cause to commit her unto the Gaolers Custody. Goodwin had no proof that could have done her any Hurt; but the Hag had not power to deny her interest in the Enchantment of the Children; and I when she was asked, Whether she believed there was a God? her Answer was too blasphemous and horrible for any Pen of mine to mention. An Experiment was made, Whether she could recite the Lords Prayer; and it was found, that tho clause after clause was most carefully repeated unto her, yet when she said it after them that prompted her, she could not Possibly avoid making Nonsense of it, with some ridiculous Depravations. This Experiment I had the curiosity since to see made upon two more, and it had the same Event. Upon Commitment of this extrordinary Woman, all the Children had some present ease,; until one (related unto her) accidentally meeting one or two of them, entertained them with her Blessing, that is, Railing; upon which Three of them fell ill again, as they were before.

Sect. VIII. It was not long before the Witch thus in the Trap, was brought upon her Tryal; at which, thro' the Efficacy of a Charm, I suppose, used upon her, by one or some of her Cruel the Court could receive Answers from her in one but the Irish, which was her Native Language; altho she under-stood the English very well, and had accustomed her whole Family to none but that Language in her former Conversation; and therefore the Communication between the Bench and the Bar, was now cheefly convey'd by two honest and faithful men that were interpreters. It was long before she could with any direct Answers plead unto her Indictment and; when she did plead, it was with Confession rather than Denial of her Guilt. Order was given to search the old womans house, from whence there were brought into the Court, several small Images, or Puppets, or Babies, made of Raggs, and stuff't with Goat's hair, and other such Ingredients. When these were produced, the vile Woman acknowledged, that her way to torment the Objects of her malice, was by wetting of her Finger with her Spittle, and streaking of those little Images. The abused Children were then present, and the Woman still kept stooping and shrinking as one that was almost prest to Death with a mighty Weight upon her. But one of the

Salem Witch Trials

Project 5—Memorable Providences, *Page 6*

Images being brought unto her, immediately she started up after an odd manner, and took it into her hand; but she had no sooner taken it, than one of the Children fell into sad Fits, before the whole Assembly. This the Judges bad their just Apprehensions at; and carefully causing the Repetition of the Experiment, found again the same event of it. They asked her, Whether she had any to stand by her: She replied, She had; and looking very pertly in the Air, she added, No, He's gone. And she then confessed, that she had One, who was her Prince, with whom she maintained, I know not what Communion. For which cause, the night after, she was heard expostulating with a Devil, for his thus deserting her; telling him that Because he had served her so basely and falsly, she had confessed all. However to make all clear, The Court appointed five or six Physicians one evening to examine her very strictly, whether she were not craz'd in her Intellectuals, and had not procured to her self by Folly and Madness the Reputation of a Witch. Diverse hours did they spend with her; and in all that while no Discourse came from her, but what was pertinent and agreeable: particularly, when they asked her, What she thought would become of her soul? she reply'd "You ask me, a very solemn Question, and I cannot well tell what to say to it." She own'd her self a Roman Catholick; and could recite her Pater Noster in Latin very readily; but there was one Clause or two alwaies too hard for her, whereof she said, " She could not repeat it, if she might have all the world." In the up-shot, the Doctors returned her Compos Mentis; and Sentence of Death was pass'd upon her.

Sect. IX. Diverse dayes were passed between her being Arraigned and Condemned. In this time one of her Neighbours had been giving in her Testimony of what another of her Neighbours had upon her Death related concerning her. It seems one Howen about Six years before, had been cruell bewitched to Death; but before she died, she called one Hughes unto her, Telling her that she laid her Death to the charge of Glover; That she had seen Glover sometimes come down her Chimney; That she should remember this, for within this Six years she might have Occasion to declare it. This Hughes now preparing her Testimony, immediately one of her children, a fine boy, well grown towards Youth, was taken ill, just in the same woful and surprising manner that Goodwins children were. One night particularly, The Boy said he saw a Black thing with a Blue Cap in the Room, Tormenting of him; and he complained most bitterly of a Hand put into the Bed, to pull out his Bowels. The next day the mother of the boy went unto Glover, in the Prison, and asked her, Why she tortured her poor lad at such a wicked rate? This Witch replied, that she did it because of wrong done to her self and her daughter. Hughes denied (as well she might) that she had done her any wrong. "Well then," sayes Glover, "Let me see your child and he shall be well again." Glover went on, and told her of her own accord, " I was at your house last night." Sayes Hughes, "In what shape?" Sayes Glover, "As a black thing with a blue Cap." Saye's Hughes, "What did you do there?" Sayes Glover, "with my hand in the Bed I tryed to pull out the boyes Bowels, but I could not." They parted; but the next day Hughes appearing at Court, had her Boy with her; and Glover passing by the Boy, expressed her good wishes for him; tho' I suppose, his Parent had no design of any mighty Respect unto the Hag, by having him with her there. But the Boy had no more Indispositions after the Condemnation of the Woman

Salem Witch Trials
Project 5—Memorable Providences, *Page 7*

Sect. X. While the miserable old Woman was under Condemnation, I did my self twice give a visit unto her. She never denyed the guilt of the Witchcraft charg'd upon her; but she confessed very little about the Circumstances of her Confederacies with the Devils; only, she said, That she us'd to be at meetings, which her Prince and Four more were present at. As for those Four, She told who they were; and for her Prince, her account plainly was, that he was the Devil. She entertained me with nothing but Irish, which Language I had not Learning enough to understand without an Interpreter; only one time, when I was representing unto her That and How her Prince had cheated her, as her self would quickly find; she reply'd, I think in English, and with passion too, "If it be so, I am sorry for that!" I offer'd many Questions unto her, unto which, after long silence, she told me, She would fain give me a full Answer, but they would not give her leave. It was demanded, "They! Who is that They?" and she return'd, that They were her Spirits, or her Saints, (for they say, the same Word in Irish signifies both). And at another time, she included her two Mistresses, as she call'd them in that They, but when it was enquired, Who those two were, she fell into, a Rage, and would be no more urged. I Sett before her the Necessity and Equity of her breaking her Covenant with Hell, and giving her self to the Lord Jesus Christ, by an everlasting Covenant; To which her Answer was, that I spoke a very Reasonable thing, but she could not do it. I asked her whether she would consent or desire to be pray'd for; To that she said, If Prayer would do her any good, shee could pray for her self. And when it was again propounded, she said, She could not unless her spirits (or angels) would give her leave. However, against her will I pray'd with her, which if it were a Fault it was in excess of Pitty. When I had done, shee thank'd me with many good Words; but I was no sooner out of her sight, than she took a stone, a long and slender stone, and with her Finger and Spittle fell to tormenting it; though whom or what she meant, I had the mercy never to understand.

Sect. XI. When this Witch was going to her Execution, she said, the Children should not be relieved by her Death, for others had a hand in it as well as she; and she named one among the rest, whom it might have been thought Natural Affection would have advised the Concealing of. It came to pass accordingly, That the Three children continued in their Furnace as before, and it grew rather Seven times hotter than it was. All their former Ails pursued them still, with an addition of (tis not easy to tell how many) more, but such as gave more sensible Demonstrations of an Enchantment growing very far towards a Possession by Evil spirits.

Sect. XII. The Children in their Fits would still cry out upon They and Them as the Authors of all their Harm; but who that They and Them were, they were not able to declare. At last, the Boy obtain'd at some times a sight of some shapes in the room. There were Three or Four of 'em, the Names of which the child would pretend at certain seasons to tell; only the Name of One, who was counted a Sager Rag than the rest, he still so stammered at, that he was put upon some Periphrasis in describing her. A Blow at the place where the Boy beheld the Spectre was alwaies felt by the Boy himself in the part of his Body that answered what might be stricken at; and this tho his Back were turn'd; which was once and again so exactly tried, that there could be no Collusion in the Business. But as a Blow at the Apparition alwaies hurt him, so it alwaies help't him too; for after the Agonies, which a Push or Stab of That had put him to, were over, (as in a minute or 2 they would be) the Boy would have a respite from his Fits a considerable while and the Hobgoblins disappear. It is very credibly reported that a wound was this way given to an Obnoxious woman in the town, whose name I will not expose: for we should be tender in such Relations lest we wrong the Reputation of the Innocent by stories not enough enquired into.

Sect. XIII. The Fits of the Children yet more arriv'd unto such Motions as were beyond the Efficacy of any natural Distemper in the World. They would bark at one another like Dogs, and again purr like so many Cats. They would sometimes complain,, that they were in a Red-hot Oven, sweating and panting at the same time unreasonably: Anon they would say, Cold water was thrown upon them, at which they would shiver very much. They would cry out of dismal Blowes with great Cudgels laid upon them; and tho' we saw no cudgels nor blowes, yet we could see the Marks left by them in Red Streaks upon their bodies afterward. And one of them would be roasted on an invisible Spit, run into his Mouth, and out at his Foot, he lying, and rolling, and groaning as if it had been so in the most sensible manner in the world; and then he would shriek, that Knives were cutting of him. Sometimes also he would have his head so forcibly, tho not visibly, nail'd unto the Floor, that it was as much as a strong man could do to pull it up. One while they would all be so Limber, that it was judg'd every Bone of them could be bent. Another while they would be so stiff, that not a joint of them could be stir'd. They would sometimes be as though they were mad, and then they would climb over high Fences, beyond the Imagination of them that look'd after them. Yea, They would fly like Geese; and be carried with an incredible Swiftness thro the air, having but just their Toes now and then upon the ground, and their Arms waved like the W'ings of a Bird. One of them, in the House of a kind Neighbour and Gentleman (Mr. Willis) flew the length of the Room, anout 20 foot, and flew just into an Infants high armed Chair; (as tis affirmed) none seeing her feet all the way touch the floor.

Sect. XIV. Many wayes did the Devils take to make the children do mischief both to themselves and others; but thro the singular Providence of God, they always fail'd in the attempts. For they could never essay the doing of any harm, unless there were somebody at hand that might prevent it; and seldome without first shrieking out, "They say, I must do such a thing!" Diverse times they went to strike furious Blowes at their tenderest and dearest friends, or to fling them down staires when they had them at the Top, but the warnings from the mouths of the children themselves, would still anticipate what the Devils did intend. They diverse times were very near Burning, or Drowning of themselves, but the Children themselves by their own pitiiful and seasonable cries for Help, still procured their Deliverance: Which made me to Consider, Whether the Little, ones had not their Angels, in the plain sense of Our Saviours Intimation. Sometimes, When they were tying their own Neck-clothes, their compelled hands miserably strangled themselves, till perhaps, the standers-by gave some Relief unto them. But if any small Mischief happen'd to be done where they were, as the

Tearing or Dirtying of a Garment, the Falling of a Cup, the breaking of a Glass or the like; they would rejoice extremely, and fall into a pleasure and Laughter very extraordinary. All which things cornpar'd with the Temper of the Children, when they are themselves, may suggest some very peculiar Thoughts unto us.

Sect. XV. They were not in a constant Torture for some Weeks, but were a little quiet, unless upon some incidental provocations; upon which the Devils would handle them like Tigres, and wound them in a manner very horrible. Particularly, Upon the least Reproof of their Parents for any unfit thing they said or did, most grievous woful Heart-breaking Agonies would they fall into. If any useful thing were to be done to them, or by them, they would have all sorts of Troubles fall upon them. It would sometimes cost one of them an Hour or Two to be undrest in the evening, or drest in the morning. For if any one went to unty a string, or undo a Button about them, or the contrary; they would be twisted into such postures as made the thing impossible. And at Whiles, they would be so managed in their Beds, that no Bed-clothes could for an hour or two be laid upon them; nor could they go to wash their Hands, without having them clasp't so odly together, there was no doing of it. But when their Friends were near tired with Waiting, anon they might do what they would unto them. Whatever Work they were bid to do, they would be so snap't in the member which was to do it, that they with grief still desisted from it. If one ordered them to Rub a clean Table, they were able to do it without any disturbance; if to rub a dirty Table, presently they would with many Torrnents be made uncapable. And sometimes, tho but seldome, they were kept from eating their meals, by having their Teeth sett when they carried any thing unto their Mouthes.

Sect. XVI. But nothing in the World would so discompose them as a Religious Exercise. If there were anv Discourse of God, or Christ, or any of the things which are not seen qnd are eternal, they would be cast into intolerable Anguishes. Once, those two Worthy Ministers Mr. Fisk and Mr. Thatcher, bestowing some gracious Counsils on the Boy, whom they there found at a Neighbours house, he immediately lost his Hearing, so that he heard not one word, but just the last word of all they said. Much more, All Praying to God, and Reading of His word, would occasion a very terrible Vexation to them: they would then stop their own Ears with their own Hands; and roar, and shriek; and holla, to drown the Voice of the Devotion. Yea, if any one in the Room took up a Bible to look into it, tho the Children could see nothing of it, as being in a croud of Spectators, or having their Faces another way, yet would they be in wonderful Miseries, till the Bible were laid aside. In short, No good thing must then be endured near those Children, Which (while they are themselves) do love every good thing in a measure that proclaims in them the Fear of God.

Sect. XVII. My Employments were such, that I could not visit this afflicted Family so often as I would; Wherefore,that I might show them what kindness I could, as also that I might have a full opportunity to observe the extraordinary Circumstances of the Children, and that I might be furnished with Evidence and Argument as a Critical Eye-Witness to confute the Saducism of this debauched Age; I took the Eldest of them home to my House. The young Woman continued well at our house, for diverse dayes, and apply'd her self to such

Salem Witch Trials
Project 5—Memorable Providences, *Page 10*

Actions not only of Industry, but of Piety, as she had been no stranger to. But on the Twentieth of November in the Fore-noon, she cry'd out, "Ah, They have found me out! I thought it would be so!" and immediately she fell into her fits again. I shall now confine my Story cheefly to Her, from whose Case the Reader may shape some Conjecture at the Accidents of the Rest.

Sect. XVIII. Variety of Tortures now siez'd upon the Girl; in which besides the forementioned Ails returning upon her, she often would cough up a Ball as big as a small Egg, into the side of her Wind-pipe, that would near choak her, till by Stroking and by Drinking it was carried down again. At the beginning of her Fits usually she kept odly Looking up the Chimney, but could not say what she saw. When I bad her Cry to the Lord Jesus for Help, her Teeth were instantly sett; upon which I added, "Yet, child, Look unto Him," and then her Eyes were presently pulled into her head, so farr, that one might have fear'd she should never have us'd them more. When I prayed in the Room, first her Arms were with a strong, tho not seen Force clap't upon her ears; and when her hands were with violence pull'd away, she cried out, "They make such a noise, I cannot hear a word!" She likewise complain'd, that Goody Glover's Chain was upon her- Leg, and when she essay'd to go, her postures were exactly sluch as the chained Witch had before she died. But the manner still was, that her Tortures in a small while would pass over, and Frolick succeed; in which she would continue many hours, nay, whole days, talking perhaps never wickedly, but alwaies wittily, beyond her self; and at certain provocations, her Tortures would renew upon her, till we had left off to give them. But she frequently told us, that if she might but steal, or be drunk, she should be well immediately.

Sect. XIX. In her ludicrous Fits, one while she would be for Flying; and she would be carried hither and thither, tho not long from the ground, yet so long as to exceed the ordinary power of Nature in our Opinion of it: another-while she would be for Diving, and use the Actions of it towards the Floor, on which, if we had not held her, she would have throwrn her self. Being at this exercise she told us, That They said, stie must go down to the Bottom of our Well, for there was Plate there, and They said, They would bring her safely up again. This did she tell us, tho she had never heard of any Plate there! and we ourselves who had newly bought the house, hardly knew of any; but the former Owner of the House just then coming in, told us there had been Plate for many Years at the Bottom of the Well. She had once a great mind to have eaten a roasted Apple, but whenever she attempted to eat it, her Teeth would be sett, and sometimes, if she went to take it up her Arm would be made so stiff, that she could not possibly bring heir hand to her Mouth: at last she said, "Now They say, I shall eat it, if I eat it quickly;" and she nimbly eat it all up. Moreover, There was one very singular passion that frequently attended her. An Invisible Chain would be clapt about her, and shee, in much pain and Fear, cry out, When They began to put it on. Once I did with my own hand knock it; off as it began to be fastned about her. But ordinarily) When it was on, shee'd be pull'd out of her seat with such violence towards the Fire, that it has been as much as one or two of us could do to keep her out. Her Eyes were not brought to be perpendicular to her feet, when she rose out of her Seat, as the Mechanism of a Humane

Body requires in them that rise, but she was one dragg'd wholly by other Hands: and once, When I gave a stamp on the Hearth, just between her and the Fire, she scream'd out, (tho I think she saw me not) that I Jarr'd the Chain, and hurt her Back.

Sect. XX. While she was in her Frolicks I was willing to try, Whether she could read or no; and I found, not only That If she went to read the Bible her Eyes would be strangely twisted and blinded, and her Neck presently broken, but also that if any one else did read the Bible in the Room, tho it were wholly out of her sight, and without the least voice or noise of it, she would be cast into very terrible Agonies. Yet once Falling into her Maladies a little time after she bad read the 59th Psalm, I said unto the standers by, "Poor child! she can't now read the Psalm she readd a little while ago," she listened her self unto something that none of us could hear and made us be silent for some few Seconds of a minute. Whereupon she said, "But I can read it, they say I shall!" So I show'd her the Psalm, and she readd it all over to us. Then said 1, "Child, say Amen to it:" but that she could not do. I added, "Read the next:" but no where else in the Bible could she read a word. I brought her a Quakers Book; and That she could quietly read whole pages of; only the Name of God and Christ she still skip't over, being unable to pronounce it, except sometimes with stammering a minute or two or more upon it. When we urged her to tell what the word was that she missed, shee'd say, "I must not speak it; They say I must not, you know what it is, it's G and O and D;" so shee'd spell the Name unto us. I brought her again one that I thought was a Good Book; and presently she was handled with intolerable Torments. But when I show'd her a JestBook, as, The Oxford Jests, or the Cambridge Jests, she could read them without any Disturbance and have witty Descants upon them too. I entertained her with a Book that pretends to prove, That there are no Witches; and that she could read very well, only the Name Devils, and Witches, could not be uttered by her without extraordinary Difficulty. I produced a Book to her that proves, That there are Witches, and that she had not power to read. When I readd in the Room the Story of Ann Cole, in my Fathers Remarkable Providences, and came to the Exclamation which the Narrative saies the Demons made upon her, "Ah she runs to the Rock!" it cast her into inexpressible Agonies; and shee'd fall into them whenever I had the Expression of, "Running to the Rock)" afterwards. A popish Book also she could endure very well; but it would kill her to look into any Book, that (in my Opinion) it might have bin profitable and edifying for her to be reading of. These Experiments were often enough repeated, and still with the same Success, before Witnesses not a few. The good Books that were found so mortal to her were cheefly such as lay ever at hand in the Room. One was the Guid to Heaven from the Word, which I had given her. Another of them was Mr. Willard's little (but precious) Treatise of Justification. Diverse Books published by my Father I also tried upon her; partictilarly, his Mystery of Christ; and another small Book of his about Faith and Repentance, and the day of Judgement. Once being very merrily talking by a Table that had this last Book upon it, she just opened the Book, and was immediately struck backwards as dead upon the floor. I hope I have not spoil'd the credit of the Books, By telling how much the Devils hated them. I shall therefore add, That my Grandfather Cottons Catechism called Milk for Babes, and The Assemblies Catechism, would bring hideous Convulsions on the Child if she look't into them; tho she had once learn't them with all the love that could be.

Sect. XXI. I was not unsensible that this Girls Capacity or incapacity to read, was no Test for Truth to be determined by, and therefore I did not proceed much further in this fanciful Business, not knowing What snares the Devils might lay for us in the Tryals. A few further Tryals, I confess, I did make; but what the event of 'em was, I shall not relate, because I would not offend. But that which most made me to wonder was, That one bringing to her a certain Prayer-Book, she not only could Read it very well, but also did read a large part of it over, and calling it Her Bible, she took in it a delight and put on it a Respect more than Ordinary. If she were going into her tortures, at the offer of this Book, she, would come out of her fits and read; and her Attendents were almost under a Temptation to use it as a Charm, to make and keep her quiet. Only, When she came to the Lords Prayer, (now and then occurring in this Book) she would have her eyes put out, so that she must turn over a new leaf, and then she could read again. Whereas also there are Scriptures in that Book, she could read them there, but if I shew'd her the very same Scriptures in the Bible, she should sooner Dy than read them. And she was likewise made unable to read the Psalms in an ancient meeter, which this prayer-book had in the same volumne with it. There were, I think I may say, no less than Multitudes of Witnesses to this odd thing; and I should not have been a faithful and honest Historian, if I had withheld from the World this part of my History: But I make no Reflections on it. Those inconsiderable men that are provoked at it (if any shall be of so little Sense as to be provoked) must be angry at the Devils, and not at me; their Malice, and not my Writing, deserves the Blame of any Aspersion which a true History may seem to cast on a Book that some have enough manifested their Concernment for.

Sect. XXII. There was another most unaccountable Circumstance which now attended her; and until she came to our House, I think, she never had Experience of it. Ever now and then, an Invisible Horse would be brought unto her, by those whom she only called, "them," and, "Her Company": upon the Approach of Which, her eyes would be still closed up; for (said she) "They say, I am a Tell-Tale, and therefore they will not let me see them." Upon this would she give a Spring as one mounting an Horse, and Settling her self in a RidingPosture-she would in her Chair be agitated as one sometimes Ambleing, sometimes Trotting, and sometimes Galloping very furiously. In these motions we could not perceive that she was stirred by the stress of her feet, upon the ground; for often she touch't it not; but she mostly continued in her Chair, though sometimes in her hard Trott we doubted she would have been tossed over the Back of it. Once being angry at his Dulness, When she said, she would cut off his head if she had a knife, I gave her my Sheath, wherewith she suddenly gave her self a stroke on the Neck, but complained, it would not cut. When she had rode a minute or two or three, shee'd pretend to be at a Rendezvous with Them, that were Her Company; there shee'd maintain a Discourse with them, and asking many Questions concerning her self, (for we gave her none of ours) shee'd Listen much, and Received Answers from them that indeed none but her self perceived. Then would she return and inform us, how They did intend to handle her for a day or two afterwards, besides some other things that she enquired of them. Her Horse would sometimes throw her, with much Violence; but she would mount again; and one of the Standers-by once imagining them that were Her Company, to be before her (for she call'd unto them to stay for her) he struck with his Cane in the Air where he thought they were, and tho her eyes were wholly shutt, yet she cry'd out, that he struck her. Her Fantastic Journeyes were mostly performed in her Chair without removing from it; but sometimes would she ride from her Chair, and be carried odly on the Floor, from one part of the Room to another, in the postures of a Riding Woman. If any of us asked her, Who her Company were? She generally replyed, I don't know. But If we were instant in our Demand, she would with some witty Flout or other turn it off. Once I said, "Child, if you can't tell their Names, pray tell me what Clothes they have on;" and the Words were no sooner out of my mouth, but she was laid for dead upon the Floor.

Sect. XXIII. One of the Spectators once ask'd her, Whether she could not ride up stairs; unto which her Answer was, That she believe'd she could, for her Horse could do very notable things. Accordingly, when her Horse came to her again, to our Admiration she Rode (that is, was tossed as one that rode) up the stairs: there then stood open the Study of one belonging to the Family, into which entring, she stood immediately upon her Feet, and cry'd out, "They are gone; they are gone! They say, that they cannot—God won't let 'em come here!" She also added a Reason for it, which the Owner of the Study thought more kind than true. And she presently and perfectly came to her self, so that her whole Discourse and Carriage was altered unto the greatest measure of Sobriety, and she satt Reading of the Bible and Good Books, for a good part of the Afternoon. Her Affairs calling her anon to go down again, the Daemons were in a quarter of a minute as bad upon her as before, and her Horse was Waiting for her. I understanding of it, immediately would have her up to the study of the young man where she had been at ease before; meerly to try Whether there had not been a Fallacy in what had newly happened: but she was now so twisted and writhen, that it gave me much trouble to get her into my Arms, and much more to drag her up the stairs. She was pulled out of my hands, and when I recovered my Hold, she was thrust so hard upon me, that I had almost fallen backwards, and her own breast was sore afterwards, by their Compressions to detain her; she seem'd heavier indeed than three of her self. With incredible Forcing (tho she kept Screaming, "They say I must not go in!") at length we pull'd her in; where she was no sooner come, but she could stand on her Feet, and with an altered tone, could thank me, saying, "now I am well." At first shee'd be somewhat faint, and say, She felt something go out of her; but in a minute or two, she could attend any Devotion or Business as well as ever in her Life; and both spoke and did as became a person of good Discretion. I was loth to make a Charm of the Room; yet some strangers that came to visit us, the Week after, desiring to see the Experiment made, I permitted more than two or three Repetitions of it; and it still succeded as I have declared. Once when I was assisting 'em in carrying of her up, she was torn out of all our hands; and to my self, she cry'd out, "Mr. M., One of them is going to push you down the stairs, have a care." I remember not that I felt any Thrust or Blow; but I think I was unaccountably made to step down backward two or three stairs, and within a few hours she told me by whom it was.

Sect. XXIV. One of those that had bin concerned for her Welfare, had newly implored the great God that the young woman might be able to declare whom she apprehended her self troubled by. Presently upon this her Horse returned, only it pestered her with such ugly paces, that she fell out with her Company, and threatned now to tell all, for their so abusing her. I was going abroad, and she said unto them that were about her, "Mr. M. is gone abroad, my horse won't come back, till he come home; and then I believe" (said she softly,) "I shall tell him all." I staid abroad an hour or two,andthen Returning, When I was just come to my Gate, before I had given the least Sign or Noise of my being there, she said, "My Horse is come!" and intimated, that I was at the Door. When I came in, I found her mounted after her fashion, upon her Aerial Steed; which carried her Fancy to the Journeys end. There (or rather then) she maintained a considerable Discourse with Her Company, Listening very attentively when she had propounded any Question, and receiving the Answers with impressions made upon her mind. She said; "Well what do you say? How many Fits more am I to have?—pray, can ye tell how long it shall be before you are hang'd for what you have done?—You are filthy Witches to my knowledge, I shall see some of you go after your sister; You would have killd me; but you can't, I don't fear you.—You would have thrown Mr Mather down stairs, but you could not.—Well! How shall I be To morrow? I Pray, What do you think of Tomorrow?Fare ye well.—You have brought me such an ugly Horse, I am angry at you; I could find in my heart to tell all." So she began her homeward-paces; but when she had gone a little way, (that is a little while) she said, "O I have forgot one Question, I must go back again;" and back she rides. She had that day been diverse times warning us, that they had been contriving to do some harm to my Wife, by a Fall or a Blow, or the like; and when she came out of her mysterious Journeys, she would still be careful concerning Her. Accordingly she now calls to her Company again, "Hark you, One thing more before we part! What hurt is it you will do to Mrs. Mather? will you do her any hurt?" Here she list'ned some time; and then clapping her hands, cry'd out, "O, I am glad on't, they can do Mrs. Mather no hurt: they try, but they say they can't." So she returns and at once, Dismissing her Horse, and opening her eyes, she call'd me to her, "Now Sir," (said she) "I'll tell you all. I have learn'd who they are that are the cause of my trouble, there's three of them," (and she named who) "if they were out of the way, I should be well. They say, they can tell now how long I shall be troubled, But they won't. Only they seem to think, their power will be broke this Week. They seem also to say, that I shall be very ill To morow, but they are themselves terribly afraid of to morrow; They fear, that to morrow we shall be delivered. They say too, that they can't hurt Mrs. Mather, which I am glad of. But they said, they would kill me to night, if I went to bed before ten a clock, if I told a word." And other things did she say, not now to be recited.

Sect. XXV. The Day following, which was, I think, about the twenty seventh of November, Mr. Morton of Charlestown, and Mr. Allen, Mr. Moody, Mr. Willard, and my self, of Boston, with some devout Neighbours, kept another Day of Prayer, at John Goodwin's house; and we had all the Children present with us there. The children were miserably tortured, while we laboured in our Prayers; but our good God was nigh unto us, in what we call'd upon Him for. From this day the power of the Enemy was broken; and the children, though Assaults after this were made upon them, yet were not so cruelly handled as before. The Liberty of the Children encreased daily more and more, and their Vexation abated by degrees; till within a little while they arrived to Perfect Ease, which for some weeks or months they cheerfully enjoyed. Thus Good it is for us to draw near to God.

Sect. XXVI. Within a day or two after the Fast, the young Woman had two remarkable Attempts made upon her, by her invisible Adversaries. Once, they were Dragging her into the Oven that was then heating, while there was none in the Room to help her. She clap't her hands on the Mantletree' to save her self; but they were beaten off; and she had been burned, if at her Out-cryes one had not come in from abroad for her Relief. Another time, they putt an unseen Rope with a cruel Noose about her Neck, Whereby she was choaked, until she was black in the Face; and though it was taken off before it had kil-l'd her, yet there were the red Marks of it, and of a Finger and a Thumb near it, remaining to be seen for a while afterwards.

Sect. XXVII. This was the last Molestation that they gave her for a While; and she dwelt at my house the rest of the Winter, having by an obliging and vertuous Conversation, made her self enough Welcome to the Family. But within about a Fortnight, she was visited with two dayes of as Extraordinary Obsessions as any we had been the Spectators of. I thought it convenient for me to entertain my Congregation with a Sermon upon the memorable Providences which these Children had been concerned in. When I had begun to study my Sermon, her Tormentors again seiz'd upon her; and all Fryday and Saturday, did they manage her with a special Design, as was plain, to disturb me in what I was about. In the worst of her extravacancies formerly, she was more dutiful to my self, than I had reason to Expect, but now her whole carriage to me was with a Sauciness that I had not been us'd to be treated with. She would knock at my Study Door, affirming, That some below would be glad to see me; when there was none that ask't for me. She would call to me with multiplyed Impertinencies, and throw small things at me wherewith she could not give me any hurt. Shee'd Hector me at a strange rate for the work I was at, and threaten me with I know not what mischief for it. She got a History that I had Written of this Witchcraft, and tho she had before this readd it over and over, yet now she could not read (I believe) one entire Sentence of it; but she made of it the most ridiculous Travesty in the World, with such a Patness and excess of Fancy, to supply the sense that she put upon it, as I was amazed at. And she particularly told me, That I should quickly come to disgrace by that History.

Sect. XXVIII. But there were many other Wonders beheld by us before these two dayes were out. Few tortures attended her, but such as were provoked; her Frolicks being the things that had most possession of her. I was in Latin telling some young Gentlemen of the Colledge, That if I should bid her Look to God, her Eyes would be put out, upon which her eyes were presently served so. I was in some surprize, When I saw that her Troublers understood Latin, and it made me willing to try a little more of their Capacity. We continually found, that if an English Bible were in any part of the Room seriously look'd into, though she saw and heard nothing of it, she would immediately be in very dismal Agonies. We now made a Tryal more than once or twice, of the Greek New Testament, and the Hebrew Old Testament; and We still found, That if one should go to read in it never so secretly and silently, it would procure her that Anguish, Which there was no enduring of. But I thought, at length, I fell upon one inferior Language which the Daemons did not seem so well to understand.

Sect. XXIX. Devotion was now, as formerly, the terriblest of all the provocations that could be given her. I could by no means bring her to own, That she desired the mercies of God, and the prayers of good men. I would have obtained a Sign of such a Desire, by her Lifting up of her hand; but she stirr'd it not: I then lifted up her hand my self, and though the standers-by thought a more insignificant thing could not be propounded, I said, " Child, If you desire those things, let your hand fall, when I take mine away:" I took my hand away, and liers continued strangely and stifiy stretched out, so that for some time, she could not take it down. During these two dayes we had Prayers oftener in our Family than at other times; and this was her usual Behavior at them. The man that prayed, usually began with Reading the Word of Cod; which once as he was going to do, she call'd to him, "Read of Mary Magdelen, out of whom the Lord cast seven Devils." During the time of Reading, she would be laid as one fast asleep; but when Prayer was begun, the Devils would still throw her on the Floor, at the feet of him that prayed. There would she lye and Whistle and sing and roar, to drown the voice of the Prayer; but that being a little too audible for Them, they would shutt close her Mouth and her cars, and yet make such odd noises in her Threat as that she her self could not hear our Cries to God for her. Shee'd also fetch very terrible Blowes with her Fist, and Kicks with her Foot at the man that prayed; but still (for he had bid that none should hinder her) hei, Fist and Foot would alwaies recoil, when they came within a few hairs breadths of him just as if Rebounding against a Wall; so that she touch'd him not, but then would beg hard of other people to strike him, and particularly she entreated them to take the Tongs and smite him; Which not being done, she cryed out of him, "He has wounded me in the Head." But before Prayer was out, she would be laid for Dead, wholly sensless and (unless to a severe Trial) Breathless; with her Belly swelled like a Drum, and sometimes with croaking Noises in it; thus would she ly, most exactly with the stiffness and posture of one that had been two Days laid out for Dead. Once lying thus, as he that was praying was alluding to the words of the Canaanitess, and saying, "Lord, have mercy on a Daughter vexed with a Devil;" there came a big, but low voice from her, saying, "There's Two or Three of them" (or us!) and the standers-by were under that Apprehension, as that they cannot relate whether her mouth mov'd in speaking of it. When Prayer was ended, she would Revive in a minute or two, and continue as Frolicksome as before. She thus continued until Saturday towards the Evening; when, after this man had been at Prayer, I charged all my Family to admit of no Diversion by her Frolicks, from such exercises as it was proper to begin the Sabbath with. They took the Counsel; and tho she essayed, with as witty and as nimble and as various an Application to each of them successively as ever I saw, to make them laugh, yet they kept close to their good Books which

Salem Witch Trials
Project 5—Memorable Providences, *Page 17*

then called for their Attention. When she saw that, immediately she fell asleep; and in two or three hours, she waked perfectly her self; weeping bitterly to remember (for as one come out of a dream she could remember) what had befallen her.

Sect. XXX. After this, we had no more such entertainments. The Demons it may be would once or twice in a Week trouble her for a few minutes with perhaps a twisting and a twinkling of her eyes, or a certain Cough which did seem to be more than ordinary. Moreover, Both she at my house, and her Sister at home, at the time which they call Christmas, were by the Daemons made very drunk, though they had no strong Drink (as we are fully sure) to make them so. When she began to feel her self thus drunk, she complain'd, "O they say they will have me to keep Christmas with them! They will disgrace me when they can do nothing else!" And immediately the Ridiculous Behaviours of one drunk were with a wonderful exactness represented in her Speaking, and Reeling, and Spewing, and anon Sleeping, till she was well again. But the Vexations of the Children otherwise abated continually. They first came to be alwaies Quiet, unless upon Provocations. Then they got Liberty to work, but not to read: then further on, to read, but not aloud, at last they were wholly delivered; and for many Weeks remained so.

Sect. XXXI. I was not unsensible, that it might be an easie thing to be too bold, and go too far, in making of Experiments: Nor was I so unphilosophical as not to discern many opportunityes of Giving and Solving many Problemes which the pneumatic Discipline is concerned in. I confess I have Learn't much more than I sought, and I have bin informed of some things relating to the invisible World, which as I did not think it lawful to ask, so I do not think it proper to tell; yet I will give a Touch upon one Problem commonly Discoursed of; that is, Whether the Devils know our Thoughts, or no? I will not give the Reader my Opinion of it, but only my Experiment. That they do not, was conjectured from this: We could cheat them when we spoke one thing, and mean't another. This was found when the Children were to be undressed. The Devils would still in wayes beyond the Force of any Imposture, wonderfully twist the part that was to be undress't, so that there was no coming at it. But, if we said, untye his neckcloth, and the parties bidden, at the same time, understood our intent to be, unty his Shooe! The Neckcloth, and not the shooe, has been made strangely inaccessible. But on the other side, That they do, may be conjectured from This. I called the young Woman at my House by her Name, intending to mention unto her some Religious Expedient whereby she might, as I thought, much relieve her self; presently her Neck was broke, and I continued watching my Opportunity to say what I designed. I could not get her to come out of her Fit, until I had laid aside my purpose of speaking what I thought, and then she reviv'd immediately. Moreover a young Gentleman visiting of me at my Study to ask my advice about curing the Atheism and Blasphemy which he complained his Thoughts were more than ordinarily then infested with; after some Discourse I carried him down to see this Girl who was then molested with her unseen Fiends; but when he came, she treated him very coursly and rudely, asking him What he came to the house for? and seemed very angry at his being there, urging him to be gone with a very impetuous Importunity.

SALEM WITCH TRIALS

Project 5—Memorable Providences, *Page 18*

Perhaps all Devils are not alike sagacious.

Sect. XXXII, The Last Fit that the young Woman had, was very peculiar. The Daemons having once again seiz'd her, they made her pretend to be Dying; and Dying truly we fear'd at last she was: She lay, she tossed, she pull'd just like one Dying, and urged hard for some one to dy with her, seeming loth to dy alone. She argued concerning Death, in strains that quite amazed us; and concluded, That though she was loth to dy, yet if God said she must, she must; adding something about the state of the Countrey, which we wondred at. Anon, the Fit went over; and as I guessed it would be, it was the last Fit she had at our House. But all my Library never afforded me any Commentary on those Paragraphs of the Gospels, which speak of Demoniacs, equal to that which the passions of this Child have given me.

Sect. XXXIII. This is the Story of Goodwins Children, a Story all made up of Wonders! I have related nothing but what I judge to be true. I was my self an Eye-witness to a large part of what I tell; and I hope my neighbours have long thought, That I have otherwise learned Christ, than to ly unto the World. Yea, there is, I believe, scarce any one particular, in this Narrative, which more than one credible Witness will not be ready to make Oath unto. The things of most Concernment in it were before many Critical Observersand the Whole happened in the Metropolis of the English America, unto a religious and industrious Family which was visited by all sorts of Persons, that had a mind to satisfy themselves. I do now likewise publish the History, While the thing is yet fresh and New; and I challenge all men to detect so much as one designed Falshood, yea, or so much as one important Mistake, from the Egg to the Apple of it. I have Writ as plainly as becomes an Historian, as truly as becomes a Christian, tho perhaps not so profitably as became a Divine. But I am resolv'd after this, never to use but just one grain of patience with any man that shall go to impose upon me a Denial of Devils, or of Witches. I shall count that man Ignorant who shall suspect, but I shall count him down-right Impudent if he Assert the Non-Existence of things which we have had such palpable. Convictions of. I am sure he cannot be a Civil, (and some will question whether he can be an honest man) that shall go to,deride the Being of things which a whole Countrey has now beheld an house of pious people suffering not a few Vexations by. But if the Sadducee, or the Atheist, have no right Impressions by these Memorable Providences made upon his mind; yet I hope those that know what it is to be sober will not repent any pains that they may have taken in perusing what Records of these Witchcrafts and Possessions, I thus leave unto Posterity.

Salem Witch Trials

Project 6–Fill in the Blank

Using the history card, fill in the missing blanks. This will help in memorizing the flashcard.

1. In 1692 Salem, Massachusetts was swept by an hysterical fear of _______________. Over 160 individuals were charged with "_________________ with evil spirits."
2. ________________ men and women were hanged for supposedly practicing diabolical arts.
3. In the ________ century, ________________ was commonplace–few denied the reality of the black arts.
4. ____________ in Salem began from an actual case involving two young girls. ____________, an Indian woman, admitted that she and two other girls had been practicing _______________.
5. This incident sparked the interest of many and soon the number of the accused exceeded _______________.
6. The government of __________________ was in the process of great change and dealt _________ with the accusations.
7. _______________ ____________ became critical of the sort of evidence the court had admitted. Eventually the ______________ influence brought the court's __________ to an end.

Salem Witch Trials
Test

1. What was the date of the Salem Witch Trials?

2. How did the hysteria in Salem begin?

3. How many individuals were charged with "covenanting with evil spirits?"

4. How many men and women were hanged for practicing the diabolical arts?

5. How did the government of Massachusetts deal with the accusations?

Salem Witch Trials

Test, Page 2

6. What finally put an end to this frenzy?

Review

1. Who sent 108 men from England to settle what was then known as Virginia?

2. After whom was Jamestown named?

3. Who were the Separatists? What did they believe?

4. How did Prince Henry take the lead in opening the African trade route to Asia?

Salem Witch Trials

Test, Page 3

5. In chronological order list all events studied to date. Next to each place the appropriate date.

13 Colonies Formed
Worksheet

1. Who originally owned all the colonies in America? What was his involvement with the colonies?

Farmer

____

____

2. Why did colonies have so much control over their own affairs?

____

____

Parson

3. What were the Navigation Acts?

____

____

4. List the original thirteen colonies. Next to each one list the dates that they were established.

Merchant

1. ____
2. ____
3. ____
4. ____
5. ____
6. ____

King

7. ____
8. ____
9. ____
10. ____
11. ____
12. ____
13. ____

Quaker

13 Colonies Formed

Project 1—Colony Comparison

Using the card and the coloring book Colonies, *by Arthur and Barbara Lampert, fill in the chart below. Then discuss the differences in the colonies. How many were formed for religious purposes? For economic or political reasons? How many years after the establishment of the first colony was the thirteenth colony formed?*

Thirteen Colonies Fact Sheet

Name	*Year Founded*	*Settled By*	*Why Settled*	*Leader*	*Place of First Settlement*
Connecticut					
Delaware					
Georgia					
Maryland					
Massachusetts					
New Hampshire					
New Jersey					
New York					
North Carolina					
Pennsylvania					
Rhode Island					
South Carolina					
Virginia					

13 Colonies Formed

Project 2—The Maryland Toleration Act (1649)

Read the Maryland Toleration Act.

Forasmuch as in a well governed and Christian Common Wealth matters concerning Religion and the honor of God ought to be in the first place bee taken, into serious consideracion and endeavored to bee settled, Be it therefore ordered and enacted by the Right Honourable Cecilius Lord Baron of Baltimore absolute Lord and Proprietary of this Province with the advise and consent of this Generall Assembly:

That whatsoever person or persons within this Province and the Islands thereunto belonging shall from henceforth blaspheme God, that is Curse him, or deny our Saviour Jesus Christ to bee the sonne of God, or shall deny the holy Trinity the father sonne and holy Ghost, or the Godhead of any of the said Three persons of the Trinity or the Unity of the Godhead, or shall use or utter any reproachfull Speeches, words or language concerning the said Holy Trinity, or any of the said three persons thereof, shalbe punished with death and confiscation or forfeiture of all his or her lands and goods to the Lord Proprietary and his heires.

And bee it also Enacted by the Authority and with the advise and assent aforesaid, That whatsoever person or persons shall from henceforth use or utter any reproachful words of Speeches concerning the blessed Virgin Mary the Mother of our Saviour or the holy Apostles or Evangelists or any of them shall in such case for the first offence forfeit to the said Lord Proprietary and his heirs Lords and Proprietaries of this Province the summe of five pound Sterling or the value thereof to be Levyed on the gods and chattells of every such person soe offending, but in case such Offender or Offenders, shall not then have goods and chattells sufficient for the satisfying of such forfeiture, or that the same bee not otherwise speedily satisfyed that then such Offender or Offenders shalbe publiquely whipt and bee imprisoned during the pleasure of the Lord Proprietary or the Lieutenant or cheife Governor of the Province for the time being. And that every such Offender or Offenders for every second offence shall forfeit ten pound sterling or the value thereof to bee levyed as aforesaid, or in case such Offender or Offenders shall not then have goods or chattells within this Province sufficient for that purpose then to bee publiquely and severly whipt and imprisoned as before is expressed. And that every person or persons before mentioned offending herein the third time, shall for such third Offence forfeit all his lands and Goods and bee for ever banished and expelled out of this Province.

And be it also further Enacted by the same authority advise and assent that whatsoever person or persons shall from henceforth uppon any occasion of the Offence or otherwise in a reproachful manner or Way declare call or denominate any person or persons whatsoever inhabiting, residing, traffiqueing, trading, or comerceing within this Province or within any the Ports, Harbors, Creeks or Havens to the same belonging an heritick, Scismatick, Idolator, puritan, Independent, Prespiterian popish prest, Jesuite, Jesuited papist, Lutheran, Calvenist, Anabaptist, Brownist, Antinomian, Barrowist, Roundhead, Separatist, or any other name or terme in a reproachful manner relating to matter of Religion shall for every such Offence forfeit and loose the somme of tenne shillings sterling or the value thereof to bee levyed on the goods and chattells of every such Offender or

13 Colonies Formed

Project 2, Page 2

Offenders, the one half thereof to be forfeited and paid unto the person and persons of whom such reproachfull words are or shalbe spoken or uttered, and the other half thereof to the Lord Proprietary and his heires Lords and Propietaries of this Province. But if such person or persons who shall at any time utter or speake any such reproachfull words or Language shall not have Goods or Chattells sufficient and overt within this Province to bee taken to satisfie the penalty aforesaid or that the same bee not otherwise speedily satisfyed, that then the person or persons soe offending shalbe publickly whipt, and shall suffer imprisonment without baile or maineprise [bail] untill hee, shee, or they respectively shall satisfy the party soe offended or greived by such reproachfull Languageby asking him or her respectively forgivenes publiquely for such his Offence before the Magistrate of cheife Officer or Officers of the Towne or place where such Offence shalbe given.

And be it further likewise Enacted by the Authority and consent aforesaid That every person and persons within this Province that shall at any time hereafter prophane that Sabbath or Lords day called Sunday by frequent swearing, drunkennes or by any uncivill or disorderly recreacion, or by working on that day when absolute necessity doth not require it shall for every first offence forfeit 2s 6d sterling or the value thereof, and for the second offence 5s sterling or the value thereof, and for the third offence and soe for every time he shall offend in like manner afterwards 10s sterling or the value thereof. And in case such offender and offenders shall not have sufficient goods or chattells within this Province to satisfy any of the said Penalties respectively hereby imposed for prophaning the Sabbath or Lords day called Sunday as aforesaid, That in every such case the partie soe offending shall for the first and second offence in that kinde be imprisoned till hee

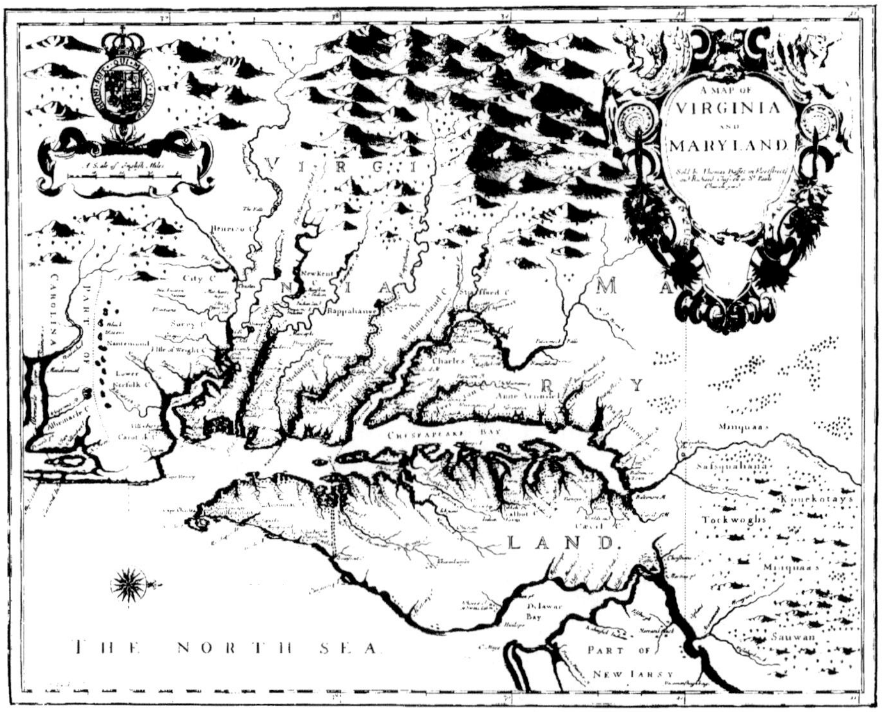

13 Colonies Formed
Project 2, Page 3

or shee shall publickly in open Court before the cheife Commander Judge or Magistrate, of that county Towne or precinct where such offence shalbe committed acknowledge that Scandall and offence he hath in that respect given against God and the good and civill Governement of this Province, And for the third offence and for every time after shall also bee publickly whipt.

And whereas the inforceing of the conscience in matters of Religion hath frequently fallen out to be of dangerous Consequence in those commonwealthes where it hath been practised, And for the more quiett and peaceable governement of this Province, and the better to preserve mutuall Love and amity amongst the Inhabitants thereof, Be it Therefore also by the Lord Propietary with the advise and consent of this Assembly Ordeyned and enacted (except as in this present Act is before Declared and sett forth) that noe person or persons whatsoever within this Province , Or the Islands, Ports, Harbors, Creekes, or havens thereunto belonging professing to beleive in Jesus Christ, shall from henceforth bee in any waies troubled, Molested or discountenanced for or in respect of his or her religion nor in the free exercise thereof within this Province or the Islands thereunto belonging nor any way compelled to the beleife or exercise of any other Religion against his or her consent, soe as they not be unfaithful to the Lord Propietary, or molest or conspire against the civill Governement established or to bee established in this Province under him or his heires. And that all and every person and persons that shall presume Contrary to the Act and the true intent and meaning thereof directly or indirectly either in person or estate willfully to wrong disturbe trouble or molest any person whatsoever within this Province professing to beleive in Jesus Christ for or in respect of his or her religion or the free exercise thereof within this Province other than is provided for in this Act that such person or persons soe offending, shalbe compelled to pay trebble damages to the party soe wronged or molested, and for every such offence shall also forfeit 20s sterling in money or the value thereof, half thereof for the use of the Lord Proprietary, and his heires Lords and Proprietaries of this Province, and the other half for the use of the party soe wronged or molested as aforesaid, Or if the partie soe offending as aforesaid shall ref se or bee unable to recompense the party soe wronged, or to satisfy such fyne or forfeiture, then such Offender shalbe severely punished by publick whipping and imprisonment during the pleasure of the Lord Proprietary, or his Lieutenant or cheife Governor of this Province for the tyme being without baile or maineprise.

And bee it further alsoe Enacted by the authority and consent aforesaid That the Sheriff or other Officer or Officers from time to time to bee appointed for that purpose, of the County Towne or precinct where every particular offence in this present Act conteyned shall happen at any time to bee committed and whereupon there is hereby a forfeiture fyne or penalty imposed shall from time to time distraine and seise the goods and estate of every such person soe offending as aforesaid against this present Act or any part thereof, and sell the same or any part thereof for the full satisfaccion of such forfeiture, fine, or penalty as aforesaid, Restoring unto the partie soe offending the Remainder or overplus of the said goods or estate after such satisfaccion soe made as aforesaid.

13 Colonies Formed

Project 3—Upon the Burning of our House

Read the following poem by Anne Bradstreet, written on July 18, 1666, then draw a picture depicting the event or rewrite the poem in prose.

In silent night when rest I took,
For sorrow near I did not look,
I waken'd was with thund'ring noise
And piteous shrieks of dreadful voice.
That fearful sound of "fire" and "fire,"
Let no man know is my Desire.
I starting up, the light did spy,
And to my God my heart did cry
To straighten me in my Distress
And not to leave me succourless.
Then coming out, behold a space
The flame consume my dwelling place.
And when I could no longer look,
I blest his grace that gave and took,
That laid my goods now in the dust.
Yea, so it was, and so 'twas just.
It was his own; it was not mine.
Far be it that I should repine,
He might of all justly bereft
But yet sufficient for us left.
When by the Ruins oft I past
My sorrowing eyes aside did cast
And here and there the places spy
Where oft I sate and long did lie.
Here stood that Trunk, and there that chest,
There lay that store I counted best,
My pleasant things in ashes lie
And them behold no more shall I.
Under the roof no guest shall sit,
Nor at thy Table eat a bit.
No pleasant talk shall 'ere be told
Nor things recounted done of old.
No Candle 'ere shall shine in Thee,
Nor bridegroom's voice ere heard shall bee.
In silence ever shalt thou lie.
Adieu, Adieu, All's Vanity.
Then straight I 'gin my heart to chide:
And did thy wealth on earth abide,
Didst fix thy hope on mouldring dust,
The arm of flesh didst make thy trust?
Raise up thy thoughts above the sky
That dunghill mists away may fly.
Thou hast a house on high erect
Fram'd by that mighty Architect,
With glory richly furnished
Stands permanent, though this be fled.
It's purchased and paid for too
By him who hath enough to do.
A price so vast as is unknown,
Yet by his gift is made thine own.
There's wealth enough; I need no more.
Farewell, my pelf; farewell, my store.
The world no longer let me love;
My hope and Treasure lies above.

13 Colonies Formed
Project 4—Tin Making

Tin was used in the colonial days for practical and decorative reasons. We will be making an ornament for Christmastime.

Supplies

hammer

nail with a large head

lids from cans (soup cans, vegetables, etc.)

permanent marker

narrow ribbon

Directions

1. Draw a simple design on the lid. Stars, circles, crescent moons, crosses work best.
2. Hammer along the line of your drawing, moving the nail about an 1/8th of an inch apart (BE CAREFUL AS THE EDGES OF THE LID CAN BE SHARP). You should be able to see through to the other side.
3. Place one nail hole at the top of your lid, then thread a ribbon through this. Tie at the top.
4. Hang your ornament on a Christmas tree.

13 Colonies Formed

Project 5—Silhouette Cutouts

Before the use of modern day photography, people would make silhouettes in order to have a "picture" of a person.

Supplies

overhead projector or a very bright light

large black and white construction paper

scissors

white chalk

Directions

1. Have a child sit in front of the overhead projector or lamp.
2. Trace the shadow of the child's face onto the black construction paper with your chalk.
3. Cut out the image.
4. Glue to white construction paper.

13 Colonies Formed

Test

1. What were the dates of the founding of the original thirteen colonies?

2. What did the king of England have to do with the original thirteen colonies?

3. What part did each colony play in their own government?

4. What were the Navigation Acts?

5. List the original thirteen colonies.

13 Colonies Formed
Test, Page 2

Review

1. After whom was the colony of Jamestown named?

2. Where did the *Mayflower* first land? How long did the passengers stay there before moving on to Plymouth?

3. Christopher Columbus was from what country?

4. What is another name that the colony of Roanoke has been given? Why?

5. In chronological order list all events studied to date. Next to each place the appropriate date.

13 Colonies Formed
Test, Page 3

5. (continued)

THE FIRST GREAT AWAKENING

Worksheet

1. What were the dates of the First Great Awakening?

____

____

____

2. Describe the First Great Awakening. Where did it take place?

____

____

____

____

____

____

____

____

____

____

3. Name two theologians that God used during this period.

____

____

4. What was the name of the famous sermon that Jonathan Edwards preached during this time?

____

____

5. In New England, Whitefield drew some ____________ hearers to the __________Common.

THE FIRST GREAT AWAKENING

Worksheet, Page 2

6. What doctrine of Wesley's did Whitefield publicly condemn?

____

____

7. Who was acknowledged as the leader of "Calvinist Methodism?"

____

____

____

8. How many of Whitefield's sermons have survived? How many is he thought to have preached?

____

____

____

The First Great Awakening

Project 1–Sinners in the Hands of an Angry God

Read and discuss the following sermon with your students. Take particular note of the urgency and severity with which he addresses his brothers in Christ.

Sinners in the Hands of an Angry God
By Jonathan Edwards

"Their foot shall slide in due time."
Deuteronomy 32:35

In this verse is threatened the vengeance of God on the wicked unbelieving Israelites, who were God's visible people, and who lived under the means of grace; but who, notwithstanding all God's wonderful works towards them, remained (as verse 28) void of counsel, having no understanding in them. Under all the cultivations of heaven, they brought forth bitter and poisonous fruit; as in the two verses next preceding the text. The expression I have chosen for my text, *Their foot shall slide in due time,* seems to imply the following things, relating to the punishment and destruction to which these wicked Israelites were exposed.

1. That they were always exposed to destruction; as one that stands or walks in slippery places is always exposed to fall. This is implied in the manner of their destruction coming upon them, being represented by their foot sliding. The same is expressed in *Psalm 73:18. "Surely thou didst set them in slippery places; thou castedst them down into destruction."*
2. It implies, that they were always exposed to sudden unexpected destruction. As he that walks in slippery places is every moment liable to fall, he cannot foresee one moment whether he shall stand or fall the next; and when he does fall, he falls at once without warning: Which is also expressed in *Psalm 73:18, 19. "Surely thou didst set them in slippery places; thou castedst them down into destruction: How they are brought into desolation as in a moment!"*
3. Another thing implied is, that they are liable to of themselves, without being thrown down by the hand of another; as he that stands or walks on slippery ground needs nothing but his own weight to throw him down.
4. That the reason why they are now fallen already, and do not fall now, is only that God's appointed time is not come. For it is said, when that due time, or appointed time comes, their foot shall slide. Then they shall be left to fall, as they are inclined by their own weight. God will not hold them up in these slippery places any longer, but will let them go; and then, at that very instant, they shall fall into destruction; as he that stands on such slippery declining ground, on the edge of a pit, he cannot stand alone, when he is let go he immediately falls and is lost.

The observation from the words that I now insist upon is this. —"There is nothing that keeps wicked men at any one moment out of hell but the mere pleasure of God"— by the mere pleasure of God, I mean, the mere pleasure of God, I mean his sovereign pleasure, his arbitrary will, restrained by no obligation, hindered by no manner of difficulty, any more than if nothing else but God's mere will had in the least degree, or in any respect whatsoever, any hand in the

The First Great Awakening
Project 1, Page 2

preservation of wicked men one moment. — The truth of this observation may appear by the following considerations.

1. There is no want of power in God to cast wicked men into hell at any moment. Men's hands cannot be strong when God rises up. The strongest have no power to resist him, nor can any deliver out of his hands. He is not only able to cast wicked men into hell, but he can most easily do it. Sometimes an earthly prince meets with a great deal of difficulty to subdue a rebel, who has found means to fortify himself, and has made himself strong by the numbers of his followers. But it is not so with God. There is no fortress that is any defence from the power of God. Though hand join in hand, and vast multitudes of God's enemies combine and associate themselves, they are easily broken into pieces. They are as great heaps of light chaff before the whirlwind; or large quantities of dry stubble before devouring flames. We find it easy to tread on and crush a worm that we see crawling on the earth; so it is easy for us to cut or singe a single thread that any thing hangs by: thus easy is it for God, when he pleases, to cast his enemies down to hell. What are we, that we should think to stand before him, at whose rebuke the earth trembles, and before whom the rocks are thrown down?
2. They deserve to be cast into hell; so that divine justice never stands in the way, it makes no objection against God's using his power at any moment to destroy them. Yea, on the contrary, justice calls aloud for an infinite punishment of their sins. Divine justice says of the tree that brings forth such grapes of Sodom, *"Cut it down, why cumbereth it the ground?" (Luke 13:7)*. The sword of divine justice is every moment brandished over their heads, and it is nothing but the hand of arbitrary mercy, and God's mere will, that holds it back.
3. They are already under a sentence of condemnation to hell. They do not only justly deserve to be cast down thither, but the sentence of the law of God, that eternal and immutable rule of righteousness that God has fixed between him and mankind, is gone out against them, and stands against them; so that they are bound over already to hell. *"He that believeth not is condemned already" (John 3:18)*. So that every unconverted man properly belongs to hell; that is his place; from thence he is. *"Ye are from beneath" (John 8:23)*. And thither he is bound; it is the place that justice, and God's word, and the sentence of his unchangeable law assign to him.
4. They are now the objects of the very same anger and wrath of God, that is expressed in the torments of hell. And the reason that they do not go down to hell at each moment, is not because God, in whose power they are, is not then very angry with them; as he is with many miserable creatures now tormented in hell, who there feel and bear the fierceness of his wrath. Yea, God is a great deal more angry with great numbers that are now on earth: yea, doubtless, with many that are now in this congregation, who it may be are at ease, than he is with many of those who are now in the flames of hell. So that it is not because God is unmindful of their wickedness, and does not resent it, that he does not let loose his hand and cut them off. God is not altogether such an one as themselves, though

they may imagine him to be so. The wrath of God burns against them, their damnation does not slumber; the pit is prepared, the fire is made ready, the furnace is now hot, ready to receive them; the flames do now rage and glow. The glittering sword is whet, and held over them, and the pit hath opened its mouth under them.

5. The devil stands ready to fall upon them, and seize them as his own, at what moment God shall permit him. They belong to him; he has their souls in his possession, and under his dominion. The Scripture represent them as his goods (Luke 11:12). The devils watch them; they are ever by them at their right hand; they stand waiting for them, like greedy hungry lions that see their prey, and expect to have it, but for the present kept back. If God should withdraw his hand, by which they are restrained, they would in one moment fly upon their poor souls. The old serpent is gaping for them; hell opens its mouth wide to receive them; and if God should permit it, they would be hastily swallowed up and lost.
6. There are in the souls of wicked men those hellish principles reigning, that would presently kindle and flame out in to hell fire, if it were not for God's restraints. There is laid in the very nature of carnal men, a foundation for the torments of hell. There are those corrupt principles, in reigning power in them, and in full possession of them, that are seeds of hell fire. These principles are active and powerful, exceeding violent in their nature, and if were not for the restraining hand of God upon them, they would soon break out, they would flame out after the same manner as the same corruptions, the same enmity does in the hearts of damned souls, and would beget the same torments as they do in them. The souls of the wicked are in Scripture compared to the troubled sea (Is. 62:20). For the present, God restrains their wickedness by his mighty power, as he does the raging waves of the troubled sea, saying, "Hitherto shalt thou come, but no further;" but if God were to withdraw that restraining power, it would soon carry all before it. Sin is the ruin and misery of the soul; it is destructive in its nature; and if God should leave it without restraint, there would need nothing else to make the soul perfectly miserable. The corruption of the heart of man is immoderate and boundless in its fury; and while wicked men live here, it is like fire pent up by God's restraints, whereas if it were let loose, it would set on fire the course of nature; and as the heart is now a sink of sin, so if sin was not restrained, it would immediately turn the soul into a fiery oven, or a furnace of fire and brimstone.
7. It is no security to wicked men for one moment, that there are no visible means of death at hand. It is no security to a natural man, that he is now in health, and that he does not see which way he should now immediately go out of the world by any accident, and that there is no visible danger in any respect in his circumstances. The manifold and continual experience of the world in all ages, shows this is no evidence, that a man is not on the very brink of eternity, and that the next step will not be into another world. The unseen, unthought-of ways and means of persons going suddenly out of this world are innumerable and inconceivable. Unconverted men walk over the pit of hell on a rotten covering, and there

The First Great Awakening

Project 1, Page 4

are innumerable places in this covering that are so weak that they will not bear their weight, and these places are not seen. The arrows of death fly unseen at noonday; the sharpest sight cannot discern them. God has so many different unsearchable ways of taking wicked men out of the world and sending them to hell, that there is nothing to make it appear, that God had need to be at the expense of a miracle, or go out of the ordinary course of his providence, to destroy any wicked man, at any moment. All the means that there are of sinners going out of the world, are so in God's hands, and so universally and absolutely subject to his power and determination, that it does not depend at all that less on the mere will of God, whether sinners shall at any moment go to hell, than if means were never made use of, or at all concerned in the case.

8. Natural men's prudence and care to preserve their own lives, or the care of others to preserve them, do not secure them a moment. To this, divine providence and universal experience do also bear testimony. There is this clear evidence that men's own wisdom is no security to them from death; that if it were otherwise we should see some difference from that wise and politic men of the world, and others, with regard to their liableness to early and unexpected death: but how is it in fact? *"How dieth the wise man? even as the fool" (Eccl. 2:16).*
9. All wicked men's pains and contrivance which they use to escape hell, while they continue to reject Christ, and so remain wicked men, do not secure them from hell one moment. Almost every natural man that hears of hell, flatters himself that he shall escape it; he depends upon himself for his own security; he flatters himself in what he has done, in what he is now doing, or what he intends to do. Every one lays out matters in his own mind how he shall avoid damnation, and flatters himself that he contrives well for himself, and that his schemes will not fail. They hear indeed that there are but a few saved, and that the greater part of men that have died heretofore are gone to hell; but each one imagines that he lays out matters better for his own escape than others have done. He does not intend to come to that place of torment; he says within himself, that he intends to take effectual care, and to order matters so for himself as not to fail. But the foolish children of men miserably delude themselves in their own schemes, and in confidence of their own strength and wisdom; they trust to nothing but a shadow. The greater part of those who heretofore have lived under the same means of grace, and are now dead, are undoubtedly gone to hell; and it was not because they were not as wise as those who are now alive: it is not because they did not lay out matters as well for themselves to secure their own escape. If we could speak with them, and inquire of them, one by one, whether they expected, when alive, and when they used to hear about hell, ever to be the subjects of that misery: we doubtless, should hear one and another reply, "No, I never intended to come here: I had laid out matters otherwise in my mind; I thought I should contrive well for myself: I thought my scheme good. I intended to take effectual care; but it came upon me unexpected; I did not look for it at that time, and in that manner; it came as a thief: Death outwitted me: God's wrath was too quick

for me. Oh, my cursed foolishness! I was flattering myself, and pleasing myself with vain dreams of what I would do hereafter; and when I was saying, Peace and safety, then suddenly destruction came upon me."

10. God has laid himself under no obligation, by any promise to keep any natural man out of hell one moment. God has certainly made no promises either of eternal life, or of any deliverance or preservation from eternal death, but what are contained in the covenant of grace, the promises that are given in Christ, in whom all the promises are yea and amen. But surely they have no interest in the promises of the covenant of grace who are not the children of the covenant, who do not believe in any of the promises, and have no interest in the Mediator of the covenant.

So that, whatever some have imagined and pretended about promises made to natural men's earnest seeking and knocking, it is plain and manifest, that whatever pains a natural man takes in religion, whatever prayers he makes, till he believes in Christ, God is under no manner of obligation to keep him a moment from eternal destruction.

So that, thus it is that natural men are held in the hand of God, over the pit of hell; they have deserved the fiery pit, and are already sentenced to it; and God is dreadfully provoked, his anger is as great towards them as to those that are actually suffering the executions of the fierceness of his wrath in hell, and they have done nothing in the least to appease or abate that anger, neither is God in the least bound by any promise to hold them up one moment; the devil is waiting for them, hell is gaping for them, the flames gather and flash about them, and would fain lay hold on them, and swallow them up; the fire bent up in their own hearts is struggling to break out: and they have no interest in any Mediator, there are no means within reach that can be any security to them. In short, they have no refuge, nothing to take hold of; all that preserves them every moment is the mere arbitrary will, and uncovenanted, unobliged forbearance of an incensed God.

Application

The use of this awful subject may be for awakening unconverted persons in this congregation. This that you have heard is the case of every one of you that are out of Christ. That world of misery, that lake of burning brimstone, is extended abroad under you. There is the dreadful pit of the glowing flames of the wrath of God; there is hell's wide gaping mouth open; and you have nothing to stand upon, nor any thing to take hold of; there is nothing between you and hell but the air; it is only the power and mere pleasure of God that holds you up.

You probably are not sensible to this; you find you are kept out of hell, but do not see the hand of God in it; but look at other things, as the goodstate of your bodily constitution, your care of your own life, and the means you use for your own preservation. But indeed these things are nothing; if God should withdraw his hand, they would avail no more to keep you from falling, than the thin air to hold up a person that is suspended in it.

Your wickedness makes you as if it were as heavy as lead, and to tend downwards with great weight and pressure towards hell; and if God should let you go, you would immediately sink and swiftly

The First Great Awakening
Project 1, Page 6

descend and plunge into the bottomless gulf, and your healthy constitution, and your own care and prudence, and best contrivance, and all your righteousness, would have no more influence to uphold you and keep you out of hell, than a spider's web would have to stop a fallen rock. Were it not for the sovereign pleasure of God, the earth would not bear you one moment; for you are a burden to it; and creation groans with you; the creature is made subject to the bondage of your corruption, not willingly; the sun does not willingly shine upon you to give you light to serve sin and Satan; the earth does not willingly yield her increase to satisfy your lusts; nor is it willingly a stage for your wickedness to be acted upon; the air does not willingly serve you for breath to maintain the flame of life in your vitals, while you spend your life in the service of God's enemies. God's creatures are good, and were made for men to serve God with, and do not willingly subserve to any other purpose, and groan when they are abused to purposes so directly contrary to their nature and end. And the world would spew you out, were it not for the sovereign hand of him who hath subjected it in hope. There are black clouds of God's wrath now hanging directly over your heads, full of the dreadful storm, and big with thunder; and were it not for the restraining hand of God, it would immediately burst forth upon you. The sovereign pleasure of God, for the present, stays his rough wind; otherwise it would come with fury, and your destruction would come like a whirlwind, and you would be like the chaff of the summer threshing floor.

The wrath of God is like great waters that are damned for the present; they increase more and more, and rise higher and higher, till an outlet is given; and the longer the stream is stopped, the more rapid and mighty is its course, when once it is let loose. It is true, that vengeance against your evil works has not been executed hitherto; the floods of God's vengeance have been withheld; but your guilt in the mean time is constantly increasing, and you are every day treasuring up more wrath; the waters are constantly rising; and waxing more and more mighty; and there is nothing but the mere pleasure of God, that holds the waters back, that are unwilling to be stopped, and press hard to go forward. If God should only withdraw his hand from the floodgate, it would immediately fly open, and the fiery floods of the fierceness and wrath of God, would rush forth with inconceivable fury, and would come upon you with omnipotent power; and if your strength were ten thousand times greater than it is, yea, ten thousand times greater than the strength of the stoutest, sturdiest devil in hell, it would be nothing to withstand or endure it.

The bow of God's wrath is bent, and the arrow made ready on the string, and justice bends the arrow at your heart, and strains the bow, and it is nothing but the mere pleasure of God, and that of an angry God, without any promise or obligation at all, that keeps the arrow one moment from being made drunk with your blood. Thus all you that never passed under a great change of heart, by the mighty power of the Spirit of God upon your souls; all you that were never born again, and made new creatures, and raised from being dead to sin, to a state of new, and before altogether unexperienced light and life, are in the hands of an angry God. However, you may have reformed your life in many things, and may have had religious affections, and may keep up a form of religion in your families and closets, and in the house of God, it is nothing but his mere

THE FIRST GREAT AWAKENING
Project 1, Page 7

pleasure that keeps you from being this moment swallowed up in everlasting destruction. However unconvinced you may now be of the truth of what you hear, by and by you will be fully convinced of it. Those that are gone from being in the like circumstances with you, see that it was so with them; for destruction came suddenly upon most of them; when they expected nothing of it, and while they were saying, Peace and safety: now they see, that those things on which they depended for peace and safety, were nothing but thin air and empty shadows.

The god that holds you over the pit of hell, much as one holds a spider, or some loathsome insect over the fire, abhors you, and is dreadfully provoked: his wrath towards you burns like fire; he looks upon you as worthy of nothing else, but to be cast into the fire; he is of purer eyes than to bear to have you in his sight; you are ten thousand times more abominable in his eyes, than the most hateful venomous serpent is in ours. You have offended him infinitely more than ever a stubborn rebel did his prince; and yet it is nothing but his hand that holds you from falling into the fire at every moment. It is to be ascribed to nothing else, that you did not go to hell last night; that you suffered to awake again in this world, after you closed your eyes to sleep. And there is no other reason to be given, why you have not dropped into hell since you arose in the morning, but that God's hand has held you up. There is no other reason to be given why you have not gone to hell, since you have sat here in the house of God, provoking his pure eyes by your sinful wicked manner of attending his solemn worship. Yea, there is nothing else that is to be given as a reason why you do not this very moment drop down into hell.

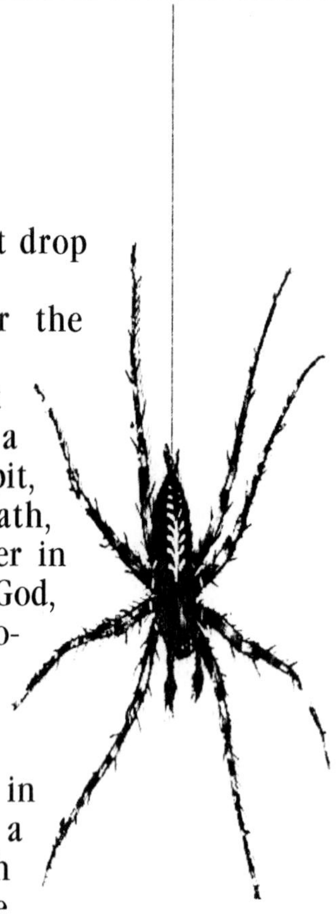

O sinner! Consider the fearful danger you are in: it is a great furnace of wrath, a wide and bottomless pit, full of the fire of wrath, that you are held over in the hand of that God, whose wrath is provoked and incensed as much against you, as against many of the damned in hell. You hang by a slender thread, with the flames of divine wrath flashing against, and ready every moment to singe it, and burn it asunder; and you have no interest in any Mediator, and nothing to lay hold of to save yourself, nothing to keep off the flames of wrath, nothing of your own, nothing that you have ever done, nothing that you can do, to induce God to spare you one moment. And consider here more particularly,

1. Whose wrath it is: it is the wrath of the infinite God. If it were only the wrath of man, though it were of the most potent prince, it would be comparatively little to be regarded. The wrath of kings is very much dreaded, especially of absolute monarchs, who have the possessions and loves of their subjects wholly in their power, to be disposed of at their mere will. *"The fear of a king is as the roaring of a lion; Who provoketh him to anger, sinneth against his own soul" (Prov. 20:2).* The subject that very much enrages an arbitrary prince, is liable to suffer the most extreme torments that human art

The First Great Awakening
Project 1, Page 8

can invent, or human power can inflict. But the greatest earthly potentates in their greatest majesty and strength, and when clothed in their greatest terrors, are but feeble, despicable worms of the dust, in comparison of the great and almighty Creator and King of heaven and earth. It is but little that they can do, when most enraged, and when they have exerted the utmost of their fury. All the kings of the earth, before God, are as grasshoppers; they are nothing, and less than nothing: both their love and their hatred is to be despised. The wrath of the great King of kings is as much more terrible than theirs, as his majesty is greater. *And I say unto you, my friends, Be not afraid of them that kill the body, and after that, have no more that they can do. But I will forewarn you whom you shall fear: fear him, which after he hath killed, hath power to cast into hell; yea, I say unto you, Fear him" (Luke 12:4, 5).*

2. It is the fierceness of his wrath that you are exposed to. We often read of the fury of God; as in *Isaiah 59:18 "According to their deeds, accordingly he will repay fury to his adversaries."* So *Isaiah 66:15 "For behold, the Lord will come with fire, and with his chariots like a whirlwind, to render his anger with fury, and his rebuke with flames of fire."* And in many other places. So, we read of *"the wine press of the fierceness and wrath of Almighty God" (Rev. 19:15).* The words are exceeding terrible. If it had only been said, "the wrath of God," the words would have implied that which is infinitely dreadful: but it is "the fierceness and wrath of God." The fury of God! the fierceness of Jehovah! Oh, how dreadful that must be! Who can utter or conceive what such expressions carry in them! But it is also "the fierceness and wrath of Almighty God." As though there would be a very great manifestation of his almighty power in what the fierceness of his wrath should inflict, as though omnipotence should be as it were enraged, and exerted, as men are wont to exert their strength in the fierceness of their wrath. Oh! then, what will be the consequence! What will become of the poor worms that shall suffer it! Whose hands can be strong? And whose heart can endure? To what a dreadful, inexpressible, inconceivable depth of misery must the poor creature be sunk who shall be the subject of this!

Consider this, you that are here present, that yet remain in an unregenerate state. That God will execute the fierceness of his anger, implies that he will inflict wrath without any pity. When God beholds the ineffable extremity of your case, and sees your torment to be so vastly disproportioned to your strength, and sees how your poor soul is crushed, and sinks down, as it were, into an infinite gloom; he will have no compassion upon you, he will not forbear the executions of his wrath, or in the least lighten his hand; there shall be no moderation or mercy, nor will God then at all stay his rough wind; he will have no regard to your welfare, nor be at all careful lest you should suffer too much in any other sense, than only that you shall not suffer beyond what strict justice requires. Nothing shall be withheld, because it is so hard for you to bear. *"Therefore will I also deal in fury: mine eye shall not spare, neither will I have pity; and though they cry in mine ears with a loud voice, yet I will not hear them" (Ezek. 8:18).* Now God stands ready to pity you; this is a day of mercy; you may cry now with some encouragement of obtaining mercy. But when once that day of mercy is past, your most lamentable and dolorous cries and shrieks will be in vain; you will be wholly lost and thrown away of God, as to any regard to your welfare. God will have no other use to put you to, but to suffer misery; you shall be continued in being to no other end; for you will be a vessel of wrath fitted to destruction; and there will be no other use of this vessel, but to be filled full of wrath. God will be so far from pitying you when you cry to him, that it is said he will only *"laugh and mock" (Prov. 1:25, 26, etc).*

How awful are those words which are the words of the great God. *"I will tread them in mine anger, and will trample them in my fury, and their blood shall be sprinkled upon my garments, and I will stain all my raiment" (Is. 63:3).* It is perhaps impossible to conceive of words that carry in them greater manifestations of these three things, viz. contempt, and hatred, and fierceness of indignation. If you cry to God to pity you, he will be so far from pitying you in your doleful case, or showing you the least regard or favour, that instead of that, he will only tread you under foot. And though he will know that you cannot bear the weight of omnipotence treading upon you, yet he will not regard that, but he will crush you under his feet without mercy; he will crush out your blood, and make it fly, and it shall be sprinkled on his garments, so as to stain all his raiment. He will not only hate you, but he will have you, in the utmost contempt: no place shall be thought fit for you, but under his feet to be trodden down as the mire of the streets.

3. The misery you are exposed to is that which God will inflict to that end, that he might show what that wrath of Jehovah is. God hath had it on his heart to show to angels and men, both how excellent his love is, and also how terrible his wrath is. Sometimes earthly kings have a mind to show how terrible their wrath is, by the extreme punishments they would execute in those that would provoke them. Nebuchadnezzar, that mighty and haughty monarch of the Chaldean empire, was willing to show his wrath when enraged with Shadrach, Meshach, and Abednego; and accordingly gave orders that the burning fiery furnace should be heated seven times hotter than it was before; doubtless, it was raised to the utmost degree of fierceness

that human art could raise it. But the great God is also willing to show his wrath, and magnify his awful majesty and mighty power in the extreme sufferings of his enemies. *"What if God, willing to show his wrath, and to make his power known, endured with much longsuffering the vessels of wrath fitted to destruction?" (Ro. 9:22).* And seeing this is his design, and what he has determined, even to show how terrible the unrestrained wrath, the fury and fierceness of Jehovah is, he will do it to effect. There will be something accomplished and brought to pass that will be dreadful with a witness. Then the great and angry God hath risen up and executed his awful vengeance on the poor sinner, and the wretch is actually suffering the infinite weight and power of his indignation, then will God call upon the whole universe to behold that awful majesty and mighty power that is to be seen in it. *"And the people shall be as the burnings of lime, as thorns cut up shall they be burnt in the fire. Hear ye that are far off, what I have done; and ye that are near, acknowledge my might. The sinners in Zion are afraid; fearfulness hath surprised the hypocrites..." (Is. 33:12-14).*

Thus it will be with you that are in an unconverted state, if you continue in it; the infinite might, and majesty, and terribleness of the omnipotent God shall be magnified upon you, in the ineffable strength of your torments. You shall be tormented in the presence of the holy angels, and in the presence of the Lamb; and when you shall be in this state of suffering, the glorious inhabitants of heaven shall go forth and look on the awful spectacle, that they may see what the wrath and fierceness of the Almighty is; and when they have seen it, they will fall down and adore that great power and majesty. *"And it shall come to pass, that from one new moon to another, and from one sabbath to another, shall all flesh come to worship before me, saith the Lord. And they shall go forth and look upon the carcasses of the men that have transgressed against me; for their worm shall not die, neither shall their fire be quenched, and they shall be an abhorring unto all flesh" (Is. 66:23, 24).*

4. It is everlasting wrath. It would be dreadful to suffer this fierceness and wrath of Almighty God one moment; but you must suffer it to all eternity. There will be no end to this exquisite horrible misery. When you look forward, you shall see a long for ever, a boundless duration before you, which will swallow up your thoughts, and amaze your soul; and you will absolutely despair of ever having any deliverance, any end, any mitigation, any rest at all. You will know certainly that you must wear out long ages, millions and millions of ages, in wrestling and conflicting with this almighty merciless vengeance; and then when you have so done, when so many ages have actually been spent by you in this manner, you will know that all is but a point to what remains. So that your punishment will indeed be infinite. Oh, who can express what the state of a soul in such circumstances is! All that we can possibly say about it, gives but a very feeble, faint representation of it; it is inexpressible and inconceivable. *For "who knows the power of God's anger?"*

How dreadful is the state of those that are daily and hourly in the danger of this great wrath and infinite misery! But this is the dismal case of every soul in this congregation that has not been born again, however moral and strict, sober and religious, they may otherwise be. Oh that you would consider it, whether you be young or old! There is reason to think, that there are many in this congregation now hearing this discourse, that will actually be the subjects of this very misery to all eternity. We know not who they are, or in what seats they sit, or what thoughts they now have. It may be that they are now at ease, and hear all these things without much disturbance, and are now flattering themselves that they are not the persons, promising themselves that they shall escape. If we knew that there was one person, and but one, in the whole congregation, that was to be the subject of this misery, what an awful thing would it be to think of! If we knew who it was, what an awful sight would it be to see such a person! How might all the rest of the congregation lift up a lamentable and bitter cry over him! But, alas! instead of one, how many is it likely will remember this discourse in hell? And it would be a wonder, if some that are now present should not be in hell in a very short time, even before this year is out. And it would be no wonder that some persons, that now sit here, in some seats of this meeting house, in health, quiet and secure, should be there before tomorrow morning. Those of you that finally continue in a natural condition, that shall keep out of hell longest will be there in a little time! your damnation does not slumber it; it will come swiftly, and, in all probability, very suddenly upon many of you. You have reason to wonder that you are not already in hell. It is doubtless the case of some whom you have seen and known, that never deserved hell more than you, and that heretofore appeared as likely to have been now alive as you. Their case is past all hope, they are crying in extreme misery and perfect despair; but here you are in the land of the living and in the house of God, and have an opportunity to obtain salvation. What would not those poor damned hopeless souls give for one day's opportunity such as you now enjoy!

And now you have an extraordinary opportunity, a day wherein Christ has thrown the door of mercy wide open, and stands in calling and crying with a loud voice to poor sinners; a day wherein many are flocking to him, and pressing into the kingdom of God. Many are daily coming from the east, west, north and south; many that were very lately in the same miserable condition that you are in, are now in a happy state, with their hearts filled with love to him who has loved them, and washed them from their sins in his own blood, and rejoicing in hope of the glory of God. How awful is it to be left behind at such a day! To see so many others feasting, while you are pining and perishing! To see so many rejoicing and singing for joy of heart, while you have cause to mourn for sorrow of heart, and howl for vexation of spirit! How can you rest one moment in such a condition? Are not your souls as precious as the souls of the people at Suffield, where they are flocking from day to day to Christ?

Are there not many here who have lived long in the world, and are not to this day born again? and so are aliens from the commonwealth of Israel, and have done nothing ever since they have lived, but treasure up wrath against the day of wrath? Oh, sirs, your case, in an especial manner, is extremely dangerous. Your guilt and hardness of heart is extremely great. Do you not see how generally persons of your years are passed over and left, in the present remarkable and wonderful dispensation of God's mercy? You

The First Great Awakening
Project 1, Page 12

have need to consider yourselves, and awake thoroughly out of sleep. You cannot bear the fierceness and wrath of the infinite God. And you, young men, and young women, will you neglect this precious season which you now enjoy, when so many others your age are renouncing all youthful vanities, and flocking to Christ? You especially have now an extraordinary opportunity; but if you neglect it, it will soon be with you as with those persons who spent all the precious days of youth in sin, and are now come to such a dreadful pass in blindness and hardness. And you, children, who are unconverted, do not you know that you are going down to hell, to bear the dreadful wrath of the God, who is now angry with you every day and every night? Will you be content to be the children of the devil, when so many other children in the land are converted, and are become the holy and happy children of the King of kings?

And let every one that is yet of Christ, and hanging over the pit of hell, whether they be old men and women, or middle aged, or young people, or little children, now hearken to the loud calls of God's word and providence. This acceptable year of the Lord, a day of such great favours to some, will doubtless be a day of some remarkable vengeance to others. Men's hearts harden, and their guilt increases apace at such a day as this, if they neglect their souls; and never was there so great danger of such persons being given up to hardness of heart and blindness of mind. God seems now to be hastily gathering in his elect in all parts of the land; and probably the greater part of adult persons that ever shall be saved, will be brought in now in a little time, and that will be as it was on the great outpouring of the Spirit upon the Jews in the apostles' days; the election will obtain, and the rest will be blinded. If this should be the case with you, you will eternally curse this day, and will curse the day that ever you were born, to see such a season of the pouring out of God's Spirit, and will wish that you had died and gone to hell before you had seen it. Now undoubtedly it is, as it was in the days of John the Baptist, the axe is in an extraordinary manner laid at the root of the trees, that every tree which brings not forth good fruit, may be hewn down and cast in to the fire.

Therefore, let every one of you that is out of Christ, now awake and fly from the wrath to come. The wrath of Almighty God is now undoubtedly hanging over a great part of this congregation: Let every one fly out of Sodom: "Haste and escape for your lives, look not behind you, escape to the mountain, lest you be consumed."

The First Great Awakening
Project 1, Page 13

Outline Jonathan Edwards' sermon Sinners in the Hand of an Angry God.

THE FIRST GREAT AWAKENING

Project 2—"No, Dear Sir, You Mistake."

A letter from George Whitefield to the Rev. Mr. John Wesley in answer to Mr. Wesley's sermon entitled "Free Grace."

John Wesley

PREFACE

I am very well aware what different effects this letter against the dear Mr. Wesley's Sermon will produce. Many of my friends who are strenuous advocates for universal redemption will immediately be offended. Many who are zealous on the other side will be much rejoiced. They who are lukewarm on both sides and are carried away with carnal reasoning will wish this matter had never been brought under debate.

The reasons I have given at the beginning of the letter, I think are sufficient to satisfy all of my conduct herein. I desire therefore that they who hold election would not triumph, or make a party on one hand (for I detest any such thing)—and that they who are prejudiced against that doctrine be not too much concerned or offended on the other.

Known unto God are all his ways from the beginning of the world. The great day will discover why the Lord permits dear Mr. Wesley and me to be of a different way of thinking. At present, I shall make no enquiry into that matter, beyond the account which he has given of it himself in the following letter, which I lately received from his own dear hands:

London, August 9, 1740

My dear brother,

I thank you for yours, May the 24th. The case is quite plain. There are bigots both for predestination and against it. God is sending a message to those on either side. But neither will receive it, unless from one who is of their own opinion. Therefore, for a time you are suffered to be of one opinion, and I of another. But when his time is come, God will do what man cannot, namely, make us both of one mind. Then persecution will flame out, and it will be seen whether we can count our lives dear unto ourselves, so that we may finish our course with joy. I am, my dearest brother,

Ever yours,
J. Wesley

Thus my honoured friend, I heartily pray God hasten the time, for his being clearly enlightened into all the doctrines of divine revelation, that we may thus be closely united in principle and judgment as well as heart and affection. And then if the Lord should call us into it, I care not if I go with him to prison, or to death. For like Paul and Silas, I hope we shall sing praises to God, and count it our highest honour to suffer for Christ's sake, and to lay down our lives for the brethren.

WHITEFIELD'S LETTER TO WESLEY:

Bethesda in Georgia, Dec. 24, 1740

Reverend and very dear brother,

God only knows what unspeakable sorrow of heart I have felt on your account since I left England last. Whether it be my infirmity or not, I frankly confess, that Jonah could not go with more reluctance against Nineveh, than I now take pen in hand to write against you. Was nature to speak, I had rather die to do it; and yet if I am faithful to God, and to my own and other's souls, I must not stand neutral any longer. I am very apprehensive that our common adversaries will rejoice to see us differing among ourselves. But what can I say? The children of God are in danger of falling into error. Nay, numbers have been misled, whom God has been pleased to work upon by my ministry, and a greater number are still calling aloud upon me to show also my opinion. I must then show that I know no man after the flesh, and that I have no respect to persons, any further than is consistent with my duty to my Lord and Master, Jesus Christ.

This letter, no doubt, will lose me many friends: and for this cause perhaps God has laid this difficult task upon me, even to see whether I am willing to forsake all for him, or not. From such considerations as these, I think it my duty to bear an humble testimony, and earnestly plead for the truths which, I am convinced, are clearly revealed in the Word of God. In the defence whereof I must use great plainness of speech, and treat my dearest friends upon earth with the greatest simplicity, faithfulness and freedom, leaving the consequences of all to God.

For some time before, and especially since my last departure from England, both in public and private, by preaching and printing, you have been propagating the doctrine of universal redemption. And when I remember how Paul reproved Peter for his dissimulation, I fear I have been sinfully silent too long. O then be not angry with me, dear and honoured Sir, if now I deliver my soul, by telling you that I think in this you greatly err.

'Tis not my design to enter into a long debate on God's decrees. I refer you to Dr. Edwards his Veritas Redux *[this refers to a work by Dr. John Edwards of Cambridge, not Jonathan Edwards, the famous American pastor-theologian],* which, I think is unanswerable—except in a certain point, concerning a middle sort between elect and reprobate, which he himself in effect afterwards condemns.

I shall only make a few remarks upon your sermon, entitled "Free Grace." And before I enter upon the discourse itself, give me leave to take a little notice of what in your Preface you term an indispensable obligation to make it public to all the world. I must own, that I always thought you were quite mistaken upon that head.

The case (you know) stands thus: When you were at Bristol, I think you received a letter from a private hand, charging you with not preaching the gospel, because you did not preach up election. Upon this you drew a lot: the answer was "preach and print." I have often questioned, as I do now, whether in so doing, you did not tempt the Lord. A due exercise of religious prudence, without [the drawing of] a lot, would have directed you in that matter. Besides, I never heard that you enquired of God, whether or not election was a gospel doctrine.

But, I fear, taking it for granted [that election was not a biblical truth], you only enquired whether you should be silent or preach and print against it.

However this be, the lot came out "preach and print; accordingly you preached and printed against election. At my desire, you suppressed the publishing of the sermon whilst I was in England; but you soon sent it into the world after my departure. O that you had kept it in! However, if that sermon was printed in answer to a lot, I am apt to think, one reason why God should so suffer you to be deceived, was, that hereby a special obligation might be laid upon me, faithfully to declare the Scripture doctrine of election, that thus the Lord might give me a fresh opportunity of seeing what was in my heart, and whether I would be true to his cause or not; as you could not but grant, he did once before, by giving you such another lot at Deal.

The morning I sailed from Deal to Gibraltar [2 February 1738], you arrived from Georgia. Instead of giving me an opportunity to converse with you, though the ship was not far off the shore, you drew a lot, and immediately set forward to London. You left a letter behind you, in which were words to this effect: "When I saw [that} God, by the wind which was carrying you out, brought me in, I asked counsel of God. His answer you have enclosed." This was a piece of paper, in which were written these words, "Let him return to London."

When I received this, I was somewhat surprised. Here was a good man telling me he had cast a lot, and that God would have me return to London. On the other hand, I knew my call was to Georgia, and that I had taken leave of London, and could not justly go from the soldiers, who were committed to my charge. I betook myself with a friend to prayer. That passage in 1 Kings 13 was powerfully impressed upon my soul, where we are told that the Prophet was slain by a lion when he was tempted to go back (contrary to God's express order) upon another Prophet's telling him God would have him do so. I wrote you word that I could not return to London. We sailed immediately.

Some months after, I received a letter from you at Georgia, wherein you wrote words to this effect: "Though God never gave me a wrong lot, yet, perhaps, he suffered me to have such a lot at that time, to try what was in your heart." I should never have published this private transaction to the world, did not the glory of God call me to it. It is plain you had a wrong lot given you here, and justly, because you tempted God in drawing one. And thus I believe it is in the present case. And if so, let not the children of God who are mine and your intimate friends, and also advocates for universal redemption, think that doctrine true—because you preached it up in compliance with a lot given out from God.

This, I think, may serve as an answer to that part of the Preface to your printed sermon, wherein you say, "Nothing but the strongest conviction, not only that what is here advanced is the truth as it is in Jesus, but also that I am indispensably obligated to declare this truth to all the world." That you believe what you have written to be truth, and that you honestly aim at God's glory in writing, I do not in the least doubt. But then, honoured Sir, I cannot but think you have been much mistaken in imagining that your tempting God, by casting a lot in the manner you did could lay you under an indispensable obligation to any action, much less to publish your sermon against the doctrine of predestination to life.

I must next observe, that as you have been unhappy in printing at all upon such an imaginary warrant, so you have been as unhappy in the choice of your text. Honoured Sir, how could it enter in to your heart to choose a text to disprove the doctrine of election out of Romans 8, where this doctrine is so plainly asserted? Once I spoke with a Quaker upon this subject, and he had no other way of evading the force of the Apostle's assertion than by saying, "I believe Paul was in the wrong." And another friend lately, who was once highly prejudiced against election, ingenuously confessed that he used to think St. Paul himself was mistaken, or that he was not truly translated.

Indeed, honoured Sir, it is plain beyond all contradiction that St. Paul, through the whole of Romans 8, is speaking of the privileges of those only who are really in Christ. And let any unprejudiced person read what goes before and what follows your text, and he must confess the word "all" only signifies those that are in Christ. And the latter part of the text plainly proves, what, I find, dear Mr. Wesley will, by no means, grant. I mean the final perseverance of the children of God: "He that spared not his own Son, but delivered him up for us all, [i.e. all Saints] how shall he not with him also freely give us all things?" (Rom. 8:32). [He shall give us] grace, in particular, to enable us to persevere, and every thing else necessary to carry us home to our Father's heavenly kingdom.

Had any one a mind to prove the doctrine of election, as well as of final perseverance, he could hardly wish for a text more fit for his purpose than that which you have chosen to disprove it! One who did not know you would suspect that you were aware of this, for after the first paragraph, I scarce know whether you have mentioned [the text] so much as once through your whole sermon.

But your discourse, in my opinion, is as little to the purpose as your text, and instead of warping, does but more and more confirm me in the belief of the doctrine of God's eternal election.

I shall not mention how illogically you have proceeded. Had you written clearly, you should first, honoured Sir, have proved your proposition: "God's grace is free to all." And then by way of inference [you might have] exclaimed against what you call the horrible decree. But you knew that people (because Arminianism, of late, has so much abounded among us) were generally prejudiced against the doctrine of reprobation, and therefore thought if you kept up their dislike of that, you could overthrow the doctrine of election entirely. For, without doubt, the doctrine of election and reprobation must stand or fall together.

But passing by this, as also your equivocal definition of the word grace, and your false definition of the word free, and that I may be as short as possible, I frankly acknowledge: I believe the doctrine of reprobation, in this view, that God intends to give saving grace, through Jesus Christ, only to a certain number, and that the rest of mankind, after the fall of Adam, being justly left to God to continue in sin, will at last suffer that eternal death which is its proper wages.

This is the established doctrine of Scripture, and acknowledged as such in the 17th article of the Church of England, as Bishop Burnet himself confesses. Yet dear Mr. Wesley absolutely denies it.

But the most important objections you have urged against this doctrine as reasons why you reject it, being seriously considered, and faithfully tried by the Word of God, will appear to be of no force at all. Let the matter be humbly and calmly reviewed, as to the following heads:

First, you say that if this be so (i.e. if there be an election) then is all preaching vain: it is needless to them that are elected; for they, whether with preaching or without, will infallibly be saved. Therefore, the end of preaching to save souls is void with regard to them. And it is useless to them that are not elected, for they cannot possibly be saved. They, whether with preaching or without, will infallibly be damned. The end of preaching is therefore void with regard to them likewise. So that in either case our preaching is in vain, and your hearing also vain. Page 10, paragraph 9.

O dear Sir, what kind of reasoning—or rather sophistry—is this! Hath not God, who hath appointed salvation for a certain number, appointed also the preaching of the Word as a means to bring them to it? Does anyone hold election in any other sense? And if so, how is preaching needless to them that are the elected, when the gospel is designated by God himself to be the power of God unto their eternal salvation? And since we know not who are elect and who reprobate, we are to preach promiscuously to all. For the Word may be useful, even to the non-elect, in restraining them from much wickedness and sin. However, it is enough to excite to the utmost diligence in preaching and hearing, when we consider that by these means, some, even as many as the Lord hath ordained to eternal life, shall certainly be quickened and enable to believe. And who that attends, especially with reverence and care, can tell but he may be found of that happy number?

Second, you say that the doctrine of election and reprobation directly tends to destroy holiness, which is the end of all the ordinances of God. For (says the dear mistaken Mr. Wesley) "it wholly takes away those first motives to follow after it, so frequently proposed in Scripture. The hope of future reward, and fear of punishment, the hope of heaven, and the fear of hell, et cetera."

I thought that one who carries perfection to such an exalted pitch as dear Mr. Wesley does, would know that a true lover of the Lord Jesus Christ would strive to be holy for the sake of being holy, and work for Christ out of love and gratitude, without any regard to the rewards of heaven, or fear of hell. You remember, dear Sir, what Scougal says, "Love's a more powerful motive that does them move." But passing by this, and granting that rewards and punishments (as they certainly are) may be motives from which a Christian may be honestly stirred up to act for God, how does the doctrine of election destroy these motives? Do not the elect know that the more good works they do, the greater will be their reward? And is not that encouragement enough to set them upon, and cause them to persevere in working for Jesus Christ? And how does the doctrine of election destroy holiness? Who ever preached any other election than what the Apostle preached, when he said, "Chosen . . . through sanctification of the Spirit?" (2 Thess. 2:13). Nay, is not holiness made a mark of our election by all that preach it? And how then can the doctrine of election destroy holiness?

The instance which you bring to illustrate your assertion, indeed, dear Sir, is quite impertinent. For you say, "If a sick man knows that he must unavoidably die or unavoidably recover, though he knows not which, it is not reasonable to take any physic at all." Dear Sir, what absurd reasoning is here? Were you ever sick in your life? If so, did not the bare probability or possibility of your recovering, though you knew it was unalterably fixed that you must live or die, encourage you to take physic? For how did you know but that very physic might be the means God intended to recover you by?

Just thus it is as to the doctrine of election. I know that it is unalterably fixed (one may say) that I must be damned or saved; but since I know not which for a certainty, why should I not strive, though at present in a state of nature, since I know not but this striving may be the means God has intended to bless, in order to bring me into a state of grace?

Dear Sir, consider these things. Make an impartial application, and then judge what little reason you had to conclude the 10th paragraph, Page 12, with these words: "So directly does this doctrine tend to shut the very gate of holiness in general, to hinder unholy men from ever approaching thereto, or striving to enter thereat."

"As directly," you say, "does the doctrine tend to destroy several particular branches of holiness, such as meekness, love, et cetera." I shall say little, dear Sir, in answer to this paragraph. Dear Mr. Wesley perhaps has been disputing with some warm narrow-spirited men that held election, and then he infers that their warmth and narrowness of spirit was owing to their principles? But does not dear Mr. Wesley know many dear children of God, who are predestinarians, and yet are meek, lowly, pitiful, courteous, tender-hearted, kind, of a catholic spirit, and hope to see the most vile and profligate of men converted? And why? because they know god saved themselves by an act of his electing love, and they know not but he may have elected those who now seem to be the most abandoned.

But, dear Sir, we must not judge of the truth of principles in general, nor of this election in particular, entirely from the practice of some that profess to hold them. If so, I am sure much might be said against your own. For I appeal to your own heart, whether or not you have not felt in yourself, or observed in others, a narrow-spiritedness, and some disunion of soul respecting those that hold universal redemption. If so, then according to your own rule, universal redemption is wrong, because it destroys several branches of holiness, such as meekness, love, et cetera. But not to insist upon this, I beg you would observe that your inference is entirely set aside by the force of the Apostle's argument, and the language which he expressly uses in Colossians 3:12-13: "Put on therefore, as the elect of God, holy and beloved, bowels of mercies, kindness, humbleness of mind, meekness, longsuffering; forbearing one another, and forgiving one another, if any man have a quarrel against any: even as Christ forgave you, so also do ye."

Here we see that the Apostle exhorts then to put on bowels of mercy, kindness, humbleness of mind, meekness, long-suffering, et cetera, upon this consideration: namely because they were the elect of God. And all who have experientially felt this doctrine in their hearts feel that these graces are the genuine effects of their being elected of God.

But perhaps dear Mr. Wesley may be mistaken in this point, and call that passion which is only zeal for God's truths. You know, dear Sir, the Apostle exhorts us to "contend earnestly for the faith once delivered to the saints" (Jude 3). Therefore you must not condemn all that appear zealous for the doctrine of election as narrow-spirited, or persecutors, just because they think it their duty to oppose you. I am sure, I love you in the bowels of Jesus Christ, and I think I could lay down my life for your sake; but yet, dear Sir, I cannot help strenuously opposing your errors upon this important subject, because I think you warmly, though not designedly, oppose the truth, as it is in Jesus. May the

The First Great Awakening
Project 2, Page 7

Lord remove the scales of prejudice from off the eyes of your mind and give you a zeal according to true Christian knowledge!

Third, says your sermon, "This doctrine tends to destroy the comforts of religion, the happiness of Christianity, et cetera."

But how does Mr. Wesley know this, who never believed election? I believe they who have experienced it will agree with our 17th article, that "the godly consideration of predestination, and election in Christ, is full of sweet, pleasant, unspeakable comfort to godly persons, and such as feel in themselves the working of the Spirit of Christ, mortifying the works of the flesh, and their earthly members, and drawing their minds to high and heavenly things, as well because it does greatly establish and confirm their faith of eternal salvation, to be enjoyed through Christ, as because it doth fervently kindle their love towards God," et cetera.

This plainly shows that our godly reformers did not think election destroyed holiness or the comforts of religion. As for my own part, this doctrine is my daily support. I should utterly sink under a dread of my impending trials, were I not firmly persuaded that God had chosen me in Christ from before the foundation of the world, and that now being effectually called, he will allow no one to pluck me out of his almighty hand.

You proceed thus: "This is evident as to all those who believe themselves to be reprobate, or only suspect or fear it; all the great and precious promises are lost to them; they afford them no ray of comfort."

In answer to this, let me observe that none living, especially none who are desirous of salvation, can know that they are not of the number of God's elect. And would dear Mr. Wesley give comfort, or dare you apply the precious promises of the gospel, being children's bread, to men in a natural state, while they continue so? God forbid! What if the doctrine of election and reprobation does put some upon doubting? So does that of regeneration. But, is not this doubting a good means to put them upon searching and striving; and that striving, a good means to make their calling and their election sure?

This is one reason among many others why I admire the doctrine of election and am convinced that it should have a place in gospel ministration and should be insisted on with faithfulness and care. It has a natural tendency to rouse the soul out of its carnal security. And therefore many carnal men cry out against it. Whereas universal redemption is a notion sadly adapted to keep the soul in its lethargic sleepy condition, and therefore so many natural men admire and applaud it.

Your 13th, 14th, and 15th paragraphs come next to be considered. "The witness of the Spirit," you say, "experience shows to be much obstructed by this doctrine."

But, dear Sir, whose experience? Not your own; for in your journal, from your embarking for Georgia, to your return to London, you seem to acknowledge that you have it not, and therefore you are not a competent judge in this matter. You must mean then the experience of others. For you say in the same paragraph, "Even in those who have tasted of that good gift, who yet have soon lost it again," (I suppose you mean lost the sense of it again) "and fallen back into doubts and fears and darkness, even horrible darkness that might be felt, et cetera." Now, as to the darkness of desertion, was not this the case of Jesus Christ himself, after he had received an unmeasurable unction of the Holy Ghost? Was not his soul exceeding sorrowful, even unto death, in the garden? And was he not surrounded with an horrible darkness, even a darkness that might be felt, when on the cross he cried out, "My God! My God! why

The First Great Awakening

Project 2, Page 8

hast thou forsaken me?"

And that all his followers are liable to the same, is it not evident from Scripture? For, says the Apostle, "He was tempted in all things like we are" (Heb. 2:15) so that he himself might be able to succour those that are tempted (Heb. 2:18). And is not their liableness thereunto consistent with that conformity to him in suffering, which his members are to bear (Phil. 3:10)? Why then should persons falling into darkness, after they have received the witness of the Spirit, be any argument against the doctrine of election?

"Yet," you ay, "many, very many of those that hold it not, in all parts of the earth, have enjoyed the uninterrupted witness of the Spirit, the continual light of God's countenance, from the moment wherein they first believed, for many months or years, to this very day." But how does dear Mr. Wesley know this? Has he consulted the experience of many, very many in all parts of the earth? Or could he be sure of what he hath advanced without sufficient grounds, would it follow that their being kept in this light is owing to their not believing the doctrine of election? No, this [doctrine], according to the sentiments of our church, "greatly confirms and establishes a true Christian's faith of eternal salvation through Christ," and is an anchor of hope, both sure and steadfast, when he walks in darkness and sees no light; as certainly he may, even after he hath received the witness of the Spirit, whatever you or others may unadvisedly assert to the contrary.

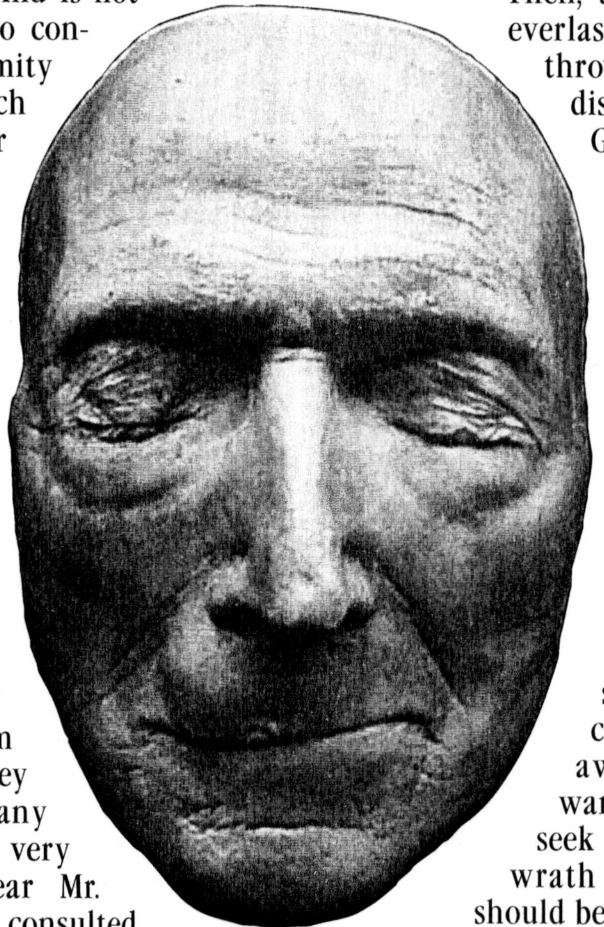

The death mask of John Wesley

Then, to have respect to God's everlasting covenant, and to throw himself upon the free distinguishing love of that God who changeth not, will make him lift up the hands that hang down, and strengthen the feeble knees.

But without the belief of the doctrine of election, and the immutability of the free love of God, I cannot see how it is possible that any should have a comfortable assurance of eternal salvation. What could it signify to a man whose conscience is thoroughly awakened, and who is warned in good earnest to seek deliverance from the wrath to come, though he should be assured that all his past sins be forgiven, and that he is now a child of God; if notwithstanding this, he may hereafter become a child of the devil, and be cast into hell at last? Could such an assurance yield any solid, lasting comfort to a person convinced of the corruption and treachery of his own heart, and of the malice, subtlety, and power of Satan? No! That which alone deserves the name of a full assurance of faith is such an assurance as emboldens the believer, under the sense of his interest in distinguishing love, to give the challenge to all his adversaries, whether men or devils, and that with regard to all their future, as well as present, attempts to destroy—saying with the Apostle,

> Who shall lay anything to the charge of God's elect? It is God that justifieth. Who is he that condemneth? It is Christ that died, yea rather, that is risen again, who is even at the right hand of God, who also maketh intercession for us. Who shall separate us from the love of Christ? shall tribulation, or distress, or persecution, or famine, or nakedness, or peril, or sword? As it is written, For thy sake we are killed all the day long, we are accounted as sheep for the slaughter. Nay, in all these things we are more than conquerors through him that loved us. For I am persuaded, that neither death, nor life, nor angels, nor principalities, nor powers, nor things present, nor things to come, nor height, nor depth, nor any other creature, shall be able to separate us from the love of God, which is in Christ Jesus our Lord (Rom. 8:33–39).

This, dear Sir, is the triumphant language of every soul that has attained a full assurance of faith. And this assurance can only arise from a belief of God's electing everlasting love. That many have an assurance they are in Christ today, but take no thought for, or are not assured they shall be in him tomorrow—nay to all eternity—is rather their imperfection and unhappiness than their privilege. I pray God to bring all such to a sense of his eternal love, that they may no longer build upon their own faithfulness, but on the unchangeableness of that God whose gifts and callings are without repentance. For those whom God has once justified, he will also glorify.

I observed before, dear Sir, it is not always a safe rule to judge of the truth of principles from people's practice. And therefore, supposing that all who hold universal redemption in your way of explaining it, after they received faith, enjoyed the continual uninterrupted sight of God's countenance, it does not follow that this is a fruit of their principle. For that I am sure has a natural tendency to keep the soul in darkness for ever, because the creature thereby is taught that his being kept in a state of salvation is owing to his own free will. And what a sandy foundation is that for a poor creature to build his hopes of perseverance upon? Every relapse into sin, every surprise by temptation, must throw him "into doubts and fears, into horrible darkness, even darkness that may be felt."

Hence it is that the letters which have been lately sent to me by those who hold universal redemption are dead and lifeless, dry and inconsistent, in comparison of those I receive from persons on the contrary side. Those who settle in the universal scheme, though they might begin in the Spirit, (whatever they may say to the contrary) are ending in the flesh, and building up a righteousness founded on their own free will: whilst the others triumph in hope of the glory of God, and build upon God's never-failing promise and unchangeable love, even when his sensible presence is withdrawn from them.

But I would not judge of the truth of election of any particular persons: if I did (O bear with me in this foolishness of boasting) I think I myself might glory in election. For these five or six years I have received the witness of God's Spirit; since that, blessed be God, I have not doubted a quarter of an hour of a saving interest in Jesus Christ: but with grief and humble shame I do acknowledge, I have fallen into sin often since that. Though I do not—dare not—allow any one transgression, yet hitherto I have not been (nor do I expect that while I am in this present world I ever shall be) able to live one day perfectly free from all defects and sin. And since the Scriptures declare that there is not a just man upon earth (no, not among those of the highest attainments in grace) that doeth good and sinneth not (Eccl. 7:20), we are sure that this will be the case of all the children of God.

The universal experience and acknowledgement of this among the godly in every age is abundantly sufficient to confute the error of those who hold in an absolute sense that after a man is born again he cannot commit sin. Especially since the Holy Spirit condemns the persons who say they have no sin as deceiving themselves, as being destitute of the truth, and as making God a liar (1 Jn. 1:8, 10). I have been also in heaviness through manifold temptations, and expect to be often so before I die. Thus were the Apostles and primitive Christians themselves. Thus was Luther, that man of God, who, as far as I can find, did not peremptorily, at least, hold election; and the great John Arndt was in the utmost perplexity, but a quarter of an hour before he died, and yet he was no predestinarian.

And if I must speak freely, I believe your fighting so strenuously against the doctrine of election and pleading so vehemently for a sinless perfection are among the reasons or culpable causes, why you are kept out of the liberties of the gospel, and from that full assurance of faith which they enjoy, who have experimentally tasted, and daily feed upon God's electing, everlasting love.

But perhaps you may say, that Luther and Arndt were no Christians, at least very weak ones. I know you think meanly of Abraham, though he was eminently called the friend of God: and, I believe, also of David, the man after God's own heart. No wonder, therefore, that in a letter you sent me not long since, you should tell me that no Baptist or Presbyterian writer whom you have read knew anything of the liberties of Christ. What? Neither Bunyan, Henry, Flavel, Halyburton, nor any of the New England and Scots divines? See, dear Sir, what narrow-spiritedness and want of charity arise from your principles, and then do not cry out against election any more on account of its being "destructive of meekness and love."

Fourth, I shall now proceed to another head. Says the dear Mr. Wesley, "How uncomfortable a thought is this, that thousands and millions of men, without any preceding offence or fault of theirs, were unchangeably doomed to everlasting burnings?"

But who ever asserted that thousands and millions of men, without any preceding offence or fault of theirs, were unchangeably doomed to everlasting burnings? Do not they who believe God's dooming men to everlasting burnings, also believe, that God looked upon them as men fallen in Adam? And that the decree which ordained the punishment first regarded the crime by which it was deserved? How then are they doomed without any preceding fault? Surely Mr. Wesley will own God's justice in imputing Adam's sin to his posterity. And also, after Adam fell, and his posterity in him, God might justly have passed them all by, without sending his own Son to be a saviour for any one. Unless you heartily agree to both these points, you do not believe original sin aright. If you do own them, then you must acknowledge the doctrine of election and reprobation to be highly just and reasonable. For if God might justly impute Adam's sin to all, and afterwards have passed by all, then he might justly pass by some. Turn on the right hand, or on the left; you are reduced to an inextricable dilemma. And, if you would be consistent, you must either give up the doctrine of the imputation of Adam's sin, or receive the amiable doctrine of election, with a holy and righteous reprobation as its consequent. For whether you can believe it or not, the Word of God abides faithful: "The election hath obtained it, and the rest were blinded" (Rom. 11:7).

Your 17th paragraph, Page 16, I pass over. What has been said on the 9th and 10th paragraphs, with a little alteration, will answer it. I shall only say, it is the doctrine of election that most presses me to abound in good works. I am willing to suffer all things for the elect's sake. This makes me to preach with comfort, because I know salvation does not depend on man's free will, but the Lord makes willing in the day of his power, and can make use of me to bring some of his elect home, when and where he pleases.

But fifth, you say, "This doctrine has a direct manifest tendency to overthrow the whole Christian religion. For," say you, "supposing that eternal, unchangeable decree, one part of mankind must be saved, though the Christian revelation were not in being."

But, dear Sir, how does that follow? Since it is only by the Christian revelation that we are acquainted with God's design of saving his church by the death of his Son. Yea, it is settled in the everlasting covenant that this salvation shall be applied to the elect through the knowledge and faith of him. As the prophet says in Isaiah 53:11, "By his knowledge shall my righteous servant justify many." How then has the doctrine of election a direct tendency to overthrow the whole Christian revelation? Who ever thought that God's declaration to Noah, that seed-time and harvest should never cease, could afford an argument for the neglect of plowing or sowing? Or that the unchangeable purpose of God, that harvest should not fail, rendered the heat of the sun, or the influence of the heavenly bodies unnecessary to produce it? No more does God's absolute purpose of saving his chosen preclude the necessity of the gospel revelation, or the use of any of the means through which he has determined the decree shall take effect. Nor will the right understanding, or the reverent belief of God's decree, ever allow or suffer a Christian in any case to separate the means from the end, or the end from the means.

And since we are taught by the revelation itself that this was intended and given by God as a means of bringing home his elect, we therefore receive it with joy, prize it highly, use it in faith, and endeavour to spread it through all the world, in the full assurance, that wherever God sends it, sooner or later, it shall be savingly useful to all the elect within its call.

How then, in holding this doctrine, do we join with modern unbelievers in making the Christian revelation unnecessary? No, dear Sir, you mistake. Infidels of all kinds are on your side of the question. Deists, Arians, and Socinians arraign God's sovereignty and stand up for universal redemption. I pray God that dear Mr. Wesley's sermon, as it has grieved the hearts of many of God's children, may not also strengthen the hands of many of his most avowed enemies!

Here I could almost lay down and weep. "Tell it not in Gath, publish it not in the streets of Askelon; lest the daughters of the Philistines rejoice, lest the daughters of the uncircumcised triumph" (2 Sam. 1:20).

Further, you say, "This doctrine makes revelation contradict itself." For instance, say you, "The assertors of this doctrine interpret that text of Scripture, Jacob have I loved, but

Esau have I hated, as implying that God, in a literal sense, hated Esau and all the reprobates from eternity!" And, when considered as fallen in Adam, were they not the objects of his hatred? And might not God, of his own good pleasure, love or show mercy to Jacob and the elect—and yet at the same time do the reprobate no wrong? But you say, "God is love." And cannot God be love, unless he shows the same mercy to all?

Again, says dear Mr. Wesley, "They infer from that text, 'I will have mercy on whom I will have mercy,' that God is merciful only to some men, viz the elect; and that he has mercy for those only, flatly contrary to which is the whole tenor of the Scripture, as is that express declaration in particular, 'The Lord is loving to every man, and his mercy is over all his works.'"

And so it is, but not his saving mercy. God is loving to every man: he sends his rain upon the evil and upon the good. But you say, "God is no respecter of persons" (Acts 10:34). No! For every one, whether Jew or Gentile, that believeth on Jesus, and worketh righteousness, is accepted of him. "But he that believeth shall not be damned" (Mk. 16:16). For God is no respecter of persons, upon the account of any outward condition or circumstances in life whatever; nor does the doctrine of election in the least suppose him to be so. But as the sovereign Lord of all, who is debtor to none, he has a right to do what he will with his own, and to dispense his favours to what objects he sees fit, merely at his pleasure. And his supreme right herein is clearly and strongly asserted in those passages of Scripture, where he says, "Moses, I will have mercy on whom I will have mercy, and I will have compassion on whom I will have compassion" (Rom. 9:15, Exod. 33:19).

Further, from the text, "the children being not yet born, neither having done any good or evil, that the purpose of God according to election might stand, not of works, but of him that calleth; it was said unto her [Rebekah], The elder shall serve the younger" (Rom. 9:11-12)—you represent us as inferring that our predestination to life in no way depends on the foreknowledge of God.

But who infers this, dear Sir? For if foreknowledge signifies approbation, as it does in several parts of Scripture, then we confess that predestination and election do depend on God's foreknowledge. But if by God's foreknowledge you understand God's fore-seeing some good works done by his creatures as the foundation or reason of choosing them and therefore electing them, then we say that in this sense predestination does not any way depend on God's foreknowledge.

But I referred you, at the beginning of this letter, to Dr. Edward's Veritas Redux, which I recommend to you also in a late letter, with Elisha Coles on God's sovereignty. Be pleased to read these, and also the excellent sermons of Mr. Cooper of Boston in New England (which I also sent you) and I doubt not but you will see all your objections answered. Though I would observe, that after all our reading on both sides the question, we shall never in this life be able to search out God's decrees to perfection. No, we must humbly adore what we cannot comprehend, and with the great Apostle at the end of our enquiries cry out, "O the depth of the riches both of the wisdom and knowledge of God! how unsearchable are his judgments, and his ways past finding out! For who hath known the mind of the Lord? or who hath been his counsellor?" (Rom. 11:33-34)—or with our Lord, when he was admiring God's sovereignty, "Even so, Father: for so it seemed good in thy sight" (Matt. 11:26).

However, it may not be amiss to take notice, that if those texts, "The Lord is . . . not willing that any should perish, but that all should come to repentance" (2 Pet. 3:9) and "I have no pleasure in the death of the wicked; but that the wicked turn from his way and live" (Ezek. 33:11)—and such like—be taken in their strictest sense, then no one will be damned.

But here's the distinction. God taketh no pleasure in the death of sinners, so as to delight simply in their death; but he delights to magnify his justice, by inflicting the punishment which their iniquities have deserved. As a righteous judge who takes no pleasure in condemning a criminal, may yet justly command him to be executed, that law and justice may be satisfied, even though it be in his power to procure him a reprieve.

I would hint further, that you unjustly charge the doctrine of reprobation with blasphemy, whereas the doctrine of universal redemption, as you set it forth, is really the highest reproach upon the dignity of the Son of God, and the merit of his blood. Consider whether it be not rather blasphemy to say as you do, "Christ not only died for those that are saved, but also for those that perish."

The text you have misapplied to gloss over this, see explained by Ridgely, Edwards, Henry; and I purposely omit answering your texts myself so that you may be brought to read such treatises, which, under God, would show you your error. You cannot make good the assertion that Christ died for them that perish without holding (as Peter Bohler, one of the Moravian brethren, in order to make out universal redemption, lately frankly confessed in a letter) that all the damned souls would hereafter be brought out of hell. I cannot think Mr. Wesley is thus minded. And yet unless this can be proved, universal redemption, taken in a literal sense, falls entirely to the ground. For how can all be universally redeemed, if all are not finally saved?

Dear Sir, for Jesus Christ's sake, consider how you dishonour God by denying election. You plainly make salvation depend not on God's free grace, but on man's free-will. And if thus, it is more than probable, Jesus Christ would not have had the satisfaction of seeing the fruit of his death in the eternal salvation of one soul. Our preaching would then be vain, and all invitations for people to believe in him would also be in vain.

But, blessed be God, our Lord knew for whom he died. There was an eternal compact between the Father and the Son. A certain number was then given him as the purchase and reward of his obedience and death. For these he prayed (Jn. 17:9), and not for the world. For these elect ones, and these only, he is now interceding, and with their salvation he will be fully satisfied.

I purposely omit making any further particular remarks on the several last pages of your sermon. Indeed had not your name, dear Sir, been prefixed to the sermon, I could not have been so uncharitable as to think you were the author of such sophistry. You beg the question, in saying that God has declared, (notwithstanding you own, I suppose, some will be damned) that he will save all—i.e., every individual person. You take it for granted (for solid proof you have none) that God is unjust, if he passes by any, and then you exclaim against the "horrible decree": and yet, as I before hinted, in holding the doctrine of original sin, you profess to believe that he might justly have passed by all.

Dear, dear Sir, O be not offended! For Christ's sake be not rash! Give yourself to reading. Study the covenant of grace. Down with your carnal reasoning. Be a little child; and then, instead of pawning your salvation, as you have done in a late hymn book, if the doctrine of universal redemption be not true; instead of talking of sinless perfection, as you

The First Great Awakening
Project 2, Page 14

have done in the preface to that hymn book, and making man's salvation to depend on his own free will, as you have in this sermon; you will compose a hymn in praise of sovereign distinguishing love. You will caution believers against striving to work a perfection out of their own hearts, and print another sermon the reverse of this, and entitle it "Free Grace Indeed." Free, not because free to all; but free, because God may withhold or give it to whom and when he pleases.

Till you do this, I must doubt whether or not you know yourself. In the meanwhile, I cannot but blame you for censuring the clergy of our church for not keeping to their articles, when you yourself by your principles, positively deny the 9th, 10th and 17th.

Dear Sir, these things ought not so to be. God knows my heart, as I told you before, so I declare again, nothing but a single regard to the honour of Christ has forced this letter from me. I love and honour you for his sake; and when I come to judgment, will thank you before men and angels, for what you have, under God, done for my soul.

There, I am persuaded, I shall see dear Mr. Wesley convinced of election and everlasting love. And it often fills me with pleasure to think how I shall behold you casting your crown down at the feet of the Lamb, and as it were filled with a holy blushing for opposing the divine sovereignty in the manner you have done.

But I hope the Lord will show you this before you go hence. O how do I long for that day! If the Lord should be pleased to make use of this letter for that purpose, it would abundantly rejoice the heart of, dear and honoured Sir,

Yours affectionate, though unworthy brother and servant in Christ,

GEORGE WHITEFIELD.

THE FIRST GREAT AWAKENING

Project 3—Edward's Spider

Read the following excerpt from Jonathan Edward's famous sermon then make the project.

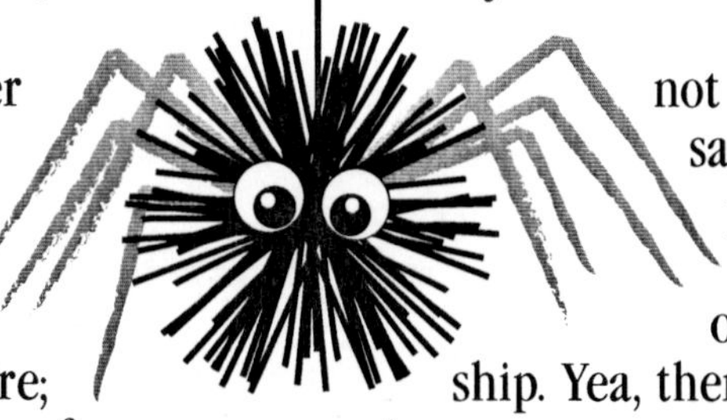

"The god that holds you over the pit of hell, much as one holds a spider, or some loathsome insect over the fire, abhors you, and is dreadfully provoked: his wrath towards you burns like fire; he looks upon you as worthy of nothing else, but to be cast into the fire; he is of purer eyes than to bear to have you in his sight; you are ten thousand times more abominable in his eyes, than the most hateful venomous serpent is in ours. You have offended him infinitely more than ever a stubborn rebel did his prince; and yet it is nothing but his hand that holds you from falling into the fire at every moment. It is to be ascribed to nothing else, that you did not go to hell last night; that you suffered to awake again in this world, after you closed your eyes to sleep. And there is no other reason to be given, why you have not dropped into hell since you arose in the morning, but that God's hand has held you up. There is no other reason to be given why you have not gone to hell, since you have sat here in the house of God, provoking his pure eyes by your sinful wicked manner of attending his solemn worship. Yea, there is nothing else that is to be given as a reason why you do not this very moment drop down into hell.

O sinner! Consider the fearful danger you are in: it is a great furnace of wrath, a wide and bottomless pit, full of the fire of wrath, that you are held over in the hand of that God, whose wrath is provoked and incensed as much against you, as against many of the damned in hell. You hang by a slender thread, with the flames of divine wrath flashing against, and ready every moment to singe it, and burn it asunder; and you have no interest in any Mediator, and nothing to lay hold of to save yourself, nothing to keep off the flames of wrath, nothing of your own, nothing that you have ever done, nothing that you can do, to induce God to spare you one moment."

Supplies

yarn

scissors

4 pipe cleaners

cardboard (3 x 2 inches)

googly eyes

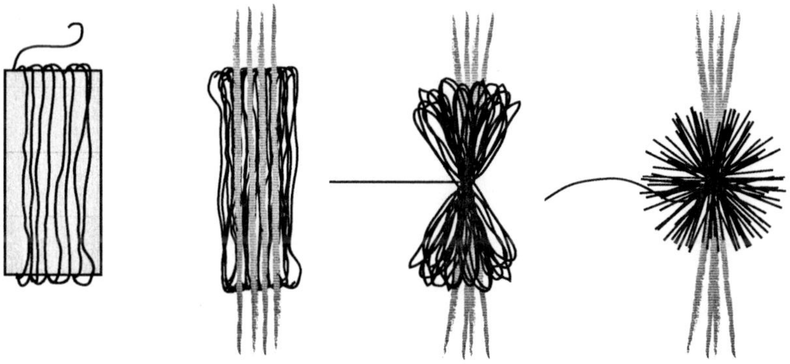

Instructions

Loosely wind a yard or two of yarn around the cardboard. Remove the yarn loops from the cardboard (keep the loops intact). Lay four pipe cleaners on top of the loops and tie a two-foot piece of yarn around the loops and the pipe cleaners. Cut the yarn loops at their edges. Trim and fluff the yarn into the shape of a pompom. Bend the pipe cleaners to look like spider legs and glue on googly eyes.

THE FIRST GREAT AWAKENING
Test

1. Who were George Whitefield and Jonathan Edwards?

2. What was the First Great Awakening?

3. Who preached the famous sermon "Sinners in the Hands of an Angry God?"

4. Who believed in the doctrine of "free grace?" Who publicly condemned this doctrine?

5. What is one of the places to which Whitefield drew many people?

6. How many sermons is Whitefield thought to have preached? How many of these sermons still survive?

7. What are the dates of the First Great Awakening?

The First Great Awakening

Test, Page 2

Review

1. Who was Ferdinand Magellan?

2. What did Champlain found? What did he discover?

3. When John White arrived at Roanoke in 1590, what did he find?

4. What agreement was signed before departing from the Mayflower?
   Who signed the document?

5. In chronological order list all events studied to date. Next to each place the appropriate date.

The First Great Awakening

Test, Page 3

5. (continued)

Colonial Trading With England

Worksheet

1. When did Colonial Trading with England occur?

____

____

____

2. From what did most of the original thirteen colonies get their authority to form?

____

____

____

3. What is mercantilism?

____

____

____

____

____

4. Even though the colonies sold items to each other, they needed to sell products to ______________ to earn money.

5. List some products sold to England.

____

____

____

____

____

Colonial Trading With England

Worksheet, Page 2

6. List some products the colonies bought from England.

7. Which two countries fought for control over trade with the colonies in the early 1700's?

8. What impact did the French and Indian Wars have on trade for the colonies?

Colonial Trading With England
Project 1—Farming and Shipping in the Colonies

After reading the following account of colonial trading and the information found in the resources mentioned on the flash card, on another sheet of paper design an advertisement for the English newspaper to market your products in the mother country.

The people who came first to North America expected to find either a way to India, or mines like those discovered farther southward. But when they found that they could not secure either the spices of India or the gold and silver of Peru, they turned their attention to the soil, to see what could be got by agriculture. But at first their plans for farming in America were as wild as their plans for getting to India. They spent much time in trying to produce silk and wine, two things which can be raised with profit only in old and well-settled countries. They also tried to raise madder, coffee, tea, olives, and the cocoa bean, from which chocolate is made.

In 1612 John Rolfe, the husband of Pocahontas, took a lesson from the Indian fields about him, and he succeeded in growing tobacco for the English market. Before this time, English smokers and snuff-takers got their tobacco from the Spaniards. The plant was well suited to the Virginia climate, and it was easy to ship tobacco from the farms, which were all on the banks of the rivers. Gold and silver coins were scarce in those days, and, in half a dozen years after John Rolfe planted the first tobacco, it had become the only money of Virginia. Almost everything bought and sold in Virginia and Maryland, before the Revolution, was paid for in tobacco.

The colony of South Carolina maintained itself in a rather poor way, during

Colonial Trading With England

Project 1, Page 2

the first twenty-six years of its existence, chiefly by shipping lumber to the West Indies and by making tar and pitch. But there was living in Charleston, in 1696, a gentleman named Thomas Smith, who had seen rice cultivated in Madagascar. One day when a sea-captain, an old friend of his, sailed into Charleston Harbor from Madagascar, Thomas Smith got from him a bag of seed-rice. This was carefully sown in a wet place in Smith's garden in Charleston. It grew, and soon Carolina was changed into a land of great rice-plantations. The raising of rice spread into Georgia when that colony was settled.

In 1741 an energetic young lady, Miss Eliza Lucas, began to try experiments in growing the indigo plant in South Carolina. A frost destroyed the first crop that she planted, and a worm cut down the next. The indigo-maker brought from the West Indies tried to deceive her afterward, but by 1745 this persevering young lady had proved that indigo could be grown in South Carolina, and in two years more, two hundred thousand pounds of it were exported. It was a leading crop for about fifty years, but, when the growing of cotton was made profitable by the invention of the cotton gin, cotton took the place of indigo.

The settlers got Indian corn from the Indians. It was unknown in Europe. From it was made most of the bread eaten by Americans before the Revolution. It was also shipped to the West Indies from Virginia and North Carolina. New York, New Jersey, and Pennsylvania formed the great wheat region of the colonial time. These colonies sent wheat, flour, and "hardtack" bread in large quantities to the West Indies and the countries on the Mediterranean Sea. Many thousands of great country wagons were employed in bringing grain to Philadelphia. Potatoes had been brought to Europe probably from South America, but they were unknown to the Indians in what is now the United States. They were taken to Virginia at the first settlement of Jamestown. Potatoes were not planted in New England fields until 1718. It was thought that if a man were to eat potatoes every day for seven years, he would die.

Cattle and hogs were brought from England very early, and were grown by thousands in the colonies. For the most part they ran in the woods, having marks on them to show to whom they belonged. Many cattle grew up without marks of ownership and were hunted as wild. There were "cowpens" established for raising cattle in the wilderness, something like the "ranches" in the Western country today. The horses of that day were small and hardy. When not in use they ran at large in the woods, and some of them quite escaped from their owners, so that after a while there came to be a race of wild horses. It was accounted rare sport to ride after a wild horse until he was tired out, and so to capture him.

The English plow of that time was very heavy, and drawn by six horses or as many oxen. Efforts were made to introduce this to the colonies, but it was not suited to a new country. The plow most used in the colonies was a clumsy thing, with thin plates of iron nailed over the rude wooden plowshares. There were many stumps and few plows. All the tools were heavy and awkward.

The Middle colonies raised wheat, the colonies on Chesapeake Bay raised tobacco, and the Southern colonies raised rice and indigo; but the soil and climate of New England were not suited to any agricultural staple of great value. So the New Englanders were driven to follow the sea. They built a great many ships, some of which they sold to English mer-

COLONIAL TRADING WITH ENGLAND

Project 1, Page 3

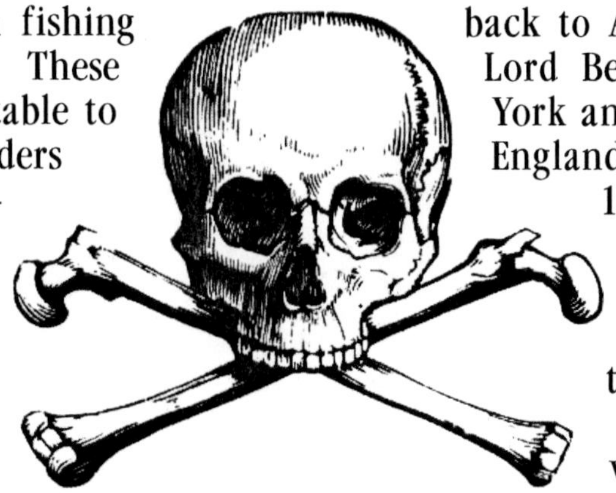

chants; others they used in fishing for codfish and mackerel. These fisheries became very profitable to them. When the Long Islanders discovered the art of whaling along the coast, the New England people learned it, and became the most prosperous whalers in the world.

The products of their fisheries were sent to many countries, and New England ships were seen in almost every sea. Boston and Newport were the chief New England seaports.

The people of New York also built many ships which were remarkable for their great size and the long voyages they made. But, before the Revolution, New York was not so large a town as Boston. Philadelphia, which was started later than the other leading cities, grew fast and became the greatest of all the cities in the colonies. But Philadelphia contained only about thirty thousand people when the Revolution broke out.

There were many pirates on the Eastern coast. The Pirates grew so numerous and bold as to interrupt trade. Some of them were caught and hanged. Captain William Kidd, of New York, was sent out in 1695 to put down the pirates that infested the Indian Ocean. The expense of his outfit was borne by certain gentlemen in America and England who were to share his spoils. Though not falling in with any pirates, he took to piratical ways himself. When he came back to America he was arrested by Lord Bellemont, Governor of New York and New England, and sent to England for trial and execution. In 1717, Steed Bonnet and Richard Worley, two pirates with their crews, had taken possession of the mouth of Cape Fear River in North Carolina, whence they committed great depredations on the commerce of South Carolina. Colonel Rhett, of South Carolina, pursued Bonnet into Cape Fear River, and, after a fight, captured him and thirty of his men. They were tried and hanged at Charleston. Governor Johnson, of South Carolina, took another vessel, and attacked Richard Worley and his pirates, who fought until all were dead but Worley and one man, and these were taken, desperately wounded, and hanged.

One of the most infamous of all the pirates of the coast was Edward Teach, who, under the name of Blackbeard, made himself the terror of all seamen on the coast from Philadelphia southward. He had his refuge also in the shallow waters of the North Carolina coast.

A little more than a year after the overthrow of Bonnet, Lieutenant Maynard sailed from Virginia and fought Blackbeard in Ocracoke Inlet. After a hand-to-hand struggle all the pirates were killed or wounded, and Maynard sailed back with Blackbeard's head hanging at his bowsprit. So many of the pirates were captured in the next half-dozen years that they gave little trouble afterward.

Colonial Trading With England

Project 1, Page 5

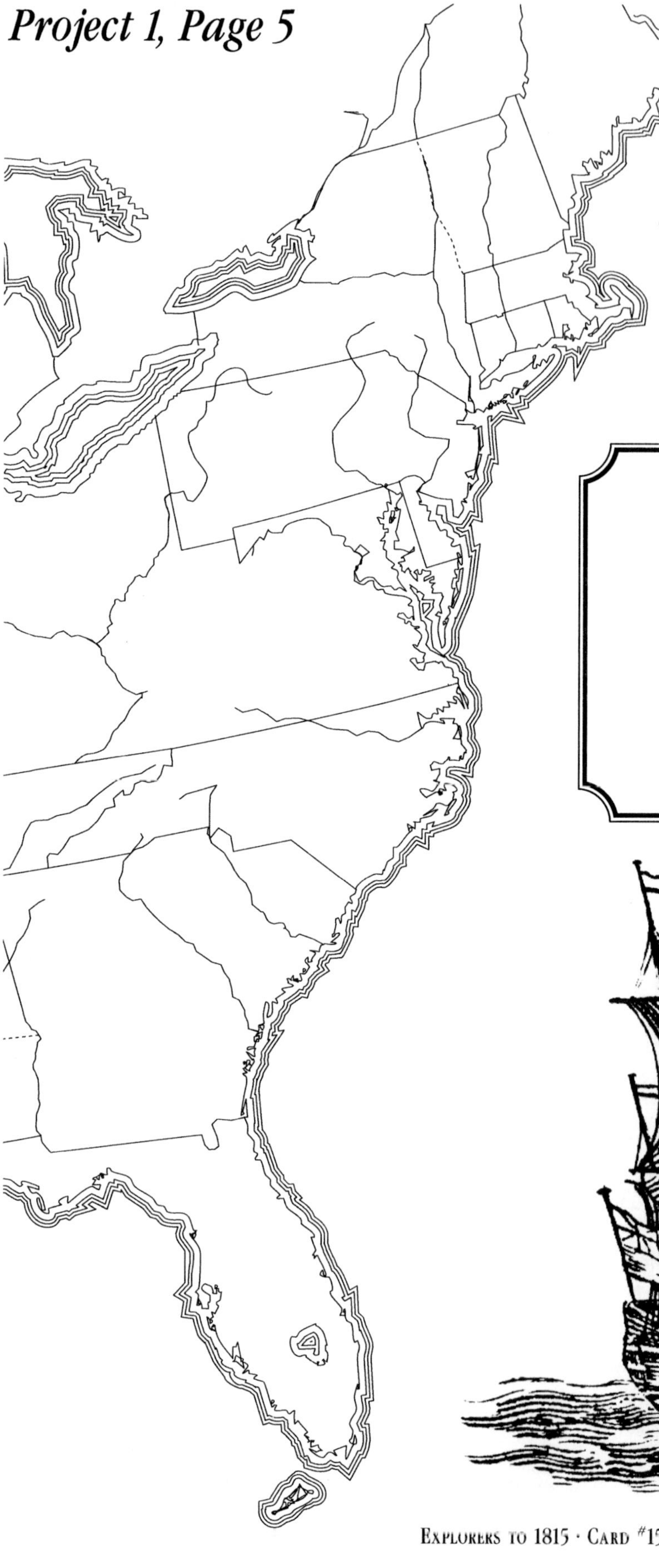

Use this map to label the products that the colonies produced. Draw a key to the symbols in the box below; for instance, use a small ship to represent ship building, a leaf to represent tobacco, etc. What were some of the hindrances to trade for the colonies? How were the hindrances dealt with?

Colonial Trading With England

Project 2—On the Misfortune of Indentured Servants

On the Misfortune of Indentured Servants (1754)

by Gottlieb Mittelberger

Both in Rotterdam and in Amsterdam the people are packed densely, like herrings so to say, in the large sea-vessels. One person receives a place of scarcely 2 feet width and 6 feet length in the bedstead, while many a ship carries four to six hundred souls; not to mention the innumerable implements, tools, provisions, water-barrels and other things which likewise occupy much space.

On account of contrary winds it takes the ships sometimes 2, 3 and 4 weeks to make the trip from Holland to . . . England. But when the wind is good, they get there in 8 days or even sooner. Everything is examined there and the custom-duties paid, whence it comes that the ships ride there 8, 10 to 14 days and even longer at anchor, till they have taken in their full cargoes. During that time every one is compelled to spend his last remaining money and to consume his little stock of provisions which had been reserved for the sea; so that most passengers, finding themselves on the ocean where they would be in greater need of them, must greatly suffer from hunger and want. Many suffer want already on the water between Holland and Old England.

When the ships have for the last time weighed their anchors near the city of Kaupp [Cowes] in Old England, the real misery begins with the long voyage. For from there the ships, unless they have good wind, must often sail 8, 9, 10 to 12 weeks before they reach Philadelphia. But even with the best wind the voyage lasts 7 weeks.

But during the voyage there is on board these ships terrible misery, stench, fumes, horror, vomiting, many kinds of sea-sickness, fever, dysentery, headache, heat, constipation, boils, scurvy, cancer, mouth-rot, and the like, all of which come from old and sharply salted food and meat, also from very bad and foul water, so that many die miserably.

Add to this want of provisions, hunger, thirst, frost, heat, dampness, anxiety, want, afflictions and lamentations, together with other trouble, as . . . the lice abound so frightfully, especially on sick people, that they can be scraped off the body. The misery reaches the climax when a gale rages for 2 or 3 nights and days, so that every one believes that the ship will go to the bottom with all human beings on board. In such a visitation the people cry and pray most piteously.

When in such a gale the sea rages and surges, so that the waves rise often like high mountains one above the other, and often tumble over the ship, so that one fears to go down with the ship; when the ship is constantly tossed from side to side by the storm and waves, so that no one can either walk, or sit, or lie, and the closely packed people in the berths are thereby tumbled over each other, both the sick and the well—it will be readily understood that many of these people, none of whom had been prepared for hardships, suffer so terribly from them that they do not survive it.

I myself had to pass through a severe illness at sea, and I best know how I felt at the time. These poor people often long for consolation, and I often entertained and comforted them with singing, praying and exhorting; and whenever it was possible and the winds and waves permitted it, I kept daily prayer-meetings with them on deck. Besides, I baptized five children in distress, because we had no ordained minister on

Colonial Trading With England

Project 2, Page 2

board. I also held divine service every Sunday by reading sermons to the people; and when the dead were sunk in the water, I commended them and our souls to the mercy of God.

Among the healthy, impatience sometimes grows so great and cruel that one curses the other, or himself and the day of his birth, and sometimes come near killing each other. Misery and malice join each other, so that they cheat and rob one another. One always reproaches the other with having persuaded him to undertake the journey. Frequently children cry out against their parents, husbands against their wives and wives against their husbands, brothers and sisters, friends and acquaintances against each other. But most against the soul-traffickers.

Many sigh and cry: "Oh, that I were at home again, and if I had to lie in my pig-sty!" Or they say: "O God, if I only had a piece of good bread, or a good fresh drop of water." Many people whimper, sigh and cry piteously for their homes; most of them get home-sick. Many hundred people necessarily die and perish in such misery, and must be cast into the sea, which drives their relatives, or those who persuaded them to undertake the journey, to such despair that it is almost impossible to pacify and console them.

No one can have an idea of the sufferings which women in confinement have to bear with their innocent children on board these ships. Few of this class escape with their lives; many a mother is cast into the water with her child as soon as she is dead. One day, just as we had a heavy gale, a woman in our ship, who was to give birth and could not give birth under the circumstances, was pushed through a loop-hole [port-hole] in the ship and dropped into the sea, because she was far in the rear of the ship and could not be brought forward.

Children from 1 to 7 years rarely survive the voyage. I witnessed misery in no less than 32 children in our ship, all of whom were thrown into the sea. The parents grieve all the more since their children find no resting-place in the earth, but are devoured by the monsters of the sea.

That most of the people get sick is not surprising, because, in addition to all other trials and hardships, warm food is served only three times a week, the rations being very poor and very little. Such meals can hardly be eaten, on account of being so unclean. The water which is served out on the ships is often very black, thick and full of worms, so that one cannot drink it without loathing, even with the greatest thirst. Toward the end we were compelled to eat the ship's biscuit which had been spoiled long ago; though in a whole biscuit there was scarcely a, piece the size of a dollar that had not been full of red worms and spiders nests.

At length, when, after a long and tedious voyage, the ships come in sight of land, so that the promontories can be seen, which the people were so eager and anxious to see, all creep from below on deck to see the land from afar, and they weep for joy, and pray and sing, thanking and praising God. The sight of the land makes the people on board the ship, especially the sick and the half dead, alive again, so that their hearts leap within them; they shout and rejoice, and are content to bear their misery in patience, in the hope that they may soon reach the land in safety. But alas!

When the ships have landed at Philadelphia after their long voyage, no one is permitted to leave them except those who pay for their passage or can give good security; the others, who cannot pay, must remain on board the ships till they are pur-

Colonial Trading With England

Project 2, Page 3

chased, and are released from the ships by their purchasers. The sick always fare the worst, for the healthy are naturally preferred and purchased first; and so the sick and wretched must often remain on board in front of the city for 2 or 3 weeks, and frequently die, whereas many a one, if he could pay his debt and were permitted to leave the ship immediately, might recover and remain alive.

The sale of human beings in the market on board the ship is carried on thus: Every day Englishmen, Dutchmen and High-German people come from the city of Philadelphia and other places, in part from a great distance, say 20, 30, or 40 hours away, and go on board the newly arrived ship that has brought and offers for sale passengers from Europe, and select among the healthy persons such as they deem suitable for their business, and bargain with them how long they will serve for their passage money, which most of them are still in debt for. When they have come to an agreement, it happens that adult persons bind themselves in writing to serve 3, 4, 5 or 6 years for the amount due by them, according to their age and strength. But very young people, from 10 to 15 years, must serve till they are 21 years old.

Many parents must sell and trade away their children like so many head of cattle; for if their children take the debt upon themselves, the parents can leave the ship free and unrestrained; but as the parents often do not know where and to what people their children are going, it often happens that such parents and children, after leaving the ship, do not see each other again for many years, perhaps no more in all their lives.

It often happens that whole families, husband, wife, and children, are separated by being sold to different purchasers, especially when they have not paid any part of their passage money.

When a husband or wife has died at sea, when the ship has made more than half of her trip, the survivor must pay or serve not only for himself or herself, but also for the deceased.

When both parents have died over halfway at sea, their children, especially when they are young and have nothing to pawn or to pay, must stand for their own and their parents' passage, and serve until they are 21 years old. When one has served his or her term, he or she is entitled to a new suit of clothes at parting; and if it has been so stipulated, a man gets in addition a horse, a woman and a cow.

When a serf has an opportunity to marry in this country, he or she must pay for each year which he or she would have yet to serve, 5 to 6 pounds. But many a one who has thus purchased and paid for his bride, has subsequently repented his bargain, so that he would gladly have returned his exorbitantly dear ware, and lost the money besides.

If some one in this country runs away from his master, who has treated him harshly, he cannot get far. Good provision has been made for such cases, so that a runaway is soon recovered. He who detains or returns a deserter receives a good reward.

If such a runaway has been away from his master one day, he must serve for it as a punishment a week, for a week a month, and for a month half a year.

Colonial Trading With England

Project 3—Candle Making

Supplies

8 packages of paraffin

small pieces of crayon or colored wax

8" cotton string per candle

Directions

1. Spray with cooking spray then melt paraffin and crayons in crock pots (use old crock pots because you may not be able to clean off all the wax).
2. Dip the string into the paraffin, leaving about 2 inches at the top.
3. Allow the wax to harden, then repeat the dipping. Candles may be dipped into several colors of wax. This activity should be done under adult supervision.

Colonial Trading With England

Project 4–Quilt Making

Supplies

old wallpaper sample books

construction paper

glue

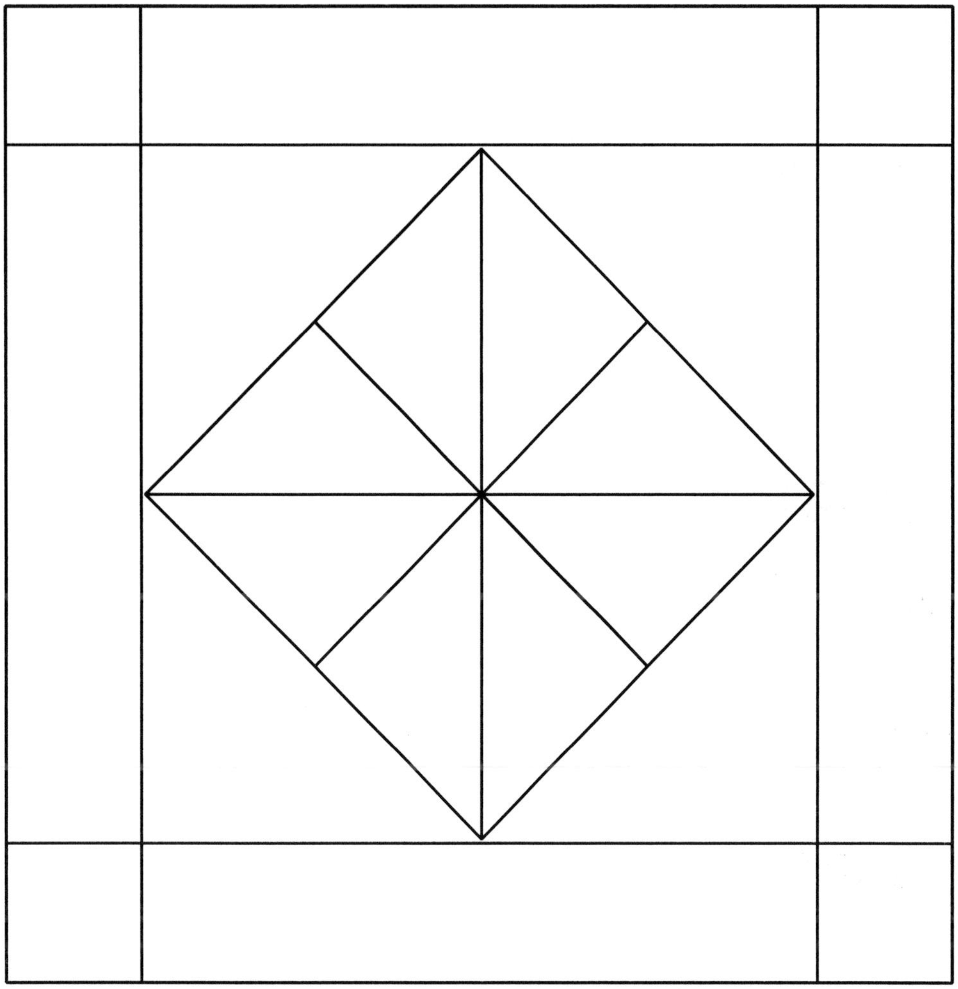

Directions

1. Using the pattern shown or utilizing patterns from a quilting book, create a wallpaper quilt.
2. Cut out sections of wallpaper in the required geometric shapes and glue to a piece of construction paper of a complementary color. Pasting or taping multiple panels together can create quite a lovely addition to your classroom's decor.

Many wallpaper stores are happy to give away old sample books just for the asking.

Colonial Trading With England

Test

1. What is the approximate date of colonial trading with England?

2. What is the term used to describe trading of goods between a "mother country" and its colonies?

3. Why did the colonies need to sell goods to England?

4. List three items sold to England from the colonies.

5. List three items the colonists would have purchased from England.

Colonial Trading With England

Test, Page 2

6. In the early 1700's what two countries fought over control of trade with the colonies?

7. After the French and Indian Wars what did England do to the colonies regarding trade?

Review

1. Who was Roger Williams and what did he found?

2. Who established the Massachusetts Bay Colony?

3. What did the Separatists, who came over on the Mayflower, believe?

Colonial Trading With England

Test, Page 3

4. Describe the colony of Jamestown. Pay particular attention to their work habits and lifestyle.

5. In chronological order list all events studied to date. Next to each place the appropriate date.

THE FRENCH AND INDIAN WARS
Worksheet

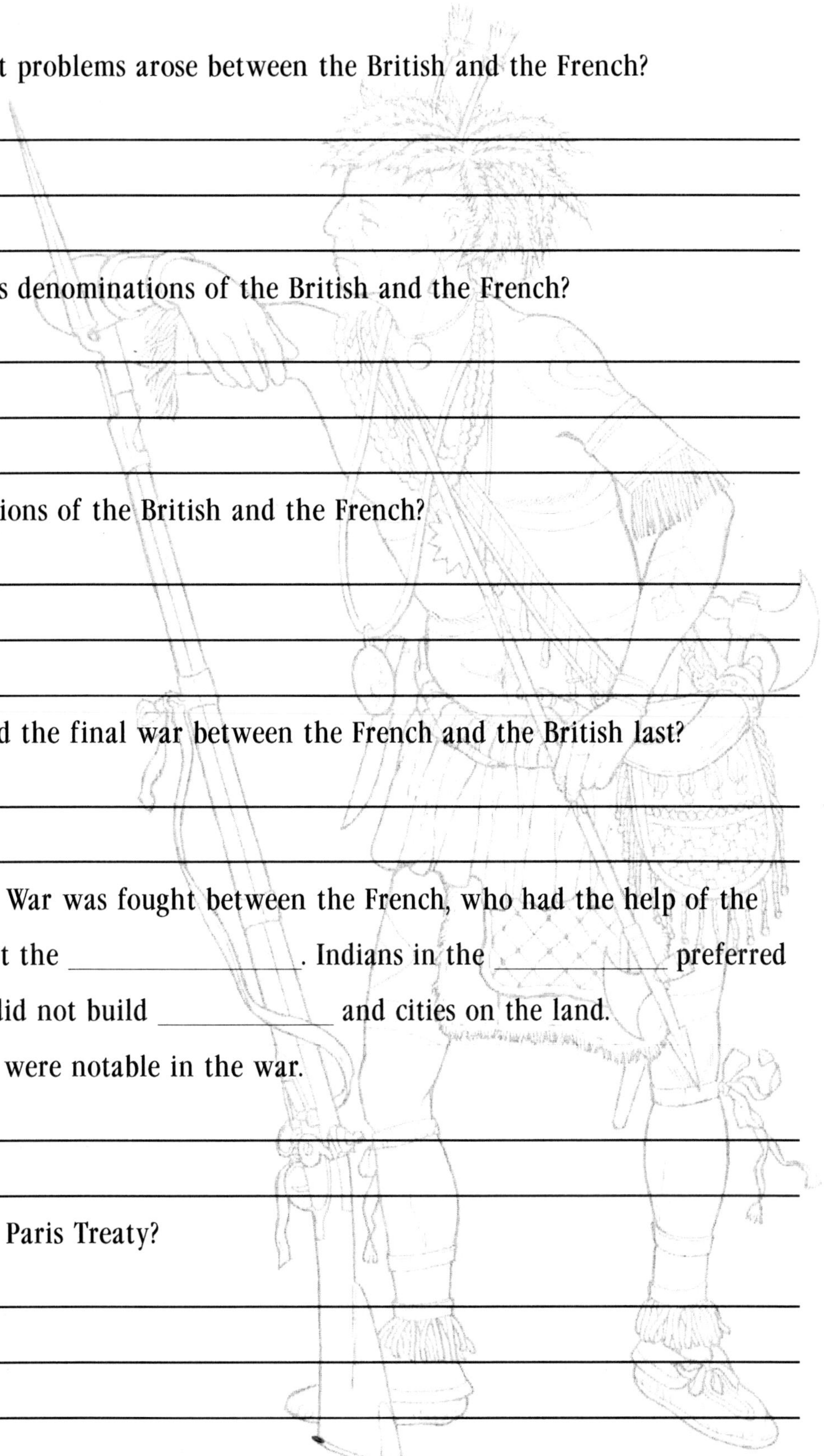

1. In the early 1700's what problems arose between the British and the French?

2. What were the religious denominations of the British and the French?

3. What were the occupations of the British and the French?

4. For how many years did the final war between the French and the British last?

5. The French and Indian War was fought between the French, who had the help of the _______________, against the _______________. Indians in the _______________ preferred the French since they did not build _______________ and cities on the land.

6. Name four people who were notable in the war.

7. What was the Peace of Paris Treaty?

THE FRENCH AND INDIAN WARS

Project—Washington, Wolfe, and Montcalm

Read the article below and discuss the questions that follow.

GEORGE WASHINGTON IN THE FRENCH AND INDIAN WAR

THE RACE FOR OHIO

There came a time when both the French and the English wanted the land along the Ohio River. The governor of Canada sent his soldiers to build forts near the head of the river. He hoped in that way to get possession of the land first and keep the English out.

Hearing what the French were doing, Governor Dinwiddie of Virginia sent a message telling the French soldiers to keep away from the Ohio because the land belonged to the English.

This race for the Ohio was the beginning of a long quarrel. It did not end until the king of France had lost every foot of land that he owned in America.

YOUNG GEORGE WASHINGTON

Governor Dinwiddie's messenger to the French was a young Virginian named George Washington. Later he became such a great man that we call him "the Father of our Country," so we shall want to learn all that we can about him.

Washington was born on a plantation in Virginia on February 22, 1732. His father died when he was eleven years old, and he was brought up by his mother and his older brothers. His brother Lawrence was like a father to him.

Washington worked hard at school and learned arithmetic so quickly and so well that he was able to survey and measure land when he was only sixteen years old.

Washington liked to write about things that he saw and did, and we can read in his own words about the first surveying trip that he made into the western part of Virginia. His diary tells us the number of acres that he surveyed each day; how he swam his horse across overflowing rivers; how he shot deer and wild turkeys. It tells us about the people that he saw, the sort of houses that he stayed in, and the Indians that he met. He says of his first surveying trip:

> On Friday, March 11, 1748, I began my journey in company with George Fairfax, and we traveled forty miles.
>
> On Tuesday, the 15th, we worked hard till night and then returned to Pennington's, got our supper, and were shown to our room. I undressed and got into bed. To my surprise I found it to be nothing but a little straw, without sheets or anything else. I was glad to get up as quickly as I could and put on my clothes. Had we not been very tired, I am sure we should not have slept much that night. I promised myself that I would never sleep in such a place again. I would rather sleep by a camp fire in the open air. But the next night, at another place, we had a good feather bed with clean sheets, which was a very agreeable change.
>
> On Friday, March 11, 1748, I began my journey in company with George Fairfax, and we traveled forty miles.
>
> On Saturday, March 26, we stopped for the night at the cabin of a settler. When we came to supper, there was neither a cloth on the table nor a knife to eat with. But as good luck would have it, we had knives of our own.

The French and Indian Wars
Project, Page 2

Tuesday, March 29, shot two wild turkeys.

Saturday, April 2: Last night was a blowing and rainy night. The straw that we were sleeping on caught fire, but luckily one of the men waked up and put out the fire before it burned us. The next night was much more blustering than the one before. The wind blew our tent entirely away, and we had to spend part of the night without shelter.

One day the young surveyor met thirty Indians coming from the warpath. They had one scalp. Washington gave them something to eat and drink, and afterward they showed him a war dance.

They built a great fire and seated themselves around it in a circle. The chief made a speech and then, Washington writes: "The best dancer jumped up, like a man just awakened from sleep. He ran and jumped about the ring in a very funny way, followed by the rest."

Their music was made by a rattle and a drum. The drum was a pot half full of water, with a deer skin stretched over it. The rattle was a gourd with shot in it "and a piece of horse's tail tied to it to make it look fine." One Indian kept rattling and another drumming all the while they were dancing.

Washington Delivers the Governor's Message

It was some years after this first surveying trip that Washington carried the governor's message to the French on the Ohio.

He was a fine looking young man at this time. People would turn to look at him when he passed. He stood six feet two inches tall in his stocking feet, and was heavily and strongly built. His eyes were blue-gray, set wide apart; his forehead was broad and high; his mouth and nose were large. His straight, thick hair was a dark, reddish brown. His face was scarred a little by smallpox; and his skin was rough and sunburned from his living in the open air.

Washington traveled through rain and snow and got to the French fort in the middle of winter. The French commander refused to move. He said: "I am here because my general told me to come, and I intend to hold the fort until he tells me to leave."

In talking to Washington the French officer said: "This country belongs to the French. No Englishman has the right to trade near the waters of the Ohio, and I have orders to make prisoners of any who attempt it."

This reply was the same as giving England a dare to drive the French out if it could. It meant war, for the English government was determined to get the valley of the Ohio for its own people.

The French and Indian Wars

Project, Page 3

The French and Indian War

The English government sent General Edward Braddock from England with a regiment of its finest soldiers to drive the French from the Ohio country. When he reached Virginia, General Braddock added several hundred colonial soldiers to his troops and appointed young Washington to be one of his officers. General Braddock did not believe that the Virginia soldiers knew how to fight. He thought they would be frightened and try to run away as soon as the battle began. He therefore divided them into small groups and scattered them among his redcoats, as the English soldiers were called. He did this so that his own well-trained soldiers could watch them and keep them in line. General Braddock would have done better to keep the Virginia soldiers separate and use them for scouts and guides. They knew much more about fighting the French and the Indians than Braddock and his English soldiers knew.

Washington tried to tell General Braddock that the French and their Indian friends would fight in the forest, hidden by brush and trees, and that the English soldiers must do the same. But the proud general would pay no attention to his young Virginia officer. He let Washington understand that he had not come to America to learn from a country surveyor how to carry on war. Battles were not fought behind brush and trees in Europe, and he let the colonists know that he had no intention of fighting that way in America.

There is an old saying that pride goes before a fall. It was true in this case, and Braddock paid dearly for his pride. Suddenly, as the men marched along in military line, they were mowed down by a hail of bullets and arrows.

As Washington had foreseen, the French and Indians keeping always out of sight in the forest, shot down the English soldiers like sheep in a pen. The English soldiers broke and ran; but the Virginia soldiers took to the brush and did what they could to save the battle.

General Braddock was killed. Washington had two horses shot under him and received four bullets through his coat while trying to stop the flight of the men, but it was all in vain. The battle was lost.

Washington was completely disgusted by the loss of the battle. He wrote Governor Dinwiddie that the English soldiers behaved like cowards. "They broke and ran," he said, "like sheep before hounds. And when we tried to stop them it was with as little success as if we had attempted to stop the wild bears of the mountains."

The truth of the matter, however, is that the soldiers were badly commanded. They were brave enough, but they did not have a good leader for the sort of fighting that had to be done in America.

The French and Indian Wars
Project, Page 4

Wolfe and Montcalm at Quebec

The English Win at Last

The war that began with the failure of the English army in the woods of western Pennsylvania ended in the complete defeat of the French and the victory of the English in Canada four years later.

The last important battle was fought in the city of Quebec, which is built on a high cliff on the north bank of the St. Lawrence River. The sides of the cliff are very steep, but the land at the top, where the city stands, is open and level. Here the French made their last stand against the English. They knew that if Quebec fell, they could no longer hold Canada or any part of America. The English knew that if they could take Quebec, they could take Canada and drive the French from America. Both sides knew that the struggle for Quebec would be fierce and terrible. France selected one of its best generals to hold the place, and England selected its best commander to take it.

Marquis de Montcalm

The French general was Marquis de Montcalm, a skillful officer who had won many victories in Europe. He was a handsome, dignified man who wore white lace cuffs and a powdered wig, as men did at that time. When he was a boy, he wrote his father that he wanted to be a brave and Christian gentleman, a good scholar, a good horseman, a good swordsman, and an obedient son. At the time of thc battle he was forty-seven years old.

When the king of France wrote Montcalm to hold Quebec at all costs, he replied, "I shall do everything to save this unhappy colony, or die."

General James Wolfe

The English commander was General James Wolfe. He seemed to be a born soldier. He had been in military service since he was a mere boy. He was over six feet tall, had delicate features, a dimple in his chin, and red hair which he would not cover with a wig. He liked to hunt, play chess and, dance. He was fond of dogs and loved children. He had a frail body, but he had an iron will.

When he once set his mind on doing a thing, he hung on like a bulldog until he got it done. He never gave up and quit.

When the king sent Wolfe to America, some men who did not like him complained that he was mad. "Mad, is he?" King George replied. "Well, I hope he will bite some of my other generals so that they too will become mad." The king knew that Wolfe would fight, and that was what he wanted him to do.

The Siege and Capture of Quebec

When General Wolfe arrived in front of Quebec, he found it defended by Montcalm with about eight thousand French soldiers and his Indian friends. Wolfe shelled the

The French and Indian Wars

Project, Page 5

town with his cannon, but could do little harm because it was so high and so well protected by the cliffs. For days and weeks the English ships lay in the river, both above and below Quebec, but there seemed no way to reach the French on the heights.

Once Wolfe captured some high French officers and, as he loved company, he had them to dine with him. In speaking of Montcalm, Wolfe said to his prisoner-guests, "If your general were a great general, he would come out and fight me." A quick-witted Frenchman replied, "General Wolfe, if you were a great general, you would make him." After a long time, Wolfe did make General Montcalm fight him and proved himself the greater of the two generals.

For a time Wolfe was quite ill, and while he was in bed he told his officers to hold a council and see if they could find a way to get to Montcalm or make him come out. The officers held the council and went over all the plans they could think of, but none of them promised much success.

While he was still on his cot, weakened with fever, Wolfe said to his doctor, "I know you cannot cure me, but patch me up so that I may be able to do my duty for a few days."

He got better and made a plan to get at the French. It was so daring that he did not tell it to any of his officers until he was ready to begin.

It was now September, and whatever was done must be done quickly before winter put an end to the fighting. Wolfe thought he had found a way to send his men up the cliff to the very gates of Quebec.

At one point there was a rough trail that led upward over rocks and through bushes to the top of the cliff. It was so steep that even a goat would have found it hard to climb in the dark, but Wolfe determined to send his men up that path at night. The French kept a small guard at the top, but they never dreamed of an attack there, because they did not believe that the enemy could reach them there.

While the gunboats kept up a steady firing from the river to hold the attention of the French, Wolfe started a little party of twenty-four men up the trail. Others and still others followed. They beat off the guards and passed the word down the line that the way was open.

The English could climb more rapidly now since they no longer had to steal up the trail without noise. When morning dawned, forty-eight hundred of Wolfe's best soldiers were in line ready to meet the French. And General Wolfe himself was there in command. He had scaled the steep cliff with his men.

The French line came on with the brave Montcalm at its head. From the French line there was continual firing, but from the English line not a shot was fired. Wolfe had told his men to wait until the French were within forty yards of them. When they were within that distance, a sharp command rang out:

"Present! Fire!"

Every gun blazed at once, and the roar was like a cannon shot. Then another volley, then scattered firing.

For an instant powder smoke covered the scene, but when it lifted, the sight in the French ranks was awful to behold. A tumbled mass of dead and dying men, twisting and groaning in pain, was seen. Then the English charged and swept all before them. The remaining French

The French and Indian Wars
Project, Page 6

soldiers were driven back.

The city surrendered a few days later. Quebec had fallen.

Both the brave generals had fallen too. Wolfe was killed in the charge. As he sank down, he was caught by one of his men.

"Support me," said Wolfe, "let not my brave fellows see me fall."

When someone wanted to call a doctor, Wolfe said, "It is useless, it is all over with me."

From the distance came the cry, "They run! they run!"

"Who run?" asked the general.

"The enemy, Sir; they give way everywhere."

Turning on his side, Wolfe murmured, "Now God be praised, I die happy."

Montcalm also was wounded, and when his doctor told him he could not live, he said, "I am glad I shall not live to see the surrender of Quebec."

The French gave up America. The peace was made in Paris in 1763. France gave up to England all of Canada and all of its territory east of the Mississippi River. At the same time the king of France gave Spain all of the land claimed by the French on the west side of the Mississippi.

All of North America was now divided between England and Spain.

Discussion questions

1. Who owned the land along the Ohio River?
2. Which was the greater leader, Wolfe or Montcalm?
3. Why would Braddock not listen to Washington?
4. Who was asked to deliver the message from the governor of Virginia to the French on the Ohio?
5. Read the following sentences out loud, filling the blanks correctly with these words: *surveying, regiment, cliff, possession, scaled*

Both France and England wanted to have ______________ of the lands along the Ohio River. Young George Washington was given the job of ______________ the land in western Virginia. England sent a ______________ of soldiers led by General Braddock to fight the French in America. In order to capture Quebec, General Wolfe and his men ______________ the ______________ and surprised the French.

The French and Indian Wars
Literature Unit 3—Duel in the Wilderness
by Karen Clafford Farley

Chapter 1: The Mission

1. Who was Major Washington ordered to appear before in Williamsburg, Virginia?
2. Why did George Washington dream of being appointed to carry out the mission?
3. Robert Dinwiddie had informed the Council of Major Washington's offer. What did Major Washington offer to do?
4. Did Robert Dinwiddie offer the mission to anyone else? If so, did they have plans to accept it?
5. Why did George Washington feel that he could not withdraw his offer of service?
6. What were the orders Governor Dinwiddie gave to Washington?
7. Before George left Logstown, he was to introduce himself to an important person and ask him for something. Who was the person, and what was he to ask of him?
8. Who was George directed to ask to be his guide into the wilderness?

Chapter 2: The Odyssey Begins

1. Who was the first person George hired as part of his mission? Why did he hire him?
2. What were the items which made Jacob Van Braam's home look like the home of a gentleman?
3. Who did George love to imitate? What did he learn from this person?
4. The amount of George's supplies gave him two concerns. What were they?
5. Traders did not venture into the deep woods anymore because of the risks. Why did George think he could reach the French alive?
6. Major Washington stated that he was serving the King. Who did Christopher Gist think George was serving?

Chapter 3: The Traders

1. What conditions did the frontiersmen seem to take as a way of life?
2. What message did Christopher Gist receive from an Indian?
3. Why did Christopher Gist not want the group to approach Mr. Frazier's cabin at once?
4. What had Tanacharison left with John Frazier for Governor Dinwiddie? What did it mean?
5. What news made George feel that he had traveled three weeks for nothing?

Chapter 4: The Indians

1. What was George to do when he was introduced to Tanacharison?
2. What were the "major traders" and how did they differ from ordinary traders?
3. Did George find Tanacharison at Logstown? Who did he meet with?
4. Who decided whether George was welcome to meet with Monachatoocha in the longhouse, and why was it this person's decision? Who invited them to sit in the longhouse?
5. Who were the Frenchmen George met at Logstown?
6. What news did George discover that was worse than Governor Dinwiddie's suspicions?

Chapter 5: The Calumet

1. Why was Tanacharison flattered by George Washington?
2. Why did George admire Tanacharison?
3. Who would decide if George gets an escort to the French?

The French and Indian Wars
Literature Unit 3—Duel in the Wilderness

4. What was the ceremony of the calumet?
5. Why did George need to wait three nights for Tanacharison before setting out again?
6. George did not understand the full importance of the wampum belts. Why then did he think the delay worthwhile?
7. Why did the council feel that their chiefs would be a better escort to George than many braves?

Chapter 6: The French
1. What did the French flag at John Frazier's represent to the traders?
2. Why did George not discuss his business with the French right away?
3. Why would Captain Joncaire not accept the letter from Governor Dinwiddie?
4. Even though the French knew the English could raise a force of two men to every one of theirs, they were still confident they could win a war. Why?
5. Joncaire greeted the Indians differently than de Marin. How was his greeting different?
6. Gist told Major Washington that the Indians felt a trap closing in on them. What was the trap the Indians felt?
7. George advised Tanacharison to give his speech to the commander at Fort Le Boeuf. Why did Tanacharison refuse?
8. How did La Force explain Captain Joncaire's insistence that he accompany George and his party to Fort Le Boeuf?

Chapter 7: The Duel
1. Why was George relieved when he was greeted by Captain Picard?
2. Why did St. Pierre not receive the papers from George immediately?
3. How many men did Currin estimate manned the French fort?
4. After St. Pierre reviewed George's letter, what did he advise him to do?
5. Why did George think it wise to split up his party?
6. Why was George insistent that the chiefs leave with him?
7. Why did George agree to stay one more day to wait for Tanacharison?

Chapter 8: Conotocarious
1. Why had Tanacharison and the other Indians stopped at the edge of the river and gone into the woods?
2. Why did George tell his companions to "dig in" to catch up to the Indians?
3. Why did George conclude they must use the horses for travel?
4. Why was Tanacharison going to continue by canoe?
5. What does Conotocarious mean, and why was this name given to George Washington?

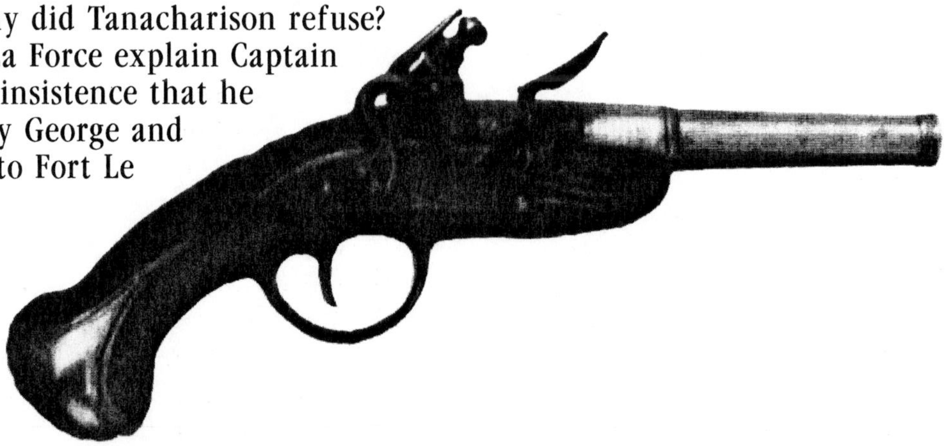

The French and Indian Wars

Literature Unit 3—Duel in the Wilderness

Chapter 9: The Assassin

1. Describe Christmas in Williamsburg.
2. Why did Gist think that Major Washington could not survive walking through the woods?
3. What does George wear to prepare himself for his walk through the snowy wilderness?
4. Why did George think that the cabin they came across in the woods was deserted?
5. Even though George noticed Gist looked worried, George thought that their meeting the Indian was a good thing. Why?

Chapter 10: The Raft and the River

1. Gist made a fire with blank sheets of paper. What was the fire for?
2. Why did Gist wish that it would snow?
3. George and Gist could not cross the Allegheny because it was not frozen the whole way across. How did George propose they cross?
4. When they arrived on the island, why wouldn't Gist let George rest through the night?
5. In the morning, George discovered how they could get off the island. What did he find?
6. When George and Gist finally arrived at Frazier's cabin, what prevented them from entering immediately?

Chapter 11: The War Party

1. Why did George think that they may not have to make a wide circle around the Iroquois Indians, that they may still be able to stop at Frazier's?
2. Why did George think they could walk through the Indian camp and not be noticed?
3. Why was George surprised to see a war party?
4. According to Frazier, why had the Indians set out, and what brought them to his cabin?
5. Why did Gist tell Frazier that George was "loyal"?
6. Whom did George and Gist pay a call to before they left? Why did George choose to do this?

Chapter 12: And the King Shall Know Your Name

1. Why did George think he would return to the wilderness as Christopher Gist did?
2. Why were the people in Williamsburg surprised to see George Washington?
3. What were the orders Dinwiddie had from King George?
4. When Dinwiddie passed George's report to the Council, what did he hope the House of Burgesses would vote for?

Epilogue

1. What did George insist on putting at the end of his report. Why?

The French and Indian Wars
Test

1. What are the dates for the French and Indian War?

2. What problems arose between the British and the French that caused the French and Indian War?

3. What were the background differences of the British and the French colonists?

4. Why did the Indians in the northeast prefer the French over the British?

5. Name one notable person on each side of the war.

The French and Indian Wars
Test, Page 2

6. How did the French and Indian War end? What was the outcome?

Review

1. What is the name of Jonathan Edward's most famous sermon?

2. What were the Salem Witch Trials?

3. List the original thirteen colonies.

The French and Indian Wars

Test, Page 3

4. Where did the Pilgrims move before coming to Plymouth?

5. In chronological order list all events studied to date. Next to each place the appropriate date.

Parliament Acts Unjustly
Worksheet

1. What did British Parliament pass that united the quarrelsome American colonies against England?

2. What was the Sugar Act of 1764?

3. What was the Stamp Act of 1765?

4. Upon what did the Stamp Act Congress agree?

5. What was the Quartering Act of 1765?

PARLIAMENT ACTS UNJUSTLY
Worksheet, Page 2

6. Why did Parliament pass a tax on tea in 1773?

____

____

____

____

7. What did the colonist do?

____

____

____

____

8. What were the Intolerable Acts?

____

____

____

____

Parliament Acts Unjustly

Project 1—Current Events, 1764–1773

Using your card and the resources listed at the bottom of the card, fill in the blanks on the next page with the event that occurred. In the boxes write a brief summary of each event.

Parliament Acts Unjustly

Project 1, Page 2

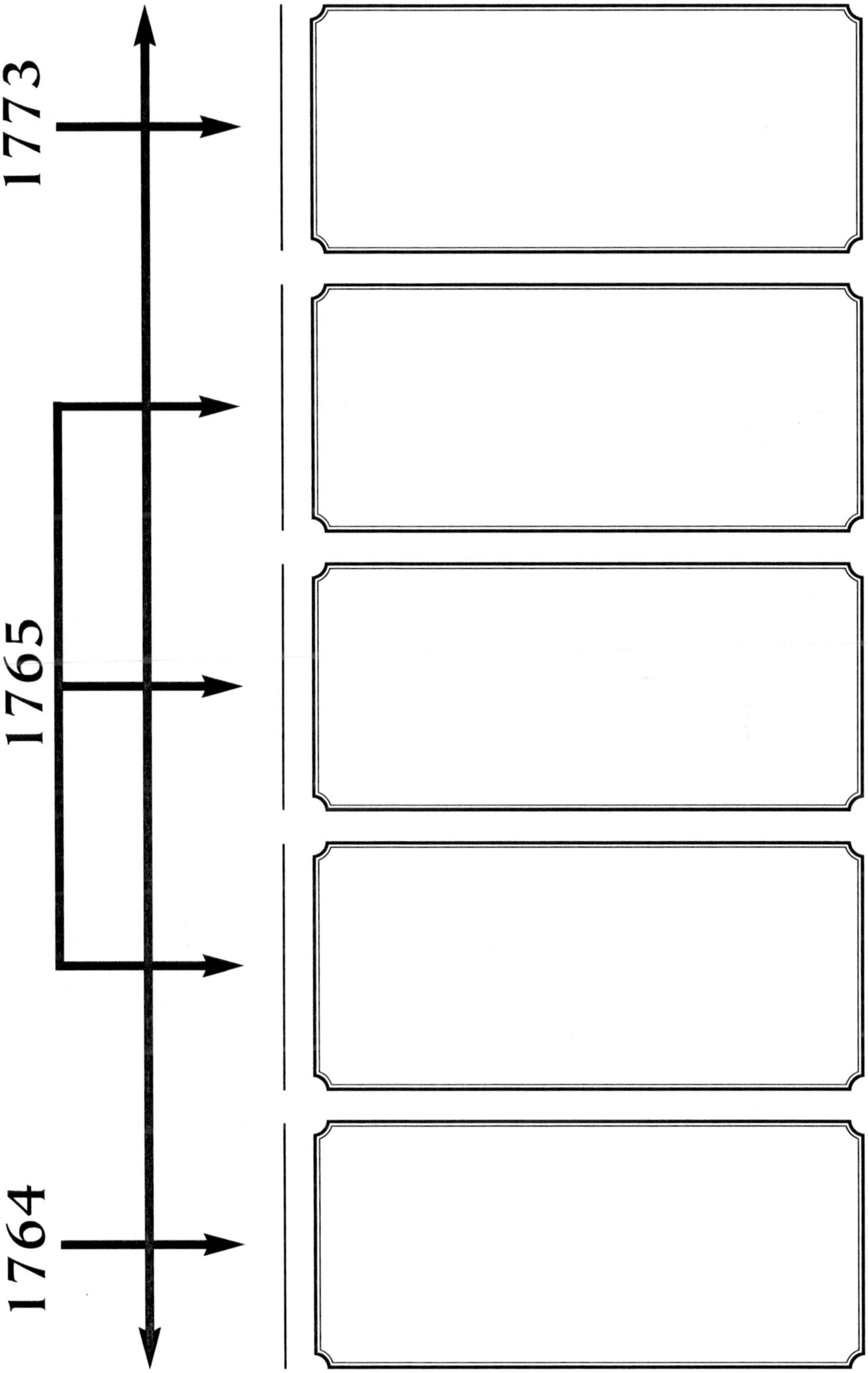

Parliament Acts Unjustly

Project 2—Resolutions of the Stamp Act Congress (October 19, 1765)

The members of this Congress, sincerely devoted, with the warmest sentiments of affection and duty to His Majesty's Person and Government, inviolably attached to the present happy establishment of the Protestant succession, and with minds deeply impressed by a sense of the present and impending misfortunes of the British colonies on this continent; having considered as maturely as time will permit the circumstances of the said colonies, esteem it our indispensable duty to make the following declarations of our humble opinion, respecting the most essential rights and liberties Of the colonists, and of the grievances under which they labour, by reason of several late Acts of Parliament.

I. That His Majesty's subjects in these colonies, owe the same allegiance to the Crown of Great-Britain, that is owing from his subjects born within the realm, and all due subordination to that august body the Parliament of Great Britain.

II. That His Majesty's liege subjects in these colonies, are entitled to all the inherent rights and liberties of his natural born subjects within the kingdom of Great-Britain.

III. That it is inseparably essential to the freedom of a people, and the undoubted right of Englishmen, that no taxes be imposed on them, but with their own consent, given personally, or by their representatives.

IV. That the people of these colonies are not, and from their local circumstances cannot be, represented in the House of Commons in Great-Britain.

V. That the only representatives of the people of these colonies, are persons chosen therein by themselves, and that no taxes ever have been, or can be constitutionally imposed on them, but by their respective legislatures.

VI. That all supplies to the Crown, being free gifts of the people, it is unreasonable and inconsistent with the principles and spirit of the British Constitution, for the people of Great-Britain to grant to His Majesty the property of the colonists.

VII. That trial by jury is the inherent and invaluable right of every British subject in these colonies.

VIII. That the late Act of Parliament, entitled, An Act for granting and applying certain Stamp Duties, and other Duties, in the British colonies and plantations in America, etc., by imposing taxes on the inhabitants of these colonies, and the said Act, and several other Acts, by extending the jurisdiction of the courts of Admiralty beyond its ancient limits, have a manifest tendency to subvert the rights and liberties of the colonists.

IX. That the duties imposed by several late acts of Parliament, from the peculiar circumstances of these colonies, will be extremely burthensome and grievous, and, from the scarcity of specie, the payment of them absolutely impracticable.

Parliament Acts Unjustly

Project 2, Page 2

X. That as the profits of the trade of Britain, to pay for the manufactures which they are obliged to take from thence, they eventually contribute very largely to all supplies granted there to the Crown.

XI. That the restrictions imposed by several late Acts of Parliament, on the trade of these colonies, will render them unable to purchase the manufactures of Great-Britain.

XII. That the increase, prosperity, and happiness of these colonies, depend on the full and free enjoyment of their rights and liberties, and an intercourse with Great-Britain mutually affectionate and advantageous.

XIII. That it is the right of the British subjects in these colonies, to petition the King, or either House of Parliament.

Lastly, That it is the indispensable duty of these colonies, to the best of sovereigns, to the mother country, and to themselves, to endeavour by a loyal and dutiful address to his Majesty, and humble applications to both Houses of Parliament, to procure the repeal of the Act for granting and applying certain stamp duties, of all clauses of any other Acts of Parliament, whereby the jurisdiction of the Admiralty is extended as aforesaid, and of the other late Acts for the restriction of American commerce.

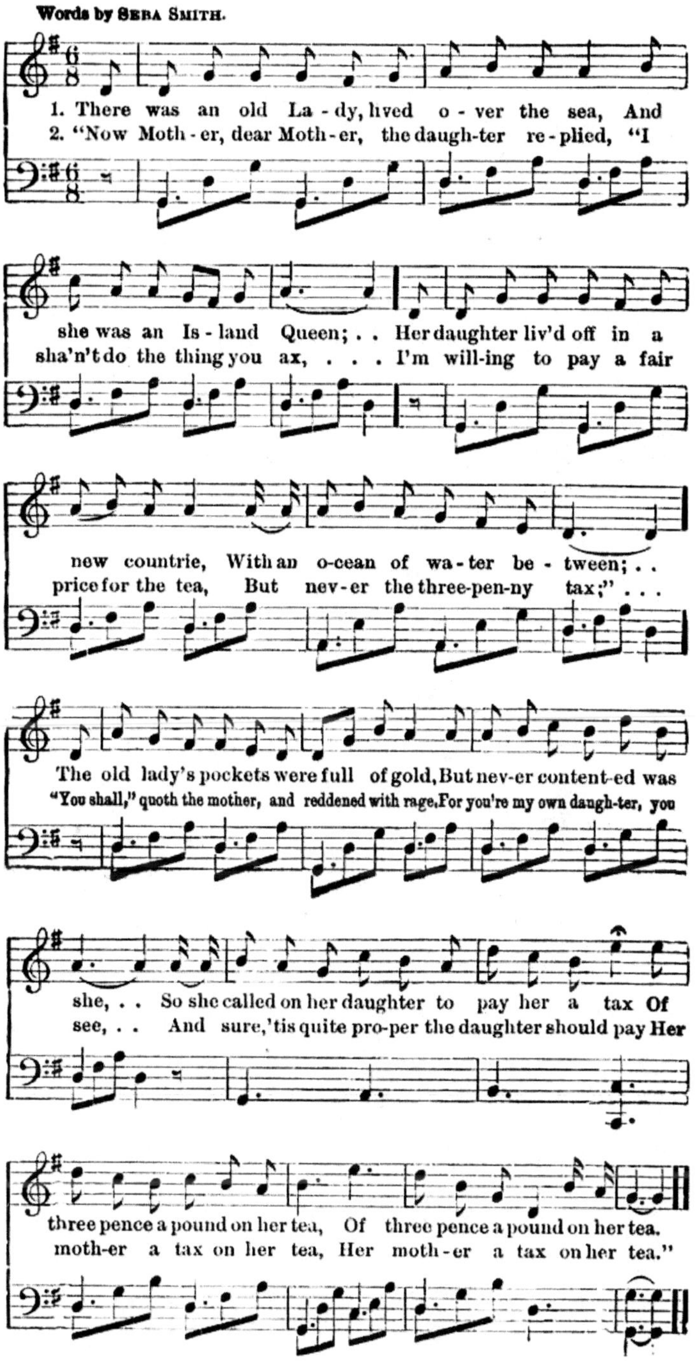

Parliament Acts Unjustly

Project 3—The Schooner Sultana

For years the schooner *Sultana* has been a popular vessel for model ship-builders, and it was her section in the book *The Colonial Schooner: 1763-1775* that caught the attention of shipwright John Swain in 1996. By 1997 Swain had sold the idea of building a reproduction of *Sultana* to a group of regional supporters, and once a shipyard and the necessary tools were found, the keel was laid in October of 1998. In spite of the concessions made to comply with U.S. Coast Guard regulations, the *Sultana* still is one of the most accurate replicas of a historic vessel in the world, and is the only living example of the Marblehead Schooners pioneered by Colonial New England Shipwrights.

The original *Sultana* was built in the yard of renowned Boston Shipwright Benjamin Hallowell in 1767, but was soon purchased to aid the Royal Navy in policing colonial merchant traffic for lead, paper, glass and tea that they might be smuggling in violation of the Townshend Duties. During her service to the Crown, the *Sultana* had had her plans drawn up to keep on file and two sets of meticulous logs kept of the vessel's position and duties for every day of her four and a half years of naval service. These, along with her muster books makes the *Sultana* one of the most well documented vessels of the colonial period.

The present-day *Sultana* inspired the writing of Veritas Press's *Squalls Before War: His Majesty's Schooner* Sultana. In this book the Great Awakening, the Boston Massacre, and even George Washington take part in the voyages of the *Sultana,* as she criss-crossed the waterways of the colonies from 1768-1771. The story offers a unique view of colonial life from the deck of a schooner as the servants of the Crown struggled among the squalls of unrest that characterized life in a land that no one dreamed would soon be in a war for independence. The plot of this book does not tell of a great romance, mighty war or treacherous quest. It merely follows the work of a boat enforcing the laws of the Crown in the middle of the eighteenth century. The sailors aboard the *Sultana* did not know that they were sailing in the headwaters of war or that they were playing a part in the formation of a new nation. They were just doing their job. *Squalls Before War* is a slice of history—showing the excitement and tedium of life on a schooner in the 1700's.

The next several pages contain projects meant to be used in conjunction with this book, though most can stand on their own. For more projects and comprehension questions, order the *Squalls Before War Comprehension Guide.* And if you live near the Chesapeake Bay, visiting the *Sultana* as a field trip is a fabulous experience. For more about the present-day *Sultana,* go to www.SchoonerSultana.org.

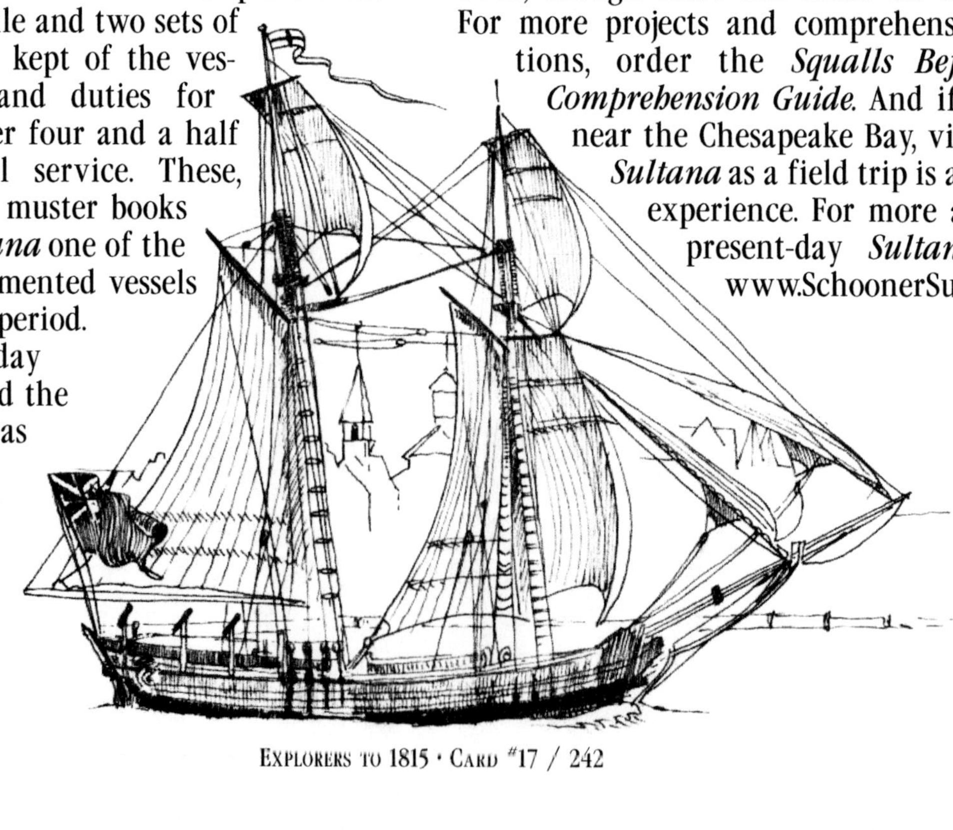

Parliament Acts Unjustly

Project 3—Nine Men's Morrice

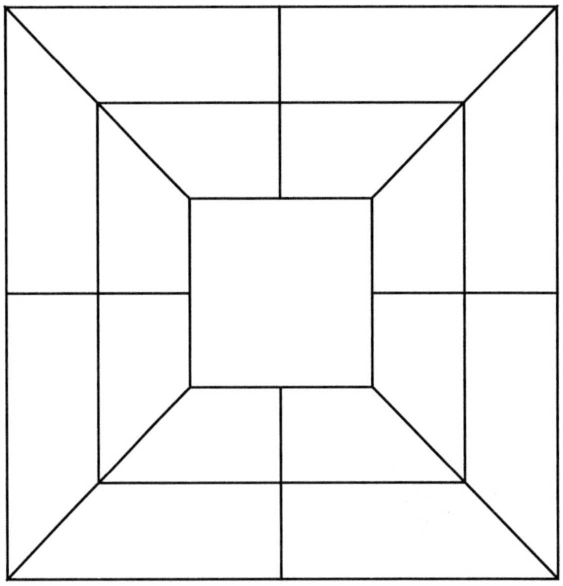

While sailing on board the Sultana *there was very little to do for entertainment. One game that was easy to assemble and play was Nine Men's Morrice. It could be played on a piece of paper or on a crate with markers as simple as corn or stones.*

Materials

18 markers
(nine of one color/style
and nine of another)

Game board
(as shown)

Instructions

Object of the Game: The object of the game is to make rows of three markers on a line, and to prevent the other player from doing the same.

1. Player A places one piece on the board on one of the intersections.
2. Player B places a piece on the board, also on an intersection. Both players continue taking turns.
3. Whenever a player gets three of his pieces in a row, he may take one of the other player's pieces.
4. When all 18 of the pieces have been placed on the intersections, the players take turns moving their pieces from one intersection to another—one intersection at a time—trying to line up three pieces in a row.
5. When a player has only two pieces left on the board, the game is over. The player with the most pieces remaining on the board wins.

Parliament Acts Unjustly

Project 3—Nautical Origins of Common Expressions

Read the following explanations for expressions in our language that have their origin in life at sea. Then draw a cartoon illustrating one of the phrases literally, or take a common phrase and make up a ficticious nautical origin for it.

Over the Barrel: The most common method of punishment aboard ship was flogging. The unfortunate sailor was tied to a grating, a mast or over the barrel of a deck cannon.

Know the Ropes: There were miles and miles of cordage in the rigging of a square rigged ship. It took an experienced seaman to know the ropes.

Footloose: The bottom portion of a sail is called the foot. If it is not secured, it is footloose and dances randomly in the wind.

First Rate: Implies excellence. A ship of 100 or more guns was a First Rate line-of-battle ship. Second Rates carried 90 to 98 guns.

Pipe Down: Means stop talking and be quiet. The Pipe Down was the last signal from the Bosun's pipe each day and meant "lights out" and "silence."

Three Sheets to the Wind: A sheet is a rope which controls the tension on the downwind side of a square sail. If, on a three-masted, fully rigged ship, the sheets of the three lower course sails are loose, the sails will flap and flutter. A ship in this condition would stagger and wander drunkenly.

Pooped: The poop is the stern section of a ship. To be pooped is to be swamped by a high, following sea.

As the Crow Flies: When lost or unsure of their position in coastal waters, ships would release a caged crow. The crow would fly straight towards the nearest land, thus giving the vessel some sort of a navigational fix. The tallest lookout platform on a ship came to be known as the crow's nest.

By and Large: Currently it means "in all cases" or "in any case." From the nautical: *by* meaning into the wind and *large* meaning with the wind: as in, "By and large the ship handled very well."

Cut and Run: If a captain of a smaller ship encountered a larger enemy vessel, he might order the crew to cut the lashings on all the sails and run away before the wind.

The Bitter End: The end of an anchor cable is fastened to the bitts at the ship's bow. If all of the anchor cable has been let out, you have come to the bitter end.

Toe the Line: When called to line up at attention, the ship's crew would form up with their toes touching a seam in the deck planking.

Slush Fund: A slurry of fat was obtained by boiling or scraping the empty salted meat storage barrels. This "slush" was often sold ashore by the ship's cook for the benefit of himself or the crew. The money so derived became known as a slush fund.

Under the Weather: If a crewman is standing watch on the weather side of the bow, he will be subject to the constant beating of the sea and the ocean spray. He will be under the weather.

Above Board: Anything on or above the open deck—in plain view.

Parliament Acts Unjustly

Project 3—Nautical Origins of Common Expressions, Page 2

Rummage Sale: From the French *arrimage* meaning "ship's cargo." Damaged cargo was sold at a rummage sale.

A Square Meal: Crews' mess was a warm meal served on square wooden platters.

Overbearing: To sail downwind directly at another ship, thus "stealing" or diverting the wind from his sails.

Taking the wind out of his sails: Sailing in a manner so as to steal or divert wind from another ship's sails.

Let the Cat Out of the Bag: In the Royal Navy the punishment prescribed for most serious crimes was flogging. This was administered by the Bosun's Mate using a whip called a cat o' nine tails. The "cat" was kept in a leather or baize bag.

Start Over with a Clean Slate: A slate tablet was kept near the helm on which the watch keeper would record the speeds, distances, headings and tacks during the watch. If there were no problems during the watch, the slate would be wiped clean so that the new watch could start over with a clean slate.

Taken Aback: A dangerous situation where the wind shifts to the wrong side of the sails, pressing them back against the mast and forcing the ship astern.

Cut of His Jib: Warships many times had their foresails or jib sails cut thinly so that they could maintain point and not be blown off course. Upon sighting thin foresails on a distant ship a captain might not like the cut of his jib and would then have an opportunity to escape.

Garbled: Garbling was the prohibited practice of mixing rubbish with the cargo. A distorted, mixed up message is said to be garbled.

Parliament Acts Unjustly
Project 3—Squalls Before War *Logbook*

Throughout the book Squalls Before War, *Master David Bruce is confronted with events and attitudes that blow him back and forth as he tries to decide whether the colonists are right or the king is right. Bruce also keeps a logbook throughout the tour of duty like Lieutenant John Inglis does, keeping track of where they were, what they were doing and the weather conditions. While you read the book keep a log of the reasons, pro and con, for supporting the colonists. Then in the end decide from these entries whether or not you agree with Bruce's final decision.*

Date	Event	Notes

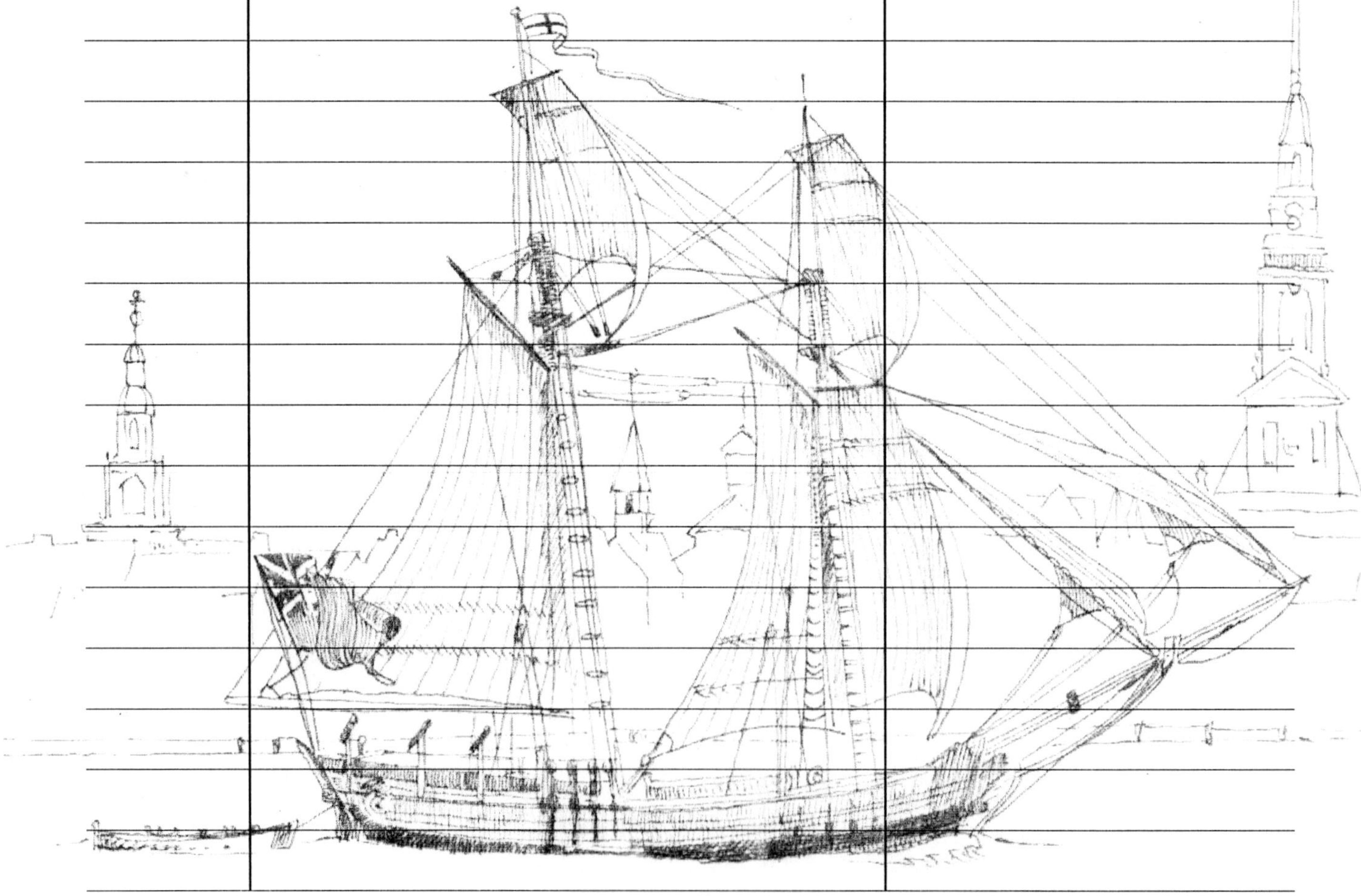

Parliament Acts Unjustly

Project 3—Squalls Before War *and the SPG*

Taxation without representation and dumping tea into the harbor in Boston were only parts of a much larger story that unfolded into the War for Independence. One factor often overlooked in all of this is the SPG. Read the following essay to learn more about this facet in the unrest that the Sultana *sailed into.*

"Let all mankind know that we came into the wilderness because we would worship God without that Episcopacy, that Common Prayer, and those unwarrantable ceremonies with which the land of our forefather's sepulchers has been defiled."
—Cotton Mather

The Society for the Propagation of the Gospel in Foreign Parts (SPG), formed in 1701, was a missionary organization of the Church of England. Around the start of the 18th century, Henry Compton, the Bishop of London, requested Rev. Dr. Thomas Bray to report on the state of the Church of England in the American colonies. Dr. Bray reported that the Anglican Church in America had "little spiritual vitality" and was "in a poor organisational condition." On June 16, 1701, King William III issued a charter establishing the SPG as "an organisation able to send priests and schoolteachers to America to help provide the Church's ministry to the colonists." The society's first missionaries started work in North America in 1702, and by the time of the American Revolution, the SPG had employed about three hundred missionaries in North America.

By the time *Sultana* sailed into the colonies, a group of Anglicans in New England had been busy for years trying to bring a bishop to America which colonists who were not members of the Church of England opposed. In 1765 and 1766 a series of conventions were held in New York involving clergy from the middle colonies. But installing a bishop required an act of Parliament. And if the Parliament made such a move, it would be breaking the compact that had been drawn up between the king and the founders of the colonies.

Articles were written, pamphlets were turned out, and eloquent sermons were delivered against this parliamentary tyranny. The argument of the colonists was that bishops were spiritual tyranny. They perverted the gospel by their hunger for power and pomp. Bishops in England were judges over the laity, and the laity in America did not want them. Had one been imposed, the Revolution might well have occurred earlier than it did.

John Adams would later say: *"[The debate] excited a general and just apprehension that bishops and dioceses and churches and priests and tithes were to be imposed on us by Parliament."*

Parliament Acts Unjustly
Test

1. What are the dates for the British Parliament acting unjustly against the Colonies?

___

___

___

2. What act was passed by Parliament in 1764 to raise revenue for England?

___

___

___

3. What was the Stamp Act of 1765?

___

___

___

___

4. When and where did the colonists formally say, "Taxation without representation is tyranny"?

___

___

___

5. What was the Quartering Act of 1765?

___

___

___

___

___

Parliament Acts Unjustly

Test, Page 2

6. In 1773, in order to save a failing tea company, Parliament passed a tax on the surplus of tea. What was the colonists response?

7. What were the Intolerable Acts?

Review

1. Of what country was Prince Henry the navigator a prince?

2. What is the relationship between Prince Henry the navigator and Christopher Columbus?

3. What countries had Spain taken over within one hundred years of Columbus's first voyage?

Parliament Acts Unjustly
Test, Page 3

4. Who was Samuel de Champlain? What did he discover?

5. In chronological order list all events studied to date. Next to each place the appropriate date.

The First Continental Congress Seeks Peace With Britain

Worksheet

1. What caused the colonies to be willing to meet in a Continental Congress in 1774?

2. Which was the only colony that did not send a delegate to Philadelphia in 1774?

3. A Declaration of Rights and Grievances was drafted at the Congress. What did it state and to whom was it written?

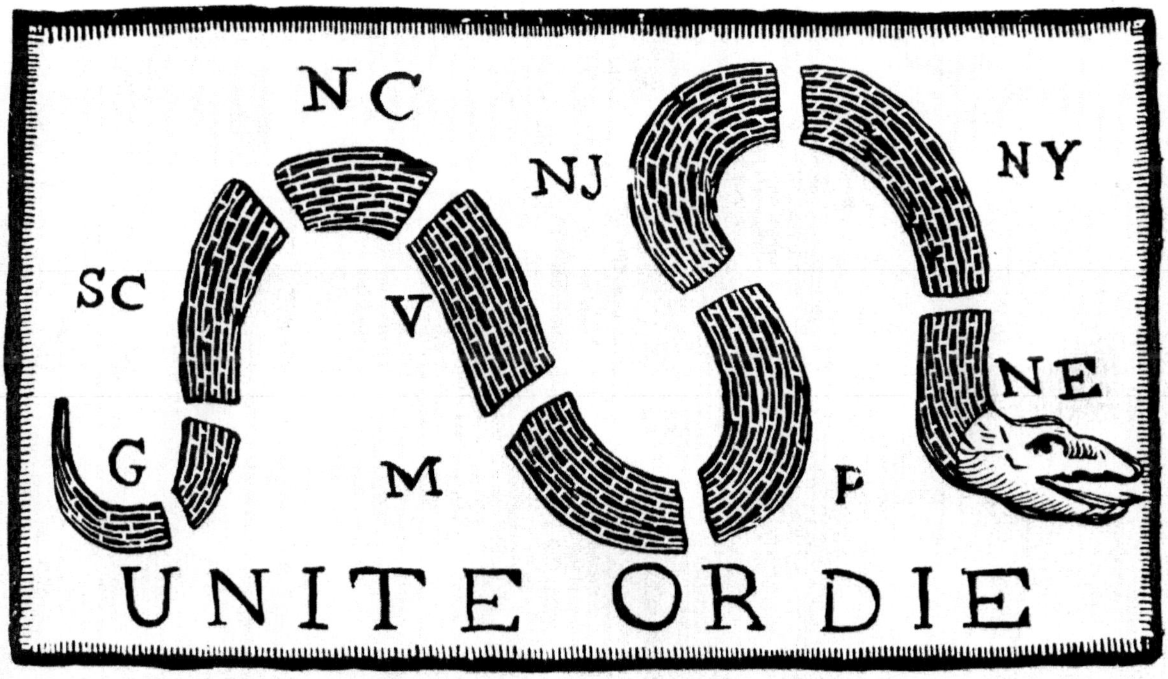

THE FIRST CONTINENTAL CONGRESS SEEKS PEACE WITH BRITAIN

Worksheet, Page 2

4. Explain the boycott the Congress established. Why did they do this?

5. How did the Congress enforce the above boycott?

6. Why were volunteer armies springing up?

The First Continental Congress Seeks Peace With Britain

Project 1—Attendee of the First Continental Congress

Using the resources listed on the card and any others you may find, use the form below to write a few paragraphs about one person who attended the First Continental Congress.

The First Continental Congress Seeks Peace With Britain

Project 2—Declaration and Resolves (October 1774)

Whereas, since the close of the last war, the British parliament, claiming a power of right to bind the people of America by statute in all cases whatsoever, hath, in some acts expressly imposed taxes on them, and in others, under various pretenses, but in fact for the purpose of raising a revenue, hath imposed rates and duties payable in these colonies, established a board of commissioners with unconstitutional powers, and extended the jurisdiction of courts of Admiralty not only for collecting the said duties, but for the trial of causes merely arising within the body of a county.

And whereas, in consequence of other statutes, judges who before held only estates at will in their offices, have been made dependent on the Crown alone for their salaries, and standing armies kept in times of peace. And it has lately been resolved in Parliament, that by force of a statute made in the thirty-fifth year of the reign of king Henry the Eighth, colonists may be transported to England, and tried there upon accusations for treasons and misprisons, or concealments of treasons committed in the colonies; and by a late statute, such trials have been directed in cases therein mentioned.

And whereas, in the last session of Parliament, three statutes were made; one entitled "An act to discontinue, in such manner and for such time as are therein mentioned, the landing and discharging, lading, or shipping of goods, wares and merchandise, at the town, and within the harbor of Boston in the province of Massachusetts-Bay, in North America;" another, entitled "An act for the better regulating the government of the province of the Massachusetts-Bay in New England;" and another, entitled "An act for the impartial administration of justice, in the cases of persons questioned for any act done by them in the execution of the law, or for the suppression of riots and tumults, in the province of the Massachusetts-Bay, in New England." And another statute was then made, "for making more effectual provision for the government of the province of Quebec, etc. All which statutes are impolitic, unjust, and cruel, as well as unconstitutional, and most dangerous and destructive of American rights.

And whereas, Assemblies have been frequently dissolved, contrary to the rights of the people, when they attempted to deliberate on grievances; and their dutiful, humble, loyal, & reasonable petitions to the crown for redress, have been repeatedly treated with contempt, by His Majesty's ministers of state:

The good people of the several Colonies of New Hampshire, Massachusetts bay, Rhode Island and Providence plantations, Connecticut, New York, New Jersey, Pennsylvania, Newcastle Kent and Sussex on Delaware, Maryland, Virginia, North Carolina, and South Carolina, justly alarmed at these arbitrary proceedings of parliament and administration, have severally elected, constituted, and appointed deputies to meet, and sit in general Congress, in the city of Philadelphia, in order to obtain such establishment, as that their religion, laws, and liberties, may not be subverted:

Whereupon the deputies so appointed being now assembled, in a full and free representation of these Colonies, taking into their most serious consideration the best means of attaining the ends aforesaid, do in the first place, as Englishmen their ancestors in like cases have usually done, for asserting and vindicating their rights and liberties, declare,

The First Continental Congress Seeks Peace With Britain

Project 2, Page 2

• That the inhabitants of the English Colonies in North America, by the immutable laws of nature, the principles of the English constitution, and the several charters or compacts, have the following Rights:

• That our ancestors, who first settled these colonies, were at the time of their emigration from the mother country, entitled to all the rights, liberties, and immunities of free and natural born subjects within the realm of England.

• That by such emigration they by no means forfeited, surrendered, or lost any of those rights, but that they were, and their descendants now are entitled to the exercise and enjoyment of all such of them, as their local and other circumstances enable them to exercise and enjoy.

• That the foundation of English liberty, and of all free government, is a right in the people to participate in their legislative council: and as the English colonists are not represented, and from their local and other circumstances, cannot properly be represented in the British parliament, they are entitled to a free and exclusive power of legislation in their several provincial legislatures, where their right of representation can alone be preserved,

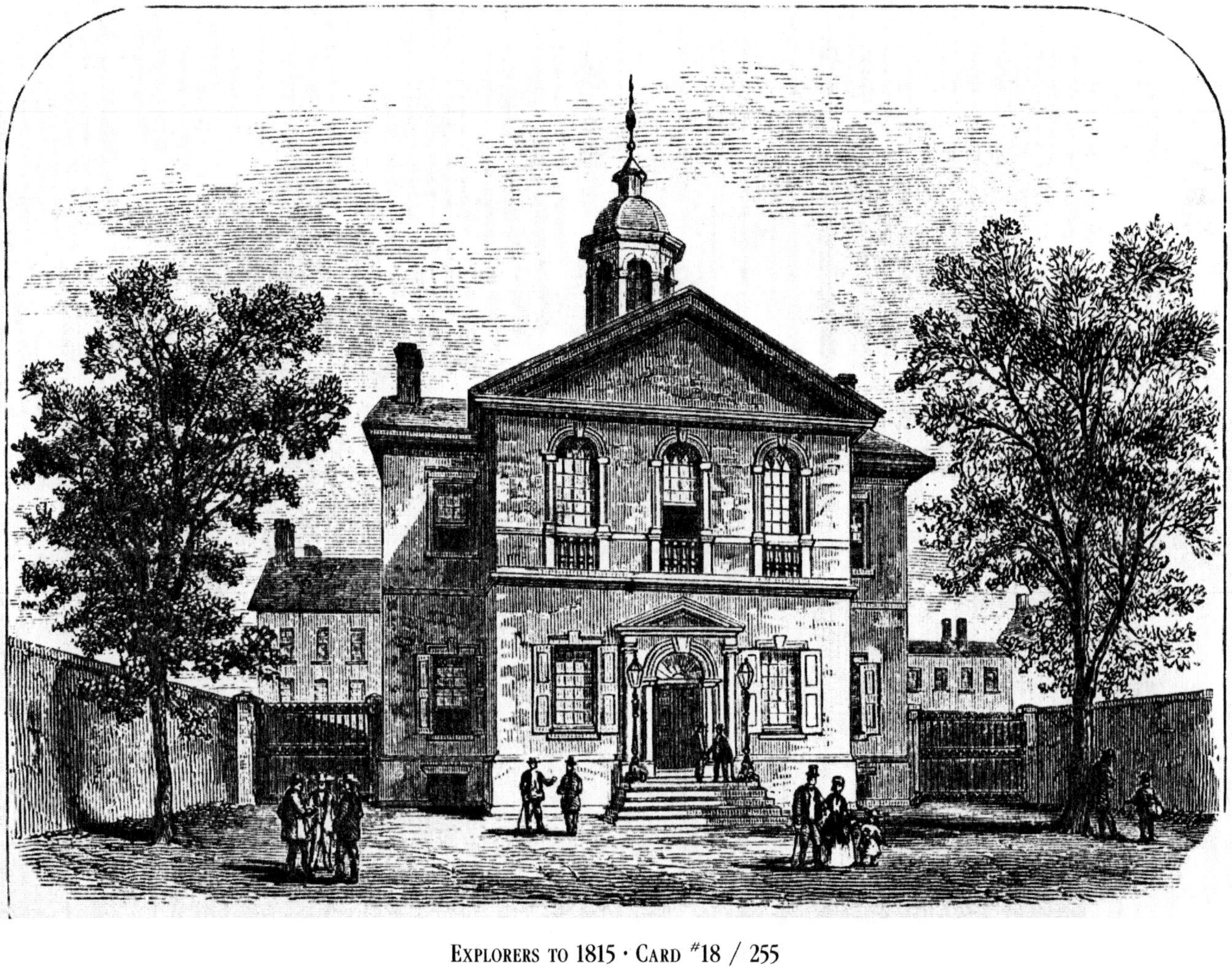

The First Continental Congress Seeks Peace With Britain

Project 2, Page 3

in all cases of taxation and internal polity, subject only to the negative of their sovereign, in such manner as has been heretofore used and accustomed. But, from the necessity of the case, and a regard to the mutual interest of both countries, we cheerfully consent to the operation of such acts of the British parliament, as are bona fide restrained to the regulation of our external commerce, for the purpose of securing the commercial advantages of the whole empire to the mother country, and the commercial benefits of its respective members excluding every idea of taxation, internal or external, for raising a revenue on the subjects in America without their consent.

· That the respective colonies are entitled to the common law of England, and more especially to the great and inestimable privilege of being tried by their peers of the vicinage, according to the course of that law

· That they are entitled to the benefit of such of the English statutes, as existed at the time of their colonization; and which they have, by experience, respectively found to be applicable to their several local and other circumstances.

· That these, his majesty's colonies, are likewise entitled to all the immunities and privileges granted and confirmed to them by royal charters, or secured by their several codes of provincial laws.

· That they have a right peaceably to assemble, consider of their grievances, and petition the King; and that all prosecutions, prohibitory proclamations, and commitments for the same, are illegal.

· That the keeping a Standing army in these colonies, in times of peace, without the consent of the legislature of that colony in which such army is kept, is against law.

· It is indispensably necessary to good government, and rendered essential by the English constitution, that the constituent branches of the legislature be independent of each other; that, therefore, the exercise of legislative power in several colonies, by a council appointed during pleasure, by the crown, is unconstitutional, dangerous, and destructive to the freedom of American legislation.

All and each of which the aforesaid deputies, in behalf of themselves, and their constituents, do claim, demand, and insist on, as their indubitable rights and liberties; which cannot be legally taken from them, altered or abridged by any power whatever, without their own consent, by their representatives in their several provincial legislatures.

In the course of our inquiry, we find many infringements and violations of the foregoing rights, which, from an ardent desire that harmony and mutual intercourse of affection and interest may be restored, we pass over for the present, and proceed to state such acts and measures as have been adopted since the last war, which demonstrate a system formed to enslave America.

Resolved, That the following acts of Parliament are infringements and violations of the rights of the colonists; and that the repeal of them is essentially necessary, in order to restore harmony between Great Britain and the American colonies, viz.:

The several Acts of 4 Geo. 3, ch. 15 & ch.

The First Continental Congress Seeks Peace With Britain

Project 2, Page 4

34; 5 Geo. 3, ch. 25; 6 Geo. 3, ch. 52; 7 Geo. 3, ch. 41 & 46; 8 Geo. 3, ch. 22; which impose duties for the purpose of raising a revenue in America, extend the powers of the admiralty courts beyond their ancient limits, deprive the American subject of trial by jury, authorize the judges' certificate to indemnify the prosecutor from damages that he might otherwise be liable to, requiring oppressive security from a claimant of ships and goods seized before he shall be allowed to defend his property; and are subversive of American rights.

Also the 12 Geo. 3, ch. 24, entitled "An act for the better preserving his Majesty's dockyards, magazines, ships, ammunition, and stores," which declares a new offense in America, and deprives the American subject of a constitutional trial by jury of the vicinage, by authorizing the trial of any person charged with the committing any offense described in the said act, out of the realm, to be indicted and tried for the same in any shire or county within the realm.

Also the three acts passed in the last session of parliament, for stopping the port and blocking up the harbor of Boston, for altering the charter & government of the Massachusetts-Bay, and that which is entitled "An Act for the better administration of Justice," &c.

Also the act passed the same session for establishing the Roman Catholic Religion in the province of Quebec, abolishing the equitable system of English laws, and erecting a tyranny there, to the great danger, from so great a dissimilarity of Religion, law, and government, of the neighboring British colonies by the assistance of whose blood and treasure the said country was conquered from France.

Also the act passed the same session for the better providing suitable quarters for officers and soldiers in his Majesty's service in North America.

Also, that the keeping a standing army in several of these colonies, in time of peace, without the consent of the legislature of that colony in which the army is kept, is against law.

To these grievous acts and measures Americans cannot submit, but in hopes that their fellow subjects in Great Britain will, on a revision of them, restore us to that state in which both countries found happiness and prosperity, we have for the present only resolved to pursue the following peaceable measures: 1st. To enter into a non-importation, non-consumption, and non-exportation agreement or association. 2. To prepare an address to the people of Great Britain, and a memorial to the inhabitants of British America, & 3. To prepare a loyal address to his Majesty, agreeable to resolutions already entered into.

The First Continental Congress Seeks Peace With Britain
Test

1. Who met in the First Continental Congress?

2. Where did the First Continental Congress meet?

3. Why did the First Continental Congress meet?

4. What did the First Continenal Congress draft?

5. Why did the Congress enforce a boycott?

The First Continental Congress Seeks Peace With Britain

Test, Page 2

6. Why did volunteer armies spring up?

Review

1. What was the name of the ship that was to accompany the *Mayflower* originally? Why did it not?

2. Who settled the Massachusetts Bay Colony?

3. Who was Roger Williams?

4. Who was Jonathan Edwards?

THE FIRST CONTINENTAL CONGRESS SEEKS PEACE WITH BRITAIN

Test, Page 2

5. In chronological order list all events studied to date. Next to each place the appropriate date.

The War for Independence Begins
Worksheet

1. What date did the War for Independence begin?

2. Why did the British blockade Boston harbor?

3. Where did the Americans stockpile arms?

4. Why were Paul Revere and William Dawes sent to Lexington?

5. What happened to Paul Revere and William Dawes?

THE WAR FOR INDEPENDENCE BEGINS

Worksheet, Page 2

6. Describe the Battle of Lexington.

____

____

____

____

____

____

7. Describe the Battle of Concord.

____

____

____

____

____

____

____

The War for Independence Begins

Project 1—Boston Massacre

Following are two accounts of the Boston Massacre. The first is from the perspective of the colonies and the second is Captain Thomas Preston's account, presenting the British side of the engagement.

Anonymous Account of the Boston Massacre

The horrid massacre in Boston, perpetrated in the evening of the fifth day of March, 1770, by soldiers of the twenty-ninth regiment which with the fourteenth regiment were then quartered there; with some observations on the state of things prior to that catastrophe

It may be a proper introduction to this narrative, briefly to represent the state of things for some time previous to the said Massacre; and this seems necessary in order to the forming a just idea of the causes of it.

At the end of the late [French and Indian] war, in which this province bore so distinguished a part, a happy union subsisted between Great Britain and the colonies. This was unfortunately interrupted by the Stamp Act; but it was in some measure restored by the repeal of it. It was again interrupted by other acts of parliament for taxing America; and by the appointment of a Board of Commissioners, in pursuance of an act, which by the face of it was made for the relief and encouragement of commerce, but which in its operation, it was apprehended, would have, and it has in fact had, a contrary effect. By the said act the said Commissioners were "to be resident in some convenient part of his Majesty's dominions in America." This must be understood to be in some part convenient for the whole. But it does not appear that, in fixing the place of their residence, the convenience of the whole was at all consulted, for Boston, being very far from the centre of the colonies, could not be the place most convenient for the whole. Judging by the act, it may seem this town was intended to be favored, by the Commissioners being appointed to reside here; and that the consequence of that residence would be the relief and encouragement of commerce; but the reverse has been the constant and uniform effect of it; so that the commerce of the town, from the embarrassments in which it has been lately involved, is greatly reduced.

The residence of the Commissioners here has been detrimental, not only to the commerce, but to the political interests of the town and province; and not only so, but we can trace from it the causes of the late horrid massacre. Soon after their arrival here in November, 1767, instead of confining themselves to the proper business of their office, they became partizans of Governor Bernard in his political schemes; and had the weakness and temerity to infringe upon one of the most essential rights of the house of commons of this province-that of giving their votes with freedom, and not being accountable therefor but to their constituents. One of the members of that house, Capt. Timothy Folgier, having voted in some affair contrary to the mind of the said Commissioners, was for so doing dismissed from the office he held under them.

These proceedings of theirs, the difficulty of access to them on office-business, and a supercilious behavior, rendered them disgustful to people in general, who in consequence thereof treated them with neglect. This probably stimulated them to resent it; and to make their resentment felt, they and their coadjutor, Governor Bernard, made such representations to his Majesty's ministers as they thought best calculated to bring the displeasure of the nation upon the town and

THE WAR FOR INDEPENDENCE BEGINS
Project 1, Page 2

province; and in order that those representations might have the more weight, they are said to have contrived and executed plans for exciting disturbances and tumults, which otherwise would probably never have existed; and, when excited, to have transmitted to the ministry the most exaggerated accounts of them.

Unfortunately for us, they have been too successful in their said representations, which, in conjunction with Governor Bernard's, have occasioned his Majesty's faithful subjects of this town and province to be treated as enemies and rebels, by an invasion of the town by sea and land; to which the approaches were made with all the circumspection usual where a vigorous opposition is expected. While the town was surrounded by a considerable number of his Majesty's ships of war, two regiments landed and took possession of it; and to support these, two other regiments arrived some time after from Ireland; one of which landed at Castle Island, and the other in the town.

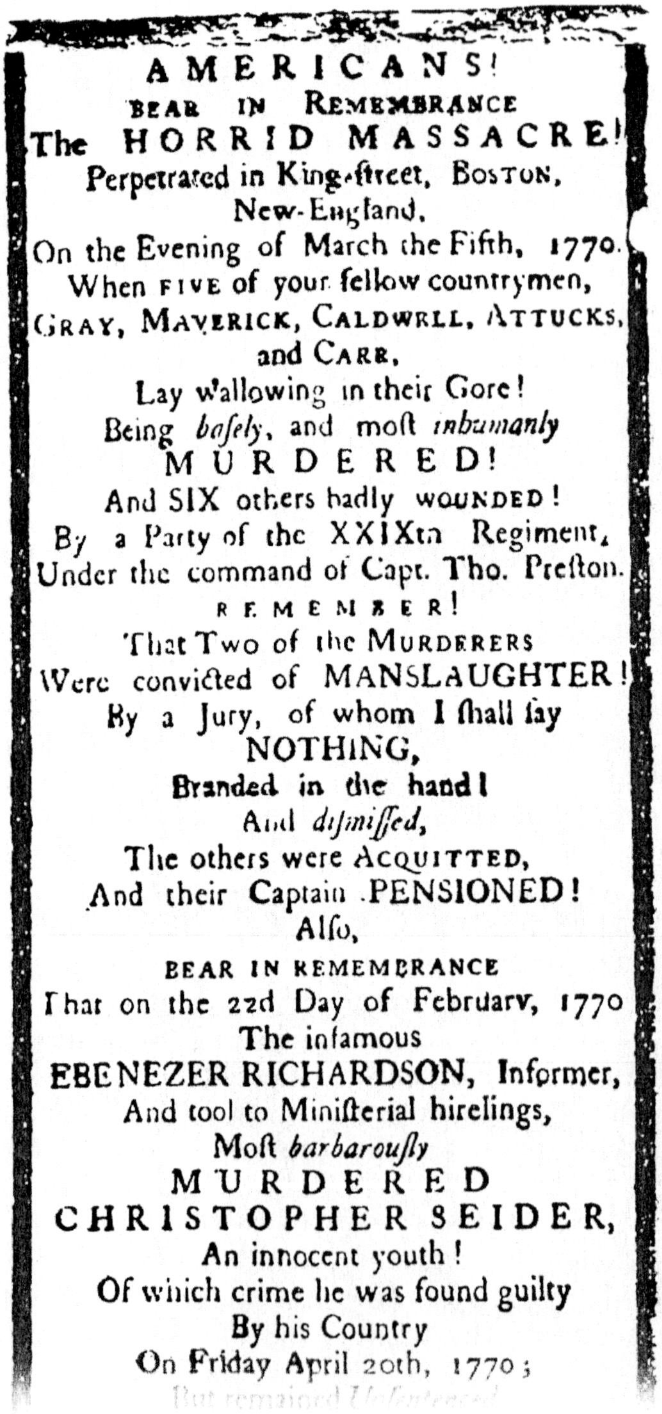

AMERICANS!
BEAR IN REMEMBRANCE
The HORRID MASSACRE!
Perpetrated in King-street, BOSTON,
New-England,
On the Evening of March the Fifth, 1770.
When FIVE of your fellow countrymen,
GRAY, MAVERICK, CALDWELL, ATTUCKS,
and CARR,
Lay wallowing in their Gore!
Being *basely*, and most *inhumanly*
MURDERED!
And SIX others badly WOUNDED!
By a Party of the XXIXth Regiment,
Under the command of Capt. Tho. Preston.
REMEMBER!
That Two of the MURDERERS
Were convicted of MANSLAUGHTER!
By a Jury, of whom I shall say
NOTHING,
Branded in the hand!
And *dismissed*,
The others were ACQUITTED,
And their Captain PENSIONED!
Also,
BEAR IN REMEMBRANCE
That on the 22d Day of February, 1770
The infamous
EBENEZER RICHARDSON, Informer,
And tool to Ministerial hirelings,
Most *barbarously*
MURDERED
CHRISTOPHER SEIDER,
An innocent youth!
Of which crime he was found guilty
By his Country
On Friday April 20th, 1770;

Thus were we, in aggravation of our other embarrassments, embarrassed with troops, forced upon us contrary to our inclination—contrary to the spirit of Magna Charta—contrary to the very letter of the Bill of Rights, in which it is declared, that the raising or keeping a standing army within the kingdom in time of peace, unless it be with the consent of parliament, is against law, and without the desire of the civil magistrates, to aid whom was the pretence for sending the troops hither; who were quartered in the town in direct violation of an act of parliament for quartering troops in America; and all this in consequence of the representations of the said Commissioners and the said Governor, as appears by their memorials and letters lately published.

As they were the procuring cause of troops being sent hither, they must therefore be the remote and a blameable cause of all the

The War for Independence Begins
Project 1, Page 3

disturbances and bloodshed that have taken place in consequence of that measure.

We shall next attend to the conduct of the troops, and to some circumstances relative to them. Governor Bernard without consulting the Council, having given up the State House to the troops at their landing, they took possession of the chambers, where the representatives of the province and the courts of law held their meetings; and (except the council chamber) of all other parts of that house; in which they continued a considerable time, to the great annoyance of those courts while they sat, and of the merchants and gentlemen of the town, who had always made the lower floor of it their exchange. They [the merchants] had a right so to do, as the property of it was in the town; but they were deprived of that right by mere power. The said Governor soon after, by every stratagem and by every method but a forcible entry, endeavored to get possession of the manufactory-house, to make a barrack of it for the troops; and for that purpose caused it to be besieged by the troops, and the people in it to be used very cruelly.

The War for Independence Begins
Project 1, Page 4

The General Court, at the first session after the arrival of the troops, viewed it in this light, and applied to Governor Bernard to cause such a nuisance to be removed; but to no purpose. The challenging the inhabitants by sentinels posted in all parts of the town before the lodgings of officers, which (for about six months, while it lasted), occasioned many quarrels and uneasiness.

Capt. Wilson, of the 59th, exciting the negroes of the town to take away their masters' lives and property, and repair to the army for protection, which was fully proved against him. The attack of a party of soldiers on some of the magistrates of the town, the repeated rescues of soldiers from peace officers, the firing of a loaded musket in a public street, to the endangering a great number of peaceable inhabitants, the frequent wounding of persons by their bayonets and cutlasses, and the numerous instances of bad behavior in the soldiery, made us early sensible that the troops were not sent here for any benefit to the town or province, and that we had no good to expect from such conservators of the peace.

It was not expected, however, that such an outrage and massacre, as happened here on the evening of the fifth instant, would have been perpetrated. There were then killed and wounded, by a discharge of musketry, eleven of his Majesty's subjects, viz.:

—Mr. Samuel Gray, killed on the spot by a ball entering his head.
—Crispus Attucks, a mulatto, killed on the spot, two balls entering his breast.
—Mr. James Caldwell, killed on the spot, by two balls entering his back.
—Mr. Samuel Maverick, a youth of seventeen years of age, mortally wounded; he died the next morning.
—Mr. Patrick Carr mortally wounded; he died the 14th instant.
—Christopher Monk and John Clark, youths about seventeen years of age, dangerously wounded. It is apprehended they will die.
—Mr. Edward Payne, merchant, standing at his door; wounded.
—Messrs. John Green, Robert Patterson, and David Parker; all dangerously wounded.

The actors in this dreadful tragedy were a party of soldiers commanded by Capt. Preston of the 29th regiment. This party, including the Captain, consisted of eight, who are all committed to jail.

There are depositions in this affair which mention, that several guns were fired at the same time from the Custom-house; before which this shocking scene was exhibited. Into this matter inquisition is now making. In the meantime it may be proper to insert here the substance of some of those depositions.

Benjamin Frizell, on the evening of the 5th of March, having taken his station near the west corner of the Custom-house in King street, before and at the time of the soldiers firing their guns, declares (among other things) that the first discharge was only of one gun, the next of two guns, upon which he the deponent thinks he saw a man stumble; the third discharge was of three guns, upon which he thinks he saw two men fall; and immediately after were discharged five guns, two of which were by soldiers on his right hand; the other three, as appeared to the deponent, were discharged from the balcony, or the chamber window of the Custom-house, the flashes appearing on the left hand, and higher than the right hand flashes appeared to be, and of which the deponent was very sensible, although his eyes were much turned to the soldiers, who were all on his right hand.

What gave occasion to the melancholy event of that evening seems to have been this. A difference having happened near Mr. Grays ropewalk, between a soldier and a man belonging to it, the soldier challenged the ropemakers to a boxing match. The challenge was accepted by one of them, and the soldier worsted. He ran to the barrack in the neighborhood, and returned with several of his companions. The fray was renewed, and the soldiers were driven off. They soon returned with recruits and were again worsted. This happened several times, till at length a considerable body of soldiers was collected, and they also were driven off, the ropemakers having been joined by their brethren of the contiguous ropewalks. By this time Mr. Gray being alarmed interposed, and with the assistance of some gentlemen prevented any further disturbance. To satisfy the soldiers and punish the man who had been the occasion of the first difference, and as an example to the rest, he turned him out of his service; and waited on Col. Dalrymple, the commanding officer of the troops, and with him concerted measures for preventing further mischief. Though this affair ended thus, it made a strong impression on the minds of the soldiers in general, who thought the honor of the regiment concerned to revenge those repeated repulses. For this purpose they seem to have formed a combination to commit some outrage upon the inhabitants of the town indiscriminately; and this was to be done on the evening of the 5th instant or soon after; as appears by the depositions of the following persons, viz.:

William Newhall declares, that on Thursday night the 1st of March instant, he met four soldiers of the 29th regiment, and that he heard them say, "there were a great many that would eat their dinners on Monday next, that should not eat any on Tuesday." Daniel Calfe declares, that on Saturday evening the 3d of March, a camp-woman, wife to James McDeed, a grenadier of the 29th, came into his father's shop, and the people talking about the affrays at the rope-walks, and blaming the soldiers for the part they had acted in it, the woman said, "the soldiers were in the right;" adding, "that before Tuesday or Wednesday night they would wet their swords or bayonets in New England people's blood." Samuel Drowne declares that, about nine o'clock of the evening of the fifth of March current, standing at his own door in Cornhill, he saw about fourteen or fifteen soldiers of the 29th regiment, who came from Murray's barracks, armed with naked cutlasses, swords, &c., and came upon the inhabitants of the town, then standing or walking in Cornhill, and abused some, and violently assaulted others as they met them; most of whom were without so much as a stick in their hand to defend themselves, as he very clearly could discern, it being moonlight, and himself being one of the assaulted persons. All or most of the said soldiers he saw go into King street (some of them through Royal Exchange lane), and there followed them, and soon discovered them to be quarrelling and fighting with the people whom they saw there, which he thinks were not more than a dozen, when the soldiers came first, armed as aforesaid. Of those dozen people, the most of them were gentlemen, standing together a little below the Town House, upon the Exchange. At the appearance of those soldiers so armed, the most of the twelve persons went off, some of them being first assaulted.

The violent proceedings of this party, and their going into King street, "quarrelling and fighting with the people whom they saw there" (mentioned in Mr. Drowne's deposi-

THE WAR FOR INDEPENDENCE BEGINS
Project 1, Page 6

tion), was immediately introductory to the grand catastrophe. These assailants, who issued from Murray's barracks (so called), after attacking and wounding divers persons in Cornhill, as abovementioned, being armed, proceeded (most of them) up the Royal Exchange lane into King street; where, making a short stop, and after assaulting and driving away the few they met there, they brandished their arms and cried out, "where are the boogers! where are the cowards!" At this time there were very few persons in the street beside themselves. This party in proceeding from Exchange lane into King street, must pass the sentry posted at the westerly corner of the Custom House, which butts on that lane and fronts on that street. This is needful to be mentioned, as near that spot and in that street the bloody tragedy was acted, and the street actors in it were stationed: their station being but a few feet from the front side of the said Custom House. The outrageous behavior and the threats of the said party occasioned the ringing of the meeting-house bell near the head of King street, which bell ringing quick, as for fire, it presently brought out a number of inhabitants, who being soon sensible of the occasion of it, were naturally led to King street, where the said party had made a stop but a little while before, and where their stopping had drawn together a number of boys, round the sentry at the Custom House. Whether the boys mistook the sentry for one of the said party, and thence took occasion to differ with him, or whether he first affronted them, which is affirmed in several depositions, however that may be, there was much foul language between them, and some of them, in consequence of his pushing at them with his bayonet, threw snowballs at him, which occasioned him to knock hastily at the door of the Custom House. From hence two persons thereupon proceeded immediately to the main-guard, which was posted opposite to the State House, at a small distance, near the head of the said street. The officer on guard was Capt. Preston, who with seven or eight soldiers, with fire-arms and charged bayonets, issued from the guardhouse, and in great haste posted himself and his soldiers in front of the Custom House, near the corner aforesaid. In passing to this station the soldiers pushed several persons with their bayonets, driving through the people in so rough a manner that it appeared they intended to create a disturbance. This occasioned some snowballs to be thrown at them which seems to have been the only provocation that was given. Mr. Knox (between whom and Capt. Preston there was some conversation on the spot) declares, that while he was talking with Capt. Preston, the soldiers of his detachment had attacked the people with their bayonets and that there was not the least provocation given to Capt. Preston of his party; the backs of the people being toward them when the people were attacked. He also declares, that Capt. Preston seemed to be in great haste and much agitated, and that, according to his opinion, there were not then present in King street above seventy or eighty persons at the extent.

The said party was formed into a half circle; and within a short time after they had been posted at the Custom House, began to fire upon the people.

Captain Preston is said to have ordered them to fire, and to have repeated that order. One gun was fired first; then others in succession and with deliberation, till ten or a dozen guns were fired; or till that number of discharges were made from the guns that were fired. By which means eleven persons were killed and wounded, as above represented.

The War for Independence Begins
Project 1, Page 7

Captain Thomas Preston's Account of the Boston Massacre (13 March 1770)

It is [a] matter of too great notoriety to need any proofs that the arrival of his Majesty's troops in Boston was extremely obnoxious to its inhabitants. They have ever used all means in their power to weaken the regiments, and to bring them into contempt by promoting and aiding desertions, and with impunity, even where there has been the clearest evidence of the fact, and by grossly and falsely propagating untruths concerning them. On the arrival of the 64th and 65th their ardour seemingly began to abate; it being too expensive to buy off so many, and attempts of that kind rendered too dangerous from the numbers [sic]

And has ever since their departure been breaking out with greater violence after their embarkation. One of their justices, most thoroughly acquainted with the people and their intentions, on the trial of a man of the 14th Regiment, openly and publicly in the hearing of great numbers of people and from the seat of justice, declared "that the soldiers must now take care of themselves, nor trust too much to their arms, for they were but a handful; that the inhabitants carried weapons concealed under their clothes, and would destroy them in a moment, if they pleased." This, considering the malicious temper of the people, was an alarming circumstance to the soldiery. Since which several disputes have happened between the townspeople and the soldiers of both regiments, the former being encouraged thereto by the countenance of even some of the magistrates, and by the protection of all the party against government. In general such disputes have

been kept too secret from the officers. On the 2d instant two of the 29th going through one Gray's ropewalk, the rope-makers insultingly asked them if they would empty a vault. This unfortunately had the desired effect by provoking the soldiers, and from words they went to blows. Both parties suffered in this affray, and finally the soldiers retired to their quarters. The officers, on the first knowledge of this transaction, took every precaution in their power to prevent any ill consequence. Notwithstanding which, single quarrels could not be prevented, the inhabitants constantly provoking and abusing the soldiery. The insolence as well as utter hatred of the inhabitants to the troops increased daily, insomuch that Monday and Tuesday, the 5th and 6th instant, were privately agreed on for a general engagement, in consequence of which several of the militia came from the country armed to join their friends, menacing to destroy any who should oppose them. This plan has since been discovered.

On Monday night about 8 o'clock two soldiers were attacked and beat. But the party of the townspeople in order to carry matters to the utmost length, broke into two meeting houses and rang the alarm bells, which I supposed was for fire as usual, but was soon undeceived. About 9 some of the guard came to me and informed me the town inhabitants were assembling to attack the troops, and that the bells were ringing as the signal for that purpose and not for fire, and the beacon intended to be fired to bring in the distant people of the country. This, as I was captain of the day, occasioned my repairing immediately to the main guard. In my way there I saw the people in great commotion, and heard them use the most cruel and horrid threats against the troops. In a few minutes after I reached the guard, about 100 people passed it and went towards the custom house where the king's money is lodged. They immediately surrounded the sentry posted there, and with clubs and other weapons threatened to execute their vengeance on him. I was soon informed by a townsman their intention was to carry off the soldier from his post and probably murder him. On which I desired him to return for further intelligence, and he soon came back and assured me he heard the mobb declare they would murder him. This I feared might be a prelude to their plundering the king's chest. I immediately sent a noncommissioned officer and 12 men to protect both the sentry and the king's money, and very soon followed myself to prevent, if possible, all disorder, fearing lest the officer and soldiers, by the insults and provocations of the rioters, should be thrown off their guard and commit some rash act. They soon rushed through the people, and by charging their bayonets in half-circles, kept them at a little distance. Nay, so far was I from intending the death of any person that I suffered the troops to go to the spot where the unhappy affair took place without any loading in their pieces; nor did I ever give orders for loading them. This remiss conduct in me perhaps merits censure; yet it is evidence, resulting from the nature of things, which is the best and surest that can be offered, that my intention was not to act offensively, but the contrary part, and that not without compulsion. The mob still increased and were more outrageous, striking their clubs or bludgeons one against another, and calling out, come on you rascals, you bloody backs, you lobster scoundrels, fire if you dare, G-d damn you,

The War for Independence Begins
Project 1, Page 9

fire and be damned, we know you dare not, and much more such language was used. At this time I was between the soldiers and the mob, parleying with, and endeavouring all in my power to persuade them to retire peaceably, but to no purpose. They advanced to the points of the bayonets, struck some of them and even the muzzles of the pieces, and seemed to be endeavouring to close with the soldiers. On which some well behaved persons asked me if the guns were charged. I replied yes. They then asked me if I intended to order the men to fire. I answered no, by no means, observing to them that I was advanced before the muzzles of the men's pieces, and must fall a sacrifice if they fired; that the soldiers were upon the half cock and charged bayonets, and my giving the word fire under those circumstances would prove me to be no officer. While I was thus speaking, one of the soldiers having received a severe blow with a stick, stepped a little on one side and instantly fired, on which turning to and asking him why he fired without orders, I was struck with a club on my arm, which for some time deprived me of the use of it, which blow had it been placed on my head, most probably would have destroyed me.

On this a general attack was made on the men by a great number of heavy clubs and snowballs being thrown at them, by which all our lives were in imminent danger, some persons at the same time from behind calling out, damn your bloods-why don't you fire. Instantly three or four of the soldiers fired, one after another, and directly after three more in the same confusion and hurry. The mob then ran away, except three unhappy men who instantly expired, in which number was Mr. Gray at whose ropewalk the prior quarrels took place; one more is since dead, three others are dangerously, and four slightly wounded. The whole of this melancholy affair was transacted in almost 20 minutes. On my asking the soldiers why they fired without orders, they said they heard the word fire and supposed it came from me. This might be the case as many of the mob called out fire, fire, but I assured the men that I gave no such order; that my words were, don't fire, stop your firing. In short, it was scarcely possible for the soldiers to know who said fire, or don't fire, or stop your firing. On the people's assembling again to take away the dead bodies, the soldiers supposing them coming to attack them, were making ready to fire again, which I prevented by striking up their firelocks with my hand. Immediately after a townsman came and told me that 4 or 5000 people were assembled in the next street, and had sworn to take my life with every man's

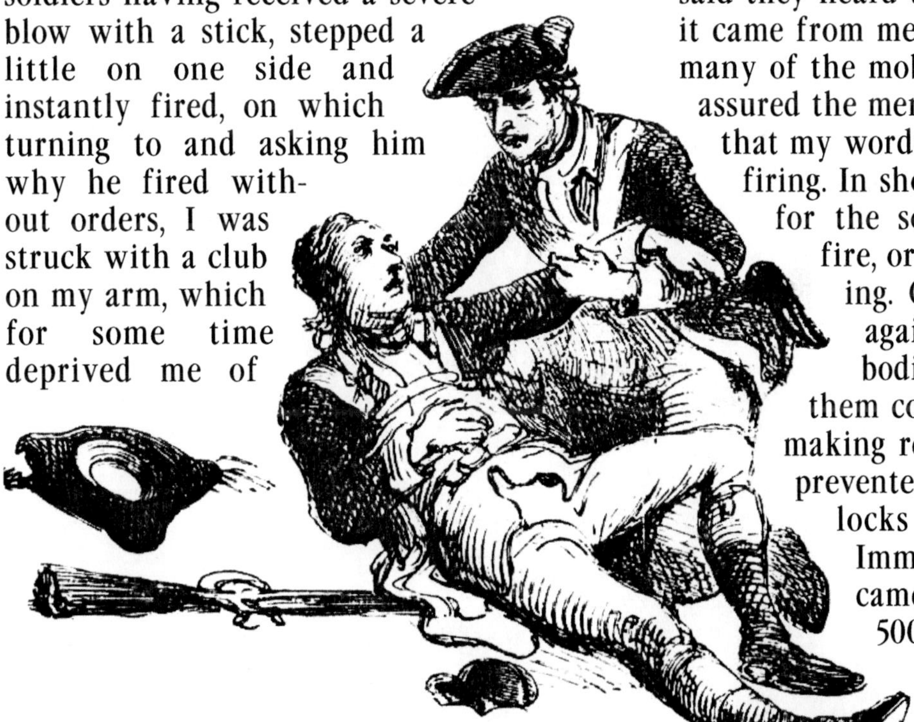

The War for Independence Begins
Project 1, Page 9

with me. On which I judged it unsafe to remain there any longer, and therefore sent the party and sentry to the main guard, where the street is narrow and short, there telling them off into street firings, divided and planted them at each end of the street to secure their rear, momently expecting an attack, as there was a constant cry of the inhabitants to arms, to arms, turn out with your guns; and the town drums beating to arms, I ordered my drums to beat to arms, and being soon after joined by the different companies of the 29th regiment, I formed them as the guard into street firings. The 14th regiment also got under arms but remained at their barracks. I immediately sent a sergeant with a party to Colonel Dalrymple, the commanding officer, to acquaint him with every particular. Several officers going to join their regiment were knocked down by the mob, one very much wounded and his sword taken from him. The lieutenant-governor and Colonel Carr soon after met at the head of the 29th regiment and agreed that the regiment should retire to their barracks, and the people to their houses, but I kept the picket to strengthen the guard. It was with great difficulty that the lieutenant-governor prevailed on the people to be quiet and retire. At last they all went off, excepting about a hundred.

A Council was immediately called, on the breaking up of which three justices met and issued a warrant to apprehend me and eight soldiers. On hearing of this procedure I instantly went to the sheriff and surrendered myself, though for the space of 4 hours I had it in my power to have made my escape, which I most undoubtedly should have attempted and could easily executed, had I been the least conscious of any guilt. On the examination before the justices, two witnesses swore that I gave the men orders to fire. The one testified he was within two feet of me; the other that I swore at the men for not firing at the first word. Others swore they heard me use the word "fire," but whether do or do not fire, they could not say; others that they heard the word fire, but could not say if it came from me. The next day they got 5 or 6 more to swear I gave the word to fire. So bitter and inveterate are many of the malcontents here that they are industriously using every method to fish out evidence to prove it was a concerted scheme to murder the inhabitants. Others are infusing the utmost malice and revenge into the minds of the people who are to be my jurors by false publications, votes of towns, and all other artifices. That so from a settled rancour against the officers and troops in general, the suddenness of my trial after the affair while the people's minds are all greatly inflamed, I am, though perfectly innocent, under most unhappy circumstances, having nothing in reason to expect but the loss of life in a very ignominous manner, without the interposition of his Majesty's royal goodness.

The War for Independence Begins
Project 2—The Midnight Ride of Paul Revere

Read The Midnight Ride of Paul Revere *by Henry Wadsworth Longfellow out loud. Then pretend you reside along Paul Revere's or William Dawe's route. Write a dialogue between yourself (you are a Patriot of course) and Revere or Dawes. Include the important information such as why you will fight, how the British will come, where the minutemen will gather, and the expected outcome. Use quotation marks to indicate direct quotes.*

Listen, my children, and you shall hear
Of the midnight ride of Paul Revere,
On the eighteenth of April, in Seventy-five;
Hardly a man is now alive'
Who remembers that famous day and year.

He said to his friend, "If the British march
By land or sea from the town to-night,
Hang a lantern aloft in the belfry arch
Of the North Church tower as a signal light,-
One, if by land, and two, if by sea;
And I on the opposite shore will be,
Ready to ride and spread the alarm
Through every Middlesex village and farm,
For the country folk to be up and to arm."

Then he said "Good-night," and with muffled oar
Silently row'd to the Charlestown shore,
Just as the moon rose over the bay,
Where swinging wide at her moorings lay
The Somerset, British man-of-war;
A phantom ship,with each mast and spar
Across the moon like a prision bar,
And a huge black hulk, that was magnified
By its own reflection in the tide.

Meanwhile his friend, through alley and street,
Wanders and watches with eager ears,
Till in the silence around him hears
The muster of men at the barrack-door,
The sound of arms, and the tramp of feet,
And the measured tread of the grenadiers
Marching down to their boats on the shore.

Then he climb'd the tower of the Old North Church,
By the wooded stairs, with stealthy tread,
To the belfry-chamber overhead,
And started the pigeons from their perch
On the sombre rafters, that round him made
Masses of moving shapes of shade,-
By the trembling ladder, steep and tall,
To the highest window in the wall,
Where he paused to listen and look down
A moment on the roofs of the town,
And the moonlight flowing over all.

Beneath, in the churchyard, lay the dead,
In their night-encampment on the hill,
Wrapp'd in silence so deep and still
That he could hear, like a sentinel's tread,
The watchful night-wind, as it went
Creeping along from tent to tent,
And seeming to whisper, "All is well!"
A moment only he feels the spell
Of the place and the hour, and the secret dread
Of the lonely belfry and the dead;
For suddenly all his thoughts are bent
On a shadowy something far away,
Where the river widens to meet the bay,-
A line of black that bends and floats
On the rising tide like a bridge of boats.

Meanwhile, impatient to mount and ride,
Booted and spurr'd, with a heavy stride
On the opposite shore walk'd Paul Revere.
Now he patted his horse's side,
Now gazed at the landscape far and near,
Then, impetuous, stamp'd the earth,
And turn'd and tighten'd his saddle-girth;
But mostly he watch'd with eager search
The belfry-tower of the Old North Church,

The War for Independence Begins

Project 2, Page 2

As it rose above the graves on the hill,
Lonely and spectral and sombre and still.
And lo! as he looks, on the belfry's height
A glimmer, and then a gleam of light!
He springs to the saddle, the bridle he turns,
But lingers and gazes, till full on his sight
A second lamp in the belfry burns.

A hurry of hoofs in a village street,
A shape in the moonlight, a bulk in the dark,
And beneath, from the pebbles, in passing, a spark
Struck out by a steed flying fearless and fleet;
That was all; and yet, through the gloom and the light,
The fate of a nation was riding that night;
And the spark struck out by that steed in his flight
Kindled the land into flame with its heat.

He has left the village and mounted the steep,
And beneath him, tranquil and broad and deep,
Is the Mystic, meeting the ocean tides,
And under the alders that skirt its edge,
Now soft on the sand, now loud on the ledge,
Is heard the tramp of his steed as he rides.

It was twelve by the village clock
When he cross'd the bridge into Medford town.
He heard the crowing of the cock,
And the barking of the farmer's dog,
And felt the damp of the river fog,
That rises after the sun goes down.

It was one by the village clock
When he galloped into Lexington.
He saw the gilded weathercock
Swim in the moonlight as he pass'd,
And the meeting-house windows, blank and bare,
Gaze at him with a spectral glare,
As if they already stood aghast
At the bloody work they would look upon.

It was two by the village clock
When he came to the bridge in Concord town.
He heard the bleating of the flock,
And the twitter of birds among the trees,
And felt the breath of the morning breeze
Blowing over the meadows brown.
And one was safe and asleep in his bed
Who at the bridge would be first to fall,
Who that day would by lying dead,
Pierced by a British musket-ball.

You know the rest; in the books you have read,
How the British regulars fired and fled,-
How the farmers gave them ball for ball,
From behind each fence and farmyard wall,
Chasing the red-coats down the land,
Then crossing the fields to emerge again
Under the trees at the turn of the road,
And only pausing to fire and load.
So through the night went his cry of alarm.
To every Middlesex village and farm,-
A cry of defiance, and not of fear,
A voice in the darkness, a knock at the door,
And a word that shall echo for evermore!
For, borne on the night-wind of the Past,
Through all our history, to the last,
In the hour of darkness, and peril, and need,
The people will waken and listen to hear,
The hurrying hoof-beats of that steed,
And the midnight message of Paul Revere.

The War for Independence Begins

Project 2, Page 3

A Dialogue with Revere or Dawes

THE WAR FOR INDEPENDENCE BEGINS

Project 3—Declaration of the Causes and Necessity of taking up Arms

JULY 6, 1775

A declaration by the Representatives of the United Colonies of North-America, now met in Congress at Philadelphia, setting forth the causes and necessity of their taking up arms.

If it was possible for men, who exercise their reason to believe, that the divine Author of our existence intended a part of the human race to hold an absolute property in, and an unbounded power over others, marked out by his infinite goodness and wisdom, as the objects of a legal domination never rightfully resistible, however severe and oppressive, the inhabitants of these colonies might at least require from the parliament of Great-Britain some evidence, that this dreadful authority over them, has been granted to that body. But a reverence for our great Creator, principles of humanity, and the dictates of common sense, must convince all those who reflect upon the subject, that government was instituted to promote the welfare of mankind, and ought to be administered for the attainment of that end.

The legislature of Great-Britain, however, stimulated by an inordinate passion for a power not only unjustifiable, but which they know to be peculiarly reprobated by the very constitution of that kingdom, and desparate [sic] of success in any mode of contest, where regard should be had to truth, law, or right, have at length, deserting those, attempted to effect their cruel and impolitic purpose of enslaving these colonies by violence, and have thereby rendered it necessary for us to close with their last appeal from reason to arms. — Yet, however blinded that assembly may be, by their intemperate rage for unlimited domination, so to slight justice and the opinion of mankind, we esteem ourselves bound by obligations of respect to the rest of the world, to make known the justice of our cause.

Our forefathers, inhabitants of the island of Great-Britain, left their native land, to seek on these shores a residence for civil and religious freedom. At the expense of their blood, at the hazard of their fortunes, without the least charge to the country from which they removed, by unceasing labor, and an unconquerable spirit, they effected settlements in the distant and inhospitable wilds of America, then filled with numerous and warlike nations of barbarians. — Societies or governments, vested with perfect legislatures, were formed under charters from the crown, and an harmonious intercourse was established between the colonies and the kingdom from which they derived their origin. The mutual benefits of this union became in a short time so extraordinary, as to excite astonishment. It is universally confessed, that the amazing increase of the wealth, strength, and navigation of the realm, arose from this source; and the minister, who so wisely and successfully directed the measures of Great-Britain in the late war, publicly declared, that these colonies enabled her to triumph over her enemies. — Towards the conclusion of that war, it pleased our sovereign to make a change in his counsels.

From that fatal moment, the affairs of the British empire began to fall into confusion, and gradually sliding from the summit of glorious prosperity, to which they had been advanced by the virtues and abilities of one man, are at length distracted by the convulsions, that now shake it to its deepest foundations. — The new ministry finding the brave foes of Britain, though frequently defeated,

The War for Independence Begins

Project 3, Page 2

yet still contending, took up the unfortunate idea of granting them a hasty peace, and then of subduing her faithful friends.

These devoted colonies were judged to be in such a state, as to present victories without bloodshed, and all the easy emoluments of statuteable plunder. – The uninterrupted tenor of their peaceable and respectful behaviour from the beginning of colonization, their dutiful, zealous, and useful services during the war, though so recently and amply acknowledged in the most honourable manner by his majesty, by the late king, and by parliament, could not save them from the meditated innovations. – Parliament was influenced to adopt the pernicious project, and assuming a new power over them, have in the course of eleven years, given such decisive specimens of the spirit and consequences attending this power, as to leave no doubt concerning the effects of acquiescence under it.

They have undertaken to give and grant our money without our consent, though we have ever exercised an exclusive right to dispose of our own property; statutes have been passed for extending the jurisdiction of courts of admiralty and vice-admiralty beyond their ancient limits; for depriving us of the accustomed and inestimable privilege of trial by jury, in cases affecting both life and property; for suspending the legislature of one of the colonies; for interdicting all commerce to the capital of another; and for altering fundamentally the form of government established by charter, and secured by acts of its own legislature solemnly confirmed by the crown; for exempting the "murderers" of colonists from legal trial, and in effect, from punishment; for erecting in a neighbouring province, acquired by the joint arms of Great-Britain and America, a despotism dangerous to our very existence; and for quartering soldiers upon the colonists in time of profound peace. It has also been resolved in parliament, that colonists charged with committing certain offences, shall be transported to England to be tried. But why should we enumerate our injuries in detail? By one statute it is declared, that parliament can "of right make laws to bind us in all cases whatsoever." What is to defend us against so enormous, so unlimited a power? Not a single man of those who assume it, is chosen by us; or is subject to our controul or influence; but, on the contrary, they are all of them exempt from the operation of such laws, and an American revenue, if not diverted from the ostensible purposes for which it is raised, would actually lighten their own burdens in proportion, as they increase ours. We saw the misery to which such despotism would reduce us. We for ten years incessantly and ineffectually besieged the throne as supplicants; we reasoned, we remonstrated with parliament, in the most mild and decent language.

Administration sensible that we should regard these oppressive measures as freemen ought to do, sent over fleets and armies to enforce them. The indignation of the Americans was roused, it is true; but it was the indignation of a virtuous, loyal, and affectionate people. A Congress of delegates from the United Colonies was assembled at Philadelphia, on the fifth day of last September. We resolved again to offer an humble and dutiful petition to the King, and also addressed our fellow-subjects of Great-Britain. We have pursued every temperate, every respectful measure: we have even proceeded to break off our commercial intercourse with our fellow-subjects, as the last peaceable admonition, that our attachment to no nation upon earth should sup-

The War for Independence Begins
Project 3, Page 3

plant our attachment to liberty. — This, we flattered ourselves, was the ultimate step of the controversy: but subsequent events have shewn, how vain was this hope of finding moderation in our enemies.

Several threatening expressions against the colonies were inserted in his majesty's speech; our petition, tho' we were told it was a decent one, and that his majesty had been pleased to receive it graciously, and to promise laying it before his parliament, was huddled into both houses among a bundle of American papers, and there neglected. The lords and commons in their address, in the month of February, said, that "a rebellion at that time actually existed within the province of Massachusetts-Bay; and that those concerned in it, had been countenanced and encouraged by unlawful combinations and engagements, entered into by his majesty's subjects in several of the other colonies; and therefore they besought his majesty, that he would take the most effectual measures to inforce due obedience to the laws and authority of the supreme legislature." — Soon after, the commercial intercourse of whole colonies, with foreign countries, and with each other, was cut off by an act of parliament; by another several of them were intirely prohibited from the fisheries in the seas near their co[a]sts, on which they always depended for their sustenance; and large reinforcements of ships and troops were immediately sent over to general Gage.

Fruitless were all the entreaties, arguments, and eloquence of an illustrious band of the most distinguis[h]ed peers, and commoners, who nobly and stren[u]ously asserted the justice of our cause, to stay, or even to mitigate the heedless fury with which these accumulated and unexampled outrages were hurried on. —Equally fruitless was the interference of the city of London,

The War for Independence Begins
Project 3, Page 4

of Bristol, and many other respectable towns in our favour. Parliament adopted an insidious manoeuvre calculated to divide us, to establish a perpetual auction of taxations where colony should bid against colony, all of them uninformed what ransom would redeem their lives; and thus to extort from us, at the point of the bayonet, the unknown sums that should be sufficient to gratify, if possible to gratify, ministerial rapacity, with the miserable indulgence left to us of raising, in our own mode, the prescribed tribute. What terms more rigid and humiliating could have been dictated by remorseless victors to conquered enemies? in our circumstances to accept them, would be to deserve them.

Soon after the intelligence of these proceedings arrived on this continent, general Gage, who in the course of the last year had taken possession of the town of Boston, in the province of Massachusetts-Bay, and still occupied it [as] a garrison, on the 19th day of April, sent out from that place a large detachment of his army, who made an unprovoked assault on the inhabitants of the said province, at the town of Lexington, as appears by the affidavits of a great number of persons, some of whom were officers and soldiers of that detachment, murdered eight of the inhabitants, and wounded many others. From thence the troops proceeded in warlike array to the town of Concord, where they set upon another party of the inhabitants of the same province, killing several and wounding more, until compelled to retreat by the country people suddenly assembled to repel this cruel aggression. Hostilities, thus commenced by the British troops, have been since prosecuted by them without regard to faith or reputation.

The inhabitants of Boston being confined within that town by the general their governor, and having, in order to procure their dismission, entered into a treaty with him, it was stipulated that the said inhabitants having deposited their arms with their own magistrates, should have liberty to depart, taking with them their other effects. They accordingly delivered up their arms, but in open violation of honour, in defiance of the obligation of treaties, which even savage nations esteemed sacred, the governor ordered the arms deposited as aforesaid, that they might be preserved for their owners, to be seized by a body of soldiers; detained the greatest part of the inhabitants in the town, and compelled the few who were permitted to retire, to leave their most valuable effects behind.

By this perfidy wives are separated from their husbands, children from their parents, the aged and sick from their relations and friends, who wish to attend and comfort them; and those who have been used to live in plenty and even elegance, are reduced to deplorable distress.

The general, further emulating his ministerial masters, by a proclamation bearing date on the 12th day of June, after venting the grossest falsehoods and calumnies against the good people of these colonies, proceeds to "declare them all, either by name or description, to be rebels and traitors, to supersede the course of the common law, and instead thereof to publish and order the use and exercise of the law martial." — His troops have butchered our countrymen, have wantonly burned Charlestown, besides a considerable number of houses in other places; our ships and vessels are seized; the necessary supplies of provisions are intercepted, and he is exerting his utmost power to spread destruction and devastation around him.

We have received certain intelligence,

THE WAR FOR INDEPENDENCE BEGINS
Project 3, Page 5

that general Carleton, the governor of Canada, is instigating the people of that province and the Indians to fall upon us; and we have but little reason to apprehend, that schemes have been formed to excite domestic enemies against us. In brief, a part of these colonies now feel, and all of them are sure of feeling, as far as the vengeance of administration can inflict them, the complicated calamities of fire, sword, and famine. We are reduced to the alternative of chusing an unconditional submission to the tyranny of irritated ministers, or resistance by force. — The latter latter is our choice. — We have counted the cost of this contest, and find nothing so dreadful as voluntary slavery. —Honour, justice, and humanity, forbid us tamely to surrender that freedom which we received from our gallant ancestors, and which our innocent posterity have a right to receive from us. We cannot endure the infamy and guilt of resigning succeeding generations to that wretchedness which inevitably awaits them, if we basely entail hereditary bondage upon them.

Our cause is just. Our union is perfect. Our internal resources are great, and, if necessary, foreign assistance is undoubtably attainable. — We gratefully acknowledge, as signal instances of the Divine favour towards us, that his Providence would not permit us to be called into this severe controversy, until we were grown up to our present strength, had been previously exercised in warlike operation, and possessed of the means of defending ourselves. With hearts fortified with these animating reflections, we most solemnly, before God and the world, declare, that exerting the utmost energy of those powers, which our beneficent Creator hath graciously bestowed upon us, the arms we have been compelled by our enemies to assume, we will, in defiance of every hazard, with unabating firmness and perseverence, employ for the preservation of our liberties; being with one mind resolved to die freemen rather than to live slaves.

Lest this declaration should disquiet the minds of our friends and fellow-subjects in any part of the empire, we assure them that we mean not to dissolve that union which has so long and so happily subsisted between us, and which we sincerely wish to see restored. —Necessity has not yet driven us into that desperate measure, or induced us to excite any other nation to war against them. —We have not raised armies with ambitious designs of separating from Great-Britain, and establishing independent states. We fight not for glory or for conquest. We exhibit to mankind the remarkable spectacle of a people attacked by unprovoked enemies, without any imputation or even suspicion of offence. They boast of their privileges and civilization, and yet proffer no milder conditions than servitude or death.

In our own native land, in defence of the freedom that is our birthright, and which we ever enjoyed till the late violation of it — for the protection of our property, acquired solely by the honest industry of our fore-fathers and ourselves, against violence actually offered, we have taken up arms. We shall lay them down when hostilities shall cease on the part of the agressors, and all danger of their being renewed shall be removed, and not before.

With an humble confidence in the mercies of the supreme and impartial Judge and Ruler of the Universe, we most devoutly implore his divine goodness to protect us happily through this great conflict, to dispose our adversaries to reconciliation on reasonable terms, and thereby to relieve the empire from the calamities of civil war.

The War for Independence Begins

*Literature Unit 5—*Johnny Tremain *by Esther Forbes*

Section I: Up and About

Chapter 1

1. Why did nobody come up to the attic for the boys?
2. Why did Dove hate Johnny?
3. Why did it seem to Dusty as if everybody liked Johnny?
4. Why did Johnny never get charcoal or water?
5. Was an apprentice like a slave? What was their life like?
6. Who did Mr. Lapham say Johnny should thank for his silversmith gift?

Chapter 2

1. Who could read in the Lapham household? Why?
2. What character trait was Mr. Lapham drawing Johnny's attention to by the Bible reading?

Chapter 3

1. What was Mr. Lapham's weakness? How did this weakness make Johnny seem cheeky?
2. Why did Mrs. Lapham send Madge to get Johnny?
3. How long did they have to fulfill the order for Mr. Hancock?
4. Why had Mr. Lapham never voted for his landlord, Mr. Hancock?

Chapter 4

1. What had Cilla and Isannah never heard of a working boy having before?

Chapter 5

1. Why did Johnny take Isannah down to the wharf?
2. Why did Johnny tell Cilla his middle name, even though he normally never would have told?
3. Why did Johnny's mother move from Townsend, Maine, to Boston?

Chapter 6

1. What emblem was on everything Merchant Lyte owned?

Section II: The Pride of Your Power

Chapter 1

1. What did Johnny take to Paul Revere's shop, and why did he take it?
2. Did Mr. Revere think Johnny's model was appropriate? If not, what advice did he give?
3. Do you think Mr. Revere was impressed with Johnny's work? Why?

Chapter 2

1. Was Johnny set to finish the handle on Sunday?
2. Why couldn't the fire be built up so that Johnny could work?
3. Mr. Lapham had a concern with regard to Johnny's character. What was it?
4. What did Johnny know the consequences might be if he worked on the Sabbath?

Chapter 3

1. Why did Dove pick the cracked crucible?
2. How did the accident happen?
3. Did Mrs. Lapham send for the doctor?

Chapter 4

1. Why did Johnny think his hand was completely useless? Would you agree?
2. What was Mr. Lapham's reaction to the "Evil that had gone on in his absence?"
3. What one pleasure did Johnny have at this time?

The War for Independence Begins
Literature Unit 5–Johnny Tremain

Chapter 5
1. Why did Mr. Lapham release Johnny from his seven-year apprentice obligations?
2. What reason did Dove give Mr. Lapham for handing Johnny the cracked crucible?

Section III: An Earth of Brass
Chapter 1
1. How had Mr. Lapham advised Johnny to look for work?
2. Why did shops hang signs with pictures only above their doors?
3. Who slipped food into Johnny's pockets and why?
4. What good character trait/skill did Rab show to the woman with a lost pig and to Johnny?
5. What work did Rab offer Johnny if he could not find work in a skilled trade?

Chapter 2
1. Why did Johnny dislike Mr. Tweedie?
2. Why did Mrs. Lapham like Mr. Tweedie?

Chapter 3
1. Why did Johnny look arrogant now?
2. People often assumed Johnny was one of two types of people. What were the two types?
3. What work did Johnny decide to pursue that he had not thought to try
4. Which merchant did Johnny apply to first and what type of work did he hope for?
5. What did Mr. Hancock have given to Johnny?

Chapter 4
1. What had been Johnny's usual diet of late?
2. What did Johnny mean by, "The kitten was no longer gnawing inside him."
3. Why did Mrs. Lapham assume that Johnny had become a thief?
4. What made Johnny feel completely happy that afternoon?

Chapter 5
1. What made Johnny able to cry?
2. After thinking about it, what did Johnny decide to do as his last resort?

Section IV: The Rising Eye
Chapter 1
1. Johnny's two 'halves' felt differently about meeting the Lytes. What were the two different feelings?
2. What did Mr. Lyte tell Johnny he should do with his cup?

Chapter 2
1. Why did Johnny need to move back to the attic?
2. What did Cilla and Isannah do that made Johnny feel happy again?
3. Why did Rab think Merchant Lyte was sly?
4. What was the difference between the Whigs and the Tories?

Chapter 3
1. What did Mr. Lyte order the sheriff to do, and why?
2. What did Sewall find out about Johnny from those at the Lapham household?

Chapter 4
1. Why was the accusation of burglary easier to take for Johnny?
2. When Rab visited Johnny, Johnny discovered something about Rab – what was it?
3. What did Mr. Lyte do that perturbed Rab?
4. Why did Johnny initially not want

The War for Independence Begins
Literature Unit 5–Johnny Tremain

Josiah Quincy to be his lawyer?

Chapter 5
1. Who arrived at the court at 11:00?
2. How did Mr. Lyte come to own four silver cups?
3. What penalty did Mr. Lyte ask to be given to Johnny, and why?
4. Whose arrival surprised the court even more so than Miss Lavinia Lyte's?
5. What did the judge tell Johnny he could bring against Mr. Lyte?

Section V—The Boston Observer
Chapter 1
1. Why did Mr. Lyte become Johnny's enemy?
2. How had Rab gotten Cilla away from Mrs. Lapham?
3. Why didn't Johnny become a cabin boy after all?
4. What did Johnny plan to do that would be disobeying his mother yet again?
5. How much did Mr. Lyte pay Johnny for his cup?
6. Given his current circumstances, what did Johnny decide to do?

Chapter 2
1. Why was Goblin difficult to ride?
2. What about Goblin and Rab gave Johnny the confidence to learn to ride?
3. What transformed Johnny into an ardent Whig?
4. Why were there so many chairs stored in the loft where Johnny and Rab slept?
5. What additional work did Johnny and Goblin take on?
6. What did Johnny do the first four days of the week?

Chapter 3
1. Why didn't Johnny ever return to the Lapham's house?
2. What was more important to Johnny than carrying the water for Cilla?

Chapter 4
1. What made Johnny become more careful about the words he spoke concerning others?
2. What were the two times Johnny saw Rab leave his customary reserved attitude?
3. Why did Rab think that Johnny's hand didn't bother anybody at the dance?

Section VI—Salt-Water Tea
Chapter 1
1. Why did the English think that the tax on tea would not be a problem for the American colonists?
2. What news caused Mr. Lorne to print on the Lord's Day?
3. What did the colonists have twenty days to accomplish?
4. Why did Johnny cross to the Lyte's stable even though he had no paper to deliver?
5. Describe James Otis.

Chapter 2
1. Was Johnny happy to see Cilla and Isannah at the pump?
2. Why did Isannah "get on Johnny's nerves"?
3. Why did Dr. Warren think that Johnny's hand was crippled from birth?

Chapter 3
1. The tea coming from England could be sold in Boston, seized and sold at auction or destroyed if not unloaded within twenty days, or the Governor could

The War for Independence Begins

Literature Unit 5–Johnny Tremain

give special permission for the ship to return to London *with* its cargo. The Observers did not want a peaceful resolution to the tea problem. Why?

2. John Adams wanted to recruit some honest, trustworthy boys for a special job. How many boys and for what job?
3. Did they need people with a certain character for this special job?

Chapter 4

1. How was Johnny going to practice his chopping?

Chapter 5

1. What would happen to the ships with the tea if they attempted to leave the harbor with their cargo?
2. Armed citizens from Boston guarded the ships. Why were they guarding the ships?

Chapter 6

1. Rab gave Johnny a special job that needed a fast runner. What was the special assignment?
2. What was the name of the volunteer "Indian" who joined the raiding party that Johnny recognized? What dishonorable thing was he doing?
3. Who did Johnny think was going to have to pay for the lost tea?

Section VII—The Fiddler's Bill

Chapter 1

1. What finally united the colonies against England?
2. What group surprisingly joined the desire to not give in to England's demand that Boston pay for the tea?
3. What right did Gage have to punish those he believed to be leaders of the rebellion?
4. Why did the soldier knock Rab out?
5. Why did Johnny agree to carry messages for the British soldiers?

Chapter 2

1. What did Johnny do with the money he earned from the British?
2. Did General Gage build a gallows in Boston?

3. Why did Cilla work at the Lyte's house?

Chapter 3

1. Why was Goblin the only horse in the stable that was not owned by the British?
2. What does commandeer mean, and what did the British soldier intend to commandeer?
3. How did Johnny prevent it?
4. Why did Johnny allow Dove to come back into his life?

Chapter 4

1. What gave Johnny cause to respect Mrs. Lapham more than he had before?
2. What groups were moving in and out of Boston?

Chapter 5

1. What did Johnny see as a bad omen at the Lapham's house?
2. Why did Johnny slap Isannah?
3. What turned Johnny against Lavinia?
4. What did he finally discover about Mrs. Bessie?

Section VIII—A World to Come

Chapter 1

1. Where was the only safe place for the Lytes to be?
2. Why was Johnny waiting at the gates to Boston?
3. Why did Cilla want to go back to Milton?
4. Why did Cilla think the silver might still be there?

Chapter 2

1. Why did Cilla light a fire in the kitchen?
2. What did Johnny discover about his relation to the Lytes?
3. Did Johnny save and treasure the paper that gave him this information?

Chapter 3

1. Why did it seem so impossible to steal a musket from the British?
2. What did Rab think enabled a man to stand up to anything?
3. How did the British punish those who attempted to steal weapons?

Chapter 4

1. Why was Mrs. Lapham forced to marry Mr. Tweedie herself?
2. How did Cilla come to know Rab?
3. Why did it bother Johnny that the apple Cilla had given to him was wormy?

Chapter 5

1. Though James Otis was one of the founders of the Observers, why was his presence no longer desired?
2. What did Sam Adams see as the problem in not getting the Minute Men out in time?
3. What did James Otis give as the reason for going to war?
4. Why did James Otis say they were lucky men?

Section IX—The Scarlet Deluge

Chapter 1

1. Why was there "no comment" from the community about the men meeting at the Green Dragon?
2. What piece of information was given to Johnny that let Mr. Lorne know the British were planning on fortifying their supply stores at Portsmouth? Who gave it to Johnny?
3. Why did Mrs. Paul Revere write a letter; pretending in the letter she was a relative writing on behalf of Paul's grandmother?

THE WAR FOR INDEPENDENCE BEGINS
Literature Unit 5—Johnny Tremain

CHAPTER 2
1. Was Dove pro-colonists or pro-British? Why?
2. Why did Rab and Johnny give Dove too much ale?
3. What was the reason Dove gave for the British King being very mad?
4. What cities were marked in red on the British map?
5. When were Johnny and Lieutenant Stranger like equals?

CHAPTER 3
1. Why did Johnny no longer ride over the countryside delivering papers?
2. What caused Goblin to bolt away from the redcoats with Johnny on his back?
3. Why did Pumpkin say the *Boston Observer* would do a lot of good with the British regulars?
4. What was the one thing Johnny wanted in return for helping Pumpkin? Why did he want it?
5. Since there was little lead, what metal did many New Englanders use to cast their bullets? Where did they get it from?

CHAPTER 4
1. What were the three reasons King George was in a fury?

CHAPTER 5
1. At first Johnny thought the eight men down by the river were fishing. What did he discover they were actually doing?
2. What event made Johnny doubt his "physical courage"? What did he think he might not have the courage to stand up to?

SECTION X—DISPERSE, YE REBELS!
CHAPTER 1
1. What was the role of the light infantry?
2. Did the British working on their boats give a definite clue as to their plans?
3. Why was Billy Dawes picked for a job?

CHAPTER 2
1. Was Rab leaving Boston because he wanted to avoid the battle?
2. Why do you think Johnny couldn't look at Rab when he was leaving?

CHAPTER 3
1. Why was information about a saddle important to Johnny?
2. How was Johnny able to figure out where Colonel Smith was headed?

CHAPTER 4
1. Why did some think that General Gage chose Colonel Smith to lead the expedition?
2. In addition to Billy, was there another gifted actor in the Dawes family?
3. Why were the people in Charlestown watching Boston that night?
4. Why did Paul Revere want Doctor Warren to leave Boston with him that night?
5. Why was Major Pitcairn sent as well?

SECTION XI—YANKEE DOODLE
CHAPTER 1
1. What was the "target practice"?
2. Why did Doctor Warren state that there will be real fighting before the day is out instead of just target practice?

The War for Independence Begins
Literature Unit 5—Johnny Tremain

Chapter 2

1. Why did Johnny think that all of them were fighting for an English cause, though they were fighting against the English?

Chapter 3

1. What order did General Gage give too late?
2. How was Mr. Lorne rescued from the British troops who came to arrest him?
3. Why does Johnny think the British suffered a defeat?
4. Had Boston changed in the last day?

Chapter 4

1. How was Johnny able to get to the Lytes' house?
2. Was the entire Lyte family returning to London?
3. How had Merchant Lyte perjured himself in court?
4. What were the consequences to be to Johnny's mother if she "ran off" with the French soldier?
5. Why did the Lytes not know Johnny by his last name?

Chapter 5

1. What idea did Johnny have to protect the Lornes?

Section XII—A Man Can Stand Up

Chapter 1

1. Why did Johnny put aside his British uniform?
2. What did Johnny see an officer do that reinforced his conviction that they were fighting for a worthy cause?
3. Why did Johnny stop himself from helping his friend, Lieutenant Stranger?
4. How did Johnny manage to get himself across to Charlestown?
5. What kept all the soldiers in Smith's command from being killed?

Chapter 2

1. What was Johnny's impression of the Minute Men after having spent so much time around British soldiers?
2. How many men was Johnny told were killed at Lexington?

Chapter 3

1. Who was Johnny trying to find, and how did he find him?
2. What did Johnny find out about Rab?

Chapter 4

1. What did Rab give to Johnny?
2. What request did Rab have for Johnny?

Chapter 5

1. What clues did Johnny see at the Silsbee farm to let him know that Grandsire was no longer there?
2. Johnny found out that there was another reason that Rab wanted Johnny to go to his family home. What was it?
3. What words of James Otis came back to Dr. Warren? What did it have to do with Rab?
6. What did Dr. Warren discover about Johnny's hand?
7. What could Dr. Warren do for Johnny?
8. As the story comes to an end, Johnny is reflecting on the people and land about him. What do you think he is feeling?

The War for Independence Begins
Test

1. When did the War for Independence begin?

2. Where did the British set up a blockade to block commerce?

3. Where did Americans stockpile arms?

4. How did Paul Revere learn if the British were attacking by land or by sea?

5. Who went with Paul Revere to Lexington and Concord to warn them that the British were coming?

6. Describe the Battle of Lexington.

The War for Independence Begins

Test, Page 2

7. Describe the Battle of Concord.

Review

1. Write a paragraph describing Roger Williams and his life.

2. Write a paragraph describing the cause and outcome of the French and Indian Wars.

THE WAR FOR INDEPENDENCE BEGINS

Test, Page 3

5. In chronological order list all events studied to date. Next to each place the appropriate date.

British Lose at Bunker Hill
Worksheet

1. What is the date of the Battle of Bunker Hill?

____

____

____

2. Where was the Battle of Bunker Hill fought?

____

____

____

3. Which direction did the British commander send his troops up the hill? Was this wise?

____

____

____

____

4. Why were the Americans told, "Don't shoot till you see the whites of their eyes!"?

____

____

____

____

5. What was the outcome of the Battle at Bunker Hill?

____

____

____

____

British Lose at Bunker Hill

Project 1—Battle of Bunker Hill (June 17)

After reading about the battle of Bunker Hill, make a model replica of the battle. Most toy stores carry inexpensive plastic figures of the War for Independence. You may want to use clay or paper mache to construct the earth works.

The patriot leader, General Ward, having learned that the British intended to fortify Bunker Hill, determined to anticipate them. A body of men, under Colonel Prescott, were accordingly assembled at Cambridge, and, after prayer by the president of Harvard College, marched to Charlestown Neck. Breed's Hill was then chosen as a more commanding site than Bunker Hill. There was bright moonlight, and they were so near Boston that the sentinel's "All's well." was distinctly heard. Yet so quietly did they work that there was no alarm. At daylight, the British officers were startled by seeing the redoubt which had been constructed.

Resolved to drive the Americans from their position, Howe, the British general, crossed the river with three thousand men and formed them at the landing. The roofs and steeples of Boston were crowded with spectators, intently watching the troops as they slowly ascended the hill. The Patriot ranks lay quietly behind their earth-works until the Redcoats were within ten rods. When Prescott shouted "Fire!" a blaze of light shot from the redoubt, and whole platoons of the British fell. The survivors, unable to endure the terrible slaughter, broke and fled. They were rallied under cover of the smoke of Charlestown, which had been wantonly fired on by the British fleet. Again they were met by deadly discharge, and again they fled. Reinforcements being received, the third time they advanced. Only one volley smote them, and then the firing ceased. The American ammunition was exhausted. The British charged over the ramparts with fixed bayonets. The Patriots gallantly resisted with clubbed muskets, but were soon driven from the field.

The effect upon the Americans of this first regular battle was that of a victory. Their untrained farmer soldiers had put to flight the British veterans. All felt encouraged, and the determination to fight for liberty was intensified.

British Lose at Bunker Hill

Project 2–Benjamin Franklin Writes to England

During the Battle of Bunker Hill, the British fleet bombarded nearby Charlestown. By nightfall the greater part of the city was in ashes.

This act roused Benjamin Franklin's indignation, and be wrote a letter to his former friend Straban, a member of the English Parliament, which showed that, though he was a man of peace, be knew when to be angry.

Below you can read what Franklin wrote in his letter to Straban. As you are reading this, keep in mind that many friendships were broken during this war.

Philadelphia, July 5, 1775

Mr. Strahan,

You are a Member of Parliament, and one of that Majority which has doomed my Country to Destruction. You have begun to burn our Towns, and murder our People. Look upon your Hands! They are stained with the Blood of your Relations!! You and I were long Friends: You are now my Enemy, and I am

Yours,

Benj.a Franklin

British Lose at Bunker Hill
Test

Write a paragraph describing the Battle of Bunker Hill. Be sure to include details.

British Lose at Bunker Hill
Test, Page 2

Review

1. What was the First Great Awakening?

2. List the original thirteen colonies.

3. How many individuals were charged with "covenanting with evil spirits" during the Salem Witch Trials?

British Lose at Bunker Hill

Test, Page 3

4. Who settled Roanoke, Virginia?

5. In chronological order list all events studied to date. Next to each place the appropriate date.

America Declares its Independence
Worksheet

1. When did America declare its independence from England?

2. In spite of the fighting, what did Americans still hope King George would do?

3. What was King George's response?

4. What was "Common Sense"?

5. What was the Declaration of Independence? Who wrote it?

6. Who signed the Declaration of Independence by the time it became effective on July 4, 1776?

7. What did the Declaration of Independence make inevitable?

America Declares its Independence

Project 1—The Declaration of Independence

Read and discuss the Declaration of Independence.

When in the Course of human events, it becomes necessary for one people to dissolve the political bands which have connected them with another, and to assume among the powers of the earth, the separate and equal station to which the Laws of Nature and of Nature's God entitle them, a decent respect to the opinions of mankind requires that they should declare the causes which impel them to the separation.

We hold these truths to be self-evident, that all men are created equal, that they are endowed by their Creator with certain unalienable Rights, that among these are Life, Liberty and the pursuit of Happiness. That to secure these rights, Governments are instituted among Men, deriving their just powers from the consent of the governed. That whenever any Form of Government becomes destructive of these ends, it is the Right of the People to alter or to abolish it, and to institute new Government, laying its foundation on such principles and organizing its powers in such form, as to them shall seem most likely to effect their Safety and Happiness. Prudence, indeed, will dictate that Governments long established should not be changed for light and transient causes; and accordingly all experience hath shown, that mankind are more disposed to suffer, while evils are sufferable, than to right themselves by abolishing the forms to which they are accustomed. But when a long train of abuses and usurpations, pursuing invariably the same Object evinces a design to reduce them under absolute Despotism, it is their right, it is their duty, to throw off such Government, and to provide new Guards for their future security. Such has been the patient sufferance of these Colonies; and such is now the necessity which constrains them to alter their former Systems of Government. The history of the present King of Great Britain is a history of repeated injuries and usurpations, all having in direct object the establishment of an absolute Tyranny over these States. To prove this, let Facts be submitted to a candid world.

He has refused his Assent to Laws, the most wholesome and necessary for the public good.

He has forbidden his Governors to pass Laws of immediate and pressing importance, unless suspended in their operation till his Assent should be obtained; and when so suspended, he has utterly neglected to attend to them.

He has refused to pass other Laws for the accommodation of large districts of people, unless those people would relinquish the right of Representation in the Legislature, a right inestimable to them and formidable to tyrants only.

He has called together legislative bodies at places unusual, uncomfortable, and distant from the depository of their public Records, for the sole purpose of fatiguing them into compliance with his measures.

He has dissolved Representative Houses repeatedly, for opposing with manly firmness his invasions on the rights of the people.

He has refused for a long time, after such dissolutions, to cause others to be elected; whereby the Legislative powers, incapable of Annihilation, have returned to the People at large for their exercise; the State remain-

America Declares its Independence

Project 1, Page 2

ing in the mean time exposed to all the dangers of invasion from without, and convulsions within.

He has endeavoured to prevent the population of these States; for that purpose obstructing the Laws for Naturalization of Foreigners; refusing to pass others to encourage their migrations hither, and raising the conditions of new Appropriations of Lands.

He has obstructed the Administration of justice, by refusing his Assent to Laws for establishing judiciary powers.

He has made judges dependent on his Will alone, for the tenure of their offices, and the amount and payment of their salaries.

He has erected a multitude of New Offices, and sent hither swarms of Officers to harrass our people, and eat out their substance.

He has kept among us, in times of peace, Standing Armies without the Consent of our legislatures.

He has affected to render the Military independent of and superior to the Civil power.

He has combined with others to subject us to a jurisdiction foreign to our constitution, and unacknowledged by our laws; giving his Assent to their Acts of pretended Legislation:

For quartering large bodies of armed troops among us:

For protecting them, by a mock Trial, from punishment for any Murders which they should commit on the Inhabitants of these States:

For cutting off our Trade with all parts of the world:

For imposing Taxes on us without our Consent:

For depriving us in many cases, of the benefits of Trial by Jury:

For transporting us beyond Seas to be tried for pretended offences:

For abolishing the free System of English Laws in a neighbouring Province, establishing therein an Arbitrary government, and enlarging its Boundaries so as to render it at once an example and fit instrument for introducing the same absolute rule into these Colonies:

For taking away our Charters, abolishing our most valuable Laws, and altering fundamentally the Forms of our Governments:

For suspending our own Legislatures, and declaring themselves invested with power to legislate for us in all cases whatsoever.

He has abdicated Government here, by declaring us out of his Protection and waging War against us.

He has plundered our seas, ravaged our Coasts, burnt our towns, and destroyed the lives of our people.

He is at this time transporting large Armies of foreign Mercenaries to compleat the works of death, desolation and tyranny, already begun, with circumstances of Cruelty & perfidy scarcely paralleled in the most barbarous ages, and totally unworthy the Head of a civilized nation.

He has constrained our fellow Citizens taken Captive on the high Seas to bear Arms against their Country, to become the executioners of their friends and Brethren; or to fall themselves by their Hands.

He has excited domestic insurrections amongst us, and has endeavoured to bring on the inhabitants of our frontiers the merciless Indian Savages, whose known rule of warfare, is an undistinguished destruction of all ages, sexes and conditions.

In every stage of these Oppressions We have Petitioned for Redress in the most humble terms: Our repeated Petitions have been answered only by repeated injury. A Prince, whose character is thus marked by every act which may define a Tyrant, is

America Declares its Independence
Project 1, Page 3

unfit to be the ruler of a free people.

Nor have We been wanting in attentions to our British brethren. We have warned them from time to time of attempts by their legislature to extend an unwarrantable jurisdiction over us. We have reminded them of the circumstances of our emigration and settlement here. We have appealed to their native justice and magnanimity, and we have conjured them by the ties of our common kindred to disavow these usurpations, which, would inevitably interrupt our connections and correspondence. They too have been deaf to the voice of justice and of consanguinity. We must, therefore, acquiesce in the necessity, which denounces our Separation, and hold them, as we hold the rest of mankind, Enemies in War, in Peace Friends.

We, therefore, the Representatives of the united States of America, in General Congress, Assembled, appealing to the Supreme Judge of the world for the rectitude of our intentions, do, in the Name, and by Authority of the good People of these Colonies, solemnly publish and declare, That these United Colonies are, and of Right ought to be Free and Independent States; that they are Absolved from all Allegiance to the British Crown, and that all political connection between them, and the State of Great Britain, is and ought to be totally dissolved; and that as Free and Independent States, they have full Power to levy War, conclude Peace, contract Alliances, establish Commerce, and to do all other Acts and Things which Independent States may of right do. And for the support of this Declaration, with a firm reliance on the protection of divine Providence, we mutually pledge to each other our Lives, our Fortunes and our sacred Honor.

America Declares its Independence

Project 1, Page 4

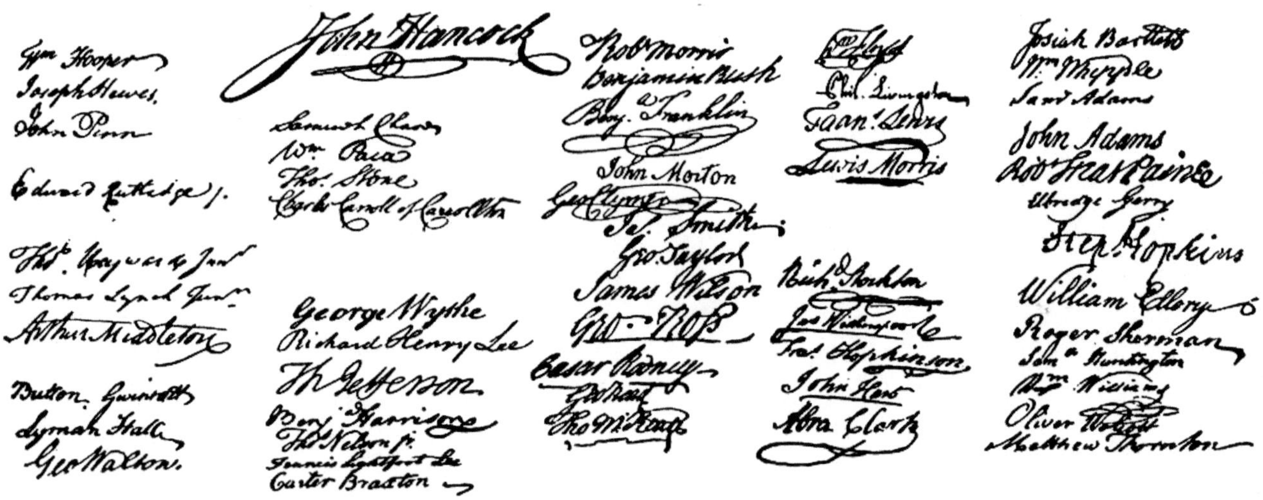

John Hancock

New Hampshire—Josiah Bartlett, William Whipple, Matthew Thornton.
Massachusetts Bay—Saml. Adams, John Adams, Robt. Treat Paine, Elbridge Gerry.
Rhode Island—Step. Hopkins, William Ellery.
Connecticut—Roger Sherman, Sam'el Huntington, Wm. Williams, Oliver Wolcott.
New York—Wm.Floyd, Phil. Livingston, Frans. Lewis, Lewis Morris.
New Jersey—Richd. Stockton, Jno. Witherspoon, Fras. Hopkinson, John Hart, Abra. Clark.
Pennsylvania—Robt. Morris, Benjamin Rush, Benja. Franklin, John Morton, Geo. Clymer, Jas. Smith, Geo. Taylor, James Wilson, Geo. Ross.
Delaware—Caesar Rodney, Geo. Read, Tho. M'Kean.
Maryland—Samuel Chase, Wm. Paca, Thos. Stone, Charles Carroll of Carrollton.
Virginia—George Wythe, Richard Henry Lee, Th. Jefferson, Benja. Harrison, Thos. Nelson Jr., Francis Lightfoot Lee, Carter Braxton.
North Carolina—Wm.Hooper, Joseph Hewes, John Penn.
South Carolina—Edward Rutledge, Thos. Heyward Junr, Thomas Lynch Junr, Arthur Middleton.
Georgia—Button Gwinnett, Lyman Hall, Geo. Walton.

America Declares its Independence

Project 2—"Common Sense"

Read the introduction to Thomas Paine's "Common Sense."

Perhaps the sentiments contained in the following pages, are not yet sufficiently fashionable to procure them general favor; a long habit of not thinking a thing wrong, gives it a superficial appearance of being right, and raises at first a formidable outcry in defence of custom. But the tumult soon subsides. Time makes more converts than reason.

As a long and violent abuse of power, is generally the Means of calling the right of it in question (and in matters too which might never have been thought of, had not the Sufferers been aggravated into the inquiry) and as the King of England had undertaken in his own Right, to support the Parliament in what he calls Theirs, and as the good people of this country are grievously oppressed by the combination, they have an undoubted privilege to inquire into the pretensions of both, and equally to reject the usurpation of either.

In the following sheets, the author hath studiously avoided every thing which is personal among ourselves. Compliments as well as censure to individuals make no part thereof. The wise, and the worthy, need not the triumph of a pamphlet; and those whose sentiments are injudicious, or unfriendly, will cease of themselves unless too much pains are bestowed upon their conversion.

The cause of America is in a great measure the cause of all mankind. Many circumstances hath, and will arise, which are not local, but universal, and through which the principles of all Lovers of Mankind are affected, and in the Event of which, their Affections are interested. The laying of a Country desolate with Fire and Sword, declaring War against the natural rights of all Mankind, and extirpating the Defenders thereof from the Face of the Earth, is the Concern of every Man to whom Nature hath given the Power of feeling; of which Class, regardless of Party Censures, is

THE AUTHOR.
Philadelphia, Feb. 14, 1776.

P.S. The Publication of this new Edition hath been delayed, with a View of taking notice (had it been necessary) of any Attempt to refute the Doctrine of Independence: As no Answer hath yet appeared, it is now presumed that none will, the Time needful for getting such a Performance ready for the Public being considerably past.

Who the Author of this Production is, is wholly unnecessary to the Public, as the Object for Attention is the Doctrine itself, not the Man. Yet it may not be unnecessary to say, That he is unconnected with any Party, and under no sort of Influence public or private, but the influence of reason and principle.

AMERICA DECLARES ITS INDEPENDENCE

Project 3—Fill in the Blank

Using the history card, fill in the missing blanks. This will help in memorizing the flashcard.

1. In spite of the fighting, Americans still hoped that ____________ ____________ would listen to their ____________ and that both sides would come to ____________ terms.
2. Instead of listening to American petitions, King George announced that American leaders were ____________, and under English law, would be ____________ and ____________ when caught.
3. Tom Paine wrote ____________ ____________, a pamphlet attacking King George and glorifying a free ____________; it became a best seller.
4. The colonies supported a public statement of their ____________ and ____________.
5. ____________ ____________ drafted the Declaration of Independence; ____________ ____________ made very few, but effective changes.
6. The Declaration was signed by a ____________ of the colonies and became effective ____________.
7. By ____________, all the colonies had signed the document.
8. The Declaration made all out _____ with Britain

America Declares its Independence
Test

1. In what year did America declare its independence from Britain?

2. What was King George's response to the American petitions?

3. What did Tom Paine write?

4. What was the Declaration of Independence? Who drafted it?

5. When did the Declaration become effective?

6. What did the Declaration of Independence make inevitable?

America Declares its Independence

Test, Page 2

Review

1. Write an essay describing three events previously covered this year that occurred since the founding of our country. Please write about them in chronological order.

2. In chronological order list all events studied to date. Next to each place the appropriate date.

America Declares its Independence
Test, Page 3

2. (continued)

WASHINGTON COMMANDS THE CONTINENTAL ARMY

Worksheet

1. What are the dates for Washington commanding the Continental Army?

2. When did George Washington become commander-in-chief of all the American armies?

3. Who won the first battles of the War for Independence? What did this cause to happen?

4. What was important about the victory at Saratoga?

5. What was John Paul Jones's involvement in the war?

6. Who was Francis Marion?

7. Why did Lord Cornwallis surrender in October 1781?

Washington Commands the Continental Army

Project 1—The Continental Soldier

The backwoods volunteers of 1775 resembled more of a mob than they did an army. The original plan was to organize 26 regiments of infantry, one regiment of artillery and one regiment of riflemen, but recruiting became, and remained, a problem. Most campaigns were waged using Continental Army units alongside local militia regiments. Through the military instruction of former Prussian officer Friedrich von Steuben, the Continental army became a first-class fighting machine.

Continental Artillery

A Light Dragoon

Continental Infantry

Friedrich Von Steuben

A Rifleman

Washington Commands the Continental Army

Project 2—Captain John Paul Jones and General Marion

Captain John Paul Jones

On a stormy afternoon in the year 1759, the villagers of the little fishing-hamlet of Arbigland, on the north coast of Solway Firth, Scotland, were gathered together in anxious groups along the shore to watch the progress of a small fishing-boat that was bravely struggling to get into the shelter of the harbor.

As the frail craft came nearer, her crew of two, man and a boy, was distinctly visible. The man was doing what sailors call "trimming the boat" by sitting on the weather-rail. The boy was making the fight, steering, handling the sheets, and commanding.

Among the watchers was one person who appeared to be especially interested in the boy in the boat. This gentleman was a shipowning merchant from Whitehaven, at the time the principal seaport on the Cumberland coast of England, and he had come to Arbigland to pick up seamen for his new brig, the "Friendship," which was ready to sail to the coast of Virginia in the colonies. His name was James Younger, and he was a Lowland Scotchman by birth.

As the northeast gale grew fiercer and the little boat tossed about in the teeth of the wind, the shipowner shook his head. "She can't weather it," he said, as he turned away. An old fisherman standing by heard the remark.

"That's my boy John conning the boat, Mr. Younger; he'll fetch her in."

It was old John Paul that spoke, the gardener of the Honorable Robert Craik, a county squire of the neighborhood; and his judgment in such matters was well known, for besides tending Mr. Craik's garden, the old man had been for many years a successful fisherman.

When, a little while after, the boat drew up alongside and was fastened, the Whitehaven merchant made haste to compliment the young sailor on his coolness and skill, and to the surprise of both father and son he then and there offered to send little John Paul as master's apprentice in the fine new vessel just about to sail for Virginia.

Old John was flattered and young John was wild with delight at the prospect, so it was soon settled between them that Mr. Younger's offer was to be accepted.

A few days later the "Friendship" sailed from Whitehaven with little John Paul aboard as a master's apprentice. Thirty-two days afterward she anchored in the Rappahannock River, near the present site of the town of Urbana in Virginia.

So it happened that the son of a humble Scotch gardener started upon a career that was to be one of the most wonderful in the naval history of the world. So it happened that the twelve-year-old boy, born at Kirkbean, Scotland, July 6, 1747, began his seafaring life on the blue water that was to be the stage of conflict and victory for the future hero of the ocean.

Being a sailor is not an easy thing now,

Washington Commands the Continental Army

Project 2, Page 2

but in 1759 it was a very hard thing indeed. Few boys of twelve years who go to school and live in comfortable homes can have any idea of the hardship of a sailor-boy's life of struggle with the winds and tides, a life of strict discipline, stern command and prompt obedience, rough work and coarse food: a hard life, but the sailor-boys loved it then and love it now.

One of John Paul's elder brothers, a long time before this, had immigrated to Virginia and had there been adopted by a Scotchman named William Jones. It chanced that when the "Friendship" dropped anchor in the Rappahannock she landed a very short distance below the plantation of this William Jones, so that little Paul found his brother, whom he had never seen before, almost immediately on his arrival in the new, strange country. William Jones took so great a liking to the master's apprentice that he offered to adopt him also. But sturdy John Paul, the sailor-boy, showed now the same determination and steadfastness of purpose that was in later life one of his chief traits of character. It was very pleasant to roam over the great plantation and exchange yarns, perhaps, with the black slave-children; pleasant to cruise about the Rappahannock in the plantation sloop; pleasant to ride across country with his elder brother, and go possum-hunting and coon-hunting with the "hands" at night when the work was done; but John Paul did not forget his resolve. He had made up his mind to follow the sea, and he could not be tempted to change his purpose. He thanked Mr. Jones, but declined the offer of adoption, and when the "Friendship" sailed off little John Paul sailed with her.

For the next ten years the young seaman continued in the merchant service, each year gaining greater skill and experience.

He was now in his twenty-seventh year, and it is not only a remarkable fact, but a lesson to every boy who has ambition, that this humbly born sailor-lad, who had had no schooling, no teacher, and indeed very little child-life, was at this time as well versed in naval history and tactical theories as any naval officer of his age in the British navy. He was also proficient in French and Spanish, and had a natural grace of manner that made him the peer of young gentlemen who had enjoyed the advantages of a college education and whose lives bad been passed in court circles.

William Jones had died in 1760, leaving the Virginia estate to John Paul, if his brother died without children, on condition that he should take the name of Jones. The brother was now dead, and by the terms of the will, to which the young heir consented, John Paul, now a captain in the merchant service, became John Paul Jones, Esquire, a Virginia planter. This happened in 1773. For two years Captain Jones lived the pleasant, free life of a colonial planter, leaving old Duncan McDean, the Scotch head farmer, or overseer, to attend to the business of the tobacco crops and other plantation affairs.

John Paul's tastes had always led him to prefer the society of cultured men and women rather than to be among the seafaring men who were to be found at the tav-

Washington Commands the Continental Army

Project 2, Page 3

ern and the coffeehouse, and John Paul Jones, by his indefatigable study, had fitted himself to take a place in such society.

The clouds from which the "lightning of Bunker Hill" was to flash were gathering thick and fast. Early in the spring Captain Jones, with his two slave-boys, Scipio and Cato, went to New York in the plantation sloop, and while there he heard the news of the battle of Lexington. This occurred on April 19, 1775.

Under date of April 27, 1775, Jones wrote a letter to his friend Mr. Hewes, copies of which were sent to Jefferson, Morris, and Livingston, in which he suggested the wisdom of "armament by land and by sea," and in which he offered his services should Congress make "provision for a naval force."

The Second Continental Congress met on June 10, and a naval commission was at once appointed. Ten days later this commission was authorized "to invite John Paul Jones, Esquire, Gent., of Virginia, Master Mariner," to give his service in the matter. From this moment John Paul Jones became the leading spirit of the commission, and by his foresight, his practical work in preparing for the conflict, as well as by the naval tactics he afterward employed, he earned and deserved the title of "Founder of the American Navy."

But there were many disappointments before him. In the first national navy list, John Paul Jones was placed as first lieutenant. After his important services this seems unjust, and many of his friends openly said he should be captain. "Let it go," said Lieutenant Jones. "Time will make all things even." And time certainly did.

On December 22, 1775, John Paul Jones, who was sixth on the list, was first to receive his commission. He was ordered to take command of the "Alfred." Obeying this order, he flung out the first American flag on a man-of-war. This was the "Pine-tree and Rattlesnake" emblem, not the Stars and Stripes. With him were Scipio and Cato, the two black boys, and an Indian boy by the name of Jeremiah, known on board the ship as "Red Cherry."

For two years Captain Jones was active in the naval service, and during this time he took so many prizes that his name was already well known to the enemy as well as to the patriots of the country and the cause he was fighting for—America and Independence.

On June 14, 1777, Congress passed two resolutions: "That the Flag of the United States of America be Thirteen Stripes, alternate red and white; that the Union be Thirteen Stars in a blue field; representing a new constellation." Also "That Captain John Paul Jones be appointed to command the ship *Range."*

Paul Jones, as people became accustomed to calling him, saw a meaning in this event. "That flag and I are twins," he said. "We cannot be parted in life or death; so long as we can float, we shall float together. If we must sink, we shall go down as one."

It is a pretty story that is told of how the first American flag, the *Ranger's* flag, was made. In old Portsmouth, where the *Ranger* was launched, a party of girls gave a "quilting-party" for the purpose of making a flag for Captain Jones, for which he had given them very particular directions. The stars were cut from the wedding-dress of Helen Seavey, who had just married a young officer of the New Hampshire Line, and the other girls cut slices off their best silk gowns for the field and stripes of the pennant, which was to win a renown that would reflect honor upon the fair hands that fashioned it. Helen Seavey, Mary

Washington Commands the Continental Army

Project 2, Page 4

Langdon, Caroline Chandler, Augusta Pierce, and Dorothy Hall (niece of the *Ranger's* second lieutenant) are the only names left to us of the historical "quilting-party." What girl today would not be proud to trace back to one of those maidens for a far off ancester!

The *Ranger* was ordered to take the news of Burgoyne's surrender to France, where our American commission was sitting with the object of gaining the aid of the French. If our French friends had not given us their help, we might not have whipped the English when and as we did. With hard work, trying duty, and terrible gales to fight, the crew of the *Ranger* found time for amusement, and Charlie Hill,the youngest midshipman, made up a song that was sung in the forecastle long after Revolutionary times:

"So now we had him hard and fast,
Burgoyne laid down his arms at last,
And that is why we brave the blast,
To carry the news to London.
Heigh-ho! Car-r-y the news
Go! Carry the news to London!
Tell old King George he's undone.
Heigh-ho! Carry the news!"

The most important part of the *Ranger's* career was her exploits on the west coast of England, where she completely destroyed the shipping of the British at Whitehaven. On the day after the descent upon the place, Captain Jones, with the *Ranger,* stood across the Irish Channel. Hearing that the English ship *Drake,* the guard-ship at Carrickfergus, was out after him, Jones determined to wait for her. The world knows the story of his famous victory, and how in reply to the *Drake's* challenge: "What ship is that?" the *Ranger's* captain said: "The American Continental ship *Ranger.* Come on! We are waiting for you." Scipio and Cato and "Red Cherry" were in this first great victory of the new sea-power, the American navy.

The young commander now tried to get a larger ship, but had to ask this of King Louis XVI of France, always America's friend. The favor was granted, the King giving him the ship *Duras,* whose name was changed to *Bonhomme Richard,* in compliment to Benjamin Franklin, who wrote under the name of "Goodman Richard."

The *Bonhomme Richard* gained one of the most remarkable victories known in history. She and her squadron took the English ship *Serapis* and her consort with a force very much inferior to the enemy's. A curious thing happened in this bloody fight. The *Bonhomme Richard* took fire from the *Serapis* and was sunk by the ship she conquered. So fierce was the struggle that at one time the English commander, Pearson, asked through the storm of shot and shell if Jones had struck. Back came the answer that has become famous all over the world: "I have not yet begun to fight."

That was the spirit of Paul Jones, and his crew was with him. Never was there a more gallant fight on both sides. Once an English officer asked of Pearson, "Has she struck?" "No," was the reply, "but we have." Brave Dick Dale, Jones's first lieutenant, was the first man over the rail of the doomed *Serapis.* The fight was over, but the *Bonhomme Richard* was sinking fast, and Captain Jones had to move his men into the conquered ship. The flag made by the Portsmouth "quilting-party" went down flying at the mast of the brave ship—the only ship on record that went down a conqueror!

The Duchess of Chartres, the richest lady in France, had given to the young American captain the watch of her grandfather, the

Washington Commands the Continental Army

Project 2, Page 5

Duke of Toulouse, and with that grace that was born in him, Jones had said: "I will consult your watch to time my victories, your Grace." After the battle, he wrote to the Duchess: "The enemy surrendered at ten forty-five. I looked at your watch to fix the moment of victory." Paul Jones was a courtier as well as a hero.

After the war with England was over, the Empress of Russia made him vice-admiral of her empire. Before that, Louis XVI had made him Chevalier of France, the only foreigner ever so honored in that country; so that in spite of many early disappointments and the jealousy of many of his brother officers, Paul Jones reaped a glorious reward for his labors.

Broken down in the prime of life, he resigned from the Russian service and went to Paris, where he died of lung trouble, July 18, 1792, at the age of forty-five. He was found lying with his face downward and holding in his hand the watch given by America's friend, the Duchess of Chartres.

For more than a century his body remained entombed in Paris. In 1905, escorted by warships of the navy whose beginnings owed so much to him, it was brought home to the United States and laid, with great honors, in one of the buildings of the Naval Academy at Annapolis.

Paul Jones had many faults, but he was a faithful friend and a true patriot. Had he lived, he would have been Admiral of France, for he was much beloved by the French people. He died in his boots and struggling. A sailor at twelve years of age, vice-admiral of an empire's navy at forty-three, Chevalier of France, patriot of America, he will live always as the ocean-hero of the world, the champion of freedom, the "Founder of the American Navy."

General Marion, the Carolina "Swamp Fox"

A hundred years ago, when boys had but few books of any kind, *The Life of General Marion* was their favorite book of adventure, because of its short stories of rare bravery and hairbreadth escapes. General Francis Marion, of whom the book tells, was a southern man, born the same year as General Washington, and a commander of some of the American troops in the War for Independence.

During that war, when the British found that they could accomplish little in the northern states, they decided to carry the war into the south. Lord Cornwallis was the British commander; under him Colonel Tarleton was a cavalry officer, notorious for bullying and cruelty, who became a terror to the whole region. Another commander of British troops in the south was a former American general, Benedict Arnold the traitor, who joined the British after he had failed to deliver West Point into the hands of the enemy.

General Horatio Gates was sent by the Congress to defend the south against the British. But General Gates was not a great or brave commander. He was defeated by Cornwallis at Camden, South Carolina. He lost two thousand men and the rest of his soldiers were scattered. Because of this terrible defeat—the worst in the whole War for Independence—the southern people were deeply discouraged.

What was to be done? In the south there were many Tories, as the people were called who believed that those who fought against England for liberty were rebels. Besides fighting in the British campaigns, the southern Tories went about in bands, shooting

Washington Commands the Continental Army

Project 2, Page 6

and injuring all the "rebels" they could. So the southern patriots gathered together in small companies to defend their families from the British and the Tories, and to prevent the British from capturing the whole southern country before Washington could send down a better general and another army.

During the months after the defeat at Camden, the fight was carried on in what was called *guerrilla* warfare (*guerrilla* being Spanish for "little war"). Small bands of Americans hid in the woods and swamps, and when they caught the British off guard, suddenly pounced upon them, taking or rescuing prisoners. The greatest leader of this kind of warfare on the American side was General Marion.

These southern soldiers had very poor weapons. Most of their guns were the kind used in shooting birds, and were loaded with shot instead of bullets. For swords they had wooden-handled saws with the teeth ground down to a smooth edge. They had but little to eat, often only potatoes which they could bake in the ashes of their campfires.

Their horses, however, were the finest and fastest in all that country. Although these men had to deny themselves food and clothing, their horses were well fed and groomed, for often the masters' lives depended on the fleetness of their steeds. And the horses sometimes acted as if they understood and enjoyed the terrible game of life and death their masters were playing.

Some of the bravest men in the South, seeing no other way to save or to serve their country, came and offered themselves to General Marion, to fight under the greatest hardships and risks in the most dangerous adventures. Among these was the famous Sergeant Jasper, who was one of the first to risk his life for the flag. Nine British ships-of-war attacked a fort in Charleston Harbor. They shot away the staff on which the American flag was flying; but Jasper jumped out, caught the banner before it touched the ground and climbed up and nailed it in place, while the guns were aimed at him as well as at the starry ensign.

While Sergeant Jasper was under General Marion he was often sent out on scout and spy duty. He had a natural talent for disguising himself. He went once to visit a sergeant in a British regiment. While he was there a number of American prisoners were brought in. Taking it for granted that a guard of ten British soldiers, with these prisoners, would pass a certain spring, Jasper left the British camp to obtain help. He found only one American who could go with him. The two hid themselves near the spring, surprised the ten Redcoats, disarmed them, and, with the former prisoners, marched gaily back to Marion's headquarters with the ten captured British soldiers.

Once when General Marion came to a river ferry, he heard that a company of ninety British regulars were taking more than two hundred captured Americans to the prison-ship at Charleston. The prisoners already in the hold of the ship were starved and neglected. Besides, smallpox had broken

WASHINGTON COMMANDS THE CONTINENTAL ARMY

Project 2, Page 7

out among them, and many of the best men among the patriots were dying of that loathsome disease. So General Marion ordered his men to ride through the darkness to the ford where the British and their prisoners had crossed the river a few hours before. Here they learned that the Redcoats and their charges were going to stay that night at a country tavern called the Blue House. The Americans approached this place with great caution. When they came to a wooden bridge, they took horse blankets and laid them down on the bridge to deaden the sound of the horses' hoofs.

Before deciding how to make an attack, General Marion sent several scouts to find out the lay of the land. With tread as sure and silent as that of moccasined Indians, the scouts returned and whispered this report:

"The officers are carousing in the house. Some of the men are outside. Many of them must be asleep, as we could not get a glimpse of them. A few sentinels are lounging about, without a thought of being attacked."

Marion told his men to lie down under the trees for a little rest. Very early in the morning, when all the British, including the sentinels, seemed to be asleep, he roused the men and ordered the attack.

The odds were over three to one against them, but Marion's men were used to that. They were taking a great risk, but there was much to be gained: guns, equipment and British prisoners who could be exchanged so as to release Americans from the prison-ship. Best of all, each man of the thirty might be the means of setting ten other Americans free.

When the men were well awake, General Marion sent a lieutenant ahead, directing him as follows:

"Take a few men with you, make a wide circle, and come in behind the house. Get as close to them as you can, and wait till I give the signal. Then close in on them and see that no one gets away. We must make quick work of this. See that your guns are all right."

To the men waiting with him he said, "Are you ready?"

"Ready, sir," they whispered back.

"Come on, then," he commanded. "Follow me. Don't make any noise. Don't speak. Watch me. Don't fire till I say the word."

They crept around the Blue House like Indians, testing every twig lest it snap, and feeling their way in the darkness. Suddenly a shot rang out in the early morning air. A sentinel on the other side of the house must have seen the lieutenant's men. The British soldiers, roused from a sound sleep, jumped about, peering this way and that in the darkness. No one knew what had happened, or what would happen next.

The officers came tumbling out, swearing and yelling. As the Americans came rushing in from all sides, shouting and shooting, the British thought they were attacked by an army instead of by thirty guerrillas. Marion's men grabbed the rifles of the British soldiers, shooting some and knocking others down. Some of the British

WASHINGTON COMMANDS THE CONTINENTAL ARMY

Project 2, Page 8

shouted, "Quarter!" and General Marion ordered his men to stop firing.

There was a wholesale surrender, and the hundreds of American prisoners were set free. Many of them joined Marion's men. When the British saw how they and their prisoners had been taken in, ten to one, they looked sheepish.

But the British leader, the bullying Colonel Tarleton, had made his escape. His motto seemed to be:

"He who fights and runs away
Will live to fight another day."

He ran away, at least, though he did not do any fighting first.

Five months after the battle of Camden, there was another battle at Cowpens. The British army, commanded by Tarleton, was only a little larger than the American. The Redcoats were so badly beaten that they lost over nine hundred men, while the American loss was only seventy-two.

One day, not long after, Tarleton was bullying a southern woman in her home, where he and some of his officers were quartered. There was, on the American side, a Colonel Washington, a distant relative of the commander-in-chief. In his insulting way, Tarleton asked, when the lady said this officer was a relative of hers, "What does Colonel Washington look like? I have never had the pleasure of meeting him."

"You might have seen him," said the lady, sweetly, "if you had looked behind you at the Battle of Cowpens!"

This polite way of calling him a coward made Tarleton very angry, but he was no match in wit for a brave and brilliant southern woman.

Though many of the wealthiest people of the south were Tories, some of them were true patriots. A widow named Motte had just built a beautiful home on a hilltop and had furnished it elegantly, when the British decided that it would make a fine fort and promptly took possession of it. General Marion and his guerrilla band surrounded the mansion and told Mrs. Motte, who was then staying in a neighbor's house, that if he could set her house afire he could "smoke out" the British and capture them. That woman patriot was glad to sacrifice her lovely home for the good of her country, so Marion burned down the mansion and made the redcoats his prisoners.

WASHINGTON COMMANDS THE CONTINENTAL ARMY

Project 2, Page 9

Have the students write a summary on either John Paul Jones or General Marion. Upon completion have the student read the summary aloud to his class or family. Have the student field questions regarding his understanding of the person about whom he wrote.

Washington Commands the Continental Army

Test

1. In what years did Washington command the Continental Army?

2. When and how did Washington become commander-in-chief of the American armies?

3. Why were many Americans enlisting in the early years?

4. Why did Americans flee to Valley Forge?

5. What was important about the victory at Saratoga?

6. Who said, "I have not yet begun to fight!" and during what circumstances did he say it?

WASHINGTON COMMANDS THE CONTINENTAL ARMY

Test, Page 2

7. Who surrendered in October of 1781?

Review

1. Who was Ferdinand Magellan? What did he do that was important?

2. Who funded Columbus's voyages?

3. What did Hernando de Soto discover?

4. Who founded Quebec?

Washington Commands the Continental Army

Test, Page 3

5. In chronological order list all events studied to date. Next to each place the appropriate date.

WINTER AT VALLEY FORGE
Worksheet

1. What is the date given for the Winter at Valley Forge?

____

____

2. Why did the American army encamp at Valley Forge?

____

____

____

3. Why did Washington himself refuse to live in comfort when the men first arrived at Valley Forge?

____

____

____

____

4. Who helped Washinton turn the army into well-trained, disciplined troops?

____

____

5. When France joined America, what did they contribute to the War?

____

____

____

6. How did Washington's army finally emerge from Valley Forge?

____

____

Winter at Valley Forge
Project 1—Correspondence from Valley Forge

Read the following two letters written by General George Washington at Valley Forge. The first is to Governor Clinton of New York asking for aid. The second letter is to the Continental Congress during the difficult winter his army spent camped at Valley Forge. Assurances from Congress that food and clothing would be sent were not fulfilled, and Washington was faced with the unpalatable choice of seizing supplies from the local population wherever he could find them.

To Governor George Clinton
Head Quarters, Valley Forge
February 16, 1778

Dear Sir:

It is with great reluctance I trouble you on a subject which does not fall within your province; but it is a subject that occasions me more distress than I have felt, since the commencement of the war; and which loudly demands the most zealous exertions of every person of weight and authority, who is interested in the success of our affairs. I mean the present dreadful situation of the army for want of provisions, and the miserable prospects before us, with respect to futurity. It is more alarming than you will probably conceive, for, to form a just idea, it were necessary to be on the spot. For some days past, there has been little less than a famine in camp. A part of the army has been a week, without any kind of flesh, and the rest for three or four days. Naked and starving as they are, we cannot enough admire the incomparable patience and fidelity of the soldiery, that they have not been ere this excited by their sufferings, to a general mutiny or dispersion. Strong symptoms, however, discontent have appeared in particular instances; and nothing but the most active efforts every where can long avert so shocking a catastrophe.

Our present sufferings are not all. There is no foundation laid for any adequate relief hereafter. All the magazines provided in the States of New Jersey, Pensylvania, Delaware and Maryland, and all the immediate additional supplies they seem capable of affording, will not be sufficient to support the army more than a month longer, if so long. Very little has been done to the Eastward, and as little to the Southward; and whatever we have a right to expect from those quarters, must necessarily be very remote; and is indeed more precarious, than could be wished. When the forementioned supplies are exhausted, what a terrible crisis must ensue, unless all the energy of the Continent is exerted to provide a timely remedy?

Impressed with this idea, I am, on my part, putting every engine to work, that I can possibly think of, to prevent the fatal consequences, we have so great a reason to apprehend. I am calling upon all those, whose stations and influence enable them to contribute their aid upon so important an occasion; and from your well-known zeal, I expect every thing within the compass of your power, and that the abilities and resources of the state over which you preside, will admit. I am sensible of the disadvantages it labours under, from having been so long the scene of war, and that it must be exceedingly drained by the great demands to which it has been subject. But, tho' you may not be able to contribute materially to our relief, you can perhaps do something towards it; and any assistance, however trifling in itself, will be of great moment at so critical a juncture, and will conduce to keeping the army together till the Commissary's department can be put upon a better footing,

Winter at Valley Forge

Project 1, Page 2

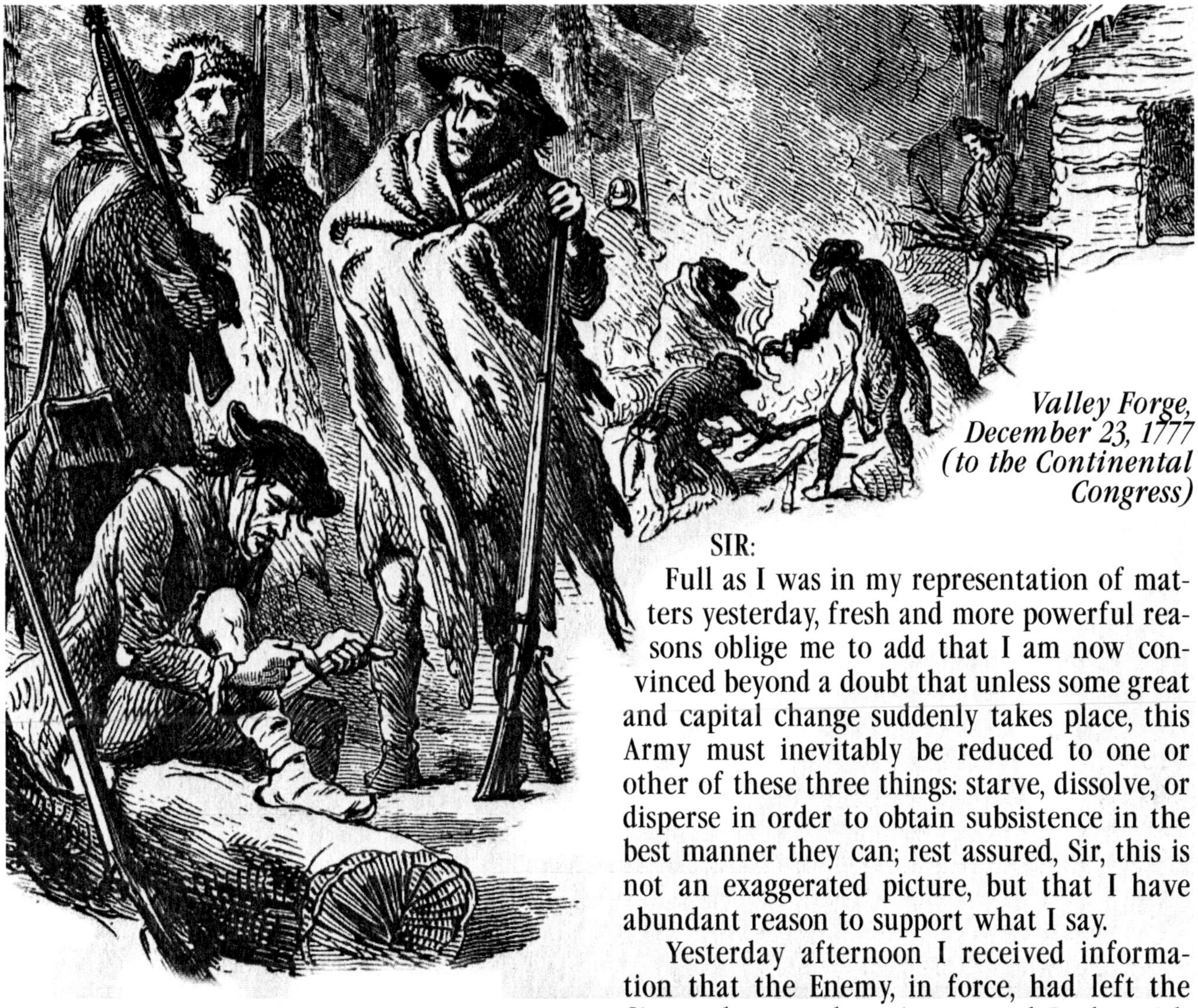

Valley Forge,
December 23, 1777
(to the Continental
Congress)

SIR:

Full as I was in my representation of matters yesterday, fresh and more powerful reasons oblige me to add that I am now convinced beyond a doubt that unless some great and capital change suddenly takes place, this Army must inevitably be reduced to one or other of these three things: starve, dissolve, or disperse in order to obtain subsistence in the best manner they can; rest assured, Sir, this is not an exaggerated picture, but that I have abundant reason to support what I say.

Yesterday afternoon I received information that the Enemy, in force, had left the City and were advancing toward Derby with apparent design to forage and draw Subsistence from that part of the Country. I order'd the Troops to be in readiness, that I might give every opposition in my power; when, behold! To my great mortification, I was not only informed but convinced that the men were unable to stir on account of Provision, and that a dangerous mutiny begun the night before and with difficulty was suppressed by the spirited exertions of some officers . . .

All I could do under these circumstances and effectual measures concerted to secure a permanent and competent supply. What methods you can take, you will be the best judge of; but, if you can devise any means to procure a quantity of cattle, or other kind of flesh, for the use of this army, to be at camp in the course of a month, you will render a most essential service to the common cause. I have the honor etc.

WINTER AT VALLEY FORGE

Project 1, Page 3

was to send out a few light parties to watch and harrass the enemy, whilst other parties were instantly detached different ways to collect, if possible, as much provision as would satisfy the present pressing wants of the Soldiery. But will this answer? No, Sir: three or four days' bad weather would prove our destruction. What then is to become of the Army this winter? And if we are as often without provisions now, what is to become of us in the Spring, when our force will be collected, with the aid perhaps of the militia, to take advantage of an early campaign before the enemy can be reinforced? These are considerations of great magnitude, meriting the closest attention, and will, when my own reputation is so intimately connected . . . justify my saying that the present commissaries are by no means equal to the execution [of their office]. Though I have been tender heretofore of giving any opinion or lodging complaints . . . it is time to speak plain in exculpation of myself. With truth, then, I can declare that no man, in my opinion, ever had his measures more impeded than I have by every department of the Army . . .

We find gentlemen, without knowing whether the army was really going into winter quarters or not, reprobating the measure [to properly supply the army] as much as if they thought the soldiers were made of rocks or stones, and equally insensible to frost and snow and moreover, as if they conceived it practicable for an inferior army under the disadvantages I have described ours to be, which is by no means exaggerated, to confine a superior one (in all respects well appointed, and provided for a winter campaign) within the city of Philadelphia, and cover from depredation and waste the states of Pennsylvania, New Jersey, etc. . . .

I can assure those gentlemen that it is a much easier and less distressing thing to draw remonstrances in a comfortable room by a good fireside than to occupy a cold, bleak hill and sleep under frost and snow, without clothes or blankets. However, although they seem to have little feeling for the naked and distressed soldiers, I feel abundantly for them and from my soul I pity those miseries which it is neither in my power to relieve nor prevent.

It is for these reasons, therefore, that I have dwelt upon the subject; and it adds not a little to my other difficulties and distress to find that much more is expected from me than is possible to be performed, and that upon the ground of safety and policy I am obliged to conceal the true state of the army from public view, and thereby expose myself to detraction and calumny . . .

In short there is as much to be done in preparing for a campaign as in the active part of it; in fine, everything depends upon the preparation that is made in the several departments in the course of this winter, and the success or misfortunes of next campaign will more than probably originate with our activity or supineness this winter.

George Washington

Winter at Valley Forge

Project 2—Weather Report at Valley Forge 1775-1782

The winter at Valley Forge was a rough one. But a winter encampment at Morristown, New Jersey, was worse. The Valley Forge Encampment was difficult because the soldiers lacked proper clothing and proper meals. There were seven winters during the Revolutionary War.

There are two excellent resources providing an account of the weather situation in the Philadelphia region during the winter of 1777-1778. One is that of Thomas Coombe, from his residence "two miles west of Philadelphia" (which would be in the city today) and that of Rev. Henry Melchior Muhlenberg, from Providence (now Trappe, approximately 10-12 miles from Valley Forge), near the Perkiomen River in Montgomery County.

The Encampment saw basically two periods of severe cold. The end of December with a low of 6 Degrees and the end of March with a low of 8 Degrees. The low in January reached 12 Degrees and February was 16 Degrees. The troops arrived at Valley Forge on the 19th of December and eight days later, the deepest single snow of the season fell, which was followed by the severest cold. They were plagued by bouts of cold, which would thaw and then refreeze. You can imagine what a muddy mess it would have been working on drills.

There were three continued snowstorms, but not of a blizzard-like quality. More moderate to heavy covering. "There was heavy snowfall" according to Dr. Muhlenberg on the 8th of February, "deeper now than we have had the whole winter," but was washed away by a heavy rainfall within the next 2 to 3 days. The heavy snowfall of the 8th, compounded by the heavy rainfall brought some flooding conditions . . . which made roads impassable.

Between the cold and freezing temperatures, there were even some above average warm temperatures during the encampment when some thaws set in. These included some days around Christmas and then approximately three periods in January lasting for several days at a time.

With a lack of proper clothing, and the inadequacies of the temporary military housing in the log huts, built during some foul weather, it was not a pleasant winter for the Continental Army. But through it all, they persevered, and we can thank them for our freedom.

Weather Report

Winters during the War for Independence:

1775-1776	Moderate
1776-1777	Moderate
1777-1778	**Moderate**
1778-1779	Mild
1779-1780	Severe
1780-1781	Mild
1781-1782	Severe

WINTER AT VALLEY FORGE

Project 3—French Alliance Brings Joy to Washington at Valley Forge

The Treaty of Alliance between France and the United States was concluded at Paris February 6, 1778 and ratified by Congress May 4, 1778. The treaty provided for a defensive alliance to aid France should England attack, and that neither France nor the United States would make peace with England until the independence of the United States was recognized. The knowledge of the Alliance came to Washington on May Day, 1778. One week later General George Washington issued the following general order:

"It having pleased the Almighty Ruler of the universe to defend the course of the United States, and finally raise up a powerful friend among the princes of the earth, to establish our Liberty and Independence upon a lasting foundation, it becomes us to set apart a day for gratefully acknowledging the Divine goodness, and celebrating the important event which we owe to His Divine interposition. The several brigades are to assemble for this purpose at nine o'clock tomorrow morning, when their chaplains will communicate the information contained in the postscript of the Pennsylvania Gazette of the 2nd instant, and offer up a thanksgiving and deliver a discourse suitable to the event. At half past ten o'clock a cannon will be fired which is to be a signal for the men to be under arms. The Brigade Inspectors will then inspect their dress and arms, and form the battalions according to the instructions given them, and announce to the commanding officers of the brigade that the battalions are formed. The commanders of the brigades will then appoint the field officers to the battalions, after which each battalion will be ordered to load and ground their arms. At half past seven o'clock a second cannon will be fired as a signal for the march; upon which the several brigades will begin their march by wheeling to the right by platoons, and proceed by the nearest way to the left of their ground by the new position. This will be pointed out by the Brigade Inspectors. A third signal will then be given, on which there will be a discharge of thirteen cannon; after which a running fire of the infantry will begin on the left of the second line and continue to the right. Upon a signal given, the whole army will huzza, 'Long Live the King of France.' The artillery then begins again and fires thirteen rounds; this will be succeeded by a second general discharge of musketry, in running fire, and a huzza, 'Long Live the Friendly European Powers.' The last discharge of thirteen pieces of artillery will be given, followed by a general running and huzza, 'The American States'."

The Commander-in-Chief and staff were the guests of the Jersey troops during the religious services of the day, after which the general officers of the command joined him at the Potts mansion, whereat was served one of those famous dinners for which Washington always manifested a fondness.

The length and breadth of Washington's exuberance upon the arrival of the good news can not be more effectively shown than in the fact that two soldiers awaiting execution in camp were pardoned and restored to the ranks by him in testimony of his joy. When we consider how rarely the Commander-in-Chief modified or reversed the finding of his courts martial, we may realize the meaning of this gift of life to men who, perhaps, did not deserve it.

Winter at Valley Forge

Project 4—Colonial Espionage

All throughout history, where there is war, there is espionage (spying). The War for Independence was no different. Following are two examples of the covert operations that occurred in the colonies at that time.

The Clark Ring

Major John Clark Jr. of Pennsylvania, Aide-de-Camp to Major General Nathaniel Greene, was born in Lancaster, and practiced law in York County. Clark developed a spy ring that gathered information on the British activities in New Jersey, Pennsylvania and Delaware. One method of obtaining information from Philadelphia was that he "counterfeited the Quaker" writing a "few lines to Sir William" Howe, the British commander, "informing him the rebels had plundered me, and that I was determined to risque my all in procuring him intelligence" in revenge; "that the bearer would give him my name," which was that of an anonymous prominent Chester Countian known to favor the British cause. Sir William gave Clark's spy a pass, which enabled the spy to walk freely about the city and gather information on British defenses, dispositions, munitions, etc., all of which he reported to Clark in great detail, forwarded in the same letter to Washington. The spy also reported that "The inhabitants" of the city "are suffering" for want of provisions.

The day after the Continental Army marched from Gulph Mills to Valley Forge, Clark notified Washington, that the enemy "intend to make another foraging excursion . . . and then pull up and destroy the bridge" at the Middle Ferry and then remain "quiet in winter quarters, for the remainder of the season." If the latter information was correct, Washington could be reassured that the enemy had little or no intention of attacking his ragged, starving army at Valley Forge. Nevertheless, he would have to remain very watchful. He also noted that "The enemy are busy turning the inhabitants of Philadelphia "out of their houses, and quartering troops in them. Many of the citizens are obliged to live in their kitchens, and permit those tyrants to occupy their houses."

The Culper Ring

Washington appointed Major Benjamin Tallmadge to organize a bureau of secret service for the colonies. He also recruited one of our nation's best spies, Robert Townsend. To Townsend and his ring was given the dangerous task of spying in and around King George's headquarters in New York. Into the patriot sport of spying Townsend (code named: Samuel Culper, Jr.) brought his friends Abraham Woodhull (Samuel Culper, Sr.), Austin Roe, and Caleb Brewster (as well as Townsend's mistress, the mysterious "355") into the ring which Tallmadge (Mr. John Bolton) managed.

Nathan Hale—America's brave (but foolhardy) spy whose amateur attempt in covert intelligence activity against the British in 1776 was so inept that it virtually assured his capture and death. Hale has gained an immortality far outweighing his usefulness to the American cause due to the inspiring dying words that are attributed to him, "I regret that I have but one life to give for my country."

WINTER AT VALLEY FORGE

Project 4, Page 2

John Jay—the brother of Sir James Jay who claimed to have invented the ink used by the colonies' secret service. James Jay forwarded the first authentic account of the British plot to force the colonies into unconditional submission. James Jay writes of his secret correspondence: "To prevent the suspicion which might arise were I to write my brother John only, who was member of congress, I write with black ink a short letter to him and likewise to one or two other persons of the family, none exceeding three or four lines in black ink. The residue of blank paper I filled up, invisibly, with such intelligence and matters as I thought would be useful to the American Cause. All these letters were left open."

To protect their espionage efforts, they used invisible ink and a complicated code that swapped letters of the alphabet and used numbers for people and places. For example, "Dqpeu Beyocpu agreeable to 28 met 723 not far from 727 & received a 356" reads as "Jonas Hawkins agreeable to appointment met Robert Townsend not far from New York." Following are some of the code numbers they used:

15 advice
286 ink
345 knowledge
355 lady
356 letter
592 ships
711 George Washington
721 John Bolton
722 Samuel Culper, Sr.
723 Samuel Culper, Jr.
724 Austin Roe
725 Caleb Brewster
727 New York
728 Long Island
729 Setauket
745 England

To run information through to General Washington, they would begin by having Austin Roe, a farmer and reknowned horseman, enter Townsend's waterfront dry-goods business at 18 Smith Street with an "order" for his neighbors. Townsend would wrap up the order with a blank sheet inside which used Jay's sympathetic stain to invisibly transmit secrets. Roe would ride back to Setauket and put the message in a drop box hidden in a field owned by Woodhull where Roe pastured his cattle. Woodhull would retrieve it, brush on the restorative solution and transcribe the note. A black petticoat and a number of handkerchiefs hanging across the bay on a clothesline would tell him where to meet Caleb Brewster's whaleboat. Brewster delivered the reconnaissance to Tallmadge in Fairfield and then the messages would be taken to Washington's headquarter's by the Hudson.

John Andre—a spy and conspirator with Benedict Arnold—was hanged at high noon on October 2, 1780. He was admired by many for his literacy, musical and artistic talents.

Space does not permit a full account of the Culper Ring or other spies of the War of Independence, like the Quakeress Lydia Darrah, Silas Town, Colonel Barton's Rhode Island militiamen and James Rivington, a New York bookseller who helped mask Washington's descent upon Cornwallis at Yorktown. Try the Culper Ring and James Jay's method of covert communication using one of the recipes for invisible ink.

Winter at Valley Forge

Project 4, Page 3

Making Invisible Ink

Heat-sensitive invisible inks are organic liquids that will appear invisible once they have dried on a sheet of paper, but will darken when held over a heat source. Lemon juice or onion juice work best, with milk or vinegar lagging close behind. They can be applied with a pen or toothpick. Allow to air dry (don't use heat to dry it). The dried paper is held some distance over a candle, or pressed with a hot iron. There is danger of the paper catching on fire with the candle, or scorching under the iron, so take the necessary precautions. It will be a little smoky, but the message should appear fairly quickly.

An alternative to the organic liquids is to use a cornstarch and water mixture. Mix about 1 tsp (5 ml) cornstarch to 1/4 cup (60 ml) of water. Cook it a bit (you can microwave it for a minute, stirring once). Let it cool, and write your message. Once dry, sponge it with a solution of iodine and water (10 or so drops in 1/4 cup of water). Your writing will appear in a dark blue, and the paper will be a lighter blue. If you substitute lemon juice for the cornstarch solution, you will end up with white text on a light blue background.

This next one is a little tricky to do, and does not always turn out completely invisible. The reacting chemical in the ink is phenolphthalein, which is a component of some laxatives. Phenolphthalein alone makes an invisible ink, but often the other components of the laxative tablet will give the ink a color. It will still produce a nice reaction.

Supplies

laxative pill (containing phenolphthalein)

washing soda (or another safe alkali)

paper

water

jar for mixing

plate

Directions

1. If the tablets you are using have a colored coating, it will need to be scraped off. Use 5 or 6 tablets. Crush the tablets with a spoon in a jar.
2. Add a couple of inches of water to the jar and mix.
3. Use this "ink" to write your secret message.
4. Allow to dry.
5. To make it visible, mix four teaspoons of washing soda with four tablespoons of hot water.
6. Lay the paper over a plate where a bit of water has been poured. You want the paper to soak up the water and saturate.
7. Carefully dribble the washing soda solution onto the paper, allowing the drops to spread over the entire surface. Don't touch the paper where the message is while it is wet, as this will smear it.
8. The writing should appear pink.

Winter at Valley Forge

Test

1. What is the date for the Winter at Valley Forge?

2. Write a paragraph describing the living conditions under which Washington and his men found themselves when they first arrived in Valley Forge and the months in which they lived there.

3. Who was General Baron von Steuben?

4. With whom did France side during the War?

Winter at Valley Forge
Test, Page 2

5. Finish the following sentence: Washington's army emerged from Valley Forge . . .

Review

1. What is cartography?

2. Why is Roanoke called the "Lost Colony"?

3. Who was John Smith?

4. In chronological order list all events studied to date. Next to each place the appropriate date.

Winter at Valley Forge

Test, Page 3

4. (continued)

Yorktown and the Treaty of Paris
Worksheet

1. Where did Washington trap the British army?

2. Who blockaded the Chesapeake Bay?

3. What song did the British play at the surrender?

4. What was the treaty called? When was it signed?

5. What did the treaty recognize?

6. How were the colonies organized?

YORKTOWN AND THE TREATY OF PARIS
Project 1—Newspaper Headlines

Write a front page newspaper story for the surrender at Yorktown and the Treaty of Paris. Look at an actual front page for layout ideas or use the grid below. A good news story answers the following questions: Who? What? When? Where? Why? *and* How? *List relevant questions before you begin to write your stories. Keep in mind the treaty was signed in 1783 even though the surrender was in 1781.*

Newspaper masthead

Headline

Yorktown and the Treaty of Paris

Project 2—The Paris Peace Treaty (1783)

Read the actual text of the Paris Peace Treaty

In the name of the most holy and undivided Trinity.

It having pleased the Divine Providence to dispose the hearts of the most serene and most potent Prince George the Third, by the grace of God, king of Great Britain, France, and Ireland, defender of the faith, duke of Brunswick and Lunebourg, arch-treasurer and prince elector of the Holy Roman Empire etc., and of the United States of America, to forget all past misunderstandings and differences that have unhappily interrupted the good correspondence and friendship which they mutually wish to restore, and to establish such a beneficial and satisfactory intercourse, between the two countries upon the ground of reciprocal advantages and mutual convenience as may promote and secure to both perpetual peace and harmony; and having for this desirable end already laid the foundation of peace and reconciliation by the Provisional Articles signed at Paris on the 30th of November 1782, by the commissioners empowered on each part, which articles were agreed to be inserted in and constitute the Treaty of Peace proposed to be concluded between the Crown of Great Britain and the said United States, but which treaty was not to be concluded until terms of peace should be agreed upon between Great Britain and France and his Britannic Majesty should be ready to conclude such treaty accordingly; and the treaty between Great Britain and France having since been concluded, his Britannic Majesty and the United States of America, in order to carry into full effect the Provisional Articles above mentioned, according to the tenor thereof, have constituted and appointed, that is to say his Britannic Majesty on his part, David Hartley, Esqr., member of the Parliament of Great Britain, and the said United States on their part, John Adams, Esqr., late a commissioner of the United States of America at the court of Versailles, late delegate in Congress from the state of Massachusetts, and chief justice of the said state, and minister plenipotentiary of the said United States to their high mightinesses the States General of the United Netherlands; Benjamin Franklin, Esqr., late delegate in Congress from the state of Pennsylvania, president of the convention of the said state, and minister plenipotentiary from the United States of America at the court of Versailles; John Jay, Esqr., late president of Congress and chief justice of the state of New York, and minister plenipotentiary from the said United States at the court of Madrid; to be plenipotentiaries for the concluding and signing the present definitive treaty; who after having reciprocally communicated their respective full powers have agreed upon and confirmed the following articles.

Article 1:

His Britannic Majesty acknowledges the said United States, viz., New Hampshire, Massachusetts Bay, Rhode Island and Providence Plantations, Connecticut, New York, New Jersey, Pennsylvania, Maryland, Virginia, North Carolina, South Carolina and Georgia, to be free sovereign and independent states, that he treats with them as such, and for himself, his heirs, and successors, relinquishes all claims to the government, propriety, and territorial rights of the same and every part thereof.

Yorktown and the Treaty of Paris
Project 2, Page 2

Article 2:

And that all disputes which might arise in future on the subject of the boundaries of the said United States may be prevented, it is hereby agreed and declared, that the following are and shall be their boundaries, viz.; from the northwest angle of Nova Scotia, viz., that angle which is formed by a line drawn due north from the source of St. Croix River to the highlands; along the said highlands which divide those rivers that empty themselves into the river St. Lawrence, from those which fall into the Atlantic Ocean, to the northwesternmost head of Connecticut River; thence down along the middle of that river to the forty-fifth degree of north latitude; from thence by a line due west on said latitude until it strikes the river Iroquois or Cataraquy; thence along the middle of said river into Lake Ontario; through the middle of said lake until it strikes the communication by water between that lake and Lake Erie; thence along the middle of said communication into Lake Erie, through the middle of said lake until it arrives at the water communication between that lake and Lake Huron; thence along the middle of said water communication into Lake Huron, thence through the middle of said lake to the water communication between that lake and Lake Superior; thence through Lake Superior northward of the Isles Royal and Phelipeaux to the Long Lake; thence through the middle of said Long Lake and the water communication between it and the Lake of the Woods, to the said Lake of the Woods; thence through the said lake to the most northwesternmost point thereof, and from thence on a due west course to the river Mississippi; thence by a line to be drawn along the middle of the said river Mississippi until it shall intersect the northernmost part of the thirty-first degree of north latitude, South, by a line to be drawn due east from the determination of the line last mentioned in the latitude of thirty-one degrees of the equator, to the middle of the river Apalachicola or Catahouche; thence along the middle thereof to its junction with the Flint River, thence straight to the head of Saint Mary's River; and thence down along the middle of Saint Mary's River to the Atlantic Ocean; east, by a line to be drawn along the middle of the river Saint Croix, from its mouth in the Bay of Fundy to its source, and from its source directly north to the aforesaid highlands which divide the rivers that fall into the Atlantic Ocean from those which fall into the river Saint Lawrence; comprehending all islands within twenty leagues of any part of the shores of the United States, and lying between lines to be drawn due east from the points where the aforesaid boundaries between Nova Scotia on the one part and East Florida on the other shall, respectively, touch the Bay of Fundy and the Atlantic Ocean, excepting such islands as now are or heretofore have been within the limits of the said province of Nova Scotia.

Article 3:

It is agreed that the people of the United States shall continue to enjoy unmolested the right to take fish of every kind on the Grand Bank and on all the other banks of Newfoundland, also in the Gulf of Saint Lawrence and at all other places in the sea, where the inhabitants of both countries used at any time heretofore to fish. And also that the inhabitants of the United States shall have liberty to take fish of every kind on such part of the coast of Newfoundland as British fishermen shall use, (but not to dry or cure the same on that island) and

Yorktown and the Treaty of Paris

Project 2, Page 3

also on the coasts, bays and creeks of all other of his Britannic

Majesty's dominions in America; and that the American fishermen shall have liberty to dry and cure fish in any of the unsettled bays, harbors, and creeks of Nova Scotia, Magdalen Islands, and Labrador, so long as the same shall remain unsettled, but so soon as the same or either of them shall be settled, it shall not be lawful for the said fishermen to dry or cure fish at such settlement without a previous agreement for that purpose with the inhabitants, proprietors, or possessors of the ground.

Article 4:

It is agreed that creditors on either side shall meet with no lawful impediment to the recovery of the full value in sterling money of all bona fide debts heretofore contracted.

Article 5:

It is agreed that Congress shall earnestly recommend it to the legislatures of the respective states to provide for the restitution of all estates, rights, and properties, which have been confiscated belonging to real British subjects; and also of the estates, rights, and properties of persons resident in districts in the possession on his Majesty's arms and who have not borne arms against the said United States. And that persons of any other description shall have free liberty to go to any part or parts of any of the thirteen United States and therein to remain twelve months unmolested in their endeavors to obtain the restitution of such of their estates, rights, and properties as may have been confiscated; and that Congress shall also earnestly recommend to the several states a reconsideration and revision of all acts or laws regarding the premises, so as to render the said laws or acts perfectly consistent not only with justice and equity but with that spirit of conciliation which on the return of the blessings of peace should universally prevail. And that Congress shall also earnestly recommend to the several states that the estates, rights, and properties, of such last mentioned persons shall be restored to them, they refunding to any persons who may be now in possession the bona fide price (where any has been given) which such persons may have paid on purchasing any of the said lands, rights, or properties since the confiscation.

And it is agreed that all persons who have any interest in confiscated lands, either by debts, marriage settlements, or otherwise, shall meet with no lawful impediment in the prosecution of their just rights.

Article 6:

That there shall be no future confiscations made nor any prosecutions commenced against any person or persons for, or by reason of, the part which he or they may have taken in the present war, and that no person shall on that account suffer any future loss or damage, either in his person, liberty, or property; and that those who may be in confinement on such charges at the time of the ratification of the treaty in America shall be immediately set at liberty, and the prosecutions so commenced be discontinued.

Article 7:

There shall be a firm and perpetual peace between his Britannic Majesty and the said states, and between the subjects of the one and the citizens of the other, wherefore all hostilities both by sea and land shall from henceforth cease. All prisoners on both sides shall be set at liberty, and his Britannic Majesty shall with all convenient

Yorktown and the Treaty of Paris
Project 2, Page 4

speed, and without causing any destruction, or carrying away any Negroes or other property of the American inhabitants, withdraw all his armies, garrisons, and fleets from the said United States, and from every post, place, and harbor within the same; leaving in all fortifications, the American artillery that may be therein; and shall also order and cause all archives, records, deeds, and papers belonging to any of the said states, or their citizens, which in the course of the war may have fallen into the hands of his officers, to be forthwith restored and delivered to the proper states and persons to whom they belong.

Article 8:

The navigation of the river Mississippi, from its source to the ocean, shall forever remain free and open to the subjects of Great Britain and the citizens of the United States.

Article 9:

In case it should so happen that any place or territory belonging to Great Britain or to the United States should have been conquered by the arms of either from the other before the arrival of the said Provisional Articles in America, it is agreed that the same shall be restored without difficulty and without requiring any compensation.

Article 10:

The solemn ratifications of the present treaty expedited in good and due form shall be exchanged between the contracting parties in the space of six months or sooner, if possible, to be computed from the day of the signatures of the present treaty. In witness whereof we the undersigned, their ministers plenipotentiary, have in their name and in virtue of our full powers, signed with our hands the present definitive treaty and caused the seals of our arms to be affixed thereto.

YORKTOWN AND THE TREATY OF PARIS
Project 3

On the map below, locate the British army, Washington's army and the French blockade. Color the British red, the Colonies' forces blue and the troops from France in green.

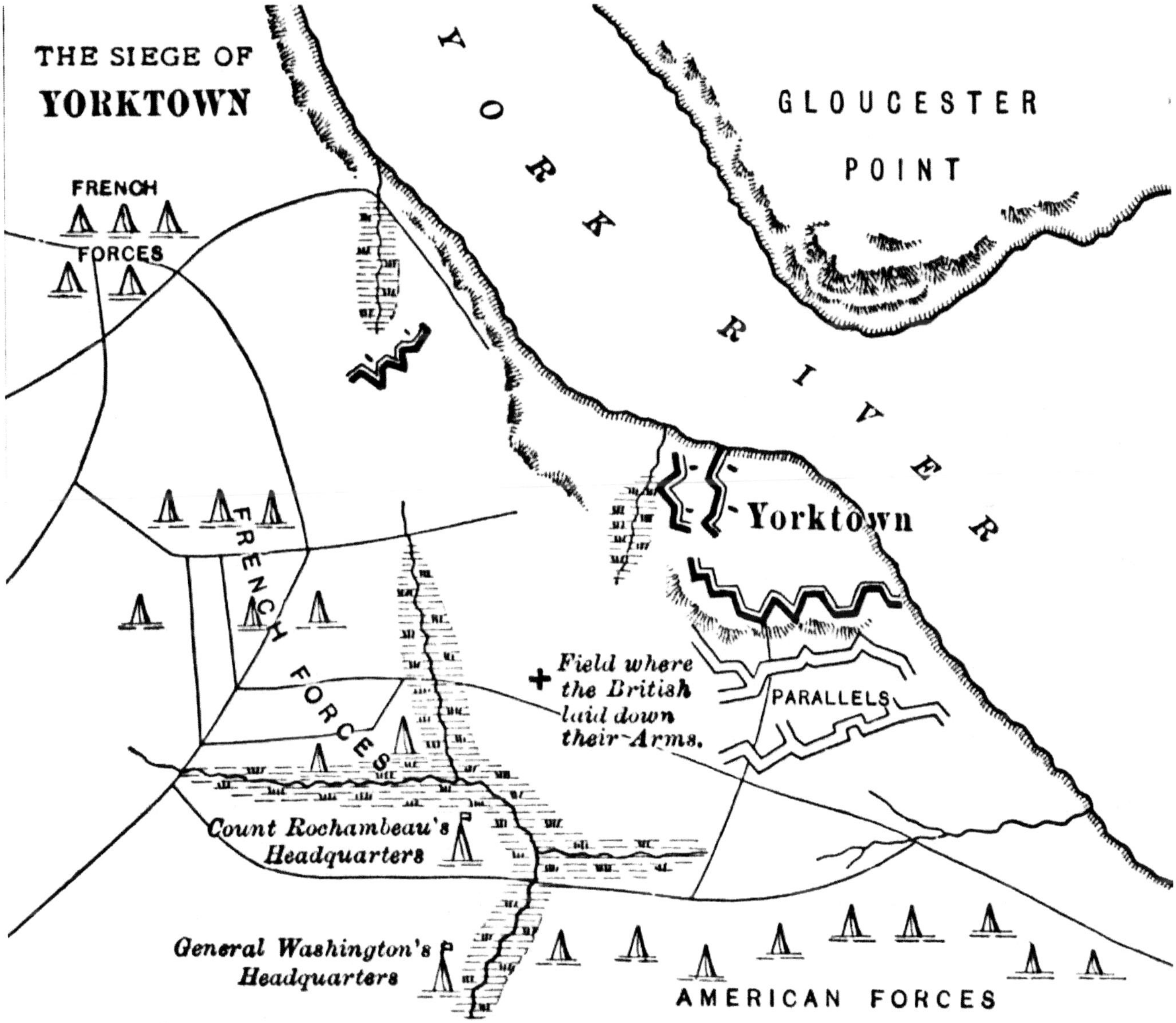

Yorktown and the Treaty of Paris

Test

1. Where did Washington trap the British army?

2. Who blockaded the Chesapeake Bay?

3. What song did the Americans play at the surrender?

4. What was the treaty called? When was is signed?

5. What did the treaty recognize?

Yorktown and the Treaty of Paris

Test, Page 2

6. How were the colonies organized?

Review

1. What did Columbus believe God had called him to do?

2. What empire did Hernando Cortes conquer?

3. Who was the colony of Jamestown named after?

4. What did the Pilgrims believe about God?

5. In chronological order list all events studied to date. Next to each place the appropriate date.

Yorktown and the Treaty of Paris
Test, Page 3

5. (continued)

The Constitutional Convention
Worksheet

1. What was the date given for the Constitutional Convention?

____

____

2. What were the Articles of Confederation?

____

____

____

3. In May 1787, ____________________ sent delegates to Philadelphia to work on a new governing document.

4. Name two famous men who attended the above meeting.

____

____

____

5. *Finish the following sentence:* The delegates agreed that a plan of government needed to

____

____

____

6. *Finish the following sentence:* They established a plan for a republic

____

____

____

7. Differences between the North and South were clear. What was the result of their compromise?

____

____

THE CONSTITUTIONAL CONVENTION
Worksheet, Page 2

8. What did the Constitution give the government the right to do?

____

____

____

____

9. Several states refused to sign the Constitution until what was included?

____

____

____

____

The Constitutional Convention

Project 1—The Articles of Confederation (1781)

Read the The Articles of Confederation.

To all to whom these presents shall come, we the undersigned delegates of the states affixed to our names, send greeting:

Whereas the delegates of the United States of America in Congress assembled, did, on the fifteenth day of November in the year of our Lord seventeen seventy-seven, and in the second year of the Independence of America, agree to Certain Articles of Confederation and perpetual union between the states of New Hampshire, Massachusetts Bay, Rhode Island and Providence Plantations, Connecticut, New York, New Jersey, Pennsylvania, Delaware, Maryland, Virginia, North Carolina, South Carolina and Georgia in the words following, viz:

Articles of Confederation and Perpetual Union Between the States of New Hampshire, Massachusetts Bay, Rhode Island and Providence Plantations, Connecticut, New York, New Jersey, Pennsylvania, Delaware, Maryland, Virginia, North Carolina, South Carolina and Georgia.

ARTICLE I. The style of this Confederacy shall be "The United States of America."

ARTICLE II. Each state retains its sovereignty, freedom and independence, and every power, jurisdiction and right which is not by this Confederation expressly delegated to the United States in Congress assembled.

ARTICLE III. The said states hereby severally enter into a firm league of friendship with each other for their common defence, the security of their liberties, and their mutual and general welfare, binding themselves to assist each other against all force offered to, or attacks made upon them, or any of them, on account of religion, sovereignty, trade, or any other pretence whatever.

ARTICLE IV. The better to secure and perpetuate mutual friendship and intercourse among the people of the different States in this Union, the free inhabitants of each of these states, paupers, vagabonds and fugitives from justice excepted, shall be entitled to all privileges and immunities of free citizens in the several states; and the people of each state shall have free ingress and regress to and from any other state, and shall enjoy therein all the privileges of trade and commerce, subject to the same duties, impositions and restrictions as the inhabitants thereof respectively; provided, that such restrictions shall not extend so far as to prevent the removal of property imported into any state, to any other state of which the owner is an inhabitant; provided also, that no imposition, duties or restriction shall be laid by any state on the property of the United States, or either of them.

If any person guilty of or charged with treason, felony, or other high misdemeanor in any state, shall flee from justice, and be found in any of the United States, he shall upon demand of the governor or executive power of the state from which he fled, be delivered up and removed to the state having jurisdiction of his offense.

Full faith and credit shall be given in each of these states to the records, acts and judicial proceedings of the courts and magistrates of every other state.

ARTICLE V. For the more convenient management of the general interests of the United States, delegates shall be annually appointed in such manner as the legislature of each state shall direct, to meet in Congress on the first Monday in November, in every year, with a power, reserved to each

The Constitutional Convention
Project 1, Page 2

state, to recall its delegates, or any of them, at any time within the year, and to send others in their stead, for the remainder of the year.

No state shall be represented in Congress by less than two, nor by more than seven members; and no person shall be capable of being a delegate for more than three years in any term of six years; nor shall any person, being a delegate, be capable of holding any office under the United States, for which he, or another for his benefit receives any salary, fees or emolument of any kind.

Each state shall maintain its own delegates in a meeting of the states, and while they act as members of the committee of the states.

In determining questions in the United States, in Congress assembled, each state shall have one vote.

Freedom of speech and debate in Congress shall not be impeached or questioned in any court, or place out of Congress, and the members of Congress shall be protected in their persons from arrests and imprisonments, during the time of their going to and from, and attendance on Congress, except for treason, felony, or breach of the peace.

ARTICLE VI. No state without the consent of the United States in Congress assembled, shall send any embassy to, or receive any embassy from, or enter into any conference, agreement, alliance or treaty with any king, prince or state; nor shall any person holding any office of profit or trust under the United States, or any of them, accept of any present, emolument, office or title of any kind whatever from any king, prince or foreign state; nor shall the United States in Congress assembled, or any of them, grant any title of nobility.

No two or more states shall enter into any treaty, confederation or alliance whatever between them, without the consent of the United States in Congress assembled, specifying accurately the purposes for which the same is to be entered into, and how long it shall continue.

No state shall lay any impost or duties, which may interfere with any stipulations in treaties, entered into by the United States in Congress assembled, with any king, prince or state, in pursuance of any treaties already proposed by Congress to the courts of France and Spain.

No vessels of war shall be kept up in time of peace by any state, except such number only as shall be deemed necessary by the United States in Congress assembled, for the defence of such state, or its trade; nor shall any body of forces be kept up by any state, in time of peace except such number only, as in the judgment of the United States, Congress assembled, shall be deemed requisite to garrison the forts necessary for the defence of such state; but every state shall always keep up a well regulated and disciplined militia, sufficiently armed and accoutered, and shall provide and constantly have ready for use, in public stores, a due number of field pieces and tents, and a proper quantity of arms, ammunition and camp equipage.

No state shall engage in any war without the consent of the United States in Congress assembled, unless such state be actually invaded by enemies, or shall have received certain advice of a resolution being formed by some nation of Indians to invade such state, and the danger is so imminent as not to admit of a delay, till the United States in Congress assembled can be consulted: nor shall any state grant commissions to any ships or vessels of war, nor letters of marque or reprisal, except it be after a declaration of war by the United States in Congress assembled, and then only against the kingdom or state and the subjects thereof, against which war has been so declared, and under such regulations as shall be established by the United States in Congress assembled, unless such state be infested by pirates, in which case vessels of war be fitted out for that occasion, and kept so long as the danger shall continue, or until the United States in Congress assembled shall determine otherwise.

ARTICLE VII. When land forces are raised by any state for the common defence, all officers of or under the rank of colonel, shall be appointed by the Legislature of each state respectively by whom such forces shall be raised, or in such manner as such state shall direct, all vacancies shall be filled up by the state which first made the appointment.

ARTICLE VIII. All charges of war, and all other expenses that shall be incurred for the common defence or general welfare, and allowed by the United States in Congress assembled, shall be defrayed out of a common treasury, which shall be supplied by the several states, in proportion to the value of all land within each state, granted to or surveyed for any person, as such land and the buildings and improvements thereon shall be estimated according to such mode as the United States in Congress assembled, shall from time to time direct and appoint.

The taxes for paying that proportion shall be laid and levied by the authority and direction of the legislatures of the several states within the time agreed upon by the United States in Congress assembled.

ARTICLE IX. The United States in Congress assembled, shall have the sole and exclusive right and power of determining on peace and war except in the cases mentioned in the sixth article; of sending and receiving ambassadors; entering into treaties and alliances; provided that no treaty of commerce shall be made whereby the legislative power of the respective states shall be restrained from imposing such imposts and

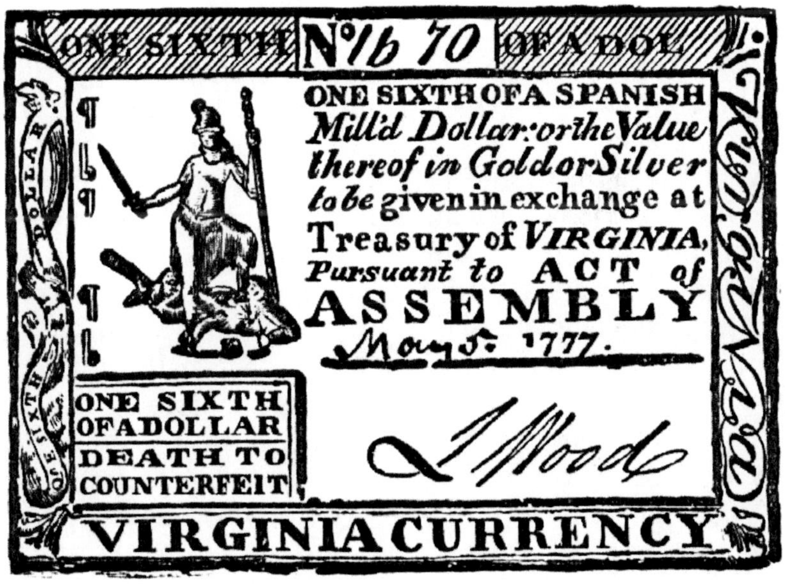

The Constitutional Convention
Project 1, Page 4

duties on foreigners, as their own people are subjected to, or from prohibiting the exportation or importation of any species of goods or commodities whatsoever; of establishing rules for deciding in all cases, what captures on land or water shall be legal, and in what manner prizes taken by land or naval forces in the service of the United States shall be divided or appropriated; of granting letters of marque and reprisal in times of peace; appointing courts for the trial of piracies and felonies committed on the high seas and establishing courts for receiving and determining finally appeals in all cases of captures, provided that no member of Congress shall be appointed a judge of any of said courts.

The United States in Congress assembled shall also be the last resort on appeal in all disputes and differences now subsisting or that hereafter may arise between two or more states concerning boundary, jurisdiction or any other cause whatever; which authority shall always be exercised in the manner following. Whenever the legislative or executive authority or lawful agent of any state in controversy with another shall present a petition to Congress, stating the matter in question and praying for a hearing, notice thereof shall be given by order of Congress to the legislative or executive authority of the other state in controversy, and a day assigned for the appearance of the parties by their lawful agents, who shall then be directed to appoint by joint consent commissioners or judges to constitute a court for hearing and determining the matter in question: but if they can not agree, Congress shall name three persons out of each of the United States, and from the list of such persons each party shall alternately strike out one, the petitioners beginning, until the number shall be reduced to thirteen; and from that number not less than seven, nor more than nine names, as Congress shall direct, shall in the presence of Congress be drawn out by lot, and the persons whose names shall be so drawn or any five of them, shall be commissioners or judges, to hear and finally determine the controversy, so always as a major part of the judges who shall hear the cause shall agree in the determination: and if either party shall neglect to attend at the day appointed, without showing reasons, which Congress judge sufficient, or being present shall refuse to strike, the Congress shall proceed to nominate three persons out of each state, and the Secretary of Congress shall strike in behalf of such party absent or refusing; and the judgment and sentence of the court to be appointed, in the manner before prescribed, shall be final and conclusive; and if any of the parties shall refuse to submit to the authority of such court, or to appear or defend their claim or cause, the court shall, nevertheless proceed to pronounce sentence, or judgment, which shall in like manner be final and decisive, the judgment or sentence and other proceeds being in either case transmitted to Congress, and lodged among the acts of Congress for the security of the parties concerned: provided that every commissioner, before he sits in judgment, shall take an oath to be administered by one of the judges of the supreme or superior court of the state where the cause shall be tried, "well and truly to hear and determine the matter in question, according to the best of his judgment without favor, affection, or hope of reward": provided also that no state shall be deprived of territory for the benefit of the United States.

All controversies concerning the private right of soil claimed under different grants of two or more states, whose jurisdiction as

The Constitutional Convention
Project 1, Page 5

they may respect such lands, and the states which passed such grants are adjusted, the said grants or either of them being at the same time claimed to have originated antecedent to such settlement of jurisdiction, shall on the petition of either party to the Congress of the United States, be finally determined as near as may be in the same manner as is before prescribed for deciding disputes respecting territorial jurisdiction between the different states.

The United States in Congress assembled shall also have the sole and exclusive right and power of regulating the alloy and value of coin struck by their own authority, or by that of respective state fixing the standard of weights and measures throughout the United States regulating the trade, and managing all affairs with the Indians, not members of any of the states, provided that the legislative right of state within its own limits be not infringed or violated; establishing and regulating post offices from one state to another, throughout all the United States, and exacting such postage on the papers passing through the same as may be requisite to defray the expenses of the said office; appointing all officers of the land forces, in the service of the United States, excepting regimental officers; appointing all the officers of the naval forces, and commissioning all officers whatever in the service of the United States; making rules for the government and regulation of said land and naval forces, and directing their operations.

The United States in Congress assembled shall have authority to appoint a committee, to sit in the recess of Congress, to be denominated "a Committee of the States," and to consist of one delegate from each state; and to appoint such other committees and civil officers as may be necessary for managing the general affairs of the United States under their direction; to appoint one of their number to preside, provided that no person be allowed to serve in the office of president more than one year in any term of three years; to ascertain the necessary sums of money to be raised for the service of the United States, and to appropriate and apply the same for defraying the public expenses; to borrow money, or emit bills on the credit of the United States, transmitting every half year to the respective states an account of the sums of money so borrowed or emitted; to build and equip a navy; to agree upon the number of land forces, and to make requisitions from each state for its quota, in proportion to the number of white inhabitants in such state; which requisition shall be binding, and therepon the legislature of each state shall appoint the regimental officers, raise the men and clothe, arm and equip them in a soldierlike manner, at the expense of the United States; and the officers and men so clothed, armed and equipped shall march to the place appointed, and within the time agreed on by the United States in Congress assembled: but if the United States in Congress assembled shall, on consideration of circumstances judge proper that any state should not raise men, or should raise a smaller number than its quota, and that any other state should raise a greater number of men than the quota thereof, such extra number shall be raised, officered, clothed, armed and equipped in the same manner as the quota of such state, unless the legislature of such state shall judge that such extra number can not be safely spared out of the same, in which case they shall raise, officer, clothe, arm and equip as many of such extra number as they judge can be safely spared. And the officers and men so clothed, armed and equipped, shall march to the place appointed, and within the time agreed on by the United States in Congress assembled.

The United States in Congress assembled shall never engage in war, nor grant letters of marque and reprisal in time of peace, nor enter into any treaties or alliances, nor coin money, nor regulate the value thereof, nor ascertain the sums and expenses necessary for the defense and welfare of the United States, or any of them, nor emit bills, nor borrow money on the credit of the United States, nor appropriate money, nor agree upon the number of vessels of war, to be built or purchased, or the number of land or sea forces to be raised, nor appoint a commander-in-chief of the army or navy, unless nine states assent to the same: nor shall a question on any other point, except for adjourning from day to day be determined, unless by the votes of a majority of the United States in Congress assembled.

The Congress of the United States shall have power to adjourn to any time within the year, and to any place within the United States, so that no period of adjournment be for a longer duration than the space of six months; and shall publish the journal of their proceedings monthly, except such parts thereof relating to treaties, alliances or military operations, as in their judgment require secrecy; and the yeas and nays of the delegates of each state on any question shall be entered on the journal, when it is desired by any delegate; and the delegates of a state, or any of them, at his or their request, shall be furnished with transcript of the said journal, except such parts as are above excepted to lay before the legislatures of the several states.

ARTICLE X. The Committee of the States, or any nine of them shall be authorized to execute, in the recess of Congress, such of the powers of Congress as the United States in Congress assembled, by the consent of nine states, shall from time to time think expedient to vest them with; provided that no power be delegated to the said committee for the exercise of which, by the Articles of Confederation, the voice of nine states in the Congress of the United States assembled is requisite.

ARTICLE XI Canada acceding to this Confederation, and joining in the measures of the United States, shall be admitted into, and entitled to all the advantages of this Union: but no other colony shall be admitted into the same, unless such admission be agreed to by nine states.

ARTICLE XII. All bills of credit emitted, moneys borrowed and debts contracted by, or under the authority of Congress, before the assembling of the United States, in pursuance of the present Confederation, shall be deemed and considered as a charge against the United States, for payment and satisfaction whereof the said United States and the public faith are hereby solemnly pledged.

ARTICLE XIII. Every state shall abide by the determinations of the United States in Congress assembled, on all quesions which by this Confederation are submitted to them. And the Articles of this Confederation shall be inviolably observed by every state, and the Union shall be perpetual; nor shall any alteration at any time hereafter be made in any of them, unless such alteration be agreed to in a Congress of the United States, and be afterwards confirmed by the legislatures of every state.

AND WHEREAS it hath pleased the Great Governor of the world to incline the hearts of the legislatures we respectively represent

The Constitutional Convention

Project 1, Page 7

in Congress, to approve of, and to authorize us to ratify the said Articles of Confederation and perpetual Union. Know ye that we the undersigned delegates, by virtue of the power and authority to us given for that purpose, do by these presents, in the name and in behalf of our respective constituents, fully and entirely ratify and confirm each and every one of the said Articles of Confederation and perpetual Union, and all and singular the matters and things therein contained: and we do further solemnly plight and engage the faith of our respective constituents, that they shall abide by the determinations of the United States Congress assembled, on all questions, which by the said Confederation are submitted to them. And that the articles thereof shall be inviolably observed by the states we respectively represent, and that the Union shall be perpetual.

IN WITNESS WHEREOF we have hereunto set our hands in Congress. Done at Philadelphia in the State of Pennsylvania the ninth day of July in the year of our Lord one thousand seven hundred and seventy-eight, and in the third year of the independence of America.

The Constitutional Convention
Project 2—Speech of Patrick Henry, 1775

While these things were taking place in New England, the patriots in other colonies were just as bold and busy.

The Second Continental Congress met at Philadelphia. The wise men and great patriots collected there said to the King: "Be just, and we will lay down our arms, and be your best friends. But know, O King that we have counted the cost of war, and find nothing so dreadful as slavery. Be just, or we will fight your fleets and armies until we become a free people."

The Congress did not wait for the King's answer, but wisely prepared for war. It appointed George Washington, the brave soldier who was with Braddock twenty years before, to be the Commander-in-Chief of the Continental armies.

Washington went immediately to Cambridge, near Boston, and there, under the shadow of a fine elm tree, he took the command of the army on the 3d of July. That army was made up of all sorts of people, with all sorts of dress and all sorts of weapons. He began at once to put them in good condition. Speeches everywhere, in favor of independence, were being made. Read the speech of Patrick Henry's which follows.

MR. PRESIDENT: No man thinks more highly than I do of patriotism. But different men often see the same subject in different lights, and therefore I hope it will not be thought disrespectful if I speak forth my sentiments freely and without reserve. This is no time for ceremony. The question before the house is one of awful moment to this country. For my part, I consider it as nothing less than a question of freedom or slavery. It is only in this way that we can hope to arrive at truth and fulfill the great responsibility which We hold to God and our country. Should I keep back my opinions at such a time, through fear of giving offense, I should consider myself as guilty of treason toward my country and of an act of disloyalty toward the Majesty of Heaven, which I revere above all earthly kings.

Mr. President, it is natural to man to indulge in the illusions of hope. We are apt to shut our eyes against a painful truth and listen to the song of that siren, till she transforms us into beasts. Is this the part of wise men, engaged in a great and arduous struggle for liberty? Are we disposed to be of the number of those who, having eyes, see not and, having ears, hear not the things which so nearly concern their temporal salvation? For my part, whatever anguish of spirit it may cost, I am willing to know the whole truth, to know the worst, and to provide for it.

I have but one lamp by which my feet are guided; and that is the lamp of experience. I know of no way of judging of the future but by the past. And judging by the past, I wish to know what there has been in the conduct of the British ministry for the last ten years, to justify those hopes with which gentlemen have been pleased to solace themselves and the house? Is it that insidious smile with which our petition has been lately received? Trust it not, sir; it will prove a snare to your feet. Suffer not yourselves to be betrayed with a kiss. Ask yourselves how this gracious reception of our petition comports with those warlike preparations which cover our waters and darken our land. Are fleets and armies necessary to a work of love and reconciliation?

Have we shown ourselves so unwilling to be reconciled, that force must be called in to win back our love? Let us not deceive our-

The Constitutional Convention

Project 2, Page 2

selves, sir. These are the implements of war and subjugation; the last arguments to which kings resort. I ask, gentlemen, sir, what means this martial array, if its purpose be not to force us to submission? Can gentlemen assign any other possible motive for it? Has Great Britain any enemy in this quarter of the world, to call for all this accumulation of navies and armies? No, sir, she has none. They are meant for us; they can be meant for no other. They are sent over to bind and rivet upon us those chains which the British ministry have been so long forging. And what have we to oppose to them? Shall we try argument? Sir, we have been trying that for the last ten years. Have we anything new to offer upon the sub'ect? Nothing., We have held the subject up in every light of which it is capable; but it has been all in vain. Shall we resort to entreaty and humble supplication? What terms shall we find, which have not been already exhausted? Let us not, I beseech you, sir, deceive ourselves longer. Sir, we have

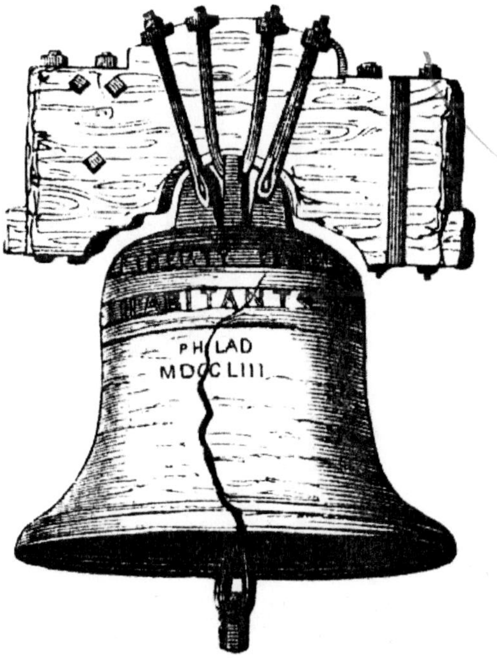

done everything that could be done to avert the storm which is now coming on. We have petitioned; we have remonstrated; we have supplicated; we have prostrated ourselves before the throne, and have implored its interposition to arrest the tyrannical hands of the ministry and Parliament. Our petitions have been slighted; our remonstrances have produced additional violence and insults; our supplications have been disregarded; and we have been spurned, with contempt, from the foot of the throne! In vain, after these things, may we indulge the fond hope of peace and reconciliation. There is no longer any room for hope. If we wish to be free—if we mean to preserve inviolate those inestimable privileges for which we have been so long contending—if we mean not basely to abandon the noble struggle in which we have been so long engaged, and which we have pledged ourselves never to abandon, until the glorious object of our contest shall be obtained—we must fight! I repeat it, sir, we must fight! An appeal to arms and to the God of Hosts is all that is left us!

They tell us, sir, that we are weak; unable to cope with so formidable an adversary. But when shall we be stronger? Will it be the next week, or the next year? Will it be when we are totally disarmed, and when a British guard shall be stationed in every house? Shall we gather strength by irresolution and inaction? Shall we acquire the means of effectual resistance, by lying supinely on our backs and hugging the delusive phantom of hope, until our enemies shall have bound us hand and foot? Sir, we are not weak, if we make a proper use of those means which the God of nature hath placed in our power. Besides, sir, we shall not fight our battles alone. There is a just God who presides over the destinies of nations, and who will raise up friends to fight our battles for us. The battle, sir, is not to the strong alone; it is to the vigilant, the active, the brave. Besides, sir, we have no election. If we were base enough to desire it, it is now too late to retire from the contest. There is no retreat, but in submission and slavery! Our chains are forged! Their clanking may be heard on the plains of Boston! The war is inevitable-and let it come! I repeat it, sir, let it come.

It is vain, sir, to extenuate the matter. Gentlemen may cry peace, peace—but there is no peace. The war is actually begun! The next gale that sweeps from the north will bring to our ears the clash of resounding arms! Our brethren are already in the field! Why stand we here idle? What is it that the gentlemen wish? What would they have? Is life so dear, or peace so sweet, as to be purchased at the price of chains and slavery? Forbid it, Almighty God! I know not what course others may take; but as for me, give me liberty, or give me death!

BE IT REMEMBERED!

THAT on the 17th of October, 1781, Lieutenant-General Earl CORNWALLIS, with above Five thouſand Britiſh Troops, ſurrendered themſelves Priſoners of War to his Excellency Gen. GEORGE WASHINGTON, Commander in Chief of the allied Forces of France and America.

LAUS DEO!

THE CONSTITUTIONAL CONVENTION
Project 3—Preamble to the Constitution

Memorize and prepare to recite the Preamble to the Constitution. Use a dictionary to define each of the italicized words in the Preamble. Record your definitions at the bottom of this paper.

We the People of the United States, in order to form a more perfect union, establish *justice,* insure *domestic tranquility,* provide for the common *defence,* promote the general *welfare,* and secure the blessings of *liberty* to ourselves and our *posterity,* do ordain and establish this Constitution for the United States of America.

justice ______________________________

____

domestic ______________________________

____

tranquility ______________________________

____

defence ______________________________

____

welfare ______________________________

____

liberty ______________________________

____

posterity ______________________________

____

____

____

____

____

____

The Constitutional Convention

Test

1. What was the date of the Constitutional Convention?

2. What were the Articles of Confederation?

3. To which city did the colonies send delegates in May 1787 to work on a new governing document?

4. Who are some of the notable people who attended this meeting mentioned in #3 above?

5. What four ideas did the delegates agree that a plan of government needed?

6. Differences in the North and South were clear. What did the compromise result in?

The Constitutional Convention

Test, Page 2

7. What three rights did the Constitution give government?

Review

1. For what was Valley Forge used during the War for Independence?

2. What was "Common Sense"? Who wrote it?

3. Of what significance was the Battle of Lexington in the War for Independence?

4. In chronological order list all events studied to date. Next to each place the appropriate date.

The Constitutional Convention
Test, Page 3

4. (continued)

AMERICA'S FOUNDING FATHERS
Worksheet

1. What is the date given for America's Founding Fathers?

2. What were four different jobs that Benjamin Franklin had during his life?

3. What was *Poor Richard's Almanac?*

4. Who was instrumental in bringing France into the War for Independence?

5. Name three things that Franklin invented.

6. Who was the principal author of the Declaration of Independence?

America's Founding Fathers
Worksheet, Page 2

7. Who was the third President of the United States?

8. Where did Jefferson send Lewis and Clark to explore?

9. Name four of Jefferson's accomplishments.

10. Who was the fourth President of the United States?

11. Who was the principal author of the Constitution?

12. What did Madison hold in highest regard?

AMERICA'S FOUNDING FATHERS

Project 1—Great War Trivia Game

Using the resources listed on the cards, create a Founding Fathers trivia game. Photocopy this page 3 times for a total of 18 cards. Cut out cards and write a question about the person who is named and pictured on the back of the card. Then mix them up and play.

BENJAMIN FRANKLIN

BENJAMIN FRANKLIN

THOMAS JEFFERSON

THOMAS JEFFERSON

JAMES MADISON

JAMES MADISON

America's Founding Fathers

Project 2—Benjamin Franklin

Read Benjamin Franklin's own account of how he became a printer in Philadelphia

My elder brothers were all put apprentices to different trades. I was put to the grammar-school at eight years of age, my father intending to devote me, as the tithe of his sons, to the service of the Church. My early readiness in learning to read (which must have been very early, as I do not remember when I could not read), and the opinion of all his friends, that I should certainly make a good scholar, encouraged him in this purpose of his. My uncle Benjamin, too, approved of it, and proposed to give me all his short-hand volumes of sermons, I suppose as a stock to set up with, if I would learn his character. I continued, however, at the grammar-school not quite one year, though in that time I had risen gradually from the middle of the class of that year to be the head of it, and farther was removed into the next class above it, in order to go with that into the third at the end of the year. But my father, in the mean time, from a view of the expense of a college education, which having so large a family he could not well afford, and the mean living many so educated were afterwards able to obtain—reasons that he gave to his friends in my hearing—altered his first intention, took me from the grammar-school, and sent me to a school for writing and arithmetic, kept by a then famous man, Mr. George Brownell, very successful in his profession generally, and that by mild, encouraging methods. Under him I acquired fair writing pretty soon, but I failed in the arithmetic, and made no progress in it. At ten years old I was taken home to assist my father in his business, which was that of a tallow-chandler and sope-boiler; a business he was not bred to, but had assumed on his arrival in New England, and on finding his dying trade would not maintain his family, being in little request. Accordingly, I was employed in cutting wick for the candles, filling the dipping mold and the molds for cast candles, attending the shop, going of errands, etc.

I disliked the trade, and had a strong inclination for the sea, but my father declared against it; however, living near the water, I was much in and about it, learnt early to swim well, and to manage boats; and when in a boat or canoe with other boys, I was commonly allowed to govern, especially in any case of difficulty; and upon other occasions I was generally a leader among the boys, and sometimes led them into scrapes.

To return: I continued thus employed in my father's business for two years, that is, till I was twelve years old; and my brother John, who was bred to that business, having left my father, married, and set up for himself at Rhode Island, there was all appearance that I was destined to supply his place, and become a tallow-chandler. But my dislikc to the trade continuing, my father was under apprehensions that if he did not find one for me more agreeable, I should break away and get to sea, as his son Josiah had done, to his great

America's Founding Fathers

Project 2, Page 2

vexation. He therefore sometimes took me to walk with him, and see joiners, bricklayers, turners, braziers, etc., at their work, that he might observe my inclination, and endeavor to fix it on some trade or other on land. It has ever since been a pleasure to me to see good workmen handle their tools; and it has been useful to me, having learnt so much by it as to be able to do little jobs myself in my house when a workman could not readily be got, and to construct little machines for my experiments, while the intention of making the experiment was fresh and warm in my mind. My father at last fixed upon the cutler's trade, and my uncle Benjamin's son Samuel, who was bred to that business in London, being about that time established in Boston, I was sent to be with him some time on liking. But his expectations of a fee with me displeasing my father, I was taken home again.

From a child I was fond of reading, and all the little money that came into my hands was ever laid out in books. Pleased with the Pilgrim's Progress, my first collection was of John Bunyan's works in separate little volumes. I afterward sold them to enable me to buy R. Burton's Historical Collections; they were small chapmen's books, and cheap, 40 or 50 in all.

This bookish inclination at length determined my father to make me a printer, though he had already one son (James) of that profession. In 1717 my brother James returned from England with a press and letters to set up his business in Boston. I liked it much better than that of my father, but still had a hankering for the sea. To prevent the apprehended effect of such an inclination, my father was impatient to have me bound to my brother. I stood out some time, but at last was persuaded, and signed the indentures when I was yet but twelve years old. I was to serve as an apprentice till I was twenty-one years of age, only I was to be allowed journeyman's wages during the last year. In a little time I made great proficiency in the business, and became a useful hand to my brother.

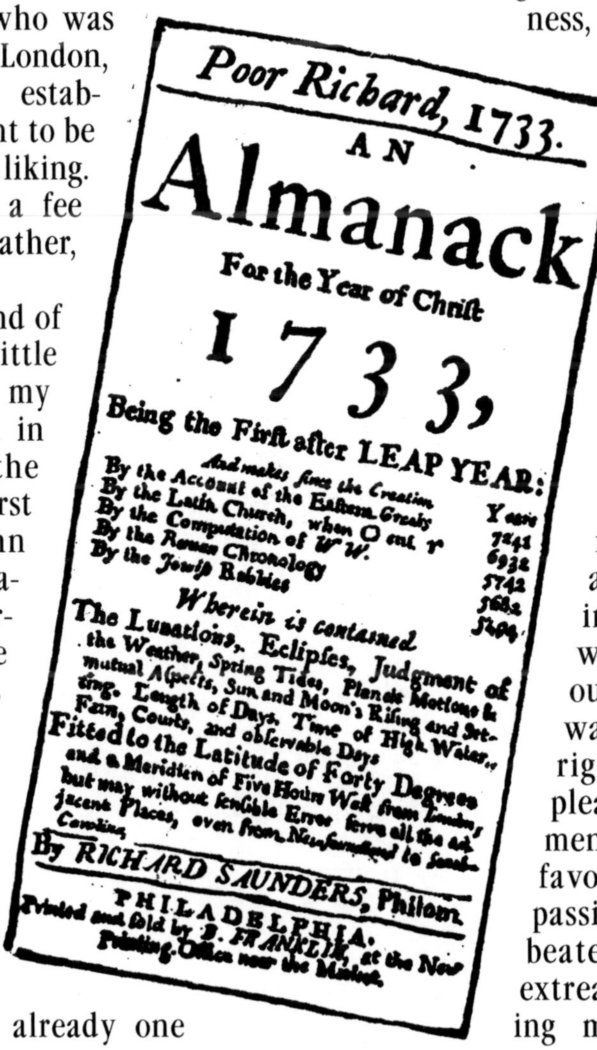
Poor Richard, 1733.
AN
Almanack
For the Year of Christ
1733,
Being the First after LEAP YEAR:
And makes since the Creation — Years
By the Account of the Eastern Greeks — 7241
By the Latin Church, when ☉ ent. ♈ — 6932
By the Computation of W. W. — 5742
By the Roman Chronology — 5682
By the Jewish Rabbies — 5494
Wherein is contained
The Lunations, Eclipses, Judgment of the Weather, Spring Tides, Planets Motions & mutual Aspects, Sun and Moon's Rising and Setting, Length of Days, Time of High Water, Fairs, Courts, and observable Days.
Fitted to the Latitude of Forty Degrees, and a Meridian of Five Hours West from London, but may without sensible Error serve all the adjacent Places, even from Newfoundland to South-Carolina.
By RICHARD SAUNDERS, Philom.
PHILADELPHIA:
Printed and sold by B. FRANKLIN, at the New Printing-Office near the Market.

Though a brother, he considered himself as my master, and me as his apprentice, and, accordingly, expected the same services from me as he would from another, while I thought he demean'd me too much in some he requir'd of me, who from a brother expected more indulgence. Our disputes were often brought before our father, and I fancy I was either generally in the right, or else a better pleader, because the judgment was generally in my favor. But my brother was passionate, and had often beaten me, which I took extreamly amiss; and, thinking my apprenticeship very tedious, I was continually wishing for some opportunity of shortening it, which at length offered in a manner unexpected.

One of the pieces in our newspaper on some political point, which I have now forgotten, gave offense to the Assembly. He [James] was taken up, censur'd, and impris-on'd for a month, by the speaker's warrant, I suppose, because he would not discover [reveal] his author. I too was taken up and examin'd before the council; but, tho' I did not give them any satisfaction, they content'd themselves with admonishing me, and dismissed me, considering me, perhaps, as an apprentice, who was bound to keep his master's secrets.

During my brother's confinement, which I resented a good deal, notwithstanding our private differences, I had the management of the paper; and I made bold to give our rulers some rubs in it, which my brother took very kindly, while others began to consider me in an unfavorable light, as a young genius that had a turn for libelling and satyr. My brother's discharge was accompany'd with an order of the House (a very odd one), that "James Franklin should no longer print the paper called the New England Courant."

There was a consultation held in our printing house among his friends, what he should do in this case. Some proposed to evade the order by changing the name of the paper; but my brother, seeing inconveniences in that, it was finally concluded on as a better way, to let it be printed for the future under the name of BENJAMIN FRANKLIN; and to avoid the censure of the Assembly, that might fall on him as still printing it by his apprentice, the contrivance was that my old indenture should be return'd to me, with a full discharge on the back of it, to be shown on occasion, but to secure to him the benefit of my service, I was to sign new indentures for the remainder of the term, which were to be kept private. A very flimsy scheme it was; however, it was immediately executed, and the paper went on accordingly, under my name for several months.

At length, a fresh difference arising between my brother and me, I took upon me to assert my freedom, presuming that he would not venture to produce the new indentures. It was not fair in me to take this advantage, and this I therefore reckon one of the first errata of my life; but the unfairness of it weighed little with me, when under the impressions of resentment for the blows his passion too often urged him to bestow upon me, though he was otherwise not an ill-natur'd man: perhaps I was too saucy and provoking.

When he found I would leave him, he took care to prevent my getting employment in any other printing-house of the town, by going round and speaking to every master, who accordingly refus'd to give me work. I then thought of going to New York, as the nearest place where there was a printer; and I was rather inclin'd to leave Boston when I reflected that I had already made myself a little obnoxious to the governing party, and, from the arbitrary proceedings of the Assembly in my brother's case, it was likely I might, if I stay'd, soon bring myself into scrapes; and farther, that my indiscrete disputations about religion began to make me pointed at with horror by good people as an infidel or atheist. I determin'd on the point, but my father now siding with my brother, I was sensible that, if I attempted to go openly, means would be used to prevent me. My friend Collins, therefore, undertook to manage a little for me. He agreed with the captain of a New York sloop for my passage, under the notion of my being a young acquaintance of his, that had got a naughty girl with child, whose friends would compel me to marry her, and therefore I could not appear or come away publicly. So I sold some of my books to raise a little money, was taken on board privately, and as we had a fair wind, in three days I found myself in New York, near 300 miles from home, a boy of but 17 without the least recommendation to, or knowledge of any person in the place, and with very little money in my pocket.

My inclinations for the sea were by this time worne out, or I might now have gratify'd them. But, having a trade, and supposing myself a pretty good workman, I offer'd my service to the printer in the place, old Mr. William Bradford, who had been the first printer in Pennsylvania, but removed from thence upon the quarrel of George Keith. He could give me no employment, having little to do, and help enough already; but says he, "My son at Philadelphia has lately lost his principal hand, Aquila Rose, by death; if you go thither, I believe he may employ you." Philadelphia was a hundred miles further; I set out, however, in a boat for Amboy, leaving my chest and things to follow me round by sea.

Then I made myself as tidy as I could, and went to Andrew Bradford the printer's. I found in the shop the old man his father whom I had seen at New York, and who, traveling on horseback, had got to Philadelphia before me. He introduc'd me to his son, who receiv'd me civilly, gave me a breakfast, but told me he did not at present want a hand, being lately suppli'd with one; but there was another printer in town, lately set up, one Keimer, who, perhaps, might employ me; if not, I should be welcome to lodge at his house, and he would give me a little work to do now and then till fuller business should offer.

I fancy his harsh and tyrannical treatment of me might be a means of impressing me with that aversion to arbitrary power that has stuck to me through my whole life.

This was in October, 1723.—B.

America's Founding Fathers
Project 3—Thomas Jefferson

Read Thomas Jefferson's First Address as President, given in Washington D.C. on Wednesday, March 4, 1801

Friends and Fellow-Citizens:

Called upon to undertake the duties of the first executive office of our country, I avail myself of the presence of that portion of my fellow-citizens which is here assembled to express my grateful thanks for the favor with which they have been pleased to look toward me, to declare a sincere consciousness that the task is above my talents, and that I approach it with those anxious and awful presentiments which the greatness of the charge and the weakness of my powers so justly inspire. A rising nation, spread over a wide and fruitful land, traversing all the seas with the rich productions of their industry, engaged in commerce with nations who feel power and forget right, advancing rapidly to destinies beyond the reach of mortal eye—when I contemplate these transcendent objects, and see the honor, the happiness, and the hopes of this beloved country committed to the issue, and the auspices of this day, I shrink from the contemplation, and humble myself before the magnitude of the undertaking. Utterly, indeed, should I despair did not the presence of many whom I here see remind me that in the other high authorities provided by our Constitution I shall find resources of wisdom, of virtue, and of zeal on which to rely under all difficulties. To you, then, gentlemen, who are charged with the sovereign functions of legislation, and to those associated with you, I look with encouragement for that guidance and support which may enable us to steer with safety the vessel in which we are all embarked amidst the conflicting elements of a troubled world.

During the contest of opinion through which we have passed the animation of discussions and of exertions has sometimes worn an aspect which might impose on strangers unused to think freely and to speak and to write what they think; but this being now decided by the voice of the nation, announced according to the rules of the Constitution, all will, of course, arrange themselves under the will of the law, and unite in common efforts for the common good. All, too, will bear in mind this sacred principle, that though the will of the majority is in all cases to prevail, that will to be rightful must be reasonable; that the minority possess their equal rights, which equal law must protect, and to violate would be oppression. Let us, then, fellow-citizens, unite with one heart and one mind. Let us restore to social intercourse that harmony and affection without which liberty and even life itself are but dreary things. And let us reflect that, having banished from our land that religious intolerance under which mankind so long bled and suffered, we have yet gained little if we countenance a political intolerance as despotic, as wicked, and capable of as bitter and bloody persecutions. During the throes and convulsions of the ancient world, during the agonizing spasms of infuriated man, seeking through blood and slaughter his long-lost liberty, it was not wonderful that the agitation of the billows should reach even this distant and peaceful shore; that this should be more felt and feared by some and less by others, and should divide opinions as to measures of safety. But every difference of opinion is not a difference of principle. We

America's Founding Fathers
Project 3, Page 2

have called by different names brethren of the same principle. We are all Republicans, we are all Federalists. If there be any among us who would wish to dissolve this Union or to change its republican form, let them stand undisturbed as monuments of the safety with which error of opinion may be tolerated where reason is left free to combat it. I know, indeed, that some honest men fear that a republican government can not be strong, that this Government is not strong enough; but would the honest patriot, in the full tide of successful experiment, abandon a government which has so far kept us free and firm on the theoretic and visionary fear that this Government, the world's best hope, may by possibility want energy to preserve itself? I trust not. I believe this, on the contrary, the strongest Government on earth. I believe it the only one where every man, at the call of the law, would fly to the standard of the law, and would meet invasions of the public order as his own personal concern. Sometimes it is said that man can not be trusted with the government of himself. Can he, then, be trusted with the government of others? Or have we found angels in the forms of kings to govern him? Let history answer this question.

Let us, then, with courage and confidence pursue our own Federal and Republican principles, our attachment to union and representative government. Kindly separated by nature and a wide ocean from the exterminating havoc of one quarter of the globe; too high-minded to endure the degradations of the others; possessing a chosen country, with room enough for our descendants to the thousandth and thousandth generation; entertaining a due sense of our equal right to the use of our own faculties, to the acquisitions of our own industry, to honor and confidence from our fellow-citizens, resulting not from birth, but from our actions and their sense of them; enlightened by a benign religion, professed, indeed, and practiced in various forms, yet all of them inculcating honesty, truth, temperance, gratitude, and the love of man; acknowledging and adoring an overruling Providence, which by all its dispensations proves that it delights in the happiness of man here and his greater happiness hereafter—with all these blessings, what more is necessary to make us a happy and a prosperous people? Still one thing more, fellow-citizens—a wise and frugal Government, which shall restrain men from injuring one another, shall leave them otherwise free to regulate their own pursuits of industry and improvement, and shall not take from the mouth of labor the bread it has earned. This is the sum of good government, and this is necessary to close the circle of our felicities.

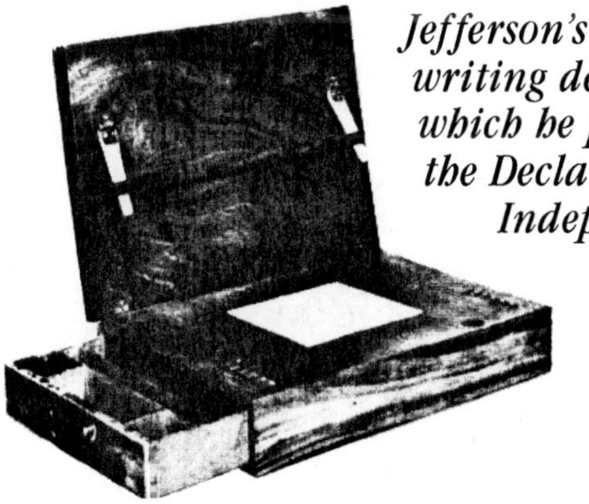

Jefferson's portable writing desk, on which he penned the Declaration of Independence

About to enter, fellow-citizens, on the exercise of duties which comprehend everything dear and valuable to you, it is proper you should understand what I deem the essential principles of our Government, and consequently those which ought to shape its Administration. I will compress them within the narrowest compass they will bear, stating the general principle, but not all its limitations. Equal and exact justice to all men, of whatever state or persuasion, religious or political; peace, commerce, and honest friendship with all nations, entangling alliances with none; the support of the State governments in all their rights, as the most competent administrations for our domestic concerns and the surest bulwarks against antirepublican tendencies; the preservation of the General Government in its whole constitutional vigor, as the sheet anchor of our peace at home and safety abroad; a jealous care of the right of election by the people—a mild and safe corrective of abuses which are lopped by the sword of revolution where peaceable remedies are unprovided; absolute acquiescence in the decisions of the majority, the vital principle of republics, from which is no appeal but to force, the vital principle and immediate parent of despotism; a well disciplined militia, our best reliance in peace and for the first moments of war, till regulars may relieve them; the supremacy of the civil over the military authority; economy in the public expense, that labor may be lightly burthened; the honest payment of our debts and sacred preservation of the public faith; encouragement of agriculture, and of commerce as its handmaid; the diffusion of information and arraignment of all abuses at the bar of the public reason; freedom of religion; freedom of the press, and freedom of person under the protection of the habeas corpus, and trial by juries impartially selected. These principles form the bright constellation which has gone before us and guided our steps through an age of revolution and reformation. The wisdom of our sages and blood of our heroes have been devoted to their attainment. They should be the creed of our political faith, the text of civic instruction, the touchstone by which to try the services of those we trust; and should we wander from them in moments of error or of alarm, let us hasten to retrace our steps and to regain the road which alone leads to peace, liberty, and safety.

I repair, then, fellow-citizens, to the post you have assigned me. With experience enough in subordinate offices to have seen the difficulties of this the greatest of all, I have learnt to expect that it will rarely fall to the lot of imperfect man to retire from this station with the reputation and the favor which bring him into it. Without pretensions to that high confidence you reposed in our first and greatest revolutionary character, whose preeminent services had entitled him to the first place in his country's love and destined for him the fairest page in the volume of faithful history, I ask so much confidence only as may give firmness and effect to the legal administration of your affairs. I shall often go wrong through defect of judgment. When right, I shall often be thought wrong by those whose positions will not command a view of the whole ground. I ask your indulgence for my own errors, which will never be intentional, and your support against the errors of others, who may condemn what they would not if seen in all its parts. The approbation implied by your suffrage is a great consolation to me for the past, and my future solicitude will be to retain the good opinion of those who have bestowed it in advance, to conciliate that of others by doing them all the good in my power, and to be instrumental to the happiness and freedom of all.

Relying, then, on the patronage of your good will, I advance with obedience to the work, ready to retire from it whenever you become sensible how much better choice it is in your power to make. And may that Infinite Power which rules the destinies of the universe lead our councils to what is best, and give them a favorable issue for your peace and prosperity.

America's Founding Fathers

Project 4—Thomas Jefferson on Slavery

Read Genesis 1:26–27 and Galatians 3:28, then read Jefferson's unbiblical thoughts on the differences of the races below. Discuss the stark contrasts between God's Word and Jefferson's position.

It will probably be asked, Why not retain and incorporate the blacks into the state, and thus save the expense of supplying, by importation of white settlers, the vacancies they will leave? Deep rooted prejudices entertained by the whites; ten thousand recollections, by the blacks, of the injuries they have sustained; new provocations; the real distinctions which nature has made; and many other circumstances, will divide us into parties, and produce convulsions, which will probably never end but in the extermination of the one or the other race. To these objections, which are political, may be added others, which are physical and moral. The first difference which strikes us is that of colour. Whether the black of the negro resides in the reticular membrane between the skin and scarf-skin, or in the scarf-skin itself; whether it proceeds from the colour of the blood, the colour of the bile, or from that of some other secretion, the difference is fixed in nature, and is as real as if its seat and cause were better known to us. And is this difference of no importance? Is it not the foundation of a greater or less share of beauty in the two races? Are not the fine mixtures of red and white, the expressions of every passion by greater or less suffusions of colour in the one, preferable to that eternal monotony, which reigns in the countenances, that immovable veil of black which covers all the emotions of the other race? Add to these, flowing hair, a more elegant symmetry of form, their own judgment in favour of the whites, declared by their preference of them, as uniformly as is the preference of the Oranootan [orang-utan] for the black women over those of his own species. The circumstance of Superior beauty, is thought worthy attention in the propagation of our horses, dogs, and other domestic animals; why not in that of man? Besides those of colour, figure, and hair, there are other physical distinctions proving a difference of race. They have less hair on the face and body. They secrete less by the kidneys, and more by the glands of the skin, which gives them a very strong and disagreeable odour. This greater degree of transpiration renders them more tolerant of heat, and less so of cold than the whites. Perhaps too a difference of structure in the pulmonary apparatus, which a late ingenious experimentalist has discovered to be the principal regulator of animal heat, may have disabled them from extricating, in the act of inspiration, so much of that fluid from the outer air, or obliged them in expiration, to part with more of it. They seem to require less sleep. A black after hard labour through the day, will be induced by the slightest amusements to sit up till midnight, or later, though knowing he must be out with the first dawn of the morning. They are at least as brave, and more adventuresome. But this may perhaps proceed from a want of forethought, which prevents their seeing a danger till it be present. When present, they do not go through it with more coolness or steadiness than the whites. They are more ardent after their female: but love seems with them to be more an eager desire, than a tender delicate mixture of sentiment and sensation. Their griefs are transient. Those numberless afflictions, which render it doubtful whether heaven has given life to us in mercy or in wrath, are less felt, and sooner forgotten with them. In general, their existence appears to participate more of sensation than reflection. To this must be ascribed their disposition to sleep when abstracted from their diversions, and unemployed in labour. An animal whose body is at rest, and who does not reflect, must be disposed to sleep of course. Comparing them by their faculties of memory, reason, and imagination, it appears to me that in memory they are equal to the whites; in reason much inferior, as I think one could scarcely be found capable of tracing and comprehending the investigations of Euclid; and that in imagination they are dull, tasteless, and anomalous. It would be unfair to follow them to Africa for this investigation.

We will consider them here, on the same stage with the whites, and where the facts are not apocryphal on which a judgment is to be formed. It will be right to make great allowances for the difference of condition, of education, of conversation, of the sphere in which they move. Many millions of them have been brought to, and born in America. Most of them indeed have been confined to tillage, to their own homes, and their own society: yet many have been so situated, that they might have availed themselves of the conversation of their masters; many have been brought up to the handicraft arts, and from that circumstance have always been associated with the whites. Some have been liberally educated, and all have lived in countries where the arts and sciences are cultivated to a considerable degree, and have had before their eyes samples of the best works from abroad.

The Indians, with no advantages of this kind, will often carve figures on their pipes not destitute of design and merit. They will crayon out an animal, a plant, or a country, so as to prove the existence of a germ in their minds which only wants cultivation. They astonish you with strokes of the most sublime oratory; such as prove their reason and sentiment strong, their imagination glowing and elevated. But never yet could I find that a black had uttered a thought above the level of plain narration; never saw even an elementary trait of painting or sculpture. In music they are more generally gifted than the whites with accurate ears for tune and time, and they have been found capable of imagining a small catch *[Jefferson's own note:* The instrument proper to them is the Banjar, which they brought hither from Africa, and which is the original of the guitar, its chords being precisely the four lower chords of the guitar.*—If Jefferson is referring to the banjo here, he is completely wrong only the ukelele-banjo has the same tone intervals as the 4 higher strings of the guitar, however the guitar is tuned in E and the ukelele-banjo in B: other four string banjo's are tuned like a violin].* Whether they will be equal to the composition of a more extensive run of melody, or of complicated harmony, is yet to be proved. Misery is often the parent of the most affecting touches in poetry. Among the blacks is misery enough, God knows, but no poetry. Love is the peculiar oestrum of the poet. Their love is ardent, but it kindles the senses only, not the imagination. Religion indeed has produced a Phyllis Whately *[a misspelled reference to Phillis Wheatley (1753-1784). She was a self-taught African slave who was a poet, fluent classicist and a fascinating and brilliant conversationalist —all before her death at the age of 31.]* but it could not produce a poet. The compositions published under her name are below the dignity of criticism. The heroes of the Dunciad are to her, as Hercules to the author of that poem. Ignatius Sancho has

America's Founding Fathers
Project 4, Page 3

approached nearer to merit in composition; yet his letters do more honour to the heart than the head. They breathe the purest effusions of friendship and general philanthropy, and show how great a degree of the latter may be compounded with strong religious zeal. He is often happy in the turn of his compliments, and his style is easy and familiar, except when he affects a Shandean fabrication of words. But his imagination is wild and extravagant, escapes incessantly from every restraint of reason and taste, and, in the course of its vagaries, leaves a tract of thought as incoherent and eccentric, as is the course of a meteor through the sky. His subjects should often have led him to a process of sober reasoning: yet we find him always substituting sentiment for demonstration. Upon the whole, though we admit him to the first place among those of his own colour who have presented themselves to the public judgment, yet when we compare him with the writers of the race among whom he lived and particularly with the epistolary class, in which he has taken his own stand, we are compelled to enrol him at the bottom of the column. This criticism supposes the letters published under his name to be genuine, and to have received amendment from no other hand; points which would not be of easy investigation.

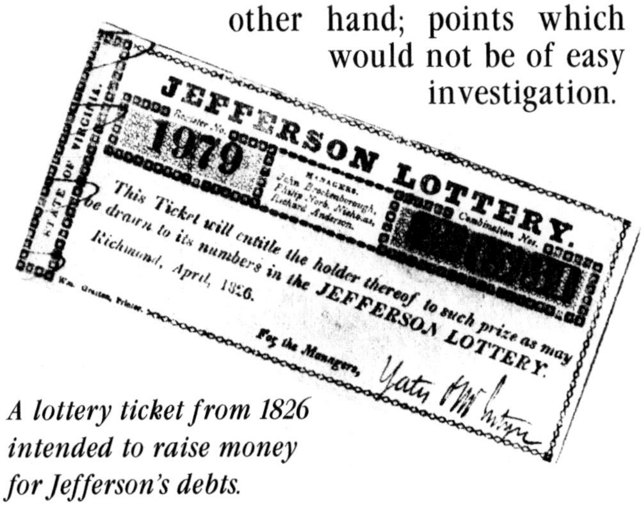

A lottery ticket from 1826 intended to raise money for Jefferson's debts.

The improvement of the blacks in body and mind, in the first instance of their mixture with the whites, has been observed by every one, and proves that their inferiority is not the effect merely of their condition of life. We know that among the Romans, about the Augustan age especially, the condition of their slaves was much more deplorable than that of the blacks on the continent of America. The two sexes were confined in separate apartments, because to raise a child cost the master more than to buy one. Cato, for a very restricted indulgence to his slaves in this particular, took from them a certain price. But in this country the slaves multiply as fast as the free inhabitants. Their situation and manners place the commerce between the two sexes almost without restraint. The same Cato, on a principle of economy, always sold his sick and superannuated slaves. He gives it as a standing precept to a master visiting his farm, to sell his old oxen, old wagons, old tools, old and diseased servants, and every thing else become useless. . . . The American slaves cannot enumerate this among the injuries and insults they receive. It was the common practice to expose in the island Esculapius, in the Tyber, diseased slaves, whose cure was like to become tedious. The emperor Claudius, by an edict, gave freedom to such of them as should recover, and first declared that if any person chose to kill rather than expose them, it should be deemed homicide. The exposing them is a crime of which no instance has existed with us; and were it to be followed by death, it would be punished capitally. We are told of a certain Vedius Pollio, who, in the presence of Augustus, would have given a slave as food to his fish, for having broken a glass. With the Romans, the regular method of taking the evidence of their slaves was under torture. Here it has been thought better never to resort to their evidence. When a master was murdered, all his slaves, in the same house, or within hearing, were condemned to death. Here punishment falls on the guilty only, and as precise proof is required against him as against a freeman. Yet notwithstanding these and other discouraging circumstances among the Romans, their slaves were often their rarest artists. They excelled too in science, insomuch as to be usually employed as tutors to their masters' children. Epictetus, Terence, and Phaedrus, were slaves. But they were of the race of whites. It is not their condition then, but nature, which has produced the distinction. Whether further observation will or will not verify the conjecture, that nature has been less bountiful to them in the endowments of the head, I believe that in those of the heart she will be found to have done them justice. That disposition to theft with which they have been branded, must be ascribed to their situation, and not to any depravity of the moral sense. The man, in whose favour no laws of property exist, probably feels himself less bound to respect those made in favour of others. When arguing for ourselves, we lay it down as a fundamental, that laws, to be just, must give a reciprocation of right; that, without this, they are mere arbitrary rules of conduct, founded in force, and not in conscience: and it is a problem which I give to the master to solve, whether the religious precepts against the violation of property were not framed for him as well as his slave? And whether the slave may not as justifiably take a little from one, who has taken all from him, as he may slay one who would slay him? That a change in the relations in which a man is placed should change his ideas of moral right or wrong, is neither new, nor peculiar to the colour of the blacks. Homer tells us it was so 2600 years ago.

Jove fix'd it certain, that whatever day
Makes man a slave, takes half his
worth away.

But the slaves of which Homer speaks were whites. Notwithstanding these considerations which must weaken their respect for the laws of property, we find among them numerous instances of the most rigid integrity, and as many as among their better instructed masters, of benevolence, gratitude and unshaken fidelity. The opinion, that they are inferior in the faculties of reason and imagination, must be hazarded with great diffidence. To justify a general conclusion, requires many observations, even where the subject may be submitted to the anatomical knife, to optical classes, to analysis by fire, or by solvents. How much more then where it is a faculty, not a substance, we are examining; where it eludes the research of all the Senses; where the conditions of its existence are various and variously combined; where the effects of those which are present or absent bid defiance to calculation; let me add too, as a circumstance of great tenderness, where our conclusion would degrade a whole race of men from the rank in the scale of beings which their Creator may perhaps have given them. To our reproach it must be said, that though for a century and a half we have had under our eyes the races of black and of red men, they have never yet been viewed by us as subjects of natural history. I advance it therefore as a suspicion only, that the blacks, whether originally a distinct race, or made distinct by time and circumstances, are inferior to the whites in the endowments both of body and mind. It is not against experience to suppose, that different Species of the same genus, or varieties of the same species, may possess different qualifications. Will not a lover of natural history then, one who views the gradations in all the races of animals with the eye of philosophy, excuse an effort to keep those in the department of man as distinct as nature has formed them?

This unfortunate difference of colour, and perhaps of faculty, is a powerful obstacle to the emancipation of these people. Many of their advocates, while they wish to vindicate the liberty of human nature are anxious also to preserve its dignity and beauty. Some of these, embarrassed by the question 'What further is to be done with them?' join themselves in opposition with those who are actuated by sordid avarice only. Among the Romans emancipation required but one effort. The slave, when made free, might mix with, without staining the blood of his master. But with us a second is necessary, unknown to history. When freed, he is to be removed beyond the reach of mixture.

It is difficult to determine on the standard by which the manners of a nation may be tried, whether catholic, or particular. It is more difficult for a native to bring to that standard the manners of his own nation, familiarized to him by habit. There must doubtless be an unhappy influence on the manners of our people produced by the existence of slavery among us. The whole commerce between master and slave is a perpetual exercise of the most boisterous passions, the most unremitting despotism on the one part, and degrading submissions on the other. Our children see this, and learn to imitate it; for man is an imitative animal. This quality is the germ of all education in him. From his cradle to his grave he is learning to do what he sees others do. If a parent could find no motive either in his philanthropy or his self love, for restraining the intemperance of passion towards his slave, it should always be a sufficient one that his child is present. But generally it is not sufficient. The parent storms, the child looks on, catches the lineaments of wrath, puts on the same airs in the circle of smaller slaves, gives a loose to the worst of passions, and thus nursed, educated, and daily exercised in tyranny, cannot but be stamped by it with odious pecularities. The man must be a prodigy who can retain his manners and morals undepraved by such circumstances. And with what execration should the statesman be loaded, who, permitting one half the citizens thus to trample on the rights of the other, transforms those into

despots, and these into enemies, destroys the morals of the one part, and the amor patriae of the other. For if a slave can have a country in this world, it must be any other in preference to that in which he is born to live and labour for another; in which he must lock up the faculties of his nature, contribute as far as depends on his individual endeavours to the evanishment of the human race, or entail his own miserable condition on the endless generations proceeding from him. With the morals of the people, their industry also is destroyed. For in a warm climate, no man will labour for himself who can make another labour for him. This is so true, that of the proprietors of slaves a very small proportion indeed are ever seen to labour. And can the liberties of a nation be thought secure when we have removed their only firm basis, a conviction in the minds of the people that these liberties are of the gift of God? That they are not to be violated but with his wrath? Indeed I tremble for my country when I reflect that God is just: that his justice cannot sleep for ever: that considering numbers, nature and natural means only, a revolution of the wheel of fortune, an exchange of situation is among possible events: that it may become probable by supernatural interference! The almighty has no attribute which can take side with us in such a contest. But it is impossible to be temperate and to pursue this subject through the various considerations of policy, of morals, of history natural and civil. We must be contented to hope they will force their way into every one's mind. I think a change already perceptible, since the origin of the present revolution. The spirit of the master is abating, that of the slave rising from the dust, his condition mollifying, the way I hope preparing, under the auspices of heaven, for a total emancipation, and that this is disposed, in the order of events, to be with the consent of the masters, rather than by their extirpation.

America's Founding Fathers
Project 5–James Madison

A Colored Man's Reminiscences of James Madison
by Paul Jennings

Paul Jennings was born a slave on President Madison's estate, in Montpelier, Va., in 1799. His reputed father was Benj. Jennings, an English trader there; his mother, a slave of Mr. Madison, and the granddaughter of an Indian. Paul was a "body servant" of Mr. Madison, till his death, and afterwards of Daniel Webster, having purchased his freedom of Mrs. Madison for $120

About ten years before Mr. Madison was President, he and Colonel Monroe were rival candidates for the Legislature. Mr. Madison was anxious to be elected, and sent his chariot to bring up a Scotchman to the polls, who lived in the neighborhood. But when brought up, he cried out: "Put me down for Colonel Monroe, for he was the first man that took me by the hand in this country." Colonel Monroe was elected, and his friends joked Mr. Madison pretty hard about his Scotch friend, and I have heard Mr. Madison and Colonel Monroe have many a hearty laugh over the subject, for years after.

When Mr. Madison was chosen President, we came on and moved into the White House; the east room was not finished, and Pennsylvania Avenue was not paved, but was always in an awful condition from either mud or dust. The city was a dreary place.

Mr. Robert Smith was then Secretary of State, but as he and Mr. Madison could not agree, he was removed, and Colonel Monroe appointed to his place. Dr. Eustis was Secretary of War – rather a rough, blustering man; Mr. Gallatin, a tip-top man, was Secretary of the Treasury; and Mr. Hamilton, of South Carolina, a pleasant gentleman, who thought Mr. Madison could do nothing wrong, and who always concurred in every thing he said, was Secretary of the Navy.

Before the war of 1812 was declared, there were frequent consultations at the White House as to the expediency of doing it. Colonel Monroe was always fierce for it, so were Messrs. Lowndes, Giles, Poydrass, and Pope–all Southerners; all his Secretaries were likewise in favor of it.

Soon after war was declared, Mr. Madison made his regular summer visit to his farm in Virginia. We had not been there long before an express reached us one evening, informing Mr. M. of Gen. Hull's surrender. He was astounded at the news, and started back to Washington the next morning.

After the war had been going on for a couple of years, the people of Washington began to be alarmed for the safety of the city, as the British held Chesapeake Bay with a powerful fleet and army. Every thing seemed to be left to General Armstrong, then Secretary of war, who ridiculed the idea that there was any danger. But, in August, 1814, the enemy had got so near, there could be no doubt of their intentions. Great alarm existed, and some feeble preparations for defense were made. Com. Barney's flotilla was stripped of men, who were placed in battery, at Bladensburg, where they fought splendidly. A large part of his men were tall, strapping negroes, mixed with white sailors and marines. Mr. Madison reviewed them just before the fight, and asked Com. Barney if his "negroes would not run on the approach of the British?" "No sir," said Barney, "they don't know how to run; they will die by their guns first." They fought till a large part of them were killed or wounded; and Barney himself wounded and taken prisoner. One or two of these negroes are still living here.

Well, on the 24th of August, sure enough, the British reached Bladensburg, and the fight began between 11 and 12. Even that very morning General Armstrong assured Mrs. Madison there was no danger. The President, with General Armstrong, General Winder, Colonel Monroe, Richard Rush, Mr. Graham, Tench Ringgold, and Mr. Duvall, rode out on horseback to Bladensburg to see how things looked. Mrs. Madison ordered dinner to be ready at 3, as usual; I set the table myself, and brought up the ale, cider, and wine, and placed them in the coolers, as all the Cabinet and several military gentlemen and strangers were expected. While waiting, at just about 3, as Sukey, the house-servant was lolling out of a chamber window, James Smith, a free colored man who had accompanied Mr. Madison to Bladensburg, gallopped up to the house, waving his hat, and cried out, "Clear out, clear out! General Armstrong has ordered a retreat!" All then was confusion. Mrs. Madison ordered her carriage, and passing through the dining-room, caught up what silver she could crowd into her old-fashioned reticule, and then jumped into the chariot with her servant girl Sukey, and Daniel Carroll, who took charge of them; Jo. Bolin drove them over to Georgetown Heights; the British were expected in a few minutes. Mr. Cutts, her brother- in-law, sent me to a stable on 14th street, for his carriage. People were running in every direction. John Freeman (the colored butler) drove off in the coachee with his wife, child, and servant; also a feather bed lashed on behind the coachee, which was all the furniture saved, except part of the silver and the portrait of Washington (of which I will tell you by-and-by).

I will here mention that although the British were expected every minute, they did not arrive for some hours; in the mean time, a rabble, taking advantage of the confusion, ran all over the White House, and stole lots of silver and whatever they could lay their hands on.

About sundown I walked over to the Georgetown ferry, and found the President and all hands (the gentlemen named before, who acted as a sort of body-guard for him) waiting for the boat. It soon returned, and we all crossed over, and passed up the road about a mile; they then left us servants to wander about. In a short time several wagons from Bladensburg, drawn by Barney's artillery horses, passed up the road, having crossed the Long Bridge before it was set on fire. As we were cutting up some planks a white wagoner ordered us away, and told his boy Tommy to reach out his gun, and he would shoot us. I told him "he had better have used it at Bladensburg." Just then we came up with Mr. Madison and his friends, who had been wandering about for some hours, consulting what to do. I walked on to a Methodist minister's, and in the evening, while he was at prayer, I heard a tremendous explosion, and, rushing out, saw that the public buildings, navy yard, ropewalks, &c., were on fire.

Mrs. Madison slept that night at Mrs. Love's, two or three miles over the river. After leaving that place she called in at a

America's Founding Fathers

Project 4, Page 3

house, and went up stairs. The lady of the house learning who she was, became furious, and went to the stairs and screamed out, "Miss Madison! if that's you, come down and go out! Your husband has got mine out fighting, and damn you, you shan't stay in my house; so get out!" Mrs. Madison complied, and went to Mrs. Minor's, a few miles further, where she stayed a day or two, and then returned to Washington, where she found Mr. Madison at her brother-in-law's, Richard Cutts, on F street. All the facts about Mrs. M. I learned from her servant Sukey. We moved into the house of Colonel John B. Taylor [Tayloe], corner of 18th street and New York Avenue, where we lived till the news of peace arrived.

In two or three weeks after we returned, Congress met in extra session, at Blodgett's old shell of a house on 7th street (where the General Post-office now stands). It was three stories high, and had been used for a theatre, a tavern, an Irish boarding house, &c.; but both Houses of Congress managed to get along in it very well, notwithstanding it had to accommodate the Patent-office, City and General Post-office, committee-rooms, and what was left of the Congressional Library, at the same time. Things are very different now.

The next summer, Mr. John Law, a large property-holder about the Capitol, fearing it would not be rebuilt, got up a subscription and built a large brick building (now called the Old Capitol, where the secesh prisoners are confined), and offered it to Congress for their use, till the Capitol could be rebuilt. This coaxed them back, though strong efforts were made to remove the seat of government north; but the southern members kept it here.

It has often been stated in print, that when Mrs. Madison escaped from the White House, she cut out from the frame the large portrait of Washington (now in one of the parlors there), and carried it off. This is totally false. She had no time for doing it. It would have required a ladder to get it down. All she carried off was the silver in her reticule, as the British were thought to be but a few squares off, and were expected every moment. John Suse' [Jean-Pierre Sioussat] (a Frenchman, then door-keeper, and still living) and Magraw, the President's gardener, took it down and sent it off on a wagon, with some large silver urns and such other valuables as could be hastily got hold of. When the British did arrive, they ate up the very dinner, and drank the wines, &c., that I had prepared for the President's party.

When the news of peace arrived, we were crazy with joy. Miss Sally Coles, a cousin of Mrs. Madison, and afterwards wife of Andrew Stevenson, since minister to England, came to the head of the stairs, crying out, "Peace! peace!" and told John Freeman (the butler) to serve out wine liberally to the servants and others. I played the President's March on the violin, John Suse' and some others were drunk for two days, and such another joyful time was never seen in Washington. Mr. Madison and all his Cabinet were as pleased as any, but did not show their joy in this manner.

Mrs. Madison was a remarkably fine woman. She was beloved by every body in Washington, white and colored. Whenever soldiers marched by, during the war, she always sent out and invited them in to take wine and refreshments, giving them liberally of the best in the house. Madeira wine was better in those days than now, and more freely drank. In the last days of her life, before Congress purchased her husband's papers, she was in a state of absolute poverty, and I think sometimes suffered for the necessaries of life. While I was a servant to Mr. Webster, he often sent me to her with a market-basket full of provisions, and told me whenever I saw anything in the house that I thought she was in need of, to take it to her. I often did this, and occasionally gave her small sums from my own pocket, though I had years before bought my freedom of her.

Mr. Madison, I think, was one of the best men that ever lived. I never saw him in a passion, and never knew him to strike a slave, although he had over one hundred; neither would he allow an overseer to do it. Whenever any slaves were reported to him as stealing or "cutting up" badly, he would send for them and admonish them privately, and never mortify them by doing it before others. They generally served him very faithfully. He was temperate in his habits. I don't think he drank a quart of brandy in his whole life. He ate light breakfasts and no suppers, but rather a hearty dinner, with which he took invariably but one glass of wine. When he had hard drinkers at his table, who had put away his choice Madeira pretty freely, in response to their numerous toasts, he would just touch the glass to his lips, or dilute it with water, as they pushed about the decanters. For the last fifteen years of his life he drank no wine at all.

After he retired from the presidency, he amused himself chiefly on his farm. At the election for members of the Virginia Legislature, in 1829 or '30, just after General Jackson's accession, he voted for James Barbour, who had been a strong Adams man. He also presided, I think, over the Convention for amending the Constitution, in 1832.

After the news of peace, and of General Jackson's victory at New Orleans, which reached here about the same time, there were great illuminations. We moved into the Seven Buildings, corner of 19th street and Pennsylvania Avenue, and while there, General Jackson came on with his wife, to whom numerous dinner-parties and levees were given. Mr. Madison also held levees every Wednesday evening, at which wine, punch, coffee, ice-cream, &c., were liberally served, unlike the present custom.

While Mr. Jefferson was President, he and Mr. Madison (then his Secretary of State) were extremely intimate; in fact, two brothers could not have been more so. Mr. Jefferson always stopped over night at Mr. Madison's, in going and returning from Washington.

I have heard Mr. Madison say, that when he went to school, he cut his own wood for exercise. He often did it also when at his farm in Virginia. He was very neat, but never extravagant, in his clothes. He always dressed wholly in black—coat, breeches, and silk stockings, with buckles in his shoes and breeches. He never had but one suit at a time. He had some poor relatives that he had to help, and wished to set them an example of economy in the matter of dress. He was very fond of horses, and an excellent judge of them, and no jockey ever cheated him. He never had less than seven horses in his Washington stables while President.

He often told the story, that one day riding home from court with old Tom Barbour (father of Governor Barbour), they met a colored man, who took off his hat. Mr. M. raised his, to the surprise of old Tom; to whom Mr. M. replied, "I never allow a negro to excel me in politeness." Though a similar story is told of General Washington, I have often heard this, as above, from Mr. Madison's own lips.

After Mr. Madison retired from the presidency, in 1817, he invariably made a visit twice a year to Mr. Jefferson—sometimes stopping two or three weeks—till Mr. Jefferson's death, in 1826.

I was always with Mr. Madison till he died, and shaved him every other day for sixteen years. For six months before his death, he was unable to walk, and spent most of his time reclined on a couch; but his mind was bright, and with his numerous visitors he talked with as much animation and strength of voice as I ever heard him in his best days. I was present when he died. That morning Sukey brought him his breakfast, as usual. He could not swallow. His niece, Mrs. Willis, said, "What is the matter, Uncle Jeames?" "Nothing more than a change of *mind*, my dear." His head instantly dropped, and he ceased breathing as quietly as the snuff of a candle goes out. He was about eighty-four years old, and was followed to the grave by an immense procession of white and colored people. The pallbearers were Governor Barbour, Philip P. Barbour, Charles P. Howard, and Reuben Conway; the two last were neighboring farmers.

Please observe that this primary source differs in much of what you may have read about Dolly Madison and her rescue of Washington's portrait. It is an interesting thing to ponder.

America's Founding Fathers
Project 6—Dress-Up Report

Dress up as one of the founding fathers and give a brief summary to the class or your family of your accomplishments. Make any props that would add to your presentation; for instance, Poor Richard's Almanac *or a kite for Franklin.*

AMERICA'S FOUNDING FATHERS
Test

On each blank write Franklin, Jefferson, or Madison to indicate who the statement describes.

__________________ 1. A writer, scientist, statesman, and printer

__________________ 2. Wrote the Declaration of Independence

__________________ 3. Popular in France

__________________ 4. Principal author of the Constitution and Bill of Rights

__________________ 5. Fourth President

__________________ 6. Sent out Lewis and Clark expedition

__________________ 7. Worked hard to see religious freedom protected

__________________ 8. Architect, scientist, and inventor of the dumbwaiter

__________________ 9. Invented bifocals and lightning rods

__________________ 10. Wrote *Poor Richard's Almanac*

WASHINGTON, OUR FIRST PRESIDENT
Worksheet

1. What is the date given for Washington, Our First President?

____

____

2. To where did Washington return after the war?

____

____

3. When was Washington unanimously elected President?

____

____

4. Washington did not feel qualified to be president, but in fact he had been in__________

   of_______________states with __________________ being the exception.

5. Name two other reasons he was a good canidate for president.

____

____

____

____

6. Where was the first capital of the United States?

____

____

____

7. With the Constitution already in place, what other things were to be set up under Washington's presidency?

____

____

____

Washington, Our First President
Worksheet, Page 2

8. Who was Vice President under Washington?

9. Who was Secretary of State under Washington?

10. Who was Secretary of the Treasury under Washington?

11. When was Washington elected to a second term?

12. Where did Washington plan for a new capital to be built?

Washington, Our First President

Project 1—Stuart's Painting, "George Washington"

Gilbert Stuart's painting "George Washington" (detail, right) has become the best known portrait of America's first President. Stuart had to duplicate this painting so often for his patrons that he ended up referring to them as his "hundred dollar bills." Draw your own portrait of Washington in the space provided below, using Stuart's painting as reference. Hint: try turning your page upside down to draw his likeness. Often you can trick your eye when drawing something inverted and end up with a much more accurate piece.

WASHINGTON, OUR FIRST PRESIDENT
Project 2—George Washington Reading

Read the following account of George Washington.

The brilliant historian of the English people, John Richard Green, has written of Washington, that "no nobler figure ever stood in the fore-front of a nation's life." In any book which undertakes to tell, no matter how slightly, the story of some of the heroic deeds of American history, that noble figure must always stand in the fore-front. But to sketch the life of Washington even in the barest outline is to write the history of the events which made the United States independent and gave birth to the American nation. Even to give a list of what he did, to name his battles and recount his acts as president, would be beyond the limit and the scope of this book. Yet it is always possible to recall the man and to consider what he was and what he meant for us and for mankind. He is worthy the study and the rememberance of all men, and to Americans he is at once a great glory of their past and an inspiration and an assurance of their future.

To understand Washington at all we must first strip off all the myths which have gathered about him. We must cast aside into the dust-heaps all the wretched inventions of the cherry-tree variety, which were fastened upon him nearly seventy years after his birth. We must look at him as he looked at life and the facts about him, without any illusion or deception, and no man in history can better stand such a scrutiny.

Born of a distinguished family in the days when the American colonies were still ruled by an aristocracy, Washington started with all that good birth and tradition could give. Beyond this, however, he had little. His family was poor, his mother was left early a widow, and he was forced after a very limited education to go out into the world to fight for himself. He had strong within him the adventurous spirit of his race. He became a surveyor, and in the pursuit of this profession plunged into the wilderness, where he soon grew to be an expert hunter and backwoodsman. Even as a boy the gravity of his character and his mental and physical vigor commended him to those about him, and responsibility and military command were put in his hands at an age when most young men are just leaving college. As the times grew threatening on the frontier, he was sent on a perilous mission to the Indians, in which, after passing through many hardships and dangers, he achieved success. When the troubles came with France it was by the soldiers under his command that the first shots were fired in the war which was to determine whether the North American continent should be French or English. In his earliest expedition he was defeated by the enemy. Later he was with Braddock, and it was he who tried to rally the broken English army on the stricken field near Fort Duquesne. On that day of surprise and slaughter he displayed not only cool courage but the

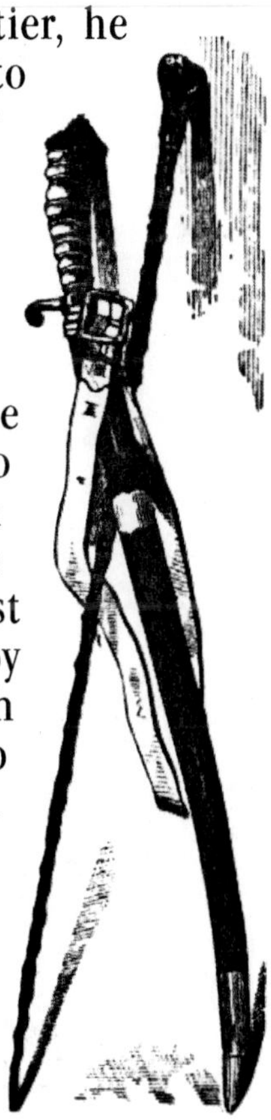

Washington, Our First President
Project 2, Page 2

reckless daring which was one of his chief characteristics. He so exposed himself that bullets passed through his coat and hat, and the Indians and the French who tried to bring him down thought he bore a charmed life. He afterwards served with distinction all through the French war, and when peace came he went back to the estate which he had inherited from his brother, as the most admired man in Virginia.

At that time he married, and during the ensuing years he lived the life of a Virginia planter, successful in his private affairs and serving the public effectively but quietly as a member of the House of Burgesses. When the troubles with the mother country began to thicken he was slow to take extreme ground, but he never wavered in his belief that all attempts to oppress the colonies should be resisted, and when he once took up his position there was no shadow of turning. He was one of Virginia's delegates to the first Continental Congress, and, although he said but little, he was regarded

by all the representatives from the other colonies as the strongest man among them. There was something about him even then which commanded the respect and the confidence of every one who came in contact with him.

It was from New England, far remoted from his own State, that the demand came for his appointment as commander-in-chief of the American army. Silently he accepted the duty, and, leaving Philadelphia, took command of the army at Cambridge. There is no need to trace him through the events that followed. From the time when he drew his sword under the famous elm tree, he was the embodiment of the American Revolution, and without him that revolution would have failed almost at the start. How he carried it to victory through defeat and trial and every possible obstacle is known to all men.

When it was all over he found himself facing a new situation. He was the idol of the country and of his soldiers. The army was unpaid, and the veteran troops, with arms in their hands, were eager to have him take control of the disordered country as Cromwell had done in England a little more than a century before. With the army at his back, and supported by the great forces which, in every community, desired order before everything else, and are ready to assent to any arrangement which will bring peace and quiet, nothing would have been easier than for Washington to have made himself the ruler of the new nation. But that was not his conception of duty, and he not only refused to have anything to do with such a movement himself, but he repressed, by his dominant personal influence, all such intentions on the part of the army. On the 23d of December, 1783, he met the Congress at Annapolis, and there resigned

Washington, Our First President
Project 2, Page 3

his commission. What he then said is one of the two most memorable speeches ever made in the United States, and is also memorable for its meaning and spirit among all speeches ever made by men. He spoke as follows :

> MR. PRESIDENT: The great events on which my resignation depended having at length taken place, I have now the honor of offering my sincere congratulations to Congress, and of presenting myself before them, to surrender into their hands the trust committed to me and to claim the indulgece of retiring from the service of my country.
>
> Happy in the confirmation of our independence and sovereignty, and pleased with the opportunity afforded the United States of becoming a respectable nation, I resign with satisfaction the appointment I accepted with diffidence; a diffidence in my abilities to accomplish so arduous a task, which, however, was superseded by a confidence in the rectitude of our cause, the support of the supreme power of the Union, and the patronage of Heaven.
>
> The successful termination of the war has verified the most sanguine expectations, and my gratitude for the interposition of Providence and the assistance I have received from my countrymen increases with every review of the momentous contest.
>
> While I repeat my obligations to the Army in general, I should do injustice to my own feelings not to acknowledge, in this place, the peculiar services and distinguished merits of the Gentlemen who have been attached to my person during the war. It was impossible that the choice of confidential officers to compose my family should have been more fortunate. Permit me, sir, to recommend in particular those who have continued in service to the present moment as worthy of the favorable notice and patronage of Congress.
>
> I consider it an indispensable duty to close this last solemn act of my official life by commending the interests of our dearest country to the protection of Almighty God, and those who have the superintendence of them to His holy keeping.
>
> Having now finished the work assigned me, I retire from the great theatre of action, and, bidding an affectionate farewell to this august body, under whose orders I have so long acted, I here offer my commission and take my leave of all the employments of public life.

The great master of English fiction, writing of this scene at Annapolis, says: "Which was the most splendid spectacle ever witnessed—the opening feast of Prince George in London, or the resignation of Washington? Which is the noble character for after ages to admire—yon fribble dancing in lace and spangles, or yonder hero who sheathes his sword after a life of spotless honor, a purity unreproached, a courage indomitable and a consummate victory?"

Washington did not refuse the dictatorship, or, rather, the opportunity to take control of the country, because he feared heavy responsibility, but solely because, as a high-minded and patriotic man, he did not believe in meeting the situation in that way.

He was, moreover, entirely devoid of personal ambition, and had no vulgar longing for personal power. After resigning his com-

Washington, Our First President

Project 2, Page 4

mission he returned quietly to Mount Vernon, but he did not hold himself aloof from public affairs. On the contrary, he watched their course with the utmost anxiety. He saw the feeble Confederation breaking to pieces, and he soon realized that that form of government was an utter failure. In a time when no American statesman except Hamilton had yet freed himself from the local feelings of the colonial days, Washington was thoroughly national in all his views. Out of the thirteen jarring colonies he meant that a nation should come, and he saw what no one else saw: the destiny of the country to the west. He wished that a nation be founded which should cross the Alleghenies, and, holding the mouths of the Mississippi, take possession of all that vast and then unknown region. For these reasons he stood at the head of the national movement, and to him all men turned who desired a better union and sought to bring order out of chaos. With him Hamilton and Madison consulted in the preliminary stages which were to lead to the formation of a new system. It was his vast personal influence which made that movement a success, and when the Constitutional Convention met at Philadelphia, he presided over its deliberations. It was his commanding will that, more than anything else, brought a constitution through difficulties and conflicting interests, which more than once made any result seem well-nigh hopeless.

When the Constitution formed at Philadelphia had been ratified by the States, all men turned to Washington to stand at the head of the new government. As he had borne the burden of the Revolution, so he now took up the task of bringing the government of the Constitution into existence. For eight years he served as president. He came into office with a paper constitution, the heir of a bankrupt, broken-down confederation. He left the United States, when he went out of office, an effective and vigorous government. When he was inaugurated, we had nothing but the clauses of the Constitution as agreed to by the Convention. When he laid down the presidency, we had an organized government, an established revenue, a funded debt, a high credit, an efficient system of banking, a strong judiciary, and an army. We had a vigorous and well-defined foreign policy; we had recovered the western posts, which, in the hands of the British, had fettered our march to the west; we had proved our power to maintain order at home, to repress insurrection, to collect the national taxes, and to enforce the laws made by Congress. Thus, Washington had shown that rare combination of the leader who could first destroy by revolution, and who, having led his country through a great civil war, was then able to build up a new and lasting fabric upon the ruins of a system which had been overthrown. At the close of his official service he returned again to Mount Vernon, and, after a few years of quiet retirement, died just as the century in which he had played so great a part was closing.

Washington stands among the greatest

WASHINGTON, OUR FIRST PRESIDENT
Project 2, Page 5

men of human history, and those in the same rank with him are very few. Whether measured by what he did, or what he was, or by the effect of his work upon the history of mankind, in every aspect he is entitled to the place he holds among the greatest of his race. Few men in all time have such a record of achievement. Still fewer can show at the end of a career so crowded with high deeds and memorable victories a life so free from spot, a character so unselfish and so pure, a fame so void of doubtful points demanding either defense or explanation. Eulogy of such a life is needless, but it is always important to recall and to freshly remember just what manner of man he was. In the first place he was physically a striking figure. He was very tall, powerfully made, with a strong, handsome face. He was remarkably muscular and powerful. As a boy he was a leader in all outdoor sports. No one could fling the bar further than he, and no one could ride more difficult horses. As a young man he became a woodsman and hunter. Day after day he could tramp through the wilderness with his gun and his surveyor's chain,

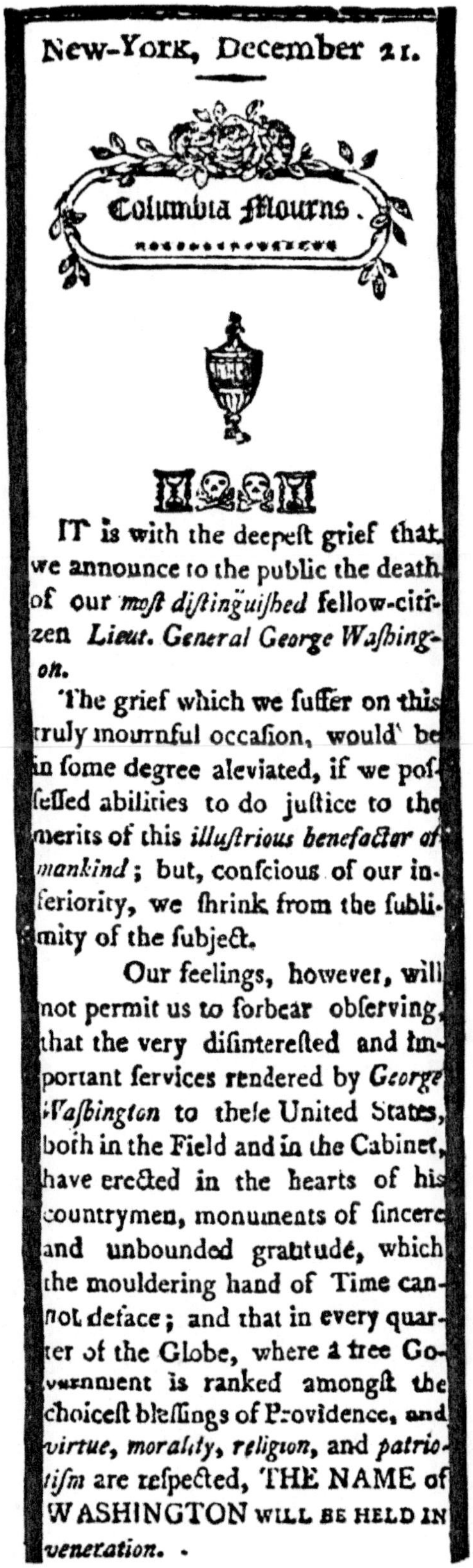

New-York, December 21.

Columbia Mourns.

IT is with the deepeſt grief that we announce to the public the death of our *moſt diſtinguiſhed* fellow-citizen *Lieut. General George Waſhington.*

The grief which we ſuffer on this truly mournful occaſion, would be in ſome degree aleviated, if we poſſeſſed abilities to do juſtice to the merits of this *illuſtrious benefactor of mankind*; but, conſcious of our inferiority, we ſhrink from the ſublimity of the ſubject.

Our feelings, however, will not permit us to forbear obſerving, that the very diſintereſted and important ſervices rendered by *George Waſhington* to theſe United States, both in the Field and in the Cabinet, have erected in the hearts of his countrymen, monuments of ſincere and unbounded gratitude, which the mouldering hand of Time cannot deface; and that in every quarter of the Globe, where a free Government is ranked amongſt the choiceſt bleſſings of Providence, and *virtue, morality, religion,* and *patriotiſm* are reſpected, THE NAME of WASHINGTON WILL BE HELD IN *veneration.*

and then sleep at night beneath the stars. He feared no exposure or fatigue, and outdid the hardiest backwoodsman in following a winter trail and swimming icy streams. This habit of vigorous bodily exercise he carried through life. Whenever he was at Mount Vernon he gave a large part of his time to fox-hunting, riding after his hounds through the most difficult country. His physical power and endurance counted for much in his success when he commanded his army, and when the heavy anxieties of general and president weighed upon his mind and heart.

He was an educated, but not a learned man. He read well and remembered what he read, but his life was, from the beginning, a life of action, and the world of men was his school. He was not a military genius like Hannibal, or Caesar, or Napoleon, of which the world has had only three or four examples. But he was a great soldier of the type which the English race has produced, like Marlborough and Cromwell, Wellington, Grant, and Lee. He was patient under defeat, capable of large combinations, a stubborn and often reckless fighter, a winner of battles,

Washington, Our First President

Project 2, Page 6

but much more, a conclusive winner in a long war of varying fortunes. He was, in addition, what very few great soldiers or commanders have ever been, a great constitutional statesman, able to lead a people along the paths of free government without undertaking himself to play the part of the strong man, the usurper, or the savior of society.

He was a very silent man. Of no man of equal importance in the world's history have we so few sayings of a personal kind. He was ready enough to talk or to write about the public duties which he had in hand, but he hardly ever talked of himself Yet there can be no greater error than to suppose Washington cold and unfeeling, because of his silence and reserve. He was by nature a man of strong desires and stormy passions. Now and again he would break out, even as late as the presidency, into a gust of anger that would sweep everything before it. He was always reckless of personal danger, and had a fierce fighting spirit which nothing could check when it was once unchained. But as a rule these fiery impulses and strong passions were under the absolute control of an iron will, and they never clouded his judgment or warped his keen sense of justice. But if he was not of a cold nature, still less was he hard or unfeeling. His pity always went out to the poor, the oppressed, or the unhappy, and he was all that was kind and gentle to those immediately about him. We have to look carefully into his life to learn all these things, for the world saw only a silent, reserved man, of courteous and serious manner, who seemed to stand alone and apart, and who impressed every one who came near him with a sense of awe and reverence. One quality he had which was, perhaps, more characteristic of the man and his greatness than any other. This was his perfect veracity of mind. He was, of course, the soul of truth and honor, but he was even more than that. He never deceived himself He always looked facts squarely in the face and dealt with them as such, dreaming no dreams, cherishing no delusions, asking no impossibilities, just to others as to himself, and thus winning alike in war and in peace. He gave dignity as well as victory 'to his country and his cause. He was, in truth, a "character for after ages to admire."

Washington, Our First President

Test

1. What is the date given for Washington, Our First President?

2. Where was Washington's home?

3. Why was Washington qualified for the job of president?

4. Where was the first capitol of the United States?

5. What other things other than the Constitution were to be set up under Washington's presidency?

6. What was John Adam's job under Washington?

Washington, Our First President

Test, Page 2

7. What was Thomas Jefferson's job under Washington?

8. What was Alexander Hamilton's job under Washington?

9. When was Washington elected to a second term as president?

10. To where did Washington plan to move the capital of the United States?

Review

1. Who was the first explorer to see the Grand Canyon?

2. What was Ponce de Leon in search of when he sailed a galleon to Florida in 1513?

Washington, Our First President

Test, Page 3

3. What was the First Great Awakening?

4. In chronological order list all events studied to date. Next to each place the appropriate date.

Washington, Our First President

Test, Page 4

4. (continued)

The Louisiana Purchase from France

Worksheet

1. What is the date given for the Louisiana Purchase from France?

____

____

____

2. The United States was growing vigorously, especially in the ____________________ ____________________ won from Great Britain.

3. What was being used to control Indian attacks?

____

____

____

4. For what did the American farmers use the Mississippi River?

____

____

____

5. What was the principal city used for shipping?

____

____

____

6. With the European conquests of Napoleon what happened to New Orleans?

____

____

____

7. What did Jefferson think about Napoleon's control of New Orleans?

____

____

THE LOUISIANA PURCHASE FROM FRANCE
Worksheet, Page 2

8. Jefferson sent ______________ ______________ to aid Robert Livingstone, a minister to France, to negotiate buying New Orleans.

9. For how much did Napoleon offer to sell the Louisiana Territory?

____

____

____

10. The purchase of Louisiana needed to be____________. Jefferson submitted the treaty directly to the ____________ where it was quickly approved.

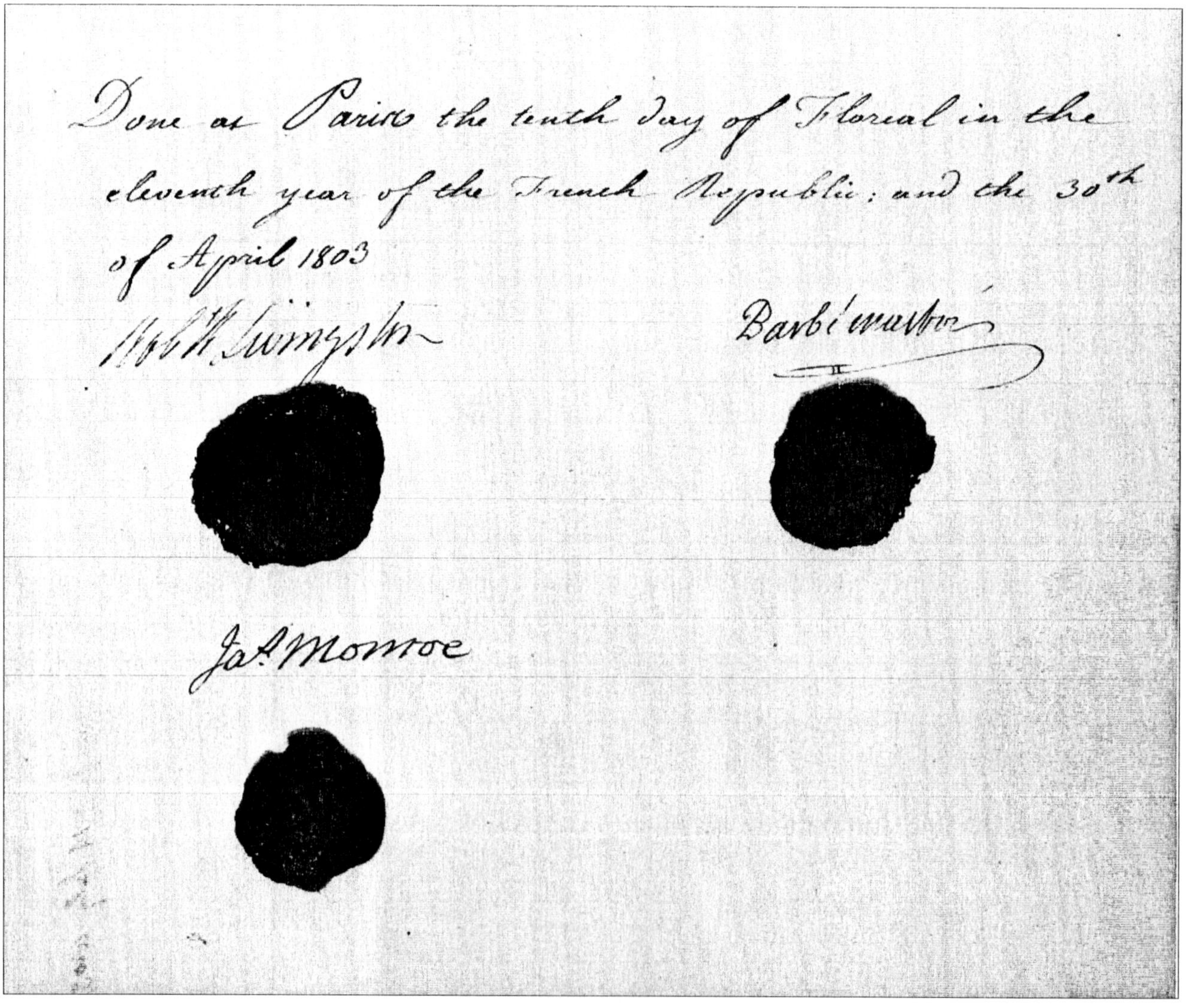
Done at Paris the tenth day of Floreal in the eleventh year of the French Republic; and the 30th of April 1803

Robt R Livingston

Barbé Marbois

Jas. Monroe

The Louisiana Purchase from France

Project 1—Primary Source Reading

Read the Treaty struck between the United States of America and the French Republic.

The President of the United States of America and the First Consul of the French Republic in the name of the French People desiring to remove all Source of misunderstanding relative to objects of discussion mentioned in the Second and fifth articles of the convention of the 8th Vende-miaire and 30th September 1800 relative to the rights claimed by the United States in virtue of the Treaty concluded at Madrid the 27 of October 1795, between His Catholic Majesty & the Said United States, & willing to Strengthen the union and friendship which at the time of the Said Convention was happily reestablished between the two nations have respectively named their Plenipotentiaries to wit The President of the United States, by and with the advice and consent of the Senate of the Said States; Robert R. Livingston Minister Plenipotentiary of the United States and James Monroe Minister Plenipotentiary and Envoy extraordinary of the Said States near the Government of the French Republic; And the First Consul in the name of the French people, Citizen Francis Barbé Marbois Minister of the public treasury who after having respectively exchanged their full powers have agreed to the following Articles.

Article I

Whereas by the Article the third of the Treaty concluded at St Ildefonso the 9th Vendê-miaire and 1st October 1800 between the First Consul of the French Republic and his Catholic Majesty it was agreed as follows.

"His Catholic Majesty promises and engages on his part to cede to the French Republic six months after the full and entire execution of the conditions and Stipulations herein relative to his Royal Highness the Duke of Parma, the Colony or Province of Louisiana with the Same extent that it now has in the hand of Spain, & that it had when France possessed it; and Such as it Should be after the Treaties

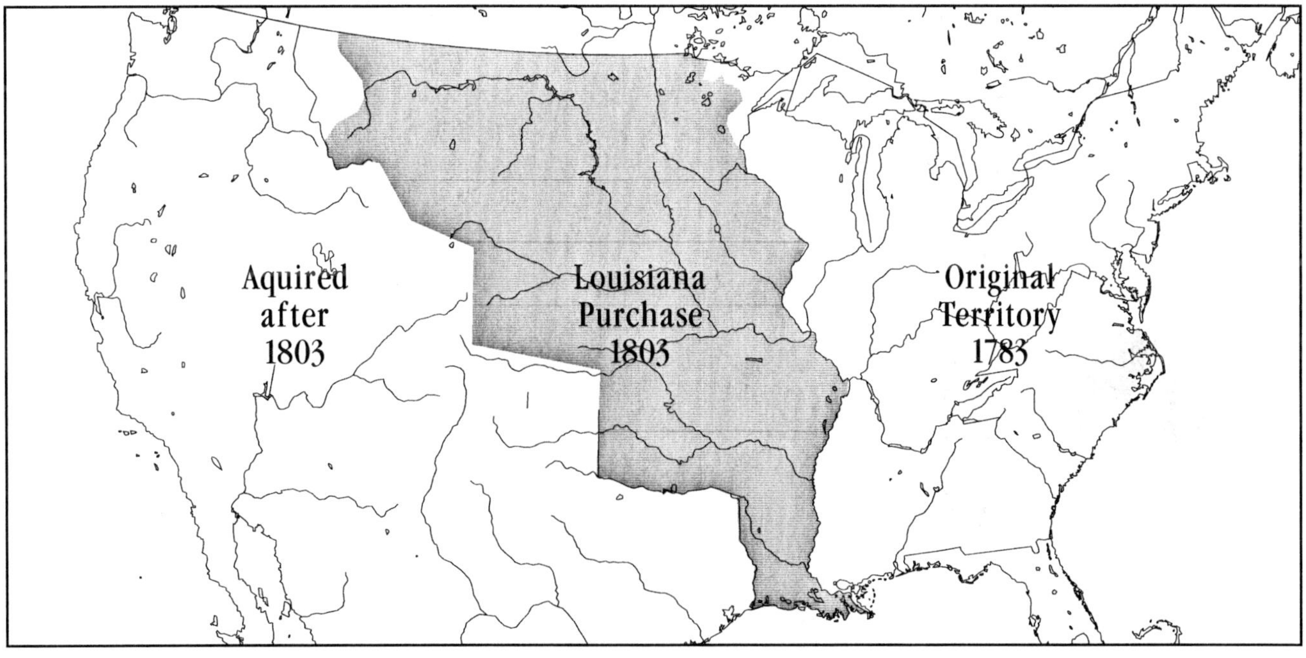

THE LOUISIANA PURCHASE FROM FRANCE
Project 1, Page 2

subsequently entered into between Spain and other States."

And whereas in pursuance of the Treaty and particularly of the third article the French Republic has an incontestible title to the domain and to the possession of the said Territory—The First Consul of the French Republic desiring to give to the United States a strong proof of his friendship doth hereby cede to the United States in the name of the French Republic for ever and in full Sovereignty the said territory with all its rights and appurtenances as fully and in the Same manner as they have been acquired by the French Republic in virtue of the above mentioned Treaty concluded with his Catholic Majesty.

Article II

In the cession made by the preceeding article are included the adjacent Islands belonging to Louisiana all public lots and Squares, vacant lands and all public buildings, fortifications, barracks and other edifices which are not private property.—The Archives, papers & documents relative to the domain and Sovereignty of Louisiana and its dependances will be left in the possession of the Commissaries of the United States, and copies will be afterwards given in due form to the Magistrates and Municipal officers of such of the said papers and documents as may be necessary to them.

Article III

The inhabitants of the ceded territory shall be incorporated in the Union of the United States and admitted as soon as possible according to the principles of the federal Constitution to the enjoyment of all these rights, advantages and immunities of citizens of the United States, and in the mean time they shall be maintained and protected in the free enjoyment of their liberty, property and the Religion which they profess.

Article IV

There Shall be Sent by the Government of France a Commissary to Louisiana to the end that he do every act necessary as well to receive from the Officers of his Catholic Majesty the Said country and its dependences in the name of the French Republic if it has not been already done as to transmit it in the name of the French Republic to the Commissary or agent of the United States.

Article V

Immediately after the ratification of the present Treaty by the President of the United States and in case that of the first Consul's shall have been previously obtained, the commissary of the French Republic shall remit all military posts of New Orleans and other parts of the ceded territory to the Commissary or Commissaries named by the President to take possession—the troops whether of France or Spain who may be there shall cease to occupy any military post from the time of taking possession and shall be embarked as soon as possible in the course of three months after the ratification of this treaty.

Article VI

The United States promises to execute Such treaties and articles as may have been agreed between Spain and the tribes and nations of Indians until by mutual consent of the United States and the said tribes or nations other Suitable articles Shall have been agreed upon.

Article VII

As it is reciprocally advantageous to the commerce of France and the United States to encourage the communication of both nations for a limited time in the country ceded by the

The Louisiana Purchase from France

Project 1, Page 3

present treaty until general arrangements relative to commerce of both nations may be agreed on; it has been agreed between the contracting parties that the French Ships coming directly from France or any of her colonies loaded only with the produce and manufactures of France or her Said Colonies; and the Ships of Spain coming directly from Spain or any of her colonies loaded only with the produce or manufactures of Spain or her Colonies shall be admitted during the Space of twelve years in the Port of New Orleans and in all other legal ports-of-entry within the ceded territory in the Same manner as the Ships of the United States coming directly from France or Spain or any of their Colonies without being Subject to any other or greater duty on merchandize or other or greater tonnage than that paid by the citizens of the United States.

During that Space of time above mentioned no other nation Shall have a right to the Same privileges in the Ports of the ceded territory—the twelve years Shall commence three months after the exchange of ratifications if it Shall take place in France or three months after it Shall have been notified at Paris to the French Government if it Shall take place in the United States; It is, however, well understood that the object of the above article is to favour the manufactures, Commerce, freight and navigation of France and of Spain So far as relates to the importations that the French and Spanish Shall make into the Said Ports of the United States without in any Sort affecting the regulations that the United States may make concerning the exportation of the produce and merchandize of the United States, or any right they may have to make Such regulations.

Article VIII

In future and for ever after the expiration of the twelve years, the Ships of France shall be treated upon the footing of the most favoured nations in the ports above mentioned.

Article IX

The particular Convention Signed this day by the respective Ministers, having for its object to provide for the payment of debts due to the Citizens of the United States by the French Republic prior to the 30th Sept. 1800 (8th Venamiaire and 9) is approved and to have its execution in the Same manner as if it had been inserted in this present treaty, and it Shall be ratified in the same form and in the Same time So that the one Shall not be ratified distinct from the other.

Another particular Convention Signed at the Same date as the present treaty relative to a definitive rule between the contracting parties is in the like manner approved and will be ratified in the Same form, and in the Same time and jointly.

Article X

The present treaty Shall be ratified in good and due form and the ratifications Shall be exchanged in the Space of Six months after the date of the Signature by the Ministers Plenipotentiary or Sooner if possible.

In faith whereof the respective Plenipotentiaries have Signed these articles in the French and English languages; declaring nevertheless that the present Treaty was originally agreed to in the French language; and have thereunto affixed their Seals.

Done at Paris the tenth day of Floreal in the eleventh year of the French Republic; and the 30th of April 1803.

Robt R Livingston
Jas. Monroe
Barbé Marbois

The Louisiana Purchase from France

Test

1. What is the date given for the Louisiana Purchase from France?

2. Where in particular was the United States growing in the year 1803?

3. What established the U.S. Army? For what was it being used?

4. How did American farmers transport goods?

5. Who came to control New Orleans? How did this occur?

6. Why was James Monroe sent by Jefferson to purchase New Orleans?

The Louisiana Purchase from France

Test, Page 2

7. How much did the United States pay for Louisiana?

8. Because the purchase needed to be quick, to whom did Jefferson submit the treaty for approval?

Review

1. What did the Puritans believe about the church of England?

2. Who was Squanto?

3. Who was Ferdinand Magellan?

The Louisiana Purchase from France

Test, Page 3

4. Who funded Christopher Columbus's voyage to the New World?

5. In chronological order list all events studied to date. Next to each place the appropriate date.

The Louisiana Purchase from France

Test, Page 4

5. (continued)

THE LEWIS AND CLARK EXPEDITION
Worksheet

1. What is the date given for The Lewis and Clark Expedition?

____

____

2. What did President Jefferson appoint Meriwether Lewis and William Clark to do? What were they to find?

____

____

____

____

3. Who was Sacajawea?

____

____

____

4. They reached the________________ ________________ in 1805 and returned to ______________ in 1806.

5. How many miles did they travel in two and one-half years?

____

____

6. What did the Lewis and Clark Journal contain?

____

____

____

7. For What did the Lewis and Clark expedition pave way?

____

____

____

The Lewis and Clark Expedition

Project 1—Expedition Scene

Read the following account and make an expedition scene using the directions at the end.

Somewhere near this point they expected to find some Snake or Shoshone Indians to guide them across the mountains.

The Indian girl, Sacajawea, knew this region, as years ago she had lived there. She had been captured by an enemy tribe and taken far away. The expedition depended on her to act as interpreter, and to secure the friendship of the Indians.

They were nearing the source of the river. Lofty mountains raised their heads close to the river's brink. The current ran faster. There were many shallow places. Across these the men had to drag the canoes. In these high altitudes game was scarce, and the meat supply began to give out.

Lewis pushed on afoot. He was anxious to meet some Indians to inquire the way. Prickly pears and thorns made traveling hard. That night Lewis outwalked his party, spending the night alone. The next morning his men found him.

They chose the middle fork. The mountains were now snowcapped. On the eleventh day the long-looked for Indian was found. He was timid and hurried away. The next day Lewis reached the source of the Missouri. It was an ice-cold spring, bursting from the mountain side.

Pressing on, Lewis crossed the divide and found the source of a tributary of the Columbia River. Here he met some Indians who took him to their camp. They agreed to furnish horses. Lewis led the way back to meet Clark. When they reached the Missouri, Clark had not yet arrived.

His absence alarmed the Indians. They thought Lewis had been lying. He had great trouble to keep them with him. Fortunately, Clark arrived and saved the day. The Indian squaw recognized the Indian chief as her long lost brother. There was an affecting scene and

THE LEWIS AND CLARK EXPEDITION
Project 1, Page 2

the friendship of these Indians was assured.

Leaving their boats they crossed the divide. The stream discovered by Lewis was too small. They started off over Indian trails to find a broad river that the Indians told about. The trail wound along the edges of the precipices, down steep mountian sides, and through rushing mountain streams. The horses stumbled and fell. Some of them had to be killed for food. A blinding snow storm swept the path. Fallen timber added to the hardships of the road.

As they descended from the mountians the heat became intense. When the plains were reached the men were exhausted. A few days' rest, then on again. New canoes were built. Their remaining horses were branded and left with a friendly Indian to keep until their return.

Game was still scarce. They lived off roots, a few fish, and dog meat bought from the Indians. Some of the Indians were hostile, but it was necessary to make them friendly for they must return over this route.

November 1st they reached tide water. The river was 5 to 7 miles wide. On November 7th they heard breakers. "Great joy in camp," wrote Lewis, "we are in view of the ocean." The river was rough, and little canoes tossed and pitched. The shores were steep and rocky. It began to rain. The storm lasted ten days.

They encamped on the rocky shores. Everything was soaked, clothing, bedding, and the travelers. For six days they were weather bound. The storm ceased and the little party pushed off once more. They rounded a high point, and the broad Pacific rolled before their delighted eyes. They had succeeded. Through many toils and dangers they had blazed the first trail across the continent.

They spent the winter on the coast, resting and preparing for the return the next spring. The remains of their huts and palisades were visible sixty years later.

Lewis and Clark spent the winter writing their journals, studying the Indians, and securing specimens to take home. The men tanned skins for clothing, split wood, hunted, and fished. A number of them spent two months making 20 gallons of salt from the sea water.

Food was scarce and their tobacco gave out. All were anxious for spring to return. On March 23rd, with snow on the ground, they broke camp and started for home.

After six months of toil, exposure, and hardships they reached St. Louis. The entire settlement turned out to greet them. Long ago they had been given up for dead. Ovations and banquets were prepared. Here they posted their letters and materials to Jefferson, and the little company of men, disbanding, left for their several homes. One of the most wonderful exploring trips in history was ended. For one year, four months, and nine days the little band of men had toiled and suffered and at last conquered.

This wonderful expedition prepared the way for settlement and gave us a stronger claim on the great Oregon Country west of the Rocky Mountians. It also told the people that this new Louisiana land was very large and very rich in natural resouces. It proved that the United States had obtained a valuable addition to its territory.

The Lewis and Clark Expedition

Project 1, Page 3—Expedition Scene

Supplies (per canoe)

2 pipe cleaners

2 eight-inch sections of brown or tan craft paper

glue

eight paperclips

salt dough (paint when dry or tint some blue, some green and brown)

twigs for trees, small rocks for staging , etc.

shoe box

Self-hardening Salt Dough Recipe
(makes about 5 cups of dough)

1 1/2 cups salt

4 cups flour

1 1/2 cups water

1 teaspoon alum

Directions for Salt Dough

1. Mix dry ingredients.
2. Add water gradually.
3. When dough forms a ball around the spoon, knead the dough well.
4. Add water if dough is crumbly. If desired, divide and tint.

Directions

1. Crumple and twist the craft paper, then flatten out again.
2. Twist one pipe cleaner to shape the upper rim of the canoe.
2. Twist the second pipe cleaner into two sections of ribbing in the canoe bottom.
3. Put glue on the long edges of the craft paper and fold long edges just over the canoe rim around the outside of the pipe cleaners.
4. Paper clip the small bit of overhang together on each side until the glue dries.
5. Trim or fold in the excess from each end and glue and paper clip in place.
6. Trim the second piece of twist paper to the line inside of the canoe and glue in place.
7. In the shoebox, make a salt dough scene for the canoes to navigate. Place twigs, rocks, etc. where desired.

The Lewis and Clark Expedition
Project 2—Lewis and Clark's Journal

Read the following excerpts from the journal of Lewis and Clark.

October 2, 1805
East of Orofino, ID

The day is very warm.

There are large numbers of Indians traveling up and down the river in canoes. It seems that the Indians are coming by to see us. Two men were sent to the village with some tobacco, ribbons, and beads to trade for food. We are eating roots. The hunters found nothing, so we killed one of the horses to eat.

Our main activity today was to continue making canoes. We have been working making five canoes for the last five days. To make a canoe we chopped down a tall, straight tree. The outside of the canoe was shaped with an ax. The inside was hollowed out by building a small fire, then chopping out the charred wood.

October 3, 1805
East of Orofino, ID

The weather today is fair. Morning winds from the east are cool, but warmer winds come from other directions later in the day.

The hunters found nothing again today. We do see small animals and birds, but our guns are not very good, and it would take many shots to get enough food for the 23 people in our party. We are eating the remains of the horse we killed yesterday.

Our main activity today was to continue making canoes. To hollow out a canoe we are using an adz. This tool is like a garden hoe, but has a short handle. It chips out little curves of wood. A man will stand on the log, or with legs spread across the log, and swing the adz between his feet. The wood is green, which makes it easier to chop, but it also helps to make a small fire to char a spot before chopping it out.

Lewis and several others in the party are ill. Mostly the problem is their stomachs, from no food, or food that isn't good for us. We have made soup from horse meat which the ill find easier to eat.

October 4, 1805
East of Orofino, ID

Warm and dry weather today.

I am hungry again today. Our horse is eaten. The hunters are not able to find game because the country here is very rough. Steep canyons rise from the river and there are only thin woods. The brush is dry and noisy and the hunters cannot stalk the deer. Several lesser chiefs from the villages down river have come to pay visits to Captains Lewis and Clark. They are very interested to trade for beads. The chicfs want to he helpful and perhaps get something in return. The chiefs see that we have many valuable possessions, including metal tools, saddles, and guns.

One of the braves got into an argument with Captain Clark after he took some tobacco from Captain Clark's sack. I understand how it looks, these white men have resources and wealth that would change the lives of my whole village. The white men see the Indians as stealing, but when the white men have so much maybe they should give more in trade.

October 5, 1805
East of Orofino, ID

Warmer today with afternoon clouds. Wind from the east again.

The hunters did not kill anything again today. We are eating dried fish and roots. Capt. Lewis and I ate boiled roots for supper.

THE LEWIS AND CLARK EXPEDITION
Project 2, Page 2

They caused us to swell so that it was hard to breathe.

Sacajawea has been helping translate when I meet the chiefs. I am very interested to learn more about the river. The chiefs draw maps of the river and explain where there are rapids, good fishing places, and greater chiefs. Today they told stories of other white men down river. We may get to the ocean in a month.

We launched two of the canoes today. They are very good little boats. We still have three to finish.

I have been supervising the men branding and cutting off the foretop from our 38 horses. We are doing this to mark the horses. Two bothers and the son of the local chief will care for our horses until we return. They will also accompany us down river for the next few days. I've given a knife and some small articles to these men in payment for their help.

October 6, 1805
East of Orofino, ID

Warm today with wind from the east. Today we finished the canoes and tested them. After dark, when the Indians were not around, we collected and buried all our saddles, along with a canister of powder and bag of balls for the guns. This cache was buried about a half mile down stream from our camp, near where Mr Shields cut the first tree for our canoes. We will return here for these supplies next spring when we head back over the pass.

I have felt unwell in the bowels since last night's supper.

The river below here is called the Koskos-kee. It is clear and shallow, with many small shoals or swift places. More open country begins a few miles down river, with trees on the left below the first creek.

October 7, 1805
East of Orofino, ID

The morning is cloudy. Clark was still ill from eating boiled roots.

We waited for the Indian Chiefs but they did not show for some reason. We put the canoes into the river, loaded them up and headed down stream. While fighting some rapids Clark's canoe was forced into a rock and sprung a leak. We stopped briefly for repairs. As we continued, we noticed several Indian camps, but we did not stop to trade.

After 19 miles we made camp for the night on the left side of the river. This was another hungry evening!

October 8, 1805
East of Lewiston, ID

Another cloudy morning.

The men reloaded the canoes and we set out 9 a.m. We passed four different islands and went through fifteen rapids which we were fortunate enough to escape. Along the way we passed many camps of Indians. At one of these camps we met up with the two Chiefs who we waited for yesterday. After a ceremony of smoking they agreed to join us.

Later during the day, Sergeant Gass's canoe nearly turned over and sprung a leak. The canoe filled with water and sunk. Many of the white men could not swim and held on to the canoe. Several Indians helped to save them. We had to stop for the night because all of the goods were soaked. Captain Lewis and Captain Clark had all of the goods spread out to dry.

They had to post guards because many of the Indians were tempted to take what they needed. The white men have so much and the Indians have so little.

I am tired. Today has been very long.

The Lewis and Clark Expedition
Project 2, Page 3

November 1, 1805
Southeast of Mt. St. Helen's

It is a very cool morning 59°; the wind is blowing hard from the NE.

The Indians who visited us last night, packed up their canoes and carried them down the great falls. We too set out after them carrying our canoes and all our baggage. We carried them by land over 940 yards. The path was rocky, wet and very slippery. The Indians carried their canoes for a total of 2 1/2 miles to avoid another falls further down. In hindsight we too should have carried our canoes as the Indians did. Instead we passed the canoes over the rocks in the river using poles. While we were attempting this, three of our men became injured. We stopped to bandage their wounds which delayed us quite a bit as we were forced to camp here for the day.

While we were stopped, several Indian canoes arrived. We visited with these men who spoke a language similar to the one spoken by our previous visitors but with a slight accent. These Indians came from the mouth of the river. They appeared healthy, however many of them have lost an eye. I assume this is a result of the dangers associated with these wild waters. Both men and women have unnaturally flat heads. I noticed several children's head in a press like device (two wooden boards tied together) used to flatten the forehead and elongate the profile. I have been informed that the flat head and long profile is a sign of beauty and high status. The women are small and homely with swollen legs. Their knees are unusually large. These Indians ask a very high price for what they sell. They claim that the whites down the river pay a much higher price for their goods and thus are reluctant to sell us anything for much less than they would usually get.

November 2, 1805
Southeast of Mt. St. Helen's

The Morning is cold.

We examined the rapid below us very carefully and decided that it would be too dangerous to pass with loaded canoes, so we sent most of the men and baggage by land. The canoes then passed the rapid safely and we were able to reload them at the foot of the rapid. Just as we were preparing to leave, seven squaws arrived bringing dried fish and bear grass. Soon after four Indians arrived in a large canoe. We had breakfast with them and so it was late in the afternoon before we again headed down stream.

After traveling several miles we passed the upper point of an island which is separated from the right shore by a narrow channel, although the channel is now dry it is apparent from the markings that it once contained an immense amount of water. We named this island Strawberry Island because the land is covered with strawberry vines. In several places on the island the Indians have been digging for roots and the whole island appears to be cultivated. We have now passed the last of the rapids on the Columbia and have reached the place where the tide waters begin and the river is much wider and calmer.

After traveling four more miles we

The Lewis and Clark Expedition
Project 2, Page 4

reached the lower point of Strawberry Island. From here we could see three small islands covered with wood. On one of these islands there is a high perpendicular rock, it is about eight hundred feet high, and four hundred feet wide, we named this Beacon Rock. These islands are covered with pine, spruce-pine, cottonwood, a species of ash, and some alder. The country before was so barren that it seems wonderful to see so many trees. We continued on for twelve miles and then stopped for the night. We will be able to eat well tonight as we were able to kill eighteen water-fowl.

November 3, 1805
Near the Mouth of the Columbia

The morning was very foggy. It was so foggy that we could not see men who were only 50 steps away.

Due to the weather, we were delayed until 10:00 am. before setting out. When we did get going, our Indian friends from a village near the great falls went with us.

We saw what we believed to be Mt. Hood, to the southeast, about 47 miles away. The mountain was snow covered and cone-shaped, but rugged. We proceeded on from there, to a large island in the middle of the river that we called Diamond Island, because of its appearance.

We landed on the north side of Diamond Island, and met 15 Indian men with 2 canoes. They told us that they had seen 3 other vessels down the river. After encamping, another canoe arrived with a man, his wife, three children, and a woman who had been taken prisoner from the Snake Indians. We could not find anyone that was able to understand her though, so we did not learn anything from her.

The Indians and the family that we met continued with us, and some of them went with Captain Lewis to a small lake on the island. They brought a canoe into the lake, and hunted for birds. They killed several birds, which brought our total for the day to 3 Swans, 8 Brant, and 5 Ducks. We made a delicious meal from these, and shared with our Indian friends.

November 4, 1805
Southeast of Mt. St. Helen's

Today was cool and fair.

Several canoes of Indians came to pay us a friendly visit. They were not dressed in their normal clothes, but instead wore overalls, sailors' jackets, shirts and hats. They brought with them bows and arrows, spears, and pistols. These Indian men were not very pleasant, but we were friendly and smoked with them anyway.

While we ate dinner, one of the Indians stole my pipe tomahawk. As I searched for that, one of them stole our interpreters coat! We found the coat by a tree near the Indian men. The Indians knew we were very displeased with them and returned to their camp. We proceeded on.

November 5, 1805
Southeast of Mt. St. Helen's

The morning is wet and chilly.

Everything is wet or damp from the rain

that started last night. I did not sleep well last night because of the dreadful racket the swans, geese, and ducks made on the small island near us.

Early in the afternoon we overtook four canoes that had about 25 or more Indians in them. The lead canoe was painted with images of bears, on the bow, and men on the stern. They told Lewis and Clark about a level place down river where we could camp.

The remainder of the day was cloudy and wet and everybody was in foul spirits. In late afternoon we made camp. Clark was able to kill an enormous grouse that I cooked for the group. This was the first night that we have been entirely clear of Indians since our arrival on the Columbia River.

November 6, 1805
Southeast of Mt. St. Helen's

A cool and wet morning 59°; winds from the Southwest.

We set out early this morning and passed two lodges only a few miles downstream. Shortly after passing the lodges several of the Indians came in their canoes to sell sundry articles and provisions. We purchased wap-pa-too roots, salmon and trout from them. I purchased two beaver skins for 5 small fish hooks.

Further downstream we overtook two canoes of Indians. One of the Indians, who spoke a few words of English, said they were going down to trade with a man named Mr. Haley. He proudly showed us his hunting bow made of iron and other items Mr. Haley gave him. We stopped to eat on a long narrow island where the woods were so thick with undergrowth that the hunters could not travel any distance into them to hunt.

The Indians traveled with us until we stopped to camp for the evening, all the better, for the cold rainy day had made us wet and disagreeable. We made large fires that we used to dry our bedding and kill the flees which collect in our blankets.

November 7, 1805
Southeast of Mt. St. Helen's

This morning the rain and fog were so thick we could not see to the other side of the river.

We broke camp and continued our journey, keeping on the right side of the river. There were many islands here. There was a large island about 5 miles long and many lower, marshy islands.

The Indians in this area seem to be of a different tribe. Their heads are flattened and they speak a different language than the people above them. Their houses are different, too. The men dress the same, but the women dress quite differently. They wear a fur robe from the arms to the hip. Below this robe they wear a skirt of white cedar bark that hangs to the knee in front and to midleg behind.

Later in the day the fog cleared and we viewed for the first time the object of our visit—the ocean! The sound of distant breakers excited us more and we continued on in high cheerfulness, despite the rain!

The steep high rocks on the north shore prevented us from camping for a considerable way. We traveled 34 miles today and wearily set up our camp in the rain.

The Lewis and Clark Expedition
Test

1. What is the date given for the Lewis and Clark expedition?

2. What did Jefferson appoint Meriweather Lewis and William Clark to do? (Give a detailed answer)

3. Who was Sacajawea?

4. About how many miles did they travel and in how many years?

5. What was the Lewis and Clark Journal?

The Lewis and Clark Expedition
Test, Page 2

6. For what did their exploration help pave the way?

Review

1. Who discovered the Mississippi River in North America?

2. Where was the battle of Bunker Hill actually fought?

3. Why did the British blockade Boston Harbor in 1775?

4. Name two acts of the British Parliament that taxed the American colonies and helped unite them against England?

The Lewis and Clark Expedition
Test, Page 3

5. In chronological order list all events studied to date. Next to each place the appropriate date.

The Lewis and Clark Expedition
Test, Page 3

5. (continued)

The Second Great Awakening
Worksheet

1. What are the dates given for the Second Great Awakening?

2. Where did the Second Great Awakening begin?

3. Camp meetings were attended by as many as ______________ people at one time.

4. What was one of the results of the Second Great Awakening?

5. When did the Second Great Awakening end?

6. How did the Second Great Awakening change the Church and evangelism in America?

The Second Great Awakening
Project 1—Revival at Reading

Following you will find an excerpt from Charles G. Finney's Autobiography. *The book begins with his birth and education. We will skip ahead a bit and pick it up with his discussion on the Revival at Reading.*

As I found myself in Philadelphia, in the heart of the Presbyterian church, and where Princeton views were almost universally embraced, I must say still more emphatically than I have done, if possible, that the greatest difficulty I met with in promoting revivals of religion, was the false instruction given to the people, and especially to inquiring sinners. Indeed, in all my ministerial life, in every place and country where I have labored, I have found this difficulty to a greater or less extent; and I am satisfied that multitudes are living in sin, who would immediately be converted if they were truly instructed. The foundation of the error of which I speak, is the dogma that human nature is sinful in itself; and that, therefore, sinners are entirely unable to become Christians. It is admitted, either expressly or virtually, that sinners may want to be Christians, and that they really do want to be Christians, and often try to be Christians, and yet somehow fail.

It had been the practice, and still is to some extent, when ministers were preaching repentance, and urging the people to repent, to save their orthodoxy by telling them that they could not repent, any more than they could make a world. But the sinner must be set to do something; and with all their orthodoxy, they could not bear to tell him that he had nothing to do. They must therefore, set him self-righteously to pray for a new heart. They would sometimes tell him to do his duty, to press forward in duty, to read his Bible, to use the means of grace; in short, they would tell him to do anything and everything, but the very thing which God commands him to do. God commands him to repent now, to believe now, to make to him a new heart now. But they were afraid to urge God's claims in this form, because they were continually telling the sinner that he had no ability whatever to do these things.

As an illustration of what I have found in this and other countries, more or less, ever since I have been in the ministry, I will refer to a sermon that I heard from the Rev. Baptist Noel, in England, a good man, and orthodox in the common acceptation of the term. His text was: "Repent and be converted, that your sins may be blotted out, when the times of refreshing shall come from the presence of the Lord." In the first place he represented repentance not as a voluntary, but as an involuntary change, as consisting in sorrow for sin, a mere state of the sensibility. He then insisted upon its being the sinner's duty to repent, and urged the claims of God upon him. But he was preaching to an orthodox congregation; and he must not, and did not, fail to remind them that they could not repent; that although God required it of them, still He knew that it was impossible for them to repent, only as He gave them repentance. "You ask, then," he said, "what you shall do. Go home," said he, in reply," and pray for repentance; and if it does not come, pray again for repentance; and still if it does not come, keep praying till it does come." Here he left them. The congregation was large, and the people very attentive; and I actually found it difficult to keep from screaming to the people, to repent, and not to think that they were doing their duty in merely praying for repentance.

Such instructions always pained me exceedingly; and much of my labor in the

The Second Great Awakening
Project 1, Page 2

ministry has consisted in correcting these views, and in pressing the sinner immediately to do just what God commands him to do. When he has inquired of me, if the Spirit of God has nothing to do with it, I have said, "Yes; as a matter of fact you will not do it of yourself. But the Spirit of God is now striving with you to lead you to do just what He would have you do. He is striving to lead you to repentance, to lead you to believe; and is striving with you, not to secure the performance of mere outward acts, but to change your heart." The church, to a very great extent, have instructed sinners to begin on the outside in religion; and by what they have called an outward performance of duty, to secure an inward change of their will and affections.

But I have ever treated this as totally wrong, unorthodox, and in the highest degree dangerous. Almost innumerable instances have occurred, in which I have found the results of this teaching, of which I have complained, to be a misapprehension of duty on the part of sinners; and I think I may say I have found thousands of sinners, of all ages, who are living under this delusion, and would never think themselves called upon to do anything more than merely to pray for a new heart, live a moral life, read their Bibles, attend meeting, use the means of grace, and leave all the responsibility of their conversion and salvation with God.

From Philadelphia in the winter of 1829-30, I went to Reading, a city about forty miles west of Philadelphia. At this place an incident occurred, which I shall mention in its place, that was a striking illustration of the kind of teaching to which I have alluded, and of its natural results. In Reading there were several German churches, and one Presbyterian church. The pastor of the latter was the Rev. Dr. Greer. At his request, and that of the elders of the church, I went out to labor there for a time.

I soon found, however, that neither Dr. Greer, nor any of his people, had any just idea of what they needed, or what a revival really was. None of them had ever seen a revival, so far as I could learn. Besides, all revival efforts, for that winter, had been forestalled, by an arrangement to have a ball every alternate week, which was attended by many of the members of the church, one of the leading elders in Dr. Greer's church being one of the managers. I could not learn that Dr. Greer had ever said anything against this. They had no preaching during the week, and I believe no religious meetings of any kind.

When I found what the state of things was, I thought it my duty to tell Dr. Greer that those balls would very soon be given up, or I should not be allowed to occupy his pulpit; that those balls, attended by his church members, and headed by one of his elders, would not long consist with my preaching. But he said, "Go on; take your own course." I did so; and preached three times on the Sabbath, and four times, I think, during the week, for about three weeks, before I said anything about any other meetings. We had no prayer meetings, I believe, for the reason that the lay members had never been in the habit of taking part in such meetings.

However, on the third Sabbath, I think, I gave notice that a meeting for inquiry would be held in the lecture room, in the basement of the church, on Monday evening. I stated as clearly as possible the object of the meeting, and mentioned the class of persons that I desired to attend; inviting those, and those only, that were seriously impressed with the state of their souls, and had made up their minds to attend immediately to the subject, and desired to receive instruction on the particular question of what they should do to be

The Second Great Awakening
Project 1, Page 3

saved. Dr. Greer made no objection to this, as he had left everything to my judgment. But I do not think he had an idea that many, if any, would attend such a meeting, under such an invitation; as to do so would be, to make an open acknowledgment that they were anxious for the salvation of their souls, and had made up their minds to attend to the subject at once.

Monday was rather a snowy, cold day. I think I observed that conviction was taking hold of the congregation; yet I felt doubtful how many would attend a meeting of inquirers. However, when evening came, I went to the meeting. Dr. Greer came in, and behold! the lecture room, a large one—I think nearly as large as the body of the church above—was full; and on looking around Dr. Greer observed that most of the impenitent persons in his congregation were present; and among them, those who were regarded as the most respectable and influential.

He said nothing publicly. But he said to me, "I know nothing about such a meeting as this; take it into your own hands, and manage it in your own way." I opened the meeting by a short address, in which I explained to them what I wished; that is to have a few moments conversation with each of them, and to have them state to me frankly how they felt on the subject, what their convictions were, what their determinations were, what their difficulties were.

I told them that if they were sick and called a physician, he would wish to know their symptoms, and that they should tell him how they were, and how they had been. I said to them, "I cannot adapt instruction to your present state of mind, unless you reveal it to me. The thing, therefore, that I want, is that you reveal, in as few words as you can, your exact state of mind at the present time. I will now pass around among you, and give each of you an opportunity to say in the fewest words, what your state of mind is." Dr. Greer said not a word, but followed me around, and stood or sat by me and heard all that I had to say. He kept near me, for I spoke to each one in a low voice, so as not to be heard by others than those in the immediate vicinity. I found a great deal of conviction and feeling in the meeting. They were greatly pressed with conviction. Conviction had taken hold of all classes, the high and the low, the rich and the poor.

Dr. Greer was greatly moved. Though he said nothing, still it was evident to me that his interest was intense. To see his congregation in such a state as that, was what he had never had any conception of. I saw that with difficulty, at times, he controlled his emotions.

When I had spent as much time as was allowed me in personal conversation, I then went back to the desk, and gave them an address; in which, according to my custom, I summed up the results of what I had found that was interesting, in the communications that they had made to me. Avoiding all personalities, I took up the representative cases, and dissected, and corrected, and taught them. I tried to strip away their misapprehensions and mistakes, to correct the impression that they had, that they must simply use means and wait for God to convert them; and in an address of perhaps a half or three-quarters of an hour, I set before them the whole situation, as clearly as I possibly could. After praying with them I called on those that felt prepared to submit, and who were willing then and there to pledge themselves to live wholly to God, who were willing to commit themselves to the sovereign mercy of God in Christ Jesus, who were willing to give up all sin, and to renounce it forever, to kneel down, and while I prayed, to commit them-

THE SECOND GREAT AWAKENING
Project 1, Page 4

selves to Christ, and inwardly to do what I exhorted them to do. I called on those only to kneel down, who were willing to do what God required of them, and what I presented before them. Dr. Greer looked very much surprised at the test I put, and the manner in which I pressed them to instant submission.

As soon as I saw that they thoroughly understood me, I called on them to kneel, and knelt myself. Dr. Greer knelt by my side, but said nothing. I presented the case in prayer to God, and held right to the point of now submitting, believing, and consecrating themselves to God. There was an awful solemnity pervading the congregation, and the stillness of death, with the exception of my own voice in prayer, and the sobs, and sighs, and weeping that were heard more or less throughout the congregation.

After spreading the case before God we rose from our knees, and without saying anything farther I pronounced the blessing and dismissed them. Dr. Greer took me cordially by the hand, and smiling said, "I will see you in the morning." He went his way, and I went to my lodgings. At about eleven o'clock, I should judge, a messenger came running over to my lodgings, and called me, and said that Dr. Greer was dead. I inquired what it meant. He said he had just retired, and was taken with a fit of apoplexy, and died immediately. He was greatly respected and beloved by his people, and I am persuaded he deserved to be. He was a man of thorough education, and I trust of earnest piety. But his theological education had not at all fitted him for the work of the ministry, that is to win souls to Christ. He was besides rather a timid man. He did not like to face his people, and resist the encroachments of sin as he needed to do. His sudden death was a great shock, and became the subject of constant conversation throughout the town.

Although I found a goodly number had, to all human appearance, submitted at the meeting on Monday evening, still the death of Dr. Greer, under such extraordinary circumstances, proved a great diversion of the public mind for a week or more. But after his funeral was over, and the usual evening services got into their proper channel, the work took on a powerful type, and went forward in a most encouraging manner.

Many very interesting incidents occurred in this revival. I recollect on one very snowy night, when the snow had already fallen deep, and was drifting in a terrible manner under a fierce gale of wind, I was called up about midnight, to go and visit a man who, they informed me, was under such awful conviction that he could not live, unless something could be done for him. The man's name was B. He was a stalwart man, very muscular, a man of great force of will and strength of nerve, physically a fine specimen of humanity. His wife was a professor of religion; but he had cared for none of these things.

He had been at the meeting that evening, and the sermon had torn him to pieces. He went home in a terrible state of mind, his convictions and distress increasing till it overcame his bodily strength; and his family feared he would die. Although it was in the midst of such a terrific storm, they dispatched a messenger for me. We had to face the storm, and walked perhaps fifty or sixty rods. I heard his moanings, or rather howlings, before I got near the house. When I entered I found him sitting on the floor, his wife, I believe, supporting his head—and what a look in his face! It was indescribable. Accustomed as I was to seeing persons under great convictions, I must confess that his appearance gave me a tremendous shock. He was writhing in agony, grinding his teeth,

THE SECOND GREAT AWAKENING
Project 1, Page 5

and literally gnawing his tongue for pain. He cried out to me, "Oh, Mr. Finney! I am lost! I am a lost soul!" I was greatly shocked and exclaimed, "If this is conviction, what is hell?" However, I recovered myself as soon as I could, and sat down by his side. At first he found it difficult to attend; but I soon led his thoughts to the way of salvation through Christ. I pressed the Savior upon his attention and upon his acceptance. His burden was soon removed. He was persuaded to trust the Savior, and he came out free and joyful in hope.

Of course, from day to day, I had my hands, my head, and my heart entirely full. There was no pastor to help me, and the work spread on every hand. The elder of the church to whom I have alluded as being one of the managers of their stated balls soon broke down his heart before the Lord, and entered into the work; and, as a consequence, his family were soon converted. The revival made a thorough sweep in the families of those members of the church that entered into the work.

I said that in this place a circumstance occurred, that illustrated the influence of that old school teaching of which I have complained. Very early one morning a lawyer, belonging to one of the most respectable families in the town, called at my room, in the greatest agitation of mind. I saw he was a man of first-rate intelligence, and a gentleman; but I had nowhere seen him, to know him. He came in and introduced himself, and said he was a lost sinner—that he had made up his mind that there was no hope for him. He then informed me that when he was in Princeton College, he and two of his classmates became very anxious about their souls. They went together to Dr. Ashbel Green, who was then president of the college, and asked him what they should do to be saved. He said the doctor told them he was very glad to have them come and make the inquiry; and then told them to keep out of all bad company, to read their Bible statedly, and to pray God to give them a new heart. "Continue this," he said, "and press forward in duty; and the Spirit of God will convert you; or else He will leave you, and you will return back to your sins again." "Well, I inquired, how did it terminate?" "Oh," said he, "we did just as he told us to do. We kept out of bad company, and prayed that God would make us a new heart. But after a little while our convictions wore away, and we did not care to pray any longer. We lost all interest in the subject;" and then bursting into tears he said, "My two companions are in drunkard's graves, and if I cannot

repent I shall soon be in one myself." This remark led me to observe that he had indications of being a man that made too free use of ardent spirits. However, this was early in the morning; and he was entirely free from drink, and in terrible anxiety about his soul.

I tried to instruct him, and to show him the error that he had fallen into, under such instructions as he had received, and that he had resisted and grieved the Spirit, by waiting for God to do what He had commanded him to do. I tried to show him that, in the very nature of the case, God could not do for him what He required him to do. God required him to repent, and God could not repent for him; required him to believe, but God could not believe for him; God required him to submit, but could not submit for him. I then tried to make him understand the agency that the Spirit of God has in giving the sinner repentance and a new heart; that it is a divine persuasion; that the Spirit leads him to see his sins, urges him to give them up and to flee from the wrath to come. He presents to him the Savior, the atonement, the plan of salvation, and urges him to accept it.

I asked him if he did not feel this urgency upon himself, in these truths revealed in his own mind; and a call, now to submit, to believe, to make himself a new heart. "Oh yes!" he said, "Oh yes! I see and feel all this. But am I not given up of God? Is not my day of grace past?" I said to him, "No! It is plain the Spirit of God is still calling you, still urging you to repentance; you acknowledge that you feel this urgency in your own mind." He inquired, "Is this, then, what the Spirit of God is doing, to show me all this?" I assured him that it was; and that he was to understand this as a divine call, and as evidence conclusive that he was not abandoned, and had not sinned away the day of grace, but that God was striving to save him still. I then asked him if he would respond to the call, if he would come to Jesus, if he would lay hold upon eternal life then and there.

He was an intelligent man, and the Spirit of God was upon and teaching him, and making him understand every word that I said. When I saw that the way was fully prepared, I called on him to kneel down and submit; and he did so, and to all human appearance, became a thorough convert right upon the spot. "Oh!" he afterwards said, "if Dr. Green had only told us this that you have told me, we should all have been converted immediately. But my friends and companions are lost; and what a wonder of mercy it is that I am saved!"

I recollect a very interesting incident in the case of a merchant in Reading, one branch of whose business was the making of whiskey. He had just been fitting up a very large distillery at a good deal of expense. He had constructed it with all the latest improvements, on a large scale, and was going deeply into the business. But as soon as he was converted, he gave up all thought of going any farther with that business. It was a spontaneous conclusion of his own mind. He said at once, "I shall have nothing to do with that. I shall tear my distillery down. I will neither work it, nor sell it to be worked."

His wife was a good woman, and a sister to Mr. B, whose conversion I have mentioned as occurring on that stormy night. The merchant's name was O'B. The revival took a powerful hold in his family, and several of them were converted. I do not recollect now how many there were; but I think every impenitent person in his household was converted. His brother also, and his brother's wife, and, I know not how many, but quite a large circle of relatives were among the converts. But Mr. O'B himself was in feeble

The Second Great Awakening
Project 1, Page 7

health, and was rapidly passing away with the consumption. I visited him frequently, and found him full of joy.

We had been examining candidates for admission to the church, and a large number were to be admitted on a certain Sabbath. Among them were those members of his own family, and those relatives of his that had been converted. Sabbath morning came. It was soon found Mr. O'B could not live through the day. He called his wife to his bedside and said to her, "My dear, I am going to spend the Sabbath in heaven. Let all the family go, and all the friends, and unite with the church below; and I will join the church above." Before meeting time he was dead. Friends were called in to lay him in his shroud; his family and relatives gathered around his corpse, and then turned away and came to meeting; and, as he had desired, united with the church militant, while he went to unite with the church triumphant.

Their pastor had but just gone before; and I think it was that morning, I had said to Mr. O'B, "Give my love to Brother Greer, when you get to heaven." He smiled with holy joy and said to me, "Do you think I shall know him?" I said, "Yes, undoubtedly you will know him. Give him my love, and tell him the work is going on gloriously." "I will, I will," said he. His wife and family sat at the communion table, showing in their countenance mingled joy and sorrow. There was a kind of holy triumph manifested, as their attention was called to the fact that the husband, and father; and brother, and friend, was sitting that day at the table of Jesus on high, while they were gathered around His table on earth.

There was much that was moving and interesting in that revival, in a great many respects. It was among a population that had had no conception of revivals of religion. The German population supposed themselves to have been made Christians by baptism, and especially by receiving the communion. Nearly every one of them, if asked when they became Christians, would reply that they took their communion at such a time of Dr. M, or some other German divine. And when I asked them if they thought that was religion, they would say, yes, they supposed it was. Indeed that was the idea of Dr. M himself. In walking with him to the grave of Dr. Greer, on the occasion of his funeral, he told me he had made sixteen hundred Christians by baptism, and giving them the communion, since he had been pastor of that church. He seemed himself to have no other idea of becoming a Christian than simply to learn the catechism, and to be baptized and partake of the communion.

The revival had to encounter that view of things; and the influence was at first, almost altogether in that direction. It was held, as I was informed, and I have no doubt of it, that for them to begin to think of being religious, by being converted, and to establish family prayer, or to give themselves to secret prayer, was not only fanaticism, but was virtually saying that their ancestors had all gone to hell; for they had done no such thing. The German ministers would preach against all those things, as I was informed by those that heard them, and speak severely of those that forsook the ways of their fathers, and thought necessary to be converted, and to maintain family and secret prayer.

The great majorities, I think, of Dr. Greer's congregation were converted in this revival. At first I had considerable difficulty in getting rid of the influence of the daily press. I think there were two or more daily newspapers published there at the time. I learned that the editors were drinking men; and were not infrequently carried home, on public

The Second Great Awakening
Project 1, Page 8

occasions, in a state of intoxication. The people were a good deal under the influence of the daily press. I mean the German population particularly. These editors began to give the people religious advice, and to speak against the revival, and the preaching. This threw the people into a state of perplexity. It went on from day to day, and from week to week, till finally the state of things became such that I thought it my duty to notice it. I therefore went into the pulpit when the house was crowded, and took for my text: "Ye are of your father the devil, and the lusts of your father ye will do." I then went on to show in what way sinners would fulfill the desires of the devil, pointing out a great many ways in which they would perform his dirty work, and do for him what he could not do for himself.

After I had got the subject well before the people, I applied it to the course pursued by the editors of those daily papers. I asked the people if they did not think that those editors were fulfilling the desires of the devil; if they did not believe the devil desired them to do just what they did? I then asked them if it was suitable and decent, for men of their character, to attempt to give religious instruction to the people? I told the people what I understood their character to be, and turned my hand upon them pretty heavily, that such men should attempt to instruct the people, in regard to their duties to God and their neighbors. I said, "If I had a family in the place I would not have such a paper in the house; I should fear to have it under my roof; I should consider it too filthy to be touched with my fingers, and would take the tongs and throw it into the street." In some way the papers got into the street the next morning, pretty plentifully, and I neither saw nor heard any more of their opposition.

I continued in Reading until late in the spring. There were many very striking conversions; and so far as I know, Dr. Greer's congregation was left entirely united, greatly encouraged and strengthened, and with large additions made to their number. I have never been in that place since.

From Reading I went to Lancaster, Pennsylvania, at that time and until his death, the home of the late President Buchanan. The Presbyterian church at Lancaster had no pastor, and I found religion in a very low state. They had never had a revival of religion, and manifestly had no just conception of what it was, or of the appropriate means of securing it. I remained at Lancaster but a very short time. However the work of God was immediately revived, the Spirit of God being poured out almost at once upon the people. I was the guest of an aged gentleman by the name of K, who was one of the elders of the church, and indeed the leading man in the church.

A fact occurred in relation to him, while I was in his family, that revealed the real state of things in a religious point of view, in that church. A former pastor of the church had invited Mr. K to join the church and hold the office of elder. I should say that the facts I am about to communicate respecting this event, were related to me by himself. One Sabbath evening after hearing a couple of very searching sermons, the old gentleman could not sleep. He was so greatly exercised in his mind, that he could not endure it until morning. He called me up in the middle of the night, stated what his convictions were, and then said that he knew he had never been converted. He said that when he was requested to join the church and become an elder, he knew that he was not a converted man. But the subject was pressed upon him till he finally consulted Rev. Dr. C, an aged minister of a Presbyterian church not far from Lancaster. He stated to him the fact that he had never been converted, and yet that he was desired to join the church that he might become an elder. Dr. C, in view of all the circumstances, advised him to join and accept the office, which he did.

His convictions at the time I speak of, were very deep. I gave him such instructions as I thought he needed, pressed him to accept the Savior; and dealt with him just as I would with any other inquiring sinner. It was a very solemn time. He professed at the time to submit and accept the Savior. Of his subsequent history I know nothing. He was certainly a gentleman of high character, and never to my knowledge did anything outwardly, to disgrace the position which he held. Those who are acquainted with the state of the church of which Dr. C was pastor, in regard to the eldership at that time, will not wonder at the advice which he gave to Mr. K.

Among the incidents that occurred, during my short stay at Lancaster, I recall the following. One evening I preached on a subject that led me to insist upon the immediate acceptance of Christ. The house was very much crowded, literally packed. At the close of my sermon I made a strong appeal to the people to decide at once; and I think I called on those whose minds were made up, and who would then accept the Savior, to rise up, that we might know who they were, and that we might make them subjects of prayer. As I learned the next day; there were two men sitting near one of the doors of the church, one of whom was very much affected under the appeal that was made, and could not avoid manifesting very strong emotion, which was observed by his neighbor. However, the man did not rise up, nor give his heart to God. I had pressed the thought upon them, that might be the last opportunity that some of them would ever have, to meet and decide this question; that in so large a congregation it was not unlikely that there were those there who would then decide their everlasting destiny, one way or the other. It was not unlikely that God would hold some of them to the decision that they then made.

After the meeting was dismissed, as I learned the next day, these two men went out together, and one said to the other, "I saw you felt very deeply under the appeals Mr. Finney made." "I did," he replied. "I never felt so before in my life; and especially when he reminded us that might be the last time we should ever have an opportunity to accept the offer of mercy." They went on conversing in this way, for some distance, and then separated, each one going to his own home. It was a dark night, and the one who had felt so deeply, and was so pressed with the conviction that he might then be rejecting his last offer, fell over the curbstone, and broke his neck. This was reported to me the next day.

I established prayer meetings in Lancaster, and insisted upon the elders of the church taking part in them. This they did at my earnest request, although, as I learned, they had never been accustomed to do it before. The interest seemed to increase from day to day, and hopeful conversions multiplied. I do not recollect now why I did not remain longer than I did; but I left at so early a period as not to be able to give anything like a detailed account of the work.

REVIVAL AT ROCHESTER, 1830

Leaving New York I spent a few weeks in Whitestown; and, as was common, being pressed to go in many directions, I was greatly at a loss what was my duty. But among others, an urgent invitation was received from the Third Presbyterian church in Rochester, of which Mr. Parker had been pastor, to go there and supply them for a season.

I inquired into the circumstances, and found that on several accounts it was a very unpromising field of labor. There were but three Presbyterian churches in Rochester. The Third church, that extended the invitation, had no minister, and religion was in a low state. The Second church, or the Brick Church, as it was called, had a pastor, an excellent man; but in regard to his preaching there was considerable division in the church, and he was restive and about to leave. There was a controversy existing between an elder of the Third church and the pastor of the First church, that was about to be tried before the presbytery. This and other matters had aroused unchristian feeling, to some extent, in both churches; and altogether it seemed a forbidding field of labor at that time. The friends at Rochester were exceedingly anxious to have me go there—I mean the members of the Third church. Being left without a pastor, they felt as if there was great danger that they would be scattered, and perhaps annihilated as a church, unless something could be done to revive religion among them.

With these pressing invitations before me, I felt, as I have often done, greatly perplexed. I remained at my father-in-law's, and considered the subject, until I felt that I must take hold and work somewhere. Accordingly we packed our trunks and went down to Utica, about seven miles distant, where I had many praying friends. We arrived there in the afternoon, and in the evening quite a number of the leading brethren, in whose prayers and wisdom I had a great deal of confidence, at my request met for consultation and prayer, in regard to my next field of labor. I laid all the facts before them in regard to Rochester; and so far as I was acquainted with them, the leading facts in respect to the other fields to which I was invited at that time. Rochester seemed to be the least inviting of them all.

After talking the matter all over, and having several seasons of prayer, interspersed with conversation, the brethren gave their opinions one after another, in relation to what they thought it wise for me to do. They were unanimous in the opinion that Rochester was too uninviting a field of labor, to be put at all in competition with New York, or Philadelphia, and some other fields to which I was then invited. They were firm in the conviction that I should go east from Utica, and not west. At the time, this was my own impression and conviction; and I retired from this meeting, as I supposed, settled not to go to Rochester, but to New York or Philadelphia. This was before railroads existed; and when we parted that evening I expected to take the canal boat, which was the most convenient way for a family to travel, and start in the morning for New York.

But after I retired to my lodging the question was presented to my mind under a different aspect. Something seemed to question me: "What are the reasons that deter you from going to Rochester?" I could readily enumerate them, but then the question returned: "Ah! but are these good reasons? Certainly you are needed at Rochester all the more because of these difficulties. Do you shun the field because there are so many things that need to be corrected, because there is so much that is wrong? But if all was right, you would not be needed." I soon came to the conclusion that we were all wrong; and that the reasons that had determined us against my going to Rochester, were the most cogent reasons for my going. I felt ashamed

The Second Great Awakening

Project 1, Page 11

to shrink from undertaking the work because of its difficulties; and it was strongly impressed upon me, that the Lord would be with me, and that was my field. My mind became entirely decided, before I retired to rest, that Rochester was the place to which the Lord would have me go. I informed my wife of my decision; and accordingly, early in the morning, before the people were generally moving in the city, the packet boat came along, and we embarked and went westward instead of eastward.

The brethren in Utica were greatly surprised when they learned of this change in our destination, and awaited the result with a good deal of solicitude.

We arrived in Rochester early in the morning, and were invited to take up our lodgings for the time with Mr. Josiah Bissell, who was the leading elder in the Third church, and who was the person that had complained to the presbytery respecting Dr. Penny. On my arrival I met my cousin, Mr. S, in the street, who invited me to his house. He was an elder in the First church, and hearing that I was expected at Rochester, was very anxious to have his pastor, Dr. Penny, meet and converse with me, and be prepared to cooperate with me in my labors. I declined his kind invitation, informing him that I was to be the guest of Mr. Bissell. But he called on me again after breakfast, and informed me that he had arranged an interview between myself and Dr. Penny, at his house. I hastened to meet the doctor, and we had a cheering Christian interview. When I commenced my labors, Dr. Penny attended our meetings, and soon invited me to his pulpit. Mr. S exerted himself to bring about a good understanding between the pastors and churches and a great change soon manifested itself in the attitude and spiritual state of the churches.

There were very soon some very marked conversions. The wife of a prominent lawyer in that city, was one of the first converts. She was a woman of high standing, a lady of culture and extensive influence. Her conversion was a very marked one. The first that I saw her, a friend of hers came with her to my room, and introduced her. The lady who introduced her was a Christian woman, who had found that she was very much exercised in her mind, and persuaded her to come and see me.

Mrs. M had been a gay worldly woman, and very fond of society. She afterward told me that when I first came there, she greatly regretted it, and feared there would be a revival; and a revival would greatly interfere with the pleasures and amusements that she had promised herself that winter. On conversing with her I found that the Spirit of the Lord was indeed dealing with her, in an unsparing manner. She was bowed down with great conviction of sin. After considerable conversation with her, I pressed her earnestly to renounce sin, and the world, and self, and everything for Christ. I saw that she was a very proud woman, and this struck me as rather the most marked feature of her character. At the conclusion of our conversation we knelt down to pray; and my mind being full of the subject of the pride of her heart, as it was manifested, I very soon introduced the text: "Except ye be converted and become as little children, ye shall in no wise enter into the kingdom of heaven." I turned this subject over in prayer; and almost immediately I heard Mrs. M, as she was kneeling by my side, repeating that text: "Except ye be converted and become as little children—as little children—Except ye be converted and become as little children." I observed that her mind was taken with that, and the Spirit of God was pressing it upon her heart. I therefore continued to pray, holding that subject

The Second Great Awakening
Project 1, Page 12

before her mind, and holding her up before God as needing that very thing, to be converted—to become as a little child.

I felt that the Lord was answering prayer. I felt sure that He was doing the very work that I asked Him to do. Her heart broke down, her sensibility gushed forth, and before we rose from our knees, she was indeed a little child. When I stopped praying, and opened my eyes and looked at her, her face was turned up toward heaven, and the tears streaming down; and she was in the attitude of praying that she might be made a little child. She rose up, became peaceful, settled into a joyous faith, and retired. From that moment she was outspoken in her religious convictions, and zealous for the conversion of her friends. Her conversion, of course, produced much excitement among that class of people to which she belonged.

I had never, I believe, except in rare instances, until I went to Rochester, used as a means of promoting revivals, what has since been called the anxious seat. I had sometimes asked persons in the congregation to stand up; but this I had not frequently done. However, in studying upon the subject, I had often felt the necessity of some measure that would bring sinners to a stand. From my own experience and observation I had found, that with the higher classes especially, the greatest obstacle to be overcome was their fear of being known as anxious inquirers. They were too proud to take any position that would reveal them to others as anxious for their souls.

I had found also that something was needed, to make the impression on them that they were expected at once to give up their hearts; something that would call them to act, and act as publicly before the world, as they had in their sins; something that would commit them publicly to the service of Christ. When I had called them simply to stand up in the public congregations I found that this had a very good effect; and so far as it went, it answered the purpose for which it was intended. But after all, I had felt for some time, that something more was necessary to bring them out from among the mass of the ungodly, to a public renunciation of their sinful ways, and a public committal of themselves to God.

At Rochester, if I recollect right, I first introduced this measure; this was years after the cry had been raised of new measures. A few days after the conversion of Mrs. M, I made a call, I think for the first time, upon all that class of persons whose convictions were so ripe that they were willing to renounce their sins and give themselves to God, to come forward to certain seats which I requested to be vacated, and offer themselves up to God, while we made them subjects of prayer. A much larger number came forward than I expected, and among them was another prominent lady; and several others of her acquaintance, and belonging to the same circle of society, came forward. This increased the interest among that class of people; and it was soon seen that the Lord was aiming at the conversion of the highest classes of society. My meetings soon became thronged with that class. The lawyers, physicians, merchants, and indeed all the most intelligent people, became more and more interested, and more and more easily influenced.

Very soon the work took effect, extensively, among the lawyers in that city. There has always been a large number of the leading lawyers of the state, resident at Rochester. The work soon got hold of numbers of these. They became very anxious, and came freely to our meetings of inquiry; and numbers of them came forward to the anx-

The Second Great Awakening
Project 1, Page 13

ious seat, as it has since been called, and publicly gave their hearts to God. I recollect one evening after preaching, three of them followed me to my room, all of them deeply convicted; and all of them had been, I believe, on the anxious seat, but were not clear in their minds, and felt that they could not go home until they were convinced their peace was made with God. I conversed with them, and prayed with them; and I believe, before they left, they all found peace in believing in the Lord Jesus Christ.

I should have said that very soon after the work commenced, the difficulties between Mr. Bissell and Dr. Penny were healed; and all the distractions and collisions that had existed there were adjusted; so that a spirit of universal kindness and fellowship pervaded all the churches.

On one occasion I had an appointment in the First church. There had been a military parade in the city that day. The militia had been called out, and I had feared that the excitement of the parade, might divert the attention of the people, and mar the work of the Lord. The house was filled in every part. Dr. Penny had introduced the services, and was engaged in the first prayer, when I heard something which I supposed to be the report of a gun, and the jingling of glass, as if a window had been broken. My thought was that some careless person from the military parade on the outside, had fired so near the window as to break a pane of glass. But before I had time to think again, Dr. Penny leaped from the pulpit almost over me, for I was kneeling by the sofa behind him. The pulpit was in the front of the church, between the two doors. The rear wall of the church stood upon the brink of the canal. The congregation, in a moment, fell into a perfect panic, and rushed for the doors and the windows, as if they were all distracted. One elderly woman held up a window in the rear of the church, where several, as I was informed, leaped out into the canal. The rush was terrific. Some jumped over the galleries into the aisles below; they ran over each other in the aisles.

I stood up in the pulpit, and not knowing what had happened, put up my hands, and cried at the top of my voice, "Be quiet! Be quiet!" Directly a couple of women rushing up into the pulpit, one on the one side, and the other on the other side, caught hold of me, in a state of distraction. Dr. Penny ran out into the streets, and they were getting out in every direction, as fast as possible. As I did not know that there was any danger, the scene looked so ludicrous to me, that I could scarcely refrain from laughing. They rushed over each other in the aisles, so that in several instances I observed men that had been crushed down, rising up and throwing off others that had rushed upon them. All at length got out.

Several were considerably hurt, but no one killed. But the house was strewn with all sorts of women's apparel. Bonnets, shawls, gloves, handkerchiefs, and parts of dresses, were scattered in every direction. The men had very generally gone out without their hats, I believe; and many persons had been seriously bruised in the awful rush.

I afterwards learned that the walls of the church had been settling for some time, the ground being very damp from its proximity to the canal. It had been spoken of, in the congregation, as not in a satisfactory state; and some were afraid that either the tower would fall, or the roof, or the walls of the building would come down. Of this I had heard nothing myself. The original alarm was created by a timber from the roof, falling end downwards, and breaking through the ceiling, above the lamp in front

The Second Great Awakening

Project 1, Page 14

of the organ.

On examining the house, it was found that the walls had spread in such a manner, that there was indeed danger of the roof falling in. The pressure that night in the gallery was so great as to spread the walls on each side, until there was real danger. At the time this occurred, I greatly feared, as I suppose others did, that the public attention would be diverted, and the work greatly hindered. But the Spirit of the Lord had taken hold of the work in earnest, and nothing seemed to stay it.

The Brick church was thrown open to us, and from that time our meetings alternated between the Second and Third churches, the people of the First church and congregation attending as far as they could get into the house. The three churches, and indeed Christians of every denomination generally, seemed to make common cause, and went to work with a will, to pull sinners out of the fire. We were obliged to hold meetings almost continually. I preached nearly every night, and three times on the Sabbath. We held our meetings of inquiry, after the work took on such a powerful type, very frequently in the morning.

One morning I recollect we had been holding a meeting of inquiry, and a gentleman was present and was converted there, who was the son-in-law of a very praying, godly woman belonging to the Third church. She had been very anxious about him, and had been spending much time in prayer for him. When he returned from the meeting of inquiry, he was full of joy and peace and hope. She had been spending the time in earnest prayer that God would convert him at that meeting. As soon as she met him and he declared his conversion to her, and from his countenance she saw that it was really so, it overcame her, and she swooned away and fell dead.

There was at that time a high school in Rochester, presided over by a Mr. B, the son of A B, then pastor of the church at Brighton, near Rochester. Mr. B was a skeptic, but was at the head of a very large and flourishing school. As the school was made up of both sexes, a Miss A was his assistant and associate in the school, at that time. Miss A was a Christian woman. The students attended the religious services, and many of them soon became deeply anxious about their souls. One morning Mr. B found that his classes could not recite. When he came to have them before him, they were so anxious about their souls that they wept, and he saw that they were in such a state, that it very much confounded him. He called his associate, Miss A, and told her that the young people were so exercised about their souls that they could not recite; and asked if they had not better send for Mr. Finney to give them instruction. She afterwards informed me of this, and said that she was very glad to have him make the inquiry, and most cordially advised him to send for me. He did so, and the revival took tremendous hold of that school. Mr. B himself was soon hopefully converted, and nearly every person in the school. A few years since, Miss A informed me that more than forty persons, that were then converted in that school, had become ministers. That was a fact that I had not known before. She named many of them to me at the time. A large number of them had become foreign missionaries.

After remaining a few weeks at Josiah Bissell's, we took lodgings in a more central position, at the house of Mr. B, a lawyer of the city, who was a professedly Christian man. His wife's sister was with them, and was an impenitent girl. She was a young woman of fine appearance, an exquisite singer, and a cultivated lady; and, as we soon learned, was engaged in marriage to a man, who was then judge of the supreme court of the state. He was a very proud man, and resisted the anxious seat, and spoke against it. He was absent a good deal from the city, in holding court, and was not that winter converted. A large number of the lawyers, however, were converted; and the young lady to whom he was engaged was converted. I mention this because the Judge afterwards married her; which no doubt led to his own conversion in a revival which occurred some ten years later, the leading particulars of which I shall mention in another part of my narrative.

This revival made a great change in the moral state and subsequent history of Rochester. The great majority of the leading men and women in the city, were converted. A great number of very striking incidents occurred, that I shall not soon forget. One day the lady who first visited me and whose conversion I have mentioned, called on me in company with a friend of hers with whom she wished me to converse. I did so, but found her to all appearance very much hardened, and rather disposed to trifle with the subject. Her husband was a merchant, and they were persons of high standing in the community. When I pressed her to attend to the subject, she said she would not do it, because her husband would not attend to it, and she was not going to leave him. I asked her if she was willing to be lost because her husband would not attend to it; and if it was not folly to neglect her soul because he did his. She replied very promptly, "If he goes to hell, I want to go. I want to go where he does. I do not want to be separated from him, at any rate." It seemed that I could make very little, if any, impression upon her. But from night to night I had been making appeals to the congregation, and calling forward those that were prepared to give their hearts to God; and large numbers were converted every evening.

As I learned afterwards, when this woman went home, her husband said to her, "My dear, I mean to go forward tonight, and give my heart to God." "What!" said she; "I have today told Mr. Finney that I would not become a Christian, or have anything to do with it; that you did not become a Christian, and I would not; and that if you went to hell, I should go with you." "Well," said he, "I do not mean to go to hell. I have made up my mind to go forward tonight, and give my heart to Christ." "Well," said she, "then I will not go to meeting, I do not want to see it. And if you have a mind after all, to become a Christian, you may; I won't." When the time came, he went to meeting alone. The pulpit was between the doors, in the front of the church. The house was a good deal crowded;

but he finally got a seat near one of the aisles, in quite the back path of the church. At the close of the meeting, as I had done at other times, I called for those that were anxious and whose minds were made up, to come forward, and take certain seats and occupy a certain space about the pulpit, where we could commend them to God in prayer. It afterward appeared that the wife herself had come to the meeting, had passed up the other aisle, and taken a seat almost opposite him, in the extreme part of the house. When I made the call, he started immediately. She was watching, and as soon as she saw him on his feet, and making his way along the crowded aisle, she also started down the other aisle, and they met in front of the pulpit, and knelt down together as subjects of prayer.

A large number obtained hope on the spot; but this husband and wife did not. They went home, too proud to say much to each other about what they had done, and spent a very restless night. The next day, about ten o'clock, he called to see me, and was shown into my room. My wife occupied a front room on the second floor; and I a room in the rear on the same floor. While I was conversing with him, the servant informed me that a lady was waiting in Mrs. Finney's room to see me. I excused myself for a few moments, and requested him to wait, while I went in to see her. I found that it was the woman who but the day before had been so stubborn, and the wife of the man who was then in my room. Neither of them knew that the other had called to see me. I conversed with her, and found that she was on the very verge of submitting to Christ. I had learned that he was also, to all appearance, in the same state. I then returned to him and said, "I am going to pray with a lady in Mrs. Finney's room, and we will go in there, if you please, and all join in prayer, together." He followed me, and found his own wife. They looked at each other with surprise, but we were both greatly affected, each to find the other there. We knelt down to pray. I had not proceeded far in prayer before she began to weep, and to pray audibly for her husband. I stopped and listened, and found that she had lost all concern for herself, and was struggling in an agony of prayer for his conversion. His heart seemed to break and give way, and just at this time the bell rang for our dinner. I thought it would be well to leave them together alone. I therefore touched my wife, and we rose silently and went down to dinner, leaving them in prayer. We took a hasty dinner and returned, and found them as mellow, and as humble, and as loving as could be desired.

I have not said much, as yet, of the spirit of prayer that prevailed in this revival, which I must not omit to mention. When I was on my way to Rochester, as we passed through a village, some thirty miles east of Rochester, a brother minister whom I knew, seeing me on the canalboat, jumped aboard to have a little conversation with me, intending to ride but a little way and return. He, however, became interested in conversation, and upon finding where I was going, he made up his mind to keep on and go with me to Rochester. We had been there but a few days when this minister became so convicted that he could not help weeping aloud, at one time, as he passed along the street. The Lord gave him a powerful spirit of prayer, and his heart was broken. As he and I prayed much together, I was struck with his faith in regard to what the Lord was going to do there. I recollect he would say, "Lord, I do not know how it is; but I seem to know that Thou art going to do a great work in this city." The spirit of prayer was poured out powerfully, so much so, that some persons stayed away from the public services to pray, being unable to restrain their feelings under preaching.

And here I must introduce the name of a man, whom I shall have occasion to mention frequently, Mr. Abel Clary. He was the son of a very excellent man, and an elder of the church where I was converted. He was converted in the same revival in which I was. He had been licensed to preach; but his spirit of prayer was such, he was so burdened with the souls of men, that he was not able to preach much, his whole time and strength being given to prayer. The burden of his soul would frequently be so great that he was unable to stand, and he would writhe and groan in agony. I was well acquainted with him, and knew something of the wonderful spirit of prayer that was upon him. He was a very silent man, as almost all are who have that powerful spirit of prayer.

The first I knew of his being at Rochester, a gentleman who lived about a mile west of the city, called on me one day, and asked me if I knew a Mr. Abel Clary, a minister. I told him that I knew him well. "Well," said he, "he is at my house, and has been there for some time, and I don't know what to think of him." I said, "I have not seen him at any of our meetings." "No," he replied, "he cannot go to meeting," he said. "He prays nearly all the time, day and night, and in such an agony of mind that I do not know what to make of it. Sometimes he cannot even stand on his knees, but will lie prostrate on the floor, and groan and pray in a manner that quite astonishes me." I said to the brother, "I understand it; please keep still. It will all come out right; he will surely prevail."

I knew at the time a considerable number of men who were exercised in the same way. A Deacon P, of Camden, Oneida county; a Deacon T, of Rodman, Jefferson county; a Deacon B, of Adams, in the same country; this Mr. Clary, and many others among the men, and a large number of women, partook of the same spirit, and spent a great part of their time in prayer. Father Nash, as we called him, who in several of my fields of labor came to me and aided me, was another of those men that had such a powerful spirit of prevailing prayer. This Mr. Clary continued in Rochester as long as I did, and did not leave it until after I had left. He never, that I could learn, appeared in public, but gave himself wholly to prayer.

I have said that the moral aspect of things was greatly changed by this revival. It was a young city, full of thrift and enterprise, and full of sin. The inhabitants were intelligent and enterprising, in the highest degree; but as the revival swept through the town, and converted the great mass of the most influential people, both men and women, the change in the order, sobriety, and morality of the city was wonderful.

At a subsequent period, which I shall mention in its place, I was conversing with a lawyer, who was converted at this revival of who I have been speaking, and who soon after had been made district attorney of the city. His business was to superintend the prosecution of criminals. From his position he was made thoroughly acquainted with the history of crime in that city. In speaking of the revival in which he was converted, he said to me, many years afterward: "I have been examining the records of the criminal courts, and I find this striking fact, that whereas our city has increased since that revival, threefold, there are not one-third as many prosecutions for crime, as there had been up to that time. This is, "he said," the wonderful influence that revival had upon the community. Indeed by the power of that revival, public sentiment has been molded. The public affairs of the city have been, in a great measure in the hands of Christian men;

and the controlling influences in the community have been on the side of Christ."

Among other conversions I must not forget to mention that of Mr. P, a prominent citizen of that place, a bookseller. Mr. P was an infidel; not an atheist, but a disbeliever in the divine authority of the Bible. He was a reader and a thinker, a man of keen, shrewd mind, strong will, and most decided character. He was, I believe, a man of good outward morals, and a gentleman highly respected. He came to my room early one morning, and said to me, "Mr. Finney, there is a great movement here on the subject of religion, but I am a skeptic, and I want you to prove to me that the Bible is true." The Lord enabled me at once to discern his state of mind, so far as to decide the course I should take with him. I said to him, "Do you believe in the existence of God?" "O yes!" he said, I am not an atheist. "Well, do you believe that you have treated God as you ought? Have you respected His authority? Have you loved Him? Have you done that which you thought would please Him, and with the design to please Him? Don't you admit that you ought to love Him, and ought to worship Him, and ought to obey Him, according to the best light you have?" "O yes!" he said, I admit all this. "But have you done so?" I asked. "Why, no," he answered, "I cannot say that I have." "Well then," I replied, "why should I give you farther information, and farther light, if you will not do your duty and obey the light you already have? Now," said I, "when you will make up your mind to live up to your convictions, to obey God according to the best light you have; when you will make up your mind to repent of your neglect thus far, and to please God just as well as you know how, the rest of your life, I will try to show you that the Bible is from God. Until then it is of no use for me to do any such thing." I did not sit down, and I think had not asked him to sit down. He replied, "I do not know but that is fair;" and retired.

I heard no more of him until the next morning. Soon after I arose, he came to my room again; and as soon as he entered, he clapped his hands and said, "Mr. Finney, God has wrought a miracle! I went down to the store," he continued, "after I left your room, thinking of what you had said; and I made up my mind that I would repent of what I knew was wrong in my relations to God, and that hereafter I would live according to the best light I had. And when I made up my mind to this," said he, "my feelings so overcame me that I fell; and I do not know but I should have died, if it had not been for Mr. —, who was with me in the store." From this time he has been, as all who know him are aware, a praying, earnest Christian man. For many years he has been one of the trustees of Oberlin College, has stood by us through all our trials, and has aided us with his means and his whole influence.

During this great revival, persons wrote letters from Rochester, to their friends abroad, giving an account of the work, which were read in different churches throughout several states, and were instrumental in producing great revivals of religion. Many persons came in from abroad to witness the great work of God, and were converted. I recollect that a physician was so attracted by what he heard of the work that he came from Newark, New Jersey, to Rochester, to see what the Lord was doing, and was himself converted there. He was a man of talents and high culture, and has been for years an ardent Christian laborer for immortal souls.

One evening, I recollect, when I made a call for the anxious to come forward and submit, a man of influence in a neighboring town came forward himself, and several

The Second Great Awakening
Project 1, Page 19

members of his family, and gave themselves to God. Indeed, the work spread like waves in every direction. I preached in as many places round about, as I had time and strength to do, while my main labors were in Rochester. I went to Canandaigua and preached several times. There the Word took effect, and many were converted. The pastor, Rev. Ansel Eddy, entered heartily into the work. A former pastor, an elderly man, an Englishmen by birth, also did what he could to forward the work. Wherever I went, the Word of God took immediate effect; and it seemed only necessary to present the law of God, and the claims of Christ, in such relations and proportions as were calculated to secure the conversion of men, and they would be converted by scores.

The greatness of the work at Rochester, at that time, attracted so much of the attention of ministers and Christians throughout the State of New York, throughout New England, and in many parts of the United States, that the very fame of it was an efficient instrument in the hands of the Spirit of God in promoting the greatest revival of religion throughout the land, that this country had then ever witnessed. Years after this, in conversing with Dr. Beecher about this powerful revival and its results, he remarked: "That was the greatest work of God, and the greatest revival of religion, that the world has ever seen, in so short a time. One hundred thousand," he remarked, "were reported as having connected themselves with churches, as the results of that great revival. This," he said, "is unparalleled in the history of the church, and of the progress of religion." He spoke of this having been done in one year; and said that in no year during the Christian era, had we any account of so great a revival of religion.

From the time of the New Lebanon convention, of which I have spoken, open and public opposition to revivals of religion was less and less manifested, and especially did I meet with much less personal opposition than I had met with before. It gradually but greatly subsided. At Rochester I felt nothing of it. Indeed the waters of salvation had risen so high, revivals had become so powerful and extensive, and people had time to become acquainted with them and their results, in such measure, that men were afraid to oppose them as they had done. Ministers had come to understand them better, and the most ungodly sinners had been convinced that they were indeed the work of God. So manifestly were the great mass of the conversions sound, the converts really regenerated and made new creatures, so thoroughly were individuals and whole communities reformed, and so permanent and unquestionable were the results, that the conviction became nearly universal, that they were the work of God.

The Second Great Awakening

Project 2—Charles Finney's Teachings

Charles Finney was born in 1792 in Connecticut. He grew up to become a well-known evangelist. Finney was strongly criticized by many leading theologians of his time. Read the following summaries of Finney's teachings, then use the information to fill in the chart comparing some of Finney's teaching to Scripture.

Finney used emotional tactics that led to fainting, weeping, and other "excitements," as he and his followers called them. Finney's "new measures" for evangelism included the "anxious bench" where people could wait and then publicly proclaim themselves to be committed to religious resolutions.

Finney taught that regeneration—the act of the Holy Spirit which creates a new nature in a sinner—is an act of the human will. In his *Autobiography* he wrote, "Instead of telling sinners to use the means of grace and to pray for a new heart, I called on them to make themselves a new heart and spirit, and pressed the duty of immediate surrender to God." Finney believed humans could choose to be corrupt or redeemed by nature because he did not believe original sin to be scriptural. Finney insisted, in his *Systematic Theology,* that "regeneration consists in the sinner changing his ultimate choice, intention, preference; or in changing from selfishness to love or benevolence."

Finney also taught that whenever a Christian commits a sin, he is precisely the same as an unbeliever. He wrote in his Systematic Theology, "Whenever a Christian sins he comes under condemnation, and must repent and do his first works, or be lost."

Furthermore, Finney believed Christ could not have died for anyone else's sins but his own. He taught that the Atonement, by Christ's example of selflessness, would motivate humans to virtue, but not atone for the sins of the elect.

The Second Great Awakening
Project 2, Page 2

On the chart below, write out Finney's position on the Doctrines listed after reading what the Bible has to say about each of them.

Doctrine	Bible	Finney
Original Sin	*Romans 5:12–14*	______________________ ______________________
Atonement	*Hebrews 9:27–28*	______________________ ______________________
Regeneration	*John 6:44*	______________________ ______________________
Justification	*Titus 3:5–7*	______________________ ______________________
Preservation	*Ephesians 1:13–14*	______________________ ______________________

The Second Great Awakening
Project 3—Finney's Effect on the Church

Read the following article to understand more about how Finney's inventive changes to Christianity infected the Church in America.

As America evolved into the world's most powerful nation, many changes occurred. The Revolution and its generation began to pass into history. Immigrants flooded into New York, and many pressed on to the western frontier. The fires of devotion, which once burned so brightly during the Great Awakening, had died down. Many Americans, especially those pushing west, had become ignorant of religion. Some families had not attended church for two or three generations. Many denominations, Methodists and Baptists in particular, began to concentrate their efforts on converting the hinterland, today's Midwest. Revivals erupted with a ferocity unparalleled by any of the earlier Edwardian rumblings of the previous century. Sinners at these "camp meetings" fell into trances, lost control of their motor functions, and made peculiar sounds in a fit of wildness known as "the jerks." As these strange apparitions began to appear in the Wilderness beyond the Appalachians, Charles Grandison Finney was born. Finney, an intelligent young man, became an up-and-coming lawyer, but ironically, he seemed to have little interest in the things of the Lord. One day, however, while reading the Scripture, he claimed a radical conversion. Instantly, he sprang into action, witnessing to and converting many of his friends. Although he lacked formal ministerial training, he felt a burden to preach. His numerical successes blinded him from his obvious doctrinal flaws and naiveté. His local Presbytery licensed him to preach the gospel, and in many ways, the gospel has never completely recovered from that fateful decision. In western New York state, he would harness the dynamic power of the prairie revivals, and become the most famous preacher of his age. The white hot flame of Finney's revivals, however, did not rekindle the faith of the Puritans, instead his revivalism radically and permanently altered American Protestantism.

The Reformed creeds basically maintain a uniform doctrine concerning the Fall of man and its effects. Calvin and his followers agreed that the Fall totally disabled man spiritually. They maintained that Adam's first sin not only severed him from an intimate relationship with his Creator, but Adam also passed on to all of his descendants the effects of his rebellion. The Westminster Shorter Catechism, a classic summation of the Reformed position, not only says that all humans are sinful, but it elucidates the punishment in store for mankind as a result of their mutiny saying, "every sin deserveth God's wrath and curse both in this life and that which is to come." Furthermore, Calvinists state that man's works will always prove ineffectual in regaining his lost holiness. The only recourse of those sinners who wanted to have peace with God consisted in crying out for mercy by the merits and blood of Christ. God did not owe man salvation. People only had the right to ask for their earned wages which consisted of wrath, death, and hell. This Monolithic condemnation of man served to humiliate and humble him before his Lord.

Finney's theology differed sharply with the majority's opinion concerning the nature of man. His odd attitude arose from the boundless optimism of America at the turn of the century. How could men who built an empire out of stark wilderness not

The Second Great Awakening
Project 3, Page 2

be able to overcome sin in their lives and at least cooperate in their own salvation? Leonard Sweet in his article *View of Man Inherent in New Measures Revivalism* notes that "Finney affirmed that human nature was not fixed but flexible. Born as a free agent, man is empowered with the 'natural ability' to discern and obey the moral law, making it theoretically as easy to choose right as to choose wrong." Finney continued to use, or abuse, the term "original sin," but the connotation that he tied to these terms differed greatly from the Westminster standards. Otto Scott, in his book *The Secret Six,* reports, that Original Sin, instead of being linked to defiance of God, was described as simple "deep seated but voluntary selfishness." Finney said to his unlearned and feverish crowds that "All sin consists in selfishness and all holiness or virtue, in disinterested benevolence."

To Finney's sharp legal mind, trained in books of law rather than in the Scripture, it seemed unconscionable that God could ever find the whole human race guilty on account of the first transgression in Eden.

After depreciating the effect of the Fall, Finney introduced a more hopeful view of man. He believed that all of man's evil originated in his wrong free choices. Expanding his idea of free will, he denied the fact of man's fallen nature. Make no mistake, Charles Finney preached on the depravity of man, but he made notable revisions to the original Calvinistic dogma. Bernard Weisberger in *They Gathered at the River,* his masterful history of American "revivalism," remarks, "Man's depravity, to (Finney), was a voluntary attitude of the mind. Man persisted in sin by a choice. . . ." Calvinists, of course, would not take issue with Finney's idea that man continued to choose to sin for they believed that fallen men by nature loved sin. Finney, however, meant more than simply affirming that natural man loved sin; he held that man could freely of his own power and prerogative choose his way out of sin.

These doctrinal differences between Finney and Calvinistic orthodoxy might seem insignificant at first glance, but their effects are far from trifling. Although Finney endowed man with the ability to save himself, he did not raise man from the dust and place him on a throne next to God, but he made an important step in that direction. The Puritan God chose his people from among the mass of sinful humanity, sent his only Son to redeem them, and indwelt them with his Holy Spirit. He controlled all things, and everyone stood in awe of Him. Men and women prayed that God would save them; they came as beggars; they worshiped in the dust. Finney still claimed that he worshiped the same God, but in many ways he inverted the relationship of God and man.

Although still beneath God, man held the ultimate power, the power of salvation. God tried to save all people; He did all that He could, but in the end the Almighty could only hope that man, his creature, would choose to repent. God yearned; hoped, but often God failed. Finney's ideas about God not only persisted; they have gained preeminence in modern Christianity. He took a crucial step that resulted in the making of God Almighty into a cosmic bellhop.

Not only did Finney discard traditional doctrines concerning the state of man, he also denied unconditional election and limited (or particular) atonement. Calvin and his followers believed that God, who could have justly sent all men into eternal hell, chose instead to save some of his wretched creatures. The Lord chose this remnant, the

The Second Great Awakening
Project 3, Page 3

elect, not for any merit that He could foresee in them or because He knew beforehand that they would accept the gospel; He chose them simply because He wanted to. Finney jettisoned this foundational axiom of Reformed Protestantism. Weisberger notes, "Finney rode hard over (his pastor's) insistence that salvation was only for the elect. It was made for all men, he insisted, although not all of them would take advantage of it, as God knew beforehand." For Finney, the God of the Bible could not be an elitist, choosing some and rejecting others simply for his own good pleasure. Finney, a man of his time, echoed the egalitarian perspective of the Jacksonian age. Calvinistic beliefs concerning the atonement logically followed from their doctrine of divine election, and these conceptions also met with Finney's consternation. In his memoirs Finney recalls, "(My pastor) held that Jesus suffered for the elect the literal penalty of Divine Law . . . I objected that this was absurd . . . he affirmed that Jesus literally paid the debt for the elect. . . On the contrary it seemed to me that Jesus only satisfied public Justice, and that that was all that the government of God could require."

Unlike other basic doctrines which Finney retained in name but denied in fact, he completely repudiated the idea of the imputation of Christ's righteousness to Christians. In his memoirs he even seems to mock the idea, calling it "that theological fiction." The thought that Christ had actually paid for any specific sins on the cross seemed preposterous to him. It might appear shocking to many that a preacher of the stature of Charles Finney would spurn the heart of the gospel—if not in heart, at least in teaching—but he unashamedly and unequivocally did.

Finney's doctrinal revisions, however, went even further, opposing the ideas of his Puritan forefathers who believed that regeneration depended wholly on a miracle of God, Finney believed that the power of salvation remained firmly gripped, not in the hand of God, but in the hands of men. His own radical conversion set the stage for his rejection of Augustinianism. His mind became convinced of two overriding facts: Salvation lay before him; he must take it up. Weisberger notes that Finney thought, "All that was needed to receive (salvation) was 'my own consent to give up my sins, and accept Christ'." Weisberger rightly concludes the story by saying, "Charles Finney had decided in that moment that salvation was up to him." In the matter of salvation he replaced the idea of the sovereignty of God with the sovereignty of the human will.

Maintaining the freedom and sovereignty of the will at all times, this bold preacher even seemed to stand in judgment over the Calvinistic God, and often found Him guilty. Human choice and ability, the mainstays of his Theology, pushed aside the idea of man's weakness before an infinite God. In his book *The Promise of the Holy Spirit* Finney says, "If (God) had a right and should actually set aside your liberty, in doing this He would render your salvation naturally impossible; for salvation without virtue is absurd, and virtue without free-agency is a contradiction." Finney in this one statement not only denied salvation by grace alone, but he also repudiated a host of other fundamental Protestant doctrines. He, however, had other charges to level against the Almighty. The notion that God dispensed salvation to whomever He chose not only contradicted Finney's reason, but he saw it as simply immoral. Finney maintains, "(God) has no right to set aside your liberty. . . ."

By giving man the "liberty" that opened

The Second Great Awakening

Project 3, Page 4

the way of salvation, Finney reduced the Puritan miracle of regeneration to an absurdly easy, fully human action. S.M. Houghton sums up the argument stating, "Calvinists complain . . . that, whereas the Bible teaches regeneration to be the work of the Holy Spirit, Finney declared it to be an act of the human will." Many have claimed that man must work his way to salvation. Pelagius, a heretical fifth century British monk, taught that man must do many mighty works to earn the favor and salvation of his God. Finney, however, taught a different type of deliverance, a way to God that consisted of only a little work. In a sense, he reached into heaven and pulled salvation down to man. He declares, "Faith is the most simple and easy exercise of the mind conceivable." On this matter Finney stood resolutely, noting, "Both faith and unbelief are volitions and are, therefore, in the highest sense within our own reach. . . ." Consistent with his general idea of human ability, Finney's doctrine of sanctification carried his belief in human ability to its logical conclusion: perfectibility. Although he did not advocate the idea that man could completely extricate himself from sin as vociferously as many of the utopians, he championed it none the less. A major portion of Finney's thoughts seem somewhat analogous to those of John Wesley who believed in a second definite work of grace. Whitney Cross reports in *The Burned-over District* that "Finney underwent his own personal reconversion to a sanctified condition." His experience and teaching, however, probably did not spring forth from a careful study of Wesley, because Finney had little time and particular contempt for the study of theology, and ironically, because he viewed most Arminians with a certain amount of contempt, Wesley held that after the second definite work of grace—entire sanctification—Christians progressed to higher and higher states of holiness. Finney believed that man not only progressed toward moral perfection, he arrived. Cross reports, "(Finney) told his wife that she might become perfect . . ."

Finney's belief in the free agency of man, however, did not keep him from strongly preaching against sin. He thought that man had to be persuaded to cease from his sinning. Much like the experience of the Nation of Israel at the foot of Mount Sinai, Finney intended to scare his listeners into repentance with verbal thunder and burning words. Later revivalists such as D.L. Moody and Billy Sunday, who could rightly be called Finney's progeny, would calmly, rationally, and even humorously appeal to sinners on the ground of free agency, but Finney never reached this level of refinement. By booming against sin, lukewarmness, and Unitarianism, Finney made himself more acceptable to the Calvinists, whose leaders often lost themselves in scholastic searches for doctrinal perfection, while allowing their own faith to slip into lethargy. Many of the people who came to hear Charles Finney's preaching never realized that he often greatly revised the hallowed doctrines of Protestantism, but some of the more theologically astute listeners railed against his new doctrines. One of the most interesting of these confrontations occurred at one of Finney's typical revival meetings where he ran into Mrs. Weatherby, a conservative Calvinist. Finney, noticing that she had been unaffected by his emotional preaching during the first few days of the revival, openly challenged her to repent. Weisberger continues the story saying, "Mrs. Weatherby believed and said, that she could not (repent without a special gift of divine grace). Again, Finney's fist supposedly shook before her face. 'You Lie! You can repent and be converted immediately!' Mrs. Weatherby resolutely would not move from her stand. Soon after this encounter, Weatherby's husband, who had not attended the revival with his wife, came to Finney's headquarters to voice his displeasure concerning the treatment of his wife. Returning Finney's fist shaking with interest added, he knocked down one of Finney's men who had begun to taunt Mr. Weatherby with threats of hell."

Charles Finney not only advocated an extremely individualistic approach to doctrinal issues, he also democratized the pulpit. Raised by non-Christian parents, he knew little of the church's doctrines during his childhood, and his knowledge expanded little during his disinterested youth, although as a young lawyer he dutifully attended services. After his conversion he attacked the established practice of maintaining a highly educated clergy. Finney openly stated that although many of the ministers of his day had fine doctrinal knowledge, their experiential Christianity lacked vitality. To a great extent this claim rang true. In many pulpits academic knowledge had become the only criterion for pastoring. Finney's cure, however, proved worse than the disease. Doctrine restricted Finney's freedom, so he gave up any attempt to approach it in a systematic way. He not only rejected the idea that all ministers of the gospel should be highly educated; he disparaged it. In his memoirs, he remarks, "The fact is that Mr. Gale's education for the ministry had been entirely defective. He had imbibed a set of opinions, both theological and practical that were a strait jacket to him. He could accomplish very little or nothing if he carried out his principles." When his presbytery examined him for ordination, they offered to pay for his education at Princeton, but Finney would have none of it. This precedent had far-reaching results. Writing in 1958, Weisberger notes, "Finney was an ordained layman and after him there would be no popular evangelist who was a graduate of a first-class university or seminary."

Finney's stubborn belief in the equality of all people increased the severity of his obvious ignorance of the teachings found in the Bible. He always attempted to understand the Bible as he would a law book. Taking the Protestant idea that every believer could interpret the Bible to an absurd extreme, he rejected all of the opinions of teachers who had come before him in favor of his own odd reasonings. In his memoirs Finney recalls, "I do not ever recollect to have ever read a page upon the (atonement) except what I had found in the

The Second Great Awakening
Project 3, Page 6

Bible." John MacArthur, Jr. offers a concise summation of the prominent preacher remarking, "Finney boldly challenged conventional doctrine and persuasively championed his own rather novel set of doctrines."

While revivals ushered in by Finney made massive revisions in the beliefs of Protestants, they also radically modified the practices of nineteenth century American churches. In truth, the firestorm that Finney unleashed supplanted the Christianity that existed before its arrival. Unlike Jonathan Edwards who called people back to their fathers' faith, Finney led a revolution. The leaders of the First Great Awakening praised God for the great work that He did in their midst. Finney not only disagreed with this opinion, he condemned it. Cross notes, "Charles Finney, for instance, believed 'no doctrine . . . more dangerous' than that revivals were miraculous." Setting aside the wisdom of the past, Finney sought to define the terms of his "awakening." He viewed the revival, not as a work of Jehovah, but as something that people could manufacture. Keith J. Hardinan in his book named after Finney records, "Any lingering unpredictability in awakenings was swept away in 1835 by Charles Finney, when he stated . . . , "A revival is not a miracle; nor dependent on a miracle, in any sense; it is a purely philosophical result of the right use of the constituted means."

Finney's anthropocentric attitudes concerning revivals matched the innovative practices which he instituted. In a fit of pragmatism he invented much of the structure that governs mass evangelism today. At the end of almost every modern camp meeting, the evangelist calls people to come forward and pray the sinner's prayer. Hardman notes that "At Rochester (Finney) brought in what was to be a staple of mass evangelism, the opportunity to respond immediately to the evangelists invitation by some overt physical activity such as walking forward." This practice served to further muddle the average public's idea of salvation. Inevitably, many people came to believe that the actions that became associated with salvation—raising a hand, walking forward, saying the sinner's prayer—worked "ex opera operato." Strangely, Finney, a man on the cutting edge, introduced many of the old heresies under the guise of new methods.

Making his own inventive changes to ancient practices, Finney used prayer as a pressure tactic. Since he thought that man could save himself simply by willing to do good and to trust in Christ, he focused on only changing men's minds. Therefore Finney believed in applying the maximum amount of stress on the sinner. Christians universally viewed prayer as an opportunity to communicate with God. With this, Finney agreed, but in practice pleadings seemed aimed not at the ears of the Lord, but at the mind of the sinner. Weisberger explains, "In (the revival) meetings sinners were 'prayed for' by name, and thus put under devastating social pressure to 'find' conviction in their hearts." He often prayed in a loud voice sometimes for people whom others asked him to "bring before God." Other times he prayed for people who had been involved in the first couple of days of the revival without any emotional reaction. He aired before the public the hardness of certain people's hearts, the blackness of their sins, and their rejection of Christ. In the villages that Finney frequented during the early years of his revival, almost everyone knew everyone else. This introduced a social strain that people of today's more individualistic world can hardly understand. Many of Finney's students, those who followed him and aided in setting up the revivals, also adopted and improvised on this method. Some would make it a point to go into the woods for "private" devotions, although they would always remain within ear shot of the village streets. They would pray ardently for recalcitrant sinners by name, shouting out all of the sins that they had supposedly committed. Weisberger records a portion of a "prayer" offered up by one of Finney disciples named Beman. Having already mentioned the sinner by name, he continued,

> O Lord! Thou knowest that he is a hardened wretch; thou seest how he has raised his crest against Thee. . . Now, Lord, don't let him boast himself against Thee; but draw thy sword and come down upon him; drive it through his heart, and let him bleed at they feet.

"Astonishingly," many sinner's quickly and radically converted.

Emotional pleas also pushed sinners toward the Kingdom of God. Finney combined the poise of a lawyer with a natural flair for the theatrical. Audiences sat spellbound as he led them on an emotional roller coaster that took them in one hour from hell and the depths of despair to the throne room of the Almighty. Edwards showed the sinner that he or she stood on unsure soil, and that at any moment God could call any person to account for their sinful life. Finney and his followers took this scenario one step further. Weisberger observes, "When some of them lagged about 'giving their hearts to God,' the preacher announced that he 'beheld . . . God sealing their eternal doom." In another instance, Weisberger comments, "After a brief introduction, he shot the question bluntly at the congregation. Would they make up their minds to become Christians? Those ready to do so please rise; those determined not to accept Christ would remain seated."

True to his theology, Finney never seemed to consider the possibility of a false conversion. Undoubtedly, his pressure tactics resulted in spurious conversions. He believed that man could choose his way into heaven, so any decision that any man or woman made, bound God to honor his promise and save them. This unbiblical view of salvation led to the spiritual destruction of many, and the hardening of others. Finney's converts often laid their crosses aside shortly after their leader departed, only to be reconverted by the next revivalist that swept through town. Western New York state received an especially large dose of emotionalism. This area, where Finney first rose to prominence, has retained the title "The Burned-Over District." Constantly traversed by fiery, emotional revivalists, this region ultimately became numb to evangelical influences, and to some extent has remained hardened to the gospel to this day.

Tragically, Finney viewed the massive effect that his preaching produced as a sign of God's favor. In his book *Revivals of Religion,* Finney sums up his method, "When the blessing evidently follows the introduction of the measure itself, the proof is unanswerable, that the measure is wise." He could not understand, nor did he ever seem to contemplate that success did not mean that God had anointed him to champion his cause. In his memoirs Finney recalls, "The more experience I had . . . the more was I confirmed in the fact that God had led me, had taught me, had given me right conception in regard to the best manner of winning souls." The reasoning puts the cart before the horse. Finney did not look to the Bible to find his practices; he experimented,

The Second Great Awakening
Project 3, Page 8

and then implemented what seemed to have the greatest effect. He failed to realize that successful heretics littered the history of God's Church.

Finney justified his doctrinal positions in the same pragmatic fashion. For him, the fact that people screamed, groaned, and fell flat meant that God endorsed what he said. In his memoirs, Finney even seems to mock those who do not have results like his by saying.

> (My Pastor Gale) followed out his views with very little practical results. I pursued mine and by the blessing of God the results were the opposite of those which he predicted. When this fact came out clearly, it completely upset his theological and practical ideas as a minister.

This statement not only reveals much about Finney, it also exposes the feeling of his age. America skyrocketed in the 1820's and 1830's. Industry exploded in the Northeast, and science and industry began to revolutionize life. Pragmatism supplanted all other philosophies, and became the *de facto* religion in America. Doctrinal stands, and submission of the heart to God became too subtle for most people to grasp. Finney received honor as a success not because he called people to a deeper understanding of the Scripture, or because he remained faithful to any Confession of Faith or Creed. Finney simply produced—he filled the churches. Finney's pastor's reaction in the above quote speaks volumes. Pastor Gale suffered mental distress because he, like the men and women of his age, assumed that if something works it must be true. Forgetting Christ's admonition to those who wanted him to do signs and wonders, America sold its soul for success.

Imitating the world, churches fell into the trap of pragmatism. They discarded the test of faithfulness of God's word and their creeds and substituted instead a truly American test: visible, measurable success. Finney delivered. Hardman notes, "Between 1800 and 1835 the proportion of Protestant church members to the national population almost doubled, from 7 to 12 1/2 percent." Considering Finney's doctrine and enthusiasm, one might imagine that he sprang out of the Methodist Church, the Baptist assemblies somewhere in the underbrush of the untamed West, or perhaps from the fringe sect of dissenters: he did not. Finney seduced the children of Calvin and Knox in the Presbyterian denomination. The teaching of Samuel Hopkins had stolen the life from the lively doctrines of Edwards. Pews emptied; numbers decreased; desperation gripped the church. Finney brought with him the vitality that early eighteenth century Calvinism lacked, but this vitality came with a price: doctrinal compromise. This fact could be clearly seen even at the outset of his career. Cross states, "When presbytery examined him for ordination he did not even know the Confession of Faith. He passed unanimously, not upon his learning but upon his already handsome reputation for conducting revivals." In his memoirs, Finney recalls, "Unexpectedly to myself they asked me if I received the Confession of the Presbyterian Church. I had not examined it. . . . I replied that I received it for substance of doctrine, so far as I understood it." Later, when he took the time to read the Westminster Confession of Faith, he repudiated it. Weisberger sums up the decision that faced the ministers that sat at Finney's ordination and at later disciplinary hearings by saying, "The choice was either orthodoxy and empty pews, or compromise and full ones."

The Second Great Awakening
Project 3, Page 9

As Finney's "success" mounted, compromise became easier and easier. Calvinists had suffered persecution in Europe. In England, they had always been opposed by the Anglicans. In Switzerland and the Netherlands they had flourished, but in divided countries. In France they had been exterminated. In America they had found a refuge from the massacres and prejudice of Europe. In America, a land where they enjoyed unquestioned ascendancy, a land of tremendous resources and unparalleled freedom, Calvinism unwittingly committed suicide. Charles Finney served as the instrument of its destruction.

The Second Great Awakening, led by Charles Grandison Finney, ushered in a religious revolution that erased the dominance of Calvinism in America. Finney insidiously subverted Calvinist doctrines by keeping many distinctive teachings by name, but radically changing their underlying meaning. He also fundamentally altered the general conception of the relationship between God and man. His over-reaction to the scholastic preaching of his day led him to repudiate the idea of a highly educated clergy with disastrous effects. Although his sincerity remains unquestioned, his self-assured ignorance can not be excused. From Finney, the forefather of countless modern religious aberrations, the Church must learn that success in Christianity can only be measured by Faithfulness to God's Word, not by full pews and coffers, and that great heresies begin with minor, seemingly harmless deviations from orthodoxy.

The Second Great Awakening
Project 4—Art Study

According to Finney, "Reason can discern divine philosophy." He was not alone in his glorification of man's mind, as can be seen in this piece of art by Francisco Goya. Look at the etching on this page and discuss the following questions:

1. The inscription on the desk the man is resting on reads "The Sleep of Reason Produces Monsters". What does the artist mean by this?
2. This etching is part of a series of images known as *Los Caprichios* (The Caprices); What is a caprice? What kind of images do you think might be considered caprices?
3. Goya lived in Spain in the late 18th and early 19th centuries; what political and religious institutions would have been in existance at the time for a liberal-minded artist such as Goya to react against ?

The Sleep of Reason Produces Monsters by Francisco Goya, 1799

The Second Great Awakening
Test

Write a paragraph describing the Second Great Awakening. Be sure to include names of those involved and the effect this event had on the Church.

____

____

____

____

____

____

____

____

____

____

____

____

____

Review

1. Puritans were those who wanted to________________the Church of England.
2. Who was the founder of Rhode Island?

____

____

3. What were the Salem Witch Trials?

____

____

____

The Second Great Awakening
Test, Page 2

4. What is mercantilism?

5. In chronological order list all events studied to date. Next to each place the appropriate date.

The Second Great Awakening

Test, Page 2

5. (continued)

THE WAR OF 1812
Worksheet

1. Despite the_________________________, Great Britain and the United States still did not get along very well.

2. With whom was Great Britain at War?

3. Who blockaded American trade with France?

4. How was the War of 1812 different from the War for Independence?

5. Who said, "We have met the enemy and they are ours"?

6. American ships challenged British naval superiority, as shown by the____________________defeat of the ___________________.

THE WAR OF 1812

Worksheet, Page 2

7. When did the British Army invade Washington, D.C.?

8. Who saved the painting of George Washington from the burning White House?

9. Where were the British troops finally stopped?

10. Who was Francis Scott Key?

THE WAR OF 1812
Project 1—The Star-Spangled Banner

Read the account below and the poem that follows, then write your own poem in tribute to our nation.

During the War of 1812, the British fleet blockaded our ports and sailed up our rivers to attack our cities and forts. Thus, they entered the Chesapeake Bay, and landed troops outside Washington City.

A battle was fought near there, but the British were not stopped from pursuing their way to the capital. The city was in great danger and the people hastened to gather their possessions and made their escape. There were only eight thousand inhabitants in Washington at that time. It was a small town, as compared with its great size and splendor today.

A messenger rode in haste to bid the people flee. He came to the White House, where Dolly Madison, the wife of President James Madison, was waiting for her husband. He called out to her, "Mr. Madison says go, or the house will be burned over your head. The British are on the way to the capital. There is no time to lose. Escape as quickly as you can."

The soldiers marched into the deserted town and burned the Treasury Building, the Public Library, and the White House. A notorious British officer named Cockburn, followed by a mob of soldiers, entered the new Capitol, climbed into the Speaker's chair and called out: "Shall this harbor of Yankee Democracy be burned?"

The mob of half-drunken soldiers called out, "Aye," and proceeded to apply the torch to the building.

Dolly Madison found refuge with her friends in the country. When she and the President returned to Washington, they had to live in a rented house.

About three weeks after the burning of the city, the British began to attack Fort McHenry, which was built to protect the harbor of Baltimore. One evening, the British sent two bomb vessels and a number of barges filled with soldiers to pass the fort and assail it in the rear. But the noise of their oars was heard in the darkness, and an order was given to open fire on them. A deadly discharge was poured out from Fort McHenry upon the creeping craft, with the result that nearly all of them were sent to the bottom.

The English suffered so much from this repulse that they abandoned the attack and sailed away.

During the bombardment, Francis Scott Key, a young lawyer, was sent, under a flag of truce, to convey a message to the British fleet. His purpose was to secure the release of several prisoners.

After delivering his message, Key and his party were on the point of departure, when an officer said, "Mr. Key, I have orders to detain you and your party until the bombardment is over. You will, therefore, remain here."

Key did not like to be held, but there was no help for it. So he and his associates were kept in a little vessel moored to the side of an English ship, under guard of a body of soldiers. Here, on the deck, they witnessed the bombardment of the fort.

The War of 1812
Project 1, Page 2

All night long the shells were fired. Key watched each one as it fell upon the fort, and listened for each explosion. Suddenly, before the morning dawned, the firing ceased.

"Has the fort surrendered, or have the British abandoned the attack?" was the anxious thought in the minds of the weary watchers.

There was no way to find out until day came. "If the flag is still flying, then the fort has not surrendered," said Key to his companions. Anxiously they paced the deck.

As day dawned, they turned their glasses toward the fort, and, to their great joy, they saw the flag was still there. Key was overcome with emotion. Drawing a letter from his pocket, he wrote on the back of it the opening lines of our national song, "The Star Spangled Banner."

Later in the day, a small boat took him back to Baltimore. On his way he completed the poem. That very night, he corrected it, and wrote it out as we now have it. The next day, he showed the poem to a friend of his, who was so pleased that he had it printed in a Baltimore paper.

When the words appeared, they were eagerly memorized by an actor, named Charles Durang, who stood on a chair and, for the first time, sang them to a crowd. Then, everybody joined in. Soon the piece was being sung all over the country. It is our greatest national song, and whenever it is played or sung, we rise, proud of our great flag and of the deeds of valor it has encouraged.

The War of 1812

Project 1, Page 3

The Star-Spangled Banner

O say, can you see, by the dawn's early light,
What so proudly we hailed at the twilight's last gleaming?
Whose broad stripes and bright stars, through the perilous fight,
O'er the ramparts we watched, were so gallantly streaming!
And the rocket's red gare, the bombs bursting in air,
Gave proof through the night that our flag was still there:
O say, does that star-spangled banner yet wave
O'er the land of the free and the home of the brave?

On the shore, dimly seen through the mists of the deep,
Where the foe's haughty host in dread silence reposes,
What is that which the breeze, o'er the towering steep,
As it fitfully blows, half conceals, half discloses?
Now it catches the gleam of the morning's first beam,
In full glory reflected now shines on the stream:
'Tis the star-spangled banner! Oh long may it wave,
O'er the land of the free and the home of the brave!

And where is that band who so vauntingly swore
That the havoc of war and the battle's confusion
A home and a country should leave us no more?
Their blood has washed out their foul footsteps' pollution.
No refuge could save the hireling and slave
From the terror of flight, or the gloom of the grave:
And the star-spangled banner in triumph doth wave
O'er the land of the free and the home of the brave.

Oh! Thus be it ever, when freemen shall stand
Between their loved homes and war's desolation!
Blest with victory and peace, may the heav'n rescued land
Praise the Power that hath made and preserved us a nation.
Then conquer we must, for our cause it is just,
And this be our motto: "In God is our trust."
And the star-spangled banner in triumph shall wave,
O'er the land of the free and the home of the brave.

The War of 1812

Project 1, Page 4

The War of 1812

Project 2—Battles of the War of 1812

After reading some of the resources on your card, look at the map below to see where many of the battles took place and highlight them with a colored marker.

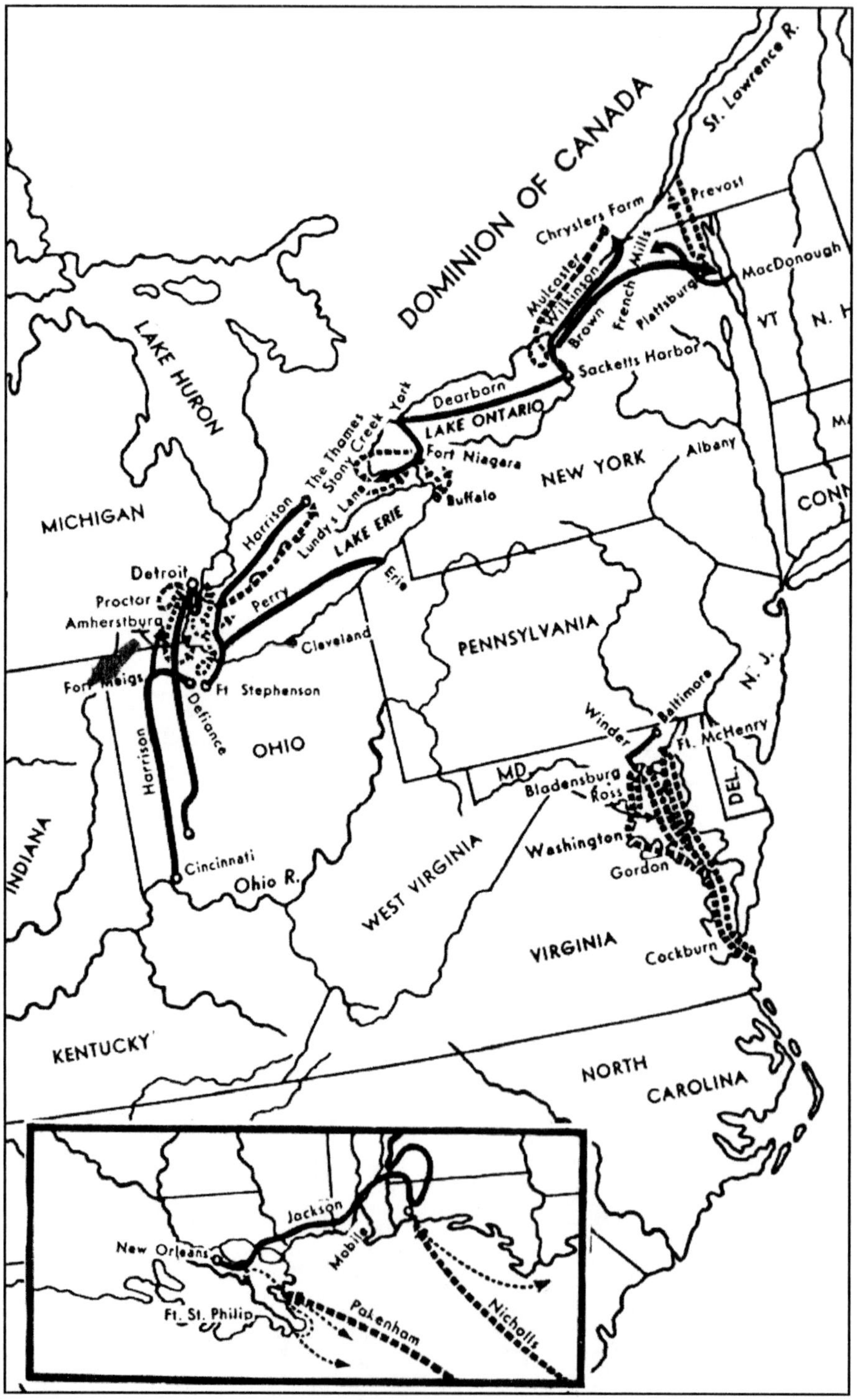

The War of 1812
Test

1. What country was the United States not getting along with?

2. Who blockaded American trade with France?

3. Where were most of the important battles fought in the War of 1812?

4. Who won a great victory on Lake Erie?

5. When did the British Army invade Washington, D.C.?

6. What did Dolly Madison save from burning in 1814?

7. Where were the British troops finally stopped?

The War of 1812

Test, Page 2

8. Who wrote the poem that would become our national anthem?

____

____

Review

1. Who was Prince Henry the Navigator?

____

____

____

2. What did Colombus believe that God had called him to do?

____

____

____

3. Who were the explorers of the Northeast?

____

____

____

4. What was the First Great Awakening?

____

____

____

The War of 1812

Test, Page 3

5. In chronological order list all events studied to date. Next to each place the appropriate date.

The War of 1812

Test, Page 4

5. (continued)

The Missouri Compromise
Worksheet

1. What is the date given for the Missouri Compromise?

____

____

____

2. In 1818 how many "free" states were there? Did most of these states represent the north or the south?

____

____

____

3. In 1818 how many "slave" states were there?

____

____

4. There was ________________ representation in Congress on slavery.

5. How did Missouri want to enter the United States?

____

____

____

6. What was the Missouri Compromise?

____

____

____

____

____

____

____

The Missouri Compromise

Project 1—Slavery Solved Forever?

Read why the North opposed the Extension of Slavery West of the Mississippi and why the South demanded it.

In 1819 the number of free states and of slave states was equal, each section having eleven. A majority of the Northern people, believing slavery to be an evil, had therefore two chief reasons for opposing its establishment west of the Mississippi in Missouri Territory:

1. They thought it would be a serious injury to that part of the country, and that it was as great of a mistake as if a farmer were to take the thistles and weeds which grew on his old land and deliberately plant them on a field of freshly cleared soil.
2. They objected to it because, if the new territory should be admitted as slave states, the South might thereby gain a majority of representatives in Congress. That section could then, by its votes, strengthen and extend slavery, and at the same time it might repeal the protective tariff (high duties to safeguard mills and American industries against foreign competion) and so permit the free importation of all kinds of manufactured goods.

On the other hand, the South argued that its prosperity depended on the extension of slave labor and on free trade with Europe; their papers boldly declared; "Slavery must have room." The people there saw that the North was rapidly outstripping them in growth of population. If, then, a part of Missouri Territory should enter the Union as a free state, the North would probably get control of Congress and of foreign trade.

Finally, a part of the Missouri Territory was set apart under the name of the state of Missouri, and applied for admission as a slave state. The South urged the measure with all its might; the North fought against it with equal determination. After nearly two years of angry debate Henry Clay of Kentucky succeeded in persuading Congress to make a compromise—that is, a bargain—in which each side agreed to give up something to the other in order to settle the dispute.

The Compromise was this:

1. The North agreed that Missouri should enter the Union as a slave state.
2. The South agreed that in all future cases the states formed out of the remainder of Missouri Territory north of the parallel of 39 degrees and 30 minutes on the map should come in free.
3. Finally, the South agreed that it would no longer oppose the effort of the North for the admission of Maine, which would, of course, come in as a free state.

This law was passed in 1820 under the name of the Missouri Compromise Act. Maine was admitted and Missouri followed (1821). This kept the political balance even, for the North now had twelve free states and the South twelve slave states.

Many people believed that the passage of the Missouri Compromise Act had settled the debate about the extension of slavery "forever." But facts proved that in this case "forever" meant only about twenty-five years.

THE MISSOURI COMPROMISE
Project 2—Free and Slave States

Color in the map, making the free states red and the slave states blue.

ORIGINAL FREE STATES
New Hampshire
Massachusetts
Connecticut
Rhode Island
New York
Pennsylvania

NEW FREE STATES
Vermont
Ohio
Indiana
Illinois
Maine

ORIGINAL SLAVE STATES
Delaware
Maryland
Virginia
North Carolina
South Carolina
Georgia

NEW SLAVE STATES
Kentucky
Tennessee
Alabama
Louisiana

The Missouri Compromise

Review Project

Choose one event studied this year that you believe you would have participated in, if you had been alive. Describe the event, in as much detail as possible, and what your involvement would have been and why you would be justified in taking the positions you chose. Would you have been a minuteman at Lexington, or an "Indian" at the Boston Tea Party, or maybe a Tory?

The Missouri Compromise
Test

1. What is the date given for the Missouri Compromise?

___

___

___

2. In 1818 how many states were "free" states and how many were "slave" states?

___

___

___

3. There was ________________ representation in Congress on slavery.

4. How did Missouri want to enter the United States?

___

___

___

5. What was the Missouri Compromise?

___

___

___

___

Review

1. Why is Roanoke called the "Lost Colony?"

___

___

___

The Missouri Compromise

Test, Page 2

2. When did the *Mayflower* land at Plymouth?

3. Who was Roger Williams?

4. List the original thirteen colonies.

5. In chronological order list all events studied to date. Next to each place the appropriate date.

The Missouri Compromise
Test, Page 3

5. (continued)

The Missouri Compromise
Test, Page 4

5. (continued)

Explorers to 1815

Memory Song Lyrics

Hear ye, hear ye, listen to the history of one nation, under God,
indivisible, with liberty and justice for all.
Let's begin in the 15th century with Prince Henry the Navigator.
Next came number two, Columbus sailed the ocean blue to the New World in 1492.
Columbus sailed in 1492.
Number three, Magellan circumnavigated the Earth.
Then came number four, Cortes, de Soto, de Leon and Coronado, Spanish explorers, all four.
Number five, explorers of the northeast were Cartier, Champlain, and Cabot.
Number six, Sir Walter Raleigh came from England and settled Roanoke, Virginia.

Then number seven, 1607, Jamestown was founded in Virginia.
Number eight was in 1620, when the Mayflower landed at Plymouth.
Number nine came the Plymouth Colony, built by the Pilgrims.
Then number 10, the Massachusetts Bay Colony was the home of the Puritans.

Number 11, Roger Williams was the founder of Rhode Island. Twelve, the witch trials of Salem.
13 the thirteen colonies; New Hampshire and Massachusetts, Rhode Island, New York, Connecticut, Pennsylvania, and New Jersey, Maryland, Delaware.
Further south you'll find Virginia, North Carolina, South Carolina. Georgia was the southernmost of thirteen colonies.

Number 14 came the First Great Awakening.
Number 15, England traded with the Colonies.
Number 16, came the French and Indian War. 17, Parliament acted unjustly.
18, the Continental Congress sought for peace with Britain.
19, the War for Independence. Number 20, the British lost at Bunker Hill.
21, America declared its independence, signed the Declaration, 17 and 76.
22, the great commander, George Washington, led the Continental Army.
23, the winter at Valley Forge. 24, the Treaty of Paris at Yorktown.
25, the Constitutional Convention. 26, the founding fathers of America.

27, came our first president, Washington in 17 and 89. 28, the Louisiana Purchase from France.
29, the Lewis and Clark expedition. Number 30, came the Second Great Awakening.
31, the War of 1812. 32, the Missouri Compromise.

Oh, how much we have learned about America!

ANSWERS

1: PRINCE HENRY THE NAVIGATOR

Worksheet

1. Portugal
2. Portugal; 1394
3. He established a school of navigation and financed voyages.
4. map making
5. the study of the celestial bodies
6. the science of getting a ship from place to place
7. more than fifty; none

Project 1

For younger and older students

Project 2

For younger and older students

Test

1. Portugal; 1394
2. Portugal
3. cartography, astronomy and navigation
4. opening the African route to Asia
5. none
6. Sierra Leone
7. one who plots a ship's direction
8. Cartography is map making, and astronomy is the study of the celestial bodies.

2: COLUMBUS SAILS TO THE NEW WORLD

Worksheet

1. Columbus learned much about navigation at Prince Henry's observatory.
2. Italy
3. Queen Isabella of Spain
4. 1492
5. three; the Nina, Pinta and Santa Maria
6. eighty-eight
7. the Indies (present day Japan); the Bahamas (off the coast of Florida)
8. four; the West Indies
9. the Indies
10. take the Gospel across the ocean and convert the people in the Indies

Project 1

For older students

Answers will vary.

Project 2

For younger and older students

Project 3

For younger and older students

Project 4

For older students

1. Just before the turn of the sixteenth century, Europe experienced something of a millenial fever. Like many in our time, people were expecting the end of the world when the year 1500 rolled around.
2. Revelation 6. From right to left they are War, Pestilence, Famine, and Death. They are closely followed by hell gobbling up the slain (including a king or bishop!).
3. By placing the lines close together, he is able to show us deep shadows and by placing them further apart he shows lighter areas.

Test

1. 1492
2. Italy
3. Queen Isabella of Spain
4. three ships and eighty-eight men
5. the Bahamas; the Indies
6. Indians
7. four
8. take the Gospel across the ocean and convert the people in the Indies

Review

1. Portugal; 1394
2. map making
3. the science of getting a ship from place to place
4. He started a school of navigation and financed voyages.
5. no

3: MAGELLAN CIRCUMNAVIGATES THE EARTH

Worksheet

1. a Portuguese sea captain
2. the first expedition that sailed around the world
3. Charles I of Spain
4. five; the Concepcion, San Antonio, Santiago, Trinidad and Victoria
5. Mutiny broke out, the mutinous leader was executed and two of his followers were marooned when the fleet sailed again.
6. a passage to the Pacific, now called the "Strait of Magellan"
7. one; 1522

ANSWERS

8. No, he was killed in the Philippines.

Project 1
For older students
Magellan's route to the Indies was too long for trade. His voyage was like Columbus's in that he was the first to explore new territory. It was different in that it actually circumnavigated the earth.

Project 2
For younger and older students

Project 3
For older students
1. He is dressed as an Augustinian monk and is still tonsured (his hair is still cut in imitation of Christ's crown of thorns). This tells us that this is an early picture of Luther and that his split from Rome is not yet a total one.
2. This is sometimes hard to tell in a picture and inferences like these are subjective; however, Luther appears strong, determined and intelligent in this picture. Additionally, history tells us that Cranach and Luther were godparents to each other's children, so we can assume that sympathies ran deep!

Test
1. 1519–1522
2. a Portuguese sea captain
3. the first expedition that sailed around the world; Charles I of Spain
4. five
5. Mutiny broke out, the mutinous leader was executed and two of his followers were marooned when the fleet sailed again.
6. a passage to the Pacific, now called the "Strait of Magellan"
7. in the Philippines
8. one
9. nearly three years

Review
1. Portugal
2. He established a school of navigation and financed voyages.
3. 1492
4. the Indies
5. to take the Gospel to the people there
6. See the master list on page 500.

4: CORTÉS, DE SOTO, DE LEON, AND CORONADO, THE SPANISH EXPLORERS

Worksheet
1. 1513–1538
2. Central America and South America
3. The Spanish Conquest
4. The Aztec Empire, it was destroyed.
5. Honduras and Baja, California
6. Hernando de Soto
7. Francisco Vasquez de Coronado, the southwest of what is now the U.S.A.
8. Ponce de Leon, the Fountain of Youth

Project 1
For older students
1. to aquire gold
2. those Indians who refused to become Christians were killed; no
3. swampy, hot and rainy

Project 2
For younger and older students
Who: Cortéz
What: conquered the Aztec empire
Where: Mexico, Honduras, Baja, California
Why: gold

Who: de Soto
What: discovered the Mississippi River
Where: southern states of what is now the U.S.A.
Why: gold

Who: Coronado
What: first to see the Grand Canyon
Where: southwest region of what is now the U.S.A.
Why: gold

Who: de Leon
What: searching for the Fountain of Youth
Where: Florida
Why: Fountain of Youth

Project 3
For younger and older students

Project 4
For younger and older students
de Soto's route begins in the southwest and de Leon's begins in Florida

Answers

Test
1. the Spanish Conquest
2. Central American and South America
3. Hernando Cortéz; Honduras, Baja, California
4. the Mississippi River
5. Coronado; the Southwest in what is now the United States
6. Florida; the Fountain of Youth

Review
1. Portugal; a school of navigation
2. map making
3. the Bahamas, the Indies
4. take the Gospel to the Indies
5. the first expedition to sail around the world
6. See the master list on page 500.

5: Explorers of the Northeast: Cartier, Champlain, and Cabot

Worksheet
1. John Cabot
2. the Indies
3. a French navigator; the Newfoundland coast, islands in the Gulf of St. Lawrence and the St. Lawrence River
4. a French explorer; the same area that Cartier had explored; Lake Champlain
5. 1497-1603

Project 1
For older students
1. John Cabot and Columbus
2. so that merchandise could be brought to Europe by a shorter route
3. Cabot
4. China, Japan, and India
5. There were no signs of the wealth and splendor which were said to exist in Japan and India.
6. the larger part of North America
7. Sebastian
8. the greatest sea captain of his time

Project 2
For older students

Project 3
For younger and older students

Test
1. Italy. He was the first European to reach the coast of North America after the end of Lief Ericson's colonies. He landed on the coast of Newfoundland.
2. the Indies
3. Newfoundland's coast, islands in the Gulf of St. Lawrence and the St. Lawrence River
4. Quebec; Lake Champlain
5. 1497-1603

Review
1. He founded a school of navigation and financed shipping voyages.
2. the Nina, Pinta and Santa Maria
3. He commanded the first expedition to sail around the world.
4. Hernando Cortes
5. See the master list on page 500.

6: Raleigh Settles Roanoke

Worksheet
1. Sir Walter Raleigh
2. 1585
3. He hoped to establish a base for raiding the Spanish empire in America.
4. Virginia Dare
5. The colony was deserted.
6. The colonists were never found, and no one knows what happened to them.
7. a tribe of Indians in southwestern North Carolina

Project 1
For older students
1. fought with the Huguenots in France, then with the Dutch against Spain; attacked by Spaniards on the way to colonize Newfoundland; commanded 100 men and fought a rebellion in Ireland
2. He spread his cloak on a muddy road for the Queen to walk on.
3. tall and handsome, dressed richly
4. They earned the ill will of the Indians and eventually abandoned the colony.
5. The colonists were probably killed by Indians.
6. their harsh treatment of the Indians

Test
1. 108; to establish a base for raiding the Spanish empire in America
2. 1585
3. Virginia Dare, Roanoke
4. The colonists were missing.
5. the "Lost Colony"
6. a tribe of Indians in southwestern North Carolina

ANSWERS

Review
1. map making
2. none
3. 1492
4. Francisco Vasquez de Coronado
5. See the master list on page 500.

7: JAMESTOWN IS FOUNDED IN VIRGINIA
Worksheet
1. King James I of England
2. 105. They were all men and boys.
3. The *Susan Constant,* the *Godspeed* (sometimes also called *Goodspeed*) and the *Discovery;* four months
4. 1607
5. adventure and easy fortune
6. They died. They wasted their time quarreling and looking for gold.
7. the third leader of the colony; "If anyone would not work, neither would they eat."
8. the "Starving Time"
9. 4,000
10. Pocahontas's husband; the cultivation of Jamestown's "cash crop" or "pay crop:" tobacco

Project 1
For younger and older students

Project 2
For younger and older students

Project 3
For older students
1. He was attracted to a life of activity and danger.
2. the London Company
3. Instead of carpenters and laborers, they were "gentlemen" in search of gold.
4. He showed them a compass and how the white people "talk on paper."
5. Pocahontas
6. He made accurate maps of the coasts of New England and the Chesapeake Bay.

Project 4
For younger and older students

Test
1. 1607
2. King James I of England
3. 105. They were all men from London.
4. adventure and easy fortune
5. They were years of quarreling, starvation and death. The men spent their time selfishly looking for gold. The period from 1609 to 1610 was called the "Starving Time."

Review
1. the Indies
2. He commanded the first expedition to sail around the world.
3. the Mississippi River
4. The colonists disappeared, and no one knows what happened to them.
5. See the master list on page 500.

8: THE MAYFLOWER LANDS AT PLYMOUTH
Worksheet
1. December, 1620
2. some Pilgrims who had been living in Holland; that they should separate from the Church of England
3. Provincetown; five weeks
4. Compact, 41, 44
5. Miles Standish
6. Plymouth Plantation

Project 1
For younger and older students

Project 2
For older students

Project 3
For younger and older students

Project 4
For older students
At 20 mph, a cruise ship will take about six and a half days. A passenger jet travelling 600 mph would cross in about six hours, and a fighter jet would take a little over two hours, if it had enough fuel.

Project 5
For older students

Project 6
For younger and older students
Answers will vary.

Literature Unit 1—Voyage to Freedom
INTRODUCTION–CHAPTER 2
1. They traveled 3000 miles on a wooden ship that

Answers

weighed only 180 tons. It was the size of six or seven family cars parked end to end and four cars parked side to side. There were 100 people on board and about 20 crew members. The journey would take approximately nine weeks.

2. in August of 1620 from the dock at Southampton
3. two; the Speedwell and the Mayflower
4. It was smaller than the Mayflower, the mast was too big for the hull and the captain of the ship, Master Reynolds, had a reputation for not being trustworthy.
5. The men were clean shaven and wore long dark stockings tucked into short black boots. On their heads they wore wide brimmed black hats with their short hair tucked into their hats. They had white collars around their necks. The ladies wore long flowing white aprons that almost covered the front of their dresses. Their black dresses had long sleeves that covered their arms and were a little longer than the apron and came almost to their shoes. On their heads they wore white caps that hid all of their hair.
6. Puritans; so that they could worship God in the way they believed the Bible instructed them
7. Matthew and Martha Lovelace, and their children, Justice and Prudence, had lived in Leyden, Holland and Scrooby, Nottinghamshire before they boarded the ship for Virginia.
8. They prayed, thanking God for His blessings and asking Him for protection during their journey.
9. Each family used the luggage they'd brought on board with them as both furniture and boundaries to their living area. Each level of the ship was only lit by candles flickering against the hull of the ship. It was very dark and smelly. The candles were made of tallow. They had no beds to sleep on and used bundles from their belongings as make shift pillows.
10. I was called Stores and held all of the water, food, and tools necessary for the journey.

Chapters 3–7

1. They looked back at the quay to their friends and family staying behind in England with sad eyes knowing they may never see them again. They looked forward with hope and faith in God to what was ahead of them. Even though they had no idea what the journey held, what life would be like on board ship, or in their new home, they knew God was going with them on this voyage.
2. They heard people snoring, babies crying, dogs snapping, groans from those who were accidentally stepped on and the hissing of water as it passed by the ship.
3. He read his Bible first thing in the morning until his family woke up. He then led them in prayer before they ate and read Scripture to them and prayed for each one individually after the meal was completed.
4. to "break" the "fast" from sleeping all night and not eating; dry biscuits (so hard they broke in their hands), salt beef (similar to our beef jerky) and hard, sour green apples.
5. When the storm began in earnest, sea water spilled down below decks. People and their belongings were thrown in every direction and soaked through. Some folks were injured from being thrown against the hull of the ship. All of this chaos was accompanied by shouting and crying.
6. They should stop shouting, gather their belongings together and restore order to their quarters so that the ungodly on board could see they trusted God for their safety.
7. All of the family was bound around the waist with strong ropes that tied them to each other and to the ship itself.
8. Psalm 46; to remind her of God's promise to be our refuge and strength in time of trouble, even in a raging sea
9. that the ship was leaking; Matthew went immediately to talk with another passenger and they decided to approach Master Reynolds after the storm abated so that they would not cause panic among the other passengers.
10. to the forbidden stores to see how it had fared in the storm; They overheard a plot to cheat the pilgrims out of their money.

Chapter 8–11

1. to sail out to sea with them for a couple of days on the leaking ship until they requested he take them back to shore and safety. He already had their money and would not refund it because the decision to turn around was theirs, not his. If they continued to Virginia anyway, he was not going to stay there with them for a year as he had promised.
2. Justice and Prudence had to confess their disobedience to their father in order for him to take care of the many families on board the Speedwell. Matthew spoke with a few other men, and they agreed to approach the Master together. At first

Answers

Master Reynolds denied the validity of their accusations, until Matthew revealed the name of the sailor who divulged the captain's treachery.
3. Dartmouth
4. He reminded the captain that he could cheat them, but he could never deceive God.
5. Master Reynolds again proved himself not to be trusted. The repairs to the Speedwell were not adequately accomplished that the pilgrim men could feel at ease for the safety of their families. Some families decided to forget going to Virginia and just set up homes in Dartmouth. The remaining passengers moved their gear from the Speedwell to the Mayflower.
6. The passengers on the Speedwell were all Puritans. On the Mayflower there were many of the Puritan families from the Speedwell along with people who were fleeing England to avoid jail sentences for crimes they had committed.
7. Saints and Strangers.
8. It was Mr. Lovelace's hope that by observing the conduct of the Saints in good times and bad, and perhaps attending their worship services, the Strangers would become Saints as God called them by His grace during their travel across the sea
9. In order to set sail, barefooted men had to climb rigging all the way up to the top to unfurl the many huge sails of the ship so that the wind could fill them and take the Mayflower and its passengers out to sea.
10. Mr. Lovelace said, "God pity that land. May King James see sense before it is too late." He was saddened that he had to uproot his family and move them to a distant, unknown land so they could worship God freely.

Chapters 12–14

1. where the friendly ship's carpenter stored his tools
2. He told them about a bird that doesn't fly, called the Great Auk. The carpenter also described how wonderful the strawberries and sweet potatoes were. He said there were many turkeys and delicious oysters "fit for a king". At the right time of year, the whole land smells of sweet magnolia.
3. Red Indians with feathers on their heads and down their backs and funny paintings on their faces. They hoop and holler and keep you awake at night.
4. hard, dry biscuits, salt beef and vegetable gruel
5. handwriting, spelling, sums (arithmetic), Bible reading, history, geography and catechism
6. because after such a time at sea the food was alive with crawling weevils; at least that way they couldn't see what they were eating. The same was true of drinking because the water was now foul, green and scummy.
7. The air in their quarters was a foul stench from the rancid tallow candles, unwashed bodies, spoiled food, and the damp musty odor of wet blankets. There was no room to play and no light of any consequence by which to see.
8. A spokesman for the group reminded the captain that they were a law-abiding people and would follow his instructions. After he departed, Matthew reminded his friends of the mercies of God and His faithfulness to them in the past. He led them in prayer for the Lord's protection of them and their vessel.
9. Mr. Howland insisted on getting air on the outside deck during the second day of the storm. Against everyone's pleading, he opened the hatch and went out. He was immediately washed overboard.
10. Mr. Lovelace tied a rope around his waist and used a boat hook to reach Mr. Howland The people below deck pulled them back through the hatch to safety.

Chapters 15–19

1. The main seam of the boat was opening.
2. a jack-screw; it forced the beam back into its spot by twisting a huge screw and applying pressure to the beam.
3. The captain said it was a stroke of luck that the farmer had his jack-screw along on the trip, but the pilgrims said it was certainly not luck, it was the providence of God.
4. The captain asked representatives of the pilgrims, of the adventurers and of his crew whether or not they should turn back. The crew was in favor of turning back, the adventurers were unsure, but the pilgrims were adamant to continue their voyage. Mr. Lovelace requested that a vote be taken among even the women and children, as they had suffered most being unfamiliar with the sea. It was unanimous to continue the journey, God had brought them this far, he would preserve them to their destination.
5. William Butten was rude, insulting and physically abusive to Mr. Howland and the Lovelace children. He stated that Mr. Howland in particular was going to die before the journey's end, and he would laugh as they threw him into the sea.
6. Romans 12

ANSWERS

7. William Butten cornered them. He threatened to harm the children, first with a knife and then with a rope.
8. Mr. Lovelace came along and witnessed his actions.
9. Justice began having nightmares of William Butten hurting him with the knife and the rope.
10. Justice's mother could tell he was having nightmares and spoke soothingly to him, assuring him that no one was going to harm him.

CHAPTERS 20–26
1. He became violently ill. He was out of his mind with fever and the sailors were unable to help him.
2. Some of the men thought that a physic should be called, others thought he should be bled. It was suggested that he be given more liquor and finally that the pilgrims should be called.
3. William Butten still cursed Mr. Lovelace in particular and all the pilgrims in general. He wanted nothing to do with God or His forgiveness. William died in this rebellious state and was buried at sea.
4. He instructed them in how a sailor could determine where they were, how fast they were traveling and how long they would continue at sea.
5. He showed them that the gulls had come out from land to welcome the ship to shore. They would see land in a few hours.
6. Unfortunately, Justice was right. They were off course by several hundred miles. Once again the pilgrims had been deceived in their journey.
7. Mr. Lovelace announced to his friends that they had been deceived yet again but that they were going to make a contract with the adventurers. This contract was in regards to governing their colony when they landed. They didn't want to arrive in their new home and still have the same bonds on their freedom that existed in England. The covenant was called the Mayflower Compact. They demanded that the ship be turned south to Virginia.
8. Jacob had been cheated by Laban, but he had still seen God's direction and control. Just as the captain and the adventurers had intended harm, they must trust that God intended this misdirection for their good.
9. to turn back to Cape Cod and make their settlement there
10. November; Prudence declared that their adventures were finally over, while Justice was sure they were just beginning!

Test
1. December, 1620
2. 35. They believed they should separate from the Church of England. They moved to Holland from Scrooby, England, where they had been persecuted.
3. Provincetown; five weeks
4. the Mayflower Compact; 41 of the 44 men
5. Miles Standish
6. the Speedwell

Review
1. cartography, astronomy and navigation
2. the Spanish Conquest
3. Newfoundland's coast, islands in the Gulf of St. Lawrence and the St. Lawrence River
4. a tribe of Indians in southwestern North Carolina
5. See the master list on page 500.

9: PILGRIMS BUILD PLYMOUTH COLONY
Worksheet
1. on the coast of Massachusetts
2. almost nothing
3. that He would provide for them
4. disease and unfamiliarity with the land
5. an Indian who taught the colony how to plant corn and showed them the best fishing streams
6. They gathered with the Indians to thank God for His provision—Thanksgiving.

Project 1
For younger and older students

Project 2
For younger and older students

Test
1. on the coast of Massachusetts
2. 1621
3. almost nothing
4. that He would provide for them
5. disease and unfamiliarity with the land
6. an Indian who taught the colony how to plant corn and showed them the best fishing streams
7. to give thanks to God for His provision; three days

Review
1. Queen Isabella of Spain
2. He was killed in the Philippines.
3. Ponce de Leon
4. King Henry VII of England
5. See the master list on page 500.

Answers

10: Massachusetts Bay Colony, Home of the Puritans

Worksheet
1. New England
2. the Puritans
3. They wanted to purify it.
4. John Endicott
5. John Winthrop; governor
6. that it was unfaithful to God; that their new society would be a "city upon a hill" and a model for Europe
7. biblical law

Project 1
For younger and older students
1. A group of English settlers who arrived in New England about ten years after the Pilgrims. They wanted to purify some forms of the English church service and church government.
2. the leader of the Puritans who arrived in 1630
3. eleven
4. It was severe, and food was scarce.
5. They thought it was so important that they established schools in every town.

Project 2
For older students

Project 3
For older students
Answers will vary.

Project 4
For older students

Test
1. Salem, Massachusetts
2. that it needed to be purified
3. John Endicott
4. Governor of the Massachusetts Bay Colony; that the Church of England was unfaithful and that the Bay Colony would be a "city upon a hill" and a model for Europe
5. biblical law

Review
1. One who plots a ship's direction
2. Queen Isabella of Spain
3. the commander of the first expedition to sail around the world
4. The Mississippi River
5. See the master list on page 500.

11: Roger Williams, Founder of Rhode Island

Worksheet
1. 1630
2. Plymouth
3. He was a proponent of extreme separation from the Church of England.
4. that he had no power to grant land in New England
5. John Cotton and Thomas Hooker
6. Rhode Island
7. that it would be religiously tolerant

Project 1
For older students

Project 2
For younger and older students
1. Jesus is confronting the woman at the well. It seems that he is telling her that he is the Messiah. the people in the background look positively scandalized that a Jew is associating with this woman who has a terrible reputation.
2. The woman is at the center of the composition and, hence, at the center of our attention—everything hinges on how she reacts to Jesus.

Test
1. 1630
2. Plymouth
3. He was a proponent of extreme separation from the Church of England.
4. That he had no power to grant land in New England
5. He was told to leave the colony.
6. Rhode Island
7. that it would be religiously tolerant

Review
1. Portugal
2. take the Gospel across the ocean and convert the people in the Indies
3. Florida; the Fountain of Youth
4. Italy. He landed on the coast of Newfoundland.
5. See the master list on page 500.

Answers

12: Salem Witch Trials

Worksheet

1. fear of witchcraft
2. over 160
3. nineteen; for supposedly practicing diabolical arts and witchcraft
4. Tituba, an Indian woman, admitted that she and two other girls had been practicing witchcraft.
5. It dealt poorly with the accusations.
6. Puritan clergy became critical of the evidence the court had admitted.

Project 1

For younger and older students

Literature Unit 2—The Witch of Blackbird Pond

Chapter 1
1. Barbados
2. 16 years
3. Kit was not used to walking on land; it felt as though the earth was moving
4. she jumped overboard to fetch a toy
5. she didn't drown, but kept afloat

Chapter 2
1. 43 miles; 9 days
2. John Holbrook
3. "walking up the river": set the anchor and pull the ship to it
4. it smelled like horses
5. her Aunt Rachel did not know she was coming to Wethersfield

Chapter 3
1. Wethersfield was not the grand place she had anticipated
2. Kit's mother, Margaret
3. Judith
4. water
5. she did not write first

Chapter 4
1. to see Kit's collection of dresses
2. slits in the sleeves
3. carding wool
4. an older man wanted to marry her
5. she overheard Judith complaining about her

Chapter 5
1. her apparel was too flamboyant
2. a group of boys
3. 2 hours
4. a small lean-to used as a temporary shelter on Sunday by families that lived too far to go home between services
5. William Ashby

Chapter 6
1. the meal had taken four days to prepare
2. the appointment of Gov. Andros
3. Mercy
4. William Ashby had asked permission to visit Kit
5. she had decided she wanted to marry John Holbrook

Chapter 7
1. he didn't talk, but only looked at her
2. Viewer of the Fences
3. he stood up to Uncle Matthew
4. he had made up his mind whom he was going to marry
5. she had to do the work meant for slaves

Chapter 8
1. a calico dress; so she wouldn't wear out her good dresses
2. the Great Meadows
3. Widow Tupper
4. they could teach school together
5. the death of his sons

Chapter 9
1. promised that Kit would tell a story
2. the students play-acted
3. Mr. Eleazer Kimberly and Rev. John Woodbridge
4. a piece of coral rock
5. a flower from the Cape of Good Hope

Chapter 10
1. they were Quakers
2. not to visit Hannah Tupper
3. smile
4. for not going to Meeting
5. Nathaniel Eaton

Chapter 11
1. she thought about the things she was able to do
2. left her flowers
3. teach her to read
4. at Hannah Tupper's house
5. Mercy

Chapter 12
1. that Kit visited Hannah Tupper
2. thatch Hannah's roof
3. all that schooling
4. reading books
5. she was a heretic and did not attend Meeting

Answers

Chapter 13
1. husking bee
2. practicing witchcraft
3. John revealed his love for Mercy
4. John and Judith were matched as a couple
5. who was to be married

Chapter 14
1. Autumn-leaves changing colors
2. woolen cloth to Hannah
3. 16 diamond-paneled windows for William Ashby's house
4. Gov. Andros was taking control of CT
5. the Dolphin was not able to sail

Chapter 15
1. pay for new land grants
2. it would not change their lives much
3. she wanted to see soldiers in uniform
4. the charter came up missing
5. she understood his magnificence

Chapter 16
1. Thanksgiving
2. put jack-o-lanterns in William's house
3. put in stocks
4. copybook, bottle of ink, quill
5. he joined the militia

Chapter 17
1. bleed her, feed her ground roasted toad
2. Dr. Bulkeley
3. Hannah Tupper
4. go warn Hannah and take her to Kit's house
5. the Dolphin sailed by in the river

Chapter 18
1. for standing up for her
2. she turned into a mouse
3. Kit's hornbook which she had given to Prudence
4. witchcraft
5. William

Chapter 19
1. her face was streaked with mud and tears
2. William
3. the copybook with Prudence's name written in it
4. wrote her name, read from the Bible
5. slander

Chapter 20
1. the first snowfall of winter
2. illness at the Wood home
3. it would take a lot of wood to heat the room
4. John Holbrook had been captured by Indians
5. she dreamed of returning to Barbados

Chapter 21
1. Dr. Bulkeley would teach John theology and medicine, but allow him to think on his own
2. sell them to pay for her passage to Barbados
3. the return of summer
4. Nat
5. The Witch

Project 2
For older students

Project 3
For older students

Project 4
For older students

Project 5
For older students

Project 6
For younger and older students
witchcraft, covenanting, Nineteen, 17th, witchcraft, Hysteria, Tituba, witchcraft, seventy, Massachusetts, poorly, Puritan clergy, clergy's, frenzy

Test
1. 1692
2. Tituba, an Indian woman, admitted that she and two other girls had been practicing witchcraft.
3. over 160
4. nineteen
5. It dealt poorly with the accusations.
6. Puritan clergy became critical of the evidence the court had admitted.

Review
1. Sir Walter Raleigh
2. King James I of England
3. a group of English Christians who believed in separation from the Church of England
4. He established a school of navigation and financed voyages.
5. See the master list on page 500.

13: 13 Colonies Formed

Worksheet
1. The King of England. He was in charge of their governments.
2. because the British Empire was divided into so

many separate units
3. laws that regulated colonial commerce
4. 1. Virginia, 1607
 2. Massachusetts, 1620
 3. New Hampshire, 1623
 4. New York, 1624
 5. Maryland, 1634
 6. Connecticut, 1635
 7. Rhode Island, 1636
 8. Delaware, 1638
 9. North Carolina, 1653
 10. New Jersey, 1664
 11. South Carolina, 1670
 12. Pennsylvania, 1682
 13. Georgia, 1733

Project 1
For older students

Project 2
For older students

Project 3
For younger and older students

Project 4
For younger and older students

Project 5
For younger and older students

Test
1. 1620–1733
2. He owned them all and was in charge of their governments.
3. Each carried out the policies and enforced the laws of England.
4. laws that regulated colonial commerce
5. Virginia, Massachusetts, New Hampshire, New York, Maryland, Connecticut, Rhode Island, Delaware, North Carolina, New Jersey, South Carolina, Pennsylvania, Georgia

Review
1. King James I of England
2. Provincetown; five weeks
3. Italy
4. the Lost Colony; because the colonists disappeared, and no knows what happened to them
5. See the master list on page 500.

14: The First Great Awakening

Worksheet
1. 1740–1742
2. It was a religious revival that emerged in the English colonies in America.
3. Jonathan Edwards and George Whitefield
4. "Sinners in the Hands of an Angry God"
5. 50,000, Boston
6. "free grace"
7. George Whitefield
8. Less than 90; 18,000

Project 1
For older students

Project 2
For older students

Project 3
For younger and older students

Test
1. They were great theologians whom God used to spark the First Great Awakening.
2. a religious revival that emerged in the English colonies in America
3. Jonathan Edwards
4. John Wesley, George Whitefield
5. Boston Commons
6. 18,000, less than 90
7. 1740–1742

Review
1. the commander of the first expedition to sail around the world
2. Quebec; Lake Champlain
3. The colony was deserted. All the colonists were missing.
4. the Mayflower Compact; 41 of the 44 men aboard the Mayflower
5. See the master list on page 500.

15: Colonial Trading with England

Worksheet
1. c. 1750
2. charters
3. trading of goods between a mother country and a colony
4. England
5. tobacco, cotton, indigo, wood products
6. Fine tools, dishes, tea, clothing

Answers

7. France and England
8. England increased its control over trade with the colonies and made it harder for the colonies to make money.

Project 1
For older students

Project 2
For older students

Project 3
For younger and older students

Project 4
For younger and older students

Test
1. c. 1750
2. mercantilism
3. to earn enough money to live
4. Answers may include: tobacco, cotton, indigo, wood products.
5. Answers may include: fine tools, dishes, tea, clothing
6. France and England
7. England increased its control over trade with the colonies and made it harder for the colonies to make money.

Review
1. a Puritan preacher; Rhode Island
2. the Puritans
3. that they should separate from the Church of England
4. Answers will vary: A group of adventurers and fortune seekers founded the colony. Many of them died while wasting their time quarreling and looking for gold. They were selfish and lazy.
5. See the master list on page 500.

16: The French and Indian Wars
Worksheet
1. They fought over who would control the land in North America.
2. The British were mostly Reformed Protestants and the French were Roman Catholics.
3. The British were farmers and settlers. The French were trappers and traders.
4. nine years (from 1754 until 1763)
5. Indians, British army, northeast, towns
6. George Washington, General Wolfe, General Montcalm, Pontiac
7. the treaty that ended the French and Indian War

Project 1
For older students
1. no one
2. Wolfe
3. He was too proud to learn anything about war from a country surveyor.
4. George Washington
5. possession, surveying, regiment, scaled, cliffs

Literature Unit 3—Duel in the Wilderness
Chapter 1
1. Governor Robert Dinwiddie and the Council.
2. If he was appointed to carry out the mission he might become an important man in the colony and realize his father's ambition to regain a seat for his family on the Council.
3. to act as diplomatic messenger to carry a letter to the French commander and learn by what right he had come into His Majesty's lands beyond the Allegheny Mountains on the River Ohio
4. Robert Dinwiddie had offered the mission to several older, more qualified gentlemen, but they had all found reasons to decline the offer.
5. because no man of pride could withdraw once his service had been offered before the Council, and because any hope to advance himself would be cut off forever
6. to go to Logstown on the River Ohio and learn where the French forces were. Then he was to take himself to that place, speak only to the highest ranking officer in that region and give him a letter from Governor Dinwiddie.
7. George was to introduce himself to an important representative of the Six Nations named Tanacharison. He was to tell him of his mission and ask for a large escort of their young men to ensure his safety.
8. George was directed to ask Christopher Gist of Will's Creek to be his guide.

Chapter 2
1. Jacob Van Braam; to be his translator to the French
2. the books on a shelf and the sword over the fireplace.
3. his older brother Lawrence. From him he learned gracious manners, swordsmanship, and

military matters.
4. that handling so many horses would be too difficult for just two men and that it would make them a tempting target for thieves
5. because he was to have a large escort of Indians. He also stated that as an emissary with a passport and a commission he had diplomatic immunity according to international law.
6. the Ohio Company

Chapter 3
1. the ever-present rain, wet tents, and having to spread pine boughs underneath their blankets to avoid direct contact with mud
2. a message from his son stating that he had fallen ill and needed his help at once.
3. He thought Frazier might not be alone. He might be a prisoner, or he might think that Christopher Gist was a hostage masking an attack.
4. Tanacharison had left a belt of wampum with a tomahawk attached to its end. It meant that Tanacharison was going to ally himself with the English and it was an invitation to make war against their common enemy.
5. The news that the French general, De Marin, was dead

Chapter 4
1. hold up his hands, palms open, to show he had no weapons
2. The major traders were men who dealt directly with merchants in the British ports along the Atlantic coast. From the merchants they obtained goods to trade to the Indians for fur. The major traders then transported the furs back to the merchants who sent them to England. They also got furs from other ordinary traders who, for various reasons, did not want to go to British settlements.
3. No. He met with Monachatoocha instead, who was second only to Tanacharison.
4. The longhouse belonged to the chief woman of the longhouse, so she had the right to decide who was welcome. It was she who invited George and his companions to sit on the buffalo robes.
5. soldiers, deserters from the French army
6. that the French were bringing reinforcements from New Orleans because they had discovered a water route between New Orleans and their settlements in Canada

Chapter 5
1. What Tanacharison told George Washington about the French was so revealing that George wanted to write it down. Tanacharison was flattered that what he had to say was so important that the "white man" would want to write it down.
2. because he was born to the role of diplomat. Tanacharison knew that the English and French were long time enemies and would never join together to fight the Indians.
3. the chiefs of the local tribes
4. The ceremony of the calumet was only used on important occasions. It involved passing a pipe, and taking two puffs on the pipe when it was your turn. To not smoke the pipe was a sign of war.
5. because Tanacharison needed to go to his hunting cabin and get the French speech-belt. In addition, the people who Tanacharison wanted to send as guard had not yet arrived, and would not arrive for another three nights.
6. While George did not understand the full importance of the wampum belts, if the returning of the wampum belts to the French meant that the Indians were canceling any agreements with the French, George felt the delay would be worthwhile.
7. That way the French would not think they were coming to make war rather than deliver a speech belt.

Chapter 6
1. the loss of their livelihoods and the capture or death of their friends
2. Much as George wanted to discuss his business right away, he could not because it was not yet time. First he had to engage in meaningless polite conversation.
3. He said he could not assume such responsibility for his government by receiving and answering a letter from a foreign governor.
4. because the French could move fast in canoes up and down the rivers which they controlled. The English would be too slow to stop them.
5. Unlike de Marin, Joncaire did not insult the Indians by calling them flies and mosquitoes, but embraced them like blood brothers and flattered them.
6. The Indians felt trapped between the English and the French. They suspected the English wanted their land just as much as the French did.
7. Tanacharison stated that his speech must be in council with Joncaire and the local Delaware chiefs because Joncaire was in charge of all

Answers

Hodenosaunee business for the French.

8. La Force told George that the French were anxious that George's company reach Fort Le Boeuf safely. As George was an official diplomat, if anything happened to him, it would cause very bad tension between the French and the English.

Chapter 7

1. because it indicated to him that the French were going to treat him as a diplomat, not a spy
2. St. Pierre told George he could not receive the papers until he got a translator.
3. at least one hundred men, not including officers.
4. to take the letter from Governor Dinwiddie to Governor Duquesne in Quebec
5. because time was very important and he had to return as quickly as possible to Williamsburg
6. The whole English alliance with the Six Nations depended upon them staying with him.
7. because it would please Tanacharison. In addition, he would only lose time, but if the French do not keep their promise to the Indians to give them guns, it would make the French look bad.

Chapter 8

1. Tanacharison and the other Indians had stopped to hunt. They came back with three bears.
2. George wanted to catch up to the Indians because three canoes with Frenchmen came down the river and passed the Englishmen. George did not want to leave the Indians in the company of the French.
3. George concluded they must use the horses for travel because going by canoe was dangerous, no faster, the river was falling and the water was freezing over.
4. because White Thunder was badly hurt and could not walk
5. *Conotocarious* means "burner of villages." Conotocarious was the name given to George's great-grandfather after he had invited five Algonquin chiefs to his camp, murdered them and burned their villages. Among the Hodenasaunee, George's family was not known as Washington, but as Conotocarious. Tanacharison said he would be known by that name until he performed his own great deeds and was given a new name among the Indians.

Chapter 9

1. During Christmastime in Williamsburg, there were candles burning in the windows, smells of roasting goose and pies. There were also balls and assemblies where young men can dance with the ladies.
2. Because he was a gentleman and used to riding a horse, he was unaccustomed to walking long distances in the woods, especially through deep snow.
3. He wore leather leggings over his knee breeches, two pairs of homespun woolen stockings and deer hide moccasins instead of his boots. He also put on a warm matchcoat made out of fur over his own hunting jacket.
4. because the door was open, and if anyone were in the cabin they would have closed the door.
5. The Indian could serve as their guide, show them the shortest route and therefore save them time.

Chapter 10

1. to make a torch, which would allow him to use his compass
2. because the snowfall would hide their tracks from any unfriendly Indians who might be trying to follow them
3. George proposed they should build a raft by felling small trees, then using a knife to get strips of bark to tie the logs together.
4. If Gist let George rest through the night, he would freeze to death.
5. that the Allegheny had completely frozen during the night
6. a war party of Indians camped around Frazier's house

Chapter 11

1. because he was a brother to the Iroquois Indians now
2. because they were dressed as Indians
3. Tanacharison had told him that his people do not make war in the winter.
4. The Indians had originally set out to make war on the Cherokees. However, the Indians came across a cabin where men, women and children had been murdered. They did not want to be blamed for it, so they turned around and were heading home. On their way home they stopped at Frazier's cabin for the night.
5. because even though George had to get to Williamsburg to complete his mission, when he saw the Indian war party he wouldn't leave, because he wouldn't leave Gist and was concerned about Frazier
6. George and Gist paid a call to Queen Alliquippa. They called on her because she was insulted

ANSWERS

when they didn't stop on their way into the Ohio Territory, and the English needed every Indian friend they could get.

CHAPTER 12

1. George thought he would return to the wilderness because he liked its incredible dangers, its loneliness and the tests of total self-reliance.
2. because they thought he was dead
3. King George had ordered Dinwiddie to inquire into the truth of whether the Indians or Europeans presumed to erect forts within the province of Virginia. If so, Dinwiddie was to ask them to leave. If they refused, he was authorized to use force.
4. the funds needed to raise an army

EPILOGUE

1. George insisted that a message of apology be printed at the end of his report, because he was horrified to learn that his hurried efforts of writing his story to the commission would be printed.

Test

1. 1754-1763
2. They disagreed and fought over who would control the land in North America.
3. The British were mostly Reformed Protestants and the French were Roman Catholics. The British were farmers and settlers, and the French were trappers and traders.
4. The French didn't build towns and cities on the land.
5. George Washington was an American, General Wolfe was British, General Montcalm was French, and Pontiac was an Indian chief.
6. The war ended with the Peace of Paris Treaty. British control was established, but England had a huge war debt that it tried to get the American colonies to help pay.

Review

1. "Sinners in the Hands of an Angry God"
2. trials in Salem, Massachusetts, in 1642 in which 160 people were charged with practicing witchcraft. Nineteen men and women were hanged as witches.
3. Virginia, Massachusetts, New Hampshire, New York, Maryland, Connecticut, Rhode Island, Delaware, North Carolina, New Jersey, South Carolina, Pennsylvania, Georgia
4. Holland
5. See the master list on page 500.

17: PARLIAMENT ACTS UNJUSTLY

Worksheet

1. A series of taxes
2. It aimed to raise revenue for England.
3. It taxed legal documents, newspapers and similar articles in the colonies.
4. The colonists agreed that "taxation without representation is tyranny"
5. It required colonists to provide quarters and supplies for British soldiers.
6. to save a failing tea company
7. When the tea arrived in Boston Harbor, they dressed as Indians, boarded the ships and threw the tea overboard.
8. They closed Boston Harbor, reduced self-rule in Massachusetts, allowed British soldiers to be quartered in private homes, and allowed British soldiers accused of crimes to be tried elsewhere.

Project 1

For younger and older students

1764: Sugar Act
1765: Stamp Act
1765: Stamp Act Congress
1765: Quartering Act
1773: Tax on Surplus Tea

Project 2

For older students

Project 3

For younger and older students

Test

1. 1764-1774
2. the Sugar Act
3. It taxed legal documents, newspapers and similar articles in the colonies.
4. in 1765 at the Stamp Act Congress
5. It required colonists to provide quarters and supplies for British soldiers.
6. They dressed as Indians, boarded the British tea ships and threw the tea overboard.
7. They closed Boston Harbor, reduced self-rule in Massachusetts, allowed British soldiers to be quartered in private homes, and allowed British soldiers accused of crimes to be tried elsewhere.

Answers

Review
1. Portugal
2. Columbus learned a lot about navigation at Prince Henry's school.
3. South America and Central America
4. a French explorer; Lake Champlain
5. See the master list on page 500.

18: The First Continental Congress Seeks Peace with Britain

Worksheet
1. concern about the injustice of Parliament
2. Georgia
3. It stated that the colonies would not buy British goods unless given their English rights, and it was written to King George.
4. The Congress told colonists not to buy British products or sell American goods to Britain. They did this because Britain depended heavily on the colonies as a market.
5. It established an effective "Association" that made the colonists obey the boycott.
6. There was growing sentiment that fighting was imminent.

Project 1
For younger and older students

Project 2
For older students

Test
1. delegates from all the colonies except Georgia
2. Philadelphia
3. They were concerned about the injustice of England's Parliament.
4. a Declaration of Rights and Grievances
5. to make use of their economic power against Britain, which depended heavily on the colonies as a market
6. There was growing sentiment that fighting was imminent.

Review
1. the Speedwell; It was found to be unseaworthy.
2. the Puritans
3. a Puritan preacher who founded Rhode Island
4. a colonial theologian whom God used to spark the First Great Awakening
5. See the master list on page 500.

19: The War for Independence Begins

Worksheet
1. 1775
2. to stop commerce
3. Lexington and Concord
4. to warn the people that the British were coming
5. They were captured.
6. On the village green, the British and Americans fought. One British soldier was killed, and eight Americans were killed.
7. The Americans fired at the British from behind fences and trees. The British lost 273 soldiers and the Americans lost 93.

Literature Unit 4–Johnny Tremain
Section I: Up and About
Chapter 1
1. Their master was too feeble and their mistress was too stout.
2. Johnny lorded his skill over him and ordered Dove about as if Johnny were the master smith.
3. Dusty thought Mr. Lapham liked Johnny because Johnny was clever at his work, that Mrs. Lapham liked Johnny because he was reliable, the Lapham girls because he sassed them so, and the neighborhood boys liked Johnny too.
4. He was so useful at his bench he could never be spared for such work.
5. An apprentice was little more than a slave. Until he had served his master seven years, he had no wages and the very clothes upon his back belonged to his master.
6. Mr. Lapham told Johnny to thank God who had seen fit to make Johnny so good an artisan.

Chapter 2
1. Only Johnny and Mr. Lapham could read. The other apprentices had never learned; Dorcas and Madge never cared to try, Mrs. Lapham could see no use to it and Cilla and Isannah had not had the chance to learn yet.
2. Johnny's pride.

Chapter 3
1. He never wrote down what was ordered or even listened very carefully. This made Johnny seem cheeky because Johnny would always have to be on hand to write down orders for the master and then would have to tell the master what to do.
2. because Mr. Hancock had come to the shop to place an order

Answers

3. one week
4. Mr. Lapham didn't agree with men who were always trying to stir up trouble between the colonies and England.

Chapter 4
1. a working boy having three names

Chapter 5
1. to get a breath of fresh air because she felt sick
2. The darkness of the night and the remoteness of the place and an affection he felt for the girls made everything seem different.
3. so Johnny would be able to learn a trade and thereby support himself, since she knew she was dying.

Chapter 6
1. the crest of the Lyte family showing an eye rising from the sea, with rays of light streaming out

Section II: The Pride of Your Power
Chapter 1
1. Johnny took the pitcher and his own wax model to ask Mr. Revere's advice. Johnny was not satisfied with his work.
2. Mr. Revere agreed with Johnny that his model wasn't, "Right." Johnny had just enlarged the handle without taking its proportion to the pitcher into account.
3. Mr. Revere must have been impressed by Johnny, because he offered him a position in his workshop if anything ever happened to his current master, Mr. Lapham.

Chapter 2
1. Johnny knew he could not finish the handle on Sunday because Mr. Lapham shut the shop for the entire day and left the furnaces cold.
2. The charcoal was all gone.
3. that Johnny was becoming too proud because he had never been up against another apprentice as good as he is and that God would send Johnny a dire punishment because of his pride.
4. Johnny knew that it was against the law as well as against his religious training. It was possible that he might be put in the stocks, and he believed it was also possible he might go to Hell for disobeying the rule.

Chapter 3
1. Dove and Dusty thought that Johnny deserved to be set back for the way he had been bossing everyone around. They thought the cracked crucible would spill silver over the top of the furnace and make Johnny look like a fool.
2. Johnny never knew exactly what happened, but while reaching for the crucible his feet went out from under him and his hand came down directly onto the furnace.
3. No. If she did they would have to confess to working on the Sabbath.

Chapter 4
1. Johnny thought his hand was completely useless because his thumb and forefinger could not meet and therefore he could no longer do silver work. As his fingers still worked, his hand was obviously not completely useless.
2. Mr. Lapham believed that Johnny had been punished for working on the Sabbath and ordered the whole pitcher to be melted down. He returned the cream pitcher to Mr. Hancock and told him the project could not be finished.
3. Swimming, for then his bad hand was just as good as his other hand. While swimming, he could forget the accident.

Chapter 5
1. Mr. Lapham had contracted with Johnny to teach him the silversmith's art in exchange for Johnny's work. However, Johnny could now no longer be taught the silversmith's art.
2. He said he wanted to teach Johnny a lesson for breaking the Sabbath.

Section III: An Earth of Brass
Chapter 1
1. Johnny was to watch until he was sure it was work that he would like. Then he was to address the master politely, show him his bad hand, and ask to be taken on.
2. Many patrons were illiterate and could only tell what the shop sold by the pictures on the sign.
3. Cilla slipped food into Johnny's pocket so that he would not be hungry while job hunting.
4. Rab showed that he was a good listener.
5. delivering papers by riding a horse

Chapter 2
1. He could not stand the look of impotence and timidity in a grown man.
2. Mr. Tweedie could save the family business and

ANSWERS

marry one of her daughters.

Chapter 3
1. He wore his hat at a rakish angle and kept his right hand thrust in his pocket.
2. either an aristocrat's son or a thief
3. the merchant field
4. Mr. Hancock; a cabin boy.
5. bag of silver

Chapter 4
1. bread, cheese, ale, and apples
2. He no longer felt hungry.
3. She knew that Johnny could not have bought the shoes with the money he had, so she assumed he had stolen the money to get the shoes or stolen the shoes.
4. forgetting his crippled hand while playing with Cilla and Isannah

Chapter 5
1. When Isannah had yelled that she hated his hand, it broke the last of his strength so that he cried on his mother's grave.
2. to visit Merchant Lyte as his mother had advised

SECTION IV: THE RISING EYE
Chapter 1
1. Half of Johnny was leaping ahead imagining great things for himself, the other half was wary. He knew it was quite possible he would receive no welcome at all.
2. that he should bring his cup to Mr. Lyte that evening at Mr. Lyte's house

Chapter 2
1. because the birth and death room had been given to Mr. Tweedie
2. They started to treat him normally—which in this case means they were throwing insults at him.
3. Merchant Lyte was one of the first to sign an agreement that he would not import any English goods until the Stamp Act was repealed, but then he imported English goods secretly and sold them under another name.
4. Whigs believed that taxation without representation is tyranny. Tories believed that all their differences with England could be settled with time, patience and a respect for government.

Chapter 3
1. to arrest Johnny, accusing him of burglary
2. When Sewall went to the Laphams, Mrs. Lapham swore that Johnny had never owned a thing except the clothes he stood in. She also stated that his indenture papers were signed "Johnny Tremain" by his mother. Mrs. Lapham also believed that he had lately taken to evil ways and that he had never owned a cup. Mr. Tweedie said that Johnny was a notorious liar.

Chapter 4
1. Isannah's squeals had broken his heart, but he felt that he was tough enough and strong enough to face the burglary accusations in court.
2. that Rab was a member of the semi-secret Sons of Liberty
3. Mr. Lyte commissioned work from the Laphams, which Rab saw as an attempt to bribe the family.
4. because he could not pay for his services

Chapter 5
1. Rab and Isannah
2. The silver cups had been made for Mr. Lyte's great grandfather. Mr. Lyte stated that four of these cups had made it to the colonies and he came into possession of the four cups.
3. that Johnny be hanged, because there was too much thieving going on around Boston and poor apprentices were getting out of hand
4. Isannah's arrival
5. a suit

SECTION V: THE BOSTON OBSERVER
Chapter 1
1. Mr. Lyte's pride had been hurt.
2. Rab had shown her a letter signed by the governor and stamped with the seal of the colony. Since Mrs. Lapham couldn't read, she had no way of knowing that the letter had nothing to do with Cilla giving testimony at the trial.
3. He didn't have the money to provide his own sea gear.
4. to sell the silver cup to Mr. Lyte
5. nothing
6. return to the print shop to ask if he can still be a horse boy

Answers

Chapter 2

1. Goblin was an extremely timid horse and would bolt at movements that startled him.
2. Rab was confident that Johnny could learn to ride and Johnny knew that Goblin was more scared than he was.
3. Johnny had gone from knowing relatively little about politics to becoming an ardent Whig due to the reading that had been doing as he delivered the papers around Boston, talking to Rab and Uncle Lorne, and listening to the leaders of the opposition.
4. They were for the secret meetings held by the Boston Observers.
5. Because the owner of the Queen liked Johnny, he recommended him for delivering letters.
6. exercising Goblin, reading, learning to write with his left hand, and delivering express letters for the Afric Queen

Chapter 3

1. He felt that Mrs. Lapham and Mr. Tweedie had been too ready to see him hang, and he was sure he would hurt Dove if he ever saw him.
2. to have a chance to talk with Cilla

Chapter 4

1. Rab challenged Johnny about Johnny's habit of going out of his way to say bad things about others.
2. The first time was when Rab was dancing and he threw himself suddenly and wildly into the dance. The second time was when he took on the butcher's boy as punishment for his threats towards the twins' cat.
3. At the dance, Johnny forgot about his hand in the fun—and therefore nobody else thought anything of it either.

Section VI: Salt-Water Tea

Chapter 1

1. The tax would be put on the tea and paid by the East India company before the tea left England, the amount of the tax was very small, the tea supplied by England was better and cheaper than other tea available, and they also did not think the colonists were not politically savvy enough to figure out exactly what was going on.
2. that England had sent ships with tea and that they would soon be landing in Boston
3. to persuade the Governor to give his permission for the ships to return to London with their cargo
4. He couldn't help himself; he was drawn to watching the Lytes.
5. James Otis was thought to be the most brilliant of the Observers because of the "largeness" of his philosophy. However, he had been going back and forth between sane and crazy over the last four years, at times being seen to leave Boston in a straightjacket with his doctor.

Chapter 2

1. No. Isannah was behaving like a vain spoiled child, and Cilla acted in a way towards him that made Johnny think that she did not recognize he was growing up and changing.
2. Isannah was becoming aware of her beauty in such a way that she showed off more and more.
3. because Johnny had answered that it was God's will that his hand was crippled.

Chapter 3

1. Many of the men did not want to mend their differences with England. Some of them would welcome a war.
2. Thirty men and boys would be needed to board the ships and dump the tea into the harbor.
3. The men and boys needed to be trustworthy so that not an ounce of the tea was stolen. The event was to be a protest, not a robbery.

Chapter 4

1. by splitting logs for firewood

Chapter 5

1. Captain Leslie had orders to fire on the ships if they attempted to return with their cargo.
2. These guards were assuring that no tea was smuggled off the ships, and that no harm was done to the ships in return.

Chapter 6

1. Johnny was to listen to Sam Adams signal. "Now may God help my country," would indicate nothing was to be done to the tea. "This meeting can do nothing more to save the country," would indicate they were to go ahead with the plan to dump the tea.
2. Johnny recognized Dove in the group of Indians. Dove was shoving tea into his breaches to smuggle off the ship.
3. the whole town of Boston

Answers

Section VII: The Fiddler's Bill

Chapter 1

1. England's punishment of Boston
2. the Tories
3. Gage had the right to send anyone to England that he believed to be a leader, or to have them hung right there in Boston.
4. He touched one of the soldiers' muskets.
5. He might learn things of use to Sam Adams, Doctor Warren and Paul Revere.

Chapter 2

1. He gave all the money to Aunt Lorne to buy food for the family.
2. No, since he was trying to befriend as many of the people in Boston as possible.
3. Isannah would not go live with them without Cilla.

Chapter 3

1. The Afric Queen had been taken over by British officers, and the owner of the tavern did not want them to "take over" his horses as well. They were sent away to the country.
2. Look up commandeer in a dictionary. The British soldier intended to commandeer Goblin, the horse.
3. He loosened the laundry drying on the line so that Goblin was startled and threw the officer off.
4. Johnny couldn't help himself. Dove needed a friend and he "[c]lung to Johnny like a drowning man." Johnny also knew that Dove's contacts with the British could be very helpful in the future.

Chapter 4

1. He remembered the times Mrs. Lapham would barter and trade to get them food. He was old enough now to recognize how valiantly she had worked to care for those for whom she was responsible.
2. The Whigs were moving out of Boston and Torie families were moving into Boston to be under the protection of the British troops.

Chapter 5

1. Mrs. Bessie, who had been with Lavinia since she was a baby, was showing no fondness or loyalty towards her.
2. Isannah was behaving in a very immodest way. Johnny slapped her not so much for himself but in honor of her grandfather.
3. He had suspected that Cilla and Isannah were treated differently, but when he saw it with his own eyes, it made him furious.
4. Mrs. Bessie was a sort of spy for Sam Adams.

Section VIII: A World to Come

Chapter 1

1. If the Lytes were scared out of their country estate, the only safe place for them to be was in Boston.
2. He was waiting for the Lytes, hoping that the girls would be okay.
3. to go get the silver that was left at the estate
4. The mob turned from the house to chase the Lytes. She thought they may not have thought to go back to the house at nighttime to loot it.

Chapter 2

1. to wash the dishes
2. that his grandfather was the younger brother of Jonathan Lyte
3. No, he shredded the paper and burned it in the fire.

Chapter 3

1. The British soldiers never left their muskets unattended.
2. a good gun
3. They were tarred and feathered.

Chapter 4

1. Mrs. Lapham's daughter, Madge, had run off to marry Sergeant Gale.
2. Rab would come to visit Cilla and buy her sweets.
3. Johnny saw the apple as a symbol of the relationship between Cilla and himself.

Chapter 5

1. When James Otis was lucid, they couldn't get him to stop talking.
2. He said the problem was in Boston itself. They did not know early enough what the plans of the troops were, but that the system of calling the Minute Men worked well.
3. He said they fought for the right of men everywhere to choose who it would be that would rule over them.
4. for the honor given to them, that they had a cause worth dying for

Section IX: The Scarlet Deluge

Chapter 1

1. They were men of humble rank. In addition, the

Answers

old stone inn was owned by Masons, and people expected Masons to meet in secrecy.

2. that the British were planning on fortifying their supply stores at Portsmouth; Lydia, the laundress at the Afric Queen
3. The British soldiers at the Neck were asking more and more questions of known Whigs, sometimes not letting them pass out of Boston. The fake letter from a relative stating that Paul Revere's grandmother was on her deathbed was to allay the soldiers' suspicions.

Chapter 2

1. Dove had become violently pro-British because he considered himself part of the British army.
2. to loosen his tongue and perhaps cause him to tell British secrets
3. because General Gage had not taken any action against the rebels
4. Worcester and Concord
5. when riding horses together

Chapter 3

1. because there was no longer any ferry from Charlestown to Boston, and the guards at the town gate were too curious
2. He stuck his spurs into Goblin.
3. A lot of them were Whigs and on the side of the Colonists.
4. Johnny wanted Pumpkin's musket. He wanted it for Rab.
5. pewter; many families donated their beautiful pewter pieces to be melted down in crucibles.

Chapter 4

1. King George was furious over the dilatory, cautious behavior of General Gage. He was also mad that rebellion had not been put down as he ordered, that few military supplies had been seized, and finally that everywhere throughout New England men were drilling when his Majesty had ordered the militias to disband.

Chapter 5

1. They were actually a firing squad.
2. the execution of Pumpkin; he did not think he had the courage to stand up to the "murderous little eyes," the ends of muskets pointed at him.

Section X—Disperse, Ye Rebels!

Chapter 1

1. They were lightly armed and did scout and flanking work.
2. No, they may have been intending to transport soldiers—but it also could have been a ruse.
3. They needed someone who could get out of town, and Billy Dawes could impersonate anybody, even a British officer.

Chapter 2

1. No, he was leaving Boston to go to Lexington to fight.
2. Answers may vary. One reason could be that Johnny was scared that Rab might be killed and didn't know how to say good-bye when it might be forever.

Chapter 3

1. Dove got into trouble for cleaning Colonel Smith's parade saddle rather than his campaign saddle. The campaign saddle had still been in storage, so the fact that he wanted it taken out and cleaned may have meant that the British were planning a movement against the colonials soon.
2. by how long the veterinarian said the horse would be fine on a boat for

Chapter 4

1. Colonel Smith had been in the service for the longest period of time.
2. Billy's mother, Mrs. Dawes, was also a gifted actor. She convinced Johnny she was full of happiness until Billy left, and then she stopped trying to look light-hearted and let her concern show.
3. They were watching for warning lights to be posted in the tower of Christ's spire warning them of a British attack.
4. Paul Revere was concerned that if fighting did break out, the British would know that Doctor Warren was part of the plan and that Gage would hang him for treason.
5. Major Pitcairn was liked by the Yankees and was a better officer than Colonel Smith.

Section XI: Yankee Doodle

Chapter 1

1. Doctor Warren stated that there were 700 British troops firing against 70 men at Lexington, and that for them it was just target practice.

ANSWERS

2. The Minute Men had been alerted and were headed towards Concord. Doctor Warren anticipated that there would be a significant battle there.

Chapter 2
1. The English flag stood for liberties beginning with the Magna Charta. Johnny thought the colonists had just expanded that idea of liberty to include that man should not be ruled or taxed except by men of his own choice. Therefore, they were all still fighting for "English liberty."

Chapter 3
1. General Gage gave the order to arrest the opposition leaders too late. Most had left Boston a month earlier.
2. Mrs. Lorne put him inside a feather bed and sewed it up.
3. He saw a British major return in partial disguise with a look of fear on his face, and he was headed towards the house were General Gage was staying. Johnny said that victors don't look like that, but British officers who are ashamed of being beaten by colonials do.
4. Yes. War had begun, the mood of the British had changed towards the "rebels," both sides were committed towards victory, and for those who thought themselves in the middle of the controversy their was fear.

Chapter 4
1. Johnny still had Pumpkin's uniform and wore it.
2. No, Mrs. Bessie and Cilla were remaining since they were declared Whigs.
3. Merchant Lyte had stated that there were only four silver cups that had come to Boston when really there were five.
4. The family said she would be cut off from them and was never to return if she married the French soldier.
5. Johnny's father was ashamed to be a prisoner, so he did not use his real last name, which was Tremain. He went by the name of Latour.

Chapter 5
1. The Lorne family could come live at the Lyte's house and pretend to be the coachman. Mrs. Bessie and Cilla would pretend they had always lived there.

SECTION XII: A MAN CAN STAND UP

Chapter 1
1. The uniform he was wearing was that of a simple soldier. A soldier like that would have been out with the fighting, and unless wounded, would not be back in Boston yet. Instead of serving as a disguise, the uniform would now attract attention.
2. He saw an officer strike a man who was screaming in pain.
3. War had divided them, and he could no longer reach out to his friend without putting himself in danger.
4. He said that he had a message for Earl Percy. The soldiers at the boat were told to take him across so he could deliver the letter.
5. At Lexington they met with Major Percy's reserve soldiers.

Chapter 2
1. Johnny was probably worried for them. He saw men with no uniforms, but more importantly, no winter clothing, no food and no gear to protect them from the elements. In addition, they may have had their guns, but no cannon and apparently no leaders.
2. eight

Chapter 3
1. Johnny's duty was to find Dr. Warren. He found him by recognizing his chaise and horse outside the Harrington house.
2. that he had stood with the Lexington men and had refused to disperse when ordered to by the British, then had been wounded very badly and would probably not live

Chapter 4
1. his musket
2. to go to his family's home.

Chapter 5
1. The first clue was that the animals had not been fed, and Grandsire had always been very careful to feed them. The second was that in the kitchen Grandsire's gun and powder horn were gone.
2. Rab knew he was going to die and didn't want Johnny to have to watch.
3. James Otis words had to do with the reason for going to war, "So that a man can stand up." Dr. Warren saw Rab as one of those brave men who stood in the face of oppression and guns and

ANSWERS

refused to give up his right for liberty, and was willing to die rather than turn away from his convictions in fear.

4. that Johnny's hand was misshapen because of a burn scar, not a deformity from birth.
5. While Dr. Warren could not promise that Johnny would be able to do silver work again, he could free his thumb from the scar tissue so that he would be able to fire a gun.
6. Answers will vary. One word that could sum it up would be patriotism. He is feeling a love for the land and for the people that makes him willing to fight for them, to feel brave for the ideas that will protect them and their freedom, so much so that he is willing to die for them if need be.

Project 1
For older students

Project 2
For younger and older students

Project 3
For older students

Test
1. 1775
2. Boston Harbor
3. Lexington and Concord
4. Two lights were lit in the steeple of Old North Church to tell him the British were coming by sea. One light would have signaled that they were coming by land.
5. William Dawes
6. On the village green, the British and Americans fought. One British soldier was killed and eight Americans were killed.
7. The Americans fired at the British from behind fences and trees. The British lost 273 soldiers and the Americans lost 93.

Review
1. Answers will vary: Roger Williams was a Puritan who came to New England in 1630. He preached in Plymouth for a year and then in Salem. He was an extreme separatist who believed that the King had no power to grant land in America. He founded the colony of Rhode Island in 1636. Rhode Island was a religiously tolerant settlement.
2. Answers will vary: The French and Indian War was fought to see who would control the land in North America. The British and the American colonies fought the French and their Indian allies. The British won the war, and British control was established, but then England had a huge war debt that it tried to get the colonies to help pay.
3. See the master list on page 500.

20: BRITISH LOSE AT BUNKER HILL

Worksheet
1. 1775
2. on Breed's Hill outside of Boston
3. in the front; no
4. They had only short-range muskets.
5. The British lost over forty percent of their men in a terrible slaughter.

Project 1
For younger and older students

Project 2
For younger and older students

Test
Answers will vary

Review
1. a religious revival that emerged in the English colonies in America
2. Virginia, Massachusetts, New Hampshire, New York, Maryland, Connecticut, Rhode Island, Delaware, North Carolina, New Jersey, South Carolina, Pennsylvania, Georgia
3. 160
4. Sir Walter Raleigh and the English
5. See the master list on page 500.

21: AMERICA DECLARES ITS INDEPENDENCE

Worksheet
1. 1776
2. listen to their petitions and come to peaceful terms
3. He called all American leaders traitors and said they would be drawn and quartered when caught.
4. a pamphlet written by Tom Paine which attacked King George and glorified a free America
5. a public statement of American rights and grievances; Thomas Jefferson and Benjamin Franklin
6. A majority of the colonies signed it by July 4, 1776. (All colonies had signed by August.)
7. all out war with Britain

Answers

Project 1
For younger and older students

Project 2
For younger and older students

Project 3
For younger and older students
King George, petitions, peaceful, traitors, drawn, quartered, Common Sense, America, rights, grievances, Thomas Jefferson, Benjamin Franklin, majority, July 4, 1776, August, war

Test
1. 1776
2. He announced that American leaders were traitors and under English law would be drawn and quartered when caught.
3. Tom Paine wrote the pamphlet "Common Sense."
4. the American colonies' public statement of their rights and grievances; Thomas Jefferson and Benjamin Frankin
5. July 4, 1776
6. all out war with Britain

Review
1. Answers will vary
2. See the master list on page 500.

22: Washington Commands the Continental Army

Worksheet
1. 1775–1781
2. May, 1775
3. America; Americans supported the war and men enlisted.
4. It formally brought France in to back the colonies.
5. He was commander of the French ship *Bonhomme Richard.* He fought and defeated the British ship *Serapis.*
6. an American guerilla fighter known as the Swamp Fox
7. He was surrounded by French ships in the Chesapeake Bay and George Washington's American troops on land.

Project 1
For younger and older students

Project 2
For older students

Test
1. 1775–1781
2. In May, 1775, the Continental Congress made George Washington commander-in-chief.
3. because Washington's army won the first battles
4. because America suffered defeats in 1777–78, and Philadelphia fell to the British
5. It finally brought France in to back the colonies.
6. John Paul Jones, when his ship was badly damaged fighting the British ship *Serapis.*
7. British commander Lord Cornwallis

Review
1. a Portuguese sea captain; he commanded the first expedition to sail around the world
2. Queen Isabella of Spain
3. the Mississippi River
4. Samuel de Champlain
5. See the master list on page 500.

23: Winter at Valley Forge

Worksheet
1. 1775–1781
2. They fled the British takeover of the colonial capital, Philadelphia, and needed shelter for the coming winter.
3. He refused to live in comfort until log cabins were built for his men first.
4. German general Baron von Steuben *(that's his picture at the top of the worksheet)*
5. sea power, commanding officers, money
6. smaller in number, but significantly better disciplined, and fortified by foreign allies

Project 1
For older students

Project 2
For younger and older students

Project 3
For older students

Project 4
For younger and older students

Test
1. 1775–1781
2. Answers will vary: The winter was unusually harsh. Many men died from exposure, disease and starvation. Log cabins had to be built for the army

ANSWERS

to live in. German general Baron Von Steuben came to help turn the army into well-trained, disciplined troops.
3. a German general who helped train the American army at Valley Forge
4. America
5. . . . smaller in number, but significantly better disciplined, and fortified by foreign allies

Review
1. map making
2. The colonists all disappeared, and no one knows what happened to them.
3. third leader of the Jamestown colony in Virginia
4. See the master list on page 500.

24: YORKTOWN AND THE TREATY OF PARIS

Worksheet
1. in the Yorktown peninsula in the Chesapeake Bay
2. the French navy
3. "The World Turned Upside Down"
4. the Treaty of Paris; 1783
5. the independence of the American colonies
6. They still were not one nation, but thirteen separate colonies which acted independently.

Project 1
For younger and older students

Project 2
For older students

Project 3
For younger and older students

Test
1. On the Yorktown peninsula in the Chesapeake Bay
2. the French navy
3. "Yankee Doodle"
4. the Treaty of Paris; 1783
5. the independence of the American colonies
6. They still were not one nation, but thirteen separate colonies which acted independently.

Review
1. take the Gospel across the ocean and convert the people of the Indies
2. the Aztec Empire
3. King James I of England
4. that He would provide for them
5. See the master list on page 500.

25: THE CONSTITUTIONAL CONVENTION

Worksheet
1. 1787
2. After the war the colonies were loosely organized under the Articles of the Confederation.
3. twelve colonies
4. George Washington, James Madison
5. . . . be workable, resemble the British system, limit central government, and protect property rights
6. . . . where majority opinion ruled, but minority rights were respected.
7. the establishment of three branches of government: judicial, executive and legislative
8. levy and collect taxes, regulate commerce between states and foreign countries, and establish a currency system
9. a Bill of Rights which included: the right to bear arms, religious freedom, freedom of speech, freedom of the press, and the right to trial by jury

Project 1
For older students

Project 2
For older students

Project 3
For younger and older students

Test
1. 1787
2. After the war the colonies were loosely organized under the Articles of the Confederation.
3. Philadelphia
4. George Washington, James Madison
5. . . . be workable, resemble the British system, limit central government, and protect property rights
6. the establishment of three branches of government: judicial, executive and legislative
7. levy and collect taxes, regulate commerce between states and foreign countries, and establish a currency system

Review
1. Shelter and a training ground for the American army during the winter of 1777
2. A pamphlet attacking King George and glorifying a free America; Tom Paine
3. It was the first battle of the war.

Answers

4. See the master list on page 500.

26: America's Founding Fathers

Worksheet

1. c. 1788
2. Writer, scientist, statesmen, printer
3. an almanac, written by Benjamin Franklin, famous for its witty and simple sayings
4. Benjamin Franklin
5. bifocals, the Franklin stove and lightning rods
6. Thomas Jefferson
7. Thomas Jefferson
8. The Louisiana Territory
9. Answers may include: wrote the Declaration of Independence, third president of the United States, was an architect, invented the dumbwaiter, sent Lewis and Clark to explore the Louisiana Territory, was a scientist
10. James Madison
11. James Madison
12. Scripture and Christian training

Project 1
For younger and older students

Project 2
For older students

Project 3
For older students

Project 4
For older students

Project 5
For older students

Project 6
For younger and older students

Test

1. Franklin
2. Jefferson
3. Franklin
4. Madison
5. Madison
6. Jefferson
7. Madison
8. Jefferson
9. Franklin
10. Franklin

27: Washington, Our First President

Worksheet

1. 1789
2. home to Mount Vernon
3. April, 1789
4. twelve, thirteen, Georgia
5. Answers may include: He knew all the American leaders of his day. He had good judgment and rarely made decisions without counsel. His integrity was unquestioned both home and abroad.
6. New York City
7. additional laws, government buildings and manpower
8. John Adams
9. Thomas Jefferson
10. Alexander Hamilton
11. 1783
12. in a location between the North and the South on land called the District of Columbia

Project 1
For younger and older students

Project 2
For older students

Test

1. 1789
2. Mount Vernon
3. Answers may include: He had been in twelve of the thirteen colonies. He knew all the American leaders of his day. He had good judgment and rarely made decisions without counsel. His integrity was unquestioned both home and abroad.
4. New York City
5. additional laws, government buildings and manpower
6. Vice President
7. Secretary of State
8. Secretary of Treasury
9. 1793
10. a location between the North and the South on land called the District of Columbia

Review

1. Francisco Vasquez de Coronado
2. the Fountain of Youth
3. a religious revival that emerged in the English colonies in America in 1740-1742
4. See the master list on page 500.

Answers

28: The Louisiana Purchase from France

Worksheet
1. 1803
2. Northwest Territory
3. the United States Army
4. to transport crops to domestic and foreign markets
5. New Orleans
6. It changed from Spanish to French control.
7. It could be disastrous for Western American commerce.
8. James Monroe
9. Napoleon offered to sell not only New Orleans but all the Louisiana Territory for $15,000,000.
10. quick, Senate

Project 1
For older students

Test
1. 1803
2. the Northwest Territory
3. the Constitution; to control Indian attacks
4. on the Mississippi River and its tributaries
5. France; it was due to the European conquests of Napoleon
6. to aid Robert Livingstone, minister to France
7. $15,000,000
8. the Senate

Review
1. it was unfaithful to God
2. an Indian who befriended the Plymouth Colony, taught them to grow corn, and showed them the best fishing streams
3. the commander of the first expedition to sail around the world
4. Queen Isabella of Spain
5. See the master list on page 500.

29: The Lewis and Clark Expedition

Worksheet
1. 1805
2. explore the territory purchased in the Louisiana Purchase; the source of the Missouri River, a waterway that connected the East and West coasts, and about Indian inhabitants and geographical features of the area
3. an Indian woman who accompanied the expedition and helped communicate with other Indian tribes
4. Pacific Ocean, St. Louis
5. almost 8,000
6. details of Indian life, botany, geography, wildlife, and the adventures of the expedition
7. eventual settlement and acquisition of the Oregon Territory

Project 1
For younger and older students

Project 2
For older students

Test
1. 1805
2. They were to explore the vast new territory of the Louisiana Purchase, to find a waterway connecting the east and west coasts, to find the source of the Missouri river, and to find out about the Indian inhabitants and the geographical features of the area.
3. an Indian woman who accompanied the expedition and helped communicate with other Indian tribes
4. 8,000 miles in two and one-half years
5. an account of the Lewis and Clark expedition which included details of Indian life, botany, geography, wildlife, and the expedition's adventures
6. eventual settlement and acquisition of the Oregon Territory

Review
1. Hernando de Soto
2. Breed's Hill
3. to stop American commerce
4. Answers may include: the Stamp Act, the Quartering Act, the Sugar Act, the Intolerable Acts
5. See the master list on page 500.

30: The Second Great Awakening

Worksheet
1. 1799–1830
2. The Western frontier and New England
3. 20,000
4. a great wave of desire among Christians to reform America
5. with Charles Finney's preaching of erroneous doctrine and the spreading of his "new measures" for evangelism
6. Camp meetings and revivals continued as a tradition in many denominations long afterwards.

Answers

Project 1
For older students

Project 2
For older students
Original Sin: Finney did not believe it was scriptural.
Atonement: Christ's Atomement did not atone for the sins of the elect. It was simply an example that should motivate Christians to selflessness.
Regeneration: This consists in the sinner changing his choice, intention or preference, not in the Holy Spirit giving us new natures.
Justification: Finney taught that we are justified by works of righteousness.
Preservation: Whenever a Christian sins, he is just like an unbeliever and needs to "do his first works" again.

Project 3
For older students

Project 4
For older students
1. When reason is ignored—allowed to sleep—then all sorts of ignorant superstitions will arise in its place. Many of these superstitions will not be benign, but will turn out to be harmful or monstrous.
2. A caprice is something done on a whim for little or no apparent reason. The Caprichios contain many satirical images lampooning foolish and vain customs prevalent in Goya's day.
3. Like many other royal courts, the royal Spanish court was corrupt and full of intrigue that was plain to see. The Spanish Inquisition was also still a very powerful force in Goya's time; he saw no value in this institution and, consequently, he skewers the Inquisition in his work.

Test
The Second Great Awakening began on the Western frontier and in New England. It was possibly the greatest period of conversions to Christianity in American history. One of the results of the Awakening was a great wave of desire among Christians to reform America. One of the later preachers of the Awakening was Charles Finney, an evangelist who changed the face of the church and evangelicalism in America.

Review
1. purify
2. Roger Williams
3. A series of trials in 1692 in Salem, Massachusetts, where 160 people were charged with "covenanting with evil spirits." Nineteen men and women were hung for supposedly practicing diabolical arts.
4. trading of goods between a mother country and her colonies.
5. See the master list on page 500.

31: The War of 1812

Worksheet
1. Treaty of Paris
2. France
3. British ships
4. Many of the important battles were on water.
5. Commodore Oliver Perry
6. *U.S.S. Constitution's, Guerriere*
7. 1814
8. Dolly Madison, the president's wife
9. Fort McHenry, Baltimore
10. The man who wrote the poem which became our national anthem: "The Star-Spangled Banner"

Project 1
For older students

Project 2
For younger and older students

Test
1. Great Britain
2. the British navy
3. on water
4. Commodore Oliver Perry
5. 1814
6. a portrait of George Washington
7. Fort McHenry, Baltimore
8. Francis Scott Key

Review
1. the Prince of Portugal, who started a school of navigation and financed voyages
2. take the Gospel across the ocean and convert the people in the Indies
3. Jacques Cartier, Samuel de Champlain and John Cabot
4. a religious revival that emerged in the English colonies in America between 1740–1742
5. See the master list on page 500.

ANSWERS

32: THE MISSOURI COMPROMISE

Worksheet

1. 1820
2. Eleven; the North
3. Eleven
4. equal
5. as a slave state
6. It allowed Missouri to be a slave state if the new state of Maine was a free state. It did not permit any slave state north of 36 degrees latitude.

Project 1

For older students

Project 2

For younger and older students

Test

1. 1820
2. Eleven free states and eleven slave states
3. equal
4. as a slave state
5. It allowed Missouri to be a slave state if the new state of Maine was a free state. It did not permit any slave state north of 36 degrees latitude.

Review

1. The colonists disappeared, and no one knows what happened to them.
2. December, 1620
3. a Puritan preacher and the founder of Rhode Island
4. Virginia, Massachusetts, New Hampshire, New York, Maryland, Connecticut, Rhode Island, Delaware, North Carolina, New Jersey, South Carolina, Pennsylvania, Georgia
5. See the master list on page 500.

EXPLORERS TO 1815 HISTORY CARDS

Master List

1: Prince Henry the Navigator | 1394-1460
2: Columbus Sails to the New World | 1492
3: Magellan Circumnavigates the Earth | 1519-1522
4: Cortez, de Soto, de Leon, and Coronado, the Spanish Explorers | 1513-1538
5: Explorers of the Northeast, Cartier, Champlain, and Cabot | 1497-1603
6: Raleigh Settles Roanoke | 1585
7: Jamestown is Founded in Virginia | 1607
8: The Mayflower Lands at Plymouth | 1620
9: Pilgrims Build Plymouth Colony | 1621
10: Massachusetts Bay Colony, Home of the Puritans | 1630
11: Roger Williams, Founder of Rhode Island | 1636
12: Salem Witch Trials | 1692
13: Thirteen Colonies Formed | 1620-1733
14: The First Great Awakening | 1740-1742
15: Colonial Trading with England | c. 1750
16: The French and Indian Wars | 1754-1763
17: Parliament Acts Unjustly | 1764-1774
18: The First Continental Congress Seeks Peace with Britain | 1774
19: The War for Independence Begins | 1775
20: British Lose at Bunker Hill | 1775
21: America Declares its Independence | 1776
22: Washington Commands the Continental Army | 1775-1781
23: Winter at Valley Forge | 1777-1778
24: Yorktown and the Treaty of Paris | 1781, 1783
25: The Constitutional Convention | 1787
26: America's Founding Fathers | c. 1788
27: Washington, Our First President | 1789
28: The Louisiana Purchase from France | 1803
29: The Lewis & Clark Expedition | 1805
30: The Second Great Awakening | 1799-1830
31: The War of 1812 | 1812
32: The Missouri Compromise | 1820

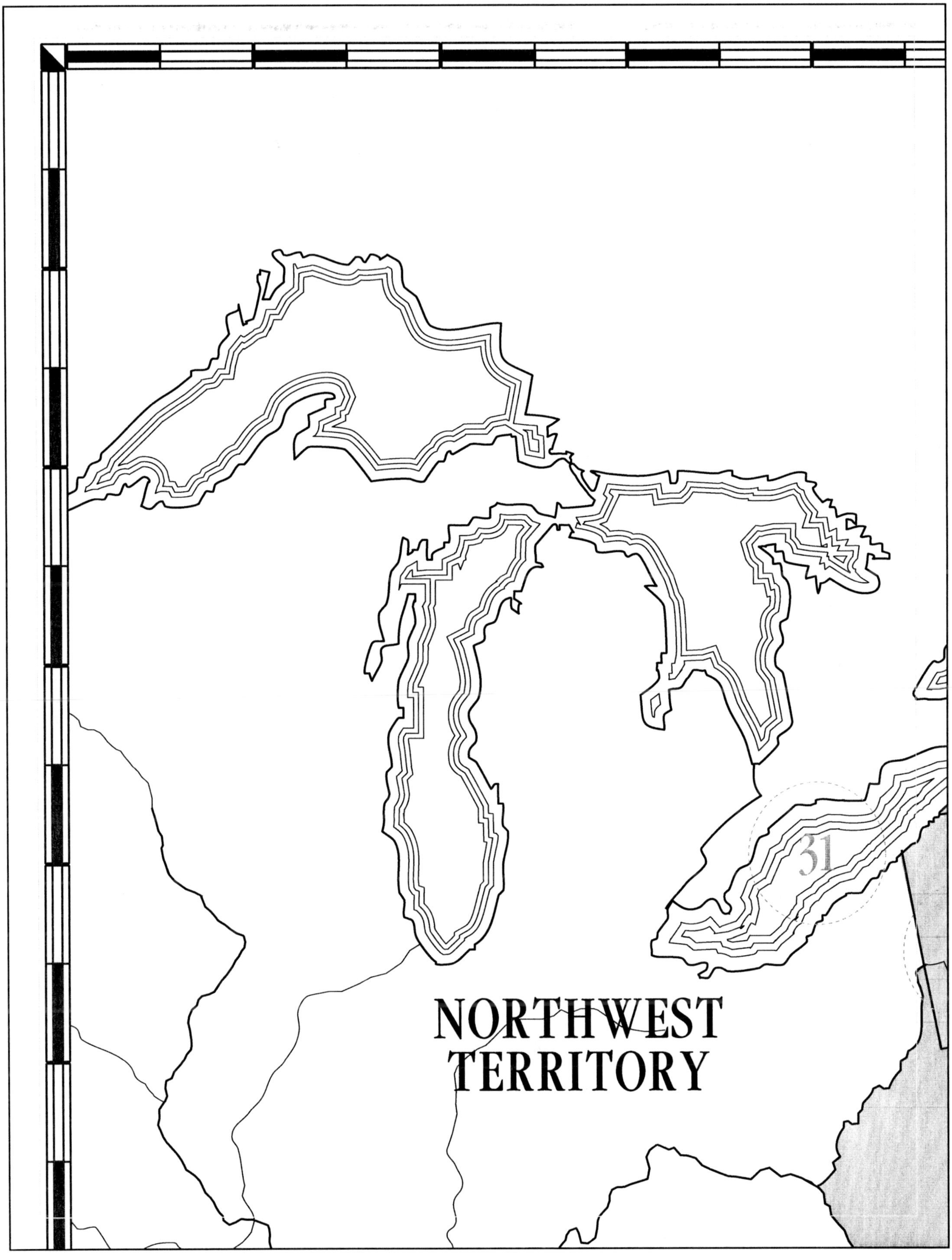
31
NORTHWEST TERRITORY

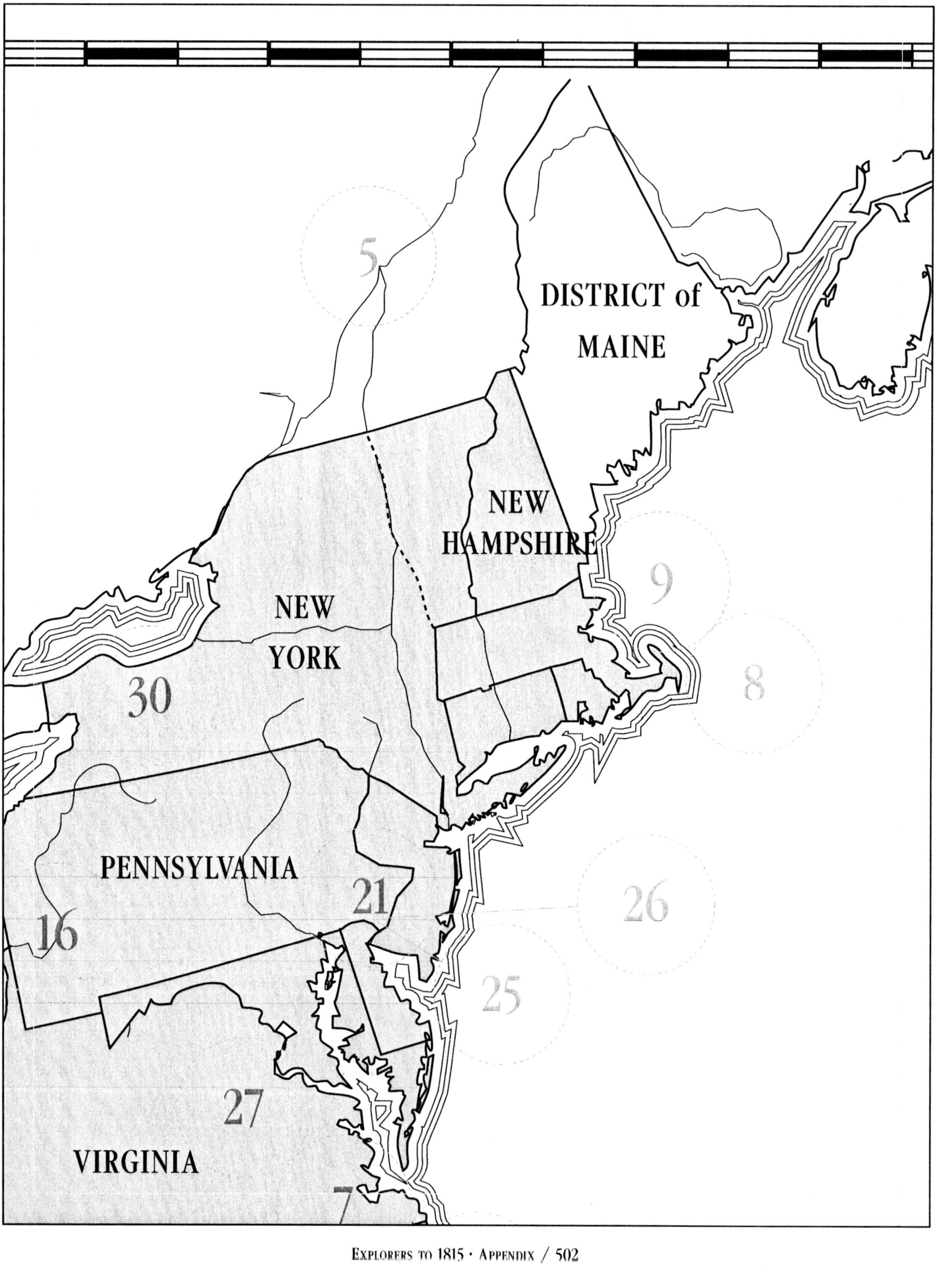
5
DISTRICT of
MAINE
NEW
HAMPSHIRE
9
8
NEW
YORK
30
PENNSYLVANIA
21
26
16
25
27
VIRGINIA
7

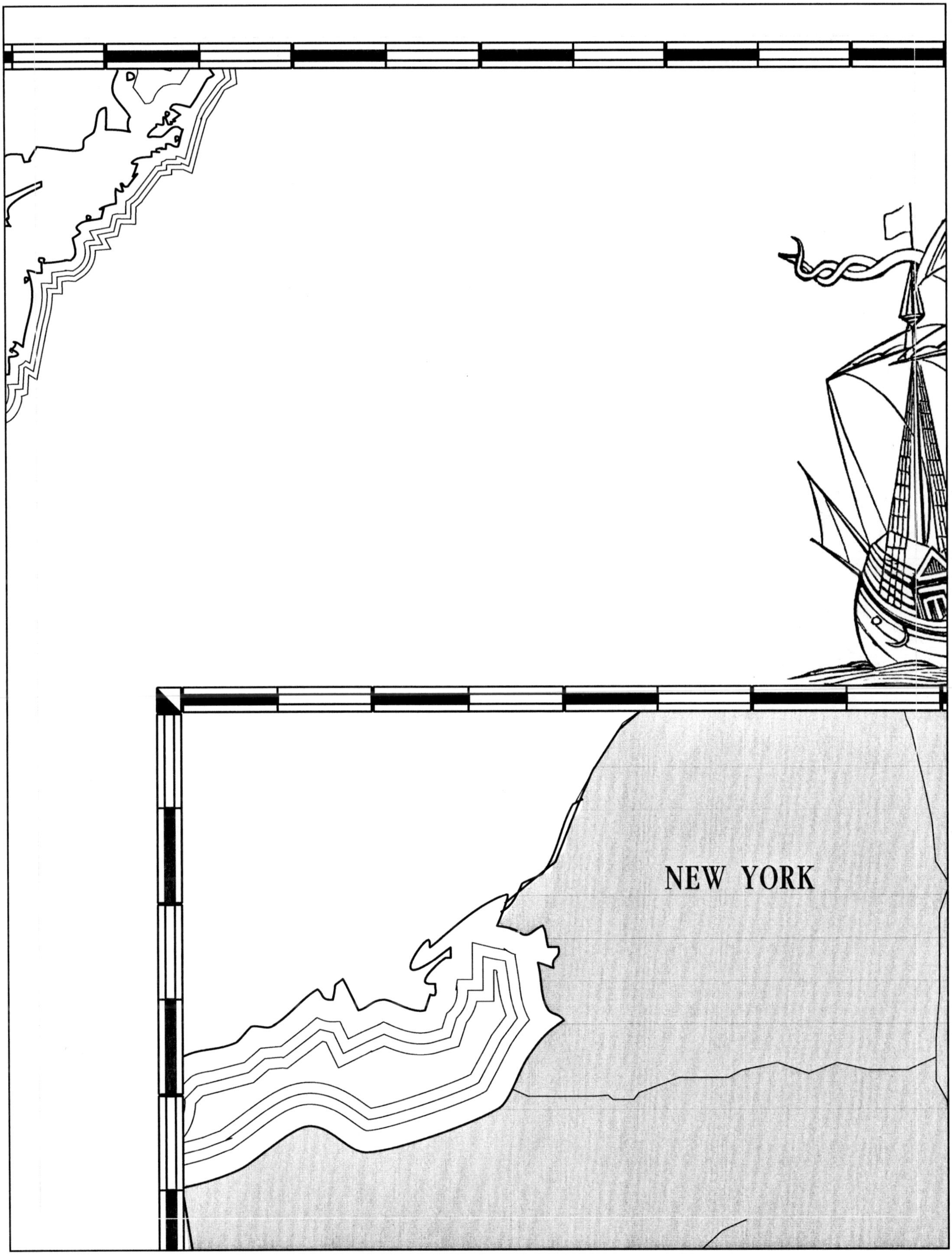
NEW YORK

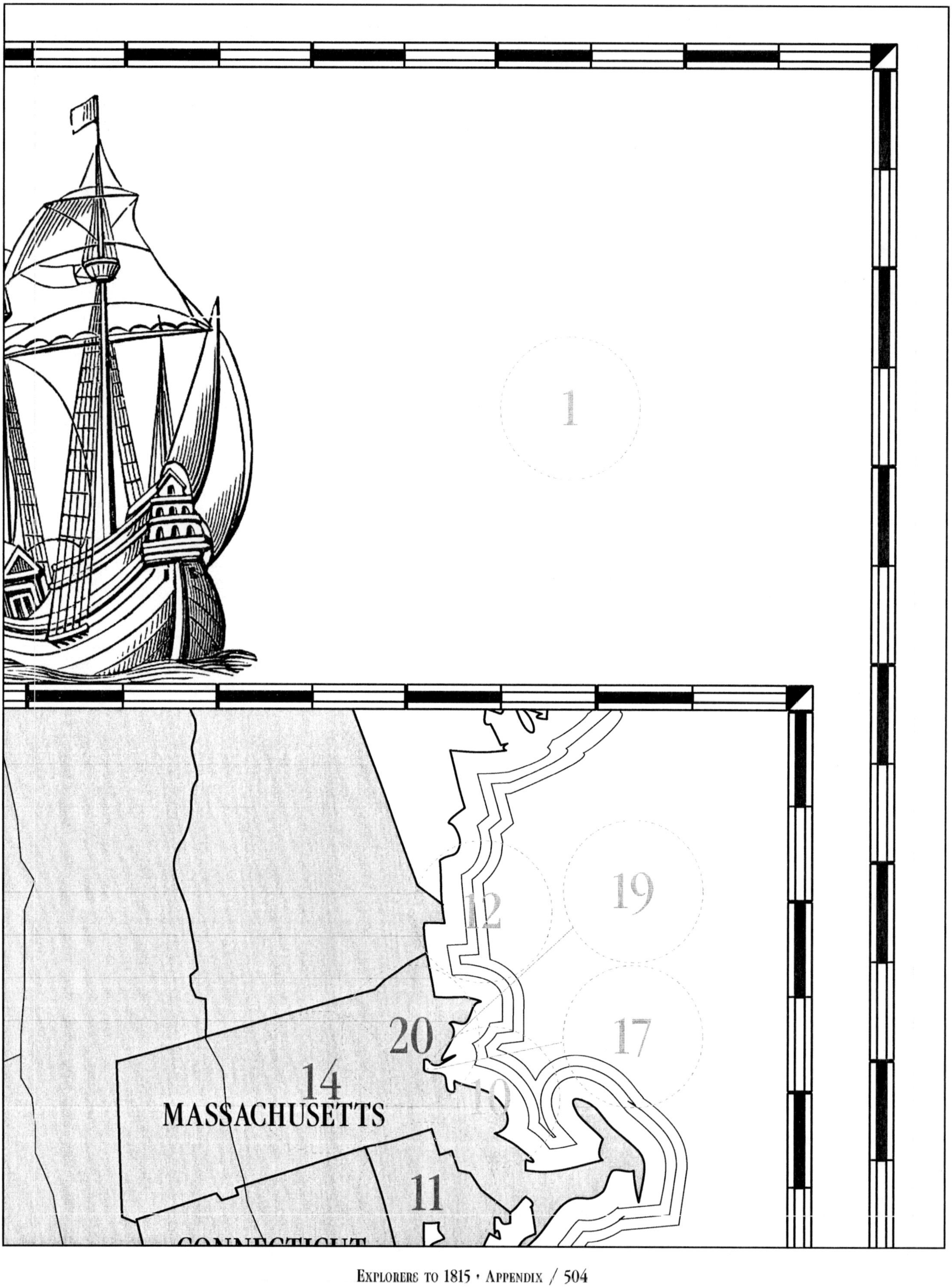
1
19
12
17
20
14
MASSACHUSETTS
10
11
CONNECTICUT

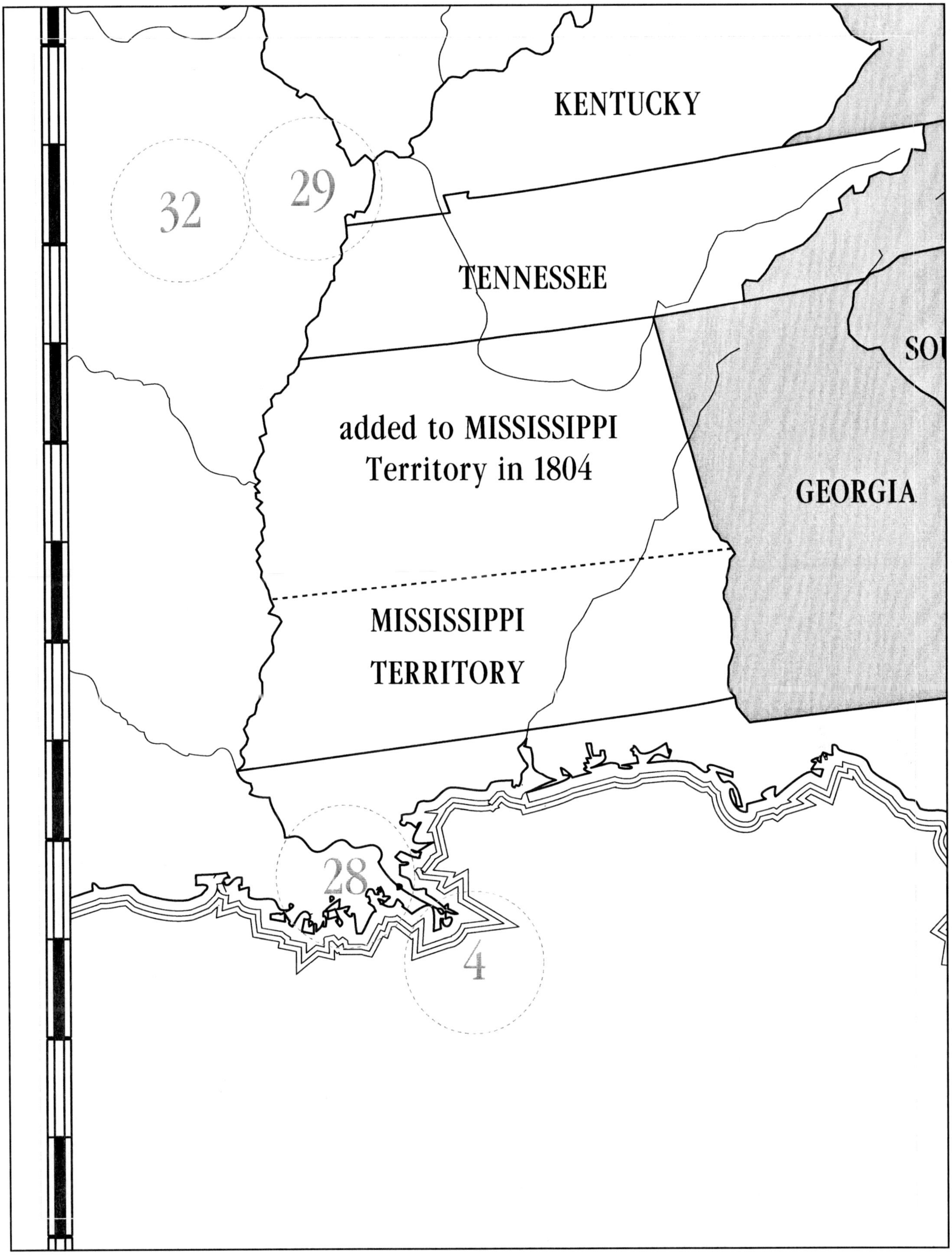
KENTUCKY
32
29
TENNESSEE
SOU
added to MISSISSIPPI
Territory in 1804
GEORGIA
MISSISSIPPI
TERRITORY
28
4

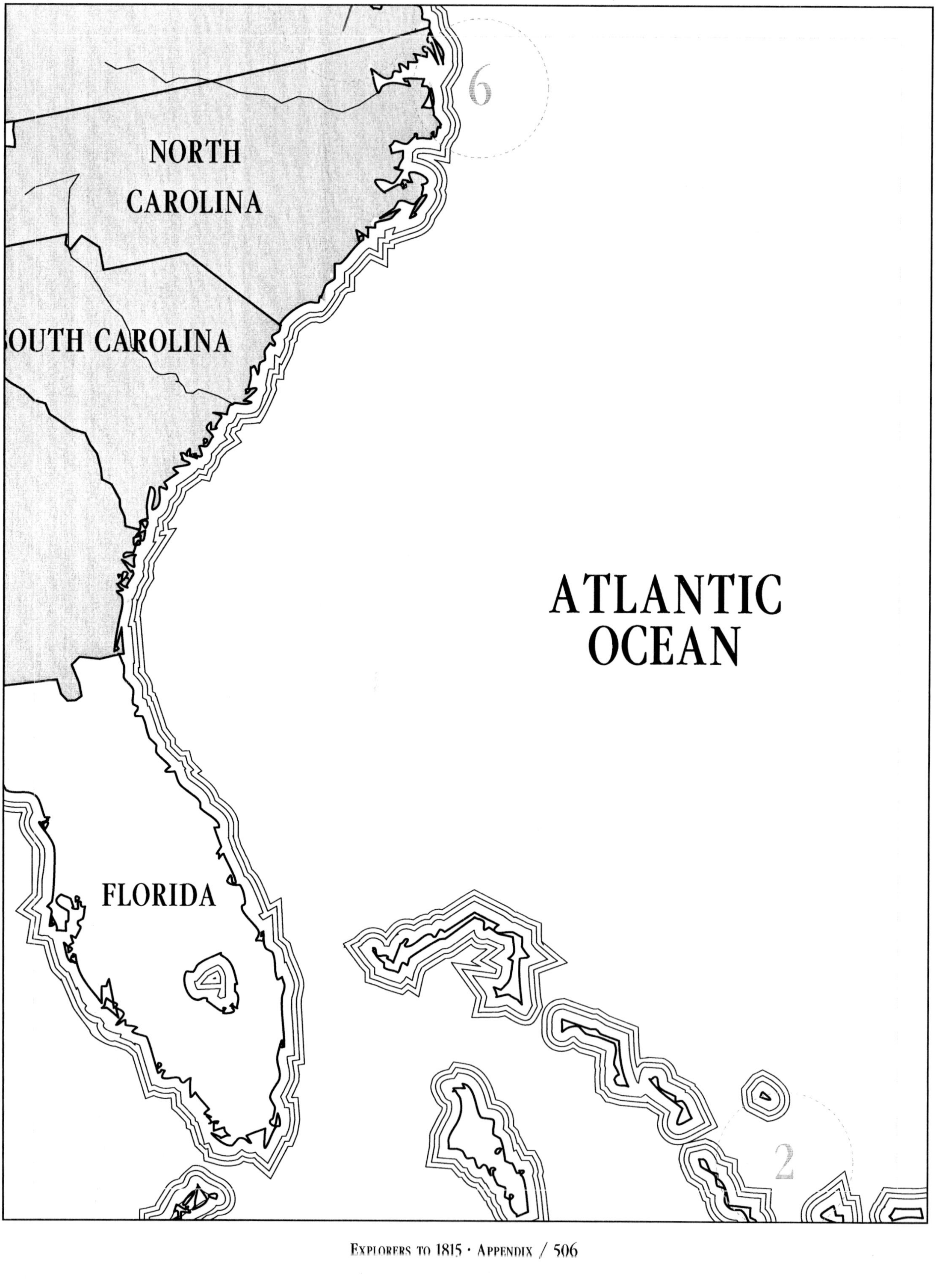
6
NORTH CAROLINA
SOUTH CAROLINA
ATLANTIC OCEAN
FLORIDA
2

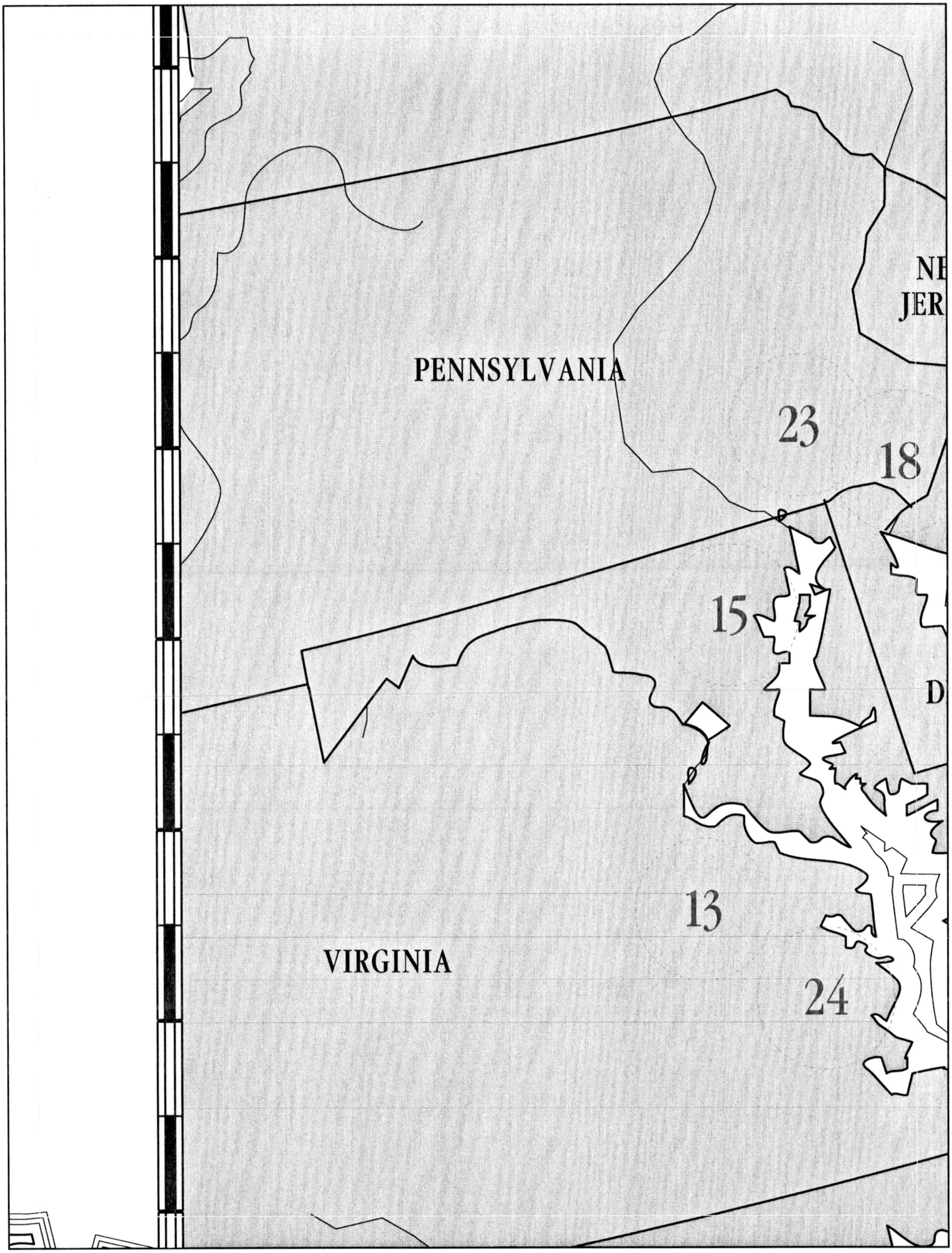

PENNSYLVANIA
NE
JER
23
18
15
D
13
VIRGINIA
24

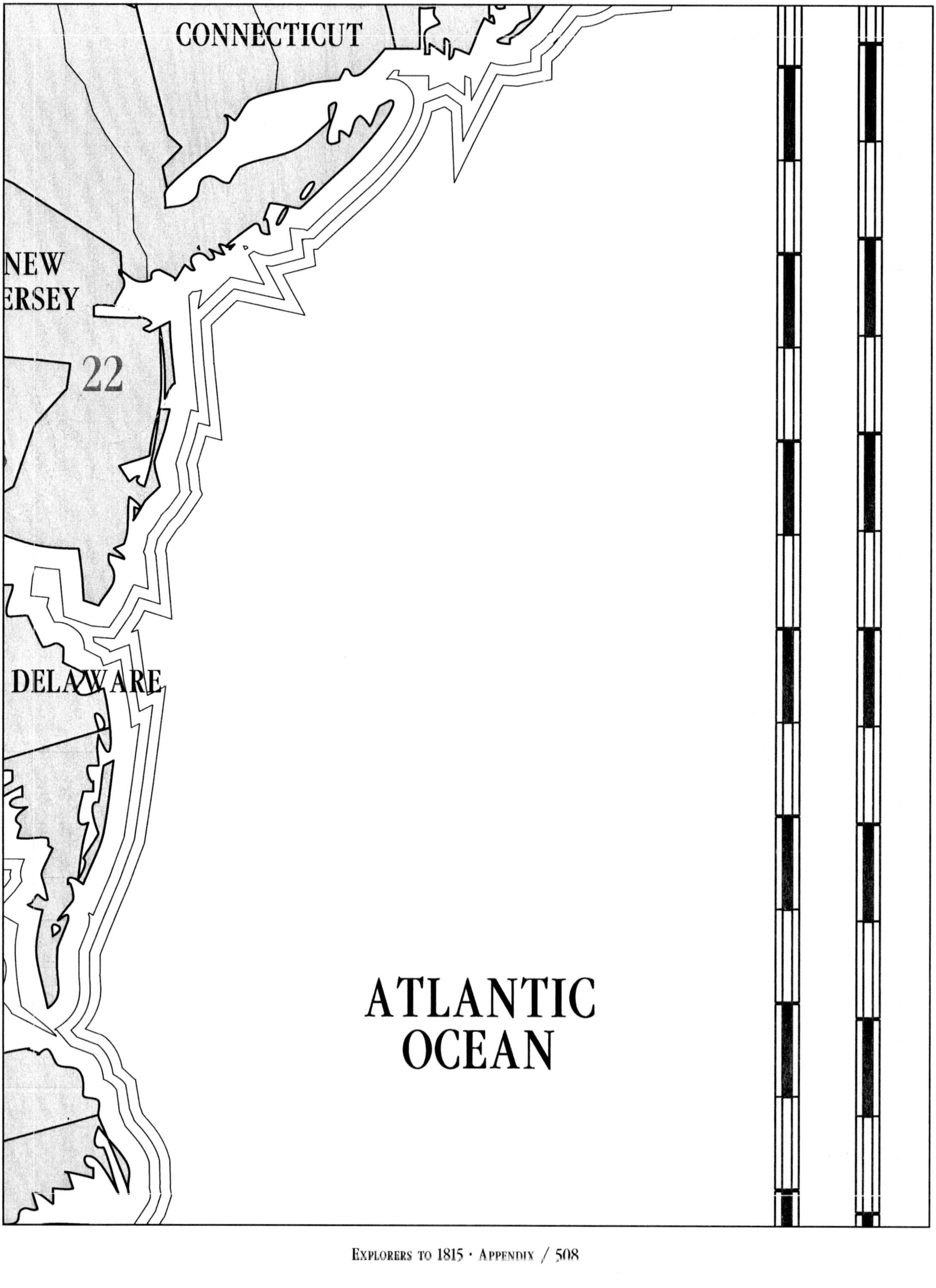
CONNECTICUT
NEW
ERSEY
22
DELAWARE
ATLANTIC
OCEAN

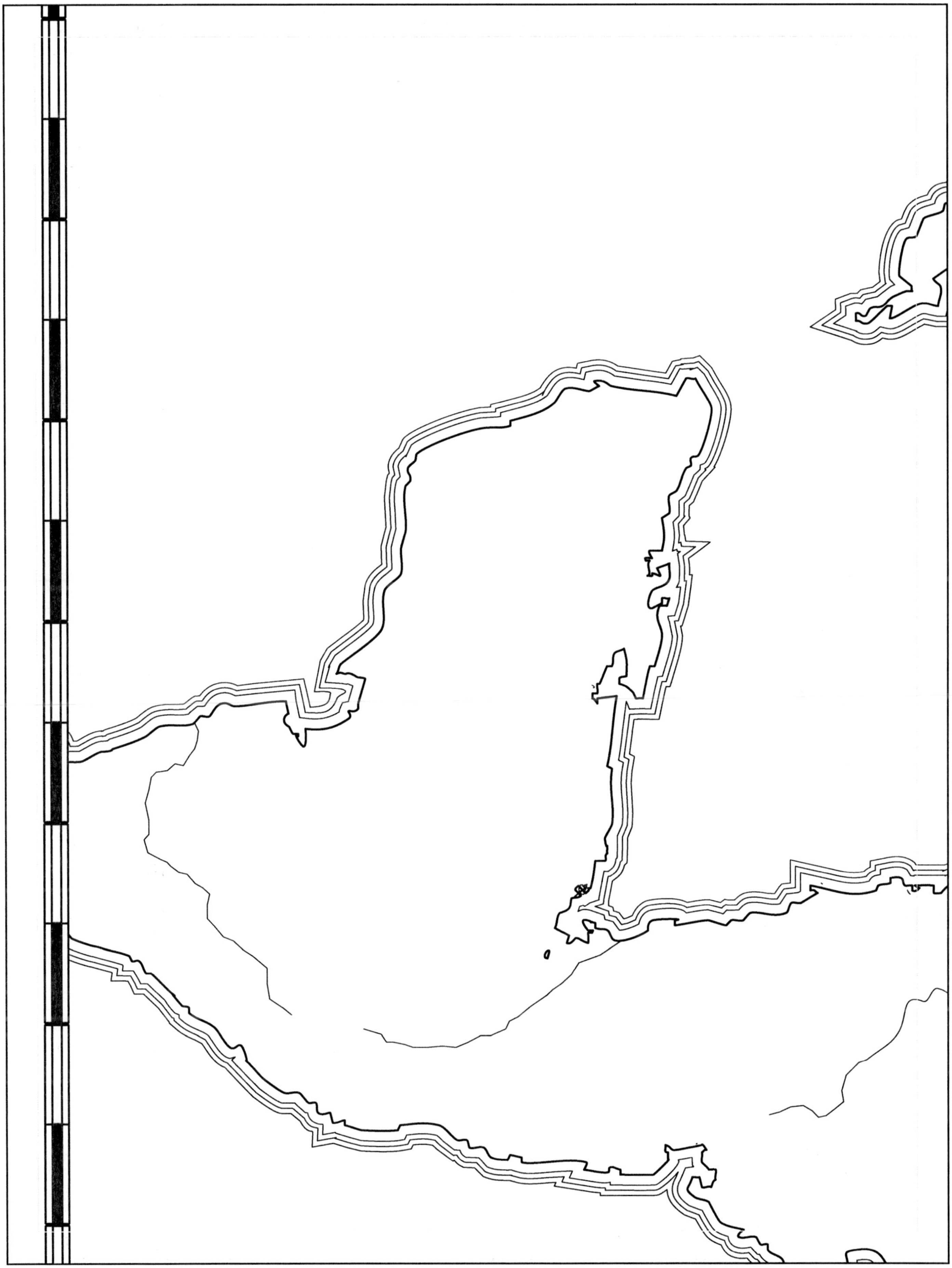

N
W
E
S

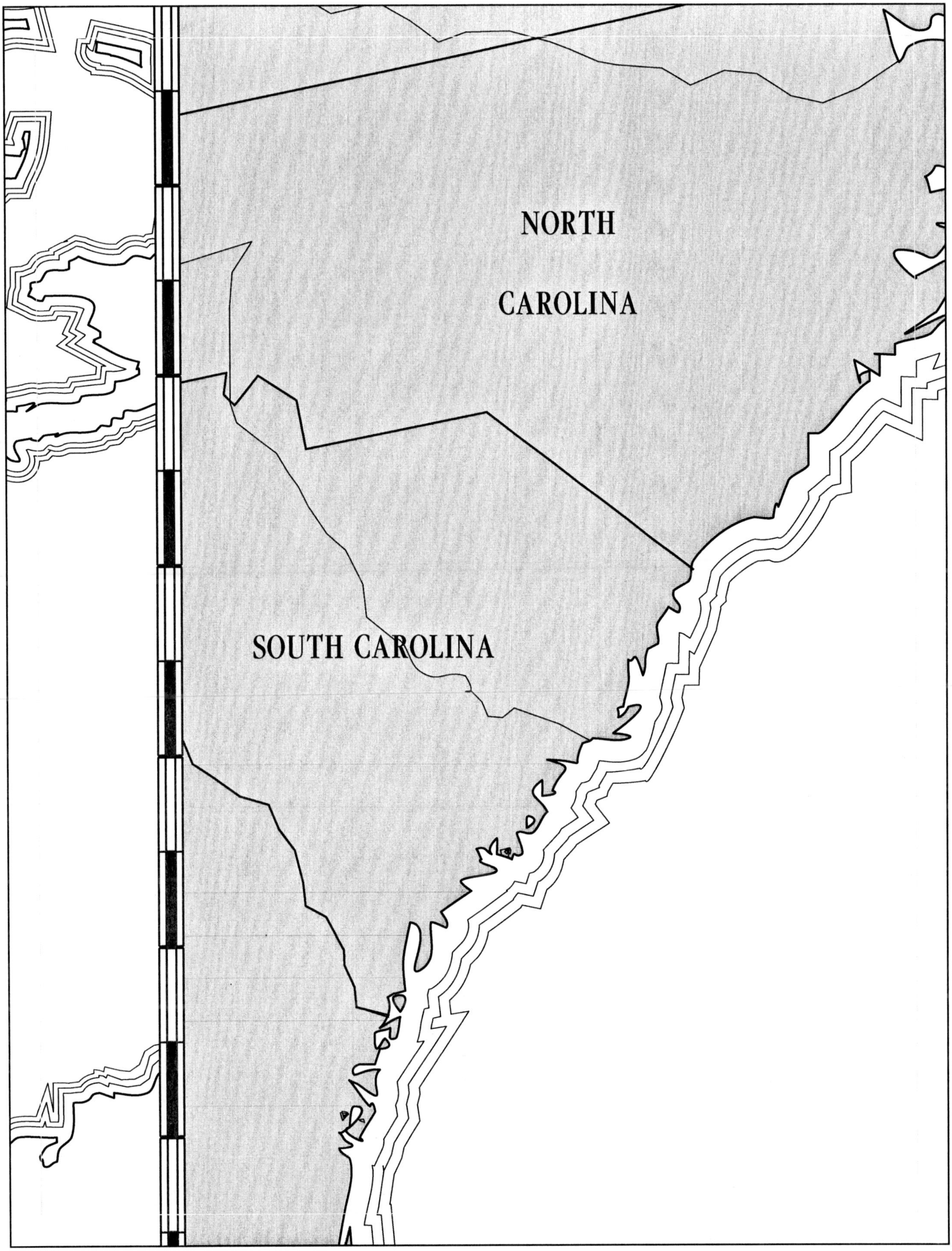
NORTH
CAROLINA
SOUTH CAROLINA

Explorers to 1815

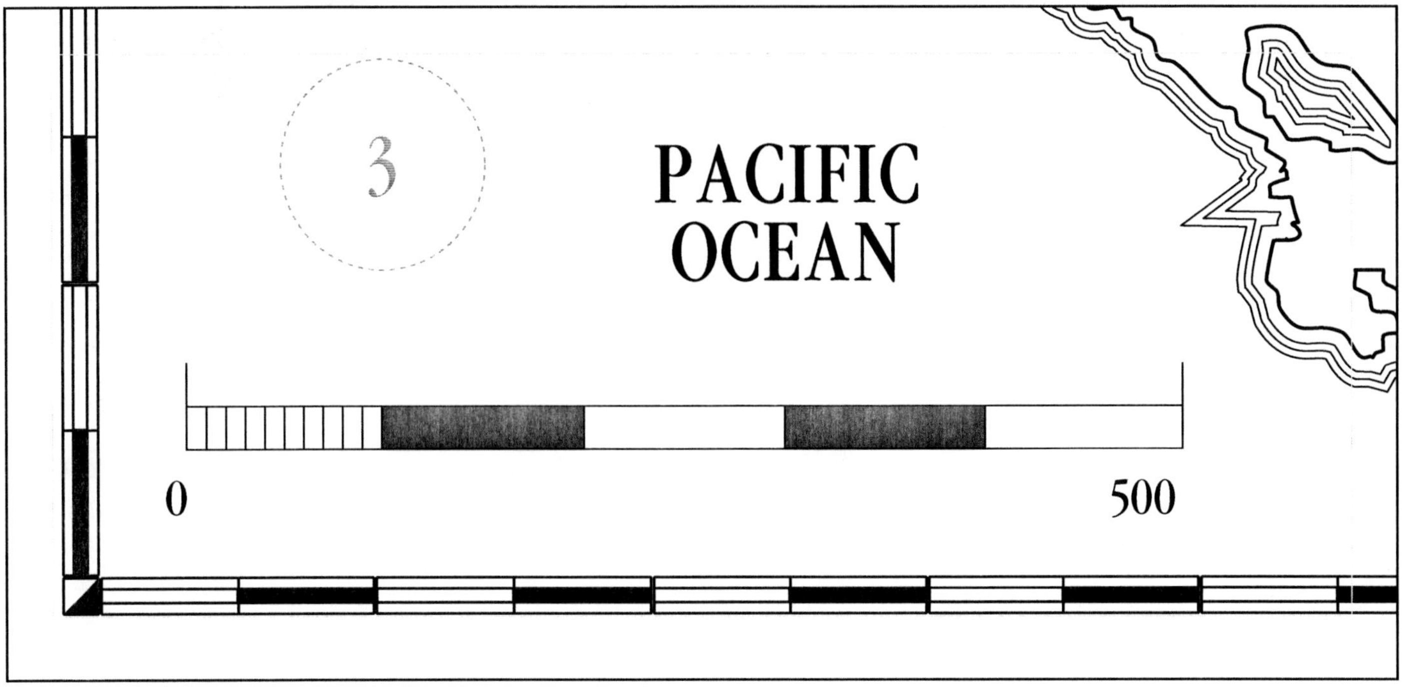
3
PACIFIC
OCEAN
0
500

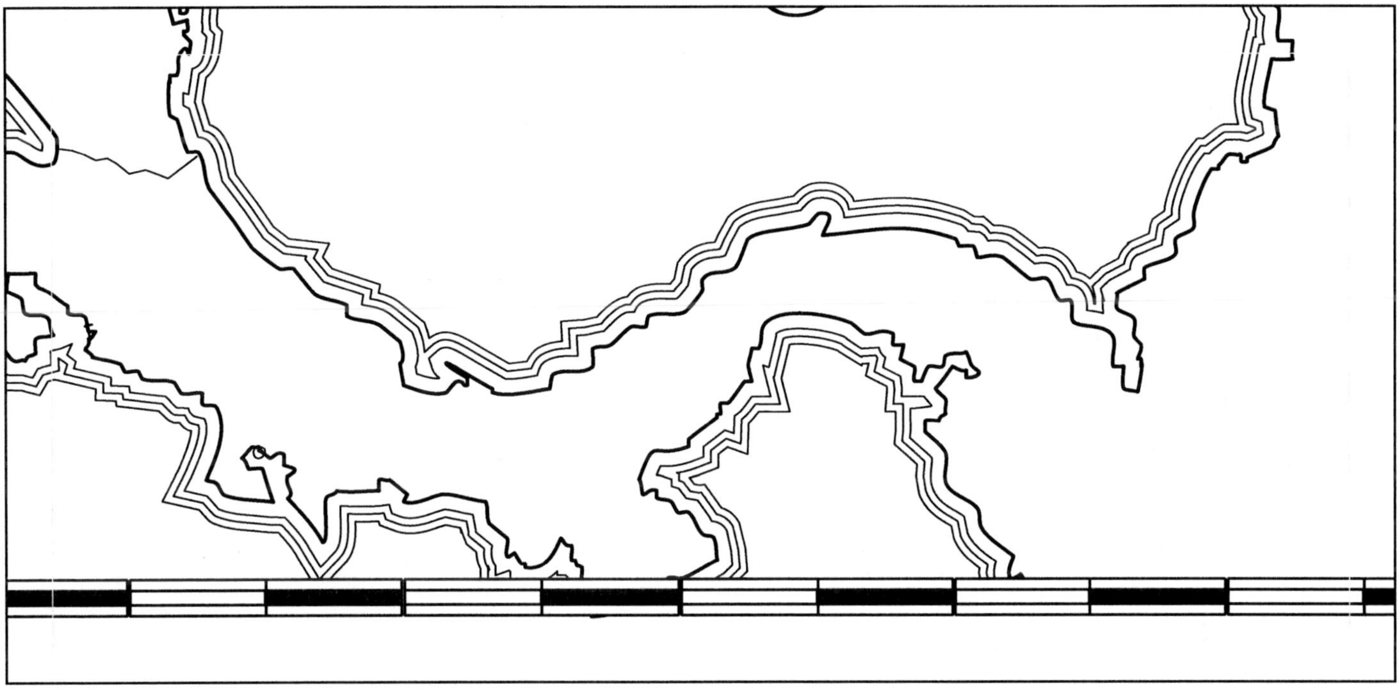

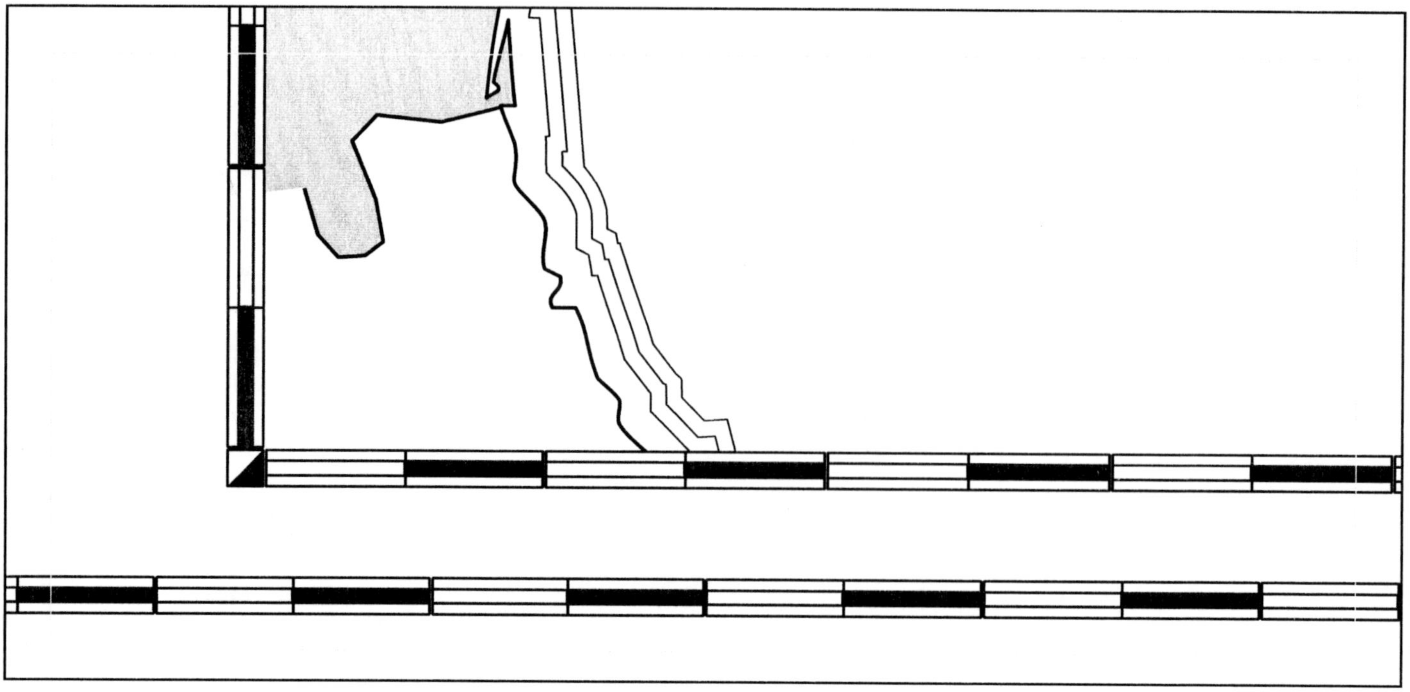

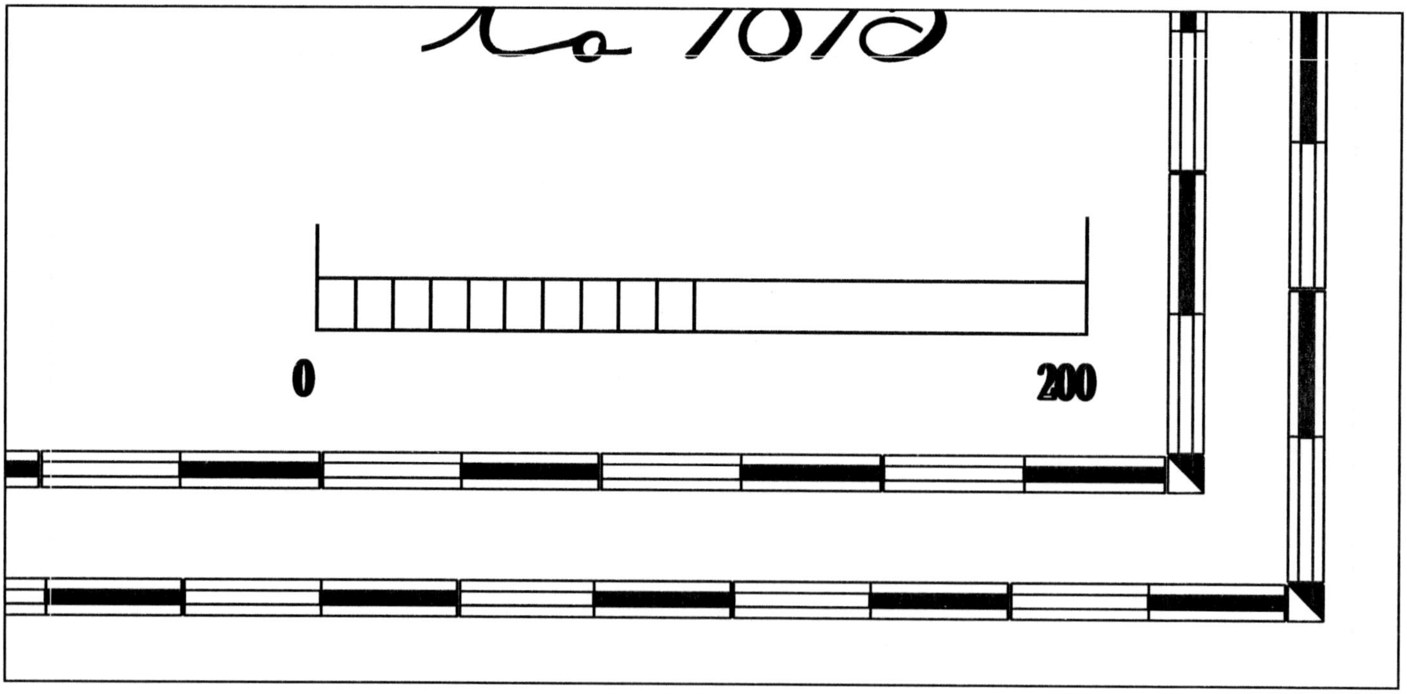
0
200

1

2

3

4

5

6

7

8

9

10

11

12

13

14
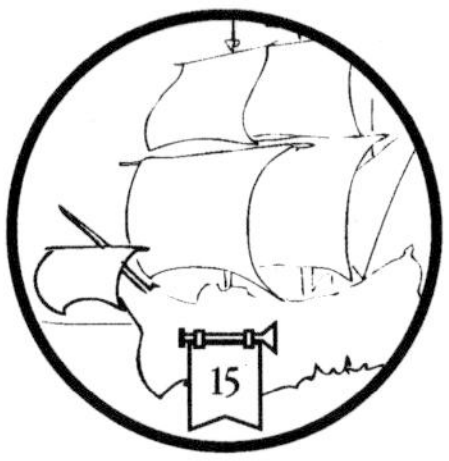
15

16

17

18

19

20

21

22

23

24

25

26

27

28

29

30

31

32

Prince Henry the Navigator

Date: ________________________________

We will encounter several themes during this year. A few of the most prominent ones are Exploration, Suffering, Prosperity and Freedom. We probably think of Prosperity and Freedom most when we think of America, and although the colonization of the New World began with voyagers in search of prosperity, it often resulted in suffering and even death. Perseverance and a vision for the future, however, kept the first Americans faithful to the calling that they believed God had given them. Much of it began with Prince Henry's establishing a school of navigation. It opened up a trade route from Africa to Asia in hopes of gaining wealth. Although he didn't directly send anyone to the New World, he opened up possibilities for future exploration and discovery. Eastward navigation had only been attempted and no one dared travel westward, into the great unknown. But as we know, America lies west of Europe, and it took some brave, fierce men willing to risk their lives for prosperity and freedom. Now, place the first history medallion in the Atlantic Ocean, the imposing frontier for those who would follow the vision of Prince Henry.

Other Events

____

____

____

____

____

____

____

The Arts/Technology

____

____

____

____

____

____

____

Columbus Sails to the New World

Date: ____________________

Place your second medallion in the islands of the Bahamas, at the southern tip of Florida. Although the voyage of Christopher Columbus began in Spain, it was here that the *Niña,* the *Pinta* and the *Santa Maria* first landed in their travels to the Indies. As a young man, Columbus was determined to find a faster route to Asia, a land flowing with gold and riches, and he believed that God had called him to Christianize the Indies. He calculated that the Indies must lie about 3,000 miles directly west across the "Sea of Darkness." But no one knew for sure what lay beyond the great sea, and no other men had ventured that far west before. Columbus wanted to be the first man to find out. He waited years before receiving approval from the king and queen of Spain, until finally his voyage was launched on August 3, 1492. He and his men endured hunger, sickness, and loss of hope that they would ever reach land. More than two months later they landed in the Bahamas, though Columbus was sure he had reached Japan. He had miscalculated the distance to the Indies by at least 8,000 miles! During his time in the "Indies," Columbus was actually discovering a new land in the countries we know today to be Haiti, Cuba, Central American, Venezuela and the islands surrounding these areas. While Columbus never found the riches he expected, he paved the way for further discovery of the Americas.

Other Events

____

____

____

____

____

____

____

The Arts/Technology

____

____

____

____

____

____

____

Magellan Circumnavigates the Earth

Date: ______________________________

Following in the footsteps of Christopher Columbus, Ferdinand Magellan set out from Spain in 1519 to find a trade route to the East by sailing west. The Spice Islands held the treasures that Magellan and other Europeans sought. Little did he know the earth was far larger than anyone had imagined. Despite the conflict he encountered with the other sailors, Magellan was determined to find a waterway through the continent of South America leading directly to the East Indies. After passing through the Strait of Magellan—near the very southern tip of South America—Magellan was perplexed to find that it merely opened up to another vast expanse of ocean. This body of water Magellan named *Mar Pacifico,* which means "Peaceful Sea" in Spanish, and is where the name Pacific Ocean originated. Place your medallion in the Pacific Ocean. Magellan didn't realize that this ocean was the largest body of water in the world. He eventually reached the Philippine Islands, which was one of his goals, but was killed by the natives there. Although he did not live to see the completion of his journey, Magellan's determination and strong will on his voyage around the world led to all kinds of new discoveries, including a more precise knowledge of the circumference of the earth.

Other Events

The Arts/Technology

Cortes, de Soto, de Leon and Coronado: The Spanish Explorers

Date: ______________________________

Spain continued to send out even more explorers following Magellan. When Hernando Cortes landed in Mexico, the Aztec Indians thought he was a god—all but Aztec ruler Montezuma, that is. Montezuma offered the strangers gold and precious gifts in hopes that they would accept them and leave. Cortes, however, had great pride in himself and his achievements as well as a desire for wealth. He did not fear the Atzec king. Thus, he and his few Spanish comrades with their guns and horses proceeded toward Tenochtitlan, the Aztec capital city, and destroyed it. Montezuma died and Cortes claimed Mexico for Spain. Cortes would go on to explore other parts of Central America and parts of North America as well. Place your next medallion at the mouth of the Mississippi. Hernando de Soto would be the first to explore the Mississippi River, and we will learn that much of the land west of the Mississippi remained Spanish territory for hundreds of years, until they gave it up to the French under Napoleonic Rule, and then to United States in the Louisiana Purchase. All of the conquests by these explorers would later affect the development of America.

Other Events

____

____

____

____

____

____

____

The Arts/Technology

____

____

____

____

____

____

____

Explorers of the Northeast: Cartier, Champlain, and Cabot

Date: ______________________________

John Cabot believed that he could reach the East Indies by a shorter route than Christopher Columbus. Many people thought that Columbus had reached the outer islands of China on his voyage, so Cabot thought that if he headed further north, he would reach mainland China. Like Columbus, Cabot miscalculated the vastness of the world, and instead of landing in the Indies, he discovered Newfoundland, now a part of Canada, northeast of Maine. Another French explorer, Samuel de Champlain, wanted to establish a French settlement in America. He founded the city of Quebec, and much of Canada was called New France. Place the fifth medallion in Quebec. The French were the first European explorers to discover much of the northeastern territory of North America. Later we will see France and England go to war over possession of much of this land.

Other Events

____

____

____

____

____

____

____

The Arts/Technology

____

____

____

____

____

____

____

Raleigh Settles Roanoke

Date: ______________________

Although we know that Roanoke is a city in Virginia, Sir Walter Raleigh didn't establish his colony where we call Roanoke, Virginia, today. Place your medallion on Roanoke Island, off the coast of North Carolina. It was this small island where Raleigh hoped to build the first English colony in America. He named it after the virgin Queen Elizabeth, who had given him permission to send men to colonize North America. After financing an unsuccessful English group in 1585, Raleigh sent John White and numerous men, women and children on a second attempt in 1587. John White's granddaughter, Virginia Dare, was the first English child born in America, and today the Virginia Dare Memorial Bridge extends from Roanoke Island to mainland North Carolina. Due to low food supplies, White had to abandon the colony and return to England for more. When he returned three years later, the island was empty—his daughter and granddaughter were nowhere to be found. There was no sign of an English colony anywhere. Raleigh's attempts to form the first English colony in America did not succeed, but today numerous memorials commemorate his efforts on Roanoke Island.

Other Events

____

____

____

____

____

____

____

The Arts/Technology

____

____

____

____

____

____

____

Jamestown is Founded in Virginia

Date: ____________________

Unlike Roanoke, Jamestown was the first English colony to survive in America. Place your medallion at Jamestown, Virginia. Again we see the English motivated by the riches and wealth that they hoped awaited their settlement of the New World; however those riches would be hard to come by until after many years of suffering. Disease, illness and Indian hostility, combined with many colonists' unwillingness to work, prevented them from filling their food stores and led to the deaths of hundreds of the English settlers. Although the Indians showed severe hostility at times, Powhatan and the Indians saved the lives of the colonists by trading food for goods (not to mention how Pocahontas is said to have saved the life of Captain John Smith). The Indians would have a significant impact on the later success of the colony. The colonists may not have found the gold that they sought in America, but the Indians introduced them to a very important resource: tobacco. The Virginians began importing tobacco from South America and traded with England. Tobacco saved the Jamestown colony and would become the major source of industry for the South. We will see (next year) how this affected American culture as it sparked the slave trade and led to the War Between the States.

Other Events

The Arts/Technology

THE *MAYFLOWER* LANDS AT PLYMOUTH

Date: ____________________________________

Freedom at last! The separatists aboard the *Mayflower* finally landed in the New World and could worship God as they saw fit. They did not come to America in search of riches; the Church of England drove this group of Christians to separate from them because of their religious practices. Thus, the separatists were treated poorly by the Anglican Church. As William Bradford wrote, “They were hunted and persecuted on every side. . . . Some were clapped into prison; others had their houses watched night and day, and escaped with difficulty; and most were obliged to fly, and leave their homes and means of livelihood.” So they were forced to leave their homes, families, and friends for Holland, where they lived several years in peace among their newly formed congregations. But even then they still faced persecution. American soil looked like their best escape for freedom. Place your medallion along the coast of Massachusetts, where in 1620, 35 of these “pilgrims” (pilgrims are those who go on a religious journey) landed to start their own colony and worship God as they chose. Freedom is one theme we’ll be studying this year, and this is just the beginning.

Other Events

____

____

____

____

____

____

____

The Arts/Technology

____

____

____

____

____

____

____

Pilgrims Build Plymouth Colony

Date: ______________________

Your next medallion will be very close to the previous one, as the Pilgrims built their colony along the coast of Massachusetts where the land is hard and rocky. The Pilgrims landed there right as winter began. They came to the land with little food, and had little time to gather any before the winter set in. By the time the harsh cold came to an end, many of the Pilgrims had died, and those who lived were in desperate need of nourishment. So when Samoset and Squanto, along with sixty or more other Indians, greeted the Pilgrims in their English tongue, they were delighted. The Pilgrims had cried out to God when they were in need, and again God provided for them through these Indians. Squanto taught them how to plant and harvest crops, to fish, and how to adapt to living in the woods and hills of Massachusetts. Without the help of the Indians (as was also true in the Jamestown settlement), America would have had a very different heritage and tradition. After a summer of plentiful sowing, the Pilgrims invited ninety Indian friends to join in their harvest feast: a Thanksgiving celebration of God's provision. Here the natives and colonists united together to feast upon the blessings of God.

Other Events

The Arts/Technology

MASSACHUSETTS BAY COLONY, HOME OF THE PURITANS

Date: ________________________

King Charles I of England was happy to see the Puritans leave his land. The Puritans had grown increasingly discontent with the King's authority over the Anglican Church, and they petitioned him to reform the Church. When Charles refused and continued to make the Church even more Roman Catholic, the Puritans had had enough. They were ready to leave. The King willingly granted them a charter, giving them permission to establish their own religious dictates in the New World. Within a 12-year time span, some 24,000 Puritans (mostly English and Scottish) immigrated to New England, settling in Salem, Massachusetts. Place your medallion at Salem, north of Plymouth Colony along the Massachusetts coast. The Puritans also faced times of starvation and death among the colony, but their fortitude during these times multiplied the colony quickly. By 1636 they had already established Harvard College for men entering the ministry of the church, and they had formed their own laws and political systems. We will see what happens when England attempts to regain control of the colonies and take away their freedoms. This will result in a great revolution.

Other Events	*The Arts/Technology*

Roger Williams, Founder of Rhode Island

Date:

We know that humans are sinful and that we tend to fight with people that we love, even our fellow Christians. The Puritans too, though they were godly people, were sinful, and disputes rose up in the church, especially when Roger Williams entered the Massachusetts Bay Colony. It is said that Williams was a kind man who had a heart for the American Indians, but not necessarily for other Puritans. He caused many disputes among the Massachusetts colonists. He thought that the Puritans were too intolerant of other religious beliefs, and he did not approve of their forcing Indians to convert to Christianity. Williams was even more of a separatist than the separatists were. He demanded that all ties with the Church of England be broken and wanted to excommunicate Christians who associated with the Anglican Church. For this the Puritans viewed Williams with skepticism, as well as for his rejection of the Bible as the standard and guide for all government law. This was central to the Puritans' beliefs, and they feared his influence upon others. So, the Puritans demanded that Williams leave the colony of Massachusetts Bay. Please place your medallion where, with twenty other people, Williams settled in the small area of Rhode Island, declaring religious liberty for all people.

Other Events

The Arts/Technology

Salem Witch Trials

Date: ____________________

Many theories exist attempting to explain the Salem witch trials. Some people believe that perhaps the young girls had eaten a food that caused them to hallucinate and convulse. The girls claimed to have eaten "witch cakes," which may have contained a fungus that acted like a potent drug. Others believe that the girls were playing foolish and deceitful pranks. But either way the Puritans, traditionally god-fearing people, allowed themselves to be swept away by the hysteria that entered Salem Village in 1692. Were the girls really demon-possessed? The court system had negated the biblical principle that requires testimonies from two witnesses before sentencing anyone to death, and instead they believed anyone who accused others of witchcraft. Thus, nineteen people accused of witchcraft were hanged, four died in prison and one man was pressed to death. The trials finally came to a halt when Increase Mather, a minister and president of Harvard, finally came to the rescue. "It is better that ten suspected witches should escape than one innocent person should be condemned," he said. Sadly, many people only associate the Puritans with the Salem witch trials, which is a poor representation of who they really were. This was only a localized and small occurrence, but was shameful nonetheless. Place your medallion near Salem, Massachusetts.

Other Events

The Arts/Technology

Thirteen Colonies Formed

Date: ______________________________

English men and women continued to settle in America for various reasons that go along with the themes for this year: to flee the suffering they experienced from religious persecution, to gain freedom from Britain, and to seek prosperity and wealth. For more than a decade the first thirteen American colonies grew and became established. Stretching from New Hampshire all the way down to Georgia, the British Empire owned these colonies. Because the British Empire was the largest in the world, the American colonies were only a small portion of British interests and were often neglected by their rulers. Thus, the king's greed only set him up for problems. When the colonies formed, they were still very different and separate entities, but as their awareness of Britain's unjust treatment grew, we will see them begin to unite as one nation. Place medallion 13 in Virginia, the first British colony formed in America.

Other Events

____

____

____

____

____

____

____

The Arts/Technology

____

____

____

____

____

____

____

The First Great Awakening

Date:

You will place your next medallion between Plymouth and Salem in Boston, Massachusetts. Thousands of people gathered at the Boston Common on one day. They pushed and forced their way to the front of the crowd just to view and listen to the new celebrity in town. Today, it could have been mistaken for an outdoor rock concert or a political campaign based on the large number of people, but these New Englanders gathered to hear the famous English preacher, George Whitefield, speak about passion for Christ. The listeners were convicted of nominalism (merely taking the name of "Christian" but not claiming Christ as their personal Savior), and when they heard Whitefield's words, they were thrown into fits of convulsion and shaking. The Holy Spirit was working in their hearts. Many brilliant preachers, in addition to Whitefield came out of the Great Awakening—Jonathan Edwards, Gilbert Tennent, Charles and John Wesley—as well as many well-known colleges: Princeton, Rutgers, Dartmouth, and Brown College. This religious revival, while it brought many people to Christ, also fractured Protestant Christianity and sparked a greater desire for political and religious independence that would push America closer to war with England.

Other Events

The Arts/Technology

Colonial Trading with England

Date: ______________________

Although the colonists discovered new resources and agricultural products in America, they still depended a lot on England for their welfare. The colonies, from New Hampshire to Georgia, had unstable economies. Each relied upon a single or very few resources. Virginia's economy, for example, depended upon the production of tobacco, but when the tobacco harvest suffered, so did the pockets of the Virginians. Thus, England supplied a majority of goods to Virginia. Place your next medallion in Baltimore, Maryland, which became one of the largest cities and harbors for commercial trading. The colonies' dependence upon England would later give the mother country more power to tighten trade regulations and would open the eyes of the Americans to see their need for independence.

Other Events

The Arts/Technology

The French and Indian Wars

Date: ______________________________

This is one of the first times that we see our heroic George Washington enter the public scene, though he could not boast of victory in his first battles. It was a time of tension and hatred between the English and French, and both tried to claim land in North America that the other wanted. When the French built Fort Duquesne (present-day Pittsburgh, Pennsylvania) on what the English considered their Virginian territory, they sent the young George Washington, then a surveyor of the land, to verify that it was indeed English territory. But the French would not leave. Washington's band of 150 Virginians killed ten Frenchmen at Fort Duquesne and ignited the sparks of war. The enraged French and their Indian allies retaliated. Disguised amongst the woods and in camouflage animal skins, the few French troops with their sly fighting tactics defeated the numerous British forces who remained in their straight lines and bright red uniforms. Place medallion 16 at Fort Duquesne, where Pittsburgh is today. Although this may have been a humiliating defeat for the British, they would end the war in victory, gaining the land east of the Mississippi from the French. Britain, however, was left with a large debt, and we will see next how they enforced taxes to make the colonists pay for Britain's help in the war.

Other Events

____

____

____

____

____

____

____

The Arts/Technology

____

____

____

____

____

____

____

Parliament Acts Unjustly

Date: ______________________________

"No taxation without representation!" The colonists had had enough of British taxes! Remember how we said mercantilism would lead England to impose themselves on the colonies? Well, first the colonies' religious freedom was in danger (England sent Anglican bishops to America to control religious affairs), then King George III demanded the colonists pay taxes on paper, stamps, sugar, paint, lead, glass and tea—basically all imported goods. The colonists wouldn't have minded paying the taxes if they had had representatives in Parliament, but it was by mere force that the King of England taxed them. He was not looking out for the welfare of the colonies, but merely wanted to keep them under his power. Thus the colonists rebelled. Place your medallion at the Boston harbor. Here thousands of colonists demonstrated their rebellion when they marched behind a band of nearly fifty men dressed up as Indians, who stormed the British merchant ships that were filled with tea. They threw more than 300 chests of English tea into Boston Harbor. The injustice of the mother country was beginning to unite the very separate and distinct American colonies and shape them into a powerful force against Britain.

Other Events

____

____

____

____

____

____

____

The Arts/Technology

____

____

____

____

____

____

____

The First Continental Congress Seeks Peace with Britain

Date: ______________________________

Philadelphia, Pennsylvania, where you will place your next medallion, was the meeting place of some of the most influential men in American history at the First Continental Congress: Peyton Randolph, John and Samuel Adams, John Dickinson, John Jay, George Washington, Patrick Henry. You may be unfamiliar with some of these names, but the last of these men you should know about. Patrick Henry was a very vocal and radical man who believed that war with Britain was inescapable, though this meeting was a last effort to seek Britain's favor. These men were Englishmen who knew Britain's own standards for freedom, and they could not compromise this privilege they were being denied. Most of the colonists wanted to make peace with England, yet they were growing more and more united in their stance against the King of England. Patrick Henry said, "The distinctions between Virginians, Pennsylvanians, New Yorkers and New Englanders, are no more. I am not a Virginian, but an American." Up until this point the American colonies were almost like separate countries, each minding its own business and caring little about their neighboring colonies. But Patrick Henry's speech reveals the changing times. The colonies were beginning to view themselves and each other as "Americans."

Other Events

____

____

____

____

____

____

____

The Arts/Technology

____

____

____

____

____

____

____

The War for Independence Begins

Date: ______________________________

"The British are coming! The British are coming!" American colonists awoke to this call early in the morning on the day that the war with Britain began. Little sleep was had by anyone as Paul Revere, William Dawes and Samuel Prescott rode through the towns of Massachusetts warning the Patriots of the nearing British soldiers. More than 700 redcoats set out on April 18, 1775 to seize American arms in the small towns of Lexington and Concord. But before the sun was even up on the following day, about 70 American minutemen were waiting on the village green in Lexington. The sound of synchronized British boots marching toward the village could be heard long before they could be seen. The mass of British soldiers marched through the town in their well-organized lines, and professional red uniforms, while the American militia was disorganized, small in number and without uniforms. Yet the colonists were determined to fight. Although more Americans than British died on Lexington Green, the minutemen outwitted the British as they traveled on to Concord. The colonists fired cannons and guns while taking cover behind trees, houses and barns; but the redcoats remained in their rigid formation, and lost three times more men as a result. Thus these two battles that ignited the fire of the revolution are marked American victories. Place your next medallion between Lexington and Concord, just northwest of Boston.

Other Events

____

____

____

____

____

____

____

The Arts/Technology

____

____

____

____

____

____

____

British Lose at Bunker Hill

Date: ______________________

Why do we call the Battle of Bunker Hill a British loss? Didn't the British take the hill and drive the colonists to retreat? Once the British reached the top of the hill, the Rebels had run out of ammunition and were using rocks and nails in their guns, and were forced back by the British. The colonists, however, had withstood two prior attempts by the British to take the hill and had sent them twice in retreat. Place your medallion on Breed's Hill where this battle actually occurred, outside of Boston. The British may have taken the hill, but nearly 1,000 men were either dead or wounded, while the American casualty count was around 400 men. The Yankees, as the colonists were called by the British, proved that they were strong enough to stand up to the army of the world's most powerful empire! This battle gave the colonists confidence. British victory was no longer seen as inevitable; the Americans had a chance to succeed in their cause for freedom.

Other Events

The Arts/Technology

America Declares its Independence

Date: ______________________

Crowds cheered, bells rang and cannons blasted as the American colonists who gathered in Philadelphia at the Pennsylvania State House celebrated their declaration of independence. The members of the Second Continental Congress had announced their approval of the document that would demand Great Britain view them as "Free and Independent States." This was America's declaration of war. No longer would the colonists petition King George III and seek peace; this time they were telling Britain that they would settle for nothing less than separation from the mother country. This was a bold move by the men who signed the Declaration of Independence. Now they were guilty of treason to England, and they risked being hanged if they were captured. But they believed they were under no obligation to obey a tyrannical and oppressive government where their interests were of no consideration to the King. So Thomas Jefferson wrote the Declaration of Independence, and it was approved by the Congress on July 4, 1776. Place your medallion near Philadelphia, where this action signaled the beginning of a war that would change the world.

Other Events

____

____

____

____

____

____

The Arts/Technology

____

____

____

____

____

____

Washington Commands the Continental Army

Date:

Did you know that George Washington did not sign the Declaration of Independence? Do you know why? He was busy training and preparing the American soldiers for war. It was a frightful task to take on the world's largest and most powerful army, but George Washington far exceeded his expectations as general. Although he was hesitant to accept his nomination to command the army, he did accept the position but he refused to be paid—he would only accept reimbursement for his expenses. He was committed to America's cause for freedom. Washington led the army in numerous battles, some defeats but many more victories. Place medallion number 22 in New Jersey. Trenton and Princeton are cities in New Jersey where Washington won two key battles during the colonies' most hopeless period of the war, due to his perseverance and hope for independence. Even when it looked like the British were winning, Washington came through victorious.

Other Events

The Arts/Technology

WINTER AT VALLEY FORGE

Date: ______________________________

Imagine being a soldier in the American Army and having just suffered a defeat by the British as they overtook the capital city, Philadelphia. Your morale and spirits are low. Now George Washington leads you and all of the soldiers 22 miles north of Philadelphia to Valley Forge, which is covered with inches of snow. You look around and see no shelter and realize that you have to build your own. All of your clothing is thin and worn, your shoes have holes in them so your feet are bleeding from frostbite, and you are extremely hungry. You haven't seen food in days. Hundreds, perhaps thousands, of soldiers have died from starvation and disease; but the faithful concern, sympathy, and hard work of General Washington has kept you determined for survival. A glimmer of hope arrives when German Baron von Steuben enters the camp intending to drill and train the American Army, but not without first caring for your physical needs. "A captain . . . must pay the greatest attention to the health of his men, their discipline, arms, accoutrements, ammunition, clothes and necessaries. His first object should be to gain the love of his men by treating them with every possible kindness." He cared for the welfare of the army and not only trained them back to health, but equipped them for war! What was the darkest period of the War for Independence soon became the brightest. Place your medallion at Valley Forge where the American Army regained hope of victory.

Other Events

The Arts/Technology

Yorktown and the Treaty of Paris

Date: ______________________

The American colonists did not fight the British on their own. We must not forget the major and significant role the French played in helping America gain its independence. Place your next medallion at Yorktown, Virginia, a peninsula on the Chesapeake Bay, where Lord Cornwallis had decided to station his army waiting for more ships to arrive from England. When General Washington received news of this, he sent the Marquis de Lafayette to surprise Cornwallis's troops, and he soon joined Lafayette when he caught word that thousands of French reinforcements were on their way. The French needed to arrive before the British in order for the plan to succeed. De Grasse and the French fleet fought British ships on their way to the Chesapeake Bay and prevented them from coming to Cornwallis's aid. When the French arrived, they and the American forces forced Cornwallis and his men to surrender. Only four days later the British fleets arrived, but it was too late. Without the help of the French, America may have had a very different story, but because of their cooperation, the colonies were now "Free and Independent States."

Other Events

The Arts/Technology

THE CONSTITUTIONAL CONVENTION

Date: ______________________________

Do you know what makes America's government different from so many other nations' governmental systems? The Constitution established three branches of government to work as a checks-and-balances system. The writers of the Constitution recognized that all men are by nature sinful, and without a system to restrain man's desire for power, a government system can easily fall into corruption and tyranny. So, the legislative, executive and judicial branches were established to prevent such corruption from happening. Representation of the people in government was also important to make sure that the nation would fulfill its role and "ensure domestic tranquility, promote the general welfare, and secure the blessings of liberty" for years to come. Our right to vote allows us to be represented by the people we elect, and this right is a great privilege that we have. George Washington, James Madison, Benjamin Franklin and the other men who met in Philadelphia, Pennsylvania, to sign the Constitution of the United States of America, had a vision for the future, and they built the nation with you and me in mind. Place medallion 25 near Philadelphia.

Other Events

____
____
____
____
____
____
____

The Arts/Technology

____
____
____
____
____
____
____

America's Founding Fathers

Date: ____________________

What do Thomas Jefferson, Benjamin Franklin and James Madison have in common? These men helped write the founding documents of American government. Jefferson and Franklin were two main composers of the Declaration of Independence, while Madison was the chief author of the Constitution and the Federalist Papers. Many of their ideas were very similar.

Place medallion 26 in Philadelphia. This city was vital in the life and prosperity of America, as it is where many of the events we are learning about took place. Indeed it was one of the largest American cities at the time and was once the capital of the country. These founding fathers met in the square of Philadelphia to compose the documents that would shape America.

Other Events

The Arts/Technology

Washington, Our First President

Date: ______________________________

George Washington didn't have to campaign for the presidency and spend millions of dollars on advertising so that he'd be elected, as all government candidates do today. In fact, being president was the last thing on his mind. What he really wanted was to go back to his home at Mount Vernon in Virginia, which was originally his half-brother's farm, and live there peaceably with his wife and children, as a farmer. However, the American people had a different idea. Before Washington was even asked to be president, the electors all agreed that Washington was the only man fit for the presidency, and they called him to take the office. Washington could not refuse. His loyalty to his countrymen compelled him to fulfill their wish. Everyone in the country knew that this man would be just that person who would "possess most wisdom to discern, and most virtue to pursue the common good of the society," as James Madison stated in the Federalist Papers. His character indeed was above reproach. Place your next medallion at Mount Vernon, where the "Father of His Country" finally retired to his serene home after a life of devotion to America.

Other Events

____

____

____

____

____

____

____

The Arts/Technology

____

____

____

____

____

____

____

The Louisiana Purchase

Date: ____________________________________

Imagine what the United States would be like if France controlled a majority of the states west of the Mississippi. Travel across the states would be restricted, and perhaps taxes would be higher if France still controlled the Mississippi River. President Jefferson realized the urgency of controlling Louisiana, in particular, with access to New Orleans and the Gulf of Mexico, for trade purposes, so he sent ambassadors to France to offer a bargain for the land. Place your next medallion near New Orleans. French ruler Napoleon was more than willing to give up Louisiana, but only if Jefferson would also purchase the rest of the Louisiana territory that France owned. For this moment of quick decision, Jefferson had to override the Constitution and approve the offer made by Napoleon. Jefferson had made a good decision. The United States territory expanded so much that the President had to send men on a voyage to explore it all.

Other Events

____

____

____

____

____

____

____

The Arts/Technology

____

____

____

____

____

____

____

The Lewis and Clark Expedition

Date: ______________________________

Place your next medallion on St. Louis, Missouri, where Meriwether Lewis and William Clark set out to explore the Louisiana Territory. Trace the route that they took to the Pacific Ocean and back. It has been a while since we have come across any explorers; but now that the United States was founded (it still only contained 13 of the 50 states) and President Jefferson had purchased much of what we call today the Midwest and Plains territories, this land needed someone to explore it. Thus, Jefferson sent two soldiers, Lewis and Clark, on a voyage to the unknown western side of the North American continent. As you read in their journal entries, they encountered many Native Americans; dangerous wildlife, climates, and terrain; they often feared starvation. Their journey was a success owing much to Sacajawea, the Indian woman who helped the explorers make peaceful agreements with other tribes. Without the success of this voyage, westward expansion may have taken a much longer time, and the West may not be what it is today.

Other Events

____

____

____

____

____

____

____

The Arts/Technology

____

____

____

____

____

____

____

The Second Great Awakening

Date: ______________________________

You will recall that many of the first settlers to America came for religious freedom in order to escape persecution in Europe and to worship God as they saw fit. So, many of them were rather serious about their religious beliefs. However, after a century and a half in America, Christianity was experiencing a decline: sin was rampant, moral standards were low, and people were indifferent to the gospel. Christianity in America was in need of revival. The Second Great Awakening, however, would have a different look than the first one. Circuit riders and camp meetings were gaining popularity as men like Francis Asbury, James McGready and Charles Finney preached convicting sermons that made people aware of their sins. Place medallion 30 in Rochester, New York, where Finney, America's leading evangelist, preached to thousands of people. This Awakening indeed had its positive effects, such as gaining thousands of converts and founding the first foreign missions organization (ABCFM), yet Charles Finney also taught many false doctrines and drastically changed Protestant Christianity.

Other Events

____

____

____

____

____

____

____

The Arts/Technology

____

____

____

____

____

____

____

THE WAR OF 1812

Date: ____________________

George Washington's Farewell Address in 1796 made clear the nation's policy on foreign affairs: "It is our true policy to steer clear of permanent alliances with any portion of the foreign world, so far, I mean, as we are now at liberty to do it. . . ." When Britain and France began fighting with one another again in 1803, President Thomas Jefferson, listening to the advice of former President Washington, tried to remain neutral as long as he could. But when both countries seized American ships, and Britain began forcing Americans into service on their ships, our country had to step in and defend itself. In 1812 President James Madison declared war on Britain, whom our country thought was a greater threat than France. It was a huge risk for the United States navy to take on Britain's, which was known as a very powerful navy. As we know, the small American forces held their own. Place your medallion on Lake Erie where American captain Oliver Perry surprisingly defeated the British fleet with a crew of Kentucky militiamen and ships that he built himself. This one small victory led to the great victory for the "land of the free and the home of the brave."

Other Events

The Arts/Technology

The Missouri Compromise

Date: ______________________________

This last event that we study will also mark the beginning of next year's studies, the rest of American history. Freedom will also be a theme for next year, though it will take a different form. While this year we saw the early Americans' glorious struggle for independence from the slavery of the King, next year's struggle will not seem so glorious, but will be a hard fight for freedom against the African slave trade. The Missouri Compromise was the beginning of the end to slavery, though it took several decades before this was accomplished. Place your final medallion in Missouri. The compromise declared that the new state of Missouri was to remain a slave state, while the new state of Maine would join as a free state. Earlier we placed a medallion in St. Louis; the same state where Lewis and Clark paved the way for exploration and freedom to the West would also be a symbol of slavery in the South. But the struggle for freedom has been present since the Fall of Man, as man is in a constant battle against sin. We know, however, that Jesus Christ paid the ultimate price for our bondage to sin, so now we are truly free.

Other Events

The Arts/Technology

EXPLORERS TO 1815
Writing Exercises

TEACHER'S INSTRUCTIONS FOR INTEGRATING HISTORY AND WRITING

1. Vocabulary: Before giving the assignment, the teacher should look at the vocabulary and make a judgment as to whether or not the students will be likely to know most of them. If the answer is yes, skip to step #2 and have them look up the vocabulary afterward. If not, have them look up the vocabulary words first.
2. Reading/note-taking: Have the students read the passage while taking notes using the "key-word method." In brief, this means **no more than 3** words from each sentence that will help the student remember what is said in it. Appropriate answers can, of course, vary, but sample answers are given in the answer key. Two general rules can help these notes to be meaningful:
   a. Distilling the grammatical core—words that are part of the grammatical core of the sentence, particularly subjects, action verbs, direct objects, predicate nouns and adjectives.
   b. Note that *linking verbs* are not listed above. Though they are just as much a part of the grammatical core, they are easy to assume (i.e., instead of writing "Alexander was brutal," it is more effective to write, "Alexander brutal").
3. Title: Have the students try to come up with a title for each paragraph. This forces them to try to look at each paragraph understand its main point. Sample titles are given in the answer key.
4. Summary paragraph: Have the students hide the page and try to reconstruct, in brief, the essence of the original on a separate sheet of paper using only their notes.
5. Improved paragraph: Have the students spruce up their paragraphs using a list of "modifiers," "power words" or grammatical constructions that can help the students to make their writing more interesting. (Andrew Pudewa's "Excellence in Writing" method is a good example of how to do this in practice.)

The following writing excercise are examples you may use as optional projects. We encourage you to make up your own for the other flashcards.

Explorers to 1815

Writing Exercises Card 1

Prince Henry, the Portuguese Empire and Exploration

I

Portugal is a very small place and it isn't particularly wealthy or populous. Yet, for about one hundred and fifty years after Prince Henry, it had one of the largest and most powerful empires in the world. The reason why such a small country was able to have such a large empire is that it had a head start, and that head start on other countries was partly because of Prince Henry.

II

Prince Henry is often called "the Navigator." A navigator is one who pilots or plans the route of a ship. Prince Henry is called this not because he actually did any navigating but because he established one of the first schools of navigation in Europe and then encouraged and financed many voyages of discovery. If he was never a navigator himself, what caused him to take such an interest in it? Though he hadn't done much sailing, he had traveled quite a bit when he was in the midst of his campaigns against the Moslems of North Africa. One thing that he had noticed was that Arab and Moorish merchants were able to make an enormous profit from selling such things as spices to Europeans. He also helped encourage the construction of a new generation of faster, more maneuverable and more seaworthy ships. Prince Henry thought that if Europeans could learn to navigate better, build better ships, and perhaps even find a better route to the East, they could take over the spice trade themselves.

III

Although Portugal did, in fact, become one of the world's great early naval and mercantile powers, it probably took longer than he expected. By the time that Columbus sailed, however, Portugal had already laid the foundation for its empire. Two years later, in 1494, Spain and Portugal confidently divided the whole world between them with the treaty of Tordesillas. The Portuguese and Spanish had little trouble dominating the Atlantic, Pacific and Indian Oceans. Their great galleons, armed with cannons, were far more powerful, more seaworthy and more suited to long journeys than the smaller north African and Asian vessels.

Explorers to 1815
Writing Exercises Card 1, Page 2

Vocabulary

1. *populous:* ____

2. *voyage:* ____

3. *Moslem:* ____

4. *Moor:* ____

5. *seaworthy:* ____

6. *naval:* ____

7. *mercantile:* ____

8. *foundation:* ____

9. *galleons:* ____

10. *campaigns:* ____

11. *maneuverable:* ____

Explorers to 1815

Writing Exercises Card 1, Page 3

Key Word Outline

I

1 __________

2 __________

3 __________

II

1 __________

2 __________

3 __________

4 __________

5 __________

6 __________

7 __________

III

1 __________

2 __________

3 __________

4 __________

5 __________

Explorers to 1815

Writing Exercises Card 1, Page 4

Answers

Vocabulary

1. *populous:* having many people
2. *voyage:* long journey
3. *Moslem:* follower of Islam
4. *Moor:* Moslem of North Africa or Spain
5. *seaworthy:* able to handle rough waters
6. *naval:* having to do with military ships
7. *mercantile:* having to do with trade
8. *foundation:* something on which other things rest
9. *galleons:* deep-drafted, high-sided, castle-like ships carrying cannons
10. *campaigns:* large military operations
11. *maneuverable:* able to be moved about with ease

Key Word Outline

I. Portugal's Head Start
   1. Portugal small
   2. largest, powerful, empire
   3. head start, Prince Henry

II. Prince Henry's Dream
   1. Navigator
   2. Plans, route, ship
   3. Because, established, schools
   4. Caused, interest ?
   5. Traveled, campaigns, North Africa
   6. Merchants, profits, spices
   7. Encouraged, construction, ships
   8. Europeans, take over, trade

III. Portugal's Empire
   1. Naval, mercantile, powers
   2. Time, Columbus, foundation
   3. Divided, world, between
   4. Dominating, oceans
   5. Galleons, powerful, seaworthy

Explorers to 1815

Writing Exercises Card 2

Columbus, the Confused Explorer

I

Columbus was a brave man and a true visionary. The fact remains, though, that he was completely wrong in his geography. The resistance to his bold plan on the part of the various courts of Europe has often been explained by saying that it was due to ignorance and superstition. In particular, it has often been incorrectly asserted that the reason was because back then nearly everyone thought that the world was "flat". While it was true that many ignorant and superstition still believed this, including, to be sure, many common sailors, educated people had long believed that the earth was round.

II

Going all the way back to the ancients, most educated people had accepted the view of the universe laid out by the Greek-Egyptian astronomer Ptolemy. While his view was wrong in assuming that the earth was the center of the universe, it was quite correct in saying that the earth was round. What is more, the geographers had come to a fairly close estimate of the Earth's size in places like Portugal, where Columbus' idea was rejected.

III

Columbus differed from conventional wisdom mainly in saying that the earth was actually smaller than the previous estimates, making his idea plausible. You see, if the earth was really as big as it was thought to be, such a trip would be suicide across nothing but open sea. Since, in reality, Columbus was actually wrong and the conventional wisdom right, Columbus was very fortunate that there was actually a huge landmass blocking his way to the East Indies. Not only did it give him the chance to explore new worlds that he hadn't imagined existed, it prevented his crew from dying of hunger and thirst on the open sea.

Explorers to 1815
Writing Exercises Card 2, Page 2

Vocabulary

1. *visionary:* ____________________

2. *geography:* ____________________

3. *ignorance:* ____________________

4. *superstition:* ____________________

5. *astronomer:* ____________________

6. *estimate:* ____________________

7. *conventional:* ____________________

8. *plausible:* ____________________

9. *suicide:* ____________________

Explorers to 1815

Writing Exercises Card 2, Page 3

Key Word Outline

I

1 ____________________

2 ____________________

3 ____________________

4 ____________________

5 ____________________

II

1 ____________________

2 ____________________

3 ____________________

III

1 ____________________

2 ____________________

3 ____________________

4 ____________________

Explorers to 1815

Writing Exercises Card 2, Page 4

Answers

Vocabulary

1. *visionary:* one with big ideas
2. *geography:* the science of mapping the earth
3. *ignorance:* lack of knowledge
4. *superstition:* the belief in unproven traditions, particularly one involving magic and the supernatural
5. *astronomer:* one who charts the stars
6. *estimate:* a thoughtful guess
7. *conventional:* generally accepted
8. *plausible:* likely
9. *suicide:* the killing of oneself

Key Word Outlines

I. The Myth of the Flat-Earth Myth
   1. Columbus, brave, visionary
   2. Completely, wrong, geography
   3. resistance, explained, ignorance
   4. asserted, reason, "flat"
   5. educated, believed, round

II. Ptolemy and the Educated Geographers
   1. Most, accepted, Ptolemy
   2. Earth, center, round
   3. Geographers, estimate, size

III. Columbus's Good Fortune
   1. Columbus, differed, smaller
   2. Thought, trip, suicide
   3. Columbus, fortunate, blocking
   4. Chance, prevented, dying

Explorers to 1815

Writing Exercises Card 16

Wars in Europe, Wars in America

I

There aren't too many things that determine the future of an entire continent, but the French and Indian Wars was one of them. When the term "French and Indian Wars" is used, there are actually two different things that could be meant, because the term is often used for a long (almost 80 years) series of wars between Britain and France over who would control North America, while, at the same time, it is also used to describe the last and most important of these wars. Of course, the name implies a British-American point of view, since from their perspective, their enemy in all of these wars was the French and their Indian allies. The American names for the other wars shows the American way of looking at things, too. In America, we call the War of the League of Augsburg (1689-1697) "King William's War", the War of Spanish Succession (1702-1713) "Queen Anne's War" and the War of Austrian Succession (1740-1748) "King George's War." Why do these names show an American perspective? Well, for the colonists, these were mostly wars that started over in Europe for reasons that they didn't understand real well or care too much about. What affected their lives was mostly the fact that every time England and France went to war, Indians that sided with the French (like the Hurons) would come and attack their homes. So what did cause all these wars? What it really boiled down to is that England and France were the two most powerful countries in Europe and they didn't like each other much, so every time a

Explorers to 1815

Writing Exercises Card 16, Page 2

major war broke out in Europe for any reason, it was pretty much guaranteed that they would take opposite sides in it. Since they both had colonies in the Americas, their European wars would "spill over" into America.

II

The last of the French and Indian Wars, also known as the French and Indian War, was different for three reasons, however. First, even though it mostly happened at the same time that the Seven Years War (1756-1763) was happening in America, it actually started two years earlier in America, so it wasn't just a "spillover" war. Second, even though the others were known as French and Indian Wars, the British and the colonists actually had many Indian allies, particularly the powerful, five-tribe Iroquois Nation. In the French and Indian War, even some of the Iroquois tribes joined in with the French, and that created a very bad situation for the colonists. Third, the dangerous situation that the British colonists were in caused them to begin to think that they had to rely more on themselves, and on each other, rather than looking to the mother country for protection. When General Braddock's army was defeated and wiped out, many of the Americans began to think that they knew more about how to fight in the wilderness environment than the British. The British colonies had many more people and were much better established than New France. Thus, in the end, when the British colonists really joined with a whole heart in the struggle and the British regulars had learned a few lessons from General Braddock, the victory of the British in North America was the natural outcome. The lesson in self-sufficiency that the colonists had learned, however, was one that they would not soon forget.

EXPLORERS TO 1815

Writing Exercises Card 16, Page 3

VOCABULARY

1. *continent:* ____________________

____

2. *perspective:* ____________________

____

3. *environment:* ____________________

____

4. *established:* ____________________

____

5. *outcome:* ____________________

____

6. *self-sufficiency:* ____________________

____

7. *wilderness:* ____________________

____

Explorers to 1815
Writing Exercises Card 16, Page 4

Key Word Outline

I

1 ____________________

2 ____________________

3 ____________________

4 ____________________

5 ____________________

6 ____________________

7 ____________________

8 ____________________

9 ____________________

10 ____________________

11 ____________________

II

1 ____________________

2 ____________________

3 ____________________

4 ____________________

5 ____________________

6 ____________________

7 ____________________

8 ____________________

9 ____________________

Explorers to 1815

Writing Exercises Card 16, Page 5

Answers

Card 16

Vocabulary

1. *continent:* one of the principal land masses of the earth
2. *perspective:* a vista or view
3. *environment:* surroundings
4. *established:* to make secure or firm
5. *outcome:* a final consequence
6. *self-sufficiency:* providing for oneself without help
7. *wilderness:* uninhabited region left in its natural condition

Key Note Outline

I. The French and Indian Wars
   1. Determine, future, continent
   2. Different, term, used
   3. Name, implies, view
   4. Names, other, too
   5. Call, war
   6. American, perspective ?
   7. Started, Europe, understand
   8. Effected, lives, Indians
   9. What, cause ?
   10. Complicated
   11. England, France, opposite
   12. European, spill, over

II. The French and Indian War
   1. Last, war, different
   2. Started, America
   3. Second, Iroquois Nation
   4. Iroquois, joined, French
   5. Rely, themselves,protection
   6. Braddock, defeated, wilderness
   7. British, more, people
   8. Thus, victory, natural
   9. Lesson learned

Explorers to 1815

Project—Example Grammar-History Sentences

Directions for History-Grammar Integration

We recommend the Shurley Grammar program as being the one which does the best job of teaching students the fundamental structure of the English sentence. Obviously, the sentences in the various sentences groups of Shurley are not all going to have any relationship with the content of their history, but we believe that making up extra practice sentences which have content culled from their history lessons can bring a beneficial "synergy" into the curriculum.

Several sentences derived from the content of the history lessons have been written and parsed as examples. Obviously, the possibilities are limitless.

It would also be worthwhile to have the children make up their own, history?related sentences. This could be done for the whole class to parse, or for their own, individual practice and improved sentences that are integral to the Shurley lessons.

```
                    SN                      V   A    ADJ      PN
1. SN LV  Prince Henry the Navigator / was an important influence
   PN P4   P  A     OP          P  A          OP
          (on the founding) (of the Portuguese Empire).
```

1. Prince Henry the Navigator was an important influence on the founding of the Portuguese Empire.
2. Who was an important influence on the founding of the Portuguese Empire? Prince Henry the Navigator / SN
3. What is being said about Prince Henry the Navigator? Prince Henry the Navigator was / V
4. Was what? influence / verify the noun
5. Does influence mean the same thing as Prince Henry the Navigator? yes
6. Influence / PN
7. was / LV
8. What kind of influence? Important / Adj
9. An / A
10. On / P
11. On What? founding / OP
12. The / A
13. Of / P
14. Of what? Portuguese Empire / OP
15. The / A
16. SN LV PN P4 check
17. LV check again
18. (on the founding), prepositional phrase
19. (of the Portuguese Empire), prepositional phrase
20. period, statement / D

Explorers to 1815

Project—Example Grammar-History Sentences

21. Go back to the verb; divide the complete subject from the complete predicate.
22. Is their an adverb exception? no
23. is this sentence in a natural or inverted order? natural / no change

CSN C A ADJ CSN
2. SN V Christopher Columbus and the Portuguese navigators
P1 V P A OP P A OP
/ disagreed (about the size) (of the earth).D

1. Christopher Columbus and the Portuguese navigators disagreed about the size of the earth.
2. Who disagreed about the size of the earth? Christopher Columbus and navigators/CSN,CSN
3. What is being said about Christopher Columbus and Navigators? Christopher Columbus and Navigators disagreed / V
4. About / P
5. About what? size / OP
6. The / A
7. Of / P
8. Of what? Earth / OP
9. The / A
10. What kind of navigators? Portuguese / Adj
11. The / A
12. And / C
13. SN V P1 check
14. (about the size), prepositional phrase
15. (of the earth), prepositional phrase
16. period, statement / D
17. Go back to the verb, divide the complete subject from the complete predicate.
18. Is their an adverb exception? no
19. Is this sentence in a natural or inverted order? natural / no change

A SN LV PA
3. SN V The Stamp Act / was unfair.D
PA P5

1. The Stamp Act was unfair.
2. What was unfair? Stamp Act / SN
3. What is being said about Stamp Act? the Stamp Act was / V

Explorers to 1815

Project—Example Grammar-History Sentences

4. Was what? unfair / PA
5. The / A
6. SN LV PA P5 check
7. Period, statement / D
8. Go back to the verb; divide the complete subject from the complete predicate.
9. Is their an adverb exception? no
10. Is this sentence in a natural or inverted order? natural / no change

SN ADV V-t A DO
4. SN V-t George Washington / valiantly fought the British
DO P2 P A OP
(during the Revolutionary War).D

1. George Washington valiantly fought the British during the Revolutionary War.
2. Who fought valiantly during the Revolutionary War? George Washington / SN
3. What is being said about George Washington? George Washington fought / V
4. Fought whom? British / verify the noun
5. Does British mean the same thing as George Washington? no
6. British / DO
7. Fought / V-t
8. Fought how? valiantly / Adv
9. The / A
10. During / P
11. During what? Revolutionary War / OP
12. The / A
13. SN V-t DO P2 check
14. (during the Revolutionary War), prepositional phrase
15. period, statement / D
16. Go back to the verb; divide the complete subject from the complete predicate.
17. Is their an adverb exception? yes / Move the line
18. Is this sentence in a natural or inverted order? natural / no change

EXPLORERS TO 1815

Project—Example Grammar-History Sentences

```
                  P    A       OP              SN    HV    ADV  V-t
5. SN      V-t (During the 18th century), Britain / did not give
   IO DO P3 A      IO      PPA  ADJ      OP
               the colonies their due representation.D
```

1. During the 18th century, Britain did not give the colonies their due representation.
2. Who did not give the colonies their due representation? Britain / SN
3. What is being said about Britain? Britain did give / V
4. Did / HV
5. Did give how? not
6. Did give what? representation / verify the noun
7. Does representation mean the same thing as Britain? no
8. Representation / DO
9. Give / V-t
10. Did give to whom? colonies / IO
11. The /A
12. What kind of representation? due / Adj
13. Whose due representation? their / PPA
14. During / P
15. During what? 18th century / OP
16. The / A
17. SN V-t IO DO P3 check
18. (during the 18th century), prepositional phrase
19. period, statement / D
20. Go back to the verb; divide the complete subject from the complete predicate.
21. Is their an adverb exception? no
22. Is this sentence in a natural or inverted order? inverted / Underline the subject parts once and the predicate parts twice.

Explorers to 1815

Great Games for History Review

Make cards with names, dates, events and places to keep in a packet. Add to the cards as more topics are studied. On review days pull out the 3x5 cards for ready-made clues. They can be helpful for many of the following games, especially when everyone's brains are tired and they just can't think of a word for hangman or a charade to act out.

Who Am I? (Where Am I? What Am I?)

A student selects a person, place or thing from his history knowledge. The student who is "It" gives clues and calls on classmates (with their hands raised) to guess. The student with the correct guess gets the next turn to be "It."

Twenty Questions

The student chooses a history person, place or thing. They announce to the class whether they are a person, place or thing. The class can ask twenty questions. All questions must be worded so that a 'yes' or a 'no' answer is given. If after twenty questions no one has guessed the correct answer, "It" identifies the person, place or thing.

Charades

Play as individuals or as teams. One person or team acts out clues to an identity or event. The remaining students or team tries to guess. Set a time limit of several minutes.

Thumbs Up or Down

The teacher asks 'yes' or 'no' questions pertaining to history. The class responds with thumbs up for yes and thumbs down for no.

Knock-Knock

Teacher says, "Knock-Knock."
Student replies, "Who's there?"
Teacher gives a fact as response. For example, "I had six wives." Student tells the name, "King Henry VIII."

Mixed-Up Story

Retell a historical event with a few of the facts incorrect. As the teacher tells the story, students raise their hands and correct the errors.

Chronological Order

Give the students one or two history flashcards. Have the students place their cards in chronological order without looking at the numbers on the back.

A B C's of History

The first student begins by naming a history person, place or thing that begins with an A and telling a fact about it. The next student follows in turn with the next letter of the alphabet. For example, A-Aristotle was a philosopher. B-Botticelli was a Renaissance artist.

Ball Toss

Teacher tosses a small soft ball to a student who answers the question posed. The student tosses the ball back to the teacher.

Baseball

This can be adapted to paper for smaller groups or for quieter times. Chair baseball can be quite noisy, but will probably be the class's favorite review game. Set up chairs in a baseball diamond. Label home, 1st, 2nd, and 3rd bases. Divide the class into two teams. Player gets a hit when they correctly answer a question. They can move around the bases as their teammates correctly answer. A run is scored when a player advances to home. Incorrect answers are outs.

Explorers to 1815

Great Games for History Review

Tic Tac Toe

This can be played in pairs or by dividing into two teams. Students choose where to place the X or 0 when they correctly answer a question.

Secret Identity

One player selects a person and tells other players the initial of the selection's last name. Other players ask questions phrased so that the chooser has to identify other people with the same initial. If the initial is H for example, the first question could be "Are you a president of the United States?" The response may be, "No, I am not William Harrison." If the chooser is stumped for a response with the proper initial, then the asker can request other information: "Are you alive?" The "stumped" questions can only be answered by a 'yes' or a 'no.' The chooser continues answering questions until someone guesses the identity.

Boxes

Set up the game with a square grid made up of dots. Ask questions of the students. Correct answers earn a horizontal or vertical line connecting two of the dots. The student who closes in a box puts his initials inside and gets another turn. He may continue adding lines as long as each line forms a new box. The student with the most boxes wins.

Categories

Select twenty categories ahead of time (colonies, items traded with England, presidents, founding fathers, famous ships, items England taxed). Each student writes names of all the categories across the top of his paper. The players have 5-10 minutes to write as many items that fit the categories as they can. When time is up, trade lists for scoring. Each correct answer is one point. An answer no one else has gets two points. The player with the most points wins.

Drawing in the Dark

Retell a history event to the class. The class should draw the events with their eyes closed. Judges can choose the most accurate, funniest, etc.

Hangman

Choose words related to history. Each student guesses a letter in turn until someone has a guess or the stickman figure is hanged.

Magazining

Collect as many old magazines as feasible. Allow students several minutes to depict a historical event by cutting out pictures and words from magazines and gluing them to blank pages. They can even compile the pages into a book to show the flow of events.

Questions

The first player asks a question. The second player must respond with another related question, and then the first player with a question, etc. If a player pauses too long between questions, forgets to ask a question or asks a nonsensical question, he is out. For example, "Did Paul Revere live in Boston?" "Didn't he look for a signal in the church tower?" "Was it one if by land, two if by sea?"

Explorers to 1815

Project—History Matching Card Game

Photocopy the artwork on the following pages (back to back) onto card stock and cut apart.

This game is best for three to six players, but it is possible for two to play. The dealer deals five cards to each player (seven each for two players). The remaining cards are placed face down to form a stock.

The player to dealer's left starts. A turn consists of asking a specific player for a specific event. The player who asks must already hold at least one of the cards requested. If the player who was asked has the card requested, he must give it to the player who asked for it. That player then places his matching cards on the table in front of him and gets another turn.

If the person asked does not have any of the card named, he says "Pick a card." The asker must then draw the top card of the undealt stock. If the drawn card is the card asked for, the asker shows it and gets another turn. If the drawn card is not the one asked for, the asker keeps it, but the turn now passes to the player who said, "Pick a card."

The game continues until either someone has no cards left in their hand or the deck runs out. The winner is the player who has the most pairs.

PRINCE HENRY THE NAVIGATOR

COLUMBUS SAILS TO THE NEW WORLD

MAGELLAN CIRCUMNAVIGATES

THE SPANISH EXPLORERS

EXPLORERS OF THE NORTHEAST

RALEIGH SETTLES ROANOKE

JAMESTOWN IS FOUNDED

THE MAYFLOWER LANDS AT PLYMOUTH

PILGRIMS BUILD PLYMOUTH COLONY

MASSACHUSETTS BAY/PURITANS

ROGER WILLIAMS

SALEM WITCH TRIALS

THIRTEEN COLONIES FORMED

THE FIRST GREAT AWAKENING

COLONIAL TRADING WITH ENGLAND

THE FRENCH AND INDIAN WARS

PARLIAMENT ACTS UNJUSTLY

FIRST CONTINENTAL CONGRESS

The War for Independence Begins

British Lose at Bunker Hill

America Declares its Independence

Washington Commands Army

Winter at Valley Forge

Yorktown/ Treaty of Paris

Constitutional Convention

America's Founding Fathers

Washington, Our First President

THE LOUISIANA PURCHASE

LEWIS & CLARK EXPEDITION

SECOND GREAT AWAKENING

THE WAR OF 1812

THE MISSOURI COMPROMISE

EXPLORERS TO 1815

The Book Critic—Biography Report

I read the biography of: ______________________________

Title: ______________________________

Author: ______________________________

Five facts about the subject of this biography:

1. ______________________________
2. ______________________________
3. ______________________________
4. ______________________________
5. ______________________________

Is this person still alive?

Yes/No (Circle One)

Did this person live in the United States of America?

Yes/No (Circle One)

Why is the subject of this book significant enough to have a book written about his life?

____

____

____

____

____

Explorers to 1815

The Book Critic—Book Reporter

Title: ______________________________

Author: ______________________________

Illustrator: ______________________________

Main characters:

____

____

____

____

____

____

____

My favorite part of the story:

____

____

____

____

____

____

____

____

____

Explorers to 1815

Grammar Dig

Veritas Press has sent in their crack archeological team to uncover the treasures hidden in the history card you are studying. Go through the description on the back of the card with each specialist and help them ask the questions that will uncover the artifacts they are interested in. Write those words in the spaces that follow.

Nigel Noun

asks "Who?"
and"What?"

Veronica Verb

asks "What is being
said about?"

Adam Adjective

asks "What kind?" "Which
one?" and "How many?"

Ashley Adverb

asks "How?" "When?"
and "Where?"

Explorers to 1815

Project—History Curiosities

Photocopy the artwork on this and the following page back-to-back, then cut apart and staple along the spine, using the artwork below for the cover. Choose an historical event and have the students write and illustrate unusual and interesting facts they find about the event. This project can be used throughout the year (if you copy enough pages) in conjunction with the flashcards' Resources sections.

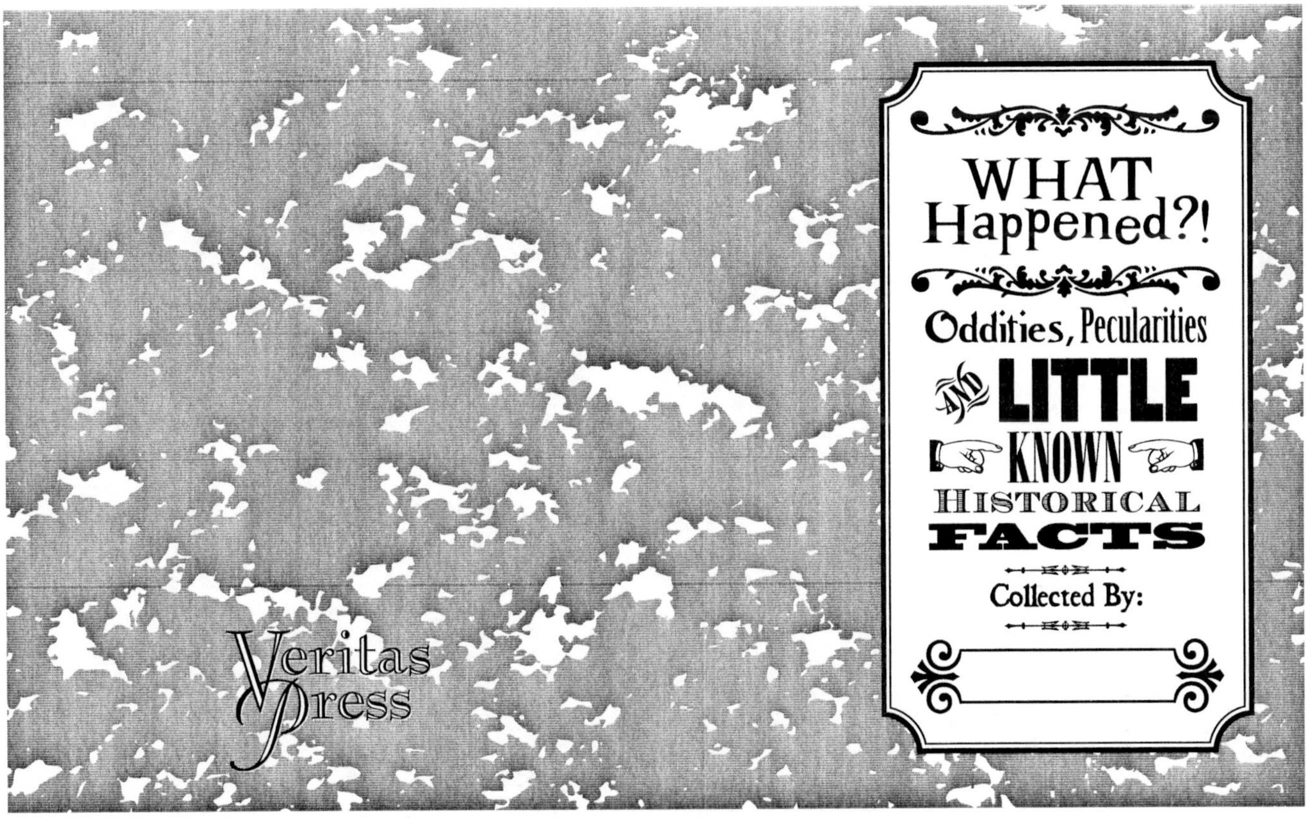

Explorers to 1815

Project—History Curiosities, Page 2

Explorers to 1815

Sequence Review 1

Event	*Date*	*Reference*

Explorers to 1815

Sequence Review 2

Mask out the information the students are supposed to review, then photocopy.

Event	*Date*
Prince Henry the Navigator	1394-1460
Columbus Sails to the New World	1492
Magellan Circumnavigates the Earth	1519-1522
Cortez, de Soto, de Leon, and Coronado, the Spanish Explorers	1513-1538
Explorers of the Northeast, Cartier, Champlain, and Cabot	1497-1603
Raleigh Settles Roanoke	1585
Jamestown is Founded in Virginia	1607
The *Mayflower* Lands at Plymouth	1620
Pilgrims Build Plymouth Colony	1621
Massachusetts Bay Colony, Home of the Puritans	1630
Roger Williams, Founder of Rhode Island	1636
Salem Witch Trials	1692
Thirteen Colonies Formed	1620-1733
The First Great Awakening	1740-1742
Colonial Trading with England	c. 1750
The French and Indian Wars	1754-1763
Parliament Acts Unjustly	1764-1774
The First Continental Congress Seeks Peace with Britain	1774
The War for Independence Begins	1775

Explorers to 1815

Sequence Review 2

Mask out the information the students are supposed to review, then photocopy.

Event	*Date*
British Lose at Bunker Hill	1775
America Declares its Independence	1776
Washington Commands the Continental Army	1775–1781
Winter at Valley Forge	1777–1778
Yorktown and the Treaty of Paris	1781, 1783
The Constitutional Convention	1787
America's Founding Fathers	c. 1788
Washington, Our First President	1789
The Louisiana Purchase from France	1803
The Lewis & Clark Expedition	1805
The Second Great Awakening	1799–1830
The War of 1812	1812
The Missouri Compromise	1820

Explorers to 1815

Project—Art History Museum

Create an art museum for your students to visit to reinforce the events studied on the history flashcards.

Building Your Collection

After completing a flashcard, photocopy an image out of the additional readings that represents that event. Color and place the picture in one of the frames below. Hang this artwork in the museum (see next page) to build a collection for that "wing" of your art museum. In the *Veritas Press Phonics Museum* reading program, additional paintings are available that would add color and variety to this project.

1815 TO THE PRESENT

Project—Art History Museum, Page 2

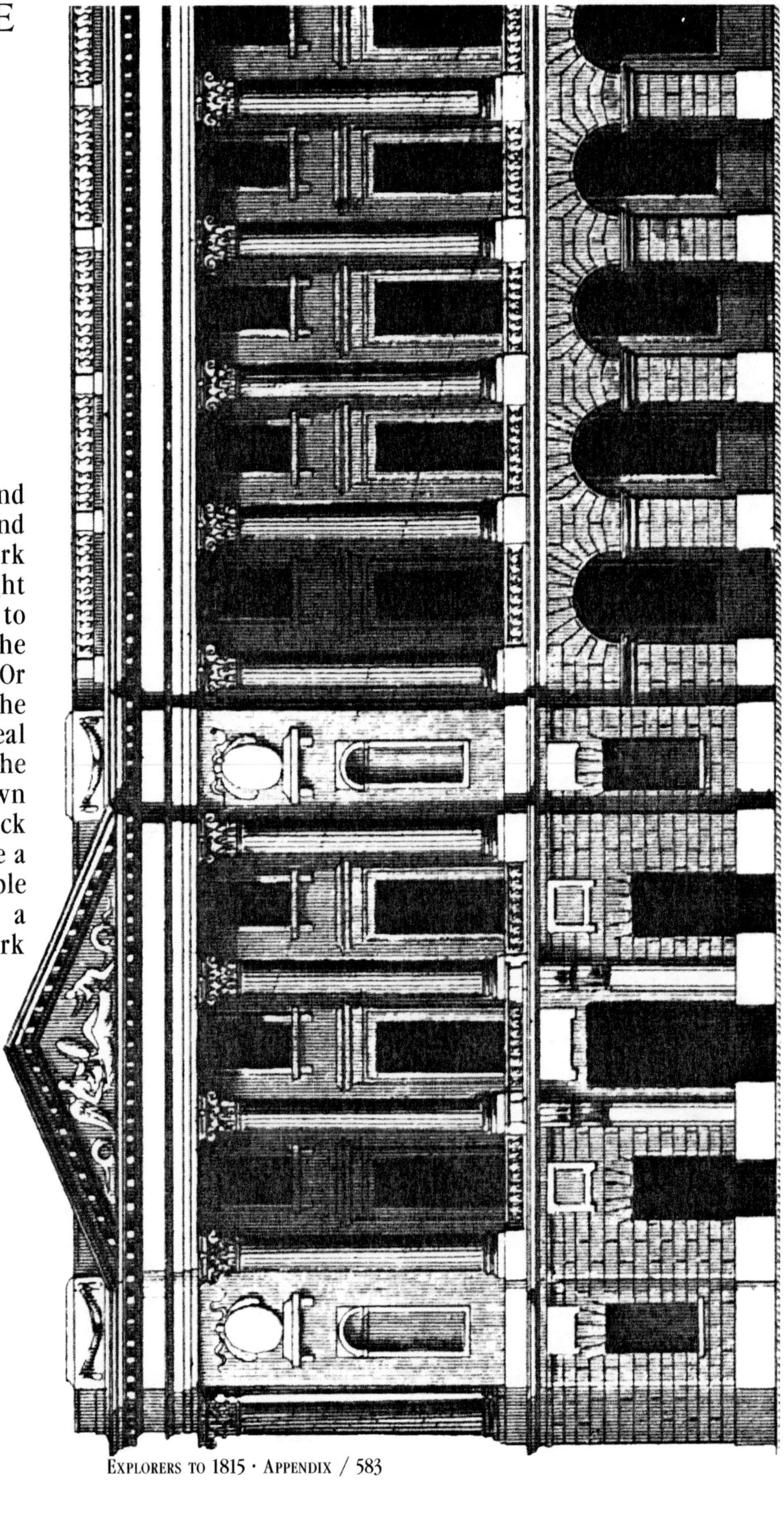

Building Your Museum

Find a cardboard box and spray paint the inside and the outside white. Artwork is provided on the right that may be photocopied to make "wallpaper" for the exterior of the museum. Or the students can design the outside to their tastes. Seal the box then cut along the top edge of the box, down the adjacent side then back along the bottom to make a "wall" of the museum able to be swung open like a door. Hang your artwork and invite visitors to enjoy it.

Explorers to 1815
Reference Report

TITLE: ______________________________

AUTHOR: ______________________________

EVENT: ______________________________

Explorers to 1815

Resource Notes—Event

Title of Resource:

____

Author:

____

What (is the event?)*:*

____

____

____

____

Who (was important in the event?)*:*

____

____

When (date)*:*

____

Where (did the event occur?)*:*

____

____

____

____

Importance:

____

____

____

____

Explorers to 1815

Resource Notes—Visual Record

Title of Resource:

____

Author:

____

Who or What:

____

____

____

Date:

____

Where:

____

____

____

____

Draw a picture to illustrate what you have studied (turn the page if you need to draw a wide picture instead of a tall picture).

EXPLORERS TO 1815
Postage Stamp

In the space provided below, design a class stamp based on an historical event studied or a literature book you have read.

Explorers to 1815

Bookmark

Supplies

One copy of the bookmark on cardstock

markers

glue stick

scissors

hole punch

yarn (4 inches)

Directions

Make a copy of this page onto card stock. Illustrate the person or event you are studying, then color and cut it out. Fold over and glue together. For best results, laminate the bookmark when you are finished to make it last longer. Using a hole punch, punch out a hole at the top of the bookmark. Take pieces of yarn and tie them through the hole.

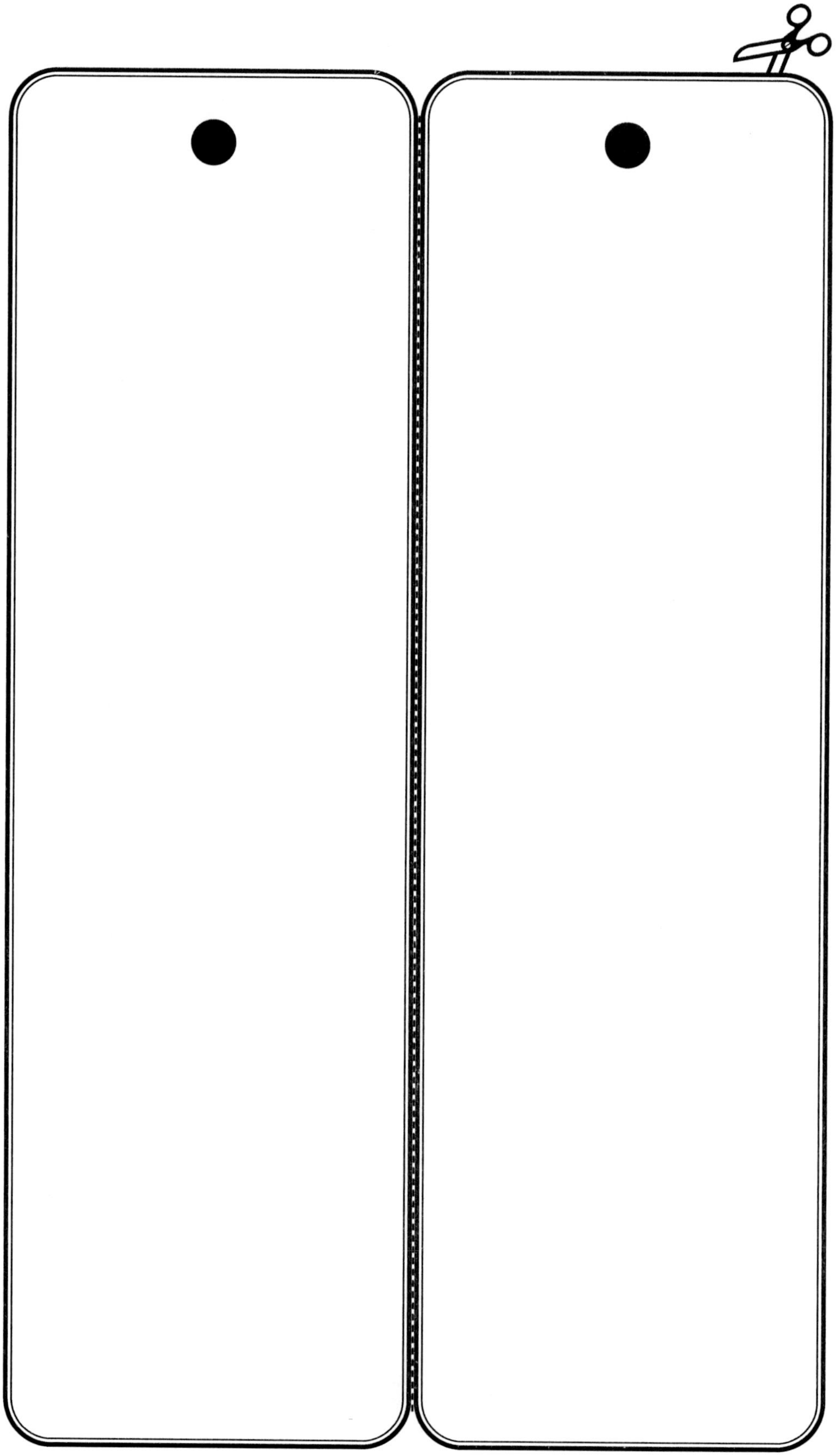

Explorers to 1815

Field Trip Postcard

In the space provided below, make an imaginary postcard based on your field trip. On the front draw a picture of the place, and on the back answer the questions provided.

POSTCARD

Where are you visiting?

What is the favorite thing you have seen?

How does this relate to what you are studying?

Wish you were here!

Explorers to 1815

Timetripper *Board Game*

In this game, the players are trapped in the past and must try to get to the present day by answering questions as they proceed forward in time.

Supplies

scissors

tape

colored pencils

Directions

Make several back-to-back copies of the question cards or glue them together. Cut out all the cards, pocket watch player tokens and the game board. Tape the game board together and then color it. Laminating the board may prove useful, as it will be used throughout the year.

Explorers to 1815

Timetripper, *Page 2*

Game Instructions

On each card write out a question and answer based on the history cards studied. To start, each player puts his token on the space marked "The Past." The players then take turns moving forward one space and following the directions on that space. If the player is directed to draw a card, a correct answer to the question entitles him to move ahead two spaces.

Oh, no! You have run into another timetripper going back in time:

SLIDE BACK THREE PLACES

Q: ______

A: ______

Q: ______

A: ______

Q: ______

A: ______

Q: ______

A: ______

Q: ______

A: ______

— a histor
The Present
Go Back 3 Spaces
Draw a Card
Lose 1 Turn
Draw a Card
Draw a Card
Draw a Card

THE PAST
DRAW A CARD
DRAW A CARD
DRAW A CARD
DRAW A CARD
FREE TURN
GO B
3 SP
TIMETR

ory game –
Draw a Card
Free Turn
Draw a Card
Lose 1 Turn
Draw a Card
Draw a Card
Go Back 2 Spaces
Draw a Card

Go Back 3 Spaces
Draw a Card
Draw a Card
Lose 1 Turn
Free Turn
Draw a Card
Draw a Card
Draw a Card
RIPPER

Explorers to 1815

Accordion Books: Art (front)

Directions

Copy the front and back pages back-to-back or glue them together. Cut out around the outer edges. Holding the book with the front page oriented for reading, lift up the second and third panels and fold over, face down to the left. Now lift the left side of the third panel and fold back over the upside down second panel. Lift and fold the slotted flaps toward the center and "lock" them together. On the other side, illustrate the booklet and give it a title. Then open and unfold to complete the questions inside.

How does the artist use light?

What do you notice first?

Artist:

Title:

Date:

Location Painted:

Explorers to 1815

Accordion Books: Art (back)

What lines can you see (visible and invisible) and where do they lead you in the painting?

Does the painting portray biblical values (ie. Bad is bad and Good is good—not is it a biblical event)?

Explorers to 1815

Accordion Books: Technology (front)

Directions

Copy the front and back pages back-to-back or glue them together. Cut out around the outer edges. Holding the book with the front page oriented for reading, lift up the second and third panels and fold over, face down to the left. Now lift the left side of the third panel and fold back over the upside down second panel. Lift and fold the slotted flaps toward the center and "lock" them together. On the other side, illustrate the booklet and give it a title. Then open and unfold to complete the questions inside.

What does this invention do?

What do you find interesting about this technological advance?

Inventor:

Name of Object:

Date of Development:

Location First Made:

Explorers to 1815

Accordion Books: Art (back)

What lines can you see (visible and invisible) and where do they lead you in the painting?

Does the painting portray biblical values (i.e., Bad is bad and Good is good—not is it a biblical event)?

EXPLORERS TO 1815

Accordion Books: Technology (front)

Directions

Copy the front and back pages back-to-back or glue them together. Cut out around the outer edges. Holding the book with the front page oriented for reading, lift up the second and third panels and fold over, face down to the left. Now lift the left side of the third panel and fold back over the upside down second panel. Lift and fold the slotted flaps toward the center and "lock" them together. On the other side, illustrate the booklet and give it a title. Then open and unfold to complete the questions inside.

What does this invention do?

What do you find interesting about this technological advance?

Inventor:

Name of Object:

Date of Development:

Location First Made:

Explorers to 1815

Accordion Books: Technology (back)

What problem did people have that this device helps solve?

Is this invention still in use?

Explorers to 1815

Accordion Books: Music (front)

Directions

Copy the front and back pages back-to-back or glue them together. Cut out around the outer edges. Holding the book with the front page oriented for reading, lift up the second and third panels and fold over, face down to the left. Now lift the left side of the third panel and fold back over the upside down second panel. Lift and fold the slotted flaps toward the center and "lock" them together. On the other side, illustrate the booklet and give it a title. Then open and unfold to complete the questions inside.

Was it to be performed vocally or instrumentally?

Why was this piece of music written?

Composer:

Musical Era:

Date Written:

Location First Performed:

Explorers to 1815

Accordion Books: Music (back)

What are the composer's most famous works?

Whose music most influenced the composer?

Explorers to 1815

Accordion Books: Other Historical Event (front)

Directions

Copy the front and back pages back-to-back or glue them together. Cut out around the outer edges. Holding the book with the front page oriented for reading, lift up the second and third panels and fold over, face down to the left. Now lift the left side of the third panel and fold back over the upside down second panel. Lift and fold the slotted flaps toward the center and "lock" them together. On the other side, illustrate the booklet and give it a title. Then open and unfold to complete the questions inside.

What do you find interesting about this event?

Describe the event.

Event:

Person(s):

Date:

Location:

Explorers to 1815

Accordion Books: Other Historical Event (back)

What else was happening in history at this time?

How does this event relate to the history card you are studying?

Explorers to 1815

Grading Chart

NUMBER OF PROBLEMS

Number Incorrect	06	07	08	09	10	11	12	13	14	15	16	17	18	19	20	21	22	23	24	25	26	27	28	29	30	31	32	33	34	35	36	37	38	39	40	41	42	43	44	45	46	47	48	49	50
1	83	86	88	89	90	91	92	92	93	93	94	94	94	95	95	95	95	96	96	96	96	96	96	97	97	97	97	97	97	97	97	97	97	97	98	98	98	98	98	98	98	98	98	98	98
2	67	71	75	78	80	82	83	85	86	87	88	88	89	89	90	90	91	91	92	92	92	93	93	93	93	94	94	94	94	94	94	95	95	95	95	95	95	95	95	96	96	96	96	96	96
3	50	57	63	67	70	73	75	77	79	80	81	82	83	84	85	86	86	87	88	88	88	89	89	90	90	90	91	91	91	91	92	92	92	92	93	93	93	93	93	93	93	94	94	94	94
4	33	43	50	56	60	64	67	69	71	73	75	76	78	79	80	81	82	83	83	84	85	85	86	86	87	87	88	88	88	89	89	89	89	90	90	90	90	91	91	91	91	91	92	92	92
5	17	29	38	44	50	55	58	62	64	67	69	71	72	74	75	76	77	78	79	80	81	81	82	83	83	84	84	85	85	86	86	86	87	87	88	88	88	88	89	89	89	89	90	90	90
6		14	25	33	40	45	50	54	57	60	63	65	67	68	70	71	73	74	75	76	77	78	79	79	80	81	81	82	82	83	83	84	84	85	85	85	86	86	86	87	87	87	88	88	88
7			13	22	30	36	42	46	50	53	56	59	61	63	65	67	68	70	71	72	73	74	75	76	77	77	78	79	79	80	81	81	82	82	83	83	83	84	84	84	85	85	85	86	86
8				11	20	27	33	38	43	47	50	53	56	58	60	62	64	65	67	68	69	70	71	72	73	74	75	76	76	77	78	78	79	79	80	80	81	81	82	82	83	83	83	84	84
9					10	18	25	31	36	40	44	47	50	53	55	57	59	61	63	64	65	67	68	69	70	71	72	73	74	74	75	76	76	77	78	78	79	79	80	80	80	81	81	82	82
10						09	17	23	29	33	38	41	44	47	50	52	55	57	58	60	62	63	64	66	67	68	69	70	71	71	72	73	74	74	75	75	76	77	77	78	78	79	79	80	80
11							08	15	21	27	31	35	39	42	45	48	50	52	54	56	58	59	61	62	63	65	66	67	68	69	69	70	71	72	73	73	74	74	75	76	76	77	77	78	78
12								08	14	20	25	29	33	37	40	43	45	48	50	52	54	56	57	59	60	61	63	64	65	66	67	68	68	69	70	71	71	72	73	73	74	74	75	76	76
13									07	13	19	24	28	32	35	38	41	43	46	48	50	52	54	55	57	58	59	61	62	63	64	65	66	67	68	68	69	70	70	71	72	72	73	73	74
14										07	13	18	22	26	30	33	36	39	42	44	46	48	50	52	53	55	58	58	59	60	61	62	63	64	65	66	67	67	68	69	70	70	71	71	72
15											06	12	17	21	25	29	32	35	38	40	42	44	46	48	50	52	53	55	56	57	58	59	61	62	63	63	64	65	66	67	67	68	69	69	70
16												06	11	16	20	24	27	30	33	36	38	41	43	45	47	48	50	52	53	54	56	57	58	59	60	61	62	63	64	64	65	66	67	67	68
17													06	11	15	19	23	26	29	32	35	37	39	41	43	45	47	48	50	51	53	54	55	56	58	59	60	60	61	62	63	64	65	65	66
18														05	10	14	18	22	25	28	31	33	36	38	40	42	44	45	47	49	50	51	53	54	55	56	57	58	59	60	61	62	63	63	64
19															05	10	14	17	21	24	27	30	32	34	37	39	41	42	44	46	47	49	50	51	53	54	55	56	57	58	59	60	60	61	62
20																05	09	13	17	20	23	26	29	31	33	35	38	39	41	43	44	46	47	49	50	51	52	53	55	56	57	57	58	59	60
21																	05	09	13	16	19	22	25	28	30	32	34	36	38	40	42	43	45	46	48	49	50	51	52	53	54	55	56	57	58
22																		04	08	12	15	19	21	24	27	29	31	33	35	37	39	41	42	44	45	46	48	49	50	51	52	53	54	55	56
23																			04	08	12	15	18	21	23	26	28	30	32	34	36	38	39	41	43	44	45	47	48	49	50	51	52	53	54
24																				04	08	11	14	17	20	23	25	27	29	31	33	35	37	38	40	41	43	44	45	47	48	49	50	51	52
25																					04	07	11	14	17	19	22	24	26	29	31	32	34	36	38	39	40	42	43	44	46	47	48	49	50
26																						04	07	10	13	16	19	21	24	26	28	30	32	33	35	37	38	40	41	42	43	45	46	47	48
27																							04	07	10	13	16	18	21	23	25	27	29	31	33	34	36	37	39	40	41	43	44	45	46
28																								03	07	10	13	15	18	20	22	24	26	28	30	32	33	35	36	38	39	40	42	43	44
29																									03	06	09	12	15	17	19	22	24	26	28	29	31	33	34	36	37	38	40	41	42
30																										03	06	09	12	14	17	19	21	23	25	27	29	30	32	33	35	36	38	39	40

NUMBER OF PROBLEMS

Number Incorrect	51	52	53	54	55	56	57	58	59	60	61	62	63	64	65	66	67	68	69	70	71	72	73	74	75	76	77	78	79	80	81	82	83	84	85	86	87	88	89	90	91	92	93	94	95
1	98	98	98	98	98	98	98	98	98	98	98	98	98	98	98	98	99	99	99	99	99	99	99	99	99	99	99	99	99	99	99	99	99	99	99	99	99	99	99	99	99	99	99	99	99
2	96	96	96	96	96	96	96	97	97	97	97	97	97	97	97	97	97	97	97	97	97	97	97	97	97	97	97	97	97	98	98	98	98	98	98	98	98	98	98	98	98	98	98	98	98
3	94	94	94	94	95	95	95	95	95	95	95	95	95	95	95	96	96	96	96	96	96	96	96	96	96	96	96	96	96	96	96	96	96	96	97	97	97	97	97	97	97	97	97	97	97
4	92	92	92	93	93	93	93	93	93	93	93	94	94	94	94	94	94	94	94	94	94	94	95	95	95	95	95	95	95	95	95	95	95	95	95	95	95	95	96	96	96	96	96	96	96
5	90	90	91	91	91	91	91	91	92	92	92	92	92	92	92	92	93	93	93	93	93	93	93	93	93	93	94	94	94	94	94	94	94	94	94	94	94	94	94	94	95	95	95	95	95
6	88	88	89	89	89	89	89	90	90	90	90	90	90	91	91	91	91	91	91	91	92	92	92	92	92	92	92	92	92	93	93	93	93	93	93	93	93	93	93	93	93	93	94	94	94
7	86	87	87	87	87	88	88	88	88	88	89	89	89	89	89	89	90	90	90	90	90	90	90	91	91	91	91	91	91	91	91	91	92	92	92	92	92	92	92	92	92	92	92	93	93
8	84	85	85	85	85	86	86	86	86	87	87	87	87	88	88	88	88	88	88	89	89	89	89	89	89	89	90	90	90	90	90	90	90	90	91	91	91	91	91	91	91	91	91	91	92
9	82	83	83	83	84	84	84	84	85	85	85	85	86	86	86	86	87	87	87	87	87	88	88	88	88	88	88	88	89	89	89	89	89	89	89	90	90	90	90	90	90	90	90	90	91
10	80	81	81	81	82	82	82	83	83	83	84	84	84	84	85	85	85	85	86	86	86	86	86	86	87	87	87	87	87	88	88	88	88	88	88	88	89	89	89	89	89	89	89	89	89
11	78	79	79	80	80	80	81	81	81	82	82	82	83	83	83	83	84	84	84	84	85	85	85	85	85	86	86	86	86	86	86	87	87	87	87	87	87	88	88	88	88	88	88	88	88
12	76	77	77	78	78	79	79	79	80	80	80	81	81	81	82	82	82	82	83	83	83	83	84	84	84	84	84	85	85	85	85	85	86	86	86	86	86	86	87	87	87	87	87	87	87
13	75	75	75	76	76	77	77	78	78	78	79	79	79	80	80	80	81	81	81	81	82	82	82	82	83	83	83	83	84	84	84	84	84	85	85	85	85	85	85	86	86	86	86	86	86
14	73	73	74	74	75	75	75	76	76	77	77	77	78	78	78	79	79	79	80	80	80	81	81	81	81	82	82	82	82	83	83	83	83	83	84	84	84	84	84	84	85	85	85	85	85
15	71	71	72	72	73	73	74	74	74	75	75	76	76	77	77	77	78	78	78	79	79	79	79	80	80	80	81	81	81	81	81	82	82	82	82	83	83	83	83	83	84	84	84	84	84
16	69	69	70	70	71	71	72	72	73	73	74	74	75	75	75	76	76	76	77	77	77	78	78	78	79	79	79	79	80	80	80	80	81	81	81	81	82	82	82	82	82	83	83	83	83
17	67	67	68	69	69	70	70	71	71	72	72	73	73	73	74	74	75	75	75	76	76	76	77	77	77	78	78	78	78	79	79	79	79	80	80	80	80	81	81	81	81	82	82	82	82
18	65	65	66	67	67	68	68	69	69	70	70	71	71	72	72	73	73	74	74	74	75	75	75	76	76	76	77	77	77	78	78	78	78	79	79	79	79	80	80	80	80	80	81	81	81
19	63	63	64	65	65	66	67	67	68	68	69	69	70	70	71	71	72	72	72	73	73	74	74	74	75	75	75	76	76	76	77	77	77	77	78	78	78	78	79	79	79	79	80	80	80
20	61	62	62	63	64	64	65	66	66	67	67	68	68	69	69	70	70	71	71	71	72	72	73	73	73	74	74	74	75	75	75	76	76	76	76	77	77	77	78	78	78	78	78	79	79
21	59	60	60	61	62	63	63	64	64	65	66	66	67	67	68	68	69	69	70	70	70	71	71	72	72	72	73	73	73	74	74	74	75	75	75	76	76	76	76	77	77	77	77	78	78
22	57	58	58	59	60	61	61	62	63	63	64	65	65	66	66	67	67	68	68	69	69	69	70	70	71	71	71	72	72	73	73	73	73	74	74	74	75	75	75	76	76	76	76	77	77
23	55	56	57	57	58	59	60	60	61	62	62	63	63	64	65	65	66	66	67	67	68	68	68	69	69	70	70	71	71	71	72	72	72	73	73	73	74	74	74	74	75	75	75	76	76
24	53	54	55	56	56	57	58	59	59	60	61	61	62	63	63	64	64	65	65	66	66	67	67	68	68	68	69	69	70	70	70	71	71	71	72	72	72	73	73	73	74	74	74	74	75
25	51	52	53	54	55	55	56	57	58	58	59	60	60	61	62	62	63	63	64	64	65	65	66	66	67	67	68	68	68	69	69	70	70	70	71	71	71	72	72	72	73	73	73	73	74
26	49	50	51	52	53	54	54	55	56	57	57	58	59	59	60	61	61	62	62	63	63	64	64	65	65	66	66	67	67	68	68	68	69	69	69	70	70	70	71	71	71	72	72	72	73
27	47	48	49	50	51	52	53	53	54	55	56	56	57	58	58	59	60	60	61	61	62	63	63	64	64	64	65	65	66	66	67	67	67	68	68	69	69	69	70	70	70	71	71	71	72
28	45	46	47	48	49	50	51	52	53	53	54	55	56	56	57	58	58	59	59	60	61	61	62	62	63	63	64	64	65	65	65	66	66	67	67	67	68	68	69	69	69	70	70	70	71
29	43	44	45	46	47	48	49	50	51	52	52	53	54	55	55	56	57	57	58	59	59	60	60	61	61	62	62	63	63	64	64	65	65	65	66	66	67	67	67	68	68	68	69	69	69
30	41	42	43	44	45	46	47	48	49	50	51	52	52	53	54	55	55	56	57	57	58	58	59	59	60	61	61	62	62	63	63	63	64	64	65	65	66	66	66	67	67	67	68	68	68

Cumulative Review

Test

Card:

Date:

Two Facts:

Card:

Date:

Two Facts:

Card:

Date:

Two Facts:

Card:

Date:

Two Facts: